CASENOTE® Legal Briefs®

CONSTITUTIONAL LAW

Keyed to Courses Using

Feldman and Sullivan's
Constitutional Law
Twenty-First Edition

Authored by: Publisher's Editorial Staff

ASPEN PUBLISHING

To contact Customer Service, e-mail customer.service@aspenpublishing.com, call 1-800-950-5259, or mail correspondence to:

Aspen Publishing
Attn: Order Department
1 Wall Street
Burlington, MA 01803

Printed in the United States of America.

1 2 3 4 5 6 7 8 9 0

ISBN 979-8-8861-4550-2

SUSTAINABLE FORESTRY INITIATIVE Certified Sourcing
www.forests.org
SFI-00756

About Aspen Publishing

Aspen Publishing is a leading provider of educational content and digital learning solutions to law schools in the U.S. and around the world. Aspen provides best-in-class solutions for legal education through authoritative textbooks, written by renowned authors, and breakthrough products such as Connected eBooks, Connected Quizzing, and PracticePerfect.

The Aspen Casebook Series (famously known among law faculty and students as the "red and black" casebooks) encompasses hundreds of highly regarded textbooks in more than eighty disciplines, from large enrollment courses such as Torts and Contracts to emerging electives such as Sustainability and the Law of Policing. Study aids such as the *Examples & Explanations* and the *Emanuel Law Outlines* series, both highly popular collections, help law students master complex subject matter.

Major products, programs, and initiatives include:

- **Connected eBooks** are enhanced digital textbooks and study aids that come with a suite of online content and learning tools designed to maximize student success. Designed in collaboration with hundreds of faculty and students, the Connected eBook is a significant leap forward in the legal education learning tools available to students.
- **Connected Quizzing** is an easy-to-use formative assessment tool that tests law students' understanding and provides timely feedback to improve learning outcomes. Delivered through CasebookConnect.com, the learning platform already used by students to access their Aspen casebooks, Connected Quizzing is simple to implement and integrates seamlessly with law school course curricula.
- **PracticePerfect** is a visually engaging, interactive study aid to explain commonly encountered legal doctrines through easy-to-understand animated videos, illustrative examples, and numerous practice questions. Developed by a team of experts, PracticePerfect is the ideal study companion for today's law students.
- The **Aspen Learning Library** enables law schools to provide their students with access to the most popular study aids on the market across all of their courses. Available through an annual subscription, the online library consists of study aids in e-book, audio, and video formats with full text search, note-taking, and highlighting capabilities.
- Aspen's **Digital Bookshelf** is an institutional-level online education bookshelf, consolidating everything students and professors need to ensure success. This program ensures that every student has access to affordable course materials from day one.
- **Leading Edge** is a community centered on thinking differently about legal education and putting those thoughts into actionable strategies. At the core of the program is the Leading Edge Conference, an annual gathering of legal education thought leaders looking to pool ideas and identify promising directions of exploration.

Format for the Casenote® Legal Brief

Nature of Case: This section identifies the form of action (e.g., breach of contract, negligence, battery), the type of proceeding (e.g., demurrer, appeal from trial court's jury instructions) or the relief sought (e.g., damages, injunction, criminal sanctions).

Fact Summary: This is included to refresh your memory and can be used as a quick reminder of the facts.

Rule of Law: Summarizes the general principle of law that the case illustrates. It may be used for instant recall of the court's holding and for classroom discussion or home review.

Facts: This section contains all relevant facts of the case, including the contentions of the parties and the lower court holdings. It is written in a logical order to give you a clear understanding of the case. The plaintiff and defendant are identified by their proper names throughout and are always labeled with a (P) or (D).

Issue: The issue is a concise question that brings out the essence of the opinion as it relates to the section of the casebook in which the case appears. Both substantive and procedural issues are included if relevant to the decision.

Palsgraf v. Long Island R.R. Co.

Injured bystander (P) v. Railroad company (D)

N.Y. Ct. App., 248 N.Y. 339, 162 N.E. 99 (1928).

NATURE OF CASE: Appeal from judgment affirming verdict for plaintiff seeking damages for personal injury.

FACT SUMMARY: Helen Palsgraf (P) was injured on R.R.'s (D) train platform when R.R.'s (D) guard helped a passenger aboard a moving train, causing his package to fall on the tracks. The package contained fireworks which exploded, creating a shock that tipped a scale onto Palsgraf (P).

RULE OF LAW
The risk reasonably to be perceived defines the duty to be obeyed.

FACTS: Helen Palsgraf (P) purchased a ticket to Rockaway Beach from R.R. (D) and was waiting on the train platform. As she waited, two men ran to catch a train that was pulling out from the platform. The first man jumped aboard, but the second man, who appeared as if he might fall, was helped aboard by the guard on the train who had kept the door open so they could jump aboard. A guard on the platform also helped by pushing him onto the train. The man was carrying a package wrapped in newspaper. In the process, the man dropped his package, which fell on the tracks. The package contained fireworks and exploded. The shock of the explosion was apparently of great enough strength to tip over some scales at the other end of the platform, which fell on Palsgraf (P) and injured her. A jury awarded her damages, and R.R. (D) appealed.

ISSUE: Does the risk reasonably to be perceived define the duty to be obeyed?

HOLDING AND DECISION: (Cardozo, C.J.) Yes. The risk reasonably to be perceived defines the duty to be obeyed. If there is no foreseeable hazard to the injured party as the result of a seemingly innocent act, the act does not become a tort because it happened to be a wrong as to another. If the wrong was not willful, the plaintiff must show that the act as to her had such great and apparent possibilities of danger as to entitle her to protection. Negligence in the abstract is not enough upon which to base liability. Negligence is a relative concept, evolving out of the common law doctrine of trespass on the case. To establish liability, the defendant must owe a legal duty of reasonable care to the injured party. A cause of action in tort will lie where harm, though unintended, could have been averted or avoided by observance of such a duty. The scope of the duty is limited by the range of danger that a reasonable person could foresee. In this case, there was nothing to suggest from the appearance of the parcel or otherwise that the parcel contained fireworks. The guard could not reasonably have had any warning of a threat to Palsgraf (P), and R.R. (D) therefore cannot be held liable. Judgment is reversed in favor of R.R. (D).

DISSENT: (Andrews, J.) The concept that there is no negligence unless R.R. (D) owes a legal duty to take care as to Palsgraf (P) herself is too narrow. Everyone owes to the world at large the duty of refraining from those acts that may unreasonably threaten the safety of others. If the guard's action was negligent as to those nearby, it was also negligent as to those outside what might be termed the "danger zone." For Palsgraf (P) to recover, R.R.'s (D) negligence must have been the proximate cause of her injury, a question of fact for the jury.

ANALYSIS

The majority defined the limit of the defendant's liability in terms of the danger that a reasonable person in defendant's situation would have perceived. The dissent argued that the limitation should not be placed on liability, but rather on damages. Judge Andrews suggested that only injuries that would not have happened but for R.R.'s (D) negligence should be compensable. Both the majority and dissent recognized the policy-driven need to limit liability for negligent acts, seeking, in the words of Judge Andrews, to define a framework "that will be practical and in keeping with the general understanding of mankind." The Restatement (Second) of Torts has accepted Judge Cardozo's view.

Quicknotes

FORESEEABILITY A reasonable expectation that change is the probable result of certain acts or omissions.

NEGLIGENCE Conduct falling below the standard of care that a reasonable person would demonstrate under similar conditions.

PROXIMATE CAUSE The natural sequence of events without which an injury would not have been sustained.

Party ID: Quick identification of the relationship between the parties.

Concurrence/Dissent: All concurrences and dissents are briefed whenever they are included by the casebook author.

Analysis: This last paragraph gives you a broad understanding of where the case "fits in" with other cases in the section of the book and with the entire course. It is a hornbook-style discussion indicating whether the case is a majority or minority opinion and comparing the principal case with other cases in the casebook. It may also provide analysis from restatements, uniform codes, and law review articles.

Holding and Decision: This section offers a clear and in-depth discussion of the rule of the case and the court's rationale. It is written in easy-to-understand language and answers the issue presented by applying the law to the facts of the case. When relevant, it includes a thorough discussion of the exceptions to the case as listed by the court, any major cites to the other cases on point, and the names of the judges who wrote the decisions.

Quicknotes: Conveniently defines legal terms found in the case.

Note to Students

Aspen Publishing is proud to offer *Casenote® Legal Briefs*—continuing thirty years of publishing America's best-selling legal briefs.

Casenote® Legal Briefs are designed to help you save time when briefing assigned cases. Organized under convenient headings, they show you how to abstract the basic facts and holdings from the text of the actual opinions handed down by the courts. Used as part of a rigorous study regimen, they can help you spend more time analyzing and critiquing points of law than on copying bits and pieces of judicial opinions into your notebook or outline.

Casenote® Legal Briefs should never be used as a substitute for assigned casebook readings. They work best when read as a follow-up to reviewing the underlying opinions themselves. Students who try to avoid reading and digesting the judicial opinions in their casebooks or online sources will end up shortchanging themselves in the long run. The ability to absorb, critique, and restate the dynamic and complex elements of case law decisions is crucial to your success in law school and beyond. It cannot be developed vicariously.

In addition to *Casenote® Legal Briefs*, Aspen Publishing offers the following study aids:

- *Casenote® Legal Briefs*
- *Emanuel® Law Outlines*
- Emanuel® *Law in a Flash* Flash Cards
- Emanuel® *CrunchTime®* Series

Each of these series is designed to provide you with easy-to-understand explanations of complex points of law. Each volume offers guidance on the principles of legal analysis and, consulted regularly, will hone your ability to spot relevant issues. We have titles that will help you prepare for class, prepare for your exams, and enhance your general comprehension of the law along the way.

To find out more about our law school tools for success, visit us at *www.AspenPublishing.com* or e-mail us at *customer.service@aspenpublishing.com*. We'll be happy to assist you.

How to Brief a Case

A. Decide on a Format and Stick to It

Structure is essential to a good brief. It enables you to arrange systematically the related parts that are scattered throughout most cases, thus making manageable and understandable what might otherwise seem to be an endless and unfathomable sea of information. There are, of course, an unlimited number of formats that can be utilized. However, it is best to find one that suits your needs and stick to it. Consistency breeds both efficiency and the security that when called upon you will know where to look in your brief for the information you are asked to give.

Any format, as long as it presents the essential elements of a case in an organized fashion, can be used. Experience, however, has led *Casenote® Legal Briefs* to develop and utilize the following format because of its logical flow and universal applicability.

NATURE OF CASE: This is a brief statement of the legal character and procedural status of the case (e.g., "Appeal of a burglary conviction").

There are many different alternatives open to a litigant dissatisfied with a court ruling. The key to determining which one has been used is to discover *who is asking this court for what.*

This first entry in the brief should be kept as *short as possible.* Use the court's terminology if you understand it. But since jurisdictions vary as to the titles of pleadings, the best entry is the one that addresses who wants what in this proceeding, not the one that sounds most like the court's language.

RULE OF LAW: A statement of the general principle of law that the case illustrates (e.g., "An acceptance that varies any term of the offer is considered a rejection and counteroffer").

Determining the rule of law of a case is a procedure similar to determining the issue of the case. Avoid being fooled by red herrings; there may be a few rules of law mentioned in the case excerpt, but usually only one is *the* rule with which the casebook editor is concerned. The techniques used to locate the issue, described below, may also be utilized to find the rule of law. Generally, your best guide is simply the chapter heading. It is a clue to the point the casebook editor seeks to make and should be kept in mind when reading every case in the respective section.

FACTS: A synopsis of only the essential facts of the case, i.e., those bearing upon or leading up to the issue.

The facts entry should be a short statement of the events and transactions that led one party to initiate legal proceedings against another in the first place. While some cases conveniently state the salient facts at the beginning of the decision, in other instances they will have to be culled from hiding places throughout the text, even from concurring and dissenting opinions. Some of the "facts" will often be in dispute and should be so noted. Conflicting evidence may be briefly pointed up. "Hard" facts must be included. Both must be *relevant* in order to be listed in the facts entry. It is impossible to tell what is relevant until the entire case is read, as the ultimate determination of the rights and liabilities of the parties may turn on something buried deep in the opinion.

Generally, the facts entry should not be longer than three to five *short* sentences.

It is often helpful to identify the role played by a party in a given context. For example, in a construction contract case the identification of a party as the "contractor" or "builder" alleviates the need to tell that that party was the one who was supposed to have built the house.

It is always helpful, and a good general practice, to identify the "plaintiff" and the "defendant." This may seem elementary and uncomplicated, but, especially in view of the creative editing practiced by some casebook editors, it is sometimes a difficult or even impossible task. Bear in mind that the *party presently* seeking something from this court may not be the plaintiff, and that sometimes only the cross-claim of a defendant is treated in the excerpt. Confusing or misaligning the parties can ruin your analysis and understanding of the case.

ISSUE: A statement of the general legal question answered by or illustrated in the case. For clarity, the issue is best put in the form of a question capable of a "yes" or "no" answer. In reality, the issue is simply the Rule of Law put in the form of a question (e.g., "May an offer be accepted by performance?").

The major problem presented in discerning what is *the* issue in the case is that an opinion usually purports to raise and answer several questions. However, except for rare cases, only one such question is really the issue in the case. Collateral issues not necessary to the resolution of the matter in controversy are handled by the court by language known as *"obiter dictum"* or merely *"dictum."* While dicta may be included later in the brief, they have no place under the issue heading.

To find the issue, ask *who wants what* and then go on to ask *why did that party succeed or fail in getting it.* Once this is determined, the "why" should be turned into a question.

The complexity of the issues in the cases will vary, but in all cases a single-sentence question should sum up the issue. *In a few cases,* there will be two, or even more rarely, three issues of equal importance to the resolution of the case. Each should be expressed in a single-sentence question.

Since many issues are resolved by a court in coming to a final disposition of a case, the casebook editor will reproduce the portion of the opinion containing the issue or issues most relevant to the area of law under scrutiny. A noted law professor gave this advice: "Close the book; look at the title on the cover." Chances are, if it is Property, you need not concern yourself with whether, for example, the federal government's treatment of the plaintiff's land really raises a federal question sufficient to support jurisdiction on this ground in federal court.

The same rule applies to chapter headings designating sub-areas within the subjects. They tip you off as to what the text is designed to teach. The cases are arranged in a casebook to show a progression or development of the law, so that the preceding cases may also help.

It is also most important to remember to *read the notes and questions* at the end of a case to determine what the editors wanted you to have gleaned from it.

HOLDING AND DECISION: This section should succinctly explain the rationale of the court in arriving at its decision. In capsulizing the "reasoning" of the court, it should always include an application of the general rule or rules of law to the specific facts of the case. Hidden justifications come to light in this entry: the reasons for the state of the law, the public policies, the biases and prejudices, those considerations that influence the justices' thinking and, ultimately, the outcome of the case. At the end, there should be a short indication of thedisposition or procedural resolution of the case (e.g., "Decision of the trial court for Mr. Smith (P) reversed").

The foregoing format is designed to help you "digest" the reams of case material with which you will be faced in your law school career. Once mastered by practice, it will place at your fingertips the information the authors of your casebooks have sought to impart to you in case-by-case illustration and analysis.

B. Be as Economical as Possible in Briefing Cases

Once armed with a format that encourages succinctness, it is as important to be economical with regard to the time spent on the actual reading of the case as it is to be economical in the writing of the brief itself. This does not mean "skimming" a case. Rather, it means reading the case with an "eye" trained to recognize into which "section" of your brief a particular passage or line fits and having a system for quickly and precisely marking the case so that the passages fitting any one particular part of the brief can be easily identified and brought together in a concise and accurate manner when the brief is actually written.

It is of no use to simply repeat everything in the opinion of the court; record only enough information to trigger your recollection of what the court said. Nevertheless, an accurate statement of the "law of the case," i.e., the legal principle applied to the facts, is absolutely essential to class preparation and to learning the law under the case method.

To that end, it is important to develop a "shorthand" that you can use to make marginal notations. These notations will tell you at a glance in which section of the brief you will be placing that particular passage or portion of the opinion.

Some students prefer to underline all the salient portions of the opinion (with a pencil or colored underliner marker), making marginal notations as they go along. Others prefer the color-coded method of underlining, utilizing different colors of markers to underline the salient portions of the case, each separate color being used to represent a different section of the brief. For example, blue underlining could be used for passages relating to the rule of law, yellow for those relating to the issue, and green for those relating to the holding and decision, etc. While it has its advocates, thecolor-coded method can be confusing and time-consuming (all that time spent on changing colored markers). Furthermore, it can interfere with the continuity and concentration many students deem essential to the reading of a case for maximum comprehension. In the end, however, it is a matter of personal preference and style. Just remember, whatever method you use, underlining must be used sparingly or its value is lost.

If you take the marginal notation route, an efficient and easy method is to go along underlining the key portions of the case and placing in the margin alongside them the following "markers" to indicate where a particular passage or line "belongs" in the brief you will write:

N	(NATURE OF CASE)
RL	(RULE OF LAW)
I	(ISSUE)
HL	(HOLDING AND DECISION, relates to the RULE OF LAW behind the decision)
HR	(HOLDING AND DECISION, gives the RATIONALE or reasoning behind the decision)
HA	(HOLDING AND DECISION, applies the general principle(s) of law to the facts of the case to arrive at the decision)

Remember that a particular passage may well contain information necessary to more than one part of your brief, in which case you simply note that in the margin. If you are using the color-coded underlining method instead of marginal notation, simply make asterisks or checks in the margin next to the passage in question in the colors that indicate the additional sections of the brief where it might be utilized.

The economy of utilizing "shorthand" in marking cases for briefing can be maintained in the actual brief writing process itself by utilizing "law student shorthand" within the brief. There are many commonly used words and phrases for which abbreviations can be substituted in your briefs (and in your class notes also). You can develop abbreviations that are personal to you and which will save you a lot of time. A reference list of briefing abbreviations can be found on page x of this book.

C. Use Both the Briefing Process and the Brief as a Learning Tool

Now that you have a format and the tools for briefing cases efficiently, the most important thing is to make the time spent in briefing profitable to you and to make the most advantageous use of the briefs you create. Of course, the briefs are invaluable for classroom reference when you are called upon to explain or analyze a particular case. However, they are also useful in reviewing for exams. A quick glance at the fact summary should bring the case to mind, and a rereading of the rule of law should enable you to go over the underlying legal concept in your mind, how it was applied in that particular case, and how it might apply in other factual settings.

As to the value to be derived from engaging in the briefing process itself, there is an immediate benefit that arises from being forced to sift through the essential facts and reasoning from the court's opinion and to succinctly express them in your own words in your brief. The process ensures that you understand the case and the point that it illustrates, and that means you will be ready to absorb further analysis and information brought forth in class. It also ensures you will have something to say when called upon in class. The briefing process helps develop a mental agility for getting to the *gist* of a case and for identifying, expounding on, and applying the legal concepts and issues found there. The briefing process is the mental process on which you must rely in taking law school examinations; it is also the mental process upon which lawyers rely in serving their clients and in making a living.

Abbreviations for Briefs

acceptance . . . acp
affirmed . . . aff
answer . . . ans
assumption of risk . . . a/r
attorney . . . atty
beyond a reasonable doubt . . . b/r/d
bona fide purchaser . . . BFP
breach of contract . . . br/k
cause of action . . . c/a
common law . . . c/l
Constitution . . . Con
constitutional . . . con
contract . . . K
contributory negligence . . . c/n
cross . . . x
cross-complaint . . . x/c
cross-examination . . . x/ex
cruel and unusual punishment . . . c/u/p
defendant . . . D
dismissed . . . dis
double jeopardy . . . d/j
due process . . . d/p
equal protection . . . e/p
equity . . . eq
evidence . . . ev
exclude . . . exc
exclusionary rule . . . exc/r
felony . . . f/n
freedom of speech . . . f/s
good faith . . . g/f
habeas corpus . . . h/c
hearsay . . . hr
husband . . . H
injunction . . . inj
in loco parentis . . . ILP
inter vivos . . . I/v
joint tenancy . . . j/t
judgment . . . judgt
jurisdiction . . . jur
last clear chance . . . LCC
long-arm statute . . . LAS
majority view . . . maj
meeting of minds . . . MOM
minority view . . . min
Miranda rule . . . Mir/r
Miranda warnings . . . Mir/w
negligence . . . neg
notice . . . ntc
nuisance . . . nus
obligation . . . ob
obscene . . . obs
offer . . . O
offeree . . . OE
offeror . . . OR
ordinance . . . ord
pain and suffering . . . p/s
parol evidence . . . p/e
plaintiff . . . P
prima facie . . . p/f
probable cause . . . p/c
proximate cause . . . px/c
real property . . . r/p
reasonable doubt . . . r/d
reasonable man . . . r/m
rebuttable presumption . . . rb/p
remanded . . . rem
res ipsa loquitur . . . RIL
respondeat superior . . . r/s
Restatement . . . RS
reversed . . . rev
Rule Against Perpetuities . . . RAP
search and seizure . . . s/s
search warrant . . . s/w
self-defense . . . s/d
specific performance . . . s/p
statute . . . S
statute of frauds . . . S/F
statute of limitations . . . S/L
summary judgment . . . s/j
tenancy at will . . . t/w
tenancy in common . . . t/c
tenant . . . t
third party . . . TP
third party beneficiary . . . TPB
transferred intent . . . TI
unconscionable . . . uncon
unconstitutional . . . unconst
undue influence . . . u/e
Uniform Commercial Code . . . UCC
unilateral . . . uni
vendee . . . VE
vendor . . . VR
versus . . . v
void for vagueness . . . VFV
weight of authority . . . w/a
weight of the evidence . . . w/e
wife . . . W
with . . . w/
within . . . w/i
without . . . w/o
without prejudice . . . w/o/p
wrongful death . . . wr/d

Table of Cases

CHAPTER 1

The Supreme Court's Authority and Role

Quick Reference Rules of Law

Marbury v. Madison

Justice (P) v. Secretary of State (D)

5 U.S. (1 Cranch) 137 (1803)

NATURE OF CASE: Writ of mandamus to compel delivery of commission.

FACT SUMMARY: President Jefferson's Secretary of State, James Madison (D), refused to deliver a commission granted to William Marbury (P) by former President Adams.

RULE OF LAW

The Supreme Court has the power, implied from Article VI, § 2, of the Constitution, to review acts of Congress and if they are found repugnant to the Constitution, to declare them void.

FACTS: On March 2, 1801, the outgoing President of the United States, John Adams, named forty-two justices of the peace for the District of Columbia under the Organic Act passed the same day by Congress. William Marbury (P) was one of the justices named. The commissions of Marbury (P) and other named justices were signed by Adams on his last day in office, March 3, and signed and sealed by the Acting Secretary of State, John Marshall. However, the formal commissions were not delivered by the end of the day. The new President, Thomas Jefferson, treated those appointments that were not formalized by delivery of the papers of commission prior to Adams's leaving office as a nullity. Marbury (P) and other affected colleagues brought this writ of mandamus to the Supreme Court to compel Jefferson's Secretary of State, James Madison (D), to deliver the commissions. John Marshall, the current Chief Justice of the Supreme Court, delivered the opinion.

ISSUE: Does the Supreme Court have the power, implied from Article VI, § 2, of the Constitution to review acts of Congress and if they are found repugnant to the Constitution, to declare them void?

HOLDING AND DECISION: (Marshall, C.J.) Yes. The Supreme Court has the power, implied from Article VI, § 2, of the Constitution, to review acts of Congress and if they are found repugnant to the Constitution, to declare them void. The government of the United States is a government of laws, not of men. The President, bound by these laws, is given certain political powers by the Constitution that he may use at his discretion. To aid him in his duties, he is authorized to appoint certain officers to carry out his orders. Their acts as officers are his acts and are never subject to examination by the courts. However, where these officers are given by law specific duties on which individual rights depend, any individual injured by breach of such duty may resort to his country's laws for a remedy. Here, Marbury (P) had a right to the commission, and Madison's (D) refusal to deliver it violated that right. The present case is clearly one for mandamus. However, should the Supreme Court be the court to issue it? The Judiciary Act of 1789 established and authorized United States courts to issue writs of mandamus to courts or persons holding office under U.S. authority. Secretary of State Madison (D) comes within the Act. If the Supreme Court is powerless to issue the writ of mandamus to him, it must be because the Act is unconstitutional. Article III of the Constitution provides that the Supreme Court shall have original jurisdiction in all cases affecting ambassadors, other public ministers and consuls, and where a state is a party. In all other cases, the Supreme Court shall have appellate jurisdiction. Marbury (P) urged that since Article III contains no restrictive words, the power to assign original jurisdiction to the courts remains in the legislature. But if Congress is allowed to distribute the original and appellate jurisdiction of the Supreme Court, as in the Judiciary Act, then the constitutional grant of Article III is form without substance. But no clause in the Constitution is presumed to be without effect. For the Court to issue a mandamus, it must be an exercise of appellate jurisdiction. The grant of appellate jurisdiction is the power to revise and correct proceedings already instituted; it does not create the cause. To issue a writ of mandamus ordering an executive officer to deliver a paper is to create the original action for that paper. This would be an unconstitutional exercise of original jurisdiction beyond the power of the Court. It is the province and duty of the judicial department to say what the law is. And any law, including acts of the legislature that is repugnant to the Constitution is void. Mandamus denied.

ANALYSIS

Judicial review of legislative acts was a controversial subject even before the Constitution was ratified and adopted. Alexander Hamilton upheld the theory of judicial review in the Federalist Papers. He argued that the judiciary, being the most vulnerable branch of the government, was designed to be an intermediary between the people and the legislature. Since the interpretation of laws was the responsibility of the judiciary, and the Constitution the supreme law of the land, any conflict between legislative acts and the Constitution was to be resolved by the court in favor of the Constitution. But

Continued on next page.

other authorities have attacked this position. In the case of *Eakin v. Raub*, 12 Serg. & Rawle 330 (1825), Justice Gibson dissented, stating that the judiciary's function was limited to interpreting the laws and should not extend to scrutinizing the legislature's authority to enact them. Judge Learned Hand felt that judicial review was inconsistent with the separation of powers. But history has supported the authority of judicial review of legislative acts. The United States survives on a tripartite government. Theoretically, the three branches should be strong enough to check and balance the others. To limit the judiciary to the passive task of interpretation would be to limit its strength in the tripartite structure. Marbury served to buttress the judiciary branch making it equal to the executive and legislative branches.

Quicknotes

APPELLATE JURISDICTION The power of a higher court to review the decisions of lower courts.

JUDICIAL REVIEW Authority of the courts to review decisions, actions, or omissions committed by another agency or branch of government.

ORIGINAL JURISDICTION The power of a court to hear an action upon its commencement.

WRIT OF MANDAMUS A court order issued commanding a public or private entity, or an official thereof, to perform a duty required by law.

Martin v. Hunter's Lessee

Heir to land (P) v. Lessee (D)

14 U.S. (1 Wheat.) 304 (1816)

NATURE OF CASE: Appeal from judgment of state's highest court in an action of ejectment.

FACT SUMMARY: After the Supreme Court reversed a Virginia Court of Appeals ruling that had held that Martin (P) had lost title to land in favor of the state, the Virginia court ruled that since the Federal Judiciary Act extended the Supreme Court's appellate jurisdiction to state courts, the Judiciary Act was unconstitutional.

RULE OF LAW

Federal courts may hear appeals brought from state court decisions.

FACTS: Martin (P), a British subject resident in England, inherited vast Virginia landholdings from his uncle, Lord Fairfax. In 1789, Virginia, pursuant to state laws confiscating land owned by British subjects, purported to grant a land patent to Hunter. Martin (P) sought to eject Hunter's lessee (D) from the land. The Virginia District Court ruled for Martin (P) on the basis of anti-confiscation clauses in the treaties of 1783 and 1794 with Great Britain. The Virginia Court of Appeals reversed on grounds that the 1796 act of compromise between the Fairfax claimants and the state settled the matter against Martin (P) and that the state's title had been perfected before the treaties. The United States Supreme Court, relying on the treaty of 1794 and without discussing the compromise, reversed and remanded. On remand, the Virginia court ruled that insofar as the Judiciary Act extended the United States Supreme Court's appellate jurisdiction to state courts, the Act was unconstitutional. Martin (P) appealed.

ISSUE: May federal courts hear appeals brought from state court decisions?

HOLDING AND DECISION: (Story, J.) Yes. Federal courts may hear appeals brought from state court decisions. The third article of the Constitution grants appellate jurisdiction to the Supreme Court where it does not have original jurisdiction except in those instances where Congress has limited federal appellate jurisdiction. The framers anticipated federal courts would not have original jurisdiction over cases that arose in state court but provided for appellate jurisdiction. Some argue that the federal courts cannot interfere with state sovereignty by taking jurisdiction over state cases, but the Constitution provides in several other instances for state obligations and intrusions into state sovereignty. State judges are not entitled to independence from the federal judicial system but are in fact subject to it pursuant to the Constitution. Federal appellate power over state cases is a necessity for uniformity because of the possibility of different state courts interpreting the same statute or treaty differently. The Supreme Court's job is not to inquire into the reasons the framers provided for federal appellate jurisdiction but to construe the Constitution as written. The Constitution expressly provides for federal appellate jurisdiction over cases arising in state courts. Reversed.

ANALYSIS

As a historical note, Chief Justice Marshall disqualified himself in the first, remanded case, *Fairfax's Devisee v. Hunter's Lessee*, 7 Cranch 603 (1813), and in the case above. Marshall, as a member of the Virginia legislature, had negotiated the 1796 act of compromise while acting for the purchasers of the Fairfax estate. Marshall also had a great financial interest in the outcome because he and his brother had organized a syndicate that had purchased, from Martin (P), 160,000 acres of the land in question.

Quicknotes

APPELLATE JURISDICTION The power of a higher court to review the decisions of lower courts.

EJECTMENT An action to oust someone in unlawful possession of real property and to restore possession to the party lawfully entitled to it.

FEDERAL JUDICIARY ACT § 34 The laws of the states shall be regarded as rules of decisions in trials at common law in the federal courts.

Cooper v. Aaron

Government officials (P) v. Court (D)

358 U.S. 1 (1958)

NATURE OF CASE: Certiorari for review of suspension of plan to desegregate public schools.

FACT SUMMARY: The Governor and Legislature of Arkansas refused to obey a federal court order to desegregate the public schools in Little Rock based on the *Brown v. Board of Education*, 344 U.S. 1 (1952), case, pending further challenges to the *Brown* decision.

RULE OF LAW

State officials may not refuse to obey federal court orders resting on constitutional grounds.

FACTS: The Governor and Legislature of the State of Arkansas acted on the premise that there was no duty on state officials to obey federal court orders resting upon Supreme Court's interpretations of the Constitution. The actions consisted of the suspension of a desegregation plan for the public schools in Little Rock. The state officials claimed that they had the right to disobey the order until the decision in *Brown v. Board of Education*, 344 U.S. 1 (1952), was further challenged. The Supreme Court reviewed the actions.

ISSUE: May state officials refuse to obey federal court orders resting on constitutional grounds?

HOLDING AND DECISION: (Warren, C.J.) No. State officials may not refuse to obey federal court orders resting on constitutional grounds. The Constitution of the United States is the "supreme law of the land." The federal judiciary is supreme in the exposition of the law of the Constitution. No state legislator or executive or judicial officer can refuse to obey a federal court order based upon a federal interpretation of the Constitution without violating the duty to support the Constitution. If such refusal were to be permitted, the fiat of the official would be the supreme law instead of the Constitution. The decision in *Brown v. Board of Education*, 344 U.S. 1 (1952), is now unanimously reaffirmed. The principles announced in that decision and the obedience of the states to them, according to the command of the Constitution, are indispensable for the protection of the freedoms guaranteed by our fundamental charter for all of us.

ANALYSIS

The Supremacy Clause of the Constitution, Article VI, § 2, requires that federal court decisions based on Supreme Court's interpretations of constitutional language govern the states' legislative, judicial, and executive branches. However, where the federal court asserts power based on anything other than the Constitution or constitutional interpretations, the doctrine announced in *Erie v. Tompkins*, 304 U.S. 64 (1938), may permit the state law, if applicable, to govern.

Quicknotes

***ERIE* DOCTRINE** Federal courts must apply state substantive law and federal procedural law.

FEDERALISM A scheme of government whereby the power to govern is divided between central and localized governments.

SUPREMACY CLAUSE Article VI, ¶ 2, of the U.S. Constitution, which provides that federal action must prevail over inconsistent state action.

Lujan v. Defenders of Wildlife

Secretary of the Interior (D) v. Environmental organizations (P)

504 U.S. 555 (1992)

NATURE OF CASE: Appeal of injunction requiring the Secretary of the Interior to promulgate a regulation.

FACT SUMMARY: Defenders of Wildlife (P) sued for an injunction ordering the Secretary of the Interior (D) to apply the Endangered Species Act to actions taken in foreign countries.

RULE OF LAW

To establish standing, a plaintiff must show injury in fact, causation, and redressability, and Congress may not create a right of standing based on a generalized grievance against government.

FACTS: The Endangered Species Act § 7(a)(2) required federal agencies to consult with the Interior Department (Interior) (D) to ensure that federal actions do not jeopardize endangered species. Interior (D) reinterpreted § 7(a)(2) to apply only in the United States or at sea. Defenders of Wildlife (Defenders) (P) sued for an injunction requiring Secretary of the Interior Lujan (the Secretary) (D) to issue a regulation restoring the interpretation that § 7(a)(2) applies worldwide. To support standing, two of the Interior's (D) members, who claimed to have observed certain endangered animals on trips to Egypt and Sri Lanka, averred that they would suffer harm from federal programs overseeing and funding projects in Egypt and Sri Lanka that threatened the animals. They also presented three novel standing theories whereby anyone anywhere with a vocational, educational, or aesthetic interest in an endangered species or "contiguous ecosystem" harmed by a federal activity would have standing. They also cited the "citizen suit" provision of the Act, which grants "any person" the right to sue to enforce any of its provisions. The Secretary (D) moved for summary judgment, claiming Defenders (P) lacked standing. The district court instead issued Defenders (P) the injunction it sought. The Eighth Circuit Court of Appeals affirmed, and the Secretary (D) appealed.

ISSUE: Can Congress create a right of standing based on a generalized grievance against government, allowing a plaintiff to establish standing without showing injury in fact, causation, and redressability?

HOLDING AND DECISION: (Scalia, J.) No. To establish standing a plaintiff must show injury in fact, causation, and redressability. Congress may not create a right of standing based on a generalized grievance against government. Defenders (P) failed to establish injury in fact. "Someday" future intentions to observe animals do not establish "actual or imminent" injury. The novel theories establish harm to the ecosystem or animals but fail to establish injury to a plaintiff. It is pure speculation that anyone anywhere is harmed by a single project affecting some portion of a species without a specific connection. The theories also failed to establish redressability. Other agencies, not being parties, would not be bound by an injunction. Moreover, there was no evidence Egypt, Sri Lanka, or any other country would reduce a project or harm to endangered species if minimal U.S. support were stopped. The Act's "citizen-suit" provision is unconstitutional. Under Article III, federal courts may not hear cases where the plaintiff merely has a generalized grievance against government. Congress may not give power to the courts that the Constitution says the courts do not have. Congress may create rights that establish injury in fact to satisfy Article III, but those rights must be individualized or there is no "case or controversy." Reversed.

CONCURRENCE: (Kennedy, J.) The Court must be sensitive to Congress's ability to create new standing rights. At a minimum, though, Congress must identify the injury it wishes to vindicate and relate the injury to a class of persons who can sue. The "citizen-suit" provision fails to do either.

CONCURRENCE: (Stevens, J.) While I do not agree with the Court's conclusion that the threatened injury is not imminent nor with the plurality additional conclusion that the injury is not redressable in this litigation, I concur in the reversal because I am not persuaded Congress intended the consultation requirement of § 7(a)(2) to apply to activities in foreign countries.

DISSENT: (Blackmun, J.) On summary judgment a plaintiff need show only a genuine issue of material fact as to standing. Many environmental injuries cause harm far from the challenged activity. The funding agencies would be bound by an injunction based on their involvement in this case. Congress imposes procedural restraints on executive power. Surely the courts do not violate separation of powers by enforcing these procedures at the mandate of Congress.

ANALYSIS

The precedential value of *Lujan* is questionable. Only four justices found that the plaintiffs had not established redressability. Only three justices agreed that there was no injury in fact and that the "citizen-suit" provision was invalid.

Continued on next page.

Quicknotes

CAUSATION The aggregate effect of preceding events that brings about a tortious result; the causal connection between the actions of a tortfeasor and the injury that follows.

GENERALIZED GRIEVANCE A class of actions that does not have standing because it does not represent a controversy for the particular plaintiff but that affects the general public.

INJURY IN FACT An injury that gives rise to standing to sue.

REDRESSABILITY Requirement that in order for a court to hear a case there must be an injury that is redressable or capable of being remedied.

STANDING The right to commence suit against another party because of a personal stake in the resolution of the controversy.

Massachusetts v. Environmental Protection Agency

State (P) v. Federal agency (D)

549 U.S. 497 (2007)

NATURE OF CASE: Appeal challenging a federal agency's alleged refusal to enforce the federal Clean Air Act against motor-vehicle emissions.

FACT SUMMARY: A state and several other parties challenged the Environmental Protection Agency's (D) failure to enforce the Clean Air Act against motor-vehicle emissions.

RULE OF LAW

A plaintiff has standing if the plaintiff demonstrates a concrete injury that is both fairly traceable to the defendant and redressable by judicial relief.

FACTS: The Environmental Protection Agency (EPA) (D) refused to enforce the Clean Air Act against motor-vehicle emissions. Massachusetts (P) and several other parties appealed the EPA's (D) refusal [by petitioning the Court of Appeals for the District of Columbia Circuit to review the Agency's (D) decision. The appellate court did not affirmatively hold that Massachusetts (P) had standing, but a majority of that court did uphold the EPA's (D) decision. Massachusetts (P) petitioned the Supreme Court for further review.]

ISSUE: Does a plaintiff have standing if the plaintiff demonstrates a concrete injury that is both fairly traceable to the defendant and redressable by judicial relief?

HOLDING AND DECISION: (Stevens, J.) Yes. A plaintiff has standing if the plaintiff demonstrates a concrete injury that is both fairly traceable to the defendant and redressable by judicial relief. A well-documented rise in global temperatures has coincided with an increase in carbon dioxide in the atmosphere, and scientists believe that the two trends are related. Calling global warming "the most pressing environmental challenge of our time," a group of states, including Massachusetts (P), alleges that the Environmental Protection Agency (EPA) has abdicated its responsibility in protecting the nation. The jurisdiction of federal courts is limited to "cases" and "controversies," and Massachusetts (P) has satisfied that threshold hurdle here. It is important to note that only one of the petitioners needs to have standing in order to permit this Court to consider the petition for review. As a state, Massachusetts (P) proceeds in its quasi-sovereign capacity, and case law supports applying different standards of justiciability for such litigants. The particularized injury for Massachusetts (P) in this case is the damage to the State's (P) coastline that will, and will continue to, occur. Further, the injury to that coastline is fairly traceable to the EPA's (D) inaction; even small effects on an injury in fact satisfy the causation requirement in federal standing analysis. Finally, Massachusetts's (P) injury can be redressed judicially, even though the outcome of a judicial remedy might be delayed while new motor-vehicle emissions are implemented. Accordingly, Massachusetts (P) has standing. [Reversed.]

DISSENT: (Roberts, C.J.) Any redress of the injuries in this case should be left to the political branches. Relaxing standing requirements for a state exists nowhere in this Court's precedents. Under normal standing analysis, Massachusetts's (P) injury fails to satisfy the requirement of a "concrete and particularized" injury; injuries to "humanity at large" do not suffice. Also, any causal connection between the Environmental Protection Agency's (EPA) (D) inaction and damage to the coastlines is so tenuous and speculative that it cannot support a finding of standing. Further, Massachusetts (P) cannot satisfy the redressability factor because emissions from other countries are likely to dwarf any reduction in emissions that might result from the EPA's (D) enforcement of the Clean Air Act. Diluting the appropriate standing requirements permits courts only to encroach upon authority that is properly committed to Congress and the President.

ANALYSIS

The three factors in the standing analysis announced by *Lujan v. Defenders of Wildlife*, 504 U.S. 555 (1992), are very clear: the complaining party must have suffered (1) an injury in fact (2) that is fairly traceable to the defendant and (3) that can be redressed by judicial relief. As the Court's five-to-four decision in this case shows, however, what is not so clear is how those three factors should apply to any specific dispute. The fundamental importance of justiciability, as Chief Justice Roberts notes in dissent, resides in the most basic questions about the kinds of disputes that courts should—and should not—hear.

Quicknotes

INJURY IN FACT An injury that gives rise to standing to sue.

REDRESSABILITY Requirement that in order for a court to hear a case there must be an injury that is redressable or capable of being remedied.

STANDING The right to commence suit against another party because of a personal stake in the resolution of the controversy.

Baker v. Carr

Resident (P) v. State (D)

369 U.S. 186 (1962)

NATURE OF CASE: Certiorari granted to review unconstitutionality of a state political reapportionment law.

FACT SUMMARY: Baker (P) alleged that because of population changes since 1901, the 1901 State Apportionment Act was obsolete and unconstitutional and that the state legislature refused to reapportion itself.

RULE OF LAW

The fact that a suit seeks protection of a political right does not mean it necessarily presents a political question.

FACTS: Between 1901 and 1961, Tennessee's population had grown substantially and had been redistributed. Baker (P) alleged that because of the population changes and the state legislature's failure to reapportion voting districts by itself, the 1901 Apportionment Act was unconstitutional, as violating equal protection, and obsolete. Baker (P) also alleged that because of the makeup of the legislature resulting from the 1901 Act, redress in the form of a state constitutional amendment was difficult or impossible. Baker (P) sought an injunction against further elections under the 1901 system and reapportionment, but the lower court denied relief.

ISSUE: Does a constitutional challenge to a state apportionment act present a political question?

HOLDING AND DECISION: (Brennan, J.) No. The fact that a suit seeks protection of a political right does not mean it necessarily presents a political question. The primary reason that political questions have been held to be nonjusticiable is the separation of powers. An analysis of any case held to involve a political question will reveal: (1) a history of the issue's management by another governmental branch; (2) a lack of judicially manageable standards for resolving it; (3) the impossibility of deciding the case without an initial policy determination calling for nonjudicial discretion; (4) the impossibility of resolving it without expressing lack of respect due other government branches; (5) an unusual need for unquestioning adherence to a political decision already made; or (6) the potentiality of embarrassment from a variety of announcements by different governmental departments on one question. The mere fact that a suit seeks protection of a political right does not mean that it involves a political question. The Court cannot reject as involving a political question a real controversy as to whether a certain action exceeded constitutional limits. Here, Baker (P) alleges that a state's actions violate his right to equal protection. None of the above-mentioned characteristics of a political question are present. Further, the nonjusticiability of claims arising under the Guaranty Clause can have no bearing on the justiciability of the equal protection claim presented here. The judgment of dismissal is reversed, and the case is remanded.

DISSENT: (Frankfurter, J.) A long line of cases has held that the Guaranty Clause is not enforceable through the courts. The present case involves all the elements that have made the Guaranty Clause cases nonjusticiable. The Equal Protection Clause provides no clearer guide for judicial examination of apportionment statutes than would the Guaranty Clause. What is actually asked here is for the Court to choose among competing theories of representation, and ultimately, among competing political philosophies, to establish an appropriate frame of government for Tennessee. To find the Court's power to make such a choice in the broad guarantee of the Equal Protection Clause is to rewrite the Constitution.

ANALYSIS

Baker v. Carr is the most important case on political questions. Traditionally, the Court refused to review cases arising from state apportionment statutes, since they were all said to present political questions. In *Colegrove v. Green*, 328 U.S. 549 (1946), it was contended that the fact that apportioned districts were not of approximate equality in population rendered the state apportionment act unconstitutional. The Court held that a political question was presented and so the case was nonjusticiable. However, in *Gomillion v. Lightfoot*, 364 U.S. 339 (1960), the Court showed some willingness to enter the area of apportionment. There, a statute apportioned a district with the obvious purpose of excluding Black votes. The Court held that a justiciable violation of equal protection had been alleged. In distinguishing *Colegrove*, it stated that there the complaint alleged only a dilution of the strength of the appellants' votes as a result of legislative inaction over a number of years, whereas in *Gomillion*, the petitioners complained that affirmative legislative action had deprived them of their votes.

Quicknotes

JUSTICIABILITY An actual controversy that is capable of determination by the court.

POLITICAL QUESTION An issue that is more appropriately left to the determination of another governmental branch and which the court declines to hear.

CHAPTER 2

Federalism: History and Principles

Quick Reference Rules of Law

McCulloch v. Maryland

Bank cashier (D) v. State (P)

17 U.S. (4 Wheat.) 316 (1819)

NATURE OF CASE: Action arising out of violation of a state statute.

FACT SUMMARY: McCulloch (D), the cashier of the Baltimore branch of the U.S. Bank, issued bank notes in violation of a Maryland (P) statute. Under the statute, banks operating in Maryland without authority from the state could issue bank notes only on stamped paper furnished.

RULE OF LAW

(1) Certain federal powers, which give Congress the discretion and power to choose and enact the means to perform the duties imposed upon it, are to be implied from the Necessary and Proper Clause.
(2) The federal Constitution and the laws made pursuant to it are supreme and control the constitutions and the laws of the states.

FACTS: A Maryland (P) statute provided that any bank operating in the state without state authority could issue bank notes only on stamped paper issued by the state. The law specified the fees payable for the paper and provided for penalties for violators. An act of Congress established a U.S. Bank. McCulloch (D), the U.S. Bank's cashier for its Baltimore branch, issued bank notes without complying with the Maryland (P) law.

ISSUE:
(1) Does Congress have the power to incorporate a bank?
(2) Does a state have the power to impose fees on the operation of an institution created by Congress pursuant to its constitutional powers?

HOLDING AND DECISION: (Marshall, C.J.)
(1) Yes. Certain federal powers, which give Congress the discretion and power to choose and enact the means to perform the duties imposed upon it, are to be implied from the Necessary and Proper Clause. It is true that this government is one of enumerated powers. However, the Constitution does not exclude incidental or implied powers. It does not require that everything be granted expressly and minutely described. To have so required would have entirely changed the character of the Constitution and made it into a legal code. The enumerated powers given to the government imply the ordinary means of execution. The power of creating a corporation may be implied as incidental to other powers or used as a means of executing them. The Necessary and Proper Clause gives Congress the power to make "all laws which shall be necessary and proper, for carrying into execution" the powers vested by the Constitution in the U.S. government. Maryland (P) argues that the word "necessary" limits the right to pass laws for the execution of the granted powers to those that are indispensable. However, in common usage, "necessary" frequently means convenient, useful, or essential. Considering the word's common usage, its usage in another part of the Constitution (Article 1, § 10), and its inclusion among the powers given to Congress, rather than among the limitations upon Congress, it cannot be held to restrain Congress. The sound construction of the Constitution must allow Congress the discretion to choose the means to perform the duties imposed upon it. As long as the end is legitimate and within the scope of the Constitution, any means that are appropriate, that are plainly adapted to that end, and that are not prohibited by the Constitution, but are consistent with its spirit, are constitutional. A bank is a convenient, useful, and essential instrument for handling national finances. Hence, it is within Congress's power to enact a law incorporating a U.S. bank.
(2) No. The federal Constitution and the laws made pursuant to it are supreme and control the constitutions and the laws of the states. The federal Constitution and the laws made in pursuance thereof are supreme. They control the constitutions and laws of the states and cannot be controlled by them. Maryland (P) is incorrect in its contention that the powers of the federal government are delegated by the states, which alone are truly sovereign. The Constitution derives its authority from the people, not from the states. Here, Maryland's (P) statute in effect taxes the operation of the U.S. Bank, a bank properly created within Congress's power. The power to tax involves the power to destroy. Here it is in opposition to the supreme congressional power to create a bank. Also, when a state taxes an organization created by the U.S. government, it acts upon an institution created by people over whom it claims no control. The states have no power, by taxation or otherwise, to impede, burden, or in any manner control the operations of constitutional laws enacted by Congress. The Maryland (P) statute is, therefore, unconstitutional and void. Reversed.

Continued on next page.

ANALYSIS

Federalism is the basis of the Constitution's response to the problem of governing large geographical areas with diverse local needs. The success of federalism depends upon maintaining the balance between the need for the supremacy and sovereignty of the federal government and the interest in maintaining independent state government and curtailing national intrusion into intrastate affairs. The U.S. federal structure allocates powers between the nation and the states by enumerating the powers delegated to the national government and acknowledging the retention by the states of the remainder. The Articles of Confederation followed a similar scheme. The Constitution expanded the enumerated national powers to remedy weaknesses of the Articles. The move from the Articles to the Constitution was a shift from a central government with fewer powers to one with more powers.

Quicknotes

FEDERALISM A scheme of government whereby the power to govern is divided and shared between national and regional governments.

NECESSARY AND PROPER CLAUSE, ART. I, § 8 OF THE U.S. CONSTITUTION Enables Congress to make all laws that may be "necessary and proper" to execute its other, enumerated powers.

United States v. Comstock

Federal government (P) v. Sexually violent prisoner (D)

560 U.S. 126 (2010)

NATURE OF CASE: Appeal in action challenging as beyond Congress's power under the Necessary and Proper Clause a federal civil-commitment statute authorizing the federal government to civilly commit "sexually dangerous persons" beyond the date it lawfully could hold them on a charge or conviction for a federal crime.

FACT SUMMARY: Congress enacted § 4248, which authorizes the federal government to civilly commit "sexually dangerous persons" beyond the date it lawfully could hold them on a charge or conviction for a federal crime. The statute was challenged as beyond Congress's power under the Necessary and Proper Clause.

RULE OF LAW

Congress has power under the Necessary and Proper Clause to enact a law authorizing the federal government to civilly commit "sexually dangerous persons" beyond the date it lawfully could hold them on a charge or conviction for a federal crime.

FACTS: Congress enacted § 4248, which authorizes the federal government to civilly commit "sexually dangerous persons" beyond the date it lawfully could hold them on a charge or conviction for a federal crime. The statute was challenged as beyond Congress's power under the Necessary and Proper Clause.

ISSUE: Does Congress have power under the Necessary and Proper Clause to enact a law authorizing the federal government to civilly commit "sexually dangerous persons" beyond the date it lawfully could hold them on a charge or conviction for a federal crime?

HOLDING AND DECISION: (Breyer, J.) Yes. Congress has power under the Necessary and Proper Clause to enact a law authorizing the federal government to civilly commit "sexually dangerous persons" beyond the date it lawfully could hold them on a charge or conviction for a federal crime. This conclusion rests on five principal considerations. First, the Clause grants Congress broad authority to pass laws in furtherance of its constitutionally enumerated powers. It makes clear that grants of specific federal legislative authority are accompanied by broad power to enact laws that are "convenient or useful" or "conducive" to the enumerated power's "beneficial exercise." In determining whether the Clause authorizes a particular federal statute, there must be "means-ends rationality" between the enacted statute and the source of federal power. Although the Constitution nowhere grants Congress express power to create federal crimes beyond those specifically enumerated, to punish their violation, to imprison violators, or to provide appropriately for those imprisoned, Congress possesses broad authority to do each of those things under the Clause. Second, the statute is a modest addition to a longstanding federal statutory framework. Third, the Government (P), as custodian of its prisoners, has the constitutional power to act in order to protect nearby (and other) communities from the danger such prisoners may pose. Moreover, § 4248 is reasonably adapted to Congress's power to act as a responsible federal custodian. Congress could have reasonably concluded that federal inmates who suffer from a mental illness that causes them to have serious difficulty in refraining from sexually violent conduct would pose an especially high danger to the public if released, since Congress could have reasonably concluded that a reasonable number of such individuals would likely not be detained by the states if released from federal custody. Fourth, § 4248 does not invade state sovereignty but seeks to accommodate state interests, since it requires the Attorney General to encourage the relevant states to take custody of the individual without inquiring into the "suitability" of their intended care or treatment, and to relinquish federal authority whenever a state asserts its own. Fifth, § 4248 is narrow in scope and does not result in Congress having a general police power, given that § 4248 has been applied to only a small fraction of federal prisoners and its reach is limited to individuals already in the Government's (P) custody. Taken together, these five considerations lead to the conclusion that the statute is a "necessary and proper" means of exercising the federal authority that permits Congress to create federal criminal laws, to punish their violation, to imprison violators, to provide appropriately for those imprisoned, and to maintain the security of those who are not imprisoned but who may be affected by the federal imprisonment of others.

CONCURRENCE: (Kennedy, J.) Under the Necessary and Proper Clause, application of a "rational basis" test should be at least as exacting as it has been in the Commerce Clause cases, which require a tangible link to commerce, not a mere conceivable rational relation. Thus, the link must be an empirically demonstrated link in fact. Also, while it is logically correct to say that if the federal Government (P) has a given power to act under the Necessary and Proper Clause then that power is not one reserved to the States, it is essential in determining whether the Government (P) has authority to exercise a

Continued on next page.

given power in the first place to consider whether state sovereignty is compromised by the federal Government's (P) assertion of that power. If state sovereignty is compromised, that suggests that the power is not one properly within the reach of federal power.

CONCURRENCE: (Alito, J.) It is necessary and proper for Congress to protect the public from dangers created by the federal criminal justice and prison systems. Given that it is necessary and proper for Congress to provide for the apprehension of escaped federal prisoners, it is similarly necessary and proper for Congress to provide for the civil commitment of dangerous federal prisoners who would otherwise escape civil commitment as a result of federal imprisonment.

DISSENT: (Thomas, J.) The Government (P) identifies no specific enumerated power or powers as a constitutional predicate for § 4248, and none are readily discernible; and not even the Commerce Clause can justify federal civil detention of sex offenders. Moreover, the Court has long recognized that the power to care for the mentally ill and, where necessary, the power to protect the community from the dangerous tendencies of some mentally ill persons, are among the numerous powers that remain with the States. Notwithstanding that a majority of the states argue that § 4248 is constitutional—because the cost of detaining such sexually dangerous persons is expensive, and they would rather the federal Government (P) bear this expense—Congress's power is fixed by the Constitution; it does not depend on the states' policy preferences or on considerations of the states' allocation of their funds. Thus, the majority's decision comes perilously close to transforming the Necessary and Proper Clause into a basis for the federal police power that the Court has always rejected.

ANALYSIS

One of the constitutional principles that the Court elaborated in this decision is that congressional authority under the Necessary and Proper Clause can be more than one step removed from an enumerated power. When the inquiry is whether a federal law has sufficient links to an enumerated power to be within the scope of federal authority, the analysis depends not on the number of links in the congressional-power chain but on the strength of the chain. Thus, concluding that a relation can be put into a verbal formulation that fits somewhere along a causal chain of federal powers is merely the beginning, not the end, of the constitutional inquiry.

Quicknotes

ENUMERATED POWERS Those powers expressly delegated by the U.S. Constitution to a particular branch of government.

NECESSARY AND PROPER CLAUSE, ART. I, § 8 OF THE U.S. CONSTITUTION Enables Congress to make all laws that may be "necessary and proper" to execute its other, enumerated powers.

POLICE POWER The power of a government to impose restrictions on the rights of private persons, so long as those restrictions are reasonably related to the promotion and protection of public health, safety, morals, and the general welfare.

U.S. Term Limits, Inc. v. Thornton

Proponents of term limits (D) v. League of Women Voters (P)

514 U.S. 779 (1995)

NATURE OF CASE: Review of summary judgment striking down state term limits.

FACT SUMMARY: Arkansas' (D) congressional term limitation law was challenged as unconstitutional.

RULE OF LAW
States may not limit the terms of members of Congress.

FACTS: In 1992, Arkansas (D) adopted by initiative a state constitutional amendment limiting the tenure of both state and federal elected officials. With respect to the United States congressional and senatorial delegations, the amendment provided that an incumbent could not have his name placed on a ballot after a set number of terms. The League of Women Voters (P) challenged this provision as contrary to the Constitution. The Arkansas Supreme Court held the amendment unconstitutional, and the United States Supreme Court granted review.

ISSUE: May states limit the terms of members of Congress?

HOLDING AND DECISION: (Stevens, J.) No. States may not limit the terms of members of Congress. The qualifications for sitting in the U.S. Congress are stated in Article I of the Constitution. The Supreme Court has already held that Congress itself cannot add to, subtract from, or otherwise change these qualifications. The issue here is whether the states can do so. First, states do not have a Tenth Amendment power in this area. The Tenth Amendment reserved to the states those powers that predated the Constitution and were not delegated to the federal government. State governments never had any powers over national elections prior to the Constitution because there were none. Consequently, the Tenth Amendment gives the states no powers here. Second, the historical record is quite clear that the notion of term limits was vigorously debated prior to adoption of the Constitution, and to add such a requirement now would violate the Framers' intent. Finally, to allow states to impose term limits would violate a fundamental principle of our system of representative democracy, to wit, that people should be free to choose those whom they please to govern them. For these reasons, term limits violate the Constitution. U.S. Term Limits, Inc. (D), however, contends that the amendment in question does not truly limit terms but only restricts ballot access. The Constitution allows states to regulate the time, manner, and place of elections. U.S. Term Limits (D) contends that the amendment constitutes such a regulation. It does not. The amendment tries to do indirectly what it cannot do in a direct manner, and this sort of form over substance argument will not be endorsed by the Court. Affirmed.

CONCURRENCE: (Kennedy, J.) The federal character of congressional elections flows from the political reality that our national government is republican in form and that national citizenship has privileges and immunities protected from state abridgement by the force of the Constitution itself.

DISSENT: (Thomas, J.) [Nothing] in the Constitution deprives the people of each state of the power to prescribe eligibility requirements for congressional candidates; it is silent in that area. "Where the Constitution is silent, it raises no bar to action by the states or the people." The Court's analysis is wrong on several counts. The Tenth Amendment protects not only those powers that predate the Constitution. All power flows from consent of the people; when the people have spoken, as they did here, and the Constitution does not countermand the will of the people, the Tenth Amendment applies. When selecting members of Congress, the people of each state have retained their independent political identity, which would allow them to determine eligibility requirements. Also, the Qualifications Clause is a bare recitation of the minimum qualifications necessary to hold office; it says nothing to the effect that these are the only qualifications that can be imposed. Finally, the Court incorrectly equates limitations on ballot access with limits on tenure.

ANALYSIS

The present case is a good illustration of two different and competing theories of constitutional interpretation. The majority's approach can be called "structural." While the Constitution did not specifically prohibit term limits, the Court invalidated them as contrary to our governmental structure. Justice Thomas, in his dissent, took a strict constructionist/literalist approach, looking to the text and nothing more.

Quicknotes

TENTH AMENDMENT The Tenth Amendment to the United States Constitution reserves those powers therein, not expressly delegated to the federal government or prohibited to the states, to the states or to the people.

CHAPTER 3

The Commerce Power and Its Federalism-Based Limits

Quick Reference Rules of Law

Gibbons v. Ogden

Ship operator (D) v. Ship operator (P)

22 U.S. (9 Wheat.) 1 (1824)

NATURE OF CASE: Certiorari to review interpretation of federal commerce power in underlying action seeking an injunction to protect an exclusive right to operate ships between New York and New Jersey.

FACT SUMMARY: [Ogden (P), after acquiring a monopoly right from the State of New York to operate ships between New York City and New Jersey, sought to enjoin Gibbons (D) from operating his ships, licensed by the federal government, between the same points.]

RULE OF LAW

If a state law conflicts with a congressional act regulating commerce, the congressional act is controlling.

FACTS: [The New York legislature granted an exclusive right to Robert Livingston and Robert Fulton to operate ships powered by fire or steam in New York waters for twenty years, which right was subsequently extended for another ten years. Ogden (P) obtained an assignment from Livingston and Fulton to operate his ships between Elizabethtown, New Jersey, and New York City. Gibbons (D) was also running two boats between these points, and his boats had been enrolled and licensed under the laws of the United States for employment in the coasting trade. Ogden (P) obtained an injunction stopping Gibbons (D) from operating his ships between the points for which Ogden (P) had received an exclusive right to operate his own ships. The case was appealed to the Supreme Court.] Ogden (P) claimed the federal government did not have exclusive jurisdiction over commerce, but that the states had retained power by which they could regulate commerce within their own states and that the exclusive right to operate his ships only concerned intrastate commerce. Gibbons (D) contended that Congress had exclusive power to regulate interstate commerce and that New York had attempted to regulate interstate commerce by granting the exclusive right and enforcing it with the injunction.

ISSUE: If a state law conflicts with a congressional act regulating commerce, is the congressional act controlling?

HOLDING AND DECISION: (Marshall, C.J.) Yes. If a state law conflicts with a congressional act regulating commerce, the congressional act is controlling. The appellee Ogden (P) seeks to limit the meaning of the word commerce and have it apply only to traffic, or the buying or selling of commodities. Commerce certainly includes those meanings but is not limited to them. Commerce is the commercial intercourse between nations or parts of nations. If commerce does not embrace navigation, the government of the Union would have no direct power over this subject, but the fact is that this power over navigation has been exercised by the government from the beginning and it is understood as a commercial regulation. The subject to which the power is applied is commerce "among the several states." Commerce among the states cannot stop at the external boundary line of each state but applies to the interior as well. However, where commerce does not concern more than one state, and where it is conducted exclusively within one state, the federal government's power does not extend to such purely intrastate commerce. The government thus has the power to regulate navigation between states as part of its general commerce power. [The Court dismissed Ogden's (P) suit to obtain an injunction against Gibbons (D)].

ANALYSIS

The federal commerce power is concurrent with state power over commerce within the state. Hence, the Court has been asked many times to define the line between federal and state power to regulate commerce. During the early history of the United States, the Court was not often called upon to determine the scope of federal power under the Commerce Clause. Instead, the early cases generally involved some state action that was claimed to discriminate against or burden interstate commerce. Hence, the Commerce Clause operated as a restraint upon state powers. Most of these cases did not involve any exercise of the commerce power by Congress at all. *Gibbons v. Ogden* stands for the important principle that even where Congress has not acted under its commerce power, state regulation affecting interstate commerce will often be foreclosed. This is called Congress's negative or dormant commerce power. Large-scale regulatory action by Congress began with the Interstate Commerce Act in 1887 and the Sherman Anti-Trust Act in 1890. Challenges to these statutes initiated the major modern confrontations between the Court and congressional authority regarding commerce.

Quicknotes

COMMERCE POWER The power delegated to Congress by the U.S. Constitution to regulate interstate commerce.

Continued on next page.

DORMANT COMMERCE CLAUSE The regulatory effect of the Commerce Clause on state activity affecting interstate commerce, where Congress itself has not acted to control the activity; a provision inferred from, but not expressly present in, the language of the Commerce Clause.

INJUNCTION A court order requiring a person to do, or prohibiting that person from doing, a specific act.

Hammer v. Dagenhart (The Child Labor Case)

U.S. Attorney General (D) v. Parent of child laborers (P)

247 U.S. 251 (1918)

NATURE OF CASE: Certiorari review of judgment enjoining enforcement of the Child Labor Act.

FACT SUMMARY: Congress passed a law prohibiting the shipment in interstate commerce of any products of any mills, mines, or factories that employed children.

RULE OF LAW
The making of goods and the mining of coal are not commerce, even if afterwards shipped or used in interstate commerce.

FACTS: Congress passed a law prohibiting the shipment in interstate commerce of any products of any mills, mines, or factories that employed children.

ISSUE: Is the making of goods and the mining of coal commerce if afterwards shipped or used in interstate commerce?

HOLDING AND DECISION: (Day, J.) No. The making of goods and the mining of coal are not commerce, even if afterwards shipped or used in interstate commerce. It is argued that the power of Congress to regulate commerce includes the power to prohibit the transportation of ordinary products in commerce. However, in cases such as *The Lottery Case*, 188 U.S. 321 (1903), the power to prohibit the carrying of lottery tickets is as to those particular objects the same as the exertion of the power to regulate. In those cases, the use of interstate commerce was necessary to the accomplishment of harmful results. Regulation over commerce could be achieved only by prohibiting the use of interstate commerce to affect the evil intended. Here, the purpose of taking this action is to deny interstate commerce facilities to those employing children within the prohibited ages. The goods shipped are of themselves harmless. The production of articles intended for interstate commerce is a matter of local regulation. The making of goods and the refining of coal are not commerce, nor does the fact that these things are to be afterwards shipped or used in interstate commerce make their production a part thereof. It is also argued that congressional regulation is necessary because of the unfair advantage possessed by manufacturers in states that have less stringent child labor laws. However, Congress has no power to require states to exercise their police powers to prevent possible unfair competition. The act is unconstitutional and the decree enjoining its enforcement is affirmed.

DISSENT: (Holmes, J.) *The Lottery Case*, 188 U.S. 321 (1903), and others following it establish that a law is not beyond Congress's commerce power merely because it prohibits certain transportation. There is no legal distinction between the evils sought to be controlled in those cases and the evil of premature and excessive child labor. The court has no right to substitute its judgment of which evils may be controlled.

ANALYSIS

After the *Hammer* decision, Congress sought to regulate child labor through the taxing power. The law was invalidated in *Bailey v. Drexel Furnishing Co.*, 259 U.S. 20 (1922). Subsequently, Congress submitted a proposed constitutional amendment to the states that authorized a national child labor law. The amendment has not been ratified, but the need for it has largely disappeared in view of *U.S. v. Darby*, 312 U.S. 100 (1941), which overruled *Hammer*.

Quicknotes

COMMERCE POWER The power delegated to Congress by the U.S. Constitution to regulate interstate commerce.

NLRB v. Jones & Laughlin Steel Corp.

Federal agency (P) v. Steel company (D)

301 U.S. 1 (1937)

NATURE OF CASE: Certiorari review of alleged unfair labor practice under the National Labor Relations Act.

FACT SUMMARY: Jones & Laughlin Steel Corp. (Jones & Laughlin) (D), a manufacturing company with subsidiaries in several states and nationwide sales, was charged with an unfair labor practice under the National Labor Relations Act. In defense, Jones & Laughlin (D) claimed that the Act was an unconstitutional attempt to regulate intrastate production.

RULE OF LAW

Under the Commerce Clause, Congress has the power to regulate any activity, even intrastate production, if the activity has an appreciable effect, either direct or indirect, on interstate commerce.

FACTS: Pursuant to a complaint filed by a labor union, the National Labor Relations Board (the Board) (P) found that Jones & Laughlin Steel Corp. (Jones & Laughlin) (D) had engaged in "unfair labor practices." The Board (P) issued a cease-and-desist order to Jones & Laughlin (D) to stop using discriminatory and coercive practices to prevent union organization at two steel plants in and around Pittsburgh. The company refused to comply, and the Board (P) went to court for judicial enforcement of its order under the authority of the National Labor Relations Act of 1935. Jones & Laughlin (D) contended that the order was an unconstitutional exercise of the Board's (P) authority since the plants were not engaged in interstate commerce, being totally manufacturing facilities. The court of appeals upheld the company's position and refused enforcement of the order on the ground that "the order lay[s] beyond the range of federal power."

ISSUE: Under the Commerce Clause, does Congress have the power to regulate any activity, even intrastate production, if the activity has an appreciable effect, either direct or indirect, on interstate commerce?

HOLDING AND DECISION: (Hughes, C.J.) Yes. Under the Commerce Clause, Congress has the power to regulate any activity, even intrastate production, if the activity has an appreciable effect, either direct or indirect, on interstate commerce. The act of the National Labor Relations Board (the Board) (P) ordering Jones & Laughlin Steel Corp. (Jones & Laughlin) (D) to cease interfering with its employees' rights of self-organization and collective bargaining is an exercise of the congressional power to regulate interstate commerce. The definitions in the National Labor Relations Act (the Act) restrict the Board's (P) actions to protecting interstate commerce in the constitutional sense, and the Board (P) is given the power to determine if the practice in question affects commerce in such a way as to be subject to federal control. Congress has the power to protect interstate commerce by all appropriate types of legislation, and the controlling question is the effect on interstate commerce, not the source of the interference. Although such legislation may result in the regulation of acts that are intrastate in character, Congress still has the power to regulate if the intrastate acts bear such a close and substantial relation to interstate commerce that control is appropriate for the protection of commerce. Congress is forbidden only from regulating acts that have a remote and indirect effect on interstate commerce. Here, even though the application of the Act results in the regulation of labor practices at Jones & Laughlin's (D) manufacturing plants, the circumstances indicate the required substantial effect on interstate commerce. If production were interrupted at one of the plants due to a labor dispute, the extensive nationwide operations of Jones & Laughlin (D) indicate that there would necessarily be an immediate effect on interstate commerce. Therefore, the Act as applied to the facts of this case is a proper exercise of Congress's power to regulate interstate commerce. Reversed.

DISSENT: (McReynolds, J.) The majority reasons that there is an effect on interstate commerce in the following manner: if the employer discharges a few employees for union activities, this will create discontent among the remaining employees which will lead to a strike which may result in reduced production which may decrease the volume of goods in interstate commerce. This is obviously only a remote and indirect effect on interstate commerce and not subject to federal regulation. Manufacturing and production are purely local activities, even if the raw materials come from another state and the finished goods are shipped across state lines.

ANALYSIS

With this case the Supreme Court retreated from its strict geographical definition of interstate commerce and the direct/indirect approach that it used in *Schecter*, 295 U.S. 495 (1935), and *Carter*, 298 U.S. 238 (1936). *Jones & Laughlin* states that under the Commerce Clause, Congress has the power to regulate any activity that has a significant effect on interstate commerce, regardless of whether that effect is direct or indirect. This new concept is often called the "affectation doctrine." Although the Court cited prior cases in its opinion and said it was

Continued on next page.

not creating new law, *Jones & Laughlin* is, in effect, a reversal of the *Schecter* line of cases. The Court now bases its opinions on a combination of the Commerce Clause and the Necessary and Proper Clause: the power to regulate interstate commerce extends to control over intrastate activities when necessary and appropriate to make regulation of interstate commerce effective.

Quicknotes

INTRASTATE Any activity that takes place entirely within a single state and thus does not trigger regulation under the Commerce Clause.

United States v. Darby

Federal government (P) v. Lumber manufacturer (D)

312 U.S. 100 (1941)

NATURE OF CASE: Appeal from denial to quash indictment for violation of Fair Labor Standards Act.

FACT SUMMARY: Darby (D) was a lumber manufacturer, some of whose goods were later shipped in interstate commerce. He was indicted for violation of the wage and hour provisions of the Fair Labor Standards Act and defended on the ground that as an intrastate producer he was not subject to federal regulation.

RULE OF LAW

Congress has the power to regulate the hours and wages of workers who are engaged in the production of goods destined for interstate commerce and can prohibit the shipment in interstate commerce of goods manufactured in violation of the wage and hour provisions.

FACTS: Darby (D) was a manufacturer of finished lumber, and a large part of the lumber he produced was shipped in interstate commerce. The purpose of the Fair Labor Standards Act (the Act) was to prevent the shipment in interstate commerce of certain products produced under substandard labor conditions. The Act set up minimum wages and maximum hours and punished the shipment in interstate commerce of goods produced in violation of the wage/hour requirements, and also punished the employment of persons in violation of those requirements. Darby (D) was arrested for both shipment of goods in violation of the Act and employment of workers in violation of the Act. The trial court dismissed the indictment on the ground that the Act was an unconstitutional regulation of manufacturing within the states.

ISSUE: Does Congress have the power to prohibit shipment in interstate commerce of goods produced in violation of the wage and hour provisions of the Fair Labor Standards Act and the power to prohibit employment of workers involved in the production of goods for interstate shipment in violation of the wage/hour provisions of the Fair Labor Standards Act?

HOLDING AND DECISION: (Stone, J.) Yes. Congress has the power to regulate the hours and wages of workers who are engaged in the production of goods destined for interstate commerce and can prohibit the shipment in interstate commerce of goods manufactured in violation of the wage and hour provisions. Both prohibitions are a constitutional exercise of Congress's commerce power. Although manufacturing itself is not interstate commerce, the shipment of goods across state lines is interstate commerce and the prohibition of such shipment is a regulation of commerce. Congress has plenary power to exclude from interstate commerce any article that it determines to be injurious to public welfare, subject only to the specific prohibitions of the Constitution. In the Fair Labor Standards Act, Congress has determined that the shipment of goods produced under substandard labor conditions is injurious to commerce and therefore has the power to prohibit the shipment of such goods, independent of the indirect effect of such prohibition on the states. The prohibition of employment of workers engaged in the production of goods for interstate commerce at substandard conditions is also sustainable, independent of the power to exclude the shipment of the goods so produced. The power over interstate commerce is not confined to the regulation of commerce among the states but includes regulation of intrastate activities that so affect interstate commerce as to make regulation of them an appropriate means to the end of regulating interstate commerce. Here, Congress has determined that the employment of workers in substandard conditions is a form of unfair competition injurious to interstate commerce, since the goods so produced will be lower priced than the goods produced under adequate conditions. Such a form of competition would hasten the spread of substandard conditions and produce a dislocation of commerce and the destruction of many businesses. Since Congress has the power to suppress this form of unfair competition and the Act is an appropriate means to that end, the wage/hour provisions are within Congress's power. It is irrelevant that only part of the goods produced will be shipped in interstate commerce; Congress has the power to regulate the whole factory even though only a part of the products will have an effect on interstate commerce. Reversed.

ANALYSIS

Darby, like the preceding case of *Jones & Laughlin*, 301 U.S. 1 (1937), is an example of the application of the affectation doctrine. It had long been the law that Congress had the power to exclude from interstate commerce harmful objects or immoral activities, such as mismarked goods or lottery tickets. This case extends the power to exclude articles produced under conditions that Congress considered harmful to the national welfare. Even though production of lumber was an entirely intrastate activity, it was a part of an economic

Continued on next page.

process that led to the eventual sale of lumber across state limits, affecting interstate commerce. The federal commerce power extends to purely intrastate transactions; the effect on commerce, not the location of the regulated act, is the basis for the exercise of the federal power. This case overruled the earlier case of *Hammer v. Dagenhart*, 247 U.S. 251 (1918), which held unconstitutional an attempt by Congress to exclude articles made by child labor from interstate commerce.

Quicknotes

COMMERCE POWER The power delegated to Congress by the U.S. Constitution to regulate interstate commerce.

PLENARY Unlimited and open; as broad as a given situation may require.

Wickard v. Filburn

Department of Agriculture (P) v. Farmer (D)

317 U.S. 111 (1942)

NATURE OF CASE: Action to enjoin enforcement of penalty provisions of the Agricultural Adjustment Act.

FACT SUMMARY: Filburn (D) was ordered to pay a penalty imposed by the Agriculture Adjustment Act for producing wheat in excess of his assigned quota. He argued that the federal regulations could not be constitutionally applied to his crops because part of his crop was intended for his own consumption, not for interstate commerce.

RULE OF LAW

Farm production that is intended for consumption on the farm is subject to Congress's commerce power, since it may have a substantial economic effect on interstate commerce.

FACTS: The purpose of the Agriculture Adjustment Act (the Act) was to control the volume of wheat moving in interstate commerce to avoid surpluses and shortages that would result in abnormally high or low prices and thereby obstruct commerce. Under the Act, the Secretary of Agriculture would set a national acreage allotment for wheat production, which would be divided into allotments for individual farms. Filburn (D) was the owner and operator of a small farm. In the past he had grown a small amount of wheat of which he sold part, fed part to poultry and livestock (some of the livestock were later sold), used part in making flour for home consumption, and kept the rest for seeding the next year. In 1940, his wheat production exceeded the maximum he was allowed under the Act and he was assessed a penalty for the excess. Filburn (D) refused to pay on the ground the Act was unconstitutional in that it attempted to regulate purely local production and consumption that, at most, had an indirect effect on interstate commerce. The Government (P) argued the Act regulated not production and consumption, but only marketing (which was defined in the Act to include the feeding of the wheat to livestock that was later sold), and even if interpreted to include production and consumption, it was a legitimate exercise of the Commerce Clause and the Necessary and Proper Clause.

ISSUE: Is farm production that is intended for consumption on the farm subject to Congress's comer power, since it may have a substantial economic effect on interstate commerce?

HOLDING AND DECISION: (Jackson, J.) Yes. Farm production that is intended for consumption on the farm is subject to Congress's commerce power, since it may have a substantial economic effect on interstate commerce. A local activity, such as production, may be reached under the Commerce Clause if it exerts a substantial economic effect on interstate commerce. The Agriculture Adjustment Act (the Act) was enacted because of the problems of the wheat market: there had been a decrease in export in recent years, causing surpluses that in turn caused congestion in the market and lower prices. It has been repeatedly held that the commerce power of Congress includes the power to regulate prices and practices affecting prices. Wheat destined for home consumption has an effect on the interstate price of wheat and is therefore subject to regulation. As the market price of wheat climbs, farmers will sell more of their crop that was intended for home consumption on the market, causing a decrease in prices. Even if the wheat is never sold, there still is a substantial effect on interstate commerce because it reduces demand for wheat; that wheat which Filburn (D) produces for his own use means he will buy less wheat on the market. Although the actual effect of Filburn's (D) overproduction will be small, the combination of all such producers does cause a substantial effect on commerce.

ANALYSIS

Wickard is yet another application of the "affectation doctrine." The Court focuses not on the nature of the regulated activity (e.g., whether it is local) but on the final economic effect of that activity. Here, although the effect of Filburn's (D) excess wheat production was insignificant on the national market, there still was some effect, at least in theory, so regulation was allowed. The Court in *Wickard* expressly rejected the old formulas for determining the extent of the commerce power such as direct/indirect and production/commerce.

Quicknotes

LOCAL ACTIVITY An activity such as mining or manufacturing that has only an indirect effect in interstate commerce because it can be conducted entirely within the boundaries of the state.

NECESSARY AND PROPER CLAUSE, ART. I, § 8 OF THE U.S. CONSTITUTION Enables Congress to make all laws that may be "necessary and proper" to execute its other, enumerated powers.

United States v. Lopez

Federal government (P) v. Student (D)

514 U.S. 549 (1995)

NATURE OF CASE: Appeal from order reversing federal firearms law violation conviction.

FACT SUMMARY: Lopez (D) was convicted under the 1990 federal Gun-Free School Zones Act, which prohibited guns near schools.

RULE OF LAW

The 1990 federal Gun-Free School Zones Act exceeded Congress's Commerce Clause regulatory powers.

FACTS: The 1990 federal Gun-Free School Zones Act (the Act) made it a federal offense for a student to carry a gun onto campus. Lopez (D) was charged and convicted under the Act. On appeal, he contended that the Act was beyond Congress's powers under the Commerce Clause. The Fifth Circuit Court of Appeals agreed and reversed. The Supreme Court granted review.

ISSUE: Did the 1990 Federal Gun-Free School Zones Act exceed Congress's Commerce Clause regulatory powers?

HOLDING AND DECISION: (Rehnquist, C.J.) Yes. The 1990 federal Gun-Free School Zones Act exceeded Congress's Commerce Clause regulatory powers. It must be remembered that the federal government is one of limited, enumerated powers. For Congress to legislate, it must do so under an express constitutional provision. Since the 1930s, the Commerce Clause (the Clause) has been the source of most of Congress's legislative power. However, this Clause is not a general grant of police power. A law passed under this Clause must relate to (1) a channel of interstate commerce, (2) an instrumentality of interstate commerce, or (3) an activity having a substantial effect on interstate commerce. In this case, the regulated activity, carrying a gun to school, has no such effect. It is a purely local matter. Granted, if one is willing to accept a lengthy series of interferences and assumptions, such an activity may affect interstate commerce. Any activity can do so. However, if the concept of limited federal government is to have any meaning, Congress's legislative power must be cut off somewhere. That somewhere is the point at which a regulated activity does not substantially affect interstate commerce, and that point has been passed here. Affirmed.

CONCURRENCE: (Kennedy, J.) It is only with great care that this Court should intervene in matters relating to the Commerce Clause, as it is a matter best left to the political sectors of government. However, when an exercise of power under the Commerce Clause unduly upsets the balance of power between the states and the national government, as does the law at issue here, it is proper for the Court to intervene.

CONCURRENCE: (Thomas, J.) The substantial effects test is a New Deal innovation that goes far beyond the original intent of the Framers, who had a much narrower view of what was regulatable commerce. In fact, it grants Congress something approaching a general police power, a result clearly at odds with the Tenth Amendment.

DISSENT: (Breyer, J.) The education of our youth has a major impact on the national economy and is a proper subject for Commerce Clause regulation. In determining whether a regulated activity has a significant impact on interstate commerce, it is necessary to consider not a single example of the regulated activity, but rather the cumulative effects of all similar instances of that conduct. Here, it is clear the cumulative impact of the possession of weapons by students on campus will, over time, have a significant impact on the national economy.

DISSENT: (Souter, J.) The Court's approach today constitutes a step backward toward the excessive judicial activism that characterized judicial review of congressional enactments during the first third of this century.

DISSENT: (Stevens, J.) Congressional power to regulate commerce in firearms incorporates power to prohibit the possession of guns at any locations based on their potentially harmful use. It therefore follows that Congress also may prohibit their possession in specific markets. In this regard, the market for handgun possession by school-age children is substantial.

ANALYSIS

Since 1937, the scope of congressional regulatory power under the Commerce Clause has grown enormously. By the 1960s, Congress's power under the Commerce Clause had increased to a level approaching a general police power. The present case represents the first significant break in this pattern and may signal a states' rights trend.

Continued on next page.

Quicknotes

COMMERCE CLAUSE Article 1, section 8, clause 3 of the U.S. Constitution, granting Congress the power to regulate commerce with foreign countries and between the states.

ENUMERATED POWERS Those powers expressly delegated by the U.S. Constitution to a particular branch of government.

POLICE POWER The power of a government to impose restrictions on the rights of private persons, so long as those restrictions are reasonably related to the promotion and protection of public health, safety, morals, and the general welfare.

REGULATORY POWER Power granting authority pursuant to statute to a government agency or body to govern a particular area.

United States v. Morrison

Federal government (P) v. Students (D)

529 U.S. 598 (2000)

NATURE OF CASE: Certiorari to review constitutionality of Violence Against Women Act.

FACT SUMMARY: [Brzonkala (P) brought suit against two football-playing male students (D) and Virginia Polytechnic University under the Violence Against Women Act.]

RULE OF LAW

Commerce Clause regulation of intrastate activity may be upheld only where the regulated activity is economic in nature.

FACTS: [Brzonkala (P), a student at Virginia Polytechnic Institute, complained that two male football-playing students raped her. Virginia Tech's Judicial Committee found insufficient evidence to punish one and then set aside the other's punishment. Brzonkala (P) then dropped out of the university and brought suit against the school and the male students (D) under the Violence Against Women Act, 42 U.S.C. § 13981, providing a federal cause of action of a crime of violence motivated by gender. Brzonkala (P) argued, inter alia, that § 13981 falls under Congress's power to regulate those activities having a substantial relation to interstate commerce. The United States Supreme Court granted certiorari.]

ISSUE: May Commerce Clause regulation of intrastate activity be upheld only where the regulated activity is economic in nature?

HOLDING AND DECISION: (Rehnquist, C.J.) Yes. Commerce Clause regulation of intrastate activity may be upheld only where the regulated activity is economic in nature. In *Lopez*, 514 U.S. 549 (1995), this Court concluded that those cases in which federal regulation of intrastate activity (based on the activity's substantial effects on interstate commerce) has been sustained have included some type of economic endeavor. Gender-motivated crimes of violence are not economic activities. While the Violence Against Women Act, 42 U.S.C. § 13981 is supported by numerous findings regarding the serious impact that gender-motivated violence has on victims and their families, the existence of congressional findings is insufficient in itself to sustain the constitutionality of Commerce Clause legislation. Whether a particular activity affects interstate commerce sufficiently to come under the constitutional power of Congress to regulate is a judicial question. The Court also rejects the argument that Congress may regulate noneconomic, violent criminal conduct based solely on that conduct's aggregate effect on interstate commerce. If such reasoning were accepted, it would allow Congress to regulate any crime, or any other area traditionally regulated by the states, so long as the nationwide, aggregate impact of the conduct had substantial effects on employment, production, transit, or consumption. Such an approach is rejected, as under the Constitution there must be a distinction between what is truly national and what is truly local. Therefore, the regulation and punishment of intrastate violence that is not directed at the instrumentalities of interstate commerce is reserved to the states.

CONCURRENCE: (Thomas, J.) The notion of a substantial effects test is inconsistent with Congress's powers and early Commerce Clause jurisprudence, perpetuating the federal government's (P) view that the Commerce Clause has no limits.

DISSENT: (Souter, J.) Congress has the power to legislate regarding activities that in the aggregate have a substantial effect on interstate commerce. The fact of the substantial effect is a question for Congress in the first instance and not the courts. Here, Congress assembled a mountain of data demonstrating the effects of violence against women on interstate commerce. The sufficiency of the evidence before Congress to provide a rational basis for its finding cannot seriously be questioned. The majority departs from the understanding, enjoyed for over half a century, that congressional power under the Commerce Clause extends to all activity that, when aggregated, has a substantial effect on interstate commerce, and that politics, not judicial review, should mediate between national and state interests. The majority also ignores state support for the the Violence Against Women Act, based on the states' inadequate response to gender-based violence, and the states' belief that national action is essential.

DISSENT: (Breyer, J.) Congress, in enacting the statute, followed procedures that work to protect the federalism issues at stake. After considering alternatives, Congress developed the federal law with the intent of compensating for documented deficiencies in state legal systems and tailored federal law to prevent its use in areas traditionally reserved to the states. This law represents the result of state and federal efforts to cooperate in order to resolve a national problem. The nation is knit together by two centuries of scientific, technological, commercial, and environmental change, which effectively means that virtually every kind of activity, no matter how local, can affect commerce or its conditions outside any given

Continued on next page.

state when considered in the aggregate. Thus, it is nearly impossible for judges to develop meaningful subject-matter categories that would exclude some kinds of local activities from ordinary Commerce Clause "aggregation" rules without, at the same time, depriving Congress of its power to regulate activities that have a genuine and important effect on interstate commerce. Because judges are ill-equipped to make these types of distinctions, Congress, not the courts, must remain the institution primarily responsible for striking the appropriate state/federal balance.

ANALYSIS

The primary issue here is that the federal government is seeking to regulate areas that have been traditionally regulated by the states alone. The majority concludes that the regulation and punishment of intrastate violence that is not directed to the instrumentalities of interstate commerce is the exclusive jurisdiction of local government. What the dissent argues here is that Congress in this case has amassed substantial findings to demonstrate that such intrastate violence does have an effect on the instrumentalities of commerce.

Quicknotes

COMMERCE CLAUSE Article 1, § 8, clause 3 of the U.S. Constitution, granting Congress the power to regulate commerce with foreign countries and between the states.

FOURTEENTH AMENDMENT Declares that no state shall make or enforce any law that shall abridge the privileges and immunities of citizens of the United States; no state shall deny to any person within its jurisdiction the equal protection of the laws.

VIOLENCE AGAINST WOMEN ACT Legislation passed in 1994 that provides harsh federal penalties for sexual assaults commonly perpetrated against women and that authorizes funding for training, counseling, and treatment programs for victims of these specific forms of violence, including battered women's shelters and projects serving victims of domestic violence and child abuse.

Gonzales v. Raich

Attorney General (D) v. Medicinal user of marijuana (P)

545 U.S. 1 (2005)

NATURE OF CASE: Certiorari review of challenge to the validity of the federal Controlled Substances Act as applied to the medicinal use of marijuana.

FACT SUMMARY: Two sufferers of serious physical ailments sought to grow and use marijuana for medicinal purposes as permitted by California law.

RULE OF LAW

The Commerce Clause permits Congress to criminalize local cultivation and medicinal use of marijuana even if those uses otherwise comply with a state's laws.

FACTS: Congress enacted the Controlled Substances Act (the CSA), which could be interpreted to proscribe possessing, obtaining, or manufacturing marijuana for personal medicinal use. Angel Raich (P) and Diane Monson (P), California residents who suffered from serious medical conditions, wanted to use marijuana for medicinal purposes, a use permitted by California law. Raich (P) and Monson (P) sued the Government (D) for injunctive and declaratory relief to prohibit the CSA from being enforced against them.

ISSUE: Does the Commerce Clause permit Congress to criminalize local cultivation and medicinal use of marijuana even if those uses otherwise comply with a state's laws?

HOLDING AND DECISION: (Stevens, J.) Yes. The Commerce Clause permits Congress to criminalize local cultivation and medicinal use of marijuana even if those uses otherwise comply with a state's laws. Congress may regulate local economic activities that substantially affect interstate commerce. As applied to Angel Raich (P) and Diane Monson (P), the CSA would comply with that standard: the statute would regulate home-grown, home-used marijuana, an activity that would substantially affect the nationwide market for marijuana. The decisions in *United States v. Morrison*, 529 U.S. 598 (2000), and *Lopez v. United States*, 514 U.S. 549 (1995), are inapposite because those cases decided challenges to entire statutes, and they involved no economic activity; the proposed use here seeks only to invalidate local enforcement of the Controlled Substances Act for a very specific purpose, and the use is also an economic activity. Vacated and remanded.

CONCURRENCE: (Scalia, J.) By itself the Commerce Clause is insufficient to support the Controlled Substances Act's (the CSA's) application against Raich (P) and Monson (P). The CSA has the essential additional support, however, in the Necessary and Proper Clause, which permits Congress to regulate local, noneconomic activity if the regulation is necessary to effectuate valid legislation enacted pursuant to the Commerce Clause. Here, congressional regulation of Raich's (P) and Monson's (P) proposed use of marijuana should be permitted as a necessary part of the CSA's overall regulatory scheme.

DISSENT: (O'Connor, J.) The Court today denies California citizens the ability to serve as a national laboratory on the question of medicinal use of marijuana. Contrary to precedent, the majority has upheld federal law under the Commerce Clause without any proof that the proposed use of marijuana constitutes economic activity or that the use substantially affects interstate commerce even if it is economic activity. Today's definition of "economic activity" is effectively unlimited because the marijuana at issue here was never remotely involved in interstate commerce. Moreover, there was no evidence that in-home medicinal use of marijuana makes up a large enough proportion of the national market for marijuana to be detected at all, let alone to be seen as "substantially affecting" the national market. Regardless of how this Court might assess the wisdom of California's laws, the state's citizens should be permitted to conduct the local experiment that they chose.

DISSENT: (Thomas, J.) This decision means that Congress can regulate almost anything under the Commerce Clause. Today's decision is wrong because merely possessing an item for personal use is not economic activity within the meaning of the Commerce Clause. The Controlled Substances Act fares no better under the Necessary and Proper Clause because regulating these proposed uses is not "necessary" based on some failure of California's law. The regulation also is not "proper" because it would undermine federalism and states' rights.

ANALYSIS

In the years since this decision was handed down, an increasing number of states have legalized the use of marijuana not only for medicinal purposes but for recreational use as well, and efforts to decriminalize marijuana at the federal level have also increased. In light of these developments and the experiences states have had with legalized marijuana, the dissenters' admonitions that there is no proof that in-state personal use

Continued on next page.

of marijuana impacts interstate commerce and that the Controlled Substances Act violates states' rights in this regard, carry stronger weight. Moreover, the Court itself has increasingly been protecting states' rights against federal interference through the Tenth Amendment, on the theory that such interference is incompatible with the system of dual sovereignty embedded in the Constitution.

Quicknotes

INJUNCTIVE RELIEF A court order issued as a remedy, requiring a person to do, or prohibiting that person from doing, a specific act.

National Federation of Independent Business v. Sebelius

Business group (P) v. Government official (D)

567 U.S. 519 (2012)

NATURE OF CASE: Appeal from judgment in action challenging the constitutionality of the "individual mandate" provision of the 2010 Patient Protection and Affordable Care Act.

FACT SUMMARY: A coalition of plaintiffs (P) challenged the constitutionality of the "individual mandate" provision of the 2010 Patient Protection and Affordable Care Act. The Government (D) contended that the individual mandate was a valid exercise of Congress's authority under the Commerce Clause and the Necessary and Proper Clause.

RULE OF LAW

The "individual mandate" provision of the Patient Protection and Affordable Care Act, which requires individuals to purchase health care insurance under certain circumstances, is not a valid exercise of Congress's power under the Commerce Clause.

FACTS: In 2010, Congress enacted the Patient Protection and Affordable Care Act (the Act) in order to increase the number of Americans covered by health insurance and decrease the cost of health care. A key provision of the Act is the individual mandate, which requires most Americans to maintain "minimum essential" health insurance coverage. For individuals who are not exempt and who do not receive health insurance through an employer or government program, the means of satisfying the requirement is to purchase insurance from a private company. Those who do not comply with the mandate must make a "shared responsibility payment" to the federal government based on income and subject to a statutory cap. A coalition of plaintiffs (P) challenged the individual mandate as unconstitutional. The Government (D) contended the individual mandate was a valid exercise of Congress's authority under the Commerce Clause and the Necessary and Proper Clause. The Government (D) asserted the health care market is characterized by a significant cost-shifting problem. This problem arises because, according to the Government (D), everyone will eventually need health care at a time and to an extent they cannot predict, but if they do not have insurance, they often will not be able to pay that care. Because state and federal laws nonetheless require hospitals to provide a certain degree of care to individuals without regard to their ability to pay, hospitals end up receiving compensation for only a portion of the services they provide. To recoup the losses, hospitals pass on the cost to insurers through higher rates, and insurers, in turn, pass on the cost to policyholders in the form of higher premiums. Congress estimated that the cost of uncompensated care raises family health insurance premiums, on average, by over $1,000 per year. To address this problem, at least in part, Congress included "guaranteed-issue" and "community-rating" provisions in the Act. These provisions together prohibit insurance companies from denying coverage to those with preexisting conditions or charging unhealthy individuals higher premiums than healthy individuals. The guaranteed-issue and community-rating reforms do not, however, address the issue of healthy individuals who choose not to purchase insurance to cover potential health care needs. In fact, the reforms sharply exacerbate that problem, by providing an incentive for individuals to delay purchasing health insurance until they become sick, relying on the promise of guaranteed and affordable coverage. The reforms also threaten to impose massive new costs on insurers, who are required to accept unhealthy individuals but prohibited from charging them rates necessary to pay for their coverage. This will lead insurers to significantly increase premiums on everyone. The individual mandate was Congress's solution to these problems. By requiring that individuals purchase health insurance, the mandate prevents cost shifting by those who would otherwise go without it. In addition, the mandate forces into the insurance risk pool more healthy individuals, whose premiums on average will be higher than their health care expenses. This allows insurers to subsidize the costs of covering the unhealthy individuals that the reforms require them to accept. The Government (D) contended, inter alia, that the individual mandate is within Congress's power because the failure to purchase insurance "has a substantial and deleterious effect on interstate commerce" by creating the cost-shifting problem. The Supreme Court granted certiorari.

ISSUE: Is the "individual mandate" provision of the Patient Protection and Affordable Care Act, which requires individuals to purchase health care insurance under certain circumstances, a valid exercise of Congress's power under the Commerce Clause?

HOLDING AND DECISION: (Roberts, C.J.) No. The "individual mandate" provision of the Patient Protection and Affordable Care Act (the Act), which requires individuals to purchase health care insurance under certain circumstances, is not a valid exercise of Congress's power under the Commerce Clause. Congress has never attempted to rely on the commerce power to

Continued on next page.

compel individuals not engaged in commerce to purchase an unwanted product—and with good reason. Congress is empowered to regulate commerce, which presupposes the existence of commercial activity to be regulated. If the power to "regulate" something included the power to create it, many of the provisions in the Constitution would be superfluous. The Constitution's language supports such a conclusion, as does the Court's precedent, which uniformly describes the commerce power as reaching "activity." The individual mandate, however, does not regulate existing commercial activity. It instead compels individuals to become active in commerce by purchasing a product, on the ground their failure to do so affects interstate commerce. Construing the Commerce Clause to permit Congress to regulate individuals precisely because they are doing nothing would open a new and potentially vast domain to congressional authority, as the Government's (D) logic would justify a mandatory purchase to solve almost any problem. People, for reasons of their own, often fail to do things that would be good for them or good for society. Those failures—joined with the similar failures of others—can readily have a substantial effect on interstate commerce. Under the Government's (D) logic, that authorizes Congress to use its commerce power to compel citizens to act as the Government (D) would have them act. Congress already possesses expansive power to regulate what people do. Upholding the Act under the Commerce Clause would give Congress the same license to regulate what people do not do. The Framers knew the difference between doing something and doing nothing. They gave Congress the power to regulate commerce, not to compel it. Ignoring that distinction would undermine the principle that the federal government is a government of limited and enumerated powers. Contrary to the Government's (D) contention, the uninsured to be affected by the individual are not "active in the market for health care." In fact, the individual mandate's regulation of the uninsured as a class is particularly divorced from any link to existing commercial activity. The mandate primarily affects healthy, often young adults who are less likely to need significant health care and have other priorities for spending their money. It is precisely because these individuals, as an actuarial class, incur relatively low health care costs that the mandate helps counter the effect of forcing insurance companies to cover others who impose greater costs than their premiums are allowed to reflect. If the individual mandate is targeted at a class, it is a class whose commercial inactivity rather than activity is its defining feature. The Commerce Clause is not a general license to regulate an individual from cradle to grave, simply because he or she will predictably engage in particular transactions. Any police power to regulate individuals as such, as opposed to their activities, remains vested in the States. The individual mandate thus cannot be sustained under Congress's power to "regulate Commerce."

DISSENT: (Scalia, J.) It is manifestly clear there are structural limitations on the commerce power and on what Congress can prescribe with respect to private conduct, and upon what it can impose upon the states. To say Congress's commerce power reaches inactivity would be to permit Congress to regulate virtually every aspect of human activity and inactivity. If the individual mandate regulates anything it is the failure to maintain minimum essential coverage. That failure is abstention from commerce, not commerce. One does not regulate commerce that does not exist by compelling its existence. The fact the proposed regulations will impose great costs on the health insurance industry does not justify pressing into service healthy individuals who could be but are not customers of the relevant industry, to offset the undesirable consequences of the regulation. Congress's desire to force these individuals to purchase insurance is motivated by the fact they are further removed from the market than unhealthy individuals with preexisting conditions, because they are less likely to need extensive care in the near future. If Congress can reach out and command even those furthest removed from an interstate market to participate in the market, then the Commerce Clause becomes a font of unlimited power. Precedent makes clear the Commerce Clause, even when supplemented by the Necessary and Proper Clause, is not carte blanche for doing whatever will help achieve the ends Congress seeks by the regulation of commerce. The precedent on which the Government (D) relies to support the individual mandate is also distinguishable, as that precedent did not represent the expansion of the federal power to direct into a broad new field. The mandating of economic activity does, and since it is a field so limitless that it converts the Commerce Clause into a general authority to direct the economy, that mandating is inconsistent with the letter and spirit of the Constitution. Moreover, in that precedent, the prohibition was the only practicable way of achieving the desired outcome. Here, in contrast, there are many ways other than the individual mandate by which the regulatory scheme's goals of reducing insurance premiums and ensuring the profitability of insurers could be achieved. For example, those who did not purchase insurance could be subjected to a surcharge when they do enter the health insurance system, or they could be denied a full income tax credit given to those who do purchase the insurance. Also, the Government's (D) argument the individual mandate regulates activities having a substantial relation to interstate commerce must be rejected. The Government (D) argues the provision directs the manner in which individuals purchase health care services and related goods, but the primary problem with this argument is it does not apply only to persons who purchase all, or most, or even any, of the health care

Continued on next page.

services or goods the mandated insurance covers. Those persons—generally healthy and young—are not participants in the health care market the individual mandate purports to regulate. Because the decision to forgo participation in an interstate market is not itself commercial activity within Congress's power to regulate, the individual mandate cannot be justified by claiming it regulates such decisions because they have a substantial and deleterious effect on interstate commerce. If the Government (D) is permitted to regulate everyone who may at some point engage in commerce, there no longer will be any limits on the Government's (D) powers. The Justice Ginsburg in her dissent dismisses the conclusion that the power to compel entry into the health-insurance market would include the power to compel entry into other types of markets. She observes that purchasers in other markets will be forced to pay for goods or services received, whereas those refusing to purchase health insurance will ultimately get treated anyway, at others' expense. However, such differences do not show that the failure to enter the health-insurance market, unlike the failure to buy other types of products or services, is an activity that Congress can "regulate."

CONCURRENCE AND DISSENT: (Ginsburg, J.) Beyond question, Congress could have provided a single-payer federal health care scheme similar to Social Security, whereby the federal government would be the only health care insurer. However, it chose to preserve a central role for private insurers and state governments. According to the majority opinion on this issue, authored by the Chief Justice, the Commerce Clause does not permit that preservation. This rigid reading of the Clause makes scant sense and is stunningly retrogressive. The problem the Patient Protection and Affordable Care Act seeks to remedy with the individual mandate is that the uninsured heavily burden the national health-care market. Those with health insurance subsidize the medical care of those without it, or, in the words of economists, the uninsured "free ride" on those who pay for health insurance. States cannot resolve the problem of the uninsured on their own. A state offering universal health care would place itself in a position of economic disadvantage as compared with neighbors or competitors: the state would have to raise taxes, private health-insurance companies would have to increase premiums, and higher taxes and increased insurance costs would, in turn, encourage businesses and healthy individuals to leave the state. Because the states cannot resolve this problem on their own, Congress stepped in with the Act to provide a national solution. However, Congress comprehended guaranteed-issue and community-rating laws alone will not work. When insurance companies are required to insure the sick at affordable prices, individuals can wait until they become ill to buy insurance. The result is those in need of immediate medical care—i.e., those who cost insurers the most—become the insurance companies' main customers. This "adverse selection" problem leaves insurers with two choices: They can either raise premiums dramatically to cover their ever-increasing costs or they can exit the market. This, in fact, is what happened in those states that implemented guaranteed-issue and community-rating laws without requiring universal acquisition of insurance coverage, and the results were disastrous. In the one state—Massachusetts—that succeeded, almost all residents were required to obtain a minimum level of health insurance. Congress passed the minimum coverage provision as a key component of the Act to address an economic and social problem that has plagued the country for decades: the large number of U.S. residents who are unable or unwilling to obtain health insurance. Congress had the prerogative to make this policy decision, which passes muster under the Commerce Clause and the Necessary and Proper Clause. As to the Commerce Clause, precedent holds Congress's authority under the Commerce Clause is dependent upon "practical" considerations, including "actual experience," and Congress is afforded the leeway "to undertake to solve national problems directly and realistically." Here, Congress had a rational basis for concluding the uninsured, as a class, substantially affect interstate commerce. The individual mandate, furthermore, bears a "reasonable connection" to Congress's goal of protecting the health-care market from the disruption caused by individuals who fail to obtain insurance. By requiring those who do not carry insurance to pay a toll, the minimum coverage provision gives individuals a strong incentive to insure. This incentive, Congress had good reason to believe, would reduce the number of uninsured and, correspondingly, mitigate the adverse impact the uninsured have on the national health-care market. The inevitable yet unpredictable need for medical care and the guarantee that emergency care will be provided when required are conditions nonexistent in other markets. In other markets consumers must pay for the products or services they use and get no "free ride" at the expense of another consumer forced to pay an inflated price. Therefore, upholding the minimum coverage provision on the ground that all are participants or will be participants in the health-care market would carry no implication that Congress may justify under the Commerce Clause a mandate to buy other products and services.

ANALYSIS

The Court's former endeavors to impose categorical limits on the commerce power did not fare well. In several pre-New Deal cases, the Court attempted to cabin Congress's Commerce Clause authority by distinguishing "commerce" from activity once conceived

Continued on next page.

to be noncommercial, notably, "production," "mining," and "manufacturing." The Court also sought to distinguish activities having a "direct" effect on interstate commerce, and for that reason, subject to federal regulation, from those having only an "indirect" effect, and therefore not amenable to federal control. These line-drawing exercises were untenable, and the Court long ago abandoned them. Accordingly, Justice Ginsburg opines the Chief Justice has failed to learn from history and instead "plows ahead" with his formalistic distinction between those who are "active in commerce," and those who are not. She also, therefore, warns hindering Congress's ability to address the health care problem is shortsighted and predicts that if history is any guide, the Court's constriction of the Commerce Clause will not endure.

Quicknotes

COMMERCE CLAUSE Article 1, section 8, clause 3 of the U.S. Constitution, granting Congress the power to regulate commerce with foreign countries and among the states.

NECESSARY AND PROPER CLAUSE, ART. I, § 8 OF THE U.S. CONSTITUTION Enables Congress to make all laws that may be "necessary and proper" to execute its other, enumerated powers.

New York v. United States

State (P) v. Federal government (D)

505 U.S. 144 (1992)

NATURE OF CASE: Appeal of dismissal of suit for declaratory judgment.

FACT SUMMARY: New York (P) sought a declaration that the Low-Level Radioactive Waste Policy Amendments Act was unconstitutional.

RULE OF LAW

The federal government may not order a state government to enact particular legislation.

FACTS: Three states had disposal sites for radioactive waste. After study and negotiation, the National Governors' Association (NGA) devised a plan that became the Low-Level Radioactive Waste Policy Amendments Act (the 1985 Act). The 1985 Act set deadlines for every state to join a regional waste compact, develop instate disposal, or find another way to dispose of its own waste. The 1985 Act assured the sited states they would not have the entire nation's waste burden and gave the other 47 states seven more years of access to active sites. The 1985 Act provided three incentives for state compliance: (1) Congress authorized sited states to impose a surcharge, part of which would go into federal escrow, with funds to be returned to complying states; (2) Congress empowered sited states to deny access to states not in compliance; and (3) Congress compelled any state not in compliance by 1992 to either take title to all waste generated in their state or become liable to instate waste generators for all damages. As of 1990 New York (P) had not joined a regional waste compact. Unable to settle on an instate site, New York (P) sought to invalidate the 1985 Act as violative of state sovereignty principles of the Tenth Amendment. The sited states intervened as defendants. The district court dismissed, the court of appeals affirmed, and New York (P) appealed.

ISSUE: May the federal government order a state government to enact particular legislation?

HOLDING AND DECISION: (O'Connor, J.) No. The federal government may not order a state government to enact particular legislation. The federal government may provide incentives for states to regulate in a certain way by tying funding to acceptance of a federal plan or by giving states a choice between enacting a federal plan or having state law preempted by federal law. Here, the first incentive is a congressional exercise of Commerce Clause power (allowing sited states to impose a surcharge on interstate commerce and imposing a federal tax on that surcharge) combined with an exercise of Spending Clause power (making return of surcharges contingent on compliance with the federal plan). The second incentive is a routine exercise of the commerce power. If a state chooses not to follow the federal plan, generators of waste within that state become subject to federal regulation authorizing states with waste sites to deny access. The burden would fall on the waste generators, not on the state, and the state would not be forced to spend funds or accede to federal direction. The third incentive, however, crossed the line to coercion. Whether a state "chooses" to take title to waste or to accept liability for disposal, the burden of not enacting the federal plan falls on the state. The strength of the federal interest is irrelevant. Federal courts may issue directives to state officials, but the Constitution expressly grants that authority. Such authority is outside Congress's enumerated powers and, for that reason, also infringes on state sovereignty reserved by the Tenth Amendment. While the 1985 Act was a creation of and compromise among the states, the states may not constitutionally consent to give up their sovereignty. Affirmed as to the first two incentives, reversed as to the third.

DISSENT: (White, J.) The Low-Level Radioactive Waste Policy Amendments Act (the 1985 Act) was the product of cooperative federalism. The states bargained among themselves to solve an imminent crisis and achieve compromises for Congress to sanction. New York (P) reaped the benefits of the 1985 Act, an agreement it helped formulate, and should not be able to sue now. The majority wrongly finds that states cannot consent to relinquish some sovereignty. Tenth Amendment restrictions on the commerce power are procedural limits designed to prevent federal destruction of state governments, not to protect substantive areas of state autonomy.

CONCURRENCE AND DISSENT: (Stevens, J.) The notion that Congress may not order states to implement federal legislation is incorrect and unsound. The federal government regulates state railroads, schools, prisons, and elections, and in time of war, Congress undoubtedly could command states to supply soldiers.

ANALYSIS

Under the Articles of Confederation, the federal government could act only by ordering states to enact legislation. The Framers decided that the federal government needed power to regulate citizens directly and

Continued on next page.

so drafted the Constitution. The Court interpreted the Framers' decision as a rejection of federal power to order states to enact legislation.

Quicknotes

ENUMERATED POWERS Those powers expressly delegated by the U.S. Constitution to a particular branch of government.

STATE SOVEREIGNTY The absolute power of self-government possessed by a state.

CHAPTER 4

The National Taxing and Spending Powers and Their Federalism-Based Limits

Quick Reference Rules of Law

Child Labor Tax Case (Bailey v. Drexel Furniture Co.)

Collector of internal revenue (D) v. Furniture company (P)

259 U.S. 20 (1922)

NATURE OF CASE: Certiorari review of the constitutionality of the Child Labor Tax Law.

FACT SUMMARY: The Child Labor Tax Law imposes a tax upon persons employing children under certain ages.

RULE OF LAW

A law passed by Congress under the pretext of executing its powers, but which is for the accomplishment of objects not within congressional power, is unconstitutional.

FACTS: The Child Labor Act provides that any company employing children in violation of its provisions shall pay a tax equal to 10 percent of its net profits. The Act provides that mines and quarries shall not employ children under the age of 16; mills, canneries, and factories shall not employ children under the age of 14; and children under the age of 16 shall not work more than eight hours a day, more than six days a week, or before 6 a.m. or after 7 p.m. Anyone employing children believing them to be of the proper age is relieved of liability. Both the Internal Revenue Service and the Labor Department are given the authority to enter and inspect any mine, quarry, mill, cannery, or factory. [Drexel Furniture Co. (P) paid an approximately $6000 tax under protest, and after rejection of its claim for a refund, brought this suit.]

ISSUE: Is a law passed by Congress under the pretext of executing its powers, but which is for the accomplishment of objects not within congressional power constitutional?

HOLDING AND DECISION: (Taft, C.J.) No. A law passed by Congress under the pretext of executing its powers, but which is for the accomplishment of objects not within congressional power, is unconstitutional. The principle announced by Marshall in *McCulloch v. Maryland*, 17 U.S. 316 (1819), is applicable here. "Should Congress, under the pretext of executing its powers, pass laws for the accomplishment of objects not entrusted to the government, it would be the painful duty of this tribunal . . . to say that such an act was not the law of the land." The Child Labor Tax Law concerns the regulation of the employment of children in the states, an exclusively state function under the Constitution. It provides a heavy extraction for a departure from a detailed and specified course of conduct in business. The amount of the tax is not to be proportioned to the degree or the frequency of the violation. Moreover, only employers who knew that the children were underage will be taxed. Scienter is associated with penalties, not taxes. Further, factories, etc., are to be subject to inspection by the Secretary of Labor as well as the Internal Revenue Service, the department normally charged with tax collection. In light of these features, "A court must be blind not to see that the so-called tax is imposed to stop the employment of children within the age limits prescribed." It is true that taxes imposed with the primary motive of obtaining revenue may have an incidental motive of discouraging the taxed activity. These taxes do not lose their character as taxes because of the incidental motives. But there is a point in the extension of the penalizing features of the tax when it loses its character as a tax and becomes a mere penalty with the characteristics of regulation and punishment. Such is the case with the Child Labor Tax Law, and for these reasons it is invalid. Affirmed.

ANALYSIS

The taxing and spending powers have close functional and doctrinal ties to the commerce power since the manner in which taxes are imposed can have significant regulatory impacts. As with commerce laws, taxing measures have been used to deal with "police" as well as economic problems. The Court in *Drexel* noted the clear analogy between that case and *Hammer v. Dagenhart*, 247 U.S. 251 (1918), the child labor case. Regulations through taxing have been resorted to when the need for legislation seemed great and the direct regulatory authority through the Commerce Clause was "under constitutional clouds," such as in the cases of child labor and of New Deal legislation in the 1930s.

Quicknotes

SCIENTER Knowledge of certain facts; often refers to "guilty knowledge" that implicates liability.

TAXING POWER The authority delegated to Congress by the U.S. Constitution to impose taxes.

National Federation of Independent Business v. Sebelius

Business group (P) v. Government official (D)

567 U.S. 519 (2012)

NATURE OF CASE: Appeal from judgment in action challenging the constitutionality of the "individual mandate" provision of the 2010 Patient Protection and Affordable Care Act.

FACT SUMMARY: A coalition of plaintiffs (P) challenged the constitutionality of the "individual mandate" provision of the 2010 Patient Protection and Affordable Care Act. The Government (D) contended, inter alia, the individual mandate was a valid exercise of Congress's taxing power, since it provided that individuals who did not purchase health care insurance would pay a penalty in the form of a tax.

RULE OF LAW

The "individual mandate" provision of the Patient Protection and Affordable Care Act, which requires that individuals who do not purchase health care insurance under certain circumstances must pay a penalty in the form of a tax, is a valid exercise of Congress's taxing power.

FACTS: In 2010, Congress enacted the Patient Protection and Affordable Care Act (the Act) in order to increase the number of Americans covered by health insurance and decrease the cost of health care. A key provision of the Act is the individual mandate, which requires most Americans to maintain "minimum essential" health insurance coverage. For individuals who are not exempt and who do not receive health insurance through an employer or government program, the means of satisfying the requirement is to purchase insurance from a private company. Those who do not comply with the mandate must make a "shared responsibility payment" to the Internal Revenue Service (IRS), which is based on factors such as income, number of dependents, and joint filing status, and is subject to a statutory cap. A coalition of plaintiffs (P) challenged the individual mandate as unconstitutional. The Government (D) contended, inter alia, the individual mandate was a valid exercise of Congress's taxing power, since the Act provided the penalty would be paid to the IRS with an individual's taxes and "shall be assessed and collected in the same manner" as tax penalties. The imposition of the individual mandate was expected to raise $4 billion per year by its third year. The Supreme Court granted certiorari.

ISSUE: Is the "individual mandate" provision of the Patient Protection and Affordable Care Act, which requires that individuals who do not purchase health care insurance under certain circumstances must pay a penalty in the form of a tax, a valid exercise of Congress's taxing power?

HOLDING AND DECISION: (Roberts, C.J.) Yes. The "individual mandate" provision of the Patient Protection and Affordable Care Act (the Act), which requires that individuals who do not purchase health care insurance under certain circumstances must pay a penalty in the form of a tax, is a valid exercise of Congress's taxing power. The individual mandate must be construed as imposing a tax on those who do not have health insurance, if such a construction is reasonable. The most straightforward reading of the individual mandate is it commands individuals to purchase insurance. However, the Government's (D) alternative argument is that the mandate may be upheld as within Congress's power to "lay and collect Taxes." In pressing its taxing power argument, the Government (D) asks the Court to view the mandate as imposing a tax on those who do not buy a health insurance product. Granting the Act the full measure of deference owed to federal statutes, it can be so read, for the following reasons. First, the exaction imposed by the Act has many of the features of a tax, is functionally like a tax, and has the essential feature of a tax insofar as it raises revenue for the Government (D). Taking such a functional approach is confirmed by precedent. Second, taking such an approach, the exaction functions more like a tax than a penalty. For most Americans, the amount due will be far less than the price of insurance, and by statute, it can never be more. Also, the individual mandate contains no scienter requirement. Further, the payment is collected solely by the Internal Revenue Service (IRS) through the normal means of taxation—except the IRS is not allowed to use those means most suggestive of a punitive sanction, such as criminal prosecution. For these reasons, the exaction may be viewed as a tax and not as a penalty. Additionally, merely because the individual mandate is designed to regulate individual conduct and encourage the purchasing of health insurance does not mean it cannot be a valid exercise of the taxing power. To some extent, all taxes are regulatory in nature. While the individual mandate clearly aims to induce the purchase of health insurance, it need not be read to declare that failing to do so is unlawful. While Congress's taxing power has limits, so exactions cannot become punitive, the individual mandate passes muster as a tax and not as a punitive penalty. Accordingly, it comes within the strict limits within which Congress can tax. Congress's

Continued on next page.

authority under the taxing power is limited to requiring an individual to pay money to the federal government; the individual retains the choice whether to do or not do a certain act, so long as he or she is willing to pay a tax levied on that choice. In contrast, under the Commerce Clause Congress can command individuals to do as it commands. The individual mandate simply imposes a cost on the choice not to obtain health care insurance. Accordingly, the individual mandate may be characterized as a tax and comes within the Constitution's requirements.

DISSENT: (Scalia, J) There is a clear line between a tax and a penalty, and it has never been held that a penalty, no matter how trivial, is a tax. Where a statute contains the criteria of wrongdoing, and then imposes a monetary penalty for violation of the statute, the statute creates a regulatory penalty, not a tax. The individual mandate cannot be characterized as a tax, and to say that it is constitutes judicial rewriting of the statute. Taxes should not be legislated by the judiciary, and tax writing must originate in the House of Representatives because that is the branch of government most accountable to the citizenry.

ANALYSIS

The issue of whether the individual mandate comes within Congress's taxing power was reached only because the majority determined the Commerce Clause did not authorize the individual mandate's command to purchase insurance. Because the statute reads more naturally as a command to buy insurance than as a tax, and because the Court held the statute was unconstitutional as a command, the Court exercised its duty to construe the statute to save it, if fairly possible, if it could be interpreted as a tax. Without deciding the Commerce Clause question, the Court would have found no basis to adopt such a saving construction. Through the exercise of its duty of statutory construction, the Court upheld the individual mandate's constitutionality but only because the Court determined the statute could reasonably be read as a tax.

Quicknotes

TAXING POWER The authority delegated to Congress by the U.S. Constitution to impose taxes.

United States v. Butler

Federal government (D) v. Receivers (P)

297 U.S. 1 (1936)

NATURE OF CASE: Certiorari review of the constitutionality of the Agricultural Adjustment Act of 1933.

FACT SUMMARY: [The Agricultural Adjustment Act of 1933 stated that there was a national economic emergency arising from the low price of agricultural products in comparison with other commodities. To remedy this situation, a tax would be collected from processors of an agricultural product. The revenue raised would be paid to farmers who curtailed their production of that product.]

RULE OF LAW

Congress may not, under the pretext of exercising the taxing power, accomplish prohibited ends, such as the regulation of matters of purely state concern and clearly beyond its national powers.

FACTS: [The Agricultural Adjustment Act of 1933 (the Act) declared that a national economic emergency had arisen due to the disparity between the prices of agricultural and other commodities, resulting in the destruction of farmers' purchasing power. To remedy this situation, a tax would be collected from processors of agricultural products. The revenue raised thereby would be paid to farmers who voluntarily curtailed their production of those crops used by the processors. The Secretary of Agriculture was to determine the crops to which the Act's plan would apply. In July 1933, the Secretary determined that the Act's plan should be applied to cotton. A tax claim was presented to Butler (P) as receivers of the Hoosac Mills Corp., as cotton processors.] The district court held the tax to be valid, but the circuit court reversed.

ISSUE: May Congress, under the pretext of exercising the taxing power, accomplish prohibited ends, such as the regulation of matters of purely state concern and clearly beyond its national powers?

HOLDING AND DECISION: (Roberts, J.) No. Congress may not, under the pretext of exercising the taxing power, accomplish prohibited ends, such as the regulation of matters of purely state concern and clearly beyond its national powers. First, Butler (P) has standing to question the validity of the tax because it is but a part of the unconstitutional plan of the Agricultural Adjustment Act (the Act). A tax, as the term is used by the Constitution, is an exaction for the support of the government. It has never been thought to mean the expropriation of money from one group for the benefit of another, as is attempted by the Act in question here. The Act is unconstitutional in that it invades the rights of the states. It is a statutory plan to regulate and control agriculture production, a matter beyond the power of the federal government. The Government (D), in attempting to defend the Act, places great reliance on the fact that the Act's plan is voluntary. However, the farmer who chooses not to comply with the plan loses benefits. The power to confer or withhold unlimited benefits is the power to coerce or destroy. Even if the plan were truly voluntary, it would not be valid. At best, it is a scheme for purchasing with federal funds submission to federal regulation of a subject reserved to the states. Contracts for the reduction of acreage and the control of production are not within Congress's power. Congress has no power to enforce the ends sought by this Act onto the farmer. Hence, it may not indirectly accomplish those ends by taxing and spending to enforce them. If this Act is valid, Congress could exercise its power to regulate all industry. It could extract money from one branch of an industry and pay it to another branch. Congress may not, under the pretext of exercising the taxing power, accomplish prohibited ends. Affirmed.

DISSENT: (Stone, J.) Courts are to be concerned only with the power to enact statutes, not with their wisdom. The constitutional power of Congress to tax the processing of agricultural products is not questioned. The present tax is held to be invalid because the use to which its proceeds are to be put is disapproved. The tax is held to be invalid because it is a step in a plan to regulate agricultural production. The Court states that state powers are infringed by the expenditure of the proceeds of the tax to compensate farmers for the curtailment of their crop production. Such a limitation is contradictory and destructive of the power to appropriate for the public welfare and is incapable of practical application. Congress's spending power is not subordinate to its legislative powers. This independent grant of power presupposes freedom of selection among diverse ends and aims and the capacity to impose such conditions as will render the choice effective. It is contradictory to say that there is a power to spend for the national welfare, while rejecting any power to impose conditions reasonably adapted to the end which justifies the expenditure. If appropriation in aid of a program of curtailment is constitutional, and it is not denied that it is, payment to farmers on condition that they reduce their crop acreage is constitutional.

Continued on next page.

ANALYSIS

The *Butler* decision contributed greatly to the pressure that produced the court-packing plan a few months later. It is called the landmark case in the area of federal regulation of local matters through taxation. However, if the tax and the appropriation provisions had not been so closely tied together, it is doubtful that the Court would have invalidated the tax. The tax appeared to have a valid revenue-raising purpose, and once separated from the taxing provisions, there would have been no one withstanding to attack the appropriation.

Quicknotes

COURT PACKING PLAN An attempt to alter the composition of a court to maximize concurrence with the appointing officer's views.

SPENDING POWER The power delegated to Congress by the U.S. Constitution to spend money in providing for the nation's welfare.

South Dakota v. Dole

State (P) v. Federal government (D)

483 U.S. 203 (1987)

NATURE OF CASE: Certiorari review of decisions upholding federal highway funding requirement.

FACT SUMMARY: Congress passed a law withholding federal highway funds to states with a minimum drinking age of less than 21 years.

RULE OF LAW

Congress may withhold federal highway funds to states with a minimum drinking age of less than 21 years.

FACTS: [In 1984, Congress enacted 23 U.S.C. § 158, which directed the Secretary of Transportation to withhold 5 percent of federal highway funds to states with a drinking age of less than 21 years of age. This was based on the perception that border-states with drinking ages of less than 21 encouraged drinking and driving. South Dakota (P) sought a declaration that the law was unconstitutional.] The district and circuit courts upheld the law, and the Supreme Court granted review.

ISSUE: May Congress withhold federal highway funds to states with a minimum drinking age of less than 21 years?

HOLDING AND DECISION: (Rehnquist, C.J.) Yes. Congress may withhold federal highway funds to states with a minimum drinking age of less than 21 years. It is well recognized that Congress may use its spending power to induce cooperation by states in areas it cannot necessarily regulate directly. Therefore, even if Congress could not directly legislate state drinking ages, it can use the threat of withheld funds to achieve its regulatory goal. South Dakota (P) argued that alcohol is a special case, as the Twenty-first Amendment specifically leaves the regulation of drinking to the states. However, this leads the analysis back to its point of origin, namely, that Congress can indirectly regulate through its spending power. That is all it has done here. Affirmed.

DISSENT: (O'Connor, J.) 23 U.S.C. § 158 cannot be justified as reasonably related to the federal highway system. It is an attempt to regulate alcoholic beverages, something Congress may not do. When Congress appropriates money to build a highway, it is entitled to insist that the highway be a safe one, but it cannot insist as a condition of the funding that the state change its regulations in other areas of the state's social and economic life because of a tangential or attenuated relationship to highway use or safety. Congress has no power under the Spending Clause to impose requirements on a grant that go beyond specifying how the money should be spent. A requirement that is not such a specification is not a condition but a regulation that is valid only if it falls within one of Congress's delegated regulatory powers.

ANALYSIS

It is not uncommon for Congress to attempt to regulate "with a carrot" rather than by direct regulation. The present case is one such action. Probably the most controversial area where this has been subject to constitutional consideration is in the area of abortions. Cases such as *Maher v. Roe*, 432 U.S. 464 (1977), and *Rust v. Sullivan*, 500 U.S. 173 (1991), have established Congress's right in this area.

Quicknotes

DECLARATORY JUDGMENT A judgment of the court establishing the rights of the parties in a controversy that does not grant damages but is binding.

GENERAL WELFARE Governmental interest or concern for the public's health, safety, morals, and well-being.

SPENDING POWER The power delegated to Congress by the U.S. Constitution to spend money in providing for the nation's welfare.

National Federation of Independent Business v. Sebelius

Business group (P) v. Government official (D)

567 U.S. 519 (2012)

NATURE OF CASE: Appeal from judgment in action challenging the constitutionality of the "Medicaid expansion" provision of the 2010 Patient Protection and Affordable Care Act.

FACT SUMMARY: A coalition of plaintiffs (P) challenged the constitutionality of the "Medicaid expansion" provision of the 2010 Patient Protection and Affordable Care Act, which expanded certain Medicaid benefits but also threatened the states that administer Medicaid, with not only the loss of funding for the increased coverage but also the loss of all federal Medicaid funds.

RULE OF LAW

That part of the "Medicaid expansion" provision of the Patient Protection and Affordable Care Act that threatens the states with a loss of all federal Medicaid funding for failing to comply with the Act's expansion of Medicaid benefits and coverage is not a valid exercise of Congress's power under the Spending Clause.

FACTS: In 2010, Congress enacted the Patient Protection and Affordable Care Act (the Act) in order to increase the number of Americans covered by health insurance and decrease the cost of health care. A key provision of the Act is the "Medicaid expansion." The current Medicaid program offers federal funding to states to assist pregnant women, children, needy families, the blind, the elderly, and the disabled in obtaining medical care. The Act would expand the scope of the Medicaid program and increase the number of individuals the states must cover. For example, the Act requires state programs to provide Medicaid coverage by 2014 to adults with incomes up to 133 percent of the federal poverty level, whereas many states now cover adults with children only if their income is considerably lower and do not cover childless adults at all. The Act increases federal funding to cover the states' costs in expanding Medicaid coverage, but if a state does not comply with the Act's new coverage requirements, it may lose not only the federal funding for those requirements but all its federal Medicaid funds. A coalition of plaintiffs (P), including some states, challenged the Medicaid expansion as unconstitutionally exceeding Congress's spending power under the Spending Clause by coercing the states to enact the statute. The Supreme Court granted certiorari.

ISSUE: Is that part of the "Medicaid expansion" provision of the Patient Protection and Affordable Care Act that threatens the states with a loss of all federal Medicaid funding for failing to comply with the Act's expansion of Medicaid benefits and coverage a valid exercise of Congress's power under the Spending Clause?

HOLDING AND DECISION: (Roberts, C.J.) No. That part of the "Medicaid expansion" provision of the Patient Protection and Affordable Care Act (the Act) that threatens the states with a loss of all federal Medicaid funding for failing to comply with the Act's expansion of Medicaid benefits and coverage is not a valid exercise of Congress's power under the Spending Clause. There is no doubt the Act dramatically increases state obligations under Medicaid. In light of the expansion in coverage mandated by the Act, the Government (D) estimates its Medicaid spending will increase by approximately $100 billion per year, nearly 40 percent above current levels. To be constitutional, Congress's power under the Spending Clause to secure state compliance with federal objectives rests on whether the state voluntarily and knowingly accepts the terms of the "contract" offered by the federal Government (D). The plaintiffs (P) claim the threat of losing Medicaid funding serves no purpose other than to force unwilling states to sign up for the dramatic expansion in health care coverage affected by the Act. Under the circumstances presented by the case, the plaintiffs (P) are correct—the Government's (D) "inducement" to participate is tantamount to a gun to the head. Respecting some states, the loss of all Medicaid funding represents a loss of as much as 10 percent of the state's entire budget. This is economic coercion that leaves the states with no real option but to acquiesce in the Medicaid expansion. The states contend the expansion is in reality a new program and Congress is forcing them to accept it by threatening the funds for the existing Medicaid program. The Government (D) counters that the Medicaid expansion is properly viewed merely as a modification of the existing program and emphasizes that the states agreed Congress could change the terms of Medicaid when they signed on in the first place. The issue is one of substance, not merely what Congress has labeled the program. Here, the Medicaid expansion accomplishes a shift in kind, not merely of degree. The original program was designed to cover medical services for four particular categories of the needy. Previous amendments to Medicaid eligibility merely altered and expanded the boundaries of these categories. Under the Act, however, Medicaid is transformed into a program to meet the health care needs of the entire nonelderly population with income below 133 percent of

Continued on next page.

the poverty level. It is no longer a program to care for the neediest among us, but rather an element of a comprehensive national plan to provide universal health insurance coverage. A state could hardly have anticipated when it signed on to the Medicaid program that Congress's reservation of the right to "alter" or "amend" the Medicaid program included the power to transform it so dramatically. The constitutional violation is fully remedied by precluding the Government (D) from withdrawing existing Medicaid funds for failure to comply with the requirements set out in the expansion. The other provisions of the Act are not affected. Congress would have wanted the rest of the Act to stand, had it known that states would have a genuine choice whether to participate in the Medicaid expansion.

CONCURRENCE AND DISSENT: (Ginsburg, J.) Here, Medicaid, and Medicaid as amended by Patient Protection and Affordable Care Act (the Act), are not two separate programs, but just one with a constant aim—to enable poor persons to receive basic health care when they need it. Moreover, the states are not entitled to Medicaid funding, and if they accept such funding, they must do so on Congress's terms. Historically, expansion has been a consistent characteristic of the Medicaid program, and the new obligations the Act will impose on the states pale in comparison to the increase in federal funding. Also, the Act does not remove the states' considerable autonomy under the Medicaid program. Moreover, the alternative to conditional federal spending would be state marginalization. Here, there are no coercion concerns because the expansion relates solely to the federally funded Medicaid program; if states choose not to comply, Congress has not threatened to withhold funds earmarked for any other program. Nor does the Act use Medicaid funding to induce states to take action Congress itself could not undertake. The Government (D) undoubtedly could operate its own health-care program for poor persons, just as it operates Medicare for seniors' health care. Contrary to the Chief Justice's opinion, the Act does not create a new program; it merely expands the number of people covered by the existing program. The Chief Justice's finding the expansion took states by surprise is also unfounded. The precedent on which he relies merely requires conditions on federal funds be unambiguously clear at the time a state receives and uses the money—not at the time, perhaps years earlier, when Congress passed the law establishing the program. In any event, from the start, the Medicaid Act put states on notice the program could be changed or even repealed. Thus, the states were on notice of the Act's proposed changes. Further, the Chief Justice does not announce a workable judicial standard for determining when a state is being coerced by the federal government. The coercion inquiry appears to involve political judgments that defy judicial calculation, and conceptions of when a state has been "coerced" are too amorphous to be judicially administrable. In sum, the Chief Justice and the joint-dissenters' position is that the states' reliance on federal funds limits Congress's authority to alter its spending programs. This gets things backwards: Congress, not the states, is tasked with spending federal money in service of the general welfare, and each successive Congress is empowered to appropriate funds as it sees fit. For all these reasons, the Medicaid expansion is within Congress's spending power. Although the Chief Justice's disposition is incorrect, in light of that disposition, the Medicaid Act's severability clause determines the appropriate remedy.

DISSENT: (Scalia, J.) Contrary to the Government's (D) argument, it is not enough to meet the anticoercion rule if states are free as a matter of law to turn down federal funds. For the average state, the annual federal Medicaid subsidy is more than one-fifth of the state's expenditures. Thus, the reality is that when a heavy federal tax is levied to support a federal program that offers large grants to the states, states may, as a practical matter, be unable to refuse to participate in the federal program and to substitute a state alternative. This is because, as a practical matter, states would have to impose a huge tax on top of the heavy tax imposed by the federal government. Acceptance of the Government's (D) interpretation of the anticoercion rule would permit Congress to dictate policy in areas traditionally governed primarily at the state or local level. The dimensions of the Medicaid program are such that refusing to agree to conditions of the Patient Protection and Affordable Care Act (the Act) is not a realistic option, since the states are far less reliant on federal funding for any other program. Under the Act, the federal government has threatened to withhold 42.3 percent of all federal outlays to the states, or around $233 billion. Further, the record shows that Congress anticipated 100 percent state participation and that no state could refuse the offer of the Medicaid expansion. Accordingly, the Medicaid expansion must fall as invalid, and it should not be rewritten to permit states that reject it to retain their pre-existing Medicaid funds.

ANALYSIS

It should be noted that the Court's decision does not strike down any provision of the Patient Protection and Affordable Care Act (the Act). It prohibits only the "application" of the Secretary of Health and Human Service's authority to withhold Medicaid funds from states that decline to conform their Medicaid plans to the Act's requirements. Thus, the Act's authorization of funds to finance the expansion remains intact, and the Secretary's authority to withhold funds for reasons other than noncompliance with the expansion remains unaffected. The joint dissenters would have held the expansion was not severable from the Medicaid

Continued on next page.

extension, and consequently would have held the entire expansion was invalid. Justice Ginsburg agreed with the Chief Justice the Medicaid Act's severability clause determined the appropriate remedy. That clause provides that "[i]f any provision of [the Medicaid Act], or the application thereof to any person or circumstance, is held invalid, the remainder of the chapter, and the application of such provision to other persons or circumstances shall not be affected thereby." 42 U.S.C. § 1303.

Quicknotes

FEDERALISM A scheme of government whereby the power to govern is divided and shared between the national and regional governments.

SPENDING CLAUSE The power delegated to Congress by the U.S. Constitution to spend money in providing for the nation's welfare.

SPENDING POWER The power delegated to Congress by the U.S. Constitution to spend money in providing for the nation's welfare.

CHAPTER 5

Federal Limits on State Regulation of Interstate Commerce

Quick Reference Rules of Law

Gibbons v. Ogden

Ship operator (D) v. Ship operator (P)

22 U.S. (9 Wheat.) 1 (1824)

NATURE OF CASE: Certiorari to review interpretation of federal commerce power in underlying action seeking an injunction to protect a state-granted exclusive right to operate ships between New York and New Jersey.

FACT SUMMARY: [Ogden (P), after acquiring a monopoly right from the State of New York to operate ships between New York City and New Jersey, sought to enjoin Gibbons (D) from operating his ships, licensed by the federal government, between the same points.]

RULE OF LAW

If a state law conflicts with a congressional act regulating commerce, the congressional act is controlling.

FACTS: [The New York legislature granted an exclusive right to Robert Livingston and Robert Fulton to operate ships powered by fire or steam in New York waters for twenty years, which was subsequently extended for another ten years. Ogden (P) obtained an assignment from Livingston and Fulton to operate his ships between Elizabethtown, New Jersey, and New York City. Gibbons (D) was also running two boats between these points, and his boats had been enrolled and licensed under the laws of the United States for employment in the coasting trade. Ogden (P) obtained an injunction stopping Gibbons (D) from operating his ships between the points for which Ogden (P) had received an exclusive right to operate his own ships. The case was appealed to the Supreme Court.]

ISSUE: If a state law conflicts with a congressional act regulating commerce, is the congressional act controlling?

HOLDING AND DECISION: (Marshall, C.J.) Yes. If a state law conflicts with a congressional act regulating commerce, the congressional act is controlling. Congress has the power to regulate navigation within the limits of every state when such regulation is for a national purpose, and therefore, the regulations that Congress passed controlling navigation within the boundaries of New York were valid. Ogden (P) argues that the states through the Tenth Amendment have the power to regulate commerce with foreign nations and among the states, because the power that the states gave up to Congress to regulate commerce was not absolute and the residue of that power remained with the states. But Congress was given all the power to regulate interstate commerce, although it is possible for the states to pass regulations that may affect some activity associated with interstate commerce. In that case, states must base such regulations on some other source of power than the commerce power (such as the police power of the state). Regardless of the source of the state power, whether it is said to be a commerce power or some other power, any time a state regulation conflicts with a federal regulation, the state regulation must yield to the federal law. Since in this case the law of New York conflicted with a federal regulation dealing with interstate commerce, the New York law is not valid. [Accordingly, the Court dismissed Ogden's (P) suit to obtain an injunction against Gibbons (D).]

ANALYSIS

The federal commerce power is concurrent with state power over commerce within the state. Hence, the Court has been asked many times to define the line between federal and state power to regulate commerce. During the early history of the United States, the court was not often called upon to determine the scope of federal power under the Commerce Clause. Instead, the early cases generally involved some state action that was claimed to discriminate against or burden interstate commerce. Hence, the Commerce Clause operated as a restraint upon state powers. Most of these cases did not involve any exercise of the commerce power by Congress at all. *Gibbons v. Ogden* expresses the important principle that even where Congress has not acted under its commerce power, state regulation affecting interstate commerce will often be foreclosed. This is called Congress's negative or dormant commerce power. However, this principle was expressed only as dicta in the case, the holding of which ultimately rested on preemption principles under the Supremacy Clause. The standard for the dormant commerce clause was developed in the years after *Gibbons* was decided. Large-scale regulatory action by Congress began with the Interstate Commerce Act in 1887 and the Sherman Anti-Trust Act in 1890. Challenges to these statutes initiated the major modern confrontations between the Court and congressional authority regarding commerce.

Quicknotes

COMMERCE POWER The power delegated to Congress by the U.S. Constitution to regulate interstate commerce.

DORMANT COMMERCE CLAUSE The regulatory effect of the Commerce Clause on state activity affecting interstate

Continued on next page.

commerce, where Congress itself has not acted to control the activity; a provision inferred from, but not expressly present in, the language of the Commerce Clause.

INJUNCTION A court order requiring a person to do, or prohibiting that person from doing, a specific act.

Philadelphia v. New Jersey

State (P) v. State (D)

437 U.S. 617 (1978)

NATURE OF CASE: Certiorari review of constitutionality of state commerce statute.

FACT SUMMARY: The New Jersey Supreme Court upheld a New Jersey law prohibiting the importation of waste originating in another state into New Jersey (D) on the basis that it protected a legitimate health interest of the state of New Jersey (D).

RULE OF LAW

State laws that are basically protectionist in nature unduly burden interstate commerce and thus are unconstitutional.

FACTS: New Jersey enacted a statute that prohibited the importation of solid or liquid waste which was collected or originated in another state. New Jersey private landfill owners challenged the law. The trial court held that the law unduly burdened interstate commerce by discriminating against products from other states. The New Jersey Supreme Court reversed, holding the law advanced legitimate health and safety concerns and thus did not unduly burden interstate commerce. The United States Supreme Court granted certiorari.

ISSUE: Do state laws that are basically protectionist in nature unduly burden interstate commerce?

HOLDING AND DECISION: (Stewart, J.) Yes. State laws that are basically protectionist in nature unduly burden interstate commerce and are unconstitutional. Even if New Jersey's (D) ultimate purpose was to protect the health and safety of its citizens, it may not accomplish this by discriminating against articles of commerce coming from outside the state. Discrimination must be based on some property of the goods other than geographic origin. This law treats inherently similar products differently based solely on place of origin. As a result, it improperly discriminates against out-of-state production and unduly burdens interstate commerce. Reversed.

DISSENT: (Rehnquist, J.) The fact that New Jersey (D) must somehow dispose of its own noxious items does not mean that it must serve as a depository for those of every other state. New Jersey (D) should be free under our past precedents to prohibit the importation of solid waste because of the health and safety problems that such waste poses to its citizens.

ANALYSIS

This case reaffirms the Court's holding in *Dean Milk Co. v. Madison*, 340 U.S. 349 (1951). It recognizes that waste is an element of commerce, and its disposal must be regulated as is all commerce. Because no federal regulation exists on the interstate transport and disposition of waste, states may regulate it only if done in a way that is not unduly burdensome. Since the *Dean Milk* decision, discrimination based on point of origin has been held unduly burdensome.

Quicknotes

CERTIORARI A discretionary writ issued by a superior court to an inferior court in order to review the lower court's decisions; the Supreme Court's writ ordering such review.

INTERSTATE COMMERCE Commercial dealings between two parties located in different states or located in one state and accomplished through a point in another state or a foreign country; commercial dealings transacted between two states.

POLICE POWER The power of a government to impose restrictions on the rights of private persons, so long as those restrictions are reasonably related to the promotion and protection of public health, safety, morals, and the general welfare.

Dean Milk Co. v. Madison

Milk products distributor (P) v. Municipality (D)

340 U.S. 349 (1951)

NATURE OF CASE: Certiorari review of validity of a city ordinance regulating the sale of milk and milk products within the municipality's jurisdiction.

FACT SUMMARY: [A Madison (D) ordinance made it unlawful to sell any milk as pasteurized unless it had been processed and bottled at an approved pasteurization plant located within five miles of the city.]

RULE OF LAW

A locality may not discriminate against interstate commerce, even to protect the health and safety of its people, if reasonable alternatives exist that do not discriminate and are adequate to conserve legitimate local interests.

FACTS: [Dean Milk Co. (P) was an Illinois corporation engaged in distributing milk products in Illinois and Wisconsin. Madison (D) is a city in Wisconsin. A Madison (D) ordinance prohibited the sale of any milk as pasteurized unless it had been processed and bottled at an approved pasteurization plant located within five miles of the city. Dean Milk (P) had pasteurization plants located 65 and 85 miles from Madison (D). Dean Milk (P) was denied a license to sell its milk products within Madison (D) solely because its pasteurization plants were more than five miles away. Dean Milk (P) contended that the ordinance imposed an undue burden on interstate commerce.]

ISSUE: May a locality discriminate against interstate commerce, even to protect the health and safety of its people, if reasonable alternatives exist that do not discriminate and are adequate to conserve legitimate local interests?

HOLDING AND DECISION: (Clark, J.) No. A locality may not discriminate against interstate commerce, even to protect the health and safety of its people, if reasonable alternatives exist that do not discriminate and are adequate to conserve legitimate local interests. The Madison (D) ordinance erects an economic barrier protecting a major local industry against competition from without the state. Hence, it plainly discriminates against interstate commerce. It must be decided whether the ordinance can be justified in view of the local interest and the available methods for protecting those interests. Reasonable and adequate alternatives do exist. Madison (D) could send its inspectors to the distant plants, or it could exclude from its city all milk not produced in conformity with standards as high as those enforced by Madison (D). It could use the local ratings checked by the U.S. Public Health Service to enforce such a provision. The Madison (D) ordinance must yield to the principle that "one state, in its dealings with another, may not place itself in a position of economic isolation." *Baldwin v. G.A.F. Seelig, Inc.*, 294 U.S. 511, 527 (1935). Reversed.

DISSENT: (Black, J.) Dean Milk Co.'s (P) personal preference not to pasteurize within five miles of Madison (D), not the ordinance, keeps its milk out of Madison (D). The lower court found the ordinance to be a good-faith attempt to safeguard public health. Never has a bona fide health law been struck down on the ground that equally good or better alternatives exist. At the very least the ordinance should not be invalidated without having the parties present evidence on the relative merits of the Madison (D) ordinance and the alternatives suggested by the court. The court can, on the basis of judicial knowledge, guarantee that the substitute methods it proposes would not lower health standards.

ANALYSIS

In *Nebbia v. New York*, 291 U.S. 502 (1934), the Court sustained the state regulation of minimum milk prices to be paid by dealers to local producers. However, in *Baldwin v. G.A.F. Seelig, Inc.*, 294 U.S. 511 (1935), the same law was challenged as applied to out-of-state producers. The Supreme Court held that application to be an unconstitutional burden on commerce since it "set a barrier to traffic between one state and another as effective as if custom duties, equal to the price differential (between the out-of-state price and the minimum price set by New York) had been laid upon the thing transported." *Baldwin* was heavily relied upon in *Dean Milk*.

Quicknotes

INTERSTATE COMMERCE Commercial dealings between two parties located in different states or located in one state and accomplished through a point in another state or a foreign country; commercial dealings transacted between two states.

UNDUE BURDEN Unlawfully oppressive or troublesome requirement.

C & A Carbone, Inc. v. Clarkstown

Recycling center (D) v. Municipality (P)

511 U.S. 383 (1994)

NATURE OF CASE: Certiorari review of municipal ordinance regulating solid waste disposal.

FACT SUMMARY: The Town of Clarkstown (P) mandated that all solid waste leaving the city be processed through a particular transfer station.

RULE OF LAW

Discrimination against interstate commerce in favor of local businesses is per se invalid unless the municipality can demonstrate under rigorous scrutiny that it has no other means to advance a legitimate local interest.

FACTS: The Town of Clarkstown (the Town) (P) entered an arrangement with a local contractor that the latter would build and operate a solid waste transfer station, which, in five years, would be sold back to the Town (P). In order to amortize the cost of the facility, the Town (P), by ordinance, mandated that all solid waste leaving the Town (P) be processed through that station. When C & A Carbone, Inc. (Carbone) (D), a recycling center in town, attempted to ship its nonrecyclable waste to another state in order to save money, the Town (P) sought an injunction to force Carbone (D) to comply with the ordinance. Carbone (D) challenged the ordinance as contrary to the Commerce Clause. The state courts rejected the challenge, and the Supreme Court granted review.

ISSUE: Is discrimination against interstate commerce in favor of local businesses per se invalid unless the municipality can demonstrate under rigorous scrutiny that it has no other means to advance a legitimate local interest?

HOLDING AND DECISION: (Kennedy, J.) Yes. Discrimination against interstate commerce in favor of local businesses is per se invalid unless the municipality can demonstrate under rigorous scrutiny that it has no other means to advance a legitimate local interest. Any ordinance that deprives nonlocal businesses from access to local markets discriminates against interstate commerce and is invalid under the [dormant] Commerce Clause. When a city designates a particular commercial entity as the sole provider of such services, nonlocal providers of the service are effectively shut out. Local governments may not use their regulatory power to favor local businesses by prohibiting patronage of out-of-state competitors. Here, the Town of Clarkstown (P) has shut out nonlocal solid waste operators, although it has a number of nondiscriminatory alternatives that would satisfy its environmental and fiscal concerns, and thus its ordinance is unconstitutional.

DISSENT: (Souter, J.) The Town of Clarkstown's (the Town's) (P) local law conforms with the Commerce Clause because the Town (P) may legitimately subject local and out-of-state investors to the same economic constraints. The Town (P) here is regulating a traditional government function, something it may legitimately do.

ANALYSIS

The essential vice in discriminatory ordinances that mandate local processing is that they bar the import of the processing service. These laws hoard a local resource, whether shrimp, milk, or solid waste, for the benefit of local businesses that treat it. The Town of Clarkstown's (P) ordinance was even more egregiously protectionist than most such laws since it favored a single local proprietor.

Quicknotes

INJUNCTION A court order requiring a person to do, or prohibiting that person from doing, a specific act.

PER SE By itself; without more; taken alone; not requiring additional evidence for proof; as a matter of law.

United Haulers Assn. v. Oneida-Herkimer Solid Waste Management Authority

Private hauler of trash (P) v. County waste authority (D)

550 U.S. 330 (2007)

NATURE OF CASE: Certiorari review of a county's "flow control" ordinance under the dormant Commerce Clause.

FACT SUMMARY: A county's "flow control" ordinance required haulers of trash to deliver the trash to facilities owned and operated by a state-created public benefit corporation.

RULE OF LAW

An ordinance requiring that trash be delivered to a state-created public benefit corporation does not violate the dormant Commerce Clause.

FACTS: The Oneida-Herkimer Solid Waste Management Authority (the WMA) (D) adopted an ordinance requiring that all trash be delivered to a state-created public benefit corporation. [United Haulers Association (United Haulers) (P) sued the WMA (D), alleging that it could deliver trash to out-of-state facilities at lower costs than those required by the WMA's (D) ordinance. The trial court agreed with United Haulers' (P) Commerce Clause argument and enjoined the WMA (D) from enforcing the ordinance. The intermediate appellate court reversed, reasoning that the ordinance was permissible because it benefited a public entity instead of private businesses.] United Haulers (P) petitioned the Supreme Court for further review.

ISSUE: Does an ordinance requiring that trash be delivered to a state-created public benefit corporation violate the dormant Commerce Clause?

HOLDING AND DECISION: (Roberts, C.J.) No. An ordinance requiring that trash be delivered to a state-created public benefit corporation does not violate the dormant Commerce Clause. The distinction between private and public facilities is constitutionally significant because laws benefiting local government may serve several legitimate purposes instead of economic protectionism. To hold otherwise—that is, to treat public and private facilities equally under the dormant Commerce Clause—would lead to much interference by federal courts in state and local affairs. Also worth noting is the injury alleged by United Haulers Association (United Haulers) (P)—more expensive waste disposal—will be borne by local citizens, not by citizens of other states. Typically, the dormant Commerce Clause is enforced to prohibit shifting expenses out of state instead of keeping them at home. United Haulers' (P) proper remedy is therefore through the local political process, not through the federal courts. [Affirmed.]

DISSENT: (Alito, J.) Benefiting public facilities does not meaningfully distinguish this ordinance from the ordinance struck down in *C & A Carbone, Inc. v. Clarkstown*, 511 U.S. 383 (1994). The difference is merely formal because the waste facility in *Carbone* was "private" only in the most technical sense of the term: when that suit was filed, the facility's title was in the process of transferring to the Town of Clarkstown. Further, Oneida-Herkimer Solid Waste Management Authority's (the WMA's) (D) ordinance here violates the market-participant doctrine, which prohibits local governments from discriminatorily regulating markets in which they participate. The ordinance here also fails to serve "legitimate goals unrelated to protectionism" because it clearly benefits local employees of the public facilities and local businesses who supply those facilities. Such preference is economic protectionism by any other name and thus deserves strict scrutiny. Finally, the fact that the WMA's (D) ordinance applies equally to in-state and out-of-state private businesses is not persuasive because case law squarely provides that such an equality of burdens cannot save legislation under the dormant Commerce Clause.

ANALYSIS

The dormant Commerce Clause usually prohibits state and local regulations that impose relatively direct, overt burdens on interstate commerce. Here, Oneida-Herkimer Solid Waste Management Authority's (the WMA's) (D) ordinance clearly imposed direct, overt burdens on interstate commerce, but it did so for public benefit. That distinction with cases that bar interstate commerce to protect local private businesses saved the WMA's (D) ordinance under the dormant Commerce Clause.

Quicknotes

DORMANT COMMERCE CLAUSE The regulatory effect of the Commerce Clause on state activity affecting interstate commerce, where Congress itself has not acted to control the activity; a provision inferred from, but not expressly present in, the language of the Commerce Clause.

Continued on next page.

INTERSTATE COMMERCE Commercial dealings between two parties located in different states or located in one state and accomplished through a point in another state or a foreign country; commercial dealings transacted between two states.

MARKET PARTICIPANT DOCTRINE Allows states acting as market participants (i.e., businesses) to be exempted from the Dormant Commerce Clause.

STRICT SCRUTINY Method by which courts determine the constitutionality of a law when a law affects a fundamental right; under the test, the legislature must have had a compelling interest to enact the law and measures prescribed by the law must be the least restrictive means possible to accomplish its goal.

South-Central Timber Development, Inc. v. Wunnicke

Timber company (P) v. State (D)

467 U.S. 82 (1984)

NATURE OF CASE: Certiorari review of congressional authorization of state regulation.

FACT SUMMARY: Alaska offered to sell large amounts of state-owned timber if the buyers, including South-Central Timber Development, Inc. (South-Central Timber) (P), agreed to process it within state boundaries, but South-Central Timber (P) wanted to buy the timber and ship it to Japan for processing.

RULE OF LAW
If a state imposes burdens on commerce within a market in which it is a participant, but which have a substantial regulatory effect outside of that particular market, those burdens are per se invalid under the federal Commerce Clause.

FACTS: Alaska offered for sale a large quantity of state-owned timber. However, it required potential purchasers to agree to process the timber within state boundaries before shipment out of Alaska. This law was enacted to protect existing timber-processing industries within the state and to obtain further revenue from the timber beyond its sale. South-Central Timber Development, Inc. (South-Central Timber) (P) wanted to buy Alaskan timber and also wanted to ship it beyond Alaska's borders to Japan for processing. South-Central Timber (P) challenged the constitutional validity of the Alaska requirement on Commerce Clause grounds. Alaska responded by asserting that the in-state processing requirement was exempt from invalidation under the Commerce Clause under the "market participant" doctrine. The Court of Appeals for the Ninth Circuit found that Congress had authorized Alaska's processing requirement, and the Supreme Court granted certiorari.

ISSUE: If a state imposes burdens on commerce within a market in which it is a participant, but which have a substantial regulatory effect outside of that particular market, are those burdens per se invalid under the federal Commerce Clause?

HOLDING AND DECISION: (White, J.) Yes. If a state imposes burdens on commerce within a market in which it is a participant, but which have a substantial regulatory effect outside of that particular market, those burdens are per se invalid under the federal Commerce Clause. The market-participant doctrine allows a state to impose burdens on interstate commerce within the market in which it is a participant but allows it to go no further. The state may not impose conditions whether by statute, regulation, or contract that have a substantial regulatory effect outside of that particular market. "Market" for Commerce Clause purposes is narrowly defined and precludes a state's exercise of leverage in the market in which it is directly participating in order to regulate a "downstream" market. Here, Alaska is a direct participant in the timber market but not in the processing market. Although Alaska may legitimately prefer its own residents in the initial disposition of goods, in other words, when it is a "private trader" in the immediate transaction, it may not attach restrictions on dispositions subsequent to the goods coming to rest in private hands after Alaska no longer has a proprietary interest in them. Alaska may not govern the private, separate economic relationships of its trading partners downstream; as a typical seller, it has no say over how the product is used after sale. Reversed and remanded.

DISSENT: (Rehnquist, J.) The distinction drawn in the plurality opinion between market participation and market regulation is unconvincing and artificial. Alaska could have chosen a number of constitutionally valid ways of requiring the buyers of its timber to process it within the state, all of which in substance are the same as the contractual provisions the plurality found violative of the Commerce Clause. For instance, Alaska could have chosen to sell its timber only to those companies that own and operate processing plants in Alaska, or the state itself could have paid to have the logs processed and then sold only processed, rather than unprocessed. The plurality approach is unduly formalistic.

ANALYSIS

The facts of this case closely resemble the facts of an earlier Supreme Court case in which the Court struck down a Louisiana law prohibiting export from the state of any shrimp from which the heads and hulls had not been removed. See *Foster-Fountain Packing Co. v. Haydel*, 278 U.S. 1 (1928). The Court rejected the claim that the fact that the shrimp were owned by the state authorized the state to impose such limitations. The case, as here, involved a natural resource that the Court noted could have been retained for use and consumption within its borders; but because Louisiana permitted its shrimp to be taken and sold in interstate commerce, it released its right to and terminated its control of the shrimp so taken.

Continued on next page.

Quicknotes

DISPOSITION A transferring of property; conveyance.

MARKET PARTICIPANT DOCTRINE Allows states acting as market participants (i.e., businesses) to be exempted from the Dormant Commerce Clause.

PER SE By itself; without more; taken alone; not requiring additional evidence for proof; as a matter of law.

PROPRIETARY INTEREST An owner's interest and rights in property.

Baldwin v. G.A.F. Seelig, Inc.

State agency (D) v. Milk dealer (P)

294 U.S. 511 (1935)

NATURE OF CASE: Certiorari review of action to enjoin enforcement of a state milk price support statute.

FACT SUMMARY: G.A.F. Seelig, Inc. (P), a New York milk dealer, sought to enjoin a New York statute establishing minimum producer-to-dealer prices on milk and prohibiting the sale in New York of milk purchased out of state at lower than the minimum price for a similar in-state purchase.

RULE OF LAW

It is a violation of the Commerce Clause for a state to regulate intrastate prices by prohibiting the importation of less expensive goods in interstate commerce.

FACTS: In addition to setting up minimum producer-to-dealer prices for the in-state sale of milk, a New York statute prohibited the sale in New York of milk bought out of state for lower prices. G.A.F. Seelig, Inc. (Seelig) (P), a New York milk dealer, bought milk in Vermont in 40-quart cans at prices below the minimums for similar in-state purchases. When New York then refused to license him to sell it, Seelig (P) brought an action seeking injunctive relief and charging an unconstitutional interference with interstate commerce. An injunction was granted as to the milk Seelig (P) wanted to sell in the original containers but not as to that milk which had been subsequently placed into bottles for sale in the New York market. The latter was deemed to have passed outside the stream of interstate commerce, thereby being subject to state regulation.

ISSUE: Is it a violation of the Commerce Clause for a state to regulate intrastate prices by prohibiting the importation of less expensive goods in interstate commerce?

HOLDING AND DECISION: (Cardozo, J.) Yes. It is a violation of the Commerce Clause for a state to regulate intrastate prices by prohibiting the importation of less expensive goods in interstate commerce. Neither the power to tax nor the police power may be used by the state of destination with the aim and effect of establishing an economic barrier against competition with the products of another state or the labor of its residents. Such is a violation of the theory upon which the Constitution was framed, that the peoples of the several states must sink or swim together and that the mutual jealousies of the states cannot be permitted to result in customs barriers and other economic retaliation. Here, the argument is made that the purpose of the regulation is to advance the health of the state's citizens, and not to securing an economic advantage over rival states. This would be to eat up the rule under the guise of an exception. Economic welfare is always related to health, for there can be no health if men are starving.

ANALYSIS

The underlying principle in *Baldwin* is that one state may not, in its dealings with another, place itself in a position of economic isolation. Such a tenet is essential to maintenance of a union of states, which is why *Baldwin* is still recognized as authority.

Quicknotes

COMMERCE CLAUSE Article 1, § 8, cl. 3 of the U.S. Constitution, granting Congress the power to regulate commerce with foreign countries and among the states.

INJUNCTION A court order requiring a person to do, or prohibiting that person from doing, a specific act.

INTERFERENCE WITH INTERSTATE COMMERCE Interference with commercial dealings between two parties located in different states or located in one state and accomplished through a point in another state or a foreign country.

H.P. Hood & Sons v. Du Mond

Milk distributor (P) v. Milk commissioner (D)

336 U.S. 525 (1949)

NATURE OF CASE: Certiorari review of constitutionality of a New York milk dealer licensing law.

FACT SUMMARY: H.P. Hood & Sons (Hood) (P), a Boston milk distributor, obtained milk from New York. Hood (P) was denied a license to establish a receiving depot in New York on the basis of a New York law that makes a condition of the issuance of a license that such issuance will not tend to be destructive of competition in a market already "adequately served."

RULE OF LAW

A state may not constitutionally enact restrictions with the purpose and effect of curtailing the volume of interstate commerce for the benefit of local economic interests.

FACTS: H.P. Hood & Sons (Hood) (P) was a Boston milk distributor that obtained its supply of milk from producers in the state of New York. Hood (P) had established three milk receiving and processing depots in New York under licenses from that state. Hood's (P) application for a license to open a fourth depot was denied. The basis for the denial was that issuance would tend to creative destructive competition in an area already adequately served. In his denial, the milk commissioner (D) stated that the fourth depot would draw milk supplies away from other existing processing plants and would tend to deprive the local market of an adequate supply of milk.

ISSUE: May a state constitutionally enact restrictions with the purpose and effect of curtailing the volume of interstate commerce for the benefit of local economic interests?

HOLDING AND DECISION: (Jackson, J.) No. A state may not constitutionally enact restrictions with the purpose and effect of curtailing the volume of interstate commerce for the benefit of local economic interests. This Court has previously denied states' attempts to advance their own economic interests by curtailing the movement of articles of commerce, while it has generally supported their right to impose restrictions in the interests of health and safety. While the State (D) insists that the denial of a license for H.P. Hood & Sons (Hood) (P) does not restrict interstate commerce, we can hardly be asked to assume that the denial of the license will not deny petitioner access to such added supplies. Since the statute, as applied to Hood (P), violates the Commerce Clause and is not authorized by federal legislation pursuant to that Clause, it cannot stand. Reversed and remanded.

DISSENT: (Black, J.) The question here is whether all local phases of interstate business are to be judicially immunized from state laws against destructive competitive business practices. The language of the state act is not discriminatory, nor does the legislative history show such intent. While I have doubt about the wisdom of this New York law, I do not conceive it to be the function of this Court to revise that state's economic judgments.

DISSENT: (Frankfurter, J.) In effect, the majority holds that no matter how important the prevention of destructive competition may be to the internal economy of a state and no matter how unimportant the interstate commerce affected, a state cannot, as a means of preventing such competition, deny an applicant access to a market within the state if that applicant intends to ship out of state.

ANALYSIS

In *Milk Control Board v. Eisenberg*, 306 U.S. 346 (1939), a New York milk dealer who bought milk from Pennsylvania producers challenged a Pennsylvania law. The law set the minimum price to be paid by dealers to milk producers. The Supreme Court upheld the law, stating that it did not attempt to regulate shipment to or sale in New York. It also found that the activity affected was essentially local in Pennsylvania, since only a fraction of the milk produced in that state is shipped out of state. The effect on interstate commerce was found to be incidental. *Baldwin*, 294 U.S. 511 (1935), was not controlling. The Court stated that that decision "condemned an enactment aimed solely at interstate commerce, attempting to affect and regulate the price of milk in a sister state" and amounted, in effect, to a tariff.

Quicknotes

PAROCHIAL Regional or narrow in scope.

POLICE POWER The power of a government to impose restrictions on the rights of private persons, so long as those restrictions are reasonably related to the promotion and protection of public health, safety, morals, and the general welfare.

Kassel v. Consolidated Freightways Corp.

State (D) v. Common carrier (P)

450 U.S. 662 (1981)

NATURE OF CASE: Certiorari review of constitutionality of state statute prohibiting specific vehicles.

FACT SUMMARY: Consolidated Freightways Corp. (P) challenged the constitutionality of an Iowa (D) statute that prohibited the use of certain large trucks within the state boundaries.

RULE OF LAW

A state safety regulation will be unconstitutional if its asserted safety purpose is outweighed by its degree of interference with interstate commerce.

FACTS: Iowa (D) passed a statute restricting the length of vehicles that may use its highways. The state law set a general length limit of 55 feet for most vehicles and 60 feet for trucks pulling two trailers (doubles). Iowa was the only state in the western or midwestern United States to outlaw the use of 65-foot doubles. Consolidated Freightways Corp. (P), one of the largest common carriers in the country, alleged that the Iowa statute unconstitutionally burdened interstate commerce. The district court and the court of appeals found the statute unconstitutional and Kassel (D), on behalf of the state, appealed.

ISSUE: Will a state safety regulation be held to be unconstitutional if its asserted safety purpose is outweighed by the degree of interference with interstate commerce?

HOLDING AND DECISION: (Powell, J.) Yes. A state safety regulation will be unconstitutional if its asserted safety purpose is outweighed by its degree of interference with interstate commerce. While bona fide state safety regulations are entitled to a strong presumption of validity, the asserted safety purpose must be weighed against the degree of interference with interstate commerce. Less deference will be given to the findings of state legislators where the local regulation has a disproportionate effect on out-of-state residents and businesses. Here, Iowa (D) failed to present any persuasive evidence that 65-foot doubles are less safe than 55-foot single trailers. Consolidated Freightways Corp. (P) demonstrated that Iowa's law substantially burdens interstate commerce by compelling trucking companies either to route 65-foot doubles around Iowa or to use the smaller trucks allowed by the state statute. Thus, the Iowa statute is in violation of the Commerce Clause. Affirmed.

CONCURRENCE: (Brennan, J.) In ruling on the constitutionality of state safety regulations, the burdens imposed on commerce must be balanced against the regulatory purposes identified by the state's lawmakers. In its analysis, a court should focus ultimately on the regulatory purposes identified by the lawmakers. The only relevant evidence concerns whether the lawmakers "could rationally have believed that the challenged regulation would foster those purposes." Iowa's (D) actual rationale for the regulation had nothing to do with the alleged safety differences in the lengths of trucks but had to do with discouraging interstate truck traffic on its highways. Protectionist legislation is unconstitutional under the Commerce Clause, even if its purpose is to promote safety rather than economic purposes.

DISSENT: (Rehnquist, J.) A sensitive consideration must be made when weighing the safety purposes of a statute against the burden on interstate commerce. A state safety regulation is invalid if its asserted safety justification is merely a pretext for discrimination against interstate commerce. The Iowa statute is a valid highway safety regulation and is entitled to the strongest presumption of validity.

ANALYSIS

Traditionally, states have been free to pass public safety regulations restricting the use of highways and railway facilities. However, state safety regulations have been struck down when only a marginal increase in safety causes a substantial burden on interstate commerce. This case simply follows this rationale.

Quicknotes

COMMERCE CLAUSE Article 1, § 8, cl. 3 of the U.S. Constitution, granting Congress the power to regulate commerce with foreign countries and among the states.

INTERSTATE COMMERCE Commercial dealings between two parties located in different states or located in one state and accomplished through a point in another state or a foreign country; commercial dealings transacted between two states.

SALUTARY Remedial or beneficial.

United Building & Construction Trades Council v. Mayor and Council of Camden

Trade council (P) v. City (D)

465 U.S. 208 (1984)

NATURE OF CASE: Certiorari review of constitutionality of a municipal residency ordinance.

FACT SUMMARY: [The New Jersey Supreme Court held that a municipal ordinance, which required that 40 percent of all workers on city construction projects be residents of the city, was not covered by the Privileges and Immunities Clause.]

RULE OF LAW

The Privileges and Immunities Clause applies to municipal ordinances that discriminate on the basis of municipal residence.

FACTS: [The City of Camden (Camden) (D), New Jersey, enacted an ordinance requiring that contractors and subcontractors working on city construction projects employ a workforce of 40 percent Camden (D) residents. The United Building & Construction Trades Council (P) sued, contending the ordinance discriminated against non-city residents in violation of the Privileges and Immunities Clause. The Supreme Court of New Jersey upheld the ordinance, holding that the Privileges and Immunities Clause did not apply to municipal ordinances that discriminate on the basis of municipal residence because the discrimination applies to both New Jersey residents outside Camden (D) as well as out-of-state residents.] The United States Supreme Court granted certiorari to review the application of the Privileges and Immunities Clause to the particular ordinance.

ISSUE: Does the Privileges and Immunities Clause apply to municipal ordinances that discriminate on the basis of municipal rather than state citizenship?

HOLDING AND DECISION: (Rehnquist, J.) Yes. The Privileges and Immunities Clause (the Clause) applies to municipal ordinances that discriminate on the basis of municipal residence. Ordinances are enacted under the municipality's power derived from the state. Thus, ordinances are not outside the Clause merely because they are enacted by a municipality. Further, although New Jersey residents living outside of the City of Camden (Camden) (D) were affected by the ordinance along with out-of-state residents, New Jersey residents had the opportunity to expand or contract municipal power by voting in state elections. Out-of-state residents had no such power. Therefore, the Clause applies. The ordinance affected the rights of non-residents to pursue a livelihood of their choosing. This is clearly a fundamental privilege protected by the Clause. Because no trial was held, it is necessary the decision of the Supreme Court of New Jersey be reversed, and the case remanded to determine whether Camden's (D) economic problems were sufficient to justify the discrimination placed on non-residents by the ordinance. Reversed and remanded.

DISSENT: (Blackmun, J.) The Court erroneously extends the scope of the Privileges and Immunities Clause (the Clause) without textual or historical support. Historically, the meaning of the Clause is well settled: absent some substantial noninvidious justification, a state cannot discriminate between its own residents and those of other states on the basis of state citizenship. Now, this Court holds that the Clause applies to laws that discriminate among state residents on the basis of municipal residence.

ANALYSIS

In this case, the Court points out that although the ordinance may have been valid under the Commerce Clause, as the City of Camden (D) was acting as a market participant, such an analysis does not apply under the Privileges and Immunities Clause. That Clause imposes a direct restraint on state action in the interest of interstate harmony.

Quicknotes

PRIVILEGES AND IMMUNITIES CLAUSE Article IV, § 2, cl. 1 of the U.S. Constitution, which states that a state cannot favor its own citizens by discriminating against other states' citizens who may come within its borders.

Pacific Gas & Elec. Co. v. State Energy Resources Conservation & Development Comm'n

Electric utility company (P) v. State agency (D)

461 U.S. 190 (1983)

NATURE OF CASE: Certiorari review of federal law preemption of state law energy act.

FACT SUMMARY: Pacific Gas & Elec. Co. (P) maintained that certain provisions of California's Warren-Alquist Act were invalid because it was preempted by Congress's passage of the Atomic Energy Act of 1954.

RULE OF LAW

In passing the Atomic Energy Act of 1954, Congress preempted state regulation of the radiological safety aspects involved in the construction and operation of nuclear plants but intended for the states to retain their traditional responsibility in the field of regulating electrical utilities for determining questions of need, reliability, cost, and other related state concerns.

FACTS: In challenging the validity of various provisions of California's Warren-Alquist State Energy Resources Conservation and Development Act, Pacific Gas & Elec. Co. (P) claimed in its declaratory judgment action that such regulation as it attempted was preempted by the Atomic Energy Act, which Congress enacted in 1954. Of particular concern was a provision imposing a moratorium on the certification of new nuclear plants until the State Energy Resources and Conservation Commission (Energy Commission) (D) "finds that there has been developed and that the United States through its authorized agency has approved and there exists a demonstrated technology or means for the disposal of high-level nuclear waste." Disposal was defined as a "method for the permanent and terminal disposition of high-level nuclear waste," a goal which was not even close to being reached. The district court held that the aforementioned nuclear moratorium provision was not preempted because it saw in certain sections of the Atomic Energy Act congressional authorization for states to regulate nuclear power plants "for purposes other than protection against radiation hazards."

ISSUE: In passing the Atomic Energy Act of 1954, has Congress preempted state regulation of the radiological safety aspects involved in the construction and operation of nuclear plants but intended for the states to retain their traditional responsibility in the field of regulating electrical utilities for determining questions of need, reliability, cost, and other related state concerns?

HOLDING AND DECISION: (White, J.) Yes. In passing the Atomic Energy Act of 1954, Congress preempted state regulation of the radiological safety aspects involved in the construction and operation of nuclear plants but intended for the states to retain their traditional responsibility in the field of regulating electrical utilities for determining questions of need, reliability, cost, and other related state concerns. The intent of Congress in passing the Atomic Energy Act of 1954 was to give the federal government exclusive regulatory power over the radiological safety aspects involved in the construction and operation of a nuclear plant. It did not intend to preempt the states from exercising their traditional responsibility in the field of regulating electrical utilities (nuclear or otherwise) for determining questions of need, reliability, cost, and other related state concerns. California has maintained that its moratorium provisions are aimed at economic problems, arguing that without a permanent nuclear waste disposal system, the nuclear waste problem could become critical and lead to unpredictably high costs to either contain the problem or shut down reactors. Accepting this avowed economic purpose as the rationale for enacting the moratorium provision, the statute lies outside the occupied field of nuclear safety regulation. It does not conflict with federal regulation of nuclear waste disposal. In fact, its very words accept that it is the federal responsibility to develop and license such technology and it nowhere seeks to impose its own state standards on nuclear waste disposal. It does not conflict with the Nuclear Regulatory Commission's (the NRC's) decision to continue licensing reactors despite the uncertainty surrounding the waste disposal problem or with Congress's recent passage of legislation directed at that problem. The NRC's imprimatur indicates only that it is safe to proceed with such plants, not that it is economically wise to do so. Since the NRC order does not and could not compel a utility to develop a nuclear plant, compliance with both it and California's challenged statutory provision is possible. Furthermore, because the NRC's regulations are aimed at insuring that plants are safe, not necessarily that they are economical, California's statutory provision does not interfere with the objective of the federal regulation. Finally, there is little doubt that a primary purpose of the Atomic Energy Act was and is the promotion of nuclear power. But, as the court of appeals noted, the promotion

Continued on next page.

of nuclear power was not intended by Congress to be accomplished "at all costs." The elaborate licensing and safety provisions and the continued preservation of state regulation in traditional areas belie that. Thus, it cannot be said that California's statutory provision "frustrates" the Atomic Energy Act's purpose of developing the commercial use of nuclear power. Quite simply, there has been no preemption with regard to the type of provision California enacted. Affirmed.

CONCURRENCE: (Blackmun, J.) It is unnecessary for the majority to rule that a state may not prohibit the construction of nuclear power plants if the state is motivated by concerns about the safety of such plants.

ANALYSIS

There are instances in which Congress explicitly preempts state authority by so stating in express terms in the federal statute itself. More often, however, Congress's intent to supersede state law altogether is to be found: (1) from a "scheme of federal regulation so pervasive as to make reasonable the inference that Congress left no room to supplement it;" or (2) because "the Act of Congress touches a field in which the federal interest is so dominant that the federal system will be assumed to preclude enforcement of state laws on the same subject;" or (3) because "the object sought to be obtained by the federal law and the character of obligations imposed by it may reveal the same purpose." *Fidelity Federal Savings & Loan Assn. v. de la Cuesta*, 458 U.S. 141 (1982).

Quicknotes

DECLARATORY JUDGMENT A judgment of the court establishing the rights of the parties in a controversy that does not grant damages but is binding.

PREEMPTION Doctrine holding that matters of national interest take precedence over matters of local interest; the federal law takes precedence over state law.

CHAPTER 6

Separation of Powers

Quick Reference Rules of Law

Youngstown Sheet & Tube Co. v. Sawyer (The Steel Seizure Case)

Steel companies (P) v. Federal government (D)

343 U.S. 579 (1952)

NATURE OF CASE: Certiorari review of underlying suit for declaratory and injunctive relief from a presidential order.

FACT SUMMARY: Faced with an imminent steel strike during the Korean War, the President ordered governmental seizure of the steel companies to prevent the strike. The companies challenged his power to take such action as being without constitutional authority or prior congressional approval.

RULE OF LAW

The President, relying on a concept of inherent powers and in his capacity as Commander-in-Chief, may not make an order that usurps the lawmaking authority of Congress on the basis of a compelling need to protect the national security.

FACTS: As a result of long, but unsuccessful, negotiations with various steel companies, the United Steelworkers of America served notice of intent to strike in April 1952. Through the last months of the negotiations the President had utilized every available administrative remedy to affect a settlement and avert a strike. Congress had engaged in extensive debate on solutions but had passed no legislation on the issue. By order of the President, the Secretary of Commerce seized the steel companies so that steel production would not be interrupted during the Korean War. The steel companies sued in federal district court to have the seizure order declared invalid and to enjoin its enforcement. The government asserted that the President had "inherent power" to make the order and that it was "supported by the Constitution, historical precedent and court decisions." The district court granted a preliminary injunction that was stayed the same day by the court of appeals. The Supreme Court granted certiorari and ordered immediate argument.

ISSUE: May the President, relying on a concept of inherent powers and in his capacity as Commander-in-Chief, make an order that usurps the lawmaking authority of Congress on the basis of a compelling need to protect the national security?

HOLDING AND DECISION: (Black, J.) No. The President, relying on a concept of inherent powers and in his capacity as Commander-in-Chief, may not make an order that usurps the lawmaking authority of Congress on the basis of a compelling need to protect the national security. There is, admittedly, no express congressional authority for these seizures, and so, if any authority for the President's act can be found, it must come from the Constitution. In the absence of express authority for the President's act, it is argued that the power can be implied from the aggregate of his express powers granted by the Constitution. This order cannot be justified by reliance on the President's role as Commander-in-Chief. Even though the term "theater of war" has enjoyed an expanding definition, it cannot embrace the taking of private property to prevent a strike. The President's powers in the area of legislation are limited to proposing new laws to Congress or vetoing laws he deems inadvisable. This order is not executive implementation of a congressional act, but a legislative act performed by the President. Only Congress may do what the President has attempted here. The Constitution is specific in vesting the lawmaking powers in Congress. Affirmed.

CONCURRENCE: (Frankfurter, J.) This decision does not attempt to define the limits of presidential authority. The President cannot act in contravention of an express congressional act, nor may he act where Congress has done nothing. Were this a case of a long history of congressional acquiescence to presidential practice our decision might be different, but no such showing has been made.

CONCURRENCE: (Jackson, J.) The power of the President to act can be viewed as three separate categories of circumstances. First, the President's power is at its maximum when he acts pursuant to express or implied congressional authority. Second, in the absence of a congressional grant of power, the President acts solely on the basis of his powers as specified in the Constitution. Third, when the President acts in contravention of congressional action, he may do so only where it can be shown that Congress has exceeded its constitutional powers and the President is acting in his own sphere of authority. It is in this last area where presidential acts are subject to the closest scrutiny. This order is clearly not in the first category. His act cannot be justified in the second category since Congress has limited seizure powers to specific instances not embracing this order. The constitutional grant of powers to the President is in specific terms that do not permit any loose aggregation to create powers not specified. There is little question that Congress could have authorized those seizures and this very power denies the same authority to the President. Finally, the President's act is justified by arguing it is the result of powers accruing to his office by custom and practice of previous administrations. Present unconstitutional acts cannot be justified

Continued on next page.

by the prior unconstitutional acts of others. Presidential power may, in fact, enlarge due to congressional inaction, but the courts will not assist or approve this process.

DISSENT: (Vinson, C.J.) The majority's opinion has left the President powerless to act at the very time the need for his independent and immediate action is greatest. From Washington to Roosevelt, history is replete with examples of needed presidential action in the face of congressional inaction. Jefferson's Louisiana Purchase, Lincoln's Emancipation Proclamation, Wilson's War Labor Board with accompanying industrial seizures, and Roosevelt's seizure of an aircraft plant to avert a strike are but a few examples of presidential action that received subsequent, not prior, congressional or judicial authorization. The President's seizure in this case is in accord with congressional intent to support the resistance of aggression in the world and is in furtherance of his duty to execute the laws of this nation. The executive is the only branch of government that may, by design, act swiftly to meet national emergencies. This decision emasculates that necessary power.

ANALYSIS

Justice Black's broad language was criticized by many scholars as being overly expansive for the case presented. However, other authorities pointed out that the broad arguments advanced by the government required a broad response. During oral argument before the court, the government counsel stated that while the Constitution imposed limits on congressional and judicial powers, no such limits were imposed on the presidency. While supplemental briefs were filed modifying this position, the damage may already have been done. The Court was faced with a paucity of judicial precedents. The President and Congress have traditionally preferred political rather than judicial solutions to their conflicts. This practice avoids the limitations imposed on future actions by binding judicial precedents. And, as can be seen by the cases of *Marbury v. Madison*, 5 U.S. 137 (1803), and *United States v. Nixon*, 418 U.S. 683 (1974), the executive branch has not fared well when it has submitted to judicial jurisdiction.

Quicknotes

EXECUTIVE ORDER An order issued by the President or another executive of government that has the force of law.

PRELIMINARY INJUNCTION A judicial mandate issued to require or restrain a party from certain conduct; used to preserve a trial's subject matter or to prevent threatened injury.

Zivotofsky v. Kerry

Minor child born to U.S. citizens abroad (P) v. United States Secretary of State (D)

576 U.S. 1 (2015)

NATURE OF CASE: Action involving the issue of whether the Foreign Relations Authorization Act may override the President's recognition powers.

FACT SUMMARY: The President had never recognized Israel as sovereign over Jerusalem, but, in 2002, Congress passed the Foreign Relations Authorization Act, Fiscal Year 2003 (the FRAA), allowing citizens born in Jerusalem to list their place of birth on documents such as passports as "Israel." Zivotofsky (P), a minor child born to U.S. citizens in Jerusalem, invoking the FRAA, challenged the State Department's refusal to record "Israel" as his place of birth on his passport, which raised the issue of whether Congress could constitutionally override the President's position on the matter.

RULE OF LAW

The President has the exclusive power to grant formal recognition to a foreign sovereign.

FACTS: Although the President has recognized Israel as a nation, no President has ever recognized any country's sovereignty over Jerusalem, which Israel considers to be its capital. The President's position on Jerusalem is reflected in State Department policy regarding passports and consular reports of birth abroad. Understanding that passports will be construed as reflections of U.S. policy, the State Department's Foreign Affairs Manual (the FAM) instructs its employees, in general, to record the place of birth on a passport as the "country [having] present sovereignty over the actual area of birth." Because the President has not recognized any country as having sovereignty over Jerusalem, the FAM instructs employees to record the place of birth of citizens born there as "Jerusalem." Congress passed the Foreign Relations Authorization Act, Fiscal Year 2003 (the FRAA), seeking, in section 214(d) of the Act, to override the FAM by allowing citizens born in Jerusalem to list their place of birth as "Israel." Zivotofsky (P), a minor child born to U.S. citizens in Jerusalem, invoking the FRAA, challenged the State Department's refusal to record "Israel" as his place of birth on his passport, which raised the issue of whether Congress could constitutionally override the President's position on the matter. The Supreme Court granted certiorari in the case.

ISSUE: Does the President have the exclusive power to grant formal recognition to a foreign sovereign?

HOLDING AND DECISION: (Kennedy, J.) Yes. The President has the exclusive power to grant formal recognition to a foreign sovereign. Recognition is a "formal acknowledgement" that a particular entity possesses the qualifications for statehood or that a particular regime is the effective government of a state. The Constitution's text and structure grant the President the power to recognize foreign nations and governments. The Reception Clause directs that the President "shall receive Ambassadors and other public Ministers," Art. II, § 3. At the time of the founding, receiving an ambassador was considered tantamount to recognizing the sending state's sovereignty. It is thus logical and proper to infer that the Reception Clause would be understood to acknowledge the President's power to recognize other nations. This inference is further supported by the President's additional Article II powers: to negotiate treaties and to nominate the Nation's ambassadors and dispatch other diplomatic agents. Though ratifying a treaty and confirming an ambassador require congressional approval, Congress lacks authority to initiate the actions without the President's involvement. The President, unlike Congress, also has the power to open diplomatic channels simply by engaging in direct diplomacy with foreign heads of state and their ministers. The Constitution thus assigns the President, not Congress, means to effect recognition on his own initiative. Functional considerations also suggest that the President's recognition power is exclusive. The nation must "speak. . .with one voice" regarding which governments are legitimate in the eyes of the United States and which are not, and only the Executive has the characteristic of unity at all times. Unlike Congress, the President is also capable of engaging in the delicate and often secret diplomatic contacts that may lead to a recognition decision, and is better positioned to take the decisive, unequivocal action necessary to recognize other states at international law. The President has also exercised unilateral recognition power since the founding, a practice endorsed by the Court. Nevertheless, Congress, which has the central role in making laws, has substantial authority regarding many policy determinations that precede and follow an act of recognition. The President's recognition determination is thus only one part of the political process. The President alone may not determine the whole content of the nation's foreign policy and is not free from the ordinary controls and checks of Congress merely because foreign affairs are at issue. Because the power to recognize foreign states resides in the President alone, Foreign Relations Authorization Act, Fiscal Year 2003, § 214(d) infringes on the Executive's consistent decision to withhold recognition with respect to Jerusalem. If the recognition power is to mean anything, it must mean that the President not

Continued on next page.

only makes the initial, formal recognition determination but also may maintain that determination in his and his agents' statements. Otherwise, Congress could command the President to state a recognition position inconsistent with his own and thus override the President's recognition determination. Although Congress may express its disagreement with the President in many ways, as, for example, by enacting an embargo or declining to confirm an ambassador, it may not force the President to contradict his earlier statement of recognition.

CONCURRENCE AND DISSENT: (Thomas, J.) The Vesting Clause of Article II of the Constitution vests all powers in the President originally understood as falling within the executive power, not just those powers expressly identified in the Constitution. Such power at founding included the foreign affairs powers and was understood to encompass all foreign affairs powers other than those otherwise allocated by the Constitution. One of those powers was the issuing and control of passports. Although this view has been criticized by Justice Scalia, he offers no other interpretation that contradicts it.

DISSENT: (Roberts, C.J.) The majority errs on the fundamental question of separation of powers presented by the case, as it has been stressed that the President's power is at its lowest when he contravenes the express will of Congress. The Reception Clause is framed as an obligation rather than as an authorization, and it appears alongside the duties imposed on the President, not the powers granted to him. Additionally, the President's powers to make treaties and appoint ambassadors are shared with Congress. Therefore, the majority's textual bases for its decision are tenuous and do not support the inference that the recognition power is exclusive. Historically, too, some Presidents have claimed an exclusive recognition power, but others have expressed uncertainty about whether such preclusive authority exists. Congress has also asserted the recognition power at various points throughout history. Thus, contrary to the majority's assertion, it cannot be said that Congress has accepted the President's exclusive recognition power, and in any event, congressional acquiescence has been held to be pertinent only when the President acts in the absence of express congressional authorization. Even assuming the President does have exclusive recognition power, he still cannot prevail in this case because the statute at issue does not implicate recognition. Congress has not disputed the Executive's assurances that Foreign Relations Authorization Act, Fiscal Year 2003, § 214(d) does not alter the longstanding United States position on Jerusalem, and diplomatic history offers no examples of official recognition accomplished via an optional passport designation. Ultimately, the only power that could support the President's position is the one the majority purports to reject: the "exclusive authority to conduct diplomatic relations." Yet even this power is not one that permits the Executive to contravene a statute, but rather may be exercised pursuant to a legislative delegation.

DISSENT: (Scalia, J.) The Constitution rejected the notion that foreign affairs would be vested exclusively in the Executive, as they had been in England's King and instead contemplated shared power in this area between the President and Congress. Congress has the power to grant American citizenship to someone born abroad under its naturalization power, Art. I, § 8, cl. 4, and this power enables Congress to furnish those citizens with papers, such as passports, that verify their citizenship. It follows that Congress may require what is placed on those documents as the citizen's place of birth. The birthplace specification promotes the document's citizenship-authenticating function and promotes other objectives. Although recording Zivotofsky's (P) birthplace as "Jerusalem" rather than "Israel" would fulfill these objectives, when faced with alternative ways to carry its powers into execution, Congress has the discretion to choose the one it deems most beneficial to the people. Therefore, for example, Congress has the right to decide that recording birthplaces as "Israel" makes for better foreign policy. Additionally, Foreign Relations Authorization Act, Fiscal Year 2003, § 214(d) has nothing to do with recognition. That provision does not require the Secretary of State (D) to make a formal declaration about Israel's sovereignty over Jerusalem, and nobody suggests that international custom infers acceptance of sovereignty from the birthplace designation on a passport or birth report, as it does from bilateral treaties or exchanges of ambassadors. Instead, the provision addresses what the government says about its citizens' identities. Even if the Constitution gives the President sole power to extend recognition, it does not give him sole power to make all decisions relating to foreign disputes over sovereignty. To the contrary, a fair reading of Article I allows Congress to decide for itself how its laws should handle such controversies. Recognition is a type of legal act, not a statement, so it is a large and illogical leap to go from exclusive authority over making legal commitments regarding sovereignty to exclusive authority over making statements or issuing documents regarding national borders. It is incorrect to suggest, as Justice Thomas does, that in areas of shared authority, it is executive policy that preempts the law. Acts of Congress are the supreme law of the land, whereas acts of the President (apart from treaties) are not. That is why it has long been held that a President who takes measures that are incompatible with the expressed or implied will of Congress may rely only upon his own constitutional powers minus any constitutional powers of Congress over the matter. Finally, Justice Thomas's approach would obliterate congressional power over foreign affairs. His

Continued on next page.

finding of broad, unenumerated "residual powers" in the President, along with his narrow reading of Congress's powers would produce a presidency more akin to a monarchy—"a presidency more reminiscent of George III than George Washington."

ANALYSIS

In *Zivotofsky*, the Court rejected the Secretary of State's (D) reliance on *United States v. Curtiss-Wright Export Corp.*, 299 U.S. 304 (1936), for the proposition that the President is "the sole organ of the federal government in the field of international relations." The Court rejected such unbounded power in the President, noting that this description of the President's powers was not necessary to the holding in *Curtiss-Wright*, and that the case dealt with congressionally authorized action, rather than a unilateral presidential determination. Thus, although the Court held that Congress has no power to make recognition determinations contrary to those of the President, it did not question Congress's substantial powers over foreign affairs in general or passports in particular.

Quicknotes

NATURALIZATION The process pursuant to which a person becomes a citizen of a country.

SEPARATION OF POWERS The system of checks and balances preventing one branch of government from infringing upon exercising the powers of another branch of government.

Dames & Moore v. Regan

Creditor (P) v. Federal government (D)

453 U.S. 654 (1981)

NATURE OF CASE: Certiorari review of appeal of decision issuing an order of attachment pursuant to a breach of contract.

FACT SUMMARY: Dames & Moore (P) filed suit to recover funds owed on a contract with the government of Iran, but the order of attachment was voided by an Executive Agreement.

RULE OF LAW

The President lacks the plenary power to settle claims against foreign governments through an Executive Agreement; however, where Congress at least acquiesces in the President's actions, the President can settle such claims.

FACTS: In November of 1979 President Carter, acting pursuant to the International Emergency Economic Powers Act (IEEPA), froze Iranian assets in the United States after Americans were taken hostage in Tehran. The Americans held hostage were subsequently released on January 20, 1981, pursuant to an Executive Agreement entered the day before. The agreement included a promise to settle all claims and litigation between the countries through arbitration. Dames & Moore (P), holders of an attachment order against Iranian assets, took exception to this agreement and filed suit. The litigation eventually reached the Supreme Court.

ISSUE: Does the President possess plenary powers to settle claims against foreign governments through an Executive Agreement?

HOLDING AND DECISION: (Rehnquist, J.) No. The President lacks the plenary power to settle claims against foreign governments through an Executive Agreement; however, where Congress at least acquiesces in the President's actions, the President can settle such claims. When Congress implicitly or explicitly authorizes presidential action, the action is given the greatest presumption of validity. Here, while the President's exact decision was not contemplated in the International Emergency Economic Powers Act (IEEPA), substantial powers to seize and handle foreign assets were conferred in the President by Congress. Dames & Moore (P) would have to show that the government as a whole lacks the power to settle claims with foreign entities when it is in the interest of the United States to do so; such a heavy burden has not been met. There is a long history of congressional acquiescence to international agreements settling claims between citizens of the United States and nationals of other countries. However, there is no independent source of presidential authority to settle such claims. Had Congress not implicitly approved of the action, the President would have been beyond his bounds. But in this case, he acted under the implied authority of Congress.

ANALYSIS

Justice Rehnquist cites the concurring opinion of Justice Jackson in the case of *Youngstown Sheet & Tube Co. v. Sawyer*, 343 U.S. 579 (1952). In that case, Justice Jackson divided presidential authority into three categories: express or implied grants of power from Congress, actions in the face of congressional silence, and actions in direct contravention to congressional legislation. When acting against the wishes of Congress, the President's power was limited to express constitutional grants in Article II. At the other extreme, presidential power was at its greatest when acting with congressional approval, as Justice Rehnquist found to be the case here.

Quicknotes

EXECUTIVE AGREEMENT An agreement with a foreign nation that is binding on the country, entered into by the President without Senate approval.

ORDER OF ATTACHMENT An order mandating the seizing of the property of one party in anticipation of, or in order to satisfy, a favorable judgment obtained by another party.

PLENARY Unlimited and open; as broad as a given situation may require.

Woods v. Cloyd W. Miller Co.

Federal government (P) v. Landlord (D)

333 U.S. 138 (1948)

NATURE OF CASE: Certiorari review of constitutionality of Housing and Rental Act of 1947.

FACT SUMMARY: When World War II ended and Congress enacted rent control regulation based upon its war power, a federal district court held the legislation unconstitutional on grounds that a Presidential Proclamation had terminated hostilities.

RULE OF LAW

Congress has the power pursuant to its war power to attempt to remedy situations caused by a war and continuing to exist after hostilities have ceased.

FACTS: A federal district court held unconstitutional Title II of the Housing and Rent Act of 1947, which regulated rents by virtue of the war power, reasoning that congressional authority to impose rent controls ended with the Presidential Proclamation terminating hostilities on December 31, 1946. The district court noted that the Proclamation announced "peace-in-fact." The court also stated that, even if the war power continued, Congress did not act under it because Congress did not specifically say that it did. Direct appeal was taken to the Supreme Court.

ISSUE: Does Congress have the power pursuant to the war power to attempt to remedy situations caused by a war and continuing to exist after hostilities have ceased?

HOLDING AND DECISION: (Douglas, J.) Yes. Congress has the power pursuant to its war power to attempt to remedy situations caused by a war and continuing to exist after hostilities have ceased. The war power includes the power to remedy evils that have arisen due to a war, and "whatever may be the consequences when war is officially terminated, the war power does not necessarily end with the cessation of hostilities." The war power is adequate to support the preservation of rights created by wartime legislation. And it has an even broader sweep. In *Hamilton v. Kentucky Distilleries Co.*, 251 U.S. 146 (1919), and *Ruppert v. Caffey*, 251 U.S. 264 (1920), prohibition laws enacted after the World War I armistice were sustained as exercises of the war power, because they conserved labor and increased efficiency of production in the critical days of demobilization and helped conserve the supply of grains and cereals depleted by the war. Following these cases, the war power sustains the Housing and Rental Act. The legislative history of the Act makes it clear that the housing shortage resulting from the war has not been eliminated. The legislative history also makes it clear that Congress is invoking the war power to sustain the Act. "The question of the constitutionality of action taken by Congress does not depend on its recitals of the power which it undertakes to exercise." Reversed.

CONCURRENCE: (Jackson, J.) The United States is still technically in a state of war. Hence the war power is a valid ground for federal rent control. However, "I would not be willing to hold that war powers last as long as the effects and consequences of war, for if so, they are permanent."

ANALYSIS

Article I, § 8 of the Constitution gives Congress the power to declare war, to raise and support armies, to provide and maintain a navy, to make rules for the government and regulation of the land and naval forces, and to provide for organizing, arming, disciplining, and calling forth the militia. Under this power, Congress's enactment of comprehensive legislation regulating the national economy during a war has been sustained. The Emergency Price Control Act of 1942 was sustained as applying to rents in *Bowies v. Willingham*, 321 U.S. 503 (1944), and as to prices in *Yakus v. U.S.*, 321 U.S. 414 (1944). The Renegotiation Act was sustained in *Lichter v. U.S.*, 334 U.S. 742 (1948). It provided for recapture of excessive profits realized on war contracts where the ultimate source of payment was the U.S. government.

Quicknotes

WAR POWERS CLAUSE Article I, § 8 of the U.S. Constitution granting Congress the power to declare war.

Missouri v. Holland

State (P) v. Federal game warden (D)

252 U.S. 416 (1920)

NATURE OF CASE: Certiorari review of constitutionality of Migratory Bird Treaty Act.

FACT SUMMARY: Missouri (P) claimed that the Migratory Bird Treaty Act was an unconstitutional interference with the rights reserved to the states by the Tenth Amendment.

RULE OF LAW

Congress may validly enact a statute to enforce a treaty even if the statute standing by itself would be unconstitutional because it interfered with the rights reserved to the states by the Tenth Amendment.

FACTS: On December 8, 1916, the United States entered a treaty with Great Britain to protect birds that migrated between Canada and the United States. Congress passed a statute to enforce the Migratory Bird Treaty Act (the Treaty), which allowed the Secretary of Agriculture to formulate regulations to enforce the Treaty. The State of Missouri (P) filed a bill in equity to prevent Holland (D), the game warden of the United States, from enforcing the treaty. Missouri (P) claimed the statute was an unconstitutional interference with the rights reserved to the states by the Tenth Amendment and it had a pecuniary interest as owner of the wild birds that was being interfered with. Before the Treaty had been entered into, Congress had attempted to regulate the killing of migratory birds within the states and that statute, standing by itself, had been declared unconstitutional. The United States contended that Congress had the power to enact the statute to enforce the treaty and that the statute and treaty were the supreme law of the land.

ISSUE: Can Congress validly enact a statute to enforce a treaty if the statute standing by itself would be unconstitutional because it interfered with the rights reserved to the states by the Tenth Amendment?

HOLDING AND DECISION: (Holmes, J.) Yes. Congress may validly enact a statute to enforce a treaty even if the statute standing by itself would be unconstitutional because it interfered with the rights reserved to the states by the Tenth Amendment. Article II, § 2, grants the President the power to make treaties and Article VI, § 2, declares that treaties shall be part of the supreme law of the land. If a treaty is a valid one, Article I, § 8, gives Congress the power to enact legislation that is a necessary and proper means to enforce the treaty. While acts of Congress are the supreme law of the land only when they are made in pursuance of the Constitution, treaties are valid when made under the authority of the United States. The Court stated that there were qualifications to the treaty-making power but felt that the qualifications must be determined by looking at the facts of each case. There are situations that require national action, which an act of Congress could not deal with, but which a treaty enforced with a congressional act could. Affirmed.

ANALYSIS

Many people were upset with the decision in this case because they feared that the Court had interpreted the treaty power so broadly that all constitutional limitations could be overridden by the use of treaties and accompanying congressional legislation. In 1954, the Bricker Amendment, which required that a treaty could become effective as internal law in the United States only through legislation that would be valid in the absence of the treaty, was narrowly defeated. This would have, in effect, overruled the decision in this case because the congressional act was not valid when standing by itself. Several other similar proposals were made during the following three years, which also failed.

Quicknotes

PECUNIARY Consisting of, or pertaining to, money.

TENTH AMENDMENT The Tenth Amendment to the U.S. Constitution reserves those powers therein, not expressly delegated to the federal government or prohibited to the states, to the states or to the people.

TREATY An agreement made between two or more independent nations; once a treaty is made into law, it becomes applicable to the states under Article IV, § 2, of the U.S. Constitution.

Ex parte Quirin

Federal government (P) v. Third Reich sabotage agents (D)

317 U.S. 1 (1942)

NATURE OF CASE: Petition for habeas corpus to Supreme Court.

FACT SUMMARY: When Third Reich sabotage agents (D) were apprehended within the United States during World War II, they argued it would be unconstitutional for them to be tried before a military tribunal. The agents (D) sought trial by jury in the civil courts.

RULE OF LAW

The detention and trial of foreign espionage and sabotage agents within the United States during time of war, by a military commission appointed by the President, is constitutional.

FACTS: During World War II, citizens of the German Reich, with which the United States was at war, after being trained at a sabotage school near Berlin, entered the United States by submarine, with explosives and plans to disrupt a variety of military targets throughout the United States. All were to receive salary payments from the German government for this operation. Prior to being able to carry out their mission, they were apprehended by the Federal Bureau of Investigation and were to be tried by a military tribunal according to the Articles of War enacted by Congress for violations of the law of war and of the Articles of Law. The federal district court denied the German sabotage agents' (D) argument that their trial before a military tribunal would be unconstitutional, and the sabotage agents (D) petitioned for habeas corpus to the Supreme Court.

ISSUE: Is the detention and trial of foreign espionage and sabotage agents within the United States during time of war, by a military commission appointed by the President, constitutional?

HOLDING AND DECISION: (Stone, C.J.) Yes. The detention and trial of foreign espionage and sabotage agents within the United States during time of war, by a military commission appointed by the President, is constitutional. By universal agreement and practice, the law of war draws a distinction between the armed forces and the peaceful populations of belligerent nations and also between those who are lawful and unlawful combatants. Lawful combatants are subject to capture and detention as prisoners of war by opposing military forces. Unlawful combatants are likewise subject to capture and detention, but in addition they are subject to trial and punishment by military tribunals for acts that render their belligerency unlawful. The latter, such as spies and those who seek to wage war through destruction of life or property, as here, are familiar examples of belligerents who are deemed not to be entitled to the status of prisoners of war, but rather are offenders against the law of war subject to trial and punishment by military tribunals. Furthermore, even citizenship in the United States of an enemy belligerent does not relieve such person from the consequences of a belligerency which is unlawful because in violation of the law of war. This Court cannot say that Congress in preparing the Fifth and Sixth Amendments intended to extend trial by jury to the cases of alien or citizen offenders against the law of war otherwise triable by a military commission. Writ of habeas corpus denied.

ANALYSIS

As explained in the *Quirin* decision, by the Articles of War, Congress had explicitly provided that military tribunals had jurisdiction to try offenders or offenses against the law of war in appropriate cases. It made no difference that the unlawful combatants in the *Quirin* case were apprehended before they had the opportunity to actually commit the espionage and sabotage which was their goal.

Quicknotes

FIFTH AMENDMENT Provides that no person shall be compelled to serve as a witness against him- or herself, be subject to trial for the same offense twice, or be deprived of life, liberty, or property without due process of law.

SIXTH AMENDMENT Provides the right to a speedy and public trial by impartial jury, the right to be informed of the accusation, the right to confront witnesses, and the right to have the assistance of counsel in all criminal prosecutions.

WRIT OF HABEAS CORPUS A proceeding in which a defendant brings a writ to compel a judicial determination of whether the defendant is lawfully being held in custody.

Hamdi v. Rumsfeld

Alleged enemy combatant (P) v. Secretary of Defense (D)

542 U.S. 507 (2004)

NATURE OF CASE: Certiorari review from the denial of right to challenge enemy-combatant status.

FACT SUMMARY: Hamdi (P), an American citizen designated as an enemy combatant, argued that he was entitled to contest such designation in court.

RULE OF LAW

Due process requires that a citizen held in the United States as an enemy combatant be given a meaningful opportunity to contest the factual basis for that detention before a neutral decisionmaker.

FACTS: Hamdi (P), an American citizen, was designated by the Government (D) an "enemy combatant" and placed into indefinite detainment. The federal court of appeals held the detention to be legally authorized and that Hamdi (P) was entitled to no further opportunity to challenge his enemy-combatant label. Hamdi (P) appealed to the Supreme Court.

ISSUE: Does due process require that a citizen held in the United States as an enemy combatant be given a meaningful opportunity to contest the factual basis for that detention before a neutral decisionmaker?

HOLDING AND DECISION: (O'Connor, J.) Yes. Due process requires that a citizen held in the United States as an enemy combatant be given a meaningful opportunity to contest the factual basis for that detention before a neutral decisionmaker. This Court understands Congress's statutory grant of authority for the use of "necessary and appropriate force" to include the authority to detain for the duration of the relevant conflict, and our understanding is based on long-standing law-of-war principles. If the practical circumstances of a given conflict are entirely unlike those of the conflicts that informed the development of the law of war, that understanding may unravel. But that is not the situation that we face as of this date. The United States may, therefore, detain, for the duration of these hostilities, Hamdi (P) and other individuals legitimately determined to be Taliban combatants who "engaged in an armed conflict against the United States." Nevertheless, the writ of habeas corpus remains available to every individual detained within the United States; the writ remains a critical check on the executive branch, ensuring that Hamdi (P) was properly brought before an Article III court to challenge his detention by this writ. On the evidence presented below, the circumstances surrounding Hamdi's (P) seizure cannot in any way be characterized as "undisputed." He may—or may not—in fact be an "enemy combatant" such as to justify his detention without trial or ultimate trial before a military tribunal. It is vital that this Court does not give short shrift to the values that this country holds dear or to the privilege that is American citizenship. Accordingly, a citizen-detainee seeking to challenge his or her classification as an enemy combatant must receive notice of the factual basis for the classification, and a fair opportunity to rebut the Government's (D) factual assertions before a neutral decisionmaker. These essential constitutional promises may not be eroded. Vacated and remanded.

CONCURRENCE AND DISSENT: (Souter, J.) The Government (D) has failed to demonstrate that the Force Resolution authorizes the detention complained of here even on the facts the Government (D) claims. If the Government (D) raises nothing further than the record now shows, the Non-Detention Act entitles Hamdi (P) to be released. The branch of government asked to counter a serious threat is not the branch on which to rest the nation's entire reliance in striking the balance between the will to win and "the cost in liberty on the way to victory."

DISSENT: (Scalia, J.) The very core of liberty secured by our Anglo-Saxon system of separated powers has been freedom from indefinite imprisonment at the will of the Executive. The gist of the Due Process Clause was to force the Government (D) to follow those common-law procedures traditionally deemed necessary before depriving a person of life, liberty, or property. Hamdi (P) is entitled to a habeas decree requiring his release unless (1) criminal proceedings are promptly brought or (2) Congress has suspended the writ of habeas corpus. Neither has here occurred. Rather than remand, the decision below should be reversed.

DISSENT: (Thomas, J.) The executive branch, acting pursuant to powers vested in the President by the Constitution and by explicit congressional approval, has determined that Hamdi (P) is an enemy combatant and should be detained. This Court lacks the expertise and capacity to second-guess that decision. As such, Hamdi's (P) habeas challenge should fail, and there is no reason to remand the case.

ANALYSIS

As made clear in the *Hamdi* decision, in cases of this type the court must balance two vital yet competing interests: on the one hand, respect for separation of powers and the fundamental importance of the nation

Continued on next page.

to be able to protect itself during time of war; on the other hand, the critical and deep-seated individual constitutional interests at stake.

Quicknotes

DUE PROCESS CLAUSE Language in the Fifth and Fourteenth Amendments to the U.S. Constitution providing that no person shall be deprived of "life, liberty, or property without due process of law."

WRIT OF HABEAS CORPUS A proceeding in which a defendant brings a writ to compel a judicial determination of whether the defendant is lawfully being held in custody.

Hamdan v. Rumsfeld

Guantanamo Bay detainee (P) v. Secretary of Defense (D)

548 U.S. 557 (2006)

NATURE OF CASE: Petition for writ of habeas corpus filed by a Guantanamo Bay detainee.

FACT SUMMARY: A Yemeni national detained by U.S. military forces at Guantanamo Bay, Cuba, was charged with conspiracy "to commit offenses triable by military commission."

RULE OF LAW

A military commission does not have jurisdiction to hear a case if the commission's structures and procedures violate the Uniform Code of Military Justice and the Geneva Conventions.

FACTS: In November 2001, the U.S. military forces in Afghanistan captured Salim Ahmed Hamdan (P), a Yemeni national. Hamdan (P) was transported to an American prison at Guantanamo Bay, Cuba, in June 2002. At some time after June 2003, President Bush (D) declared Hamdan (P) subject to trial by military commission for crimes that the President (D) did not specify at that time. More than a year later, Hamdan (P) was charged with conspiring, from 1996 to November 2001, "to commit. . .offenses triable by military commission." Hamdan (P) sued the Government (D), filing a petition for writ of habeas corpus to challenge the validity of his detention. [The trial court agreed with Hamdan (P) that the military commission convened to hear his case lacked authority because it failed to comply with the Uniform Code of Military Justice and the Geneva Conventions.] The intermediate appellate court reversed, and Hamdan (P) petitioned the Supreme Court for further review.

ISSUE: Does a military commission have jurisdiction to hear a case if the commission's structures and procedures violate the Uniform Code of Military Justice and the Geneva Conventions?

HOLDING AND DECISION: (Stevens, J.) No. A military commission does not have jurisdiction to hear a case if the commission's structures and procedures violate the Uniform Code of Military Justice (UCMJ) and the Geneva Conventions. Congress generally approved military commissions in 1916, but only on the express condition that the President (D) follow the law of war. But more recent congressional action—the joint resolution authorizing the use of military force (the Authorization for Use of Military Force [the AUMF]) and the Detainee Treatment Act (DTA)—did not expand executive power to create military commissions. Such commissions generally are permitted in three circumstances: (1) to substitute for civilian law after martial law has been declared; (2) to substitute for civilian law during times of temporary military government, whether the territory in question is or is not occupied by an enemy; and (3) in a situation usually occurring on the battlefield, to decide whether the defendant has violated the law of war. Only the third situation applies here because Guantanamo Bay is not under martial law and is not territory occupied by the enemy. That holding in turn leads to the conclusion that the military commission convened to hear Hamdan's (P) conspiracy charge lacks jurisdiction. Conspiracy has almost never, if ever, been tried by a law-of-war military commission, and conspiracy is not seen internationally as violating the law of war. Moreover, the procedures to be used by the commission hearing Hamdan's (P) trial undermine the commission's authority by failing to comply with the UCMJ and the Geneva Conventions. The commission in this case would be permitted to try Hamdan (P) while preventing him from knowing what evidence was introduced against him. The rules of courts-martial, however, apply to military commissions unless such application is impracticable, and those rules grant an accused the right to be present. Here, the Government (D) has made no showing that the rules of courts-martial would be impracticable in this case. Those rules therefore must apply to Hamdan's (P) trial. Further, Article 3 of the Geneva Conventions provides that military commissions are permitted only if some demonstrated practical need to deviate from normal courts-martial exists. Again, the Government (D) has failed to make the requisite showing of need, and the military commission here thus also fails under the Geneva Conventions. The right to be present, which is guaranteed by the Conventions, therefore applies in this case under international law, too. Reversed.

CONCURRENCE: (Breyer, J.) Congress did not grant the President (D) unlimited authority to fight the war on terror. If no emergency warrants the President's (D) failure to consult with Congress, then the Court's insistence on such consultation does not undermine the war effort.

CONCURRENCE: (Kennedy, J.) Congressional action establishes boundaries in this case that the President (D) has exceeded. The military commission's structure and procedure in this case raise severe separation-of-powers issues: the executive branch can define, prosecute, and hear the charges against Hamdan (P) without any oversight or review from the other two branches of government. Additionally, this record shows no special

Continued on next page.

urgency to justify trial by military commission because Hamdan (P) now has been detained for approximately four years. For all these reasons, the military commission in this case is not regularly constituted under U.S. law as required by the Uniform Code of Military Justice. There is therefore no reason to decide whether the commission complies with the Geneva Conventions or whether (as the dissent undertakes) Hamdan's (P) conspiracy charge is valid.

DISSENT: (Thomas, J.) This decision substitutes the Court's discretion for the President's (D), contrary to our constitutional order. In the Authorization for Use of Military Force, Congress authorized the President (D) to use his discretion in using force to combat international terrorism. The military commission convened here easily complies with that authorization and with the requirement that such commissions hear charges of offenses "committed within the field of the command of the convening commander." The President (D) has deemed this conflict to have roots stretching back into the 1990s, and this Court cannot question that conclusion. But whether the Court applies the correct, flexible approach to military commissions or today's more rigid analysis, Hamdan (P) can be tried by military commission because he is an alleged member of a criminal enterprise and he allegedly conspired to commit war crimes. Countering these clear grounds for upholding the military commission in this case, the plurality can only substitute its own impression of "military necessity" for the President's (D) own discretionary judgment. The Uniform Code of Military Justice does not support this decision, and the Geneva Conventions are not judicially enforceable. Even if they were, though, Hamdan (P) should not prevail on his petition because, consistent with the Conventions, the Government (D) may not deprive him of the right to be present if doing so would subject him to an unfair trial.

DISSENT: (Alito, J.) Hamdan's (P) military commission is a "regularly constituted court," and it therefore complies with the laws applied by the plurality to invalidate the commission. The commission here provides trial procedures, administrative review, and even opportunity for formal appellate review. Contrary to today's decision, such a procedure affords an accused much more than "summary justice."

ANALYSIS

Justice Kennedy's concurrence highlights the grave separation-of-powers issues generated by the military commission in *Hamdan*. Here the executive branch tried (1) to perform legislative functions by creating a previously unknown crime subject to hearing by military commission, (2) to perform executive functions by prosecuting the alleged violation of the new crime, and (3) to perform judicial functions by adjudicating the prosecution of the alleged violation of the new crime in a forum over which the executive branch held great control. Such goals are the classic ingredients for violations of the doctrine of the separation of powers.

Quicknotes

CONSPIRACY Concerted action by two or more persons to accomplish some unlawful purpose.

GENEVA CONVENTION International agreement that governs the conduct of warring nations.

SEPARATION OF POWERS The system of checks and balances preventing one branch of government from infringing upon exercising the powers of another branch of government.

WRIT OF HABEAS CORPUS A proceeding in which a defendant brings a writ to compel a judicial determination of whether the defendant is lawfully being held in custody.

Boumediene v. Bush

Guantanamo detainees (P) v. Federal government (D)

553 U.S. 723 (2008)

NATURE OF CASE: Review of federal appeals court judgment.

FACT SUMMARY: Lakhdar Boumediene (P) and other detainees (P) held at Guantanamo Bay, Cuba, petitioned the court for a writ of habeas corpus. The federal appeals court ruled in favor of the U.S. Government (D).

RULE OF LAW

(1) The Military Commissions Act of 2006 strips federal courts of jurisdiction over habeas petitions filed by foreign citizens detained at Guantanamo Bay.

(2) Detainees are not barred from seeking habeas or invoking the Suspension Clause simply because they had been designated as enemy combatants or held at Guantanamo Bay.

(3) The Military Commissions Act of 2006 is a violation of the Suspension Clause of the Constitution.

FACTS: Bosnian police captured Lakhdar Boumediene (P) and five other Algerian natives after U.S. intelligence officers suspected them of plotting to attack the U.S. embassy there. The U.S. Government (D) classified the men as enemy combatants in the war on terror and held them at the Guantanamo Bay. Boumediene (P) filed a petition for a writ of habeas corpus, claiming that the U.S. Government (D) violated the Due Process Clause of the U.S. Constitution, various statutes and treaties, the common law, and international law. A district court judge granted the Government's (D) motion to have all of the claims dismissed on the ground that Boumediene (P), as an alien held at an overseas military base, had no right to a habeas petition. The Court of Appeals for the D.C. Circuit affirmed, but the Supreme Court reversed in *Rasul v. Bush*, 542 U.S. 466 (2004), holding that the habeas statute extends to noncitizen detainees at Guantanamo. In 2006, Congress passed the Military Commissions Act of 2006 (MCA), which withdrew the jurisdiction of federal courts to hear habeas applications from detainees classified as enemy combatants under the Detainee Treatment Act of 2005. The case was appealed to the D.C. Circuit for the second time, and this time the detainees (P) argued that the MCA did not apply to their petitions, and that if it did, it was unconstitutional under the Suspension Clause. The D.C. Circuit ruled in favor of the Government (D) on both points, holding that the MCA applied to "all cases, without exception," that pertain to aspects of detention. One of the purposes of the MCA, according to the court, was to overrule the Supreme Court's opinion in *Hamdan v. Rumsfeld*, 548 U.S. 557 (2006), which had allowed petitions like Boumediene's (P) to go forward. The D.C. Circuit held that the Suspension Clause protects only the writ of habeas corpus as it existed in 1789, and that the writ would not have been understood in 1789 to apply to an overseas military base leased from a foreign government. Constitutional rights do not apply to aliens outside of the United States, the court held, and the leased military base in Cuba does not qualify as inside the geographic borders of the United States. The Supreme Court granted certiorari after initially denying review, three months earlier.

ISSUE:

(1) Does the Military Commissions Act of 2006 strip federal courts of jurisdiction over habeas petitions filed by foreign citizens detained at Guantanamo Bay?

(2) Are detainees barred from seeking habeas or invoking the Suspension Clause simply because they had been designated as enemy combatants or held at Guantanamo Bay?

(3) Is the Military Commissions Act of 2006 a violation of the Suspension Clause of the Constitution?

HOLDING AND DECISION: (Kennedy, J.)

(1) Yes. The Military Commissions Act of 2006 (the MCA) strips federal courts of jurisdiction over habeas petitions filed by foreign citizens detained at Guantanamo Bay. If the MCA is considered valid, its legislative history requires that the detainees' cases be dismissed.

(2) No. Detainees are not barred from seeking habeas or invoking the Suspension Clause simply because they had been designated as enemy combatants or held at Guantanamo Bay. The Suspension Clause provides that the "Privilege of the Writ of Habeas Corpus shall not be suspended, unless when in Cases of Rebellion or Invasion the public Safety may require it." The Framers thought the writ was an essential mechanism in the separation-of-powers scheme. Moreover, the Suspension Clause applies to Guantanamo, despite the fact that the United States (D) does not claim sovereignty over the place of detention. Even when the United States (D) acts outside its borders, its powers are subject to the Constitution.

(3) Yes. The Military Commissions Act of 2006 (the MCA) is a violation of the Suspension Clause of the Constitution. Because the procedures laid out in the Detainee Treatment Act are not adequate substitutes

Continued on next page.

for the habeas writ, the MCA operates as an unconstitutional suspension of that writ. Reversed.

CONCURRENCE: (Souter, J.) Two additional points are worth mentioning: First, the jurisdictional question answered in this case would be answered in the same way in purely constitutional cases. Second, the prisoners involved in this case have been held at Guantanamo for six years, without habeas scrutiny, and while the military should handle such cases within some reasonable period of time, it was appropriate for the courts to step in where the military had failed after six years.

DISSENT: (Roberts, C.J.) The procedural protections offered aliens who are detained by this country as enemy combatants were generous under the Detainee Treatment Act, and the court rejects them out of hand without stating what due process rights the detainees hold. The majority also fails to delineate the procedures that should be followed by the judiciary in reviewing cases deemed appropriate. The majority's opinion is not really about the detainees but about control of federal policy regarding enemy combatants.

DISSENT: (Scalia, J.) The Court's grant of constitutional right to habeas corpus to alien enemies detained abroad by military forces occurs in the course of an ongoing war, but the writ of habeas corpus does not, and never has, run in favor of aliens abroad. The Suspension Clause has no application, and the court's intervention is ultra vires.

ANALYSIS

President Bush agreed to honor the ruling. At a June 2008 town hall meeting, then-Republican presidential nominee John McCain said the ruling was "one of the worst decisions in the history of this country." He said that "[t]hese are people who are not citizens. They do not and never have been given the rights that citizens in this country have." Then-Democratic presidential nominee Barack Obama described the ruling as "a rejection of the Bush administration's attempt to create a legal black hole at Guantanamo" and "an important step toward re-establishing our credibility as a nation committed to the rule of law."

Quicknotes

DUE PROCESS The constitutional mandate requiring the courts to protect and enforce individuals' rights and liberties consistent with prevailing principles of fairness and justice and prohibiting the federal and state governments from such activities that deprive its citizens of life, liberty, or property interest.

DUE PROCESS CLAUSE Language in the Fifth and Fourteenth Amendments to the U.S. Constitution providing that no person shall be deprived of "life, liberty, or property without due process of law."

HABEAS CORPUS A proceeding in which a defendant brings a writ to compel a judicial determination of whether he or she is lawfully being held in custody.

SUSPENSION CLAUSE A clause found in Article I of the U.S. Constitution that protects against arbitrary suspensions of the writ of habeas corpus.

INS v. Chadha

Federal agency (D) v. Deportable alien (P)

462 U.S. 919 (1983)

NATURE OF CASE: Consolidated actions challenging the constitutionality of a federal statute.

FACT SUMMARY: Chadha (P) and others challenged the constitutionality of a federal statute that purported to authorize one House of Congress, by resolution, to invalidate the decision of the Attorney General (made under authority delegated by Congress) to allow a particular deportable illegal immigrant to remain in the United States.

RULE OF LAW

The Constitution does not permit Congress to statutorily authorize a one-house veto of a decision the Attorney General makes, pursuant to authority delegated to him by Congress, to allow a particular deportable alien to remain in the United States.

FACTS: Three cases consolidated on appeal all presented the question of the constitutionality of a federal statute that authorized either House of Congress, by resolution, to invalidate the decision of the Attorney General (made pursuant to authority delegated by Congress) to allow a particular deportable alien to remain in the United States. After such a one-house veto effectively overturned the Attorney General's decision to let Chadha (P) and certain other individuals remain in the United States, each instituted action challenging the constitutionality of the aforesaid statute. Chadha (P) filed a petition for a review of his deportation order, with the Immigration and Naturalization Service (D) actually agreeing with his contention that the statute was unconstitutional. The court of appeals held that the statute violated the doctrine of separation of powers.

ISSUE: Is it constitutional for Congress to statutorily authorize a one-house veto of a decision the Attorney General makes, pursuant to authority delegated to him by Congress, to allow a particular deportable alien to remain in the United States?

HOLDING AND DECISION: (Burger, C.J.) No. The Constitution does not permit Congress to statutorily authorize a one-house veto of a decision the Attorney General makes, pursuant to authority delegated to him by Congress, to allow a particular deportable alien to remain in the United States. Such an action is clearly an exercise of legislative power, which makes it subject to the bicameralism and presentment requirements of Article I of the Constitution unless one of the express constitutional exceptions authorizing one House to act alone applies. None of them apply. Thus, to accomplish what has been attempted by one House of Congress in this case requires action in conformity with the express procedures of the Constitution's prescription for legislative action, passage by a majority of both Houses, and presentment to the President (for his signing or his veto). Such requirements were built into the Constitution to act as enduring checks on each branch and to protect the people from the improvident exercise of power by mandating certain prescribed steps. In attempting to bypass those steps, Congress has acted unconstitutionally. Affirmed.

CONCURRENCE: (Powell, J.) This case should be decided on the narrower ground that Congress assumes a judicial function in violation of the principle of separation of powers when it finds that a particular person does not satisfy the statutory criteria for permanent residence in this country. The Framers were concerned that a trial by the legislature lacks the safeguards necessary to prevent the abuse of power. The legislature here has undertaken the type of decision that has normally been left to other branches.

DISSENT: (White, J.) Today's decision sounds the death knell for nearly two hundred statutory provisions in which Congress has reserved a "legislative veto," which has become a central means by which Congress secures the accountability of executive and independent agencies. Without this particular tool, Congress faces a Hobson's choice: either to refrain from delegating the necessary authority, leaving itself with a hopeless task of writing laws with the requisite specificity to cover endless special circumstances across the entire policy landscape, or, in the alternative, to abdicate its lawmaking function to the executive branch and independent agencies. Thus, the apparent sweep of the Court's decision today, which appears to invalidate all legislative vetoes irrespective of form or subject, is regrettable. Furthermore, the Court's decision fails to recognize that the legislative veto is not the type of action subject to the bicameralism and presentment requirements of Article I. Only bills and their equivalent are subject to such requirements. The initial legislation delegating to the Attorney General the power to make a decision on the deportation of a particular alien complied with the Article I requirements. Congress's power to exercise a legislative veto over that decision cannot be viewed, then, as the power to write new law without bicameral approval or presidential consideration. If Congress can delegate lawmaking power to executive

Continued on next page.

agencies, it is most difficult to understand Article I as forbidding Congress from simply reserving a check on legislative power for itself. Without the veto, agencies to whom power has been delegated may issue regulations having the force of law without bicameral approval and without the President's signature. It is thus not apparent why the reservation of a veto over the exercise of that legislative power must be subject to a more exacting test. In both cases, it is enough that the initial statutory authorizations comply with the Article I requirements.

ANALYSIS

It is only within the past 50 years that the legislative veto has come into widespread use. When the federal government began its massive growth in response to the Depression, the legislative veto was "invented" as one means of keeping a check on the sprawling new structure. While many commentators, upon the Court's announcement of this decision, opined that the result was a major shift of power from the legislative branch to the executive branch, Congress, through more restrictive draftsmanship, should actually see a minimal diminishment of its control over those areas in which it desires to retain control.

Quicknotes

BICAMERALISM The necessity for approval by a majority of both houses of Congress when ratifying legislation or approving other legislative action.

LEGISLATIVE VETO A statutory provision that contemplates the congressional ability to require the President or another part of the executive branch to act or to refrain from taking action.

PRESENTMENT Act of bringing a congressional decision before the President for approval or veto.

Clinton v. New York

President of the United States (D) v. City government et al. (P)

524 U.S. 417 (1998)

NATURE OF CASE: Challenge to the constitutionality of new presidential powers.

FACT SUMMARY: The Line Item Veto Act of 1996 allowed the President to cancel provisions that have been signed into law. Parties affected by President Clinton's cancellation of a provision of the Balanced Budget Act of 1997 challenged the constitutionality of the Act.

RULE OF LAW

The cancellation provisions authorized by the Line Item Veto Act are not constitutional.

FACTS: [President Clinton used his authority under the Line Item Veto Act of 1996 to cancel a provision of the Balanced Budget Act of 1997. This forced New York to repay certain funds to the federal government under the Medicaid program and removed a tax benefit to food processors acquired by farmers' cooperatives. New York City and several private organizations challenged the constitutionality of the Medicaid cancellation, and the Snake River Potato Growers (a farmers' cooperative) challenged the food processors provision.]

ISSUE: Are the cancellation provisions authorized by the Line Item Veto Act constitutional?

HOLDING AND DECISION: (Stevens, J.) No. The cancellation provisions authorized by the Line Item Veto Act are not constitutional. The Line Item Veto Act gives the President the power to "cancel in whole" three types of provisions that have already been signed into law: (1) any dollar amount of discretionary budget authority; (2) any item of new direct spending; or (3) any limited tax benefit. With respect to each cancellation, the President must determine that it will (i) reduce the federal budget deficit, (ii) not impair any essential government functions, and (iii) not harm the national interest. A cancellation takes effect upon receipt by Congress of the notification of the cancellation. However, a majority vote of both Houses is sufficient to make the cancellation null and void. Although the Constitution expressly authorizes the President to veto a bill under Article I, § 7, it is silent on the subject of unilateral presidential action that repeals or amends parts of duly enacted statues as authorized under the Line Item Veto Act. Constitutional silence should be construed as express prohibition. If there is to be a new role for the President in the procedure to determine the final text of a law, such a change must come through the amendment procedures and not by legislation. Affirmed.

CONCURRENCE: (Kennedy, J.) Separation of powers was designed to protect liberty, because the concentration of power in any single branch is a threat to liberty.

DISSENT: (Breyer, J.) Given how complex our nation has become, Congress cannot divide bills into thousands or tens of thousands of separate appropriations bills, each of which the President would have to veto or sign separately. Therefore, the Line Item Veto may help representative government work better.

ANALYSIS

The majority did not comment on the wisdom of the Line Item Veto Act, because they found this step unnecessary given their finding that the Act was unconstitutional. Justice Kennedy did not let that stop him, since he felt that the Line Item Veto Act affected the separation of powers, which in turn threatened liberty.

Quicknotes

LINE ITEM VETO ACT Authorizes a government official to veto specified items in appropriation bills.

SEPARATION OF POWERS The system of checks and balances preventing one branch of government from infringing upon exercising the powers of another branch of government.

Bowsher v. Synar

Federal government (D) v. Challenger to legislation (P)

478 U.S. 714 (1986)

NATURE OF CASE: Direct appeal to consider constitutionality of "Gramm-Rudman-Hollings Act" reporting provisions.

FACT SUMMARY: Bowsher (D) took a direct appeal to the Supreme Court from a district court ruling invalidating the reporting provisions of the "Gramm-Rudman-Hollings" deficit control act, finding the assignment of certain functions under the Act to the Comptroller General violated the doctrine of separation of powers.

RULE OF LAW

The assignment of executive powers to an agent or officer of the legislative branch violates the doctrine of separation of powers.

FACTS: [In 1985, the President signed into law the Gramm-Rudman-Hollings Deficit Control Act (the Act). The Act called for automatic reductions through the implementation of the so-called reporting provisions of the Act. Under these provisions, deficits are estimated, and if excessive, the Directors of the Office of Management and Budget and the congressional Budget Office are to calculate necessary, program-by-program reductions, which are reported to the Comptroller General. After reviewing these figures, the Comptroller General reports his conclusions to the President, who is required to implement the reductions specified in the report. Anticipating constitutional challenge, the Act contained a fallback reporting provision, whereby the Directors would report to a specially created Committee on Deficit Reduction, which in turn would report a joint resolution to both houses, which would then be voted on and amended. If the resolution were passed and signed by the President, the resolution would become the basis of the mandated reductions. Hours after the Act was signed, Synar (P) filed a complaint seeking declaratory relief that the Act was unconstitutional. The district court invalidated the reporting provisions, and a direct appeal was taken to the Supreme Court.]

ISSUE: Does the assignment of executive powers to an agent or officer of the legislative branch violate the doctrine of separation of powers?

HOLDING AND DECISION: (Burger, C.J.) Yes. The assignment of executive powers to an agent or officer of the legislative branch violates the doctrine of separation of powers. [The Court quickly disposed of standing issues.] The Constitution does not contemplate an active role for Congress in the supervision of officers charged with the execution of the laws. Congress would thereby retain a sort of congressional veto. The Comptroller General is subject to removal by Congress, and these removal powers dictate that the Comptroller General will be subservient to congressional control. Further, Congress has consistently viewed the Comptroller General as an officer of the legislative branch. There is no question that the Comptroller General acts in an executive capacity by executing the Gramm-Rudman-Hollings Deficit Control Act's (the Act) reduction reporting provisions. By law, the President is required to implement the reductions of the Comptroller General. By placing the execution of the Act in the hands of an officer controlled by Congress, the doctrine of separation of powers is violated. Affirmed.

DISSENT: (White, J.) The majority's conclusion rests on the premise that any direct involvement of Congress in the removal of officers charged with the execution of laws violates the separation of powers. It is unrealistic to think that the Comptroller General is subservient to Congress. The Gramm-Rudman-Hollings Deficit Control Act (the Act) itself represents a congressional choice as to how to execute the Act, and the President has chosen not to upset the choice. Since there is no threat to the balance of authority, the Act need not be struck down.

ANALYSIS

One of the alternatives posited by the dissent ignores the 60-year evolution of the office of the Comptroller General. To invalidate the congressional removal provisions would presumably leave removal in the hands of the executive branch and would wreak havoc with the office as to any number of legislative functions the Comptroller General's office performs.

Quicknotes

CONGRESSIONAL VETO The authority vested in Congress to engage in decision-making ability over the executive branch of government.

DECLARATORY RELIEF Request to a court for determination of legal status, rights, or ownership of a thing.

SEPARATION OF POWERS The system of checks and balances preventing one branch of government from infringing upon exercising the powers of another branch of government.

Morrison v. Olson

Federal government (D) v. Subject of special prosecutor investigation (P)

487 U.S. 654 (1988)

NATURE OF CASE: Certiorari review of invalidation of the Ethics in Government Act.

FACT SUMMARY: The Ethics in Government Act, which created the independent counsel/special prosecutor, was challenged as unconstitutional.

RULE OF LAW

Congress's creation of the independent counsel was not an unconstitutional usurpation of power.

FACTS: In 1978, Congress passed the Ethics in Government Act (the Act). One facet of this legislation was the creation of the office of the independent counsel. The pertinent provisions mandated that upon receipt of certain information, the Attorney General may determine whether evidence of official wrongdoing warrants appointment of a special prosecutor. The results are reported to a special court. The court is empowered to appoint a special prosecutor, who would be given broad investigative powers. The only power to remove the prosecutor lay in impeachment or by the Attorney General, after a showing of good cause. The Act contained certain requirements of reporting to Congress. Olson (P), a subject of an inquiry by a special prosecutor, challenged the Act as violative of the Appointments Clause and separation of powers. The district court upheld the law, but the court of appeals reversed. The Supreme Court granted review.

ISSUE: Was Congress's creation of the independent counsel an unconstitutional usurpation of power?

HOLDING AND DECISION: (Rehnquist, C.J.) No. Congress's creation of the independent counsel was not an unconstitutional usurpation of power. The Appointments Clause mandates that only the President may appoint "principal" United States officers. However, Congress may invest in the judiciary the power to appoint inferior officers. This Court is of the opinion that independent counsels are inferior officers. Independent counsel is subordinate to the Attorney General; counsel's role is restricted to the investigation and possible prosecution of a number of federal crimes, and counsel's tenure is limited. Also, this Court rejects the argument that the Appointments Clause does not permit "inter-branch" appointments, exemplified by the Ethics in Government Act's (the Act's) provision of a judicial body appointing an executive officer. No restriction is to be found in the Appointments Clause. This Court further rejects the argument that the Act violates the longstanding prohibition on vesting in courts' executive powers. The special court does have certain supervisory powers, but it is the special prosecutor, not the special court, that carries out executive functions. Finally, this Court rejects the argument that the Act violates separation of powers. Congress, in passing the Act, did not attempt to usurp executive or judicial authority. Rather than take such authority unto itself, it created an executive and judicial office not unduly beholden to itself. This was not a violation of separation of powers. This being so, the Act is valid. Reversed.

DISSENT: (Scalia, J.) The Ethics in Government Act (the Act) is a clear violation of the concept of separation of powers. The only relevant questions are: (1) Is the investigation/prosecution of a federal crime an exercise of purely executive power and (2) Does the statute deprive the President of exclusive control over the exercise of that power? The Constitution and precedent mandate an affirmative answer to the former question, and any reasonable reading of the act requires a similar answer to the latter. This being so, the Act violates separation of powers.

ANALYSIS

The Court has made some important separation of powers decisions in recent years. Probably the most important other decision was *INS v. Chadha*, 462 U.S. 919 (1983). This decision struck down legislation review of executive actions. In the present case, the Court distinguished *Chadha* by holding that the Ethics in Government Act did not directly give Congress more power.

Quicknotes

APPOINTMENTS CLAUSE Article II, § 2, cl. 2 of the U.S. Constitution conferring power upon the President to appoint ambassadors, public ministers and consuls, judges of the Supreme Court, and all other officers of the United States with the advice and consent of the Senate.

ETHICS IN GOVERNMENT ACT Allows for the appointment of special independent counsel to investigate high-ranking government officials.

INDEPENDENT COUNSEL An attorney whose appointment is authorized by the Ethics in Government Act and who is charged with the investigation of possible criminal activity by high-level government officials.

INFERIOR OFFICERS Members of the executive branch having less power or authority in relation to others.

SEPARATION OF POWERS The system of checks and balances preventing one branch of government from infringing upon exercising the powers of another branch of government.

United States v. Nixon

Federal government (P) v. President of the United States (D)

418 U.S. 683 (1974)

NATURE OF CASE: Certiorari granted after denial of a motion to quash a third-party subpoena *duces tecum*.

FACT SUMMARY: Nixon (D) challenges a subpoena served on him as a third party requiring the production of tapes and documents for use in a criminal prosecution.

RULE OF LAW

Absent a claim of need to protect military, diplomatic, or sensitive national security secrets, an absolute, unqualified presidential privilege of immunity from judicial process under all circumstances does not exist.

FACTS: After the grand jury returned an indictment charging seven defendants with various offenses relating to Watergate, Special Prosecutor Jaworski moved for the issuance of a subpoena *duces tecum* to obtain Watergate-related tapes and documents from Nixon (D). Jaworski claimed that the materials were important to the Government's proof at the criminal proceeding against the seven defendants. The subpoena was issued, and Nixon (D) turned over some materials. His lawyer then moved to quash the subpoena. Nixon (D) contended that the separation of powers doctrine precludes judicial review of a presidential claim of privilege and that the need for confidentiality of high-level communication requires an absolute privilege as against a subpoena. The U.S. District Court for the District of Columbia denied the petition.

ISSUE: Absent a claim of need to protect military, diplomatic, or sensitive national security secrets, does the President possess an absolute executive privilege that is immune from judicial review?

HOLDING AND DECISION: (Burger, C.J.) No. Absent a claim of need to protect military, diplomatic, or sensitive national security secrets, an absolute, unqualified presidential privilege of immunity from judicial process under all circumstances does not exist. First, Nixon (D) claimed the court lacks jurisdiction to issue the subpoena because the matter was an intra-branch dispute within the executive branch. However, courts must look behind names that symbolize the parties to determine whether a justiciable case or controversy exists. Here, the Special Prosecutor, with his asserted need for the subpoenaed material, was opposed by the President with his assertion of privilege against disclosure. This setting assures that there is the necessary concreteness and adversity to sharpen the presentation of the issues. Against Nixon's (D) claim of absolute privilege immune from judicial review, this court reaffirms the holding of *Marbury v. Madison*, 5 U.S. 137 (1803), that "it is emphatically the province. . .of the Judicial Department to say what the law is," and this is true with respect to a claim of executive privilege. Absent a claim of need to protect military, diplomatic, or sensitive national security secrets, neither the doctrine of the separation of powers nor the generalized need for the confidentiality of high-level communications, without more, can sustain an absolute unqualified presidential privilege. Now that the court has decided that legitimate needs of judicial process may outweigh presidential privilege, it is necessary to resolve those competing interests in this case. It is true that the need for confidentiality justifies a presumptive privilege for presidential communications. However, our criminal justice system depends on a complete presentation of all relevant facts. To ensure this presentation, compulsory process must be available. Here, Jaworski has demonstrated a specific need at a criminal trial for the material sought. Nixon (D) has not based his claim of privilege on the military or diplomatic content of the materials but rather on a generalized interest in confidentiality. The allowance of this privilege based on only a generalized interest in confidentiality to withhold relevant evidence in a criminal trial would cut deeply into the guarantee of due process and cannot prevail. Affirmed.

ANALYSIS

On July 16, 1973, Alexander Butterfield testified before the Senate Select Committee on presidential campaign activities that conversations in President Nixon's offices had been recorded automatically at Nixon's (D) direction. Nixon (D) declined to comply with requests for the tapes from Special Prosecutor Cox and the Senate Select Committee. Nixon (D) maintained that the tapes would remain under his personal control. When a subpoena for the tapes was issued, Nixon (D) replied that he asserted executive privilege and that the President is not subject to compulsory process from the courts. The grand jury then instructed the Special Prosecutor to seek an order for production of the tapes. It was that enforcement proceeding which produced the first ruling in the case. Judge Sirica ordered the President to produce the items for in-camera inspection. The court of appeals affirmed. *Nixon v. Sirica*, 487 F.2d 700 (1973).

Continued on next page.

Quicknotes

ABSOLUTE PRIVILEGE Unconditional or unqualified immunity enjoyed by a person.

EXECUTIVE PRIVILEGE The right of the executive branch to refuse to disclose confidential communications if such exemption is necessary for the effective discharge of its official duties.

SUBPOENA *DUCES TECUM* A court mandate compelling the production of documents under a witness's control.

Trump v. Mazars USA, LLP

President of the United States (P) v. President's personal accounting firm (D)

140 S. Ct. 2019 (2020)

NATURE OF CASE: Appeal in action brought by the sitting President in a personal capacity contesting the enforcement of subpoenas issued by the U.S. House of Representatives (the House) seeking information about his finances, his children, and his business affiliates, on the grounds that the subpoenas exceeded the House's constitutional authority.

FACT SUMMARY: The U.S. House of Representatives (the House) issued subpoenas seeking information about the finances of President Donald Trump (Trump) (P), his children, and affiliated businesses, asserting the information it sought was for legislative purposes. Trump (P) contended that the subpoenas exceeded the House's constitutional authority.

RULE OF LAW

When Congress issues a subpoena, purportedly in furtherance of legislative purposes, for the President's personal, nonprivileged papers, a court being asked to enforce such a subpoena must take into account the significant separation of powers concerns implicated by such a subpoena by inquiring, at the least, as to whether: (1) the asserted legislative purpose warrants the significant step of involving the President and the President's papers; (2) the subpoena is no broader than reasonably necessary to support Congress's legislative objective; (3) the evidence offered by Congress to establish that a subpoena advances a valid legislative purpose is detailed and substantial; and (4) the burdens imposed on the President are excessive.

FACTS: Three committees of the U. S. House of Representatives (the House) issued four subpoenas seeking information about the finances of President Donald Trump (Trump) (P), his children, and affiliated businesses. The House Committee on Financial Services issued a subpoena to Deutsche Bank seeking any document related to account activity, due diligence, foreign transactions, business statements, debt schedules, statements of net worth, tax returns, and suspicious activity identified by Deutsche Bank. It issued a second subpoena to Capital One for similar information. The Permanent Select Committee on Intelligence issued a subpoena to Deutsche Bank that mirrored the subpoena issued by the Financial Services Committee, and the House Committee on Oversight and Reform issued a subpoena to Trump's (P) personal accounting firm, Mazars USA, LLP (Mazars) (D), demanding information related to Trump (P) and several affiliated businesses. Although each of the committees sought overlapping sets of financial documents, each supplied different justifications for the requests, explaining that the information would help guide legislative reform in areas ranging from money laundering and terrorism to foreign involvement in U.S. elections. Trump (P) in his personal capacity, along with his children and affiliated businesses, contested the subpoenas, contending that they were issued to harass Trump (P), expose Trump's (P) personal matters, and conduct law enforcement activities beyond the House's authority, thus exceeding the House's constitutional authority. The United States Supreme Court granted certiorari in the case.

ISSUE: When Congress issues a subpoena, purportedly in furtherance of legislative purposes, for the President's personal, nonprivileged papers, must a court being asked to enforce such a subpoena take into account the significant separation of powers concerns implicated by such a subpoena by inquiring, at the least, as to whether: (1) the asserted legislative purpose warrants the significant step of involving the President and the President's papers; (2) the subpoena is no broader than reasonably necessary to support Congress's legislative objective; (3) the evidence offered by Congress to establish that a subpoena advances a valid legislative purpose is detailed and substantial; and (4) the burdens imposed on the President are excessive?

HOLDING AND DECISION: (Roberts, C.J.) Yes. When Congress issues a subpoena, purportedly in furtherance of legislative purposes, for the President's personal, nonprivileged papers, a court being asked to enforce such a subpoena must take into account the significant separation of powers concerns implicated by such a subpoena by inquiring, at the least, as to whether: (1) the asserted legislative purpose warrants the significant step of involving the President and the President's papers; (2) the subpoena is no broader than reasonably necessary to support Congress's legislative objective; (3) the evidence offered by Congress to establish that a subpoena advances a valid legislative purpose is detailed and substantial; and (4) the burdens imposed on the President are excessive. Historically, for over two centuries, disputes over congressional demands for presidential documents have been resolved by the political branches through negotiation and compromise without ever before involving the Court. This is the first time such a dispute reaches the Court and represents a significant departure

Continued on next page.

from historical practice. Because in the past Congress and Presidents have been able to resolve such disputes without the Court's intervention, the Court must tread very carefully to ensure that it does not needlessly disturb the compromises and working arrangements previously reached by those branches of government. Although Congress has no enumerated constitutional power to conduct investigations or issue subpoenas, the Court has held that each House of Congress has the power to secure needed information for the purpose of legislating. This power is "indispensable" because, without information, Congress would be unable to legislate wisely or effectively. Nevertheless, because this power is justified solely as an adjunct to the legislative process, it is subject to several limitations. Most importantly, a congressional subpoena is valid only if it is related to, and in furtherance of, a legitimate task of the Congress, and the subpoena must serve a valid legislative purpose. Also, Congress may not issue a subpoena for the purpose of law enforcement, because that power is assigned to the President and the judiciary. Finally, recipients of congressional subpoenas retain their constitutional rights and various privileges throughout the course of an investigation. Trump (P) contends, as does the Solicitor General on behalf of the United States, that these usual rules for congressional subpoenas should not apply in a case such as the one at bar that involves the President's papers, and that a more exacting standard should be applied. That standard, which the Court has applied where the President asserts executive privilege, would require Congress to show that the requested information satisfies a "demonstrated, specific need," and is "demonstrably critical" to a legislative purpose. Because executive privilege safeguards the public interest in candid, confidential deliberations within the executive branch, information subject to the privilege deserves the greatest protection consistent with the fair administration of justice. However, such protection is not necessary in cases involving nonprivileged, private information, which by definition does not implicate sensitive executive branch deliberations, and such a heightened standard, if applied outside the context of privileged information, would risk seriously impeding Congress in carrying out its responsibilities, giving short shrift to its important interests in conducting inquiries to obtain information needed to legislate effectively. On the other hand, the separation of powers issues raised when Congress seeks the President's nonprivileged papers requires more than applying the rules already in place for legislative subpoenas. Otherwise, there would be essentially no limits on the congressional power to subpoena the President's personal records. A limitless subpoena power could transform the established practice of the political branches and allow Congress to aggrandize itself at the President's expense. These separation of powers concerns are unmistakably implicated by the subpoenas here, which represent not a run-of-the-mill legislative effort but rather a clash between rival branches of government over records of intense political interest for all involved. The interbranch conflict does not vanish simply because the subpoenas seek personal papers or because the President has sued in a personal capacity. Nor are separation of powers concerns less palpable because the subpoenas are issued to third parties. Neither side identifies an approach that adequately accounts for these weighty separation of powers concerns. Such concerns require a balanced approach. Therefore, in assessing whether a subpoena directed at a President's personal information is "related to, and in furtherance of, a legitimate task of the Congress," courts must take adequate account of the separation of powers principles at stake, including both the significant legislative interests of Congress and the unique position of the President. Several special considerations inform such an analysis. First, courts should carefully assess whether the asserted legislative purpose warrants the significant step of involving the President and the President's papers. Because occasions for constitutional confrontation between the two branches should be avoided whenever possible, Congress may not rely on the President's information if other sources could reasonably provide Congress the information it needs in light of its particular legislative objective. Second, to narrow the scope of possible conflict between the branches, courts should insist on a subpoena no broader than reasonably necessary to support Congress's legislative objective, and the specificity of the subpoena's request should serve as an important safeguard against unnecessary intrusion into the operation of the office of the President. Third, courts should be attentive to the nature of the evidence offered by Congress to establish that a subpoena advances a valid legislative purpose—the more detailed and substantial, the better. That is particularly true when Congress contemplates legislation that raises sensitive constitutional issues, such as legislation concerning the presidency. Fourth, courts should assess the burdens imposed on the President by a subpoena, particularly because they stem from a rival political branch that has an ongoing relationship with the President and incentives to use subpoenas for institutional advantage. Other considerations may be pertinent as well; one case every two centuries does not afford enough experience for an exhaustive list. Vacated and remanded.

DISSENT: (Thomas, J.) Congress lacks the power to issue a subpoena for private documents, regardless of whether they belong to the President or anyone else because the scope of its implied powers is very limited. As a matter of history, at the time of the founding, such power was not included by necessary implication in any of Congress's legislative powers, and there is no support

Continued on next page.

in the Constitution for Congress to issue subpoenas for nonofficial documents. Congress argues that at the time of the founding, Congress had the same investigatory powers that the British Parliament had. However, Parliament was supreme, whereas Congress is not, and the protections of the Bill of Rights, such as the prohibition on unreasonable searches and seizures, constrain Congress's power to compel documents from private citizens. Also, as a matter of history, the colonial legislatures did not issue subpoenas for private, nonofficial documents. The first the time the Court considered such a subpoena, the Court declined to uphold it because it failed to see how such a subpoena was necessary for Congress to carry out its legislative duties and because the subpoena impermissibly sought to inquire into the private affairs of citizens. A half a century later, in 1927, in *McGrain v. Daugherty,* 273 U.S. 135 (1927), the Court ruled that Congress has the power to issue subpoenas for private documents, but only if they are relevant to a legislative power. That case was decided incorrectly, as it had no support in the Constitution's text or in historical practice. Following *McGrain,* the Court pared back Congress's authority to compel testimony and documents. Instead of trying to compensate for *McGrain,* as the majority does with its four-part test, the Court should discard it altogether as unsupported precedent.

DISSENT: (Alito, J.) Legislative subpoenas are inherently suspicious because they are rarely used for considering potential legislation but can easily be used for improper non-legislative purposes. Accordingly, courts must be highly sensitive to separation of powers issues when asked to approve the enforcement of such subpoenas, especially when the subpoena is issued to a third party. In such instances, Congress must be required to provide more than a perfunctory explanation of its legislative need and how the requested documents will further the stated legislative goals. To that end, Congress should be required to specify the type of legislation being considered, its authority to enact such legislation, and why the subpoenaed information, rather than information available from other sources, is necessary. These are the types of questions the district court should be required to make on remand, and, absent a satisfactory showing by Congress regarding such questions, enforcement of the subpoenas should not be ordered.

ANALYSIS

The majority in this case affirmed Congress's broad power to investigate, and also affirmed that the scope of that power is coextensive with the scope of Congress's power to legislate. In *Watkins v. United States,* 354 U.S. 178 (1957), the Court held that Congress's power to investigate encompasses "inquiries concerning the administration of existing laws as well as proposed or possibly needed statutes" and "surveys of defects in our social, economic, or political system for the purpose of enabling the Congress to remedy them." The majority further affirmed that Congress's broad investigatory powers permit it to investigate the executive branch and even the President where such investigation is related to legitimate legislative purposes. In this case, for example, the House Oversight Committee asserted that it issued its subpoena after it received information that President Trump (P) might have failed to disclose certain financial holdings in his required federal disclosures, so that Congress had an interest in obtaining more information about his finances to guide its consideration about whether to strengthen financial disclosure laws and impose new restrictions on presidential conflicts of interest. Under the Court's precedents, such a purpose clearly serves a legitimate legislative interest.

Quicknotes

SEPARATION OF POWERS The system of checks and balances preventing one branch of government from infringing upon exercising the powers of another branch of government.

SUBPOENA A command issued by court to compel a witness to appear at trial.

Clinton v. Jones

President of the United States (D) v. Female state employee (P)

520 U.S. 681 (1997)

NATURE OF CASE: Review of judgment denying presidential immunity and request to postpone trial in sexual harassment case.

FACT SUMMARY: Jones (P) claimed Clinton (D) sexually harassed her during events that took place prior to Clinton (D) assuming the presidency.

RULE OF LAW

Presidential immunity does not apply to civil damages litigation arising out of unofficial events occurring prior to the assumption of office.

FACTS: In May of 1991, Jones (P) worked as a state employee at a conference for which Clinton (D) gave a speech. Jones (P) claimed that a state police officer persuaded her to go to Clinton's (D) hotel room, where Clinton (D) proceeded to make sexual advances toward her. Jones (P) allegedly experienced on-the-job retaliation because she rejected these advances. When Clinton (D) was elected President in 1992, Jones (P) claimed she was defamed when spokesmen for Clinton (D) denied her allegations, branding Jones (P) a liar. On May 6, 1994, Jones (P) filed suit in district court, and Clinton (D) filed a motion to dismiss based on presidential immunity. The district court denied the motion to dismiss but delayed the trial until after Clinton (D) left office. Both parties appealed and the court of appeals affirmed the denial of the motion to dismiss but reversed the delay in the trial. Clinton (D) appealed.

ISSUE: Does presidential immunity apply to civil damages litigation arising out of unofficial events occurring prior to the assumption of office?

HOLDING AND DECISION: (Stevens, J.) No. Presidential immunity does not apply to civil damages litigation arising out of unofficial events occurring prior to the assumption of office. Here, Clinton (D) cannot claim presidential immunity because his actions occurred in an unofficial capacity during a time prior to his assuming the presidency. Because the conduct occurred in an unofficial capacity, this ruling will not make any president unduly cautious in the discharge of his official duties. With respect to the separation of powers, the litigation of questions that relate entirely to the unofficial conduct of the individual who happens to be President poses no perceptible risk of misallocation of either judicial power or executive power. Affirmed.

CONCURRENCE: (Breyer, J.) Although the Constitution does not automatically grant Clinton (D) an immunity from civil lawsuits, a federal judge may not interfere with Clinton's (D) discharge of his public duties once Clinton (D) sets forth and explains how they conflict with judicial proceedings.

ANALYSIS

Intergovernmental immunity generally applies in situations where states attempt to regulate and tax the property and activities of the federal government. The federal government's power is derived from the Supremacy Clause and, generally, the federal government is given greater immunity than state governments. This case brings up an unexplored area where the limits of presidential immunity extend as it relates to the private, unofficial acts of the President.

Quicknotes

EXECUTIVE PRIVILEGE The right of the executive branch to refuse to disclose confidential communications if such exemption is necessary for the effective discharge of its official duties.

SUPREMACY CLAUSE Article VI, ¶ 2 of the U.S. Constitution, which provides that federal action must prevail over inconsistent state action.

Trump v. Vance

President of the United States (P) v. Municipal district attorney (D)

519 U.S. ___, 140 S. Ct. 2412 (2020)

NATURE OF CASE: Appeal from affirmance of denial of injunction in action brought by sitting President of the United States to enjoin enforcement of grand jury subpoena for records related to the President and business organizations affiliated with him.

FACT SUMMARY: After the New York County District Attorney's Office—acting on behalf of a grand jury—served a subpoena *duces tecum* on Mazars USA, LLP (Mazars) (D), the personal accounting firm of President Donald Trump (Trump) (P), for financial records relating to Trump (P) and his businesses, Trump (P) sued the district attorney (D) and Mazars (D) to enjoin enforcement of the subpoena, arguing that a sitting President enjoys absolute immunity from state criminal process under Article II and the Supremacy Clause.

RULE OF LAW

(1) A sitting President does not under Article II or the Supremacy Clause categorically have absolute immunity from a state grand jury subpoena seeking the President's private papers.

(2) Neither Article II nor the Supremacy Clause requires a heightened standard for the issuance of a state criminal subpoena seeking the private papers of a sitting President.

FACTS: In 2019, the New York County District Attorney's Office—acting on behalf of a grand jury—served a subpoena *duces tecum* on Mazars USA, LLP (Mazars) (D), the personal accounting firm of President Donald J. Trump (Trump) (P), for financial records relating to Trump (P) and his businesses. Trump (P), acting in his personal capacity, sued the district attorney (D) and Mazars (D) in federal district court to enjoin enforcement of the subpoena, arguing that a sitting President enjoys absolute immunity from state criminal process under Article II and the Supremacy Clause. The district court denied injunctive relief, and the Second Circuit Court of Appeals affirmed. The Supreme Court granted certiorari.

ISSUE:

(1) Does a sitting President under Article II or the Supremacy Clause categorically have absolute immunity from a state grand jury subpoena seeking the President's private papers?

(2) Does either Article II or the Supremacy Clause require a heightened standard for the issuance of a state criminal subpoena seeking the private papers of a sitting President?

HOLDING AND DECISION: (Roberts, C.J.)

(1) No. A sitting President does not under Article II or the Supremacy Clause categorically have absolute immunity from a state grand jury subpoena seeking the President's private papers. In 1807, Chief Justice Marshall ruled that a sitting President is not exempt from the Sixth Amendment's guarantee that the accused have compulsory process for obtaining witnesses for their defense. *United States v. Burr,* 25 F.Cas. 30 (CC Va. 1807). Marshall also concluded that the Sixth Amendment's guarantee extended to the production of documents, since the propriety of introducing any documents depends on the nature of the document and not the character of the person who holds it, and since the court may decide whether introducing the document is appropriate after the document is produced. In the two centuries following *Burr,* successive Presidents accepted Marshall's ruling that the President is subject to subpoena, and uniformly agreed to testify when called in criminal proceedings. In 1974, the question whether to compel the disclosure of official communications over the President's objection came to a head when the Watergate Special Prosecutor secured a subpoena *duces tecum* directing President Nixon to produce, among other things, tape recordings of Oval Office meetings. The Court rejected Nixon's claim of an absolute privilege of confidentiality for all presidential communications. Recognizing that "compulsory process" was imperative for both the prosecution and the defense, the Court held that the President's "generalized assertion of privilege must yield to the demonstrated, specific need for evidence in a pending criminal trial." *United States v. Nixon,* 418 U.S. 683 (1974). President Nixon dutifully released the tapes. This history all involved federal criminal proceedings. Here, the President (P) claims that the Supremacy Clause gives a sitting President absolute immunity from state criminal subpoenas because compliance with such subpoenas would categorically impair the performance of the President's Article II functions. The Solicitor General, arguing on behalf of the United States, claims that a state grand jury subpoena for a sitting President's personal records (it was agreed that the records at issue belonged to Trump (P) and that Mazars USA, LLP (D) was merely their custodian) must, at the very least, meet

Continued on next page.

a heightened standard of need—a standard that according to the Solicitor General was not met here. It is well established that federal criminal subpoenas do not impermissibly impair the President's ability to perform the Executive's constitutionally mandated functions. Here, Trump (P) argues that state criminal subpoenas categorically impair that function and are impermissibly burdensome on grounds of diversion, stigma, and harassment. Trump (P) contends that complying with state criminal subpoenas would necessarily distract the Chief Executive from the Executive's duties. Trump (P) grounds that concern in *Nixon v. Fitzgerald*, 457 U.S. 731 (1982), which recognized a President's "absolute immunity from damages liability predicated on his official acts." However, contrary to Trump's (P) suggestion, that case did not hold that distraction was sufficient to confer absolute immunity. Indeed, the Court expressly rejected immunity based on distraction alone 15 years later in *Clinton v. Jones*, 520 U.S. 681 (1997), when President Clinton sought absolute immunity from civil liability for private acts. As the Court explained, *Fitzgerald's* principal concern was not mere distraction but the distortion of the Executive's "decisionmaking process." The prospect that a President may become "preoccupied by pending litigation" did not ordinarily implicate constitutional concerns. Two centuries of experience likewise confirm that a properly tailored criminal subpoena will not normally hamper the performance of a President's constitutional duties. The President (P) claims this case is different. He believes that he is under investigation and argues that the toll will necessarily be heavier in that circumstance. But Trump (P) is not seeking immunity from the diversion occasioned by the prospect of future criminal liability. He concedes that he may be investigated while in office. His objection is instead limited to the additional distraction caused by the subpoena itself. That argument, however, runs up against the 200 years of precedent establishing that Presidents, and their official communications, are subject to judicial process, even when the President is under investigation. Trump (P) next claims that the stigma of being subpoenaed will undermine his leadership at home and abroad. However, even if a tarnished reputation were a cognizable impairment, there is nothing inherently stigmatizing about a President performing the citizen's normal duty of furnishing information relevant to a criminal investigation. Nor can the risk of association with persons or activities under criminal investigation absolve a President of such an important public duty. The consequences for a President's public standing will likely increase if he is the one under investigation, but Trump (P) concedes that such investigations are permitted under Article II and the Supremacy Clause. Additionally, the receipt of a subpoena would not seem to categorically magnify the harm to Trump's (P) reputation. Additionally, in the grand jury context, longstanding secrecy rules aim to prevent the very stigma Trump (P) anticipates. Finally, Trump (P) argues that subjecting Presidents to state criminal subpoenas will make them targets for harassment. The Court rejected a nearly identical argument in *Clinton*, concluding that the risk posed by harassing civil litigation was not "serious" because federal courts have the tools to deter and dismiss vexatious lawsuits. Harassing state criminal subpoenas could, under certain circumstances, threaten the independence or effectiveness of the Executive, but the law already seeks to protect against such abuse. First, grand juries are prohibited from engaging in "arbitrary fishing expeditions" or initiating investigations "out of malice or an intent to harass," and federal courts may intervene in state proceedings that are motivated by or conducted in bad faith. *Huffman v. Pursue, Ltd.*, 420 U.S. 529, 611 (1975). Second, because the Supremacy Clause prohibits state judges and prosecutors from interfering with a President's official duties, any effort to manipulate a President's policy decisions or to retaliate against a President for official acts through issuance of a subpoena would be unconstitutional. Finally, federal law allows a President to challenge any such allegedly unconstitutional influence in a federal forum. Given these safeguards and the Court's precedents, absolute immunity from a state grand jury subpoena seeking a President's private papers for a sitting President is neither necessary not appropriate under Article II nor the Supremacy Clause.

(2) No. Neither Article II nor the Supremacy Clause requires a heightened standard for the issuance of a state criminal subpoena seeking the private papers of a sitting President. First, although a President cannot be treated as an "ordinary individual" when executive communications are sought, *Burr* teaches that, with regard to private papers, a President is similarly situated to any other individual. Second, there has been no showing here that heightened protection against state subpoenas is necessary for the Executive to fulfill Article II functions. Finally, absent a need to protect the Executive, the public interest in fair and effective law enforcement cuts in favor of comprehensive access to evidence. Rejecting a heightened need standard does not leave Presidents without recourse. A President may take advantage of the same protections available to every other citizen, including the right to challenge the subpoena on any grounds permitted by state law, which usually include bad faith and undue burden or breadth. When the President

Continued on next page.

invokes such protections, the high respect that is owed to the President's office should inform the conduct of the entire proceeding, including the timing and scope of discovery. In addition, a President can raise subpoena-specific constitutional challenges in either a state or a federal forum. For example, a President can challenge the subpoena as an attempt to influence the performance of the President's official duties, in violation of the Supremacy Clause. In addition, a President can argue that compliance with a particular subpoena would impede the President's constitutional duties. Affirmed and remanded.

CONCURRENCE: (Kavanaugh, J.) *United States v. Nixon,* 418 U.S. 683 (1974), requires that a prosecutor establish a "demonstrated, specific need" for privileged executive branch information, including a President's information. This requirement accommodates the interests of the criminal process and the Article II interests of the Executive and seeks to avoid diversion or harassment of a sitting President by a state prosecutor. The majority did not apply the *Nixon* requirement to this case, but it should have. Nonetheless, the majority accounted for some of the important concerns that were raised in *Nixon* and explained existing constraints on a prosecutor issuing a subpoena to a sitting President. Moreover, there is unanimity of opinion on the Court that a President may raise objections to a state criminal subpoena not just in state court, but also in federal court. Regardless, whether in the future the majority's standard is applied, or *Nixon's* "demonstrated, specific need" standard is used, a court will have to first delve into why the state wants the information; why and how much the state needs the information, including whether the state could obtain the information elsewhere; and whether compliance with the subpoena would unduly burden or interfere with a President's official duties.

DISSENT: (Thomas, J.) There is no dispute that a President is not entitled to absolute immunity from the issuance of a state criminal subpoena, but a President may be entitled to relief against the subpoena's enforcement, if the President can demonstrate that presidential duties require all of the President's time—until the end of the President's term or until the President is removed from office. This standard applies with equal force to federal and state subpoenas, and a federal court may provide injunctive and declaratory relief to stay enforcement of a state subpoena when a President meets this standard. Here, Trump (P) has requested such relief. Accordingly, the Court should have vacated and remanded (instead of affirming and remanding) so the district court could determine whether Trump (P) has met this standard, and, thus, whether enforcement of the subpoena should be enjoined. As to the issue of whether a grand jury must make a showing of heightened need, under a heightened-need standard, a grand jury with only the usual need for particular information would be refused the information when the President is perfectly able to comply, whereas a grand jury with a heightened need would be entitled to the information even if compliance would place undue obligations on the President. This result makes little sense and lacks any basis in the original understanding of the Constitution. The questions of the grand jury's need should thus be left to state law.

DISSENT: (Alito, J.) This case raises important constitutional issues, and the specific issue before the Court cannot be answered without considering the broader question of whether the Constitution restricts a state's use of its criminal law enforcement powers against a sitting President. One consideration is that there is not always a clear line between a President's personal and official affairs. Another is that a President must be able to carry out the responsibilities of the office at all times. Although the states retain many powers under the Constitution, they may not block or interfere with the federal government's lawful work. It is clear, based on these considerations and well-established principles, that a state may not prosecute a sitting President. This conclusion is bolstered by the Constitution's impeachment provisions. However, these considerations apply not only to a state's prosecution of a sitting President, but also to any legal proceedings against a sitting President. The key is that the responsibilities and demands of the Executive Office must be taken into account; the nature of the office demands in some instances that the application of laws be adjusted at least until the person's term in office ends. This should be true of subpoenas issued to a sitting President, and a uniform rule should be articulated regarding such issuance. Such a rule should take into account both the effect of subpoenas on the functioning of the presidency and the risk that they will be used for harassment. First, even if a President suspects that he may be criminally prosecuted, that alone will sap the President's energy and impair his ability to perform their constitutional duties. Second, the use by local prosecutors of a criminal subpoena aimed at the President could be a political strategy, which would undermine the constitutional structure. The majority's approach relegates a President to the "meager defenses" that are available to all citizens when an ordinary grand jury subpoena is challenged. Instead, the presidency deserves greater protection. For these reasons, a prosecutor should be required (1) to provide at least a general description of the possible offenses that are under investigation, (2) to outline how the subpoenaed records relate to those offenses, and (3) to explain why it is important that the records be produced and why it is necessary for production to occur while the President is still in office. The prosecutor's response must be detailed and specific

Continued on next page.

and must address concerns for the President's ability to carry out the President's official duties before a subpoena will be enforced during the President's term. In sum, the Court's decision threatens to impair the functioning of the presidency and provides the presidency no real protection against the use of the subpoena power by the nation's more than 2,300 local prosecutors.

ANALYSIS

The assertion that President Trump (P) made in this case was extraordinary. Had his claim of absolute immunity from criminal process prevailed, there potentially would have been limitless immunity from criminal process not only for a President during the President's term of office, but also for the President's family members and associates. As the district court observed, presidential immunity would stretch to cover every phase of criminal proceedings, including investigations, grand jury proceedings and subpoenas, indictment, prosecution, arrest, trial, conviction, and incarceration. Such immunity presumably would encompass any conduct, at any time, in any forum, whether federal or state, and whether the President acted alone or in concert with other individuals. The President's exemption from criminal proceedings would extend not only to matters arising from performance of the President's duties and functions in the President's official capacity, but also to matters arising from the President's private affairs, financial transactions, and all other conduct undertaken by the President as an ordinary citizen, both during and before the President's tenure in office. The practical implications and actual effects of such categorical immunity could be far-reaching. In some circumstances, applicable statutes of limitations could run, barring further investigation and prosecution of serious criminal offenses, thus potentially enabling both the President and any accomplices to escape being brought to justice. Temporally, such immunity would operate to frustrate the administration of justice by insulating from criminal law scrutiny and judicial review, whether by federal or state courts, not only matters occurring during the President's tenure in office, but potentially also records relating to transactions and illegal actions the President and others may have committed before the President assumed the presidency. However, Trump's (P) claim did not prevail. All the courts to review the claim, as well as all the Supreme Court justices, agreed that there is nothing in the Constitution, in the constitutional balance of power between the respective branches of government, or in the Supreme Court's precedents that absolutely immunizes a sitting President from criminal process during the President's term. As Chief Justice Roberts notes in the majority opinion, the Founders shunned the concept of the inviolability of the King of England and the bounds of the monarch's protective screen covering the Crown's actions from legal scrutiny, and, therefore, disclaimed any notion that the Constitution generally conferred similarly all-encompassing immunity upon the President. The wisdom of that view has been tested before the courts on various occasions and has been roundly and consistently reaffirmed by the Supreme Court and lower courts, which, in numerous rulings, have circumscribed claims of presidential immunity in multiple ways. As the district court put it, the proposition advanced by President Trump (P) is "repugnant to the nation's governmental structure and constitutional values." *Trump v. Vance,* 395 F. Supp. 3d 283, 290 (S.D.N.Y. 2019).

Quicknotes

GRAND JURY A group summoned to investigate, inform, and accuse persons of crimes when sufficient evidence exists to do so.

IMMUNITY Exemption from a legal obligation.

INJUNCTIVE RELIEF A court order issued as a remedy, requiring a person to do, or prohibiting that person from doing, a specific act.

SUBPOENA *DUCES TECUM* A court mandate compelling the production of documents under a witness's control.

SUPREMACY CLAUSE Article VI, ¶ 2 of the U.S. Constitution, which provides that federal action must prevail over inconsistent state action.

CHAPTER 7

The Post-Civil War Amendments and the "Incorporation" of Fundamental Rights

Quick Reference Rules of Law

Barron v. Mayor and City Council of Baltimore

Wharf owner (P) v. Municipality (D)

32 U.S. (7 Pet.) 243 (1833)

NATURE OF CASE: Certiorari review of underlying action to recover damages.

FACT SUMMARY: Barron (P) claimed that the City (D) made his wharf useless by diverting the streams during its construction work.

RULE OF LAW

State legislation is not subject to the limitations imposed by the amendments to the United States Constitution.

FACTS: Barron (P) sued the City (D) for making his wharf in Baltimore Harbor useless. He claimed that the City (D) had diverted the flow of streams during its street construction and that this diversion had deposited earth near the wharf, causing the water to become too shallow for most vessels. Barron (P) claimed that the action violated the Fifth Amendment guarantee that property will not be taken without just compensation.

ISSUE: Is state legislation subject to the limitations imposed by the amendments to the United States Constitution?

HOLDING AND DECISION: (Marshall, C.J.) No. State legislation is not subject to the limitations imposed by the amendments to the United States Constitution. The amendments to the Constitution were intended as limitations solely on the exercise of power by the U.S. Government and are not applicable to the legislation of the states. The Constitution and its amendments were established by the people of the United States for themselves, for their own government, and not for the governments of the states. The people and each state established their own constitution. The constitutional amendments restrain only the power of the federal government and are not applicable to the actions of the state governments. Article I, § 10 expressly lists the restrictions upon the state governments. We find no reason why if the amendments were to apply to the states, there are not express words so stating. The amendments contain no expression indicating intent to apply them to the states. Hence, because there is no conflict here between the City (D) and state's action and the federal Constitution, this court has no jurisdiction over this action. Dismissed.

ANALYSIS

There were relatively few references to individual rights in the original Constitution. Its major concern was with governmental structures and relationships. The most important limitation on state power protective of individual rights was the Contract Clause. Nor was there a significant broader spectrum of individual rights restrictions on the national government. In response to the demand for additional constitutional protection of individual as well as states' rights, the first ten amendments were proposed and ratified. Since federal criminal decisions were not ordinarily reviewable by the Supreme Court, it had little occasion for interpretation of the Bill of Rights prior to the Civil War.

Quicknotes

CONTRACT CLAUSE Article 1, § 10 of the U.S. Constitution prohibiting states from passing any "law impairing the Obligation of Contracts."

JUST COMPENSATION The right guaranteed by the Fifth Amendment to the U.S. Constitution that when property is taken for public use by the state, a person is to receive adequate compensation in order to restore the person to the position he or she enjoyed prior to the appropriation.

TAKING A governmental action that substantially deprives an owner of the use and enjoyment of his or her property, requiring compensation.

Dred Scott v. Sandford

Former slave (P) v. Administrator (D)

60 U.S. (19 How.) 393 (1857)

NATURE OF CASE: Action in trespass.

FACT SUMMARY: Dred Scott (P) claimed to have been freed from his slave status by his travels to free states with his master, but Sanford (D) insisted Scott (P) could not bring a federal court action pressing the point because former slaves and their descendants are not "citizens."

RULE OF LAW

Since they are not "citizens" in the sense in which that word is used in the Constitution, Black people who were slaves in this country, or who are the descendants of such slaves, cannot bring suit in federal court.

FACTS: Dred Scott (P), a slave, was taken along on his master's sojourns to the free state of Illinois and the free part of the Missouri Territory (according to the Missouri Compromise). It was after they returned to the slave state of Missouri that the master died, and Sanford (D) became the administrator of his estate. Scott (P) attempted to bring a diversity action in federal court based on his claim that his "residence" in the aforementioned free jurisdictions had liberated him from his status as a slave. He was, he insisted, thus properly considered a "citizen" of Missouri and was therefore entitled to bring suit in federal court against Sanford (D), who was a citizen of another state (New York). Sanford (D) argued that a former slave could not be considered a citizen of the United States or of Missouri. The lower court agreed with him. Scott (P) appealed.

ISSUE: Can a former slave be a "citizen" so as to qualify to bring an action in federal court?

HOLDING AND DECISION: (Taney, C.J.) No. Black people who were slaves in this country, or who are the descendants of such slaves, are not "citizens" in the sense in which that word is used in the Constitution and are thus not entitled to maintain an action in federal court. A review of history reveals quite readily that neither class of persons who had been imported as slaves nor their descendants, whether they had become free or not, were acknowledged as part of the "people" but were rather considered as mere property. They simply were not among those who were "citizens" of the several states when the Constitution was adopted, and that is the time frame that must be utilized in determining who was included as a "citizen" in the Constitution. Because he is not a "citizen," Scott (P) cannot maintain this action. Affirmed.

DISSENT: (Curtis, J.) To determine whether individuals who were free when the Constitution was adopted were citizens, even though those individuals were the descendants of slaves, the only necessary inquiry is whether those free individuals were citizens of any of the states under the Confederation at the time of the Constitution's adoption. It is a fact that at the time the Articles of Confederation were ratified, all free native-born inhabitants of five states were citizens of those states, notwithstanding that they were descended from African slaves. There is nothing in the Constitution that deprived those who were citizens of the United States at the time of its adoption of their citizenship, especially given that those citizens established the Constitution. The Constitution also contains nothing that deprives native-born citizens of any state of their citizenship. Finally, there is nothing in the Constitution that empowers Congress to disenfranchise any state citizen of that citizenship. Therefore, every free person born on the soil of a state, who is a citizen of that state by force of its Constitution or laws, is also a citizen of the United States. This is also true of states that came into being after the Constitution was adopted. When the Constitution was framed, it was expected that some of the states would cede their claims to what were then their territories and that those territories, and new states formed therefrom, would be subject to the Constitution. Slavery itself is regulated by municipal law, and the Framers of the Constitution, who recognized this, and who knew that a slave was property only in those states where laws so provided, intended that Congress in its discretion would determine what regulations, if any, should be made concerning slavery. This intent can be gleaned from the fact the Constitution is silent as to the regulation of slavery and expresses no intent to interfere with or to displace these principles. Finally, there is nothing in the Constitution that supports the proposition that prohibiting slave owners from bringing their slaves into a Territory deprives the owners of their property without due process of law.

ANALYSIS

The justices all knew this was a historically important case; each one took the time to write an opinion. In addition to the primary opinion by Chief Justice Taney, there were six concurring and two dissenting opinions. No longer doctrinally important because of subsequent amendments to the Constitution resolving of the slavery

Continued on next page.

issues, this case still serves as a prime example of the view that the Constitution, as Chief Justice Taney put it, forever speaks "not only in the same words, but with the same meaning and intent with which it spoke when it came from the hands of the Framers." It is a view that has been roundly criticized as too rigid and formalistic an approach to take toward a document that must be flexible enough to provide effective and operable guidelines and governing principles for an ever-evolving society.

Quicknotes

ACTION OF TRESPASS An action to recover damages resulting from the wrongful interference with a party's person, property, or rights.

DIVERSITY ACTION An action commenced by a citizen of one state against a citizen of another state or against an alien, involving an amount in controversy set by statute, over which the federal court has jurisdiction.

Slaughter-House Cases

Butchers (P) v. State (D)

83 U.S. (16 Wall.) 36 (1873)

NATURE OF CASE: Certiorari review of state enforcement of a monopoly.

FACT SUMMARY: Louisiana created a 25-year slaughter-house monopoly to which several butchers (P) who were not included objected.

RULE OF LAW

The Fourteenth Amendment protects the privileges and immunities of national, not state, citizenship; and neither the Equal Protection, Due Process, nor Privileges and Immunities Clauses of that amendment may be used to interfere with state control of the privileges and immunities of state citizenship.

FACTS: [A Louisiana law of 1869 granted a monopoly to a slaughter-house company created by the legislature for the three largest parishes in that state. Butchers (P) who were not included in the monopoly challenged the law creating it on the grounds that it violated the Thirteenth Amendment ban on involuntary servitude and the Fourteenth Amendment protections of the privileges and immunities of national citizenship and equal protection and due process of law. From a judgment sustaining the law, the butchers (P) appealed.]

ISSUE: Does the Fourteenth Amendment Privileges and Immunities Clause make all privileges and immunities of citizenship federal rights subject to federal enforcement?

HOLDING AND DECISION: (Miller, J.) No. The Fourteenth Amendment protects the privileges and immunities of national, not state, citizenship; and neither the Equal Protection, nor Due Process, nor Privileges and Immunities Clauses of that Amendment may be used to interfere with state control of the privileges and immunities of state citizenship. The underlying purpose of all three of the post-Civil War amendments was to eliminate the remnants of African slavery, not to effect any fundamental change in the relations of the government. The Fourteenth Amendment expressly was adopted to assure only that states would not "abridge the privileges and immunities of citizens of the United States" (i.e., Black citizens in their pursuit of national rights such as the right to protection on the high seas). Similarly, the Equal Protection and Due Process Clauses of that Amendment were drawn to protect former slaves from state denial of federal rights. No interpretation of this Amendment (or the Thirteenth, which is an even clearer case) may be used to prevent Louisiana from exercising its police power (here, to promote public health in slaughterhouses) to define particular privileges and immunities of its citizens. Affirmed.

DISSENT: (Field, J.) The Fourteenth Amendment is protection for all citizens of the fundamental rights of free government from abridgment by the states. Among such rights clearly is the right to an equal opportunity to pursue employment.

DISSENT: (Bradley, J.) The Fourteenth Amendment is a ban upon state deprivation of life, liberty, or property without due process of law. The purpose of its passage was preventing future insubordination to government by law that fostered the Civil War.

ANALYSIS

The effect of this decision was to render the Fourteenth Amendment Privileges or Immunities Clause a nullity for the purpose of protecting individual rights from state abridgment. In addition, it ruled out the possibility that the Bill of Rights could be enforced upon the states as privileges and immunities of national citizenship. Subsequently, of course, the Court adopted the position of Justice Bradley and began selectively incorporating parts of those Amendments into the Fourteenth Amendment Due Process Clause. In addition, the Equal Protection Clause has been used extensively to prohibit state action that is discriminatory in any irrational way (i.e., the rational basis test). Note, finally, that even the Thirteenth Amendment, summarily treated above, has been expanded to bar private discriminatory action that can be identified as a badge of slavery.

Quicknotes

EQUAL PROTECTION CLAUSE A constitutional provision that each person be guaranteed the same protection of the laws enjoyed by other persons in like circumstances.

INVOLUNTARY SERVITUDE Being in a state of forced labor for the benefit of another person.

MONOPOLY A privilege or right conferred upon an individual or entity granting it the exclusive power to manufacture, sell, and distribute a particular service or commodity; a market condition in which one or a few companies control the sale of a product or service thereby restraining competition in respect to that article or service.

PRIVILEGES OR IMMUNITIES CLAUSE Section 1 of the Fourteenth Amendment of the U.S. Constitution; prohibits state laws that abridge the privileges or immunities of U.S. citizens.

Saenz v. Roe

[Parties not identified.]

526 U.S. 489 (1999)

NATURE OF CASE: Certiorari review of a state statute.

FACT SUMMARY: When California (D) discriminated against citizens who had resided in the state for less than one year in distributing welfare benefits, the state statute was challenged and held to be unconstitutional.

RULE OF LAW

Durational residency requirements violate the fundamental right to travel by denying a newly arrived citizen the same privileges and immunities enjoyed by other citizens in the same state.

FACTS: In 1992, California (D) enacted a statute limiting the maximum first-year welfare benefits available to newly arrived residents to the amount they would have received in the state of their prior residence. California residents who were eligible for such benefits challenged the constitutionality of the durational residency requirement, alleging their right to travel was violated. The district court preliminarily enjoined implementation of the statute and the court of appeals affirmed. Congress enacted the Personal Responsibility and Work Opportunity Reconciliation Act of 1996, which expressly authorized states to apply the rules (including benefit amounts) of another state if the family has resided in the state for less than twelve months. California (D) appealed, alleging that the statute should be upheld if it has a rational basis and that the state's (D) legitimate interest in saving over $10 million a year satisfied that test.

ISSUE: Do durational residency requirements violate the fundamental right to travel by denying a newly arrived citizen the same privileges and immunities enjoyed by other citizens in the same state?

HOLDING AND DECISION: (Stevens, J.) Yes. Durational residency requirements violate the fundamental right to travel by denying a newly arrived citizen the same privileges and immunities enjoyed by other citizens in the same state. The first sentence of Article IV, § 2, provides that the citizens of each state shall be entitled to all privileges and immunities of citizens in the several states. The right of a newly arrived citizen to the same privileges and immunities enjoyed by other citizens of the same state is protected not only by the new arrival's status as a state citizen but also by her status as a citizen of the United States. The Citizenship Clause of the Fourteenth Amendment protects all citizens' right to choose to be citizens of the state wherein they reside. Neither mere rationality nor some intermediate standard of review should be used to judge the constitutionality of a state rule that discriminates against some of its citizens because they have been domiciled in the state for less than a year. The state's legitimate interest in saving money provides no justification for its decision to discriminate among equally eligible citizens. Affirmed.

DISSENT: (Rehnquist, C.J.) If states can require an individual to reside in-state for a year before exercising the right to educational benefits, the right to terminate a marriage, or the right to vote in primary elections that all other state citizens enjoy, then they may surely do the same for welfare benefits. California has reasonably exercised its power to protect state resources through an objective, narrowly tailored residence requirement. There is nothing in the Constitution that should prevent the enforcement of that requirement.

DISSENT: (Thomas, J.) The majority attributes a meaning to the Privileges or Immunities Clause that likely was unintended when the Fourteenth Amendment was enacted and ratified. At that time, people understood "privileges or immunities of citizens" to be their fundamental right rather than every public benefit established by positive law.

ANALYSIS

The Court in this case found a state violated the Privileges or Immunities Clause when it discriminated against citizens who had been residents for less than one year. The Thomas dissent alleged that this was contrary to the original understanding at the time the Fourteenth Amendment was enacted. The Rehnquist dissent went on to point out that a welfare subsidy is as much an investment in human capital as is a tuition subsidy and its attendant benefits are just as portable.

Quicknotes

FOURTEENTH AMENDMENT Declares that no state shall make or enforce any law that shall abridge the privileges and immunities of citizens of the United States; no state shall deny to any person within its jurisdiction the equal protection of the laws.

FUNDAMENTAL RIGHT A liberty that is either expressly or impliedly provided for in the U.S. Constitution, the

Continued on next page.

deprivation or burdening of which is subject to a heightened standard of review.

PRIVILEGES OR IMMUNITIES CLAUSE Section 1 of the Fourteenth Amendment of the U.S. Constitution; prohibits state laws that abridge the privileges or immunities of U.S. citizens.

RATIONAL BASIS REVIEW A test employed by the court to determine the validity of a statute in equal protection actions, whereby the court determines whether the challenged statute is rationally related to the achievement of a legitimate state interest.

STRICT SCRUTINY Method by which courts determine the constitutionality of a law when a law affects a fundamental right; under the test, the legislature must have had a compelling interest to enact law and measures prescribed by the law must be the least restrictive means possible to accomplish its goal.

Duncan v. Louisiana

Criminal defendant (D) v. State (P)

391 U.S. 145 (1968)

NATURE OF CASE: Appeal from conviction of battery and sentence of 60 days with a $150 fine.

FACT SUMMARY: Louisiana's constitution granted jury trials only in cases in which capital punishment or imprisonment at hard labor may be granted.

RULE OF LAW

The Fourteenth Amendment guarantees a right of jury trial in all criminal cases that would, were they to be tried in a federal court, come within the Sixth Amendment's guarantee.

FACTS: Duncan (D) was charged with simple battery, which in Louisiana was punishable by a maximum of two years' imprisonment and a $300 fine. The trial court denied his request for a jury trial because the Louisiana (P) constitution granted jury trials only in cases in which capital punishment or imprisonment at hard labor may be imposed.

ISSUE: Does the Fourteenth Amendment guarantee a right of jury trial in all criminal cases that would, were they to be tried in a federal court, come within the Sixth Amendment's guarantee?

HOLDING AND DECISION: (White, J.) Yes. The Fourteenth Amendment guarantees a right of jury trial in all criminal cases that would, were they to be tried in a federal court, come within the Sixth Amendment's guarantee. The right to a jury trial in serious criminal cases punishable by at least two years in prison is a fundamental right that must be recognized by the states as part of their obligation to extend due process of law to all persons within their jurisdiction. A right to jury trial is granted to a criminal defendant in order to guard against an overzealous or corrupt prosecutor and the compliant, biased, or eccentric judge. A holding that due process assures a right to jury trial will not cast doubt on the integrity of every trial conducted without a jury. Thus, there is no constitutional problem with accepting waivers, and prosecuting petty crimes without extending the right where defendants are satisfied with bench trials, judicial or prosecutorial unfairness is less likely. What controls will be the maximum possible sentence and not the punishment actually meted out. The exact line between petty and serious crimes need not be settled here. Reversed and remanded.

CONCURRENCE: (Black, J.) Both total and selective incorporation of the Bill of Rights are to be preferred to assigning no settled meaning to the term "due process" as this will shift from time to time in accordance with changing theories.

DISSENT: (Harlan, J.) The Due Process Clause requires only that state procedures be fundamentally fair in all respects. There is no historical support for the total incorporation theory. The Framers of the Fourteenth Amendment intended that the meaning of "due process" will change as does the experience and conscience of the American people. Selective incorporation lacks guiding standards. The definition of "fundamental" used by the majority is circular, since it means "old," "much praised," and "found in the Bill of Rights." Here, there was no indication that Duncan's (D) trial was not a fair one.

ANALYSIS

One commentator has suggested that after *Duncan*, the Court, although describing its test as a "fundamental rights" approach, has actually embraced "selective incorporation," in which all the Bill of Rights, one provision at a time, has been incorporated in fact. Nevertheless, it is still unclear whether by "specific" provisions the Court means only the text of the actual amendments or judicial interpretations in decisions involving those rights.

Quicknotes

DUE PROCESS The constitutional mandate requiring the courts to protect and enforce individuals' rights and liberties consistent with prevailing principles of fairness and justice and prohibiting the federal and state governments from such activities that deprive its citizens of life, liberty, or property interest.

FUNDAMENTAL RIGHT A liberty that is either expressly or impliedly provided for in the U.S. Constitution, the deprivation or burdening of which is subject to a heightened standard of review.

RIGHT TO TRIAL BY JURY The right guaranteed by the Sixth Amendment to the federal constitution that in all criminal prosecutions the accused has a right to a trial by an impartial jury of the state and district in which the crime was allegedly committed.

SELECTIVE INCORPORATION Doctrine providing that the Bill of Rights is incorporated by the Due Process Clause

Continued on next page.

only to the extent that the Supreme Court decides that the privileges and immunities therein are so essential to fundamental principles of due process that they should be preserved against both state and federal action.

SIXTH AMENDMENT Provides the right to a speedy and public trial by impartial jury, the right to be informed of the accusation, the right to confront witnesses, and the right to have the assistance of counsel in all criminal prosecutions.

McDonald v. City of Chicago

Citizens (P) v. City (D)

561 U.S. 742 (2010)

NATURE OF CASE: Appeal from affirmance of judgment that the Second Amendment does not apply to the states.

FACT SUMMARY: [Several plaintiffs (P) challenged a ban on handguns in Chicago, contending that the ban was unconstitutional because the Second Amendment applies to the states.]

RULE OF LAW

The Second Amendment applies to the states by incorporation through the Due Process Clause.

FACTS: [The cities of Chicago (D) and Oak Park (D) in Illinois had gun bans. Several lawsuits were filed against the cities challenging those bans after the United States Supreme Court decided *District of Columbia v. Heller*, 554 U.S. 570 (2008), wherein the Court held that a District of Columbia (D.C.) handgun ban violated the Second Amendment because the D.C. law was enacted under the authority of the federal government and, therefore, the Second Amendment was applicable. The plaintiffs (P) in this case argued that the Second Amendment also applies to the states, and because it does, the Chicago (D) handgun bans were unconstitutional. The district court dismissed the suits, and, on appeal, the court of appeals affirmed. The United States Supreme Court granted certiorari.]

ISSUE: Does the Second Amendment apply to the states by incorporation through the Due Process Clause?

HOLDING AND DECISION: (Alito, J.) Yes. The Second Amendment applies to the states by incorporation through the Due Process Clause. As a threshold matter, the Privileges or Immunities Clause does not incorporate the Second Amendment. The issue, then, is whether the Amendment is incorporated through the Due Process Clause. In *Heller*, it was decided that the right to self-defense is a right that is "fundamental to the Nation's scheme of ordered liberty" and "deeply rooted in this Nation's history and tradition." Throughout the nation's history, Congress has upheld the right to bear arms as a fundamental right, and arguments to the contrary are not supported by history. The question is not whether a civilized society can exist without recognizing this particular right; it's whether the civilized society of our nation (as opposed to those of other nations) must recognize the right. If this were not so, for example, many of the criminal protections of the Bill of Rights, which are unique to our country, would not be incorporated against the states. The Due Process Clause of the Fourteenth Amendment incorporates the Second Amendment right recognized in *Heller*, a fundamental, deeply rooted right. Reversed and remanded.

CONCURRENCE: (Scalia, J.) While it is not clear that the Court should rely on principles of substantive due process, the decision here is supportable because the Court's incorporation of certain guarantees in the Bill of Rights is both long established and narrowly limited.

CONCURRENCE: (Thomas, J.) The judgment is correct, and the Fourteenth Amendment incorporates the Second Amendment against the states, but the Due Process Clause is not the appropriate mechanism for incorporation. Instead, the Privileges or Immunities Clause is the more appropriate avenue for incorporation. The framers of the Privileges or Immunities Clause and the ratifying-era public understood that the right to keep and bear arms was essential to the preservation of liberty. A constitutional provision that guarantees only "process" before a person is deprived of life, liberty, or property cannot define the substance of rights not mentioned in the Constitution. Neither the Due Process Clause's text nor its history suggests that it protects the many substantive rights this Court's cases now claim it does. However, reexamining the issue under the Privileges or Immunities Clause leads to the conclusion that the right to keep and bear arms is a privilege of American citizenship that is guaranteed by the Fourteenth Amendment.

DISSENT: (Stevens, J.) The core issue to be resolved here is whether the Second Amendment guarantees individuals a fundamental right, enforceable against the states, to possess a functional, personal firearm, including a handgun, within the home. That is a different question than the incorporation question, which was already decided in the late 19th century, and which is why the Court is correct in rejecting the argument that the Second Amendment is incorporated via the Privileges and Immunities Clause. The Second Amendment has not been incorporated. Thus, the issue is whether the right to bear arms applies to the states through the Fourteenth Amendment as encompassed by the idea of "liberty." First, firearms have a fundamentally ambivalent relationship to liberty. Just as they can help homeowners defend their families and property from intruders, they can help thugs and insurrectionists and other criminals murder innocent victims, thus lessening the liberty interests of those victims. Second, owning a handgun or any particular type

Continued on next page.

of firearm is not critical to leading a life of autonomy, dignity, or political equality. Further, the experience of other advanced democracies, including those that share our British heritage, undercuts the notion that an expansive right to keep and bear arms is intrinsic to ordered liberty, as those countries place stricter restrictions on firearms than does the United States. Finally, the Court's imposition of a national standard is unwise because, as part of the democratic process, elected officials have shown they are perfectly capable of safeguarding the interest in keeping and bearing arms. Gun control matters should be left to the states and localities, where citizens will be able to decide through the democratic process whether certain gun control measures are "improvident" or not.

DISSENT: (Breyer, J.) There is nothing in the Second Amendment's text, history, or purpose that would render it a fundamental right, insofar as carrying arms for personal self-defense is concerned. There is also nothing in the Constitution that warrants transferring regulatory authority over firearms from the legislative branch to the judicial branch or from the states to the federal government. Therefore, the Fourteenth Amendment does not incorporate the Second Amendment's right to keep and bear arms.

ANALYSIS

Most scholars agree that when the Bill of Rights was adopted, it was intended to limit the federal, not state, government. After the adoption of the Fourteenth Amendment in 1868, the Supreme Court held that rights from the Bill of Rights may be selectively applied, or "incorporated," through the Due Process Clause. In *McDonald*, the Court stated that provisions of the Bill of Rights may be incorporated only if they are "fundamental to our scheme of ordered liberty," or "deeply rooted in this Nation's history and tradition." The case therefore represents a restriction on the application of the Due Process Clause.

Quicknotes

DUE PROCESS CLAUSE Language in the Fifth and Fourteenth Amendments to the U.S. Constitution, providing that no person shall be deprived of "life, liberty, or property, without due process of law."

FOURTEENTH AMENDMENT Declares that no state shall make or enforce any law that shall abridge the privileges and immunities of citizens of the United States. No state shall deny to any person within its jurisdiction the equal protection of the laws.

PRIVILEGES OR IMMUNITIES CLAUSE Section 1 of the Fourteenth Amendment of the U.S. Constitution; prohibits state laws that abridge the privileges or immunities of U.S. citizens.

New York State Rifle & Pistol Association, Inc. v. Bruen

Gun rights organization (P) v. State official (D)

597 U.S. ___, 142 S. Ct. 2111 (2022)

NATURE OF CASE: Appeal from judgment upholding a state's requirement that an applicant for a license to carry a gun outside the home must demonstrate a special need for self-protection distinguishable from that of the general community.

FACT SUMMARY: New York state required an applicant for a license to carry a gun outside the home to demonstrate a special need for self-protection distinguishable from that of the general community. The requirement was challenged as violating the Second Amendment.

RULE OF LAW

(1) Where the government seeks to regulate an individual's conduct covered by the Second Amendment, the government must justify its regulation by demonstrating that the regulation is consistent with the nation's historical tradition of firearm regulation, rather than positing that the regulation promotes an important governmental interest.

(2) A state's "proper-cause" requirement for issuing gun licenses for carrying guns in public, whereby a license applicant must demonstrate to the state that the applicant has a special need for self-protection distinguishable from that of the general community, violates the Second Amendment as applied to the states by the Fourteenth Amendment.

FACTS: New York state required an applicant for a license to carry a gun outside the home to have a "proper cause," which required the applicant to demonstrate a special need for self-protection distinguishable from that of the general community. The requirement was challenged as violating the Second Amendment. The Second Circuit Court of Appeals upheld the proper-cause requirement, and the Supreme Court granted certiorari.

ISSUES:

(1) Where the government seeks to regulate an individual's conduct covered by the Second Amendment, must the government justify its regulation by demonstrating that the regulation is consistent with the nation's historical tradition of firearm regulation, rather than positing that the regulation promotes an important governmental interest?

(2) Does a state's "proper-cause" requirement for issuing gun licenses for carrying guns in public, whereby a license applicant must demonstrate to the state that the applicant has a special need for self-protection distinguishable from that of the general community, violate the Second Amendment as applied to the states by the Fourteenth Amendment?

HOLDING AND DECISION: (Thomas, J.)

(1) Yes. Where the government seeks to regulate an individual's conduct covered by the Second Amendment, the government must justify its regulation by demonstrating that the regulation is consistent with the nation's historical tradition of firearm regulation, rather than positing that the regulation promotes an important governmental interest. The Court's precedents do not support applying means-end scrutiny in the Second Amendment context. Federal courts tasked with making difficult empirical judgments regarding firearm regulations under the banner of "intermediate scrutiny" often defer to the determinations of legislatures. While judicial deference to legislative interest balancing is understandable—and, elsewhere, appropriate—it is not deference that the Constitution demands here. The Second Amendment elevates above all other interests the right of law-abiding, responsible citizens to use arms for self-defense. Even though the Second Amendment's definition of "arms" is fixed according to its historical understanding, that general definition covers modern instruments that facilitate armed self-defense. In reviewing government's arms regulations, two metrics are key: how and why the regulations burden a law-abiding citizen's right to bear arms for self-defense, even in public (i.e., "public carry"), which is a right guaranteed by the Second Amendment. In applying the requisite historical analysis, where a governmental practice has been open, widespread, and unchallenged since the early days of the Republic, the practice should guide the court, but to the extent later history contradicts what the Constitution's text says, the text controls, since liquidating indeterminacies in written laws is far removed from expanding or altering them. Also, in applying a historical analysis, courts may apply either the public's understanding of the right to keep and bear arms that was in place in 1791, when the Second Amendment was adopted, or in 1868, when the Fourteenth Amendment was ratified and made the Second Amendment (along with the other Amendments included in the Bill of Rights) applicable to the states, because, for all relevant

Continued on next page.

purposes, those understandings were the same with respect to public carry.

(2) Yes. A state's "proper-cause" requirement for issuing gun licenses for carrying guns in public, whereby a license applicant must demonstrate to the state that the applicant has a special need for self-protection distinguishable from that of the general community, violates the Second Amendment as applied to the states by the Fourteenth Amendment. A thorough review of the historical record unambiguously indicates that the Second Amendment guarantees to all Americans the right to bear commonly used arms in public subject to certain reasonable, well-defined restrictions. Those restrictions, for example, limited the intent for which one could carry arms, the manner by which one carried arms, or the exceptional circumstances under which one could not carry arms, such as before justices of the peace and other government officials. Apart from a few late-nineteenth-century outlier jurisdictions, American governments simply have not broadly prohibited the public carry of commonly used firearms for personal defense. Nor, subject to a few late-in-time outliers, have American governments required law-abiding, responsible citizens to "demonstrate a special need for self-protection distinguishable from that of the general community" in order to carry arms in public. The constitutional right to bear arms in public for self-defense is no different from other constitutional guarantees, and the exercise of no other constitutional right may be conditioned on an individual's demonstrating to government officers some special need. For these reasons, New York's proper-cause requirement violates the Fourteenth Amendment by preventing law-abiding citizens with ordinary self-defense needs from exercising their Second Amendment right to keep and bear arms in public for self-defense. [Reversed and remanded.]

CONCURRENCE: (Alito, J.) The dissent's recounting of mass shootings that have occurred in recent years is irrelevant to the issue presented. Although the dissent notes that there are nearly 400 million guns in private hands, it does not explain how that statistic bears on the question of whether a person, who already has the right to keep a gun in the home for self-defense is likely to be deterred from acquiring a gun by the knowledge that the gun cannot be carried outside the home. Although the dissent seemingly thinks that the ubiquity of guns and our country's high level of gun violence provide reasons for sustaining New York's proper-cause law, the dissent appears not to understand that it is these very facts that cause law-abiding citizens to feel the need to carry a gun for self-defense.

CONCURRENCE: (Barrett, J.) The Court does not decide two methodological issues. First, the Court does not conclusively determine the manner and circumstances in which post-ratification practice may bear on the original meaning of the Constitution. Second, the Court avoids entering the debate as to whether courts should primarily rely on the prevailing understanding of an individual right when the Fourteenth Amendment was ratified in 1868 or when the Bill of Rights was ratified in 1791. Therefore, the Court's decision should not be understood to endorse freewheeling reliance on historical practice from the mid-to-late 19th century to establish the original meaning of the Bill of Rights.

DISSENT (Breyer, J.): The majority wrongly limits its analysis to focus nearly exclusively on history. It refuses to consider the government interests that justify a challenged gun regulation, regardless of how compelling those interests may be. Because the majority decides the case on the basis of the pleadings, it ignores the benefit of discovery or an evidentiary record, which, in part, would show that the nation has recently experienced an unprecedented number of mass shootings and killings by firearms. However, the Constitution contains no such limitation, and neither do the Court's precedents, and, in any event, the majority itself demonstrates the practical problems with its history-only approach. In applying that approach to New York's law, the majority fails to correctly identify and analyze the relevant historical facts. Contrary to the majority's position, when courts interpret the Second Amendment, it is constitutionally proper, indeed often necessary, for them to consider the serious dangers and consequences of gun violence that lead states to regulate firearms. Moreover, the question of firearm regulation presents a complex problem that should be solved by legislatures rather than courts. Because different states have different interests around firearm regulation, the majority's one-size-fits-all approach is inappropriate and "goes much too far." As far as the majority's departure from precedent goes, applying means-end scrutiny to laws that regulate the Second Amendment right to bear arms would not create a constitutional anomaly; instead, it is the majority's rejection of means-end scrutiny and adoption of a rigid history-only approach that is anomalous, as well as highly impractical. Judges are practiced in weighing ends against means, but not at resolving difficult historical questions. Therefore, the majority's history-only approach raises many troubling questions. For example, do lower courts have the research resources necessary to conduct exhaustive historical analyses in every Second Amendment case? How will judges determine which historians have the better view of close historical questions? Will the meaning of the Second Amendment change if or when new historical evidence becomes available? And, most importantly, will the majority's approach permit judges to reach the

Continued on next page.

outcomes they prefer and then cloak those outcomes in the language of history? In sum, the majority's approach gives the lower courts extremely little guidance as to how to resolve modern constitutional questions based almost entirely on history, and, given that the majority itself provides numerous justifications for rejecting certain historical evidence, the majority green-lights lower court judges picking and choosing the historical evidence they favor. At worst, the majority's approach creates a one-way ratchet that will disqualify virtually any representative historical analogue and make it nearly impossible to sustain common-sense regulations necessary to our nation's safety and security. This problem will be even more acute when it comes to modern-day circumstances that the framers could not have anticipated. Laws addressing repeating crossbows, launcegays, dirks, dagges, skeines, stilladers, and other ancient weapons will be of little help to courts confronting modern problems. As technological progress pushes society ever further beyond the bounds of the framers' imaginations, attempts at "analogical reasoning" will become increasingly tortured.

ANALYSIS

Although the majority applies a history-based, analogical-reasoning approach to evaluating regulations that implicate the Second Amendment, even the majority concedes that even if a modern-day firearm regulation is not a dead ringer for historical precursors, it still may be analogous enough to pass constitutional muster. The majority notes that schools and government buildings were "sensitive places" where arms carrying could be prohibited consistent with the Second Amendment, so that courts can use analogies to those historical regulations of "sensitive places" to determine that modern regulations prohibiting the carry of firearms in new and analogous sensitive places are constitutionally permissible. However, the majority also rejected New York's proper-cause regulation as a justifiable "sensitive place" regulation, concluding that expanding the category of "sensitive places" simply to all places of public congregation that were not isolated from law enforcement would define the category of "sensitive places" far too broadly, as it would in effect exempt cities from the Second Amendment and would eviscerate the general right to publicly carry arms for self-defense.

Quicknotes

INTERMEDIATE SCRUTINY A standard of reviewing the propriety of classifications pertaining to gender or legitimacy under the Equal Protection Clause of the U.S. Constitution that requires a court to ascertain whether the classification furthers an important state interest and is substantially related to the attainment of that interest.

MEANS-END SCRUTINY The most common form of analysis used by courts in enforcing constitutional limits on government action, it examines the justification for government action by assessing whether the asserted purposes (ends) for the government action are furthered by the methods chosen (means) to accomplish those purposes to determine whether the government's justification meets or violates a constitutional limit.

CHAPTER 8

Due Process

Quick Reference Rules of Law

CHAPTER 8

16. *Home Building & Loan Ass'n v. Blaisdell.* A state may affect the obligations between two contracting parties so long as: (1) an emergency exists; (2) the legislation is addressed to a legitimate end; (3) the relief afforded and justified by the emergency could only be of a character appropriate to that emergency; (4) the conditions upon which relief is granted do not appear to be unreasonable; and (5) the legislation is temporary in operation. 145

Lochner v. New York

Employer bakery (D) v. State (P)

198 U.S. 45 (1905)

NATURE OF CASE: Certiorari review of labor law and underlying conviction for violation.

FACT SUMMARY: A state labor law prohibited employment in bakeries for more than 60 hours a week or more than 10 hours a day. Lochner (D) permitted an employee in his bakery to work over 60 hours in one week.

RULE OF LAW

To be a fair, reasonable, and appropriate use of a state's police power, an act must have a direct relation, as a means to an end, to an appropriate and legitimate state objective.

FACTS: [Lochner (D) was fined for violating a state labor law. The law prohibited employment in bakeries for more than 60 hours a week or more than 10 hours a day. Lochner (D) permitted an employee to work in his bakery for more than 60 hours in one week.]

ISSUE: To be a fair, reasonable, and appropriate use of a state's police power, must an act have a direct relation, as a means to an end, to an appropriate and legitimate state objective?

HOLDING AND DECISION: (Peckham, J.) Yes. To be a fair, reasonable, and appropriate use of a state's police power, an act must have a direct relation, as a means to an end, to an appropriate and legitimate state objective. The general right to make a contract in relation to one's business is part of the liberty of the individual protected by the Fourteenth Amendment. The right to purchase or sell labor is part of the liberty protected by this Amendment. However, the states do possess certain police powers relating to the safety, health, morals, and general welfare of the public. If the contract is one that the state in the exercise of its police power has the right to prohibit, the Fourteenth Amendment will not prevent the state's prohibition. When, as here, the state acts to limit the right to labor or the right to contract, it is necessary to determine whether the rights of the state or the individual shall prevail. The Fourteenth Amendment limits the state's exercise of its police power; otherwise, the state would have unbounded power once it stated that legislation was to conserve the health, morals, or safety of its people. It is not sufficient to assert that the act relates to public health. Rather, it must have a more direct relation, as a means to an end, to an appropriate state goal, before an act can interfere with an individual's right to contract in relation to his or her labor. In this case, there is no reasonable foundation for holding the act to be necessary to the health of the public or of bakery officials. Statutes such as this one are merely meddlesome interferences with the rights of the individual. They are invalid unless there is some fair ground to say that there is material danger to the public health or to the employees' health if the labor hours are not curtailed. It cannot be said that the production of healthy bread depends upon the hours that the employees work. Nor is the trade of a baker an unhealthy one to the degree that would authorize the legislature to interfere with the rights to labor and of free contract. Lochner's (D) conviction is reversed.

DISSENT: (Harlan, J.) Whether or not this is wise legislation is not a question for this Court. It is impossible to say that there is not substantial or real regulation between the statute and the state's legitimate goals. This decision brings under the Court's supervision matters that supposedly belonged exclusively to state legislatures.

DISSENT: (Holmes, J.) The word "liberty" in the Fourteenth Amendment should not invalidate a statute unless it can be said that a reasonable person would say that the statute infringes fundamental principles of our people and our law. A reasonable person might think this statute valid. Citizens' liberty is regulated by many state laws that have been held to be valid, i.e., the Sunday laws, the lottery laws, laws requiring vaccination.

ANALYSIS

From the *Lochner* decision in 1905 to the 1930s the Court invalidated a considerable number of laws on substantive due process grounds, such as laws fixing minimum wages, maximum hours and prices and law regulating business activities. The modern Court claims to have rejected the *Lochner* doctrine. It has withdrawn careful scrutiny in most economic areas but has maintained and increased intervention with respect to a variety of non-economic liberties. However, not only economic regulations were struck down under *Lochner*. That doctrine formed the basis for absorbing rights such as those in the First Amendment into the Fourteenth Amendment's concept of liberty. *Lochner* also helped justify other non-economic rights such as the right to teach in a foreign language, *Meyers v. Nebraska*, 262 U.S. 390 (1923). *Meyers* was to be relied upon in the birth control decision, *Griswold v. Connecticut*, 381 U.S. 479 (1965).

Continued on next page.

Quicknotes

POLICE POWER The power of a government to impose restrictions on the rights of private persons, so long as those restrictions are reasonably related to the promotion and protection of public health, safety, morals, and the general welfare.

SUBSTANTIVE DUE PROCESS A constitutional safeguard limiting the power of the state, irrespective of how fair its procedures may be; substantive limits placed on the power of the state.

Nebbia v. New York

Grocery store proprietor (D) v. State (P)

291 U.S. 502 (1934)

NATURE OF CASE: Certiorari review of Milk Board order and underlying conviction for violation of the order.

FACT SUMMARY: The State Milk Board fixed nine cents as the price to be charged for a quart of milk. Nebbia (D) sold two quarts of milk and a loaf of bread for eighteen cents.

RULE OF LAW

When the occasion is proper and by appropriate measures, a state may regulate a business in any of its aspects, including fixing prices.

FACTS: In 1933, the New York legislature established a Milk Control Board (the Board). The Board was given the power to fix minimum and maximum retail prices to be charged by stores to consumers. The Board fixed the price of a quart of milk at nine cents. Nebbia (D), a grocery store proprietor, charged eighteen cents for two quarts of milk and a five-cent loaf of bread. The law establishing the Board was based on a legislative finding that, "Milk is an essential item of diet. Failure of producers to receive a reasonable return threatens a relaxation of vigilance against contamination. The production of milk is a paramount industry of the state, and largely affects the health and prosperity of its people."

ISSUE: When the occasion is proper and by appropriate measures, may a state regulate a business in any of its aspects, including fixing prices?

HOLDING AND DECISION: (Roberts, J.) Yes. When the occasion is proper and by appropriate measures, a state may regulate a business in any of its aspects, including fixing prices. The general rule is that both the use of property and the making of contracts shall be free from government interference. However, neither property rights nor contract rights are absolute. Equally fundamental with the private interest is the public's right to regulate it in the common interest. The Fifth and Fourteenth Amendments do not prohibit governmental regulation for the public welfare. They guarantee only that regulation shall be consistent with due process. The guarantee of due process demands only that the law shall not be unreasonable, arbitrary, or capricious and that the means selected shall have a real and substantial relation to the object sought to be attained. If an industry is subject to regulation in the public interest, its prices may be regulated. An industry that is "affected with a public interest" is one that is subject to police powers. A state is free to adopt whatever economic policy may be reasonably deemed to promote the public welfare. The courts are without authority to override such policies. If the laws passed have a rational relation to a legitimate purpose and are neither arbitrary nor discriminatory, the requirements of due process are satisfied. Price control may fulfill these requirements as well as any other type of regulation. The New York law creating the Milk Control Board and giving it power to fix prices does not conflict with the due process guarantees and is constitutionally valid. Nebbia's (D) conviction is affirmed.

DISSENT: (McReynolds, J.) The Legislative Committee pointed out as the cause of decreased consumption of milk the consumer's reduced buying power. Higher store prices will not enlarge this power, nor will they increase production. This statute arbitrarily interferes with citizens' liberty since the means adopted do not reasonably relate to the end sought, the promotion of the public welfare.

ANALYSIS

The early attitude of the Court had been that the states could regulate selling prices only for industries that affect the public interest. Regulation of prices and rates charged by public utilities, dairies, grain elevators, etc., were upheld but regulation of the prices of theater tickets or ice was not. *Nebbia* held that price control regulation was to be treated the same as other police powers and a rational relation to a legitimate goal was all that was necessary. The dissent, representing the Court's earlier position, does not want to treat the legislation with the deference exercised by the majority. In its judgment, the method adopted by New York does not rationally relate to its goal. *Nebbia* represents the modern position of the Court, which is to presume the propriety of the legislation.

Quicknotes

DUE PROCESS The constitutional mandate requiring the courts to protect and enforce individuals' rights and liberties consistent with prevailing principles of fairness and justice and prohibiting the federal and state governments from such activities that deprive its citizens of a life, liberty, or property interest.

PRICE FIXING A collaboration by competing companies to uniformly set price levels.

RATIONAL-BASIS REVIEW A test employed by the court to determine the validity of a statute in equal protection actions, whereby the court determines whether the challenged statute is rationally related to the achievement of a legitimate state interest.

Williamson v. Lee Optical Co.

State (P) v. Optical company (D)

348 U.S. 483 (1955)

NATURE OF CASE: Certiorari review of constitutionality of state ophthalmology law.

FACT SUMMARY: A state law prohibited any person from fitting or duplicating lenses without a prescription from an ophthalmologist or optometrist. It also prohibited soliciting the sale of frames and the renting of space in a retail store to any person purporting to do eye examinations.

RULE OF LAW

The Due Process Clause may no longer be used to strike down state laws regulating business and industrial conditions because they may be unwise, improvident, or out of harmony with a particular school of thought.

FACTS: A state law prohibited any person who was not a licensed ophthalmologist or optometrist from fitting or duplicating lenses without a prescription from a licensed optometrist or ophthalmologist. Opticians are artisans qualified to grind lenses, fill prescriptions, and fit frames. The effect of the provision was to prevent opticians from fitting old glasses into new frames or duplicating a lost or broken lens without a prescription. Two other sections of the law prohibited soliciting the sale of frames, mountings, or other optical appliances and the renting of space in a retail store to one purporting to do eye examinations.

ISSUE: May the Due Process Clause be used to strike down state laws regulating business and industrial conditions because they may be unwise, improvident, or out of harmony with a particular school of thought?

HOLDING AND DECISION: (Douglas, J.) No. The Due Process Clause may no longer be used to strike down state laws regulating business and industrial conditions because they may be unwise, improvident, or out of harmony with a particular school of thought. For protection against abuses by the legislature, the people must resort to the polls, not the courts. The state law in question here may exact needless wasteful requirements in many cases. But it is for the legislatures, not the courts, to balance the advantages and disadvantages of the new requirement. The legislature may have concluded that the cases in which prescriptions are essential are frequent enough to justify requiring one in every case. Since frames and mountings are used only in conjunction with lenses, and lenses enter the field of health, the legislature might have concluded that to regulate one it had to regulate the other. Finally, the last provision appeared to be an attempt to rid the profession of commercialism. Hence, it cannot be said that the regulation had no rational relation to legitimate objectives. Reversed.

ANALYSIS

An example of the Court's deference to legislative judgments is *Ferguson v. Skrupa*, 372 U.S. 726 (1963), where the Court reversed the invalidation of a state statute regulating the business of debt-adjusting. The law prohibited that business except as an incident to the practice of law. The Supreme Court spoke of its abandonment of the use of the vague contours of the Due Process Clause to nullify laws that a majority of the Court believed to be economically unwise. "We refuse to sit as a super legislature to weigh the wisdom of legislation," the Court stated.

Quicknotes

COMMERCIALISM Relating to advertisement or profit.

DUE PROCESS CLAUSE Language in the Fifth and Fourteenth Amendments to the U.S. Constitution providing that no person shall be deprived of "life, liberty, or property, without due process of law."

LEGISLATIVE OBJECTIVES The goal or purpose motivating the legislature in enacting a particular law.

Griswold v. Connecticut

Doctor/director (D) v. State (P)

381 U.S. 479 (1965)

NATURE OF CASE: Certiorari review of state statute prohibiting the counseling of married persons to take contraceptives.

FACT SUMMARY: A doctor (D) and a layman (D) were prosecuted for advising married persons on the means of preventing conception.

RULE OF LAW

The right to mental privacy, although not explicitly stated in the Bill of Rights, is one of the penumbras emanating from those amendments, formed by certain other explicit guarantees, and it is protected against state regulation that sweeps unnecessarily broad.

FACTS: Griswold (D), the Executive Director of the Planned Parenthood League of Connecticut, and Dr. Buxton (D) were convicted under a Connecticut law that made counseling of married persons to take contraceptives a criminal offense.

ISSUE: Is the right to mental privacy, although not explicitly stated in the Bill of Rights, one of the penumbras emanating from those amendments, formed by certain other explicit guarantees, and is it protected against state regulation that sweeps unnecessarily broad?

HOLDING AND DECISION: (Douglas, J.) Yes. The right to mental privacy, although not explicitly stated in the Bill of Rights, is one of the penumbras emanating from those amendments, formed by certain other explicit guarantees, and it is protected against state regulation that sweeps unnecessarily broad. The various guarantees that create penumbras, or zones, of privacy include the First Amendment's right of association, the Third Amendment's prohibition against the peacetime quartering of soldiers, the Fourth Amendment's prohibition against unreasonable searches and seizures, the Fifth Amendment's Self-Incrimination Clause, and the Ninth Amendment's reservation to the people of unenumerated rights. The Connecticut law, by forbidding the use of contraceptives rather than regulating their manner or sale, seeks to achieve its goals by means having a maximum destructive impact upon that relationship. Reversed.

CONCURRENCE: (Goldberg, J.) The Ninth Amendment, while not constituting an independent source of rights, suggests that the list of rights in the first eight amendments is not exhaustive. This right is a "fundamental" one that cannot be infringed on the state's slender justification in protecting marital fidelity.

CONCURRENCE: (Harlan, J.) The Court, instead of approaching the issue as if the Due Process Clause of the Fourteenth Amendment does not touch this statute unless the enactment is found to violate some penumbra of the Bill of Rights, should have instead relied on the Due Process Clause in finding this law violative of basic values "implicit in the concept of ordered liberty." Doing this would prevent judges from interpolating into the Constitution an "artificial and largely illusory restriction on the content of due process."

CONCURRENCE: (White, J.) The Due Process Clause should be the test in determining whether such laws are reasonably necessary for the effectuation of a legitimate and substantial state interest and are not arbitrary or capricious in application. Here, the causal connection between married persons engaging in extramarital sex and contraceptives is too tenuous.

DISSENT: (Black, J.) While the law is offensive, neither the Ninth Amendment nor the Due Process Clause invalidates it. Both lead the Court into imposing its own notions as to what are wise or unwise laws. What constitutes "fundamental" values this court is incapable of determining. Keeping the Constitution "in tune with the times" is accomplished only through the amendment process. Similarly, the Due Process Clause is too imprecise and lends itself to subjective interpretation.

DISSENT: (Stewart, J.) The Due Process Clause is not the "guide" because there was no claim here that the statute is unconstitutionally vague or that the defendants were denied any of the elements of procedural due process at their trial. The Ninth Amendment simply restricts the federal government to a government of express and limited powers. Finally, the Constitution is silent on the "right to privacy."

ANALYSIS

Although the theory of "substantive due process" has declined as a means to review state economic regulation – at least since 1937 – the Court, as here, has freely applied strict scrutiny when dealing with state laws that affect social areas.

Continued on next page.

Quicknotes

DUE PROCESS CLAUSE Language in the Fifth and Fourteenth Amendments to the U.S. Constitution providing that no person shall be deprived of "life, liberty, or property, without due process of law."

NINTH AMENDMENT The Ninth Amendment to the U.S. Constitution provides that the enumeration of any rights contained therein is not to be construed as denying or disparaging other rights retained by the people.

PENUMBRA A doctrine whereby authority of the federal government is implied pursuant to the Necessary and Proper Clause; one implied power may be inferred from the conferring of another implied power.

RIGHT TO PRIVACY An individual's right to be protected against unwarranted interference in his or her personal affairs, falling into one of four categories: (1) appropriating the individual's likeness or name for commercial benefit; (2) intrusion into the individual's seclusion; (3) public disclosure of private facts regarding the individual; and (4) disclosure of facts placing the individual in a false light.

SUBSTANTIVE DUE PROCESS A constitutional safeguard limiting the power of the state, irrespective of how fair its procedures may be; substantive limits placed on the power of the state.

Roe v. Wade

Single pregnant woman (P) v. State (D)

410 U.S. 113 (1973)

NATURE OF CASE: Certiorari review of state laws making it a crime to procure an abortion except by medical advice to save the life of the mother.

FACT SUMMARY: Roe (P), a single woman, wished to have her pregnancy terminated by an abortion.

RULE OF LAW
The right of privacy found in the Fourteenth Amendment's concept of personal liberty and restrictions upon state action are broad enough to encompass a woman's decision to terminate her pregnancy.

FACTS: The Texas abortion laws challenged here were typical of those adopted by most states. The challengers were Roe (P), a single pregnant woman, a childless couple with the wife not pregnant (J and M Doe), and a licensed physician with two criminal charges pending (Halford). Only Roe (P) was found to be entitled to maintain the action. Although her 1970 pregnancy had been terminated, her case was not found moot since pregnancy "truly could be capable of repetition, yet evading review."

ISSUE: Does the constitutional right of privacy include a woman's right to choose to terminate her pregnancy?

HOLDING AND DECISION: (Blackmun, J.) Yes. The right of privacy found in the Fourteenth Amendment's concept of personal liberty and restrictions upon state action are broad enough to encompass a woman's decision to terminate her pregnancy. While the Constitution does not explicitly mention any right of privacy, such a right has been recognized. This right of privacy, whether founded in the Fourteenth Amendment's concept of personal liberty and restrictions upon state action, as this court feels it is, or in the Ninth Amendment's reservation of rights to the people, is broad enough to encompass a woman's decision to terminate her pregnancy. A statute regulating a fundamental right, such as the right to privacy, may be justified only by a compelling state interest and such statutes must be narrowly drawn. Here, Texas (D) argued that the fetus is a person within the meaning of the Fourteenth Amendment, whose right to life is guaranteed by that Amendment. However, there are no decisions indicating such a definition for "fetus." The unborn have never been recognized in the law as persons in the whole sense. Texas (D) may not, by adopting one theory of life, override the rights of the pregnant woman that are at stake. However, neither are the woman's rights to privacy absolute. The state does have a legitimate interest in preserving the health of the pregnant woman and in protecting the potentiality of life. Each of these interests grows in substantiality as the woman approaches term, and at a point, each becomes compelling. During the first trimester, mortality in abortion is less than mortality in childbirth. After that point, in promoting its interest in the mother's health, the state may regulate the abortion procedure in ways related to maternal health (i.e., licensing of physicians, facilities, etc.). Prior to viability, the physician, in consultation with the pregnant woman, is free to decide that a pregnancy should be terminated without interference by the state. Subsequent to viability, the state, in promoting its interest in the potentiality of life, may regulate and even prescribe abortion, except where necessary to save the mother's life. Because the Texas (D) statute makes no distinction between abortions performed in early pregnancy and those performed later, it sweeps too broadly and is therefore invalid.

CONCURRENCE: (Stewart, J.) The Texas statute invaded "liberty" protected by the Fourteenth Amendment's Due Process Clause. Substantive due process has been resurrected.

DISSENT: (White, J.) This issue, for the most part, should be left with the people. There is nothing in the language or history of the Constitution to support the Court's opinion. The Texas statute is not constitutionally infirm because it denies abortions to those who seek to serve only their own convenience rather than to protect their life or health.

DISSENT: (Rehnquist, J.) The test to be applied is whether the abortion law has a rational relation to a valid state objective. Here, the court applies the compelling state interest test. The application of this test requires the court to examine the legislative policies and pass on the wisdom of those policies, tasks better left to the legislature.

ANALYSIS

The Court in *Dobbs v. Jackson Women's Health Organization,* 142 S. Ct. 2228 (2022), overruled *Roe*, concluding that *Roe* was "egregiously wrong from the start. Its reasoning was exceptionally weak, and the decision has had damaging consequences." The Court held that there is no abortion right in the Constitution, and that any challenged abortion regulation would be subject to a rational-basis standard of review. The Court indicated it was acting to return the abortion issue to the states,

Continued on next page.

so the issue could be determined locally and democratically. In doing so, the Court sidestepped stare decisis principles, applied a novel test based almost exclusively on history, and effectively left the door open to jettisoning substantive due process doctrine in future cases.

Quicknotes

MOOTNESS Judgment on the particular issue would not resolve the controversy.

RATIONAL-BASIS REVIEW A test employed by the court to determine the validity of a statute in equal protection actions, whereby the court determines whether the challenged statute is rationally related to the achievement of a legitimate state interest.

STARE DECISIS Doctrine whereby courts follow legal precedent unless there is good cause for departure.

Planned Parenthood of Southeastern Pa. v. Casey

Clinics/doctors (P) v. State (D)

505 U.S. 833 (1992)

NATURE OF CASE: Certiorari review of state abortion statutes.

FACT SUMMARY: Planned Parenthood of Southeastern Pa. (P) challenged the constitutionality of Pennsylvania's (D) abortion law.

RULE OF LAW

A law is unconstitutional as an undue burden on a woman's right to choose an abortion before fetal viability if the law places a substantial obstacle in the path of a woman seeking to exercise that right.

FACTS: The Pennsylvania Abortion Control Act (the Act) required (a) a doctor to provide a woman seeking an abortion with information designed to persuade her against abortion and imposed a waiting period of at least 24 hours between provision of the information and the abortion; (b) a minor to obtain consent of one parent or a judge's order before having an abortion; (c) a married woman to sign a statement averring that her husband had been notified, her husband was not the father, her husband forcibly had impregnated her, or that she would be physically harmed if she notified her husband; and (d) a public report on every abortion, detailing information on the facility, physician, patient, and steps taken to comply with the Act. The name of the patient was confidential. The Act provided the first three provisions would not apply in a "medical emergency," i.e., a condition a doctor determines to require immediate abortion to avert death or serious risk of substantial, irreversible impairment of a major bodily function. Five clinics (P), including Planned Parenthood (P), and five doctors (P) sued Pennsylvania (D), including Governor Casey (D), claiming the Act was unconstitutional on its face. The district court held the entire Act invalid under *Roe v. Wade*, 410 U.S. 113 (1973). The court of appeals reversed, upholding the entire Act except the husband-notification requirement. Planned Parenthood et al. (P) appealed.

ISSUE: Is a law an unconstitutionally undue burden on a woman's right to choose an abortion before fetal viability if the law places a substantial obstacle in the path of a woman seeking to exercise that right?

HOLDING AND DECISION: (O'Connor, J.) Yes. A law is unconstitutional as an undue burden on a woman's right to choose an abortion before fetal viability if the law places a substantial obstacle in the path of a woman seeking to exercise that right. For two decades people have organized lives relying on the availability of abortion. The Court rarely resolves a controversy as intensely divisive as in *Roe v. Wade*, 410 U.S. 113 (1973). Such a decision should be overturned only if it proves unworkable or if new information arises that renders the decision unjustified in the present. *Roe* is neither unworkable nor based on outdated assumptions. Medical technology has altered the age of viability, but that does not affect the validity of viability as a dividing line. Viability is the point at which a fetus can be said to be an independent life so that the state's interest in protecting it then outweighs the mother's decision-making interest. The Court and the nation would be seriously damaged if the Court were to overturn *Roe* simply on the basis of a philosophical disagreement with the 1973 Court or as surrender to political pressure. The liberty rights of women and the personal, intimate nature of childbearing sharply limit state power to insist a woman carry a child to term or accept the state's vision of her role in society. Thus, the integrity of the Court, stare decisis, and substantive due process require the central principle of *Roe* to be reaffirmed: a state may not prevent a woman from making the ultimate decision to terminate her pregnancy before viability. *Roe* also recognized the state interest in maternal health and in protecting potential life. Application of the rigid trimester framework often ignored state interests, leading to striking down abortion regulations that in no real sense deprived women of the ultimate decision. Therefore, the trimester framework must be rejected, and undue-burden analysis put in its place. Here, the information requirement is not an undue burden. Truthful, non-misleading information on the nature of abortion procedure, health risks, and consequences to the fetus are reasonable to ensure informed choice, one that might cause a woman to choose childbirth. The 24-hour waiting period does not create a health risk and reasonably furthers the state interest in protecting the unborn. Requiring a period of reflection to make an informed decision is reasonable. A waiting period may increase cost and risk of delay, but on a facial challenge it cannot be called a substantial obstacle. Prior cases establish that a state may require parental consent before abortions by minors, provided there is a judicial bypass procedure. On its face, the statute's definition of "medical emergency" is not too narrow. The reporting requirement is reasonably directed to the preservation of maternal health and the provision of a vital element of medical research, and the statute protects patient confidentiality. The husband-notification requirement imposes an undue burden on abortion rights of the abused women who fear for their

Continued on next page.

safety and the safety of their children and are likely to be deterred from procuring an abortion as surely as if the state outlawed abortion. A husband has a strong interest in his wife's pregnancy, but before birth it is a biological fact that regulation of the fetus has a far greater impact on the woman. The husband-notification requirement is unconstitutional, and the rest of the statute is valid. Affirmed.

CONCURRENCE AND DISSENT: (Stevens, J.) The Court is correct in determining that stare decisis should have controlling significance in a case like this. *Roe v. Wade*, 410 U.S. 113 (1973), is an integral part of a "correct understanding of both the concept of liberty and the basic equality of men and women." States must not interfere with the decisional autonomy of the woman to choose even where they think it acts in the best interests of all.

CONCURRENCE AND DISSENT: (Blackmun, J.) The Court correctly reaffirms a woman's right to abortion. However, that right should remain fundamental, and any state-imposed burden upon it should be subjected to the strictest judicial scrutiny. Categorizing a woman's right to abortion as merely a "liberty interest" is not sufficient. In striking down the husband-notification requirement the Court sets up a framework for evaluating abortion regulations in the social context of women facing issues of reproductive choice. The Court failed to strike down the information, waiting period, parental consent, and reporting requirements on their face, but the Court's standard at least allows future courts to hold that in practice such regulations are undue burdens. The reporting requirement does not further maternal health. Fearing harassment, many doctors will stop performing abortions if their names appear on public reports. However, none of these requirements would survive under the strict-scrutiny standard of review. The trimester framework should be maintained. No other approach better protects a woman's fundamental right while accommodating legitimate state interests. The Court's cases do not create a list of personal liberties: they are a principled account of how these rights are grounded in a general right of privacy.

CONCURRENCE AND DISSENT: (Rehnquist, C.J.) *Roe v. Wade*, 410 U.S. 113 (1973), was wrongly decided, has led to a confusing body of law, and should be overturned. The Court's decision, replacing *Roe's* strict scrutiny standard and trimester framework with a new, unworkable undue burden test, cannot be justified by stare decisis. Authentic principles of stare decisis do not require erroneous decisions to be maintained. The Court's integrity is enhanced when it repudiates wrong decisions. Americans have grown accustomed to *Roe*, but that should not prevent the Court from correcting a wrong decision. The Fourteenth Amendment's concept of liberty does not incorporate any all-encompassing right of privacy. Unlike marriage, procreation, and contraception, abortion terminates potential life and must be analyzed differently. Historic traditions of the American people, critical to an understanding of fundamental rights, do not support a right to abortion. A woman's interest in having an abortion is liberty protected by due process, but states may regulate abortion in ways rationally related to a legitimate state interest. All provisions of the Pennsylvania law do so and are constitutional. The husband-notification requirement is reasonably related to promoting state interests in protecting the husband's interests, potential life, and the integrity of marriage.

CONCURRENCE AND DISSENT: (Scalia, J.) Applying the rational basis test, the Pennsylvania statute in its entirety should be upheld. The Court's description of the place of *Roe v. Wade*, 410 U.S. 113 (1973), in the social history of the United States is unrecognizable. Not only did *Roe* not resolve the deeply divisive issue of abortion, it did more than anything else to nourish it by elevating it to the national level where it is infinitely more difficult to resolve. *Roe* fanned into life an issue that has inflamed our national politics in general and has obscured with its smoke the selection of Justices to this Court in particular, ever since.

ANALYSIS

The Court in *Dobbs v. Jackson Women's Health Organization*, 142 S. Ct. 2228 (2022), overruled *Casey*, concluding that *Roe v. Wade*, 410 U.S. 113 (1973), was "egregiously wrong from the start." Having found that *Roe* was decided as an abuse of judicial authority, the Court reasoned that stare decisis, the doctrine on which *Casey's* controlling opinion (*Roe*) was based, did not compel unending adherence to *Roe*. The Court held that there is no abortion right in the Constitution, and that any challenged abortion regulation would be subject to a rational-basis standard of review. The Court indicated it was acting to return the abortion issue to the states, so the issue could be determined locally and democratically. In doing so, the Court sidestepped stare decisis principles, applied a novel test based almost exclusively on history, and effectively left the door open to jettisoning substantive due process doctrine in future cases.

Quicknotes

FUNDAMENTAL RIGHT A liberty that is either expressly or impliedly provided for in the U.S. Constitution, the deprivation or burdening of which is subject to a heightened standard of review.

Continued on next page.

RATIONAL-BASIS REVIEW A test employed by the court to determine the validity of a statute in equal protection actions, whereby the court determines whether the challenged statute is rationally related to the achievement of a legitimate state interest.

STARE DECISIS Doctrine whereby courts follow legal precedent unless there is good cause for departure.

STRICT SCRUTINY Method by which courts determine the constitutionality of a law when a law affects a fundamental right; under the test, the legislature must have a compelling interest to enact law and measures prescribed by the law must be the least restrictive means possible to accomplish goal.

SUBSTANTIVE DUE PROCESS A constitutional safeguard limiting the power of the state, irrespective of how fair its procedures may be; substantive limits placed on the power of the state.

UNDUE BURDEN Unlawfully oppressive or troublesome requirement.

VIABILITY The point at which an unborn child is capable of living outside its mother's womb.

Gonzales v. Carhart

Attorney General (D) v. Abortion doctor (P)

550 U.S. 124 (2007)

NATURE OF CASE: Certiorari review of constitutionality of the federal Partial-Birth Abortion Ban Act.

FACT SUMMARY: Congress passed a statute that criminalized doctors' performance of partial-birth abortions.

RULE OF LAW

The Partial-Birth Abortion Ban Act does not place a substantial obstacle to late-term but pre-viability abortions.

FACTS: In 2003, Congress enacted the Partial-Birth Abortion Ban Act (the Act), which criminalized doctors' performance of partial-birth abortions. The Act explicitly and precisely defined "partial-birth abortion," in part, as an abortion following the "deliver[y] [of] a living fetus." [Carhart (P), a doctor who performed partial-birth abortions, filed suit for injunctive relief to prohibit the Act from being applied against him. The trial court granted the injunction, and the intermediate appellate court affirmed.] The Government (D) sought further review in the Supreme Court.

ISSUE: Does the Partial-Birth Abortion Ban Act place a substantial obstacle to late-term but pre-viability abortions?

HOLDING AND DECISION: (Kennedy, J.) No. The Partial-Birth Abortion Ban Act (the Act) does not place a substantial obstacle to late-term but pre-viability abortions. The Act can be construed as not prohibiting the standard form of partial-birth abortion invalidated in *Stenberg v. Carhart*, 530 U.S. 914 (2000), and the Act therefore is not facially invalid on that basis. Further, instead of placing a substantial obstacle to a partial-birth abortion, the Act simply respects human life—an objective that lies within the legislative power. The Act advances that objective by ensuring that women will be fully informed about the methods of abortion to which they consent. Moreover, Congress can legitimately legislate even in the face of the medical uncertainty whether such a prohibition on one form of abortion subjects women "to significant health risks." Such uncertainty does not support a facial challenge to the Act. The proper way to attack the Act would be through an as-applied challenge that would permit review of a more precise factual scenario. Reversed.

CONCURRENCE: (Thomas, J.) The Court correctly applies existing law, but the Constitution provides no basis at all for the Court's abortion jurisprudence.

DISSENT: (Ginsburg, J.) This decision mocks *Planned Parenthood of Southeastern Pa. v. Casey*, 505 U.S. 833 (1992), and *Stenberg v. Carhart*, 530 U.S. 914 (2000), and it flies in the face of medical approval of abortion procedures. The Partial-Birth Abortion Ban Act (the Act) does subject women to significant health risks by forcing them to choose less-safe methods of abortion, and in the process, the statute does not save even one fetus because the Act criminalizes merely a method of abortion, not abortion itself. As the Court suggests, the real basis for today's decision is "moral concerns" for what the majority sees as emotionally fragile women. This rationale circumvents the concerns for stare decisis that have supported our prior decisions in this area. Today's decision is actually a veiled attempt to undermine, in a piecemeal fashion, a woman's established right to an abortion.

ANALYSIS

The Court in *Dobbs v. Jackson Women's Health Organization*, 142 S. Ct. 2228 (2022), overruled *Roe v. Wade*, 410 U.S. 113 (1973), and *Planned Parenthood of Southeastern Pa. v. Casey*, 505 U.S. 833 (1992), concluding that *Roe* was "egregiously wrong from the start." Having found that *Roe* was decided as an abuse of judicial authority, the Court reasoned that stare decisis, the doctrine on which *Casey's* controlling opinion (*Roe*) was based, did not compel unending adherence to *Roe*. The Court held that there is no abortion right in the Constitution, and that any challenged abortion regulation would be subject to a rational-basis standard of review. The Court indicated it was acting to return the abortion issue to the states, so the issue could be determined locally and democratically. In doing so, the Court sidestepped stare decisis principles, applied a novel test based almost exclusively on history, and effectively left the door open to jettisoning substantive due process doctrine in future cases.

Quicknotes

DUE PROCESS The constitutional mandate requiring the courts to protect and enforce individuals' rights and liberties consistent with prevailing principles of fairness and justice and prohibiting the federal and state governments from such activities that deprive its citizens of life, liberty, or property interest.

Continued on next page.

INJUNCTION A court order requiring a person to do, or prohibiting that person from doing, a specific act.

INJUNCTIVE RELIEF A court order issued as a remedy, requiring a person to do, or prohibiting that person from doing, a specific act.

RATIONAL-BASIS REVIEW A test employed by the court to determine the validity of a statute in equal protection actions, whereby the court determines whether the challenged statute is rationally related to the achievement of a legitimate state interest.

STARE DECISIS Doctrine whereby courts follow legal precedent unless there is good cause for departure.

Dobbs v. Jackson Women's Health Organization

State official (D) v. Abortion clinic (P)

597 U.S. ___, 142 S. Ct. 2228 (2022)

NATURE OF CASE: Appeal in action challenging a state's restrictions on abortion.

FACT SUMMARY: A Mississippi law provided that "except in a medical emergency or in the case of a severe fetal abnormality, a person shall not intentionally or knowingly perform . . . or induce an abortion of an unborn human being if the probable gestational age of the unborn human being has been determined to be greater than fifteen (15) weeks." Miss. Code Ann. § 41-41-191. Jackson Women's Health Organization (P), an abortion clinic and one of its doctors, challenged the law as violating *Roe v. Wade,* 410 U.S. 113 (1973), and *Planned Parenthood of Southeastern Pa. v. Casey*, 505 U.S. 833 (1992). Mississippi argued that *Roe* and *Casey* were wrongly decided, and that its law satisfied rational-basis review.

RULE OF LAW

The Constitution does not confer a right to abortion.

FACTS: Mississippi's Gestational Age Act (the Act) provided that "[e]xcept in a medical emergency or in the case of a severe fetal abnormality, a person shall not intentionally or knowingly perform . . . or induce an abortion of an unborn human being if the probable gestational age of the unborn human being has been determined to be greater than fifteen (15) weeks." Miss. Code Ann. § 41-41-191. Jackson Women's Health Organization (P), an abortion clinic, and one of its doctors challenged the Act, alleging that it violated the U.S. Supreme Court's precedents establishing a constitutional right to abortion, in particular *Roe v. Wade,* 410 U.S. 113 (1973), and *Planned Parenthood of Southeastern Pa. v. Casey*, 505 U.S. 833 (1992). The lower courts ruled in favor of Jackson Women's Health Organization (P), and Mississippi (D) appealed, arguing that *Roe* and *Casey* were wrongly decided and that the Act was constitutional because it satisfied rational-basis review. The United States Supreme Court granted certiorari.

ISSUE: Does the Constitution confer a right to abortion?

HOLDING AND DECISION: (Alito, J.) No. The Constitution does not confer a right to abortion. The Constitution makes no reference to abortion, and no such right is implicitly protected by any constitutional provision, including the Due Process Clause of the Fourteenth Amendment. That provision has been held to guarantee some rights that are not mentioned in the Constitution, but any such right must be deeply rooted in this Nation's history and tradition and implicit in the concept of ordered liberty. The right to abortion does not fall within this category. Until the latter part of the 20th century, such a right was entirely unknown in American law, and, in fact, abortion was mostly criminalized. Defenders of the abortion right argue that is similar to the rights recognized in past decisions involving matters such as intimate sexual relations, contraception, and marriage, but abortion is fundamentally different because it destroys "fetal life" and what the Mississippi law describes as an "unborn human being." *Roe v. Wade,* 410 U.S. 113 (1973), therefore, was an abuse of judicial power, and must be overruled. Because *Roe* was wrongly decided, the principle of stare decisis does not require the Court to adhere to *Roe* as binding precedent. It has been suggested that support can be found for the abortion right in the Fourteenth Amendment's Equal Protection Clause, but that theory is squarely foreclosed by the Court's precedents, which establish that the regulation of abortion is not a sex-based classification and is thus not subject to the heightened scrutiny that applies to such classifications. Rather, regulations and prohibitions of abortion are governed by the same standard of review as other health and safety measures, i.e., rational-basis review. Next, the Court examines whether the right to obtain an abortion is rooted in the Nation's history and tradition and whether it is an essential component of "ordered liberty." The Court finds that the right to abortion is not deeply rooted in the Nation's history and tradition. There was no such right at common law, and it was only a very short time before *Roe* was decided that it was even suggested that such right should be recognized. In the late 1800s, in fact, the vast majority of states enacted statutes criminalizing abortion at all stages of pregnancy. By 1868, the year when the Fourteenth Amendment was ratified, three-quarters of the states had enacted statutes making abortion a crime even if it was performed before quickening. By 1910, all but one state had done so. This overwhelming consensus endured until the day *Roe* was decided. The privacy right described in *Planned Parenthood of Southeastern Pa. v. Casey*, 505 U.S. 833 (1992), to make "intimate and personal choices" that are "central to personal dignity and autonomy" is not absolute and does not give a person the right to do anything they want or believe. Such a right is not part of ordered liberty. Otherwise, illicit drug use, prostitution, and the like would be licensed. In this regard, the dissent strongly errs, because it does not accord legitimacy to a

Continued on next page.

state's interest in protecting fetal life, or the destruction of a potential life. Stare decisis is not an inexorable command, and it "is at its weakest when this Court interprets the Constitution." When one of this Court's constitutional decisions goes astray, the country is usually stuck with the bad decision unless the Court corrects the mistake. As some of the Court's precedents demonstrate, a particular iteration of the Court is entitled to overrule decisions it deems were previously erroneously decided, especially when doing so returns decisions to the people to decide that were wrongfully removed from the democratic process. *Roe* was not grounded in history, text, or precedent, and, even worse, its reasoning was weak and remarkably standardless. Moreover, the Court's precedents over the last half century have diluted numerous doctrines and legal principles. Whatever reliance interests were found in *Casey* were in an intangible form, one that courts do not have the expertise, or authority, to adjudicate. The Court's previous abortion decisions were unworkable, and this decision only addresses the right to abortion, and no other rights that may have been wrongly decided by prior iterations of this Court. The Court should not allow its decisions to be affected by what is going on in the Nation, or how its decisions might affect the public. Instead, the Court should assess cases before it only in light of the Constitution's text, and in light of history and practices that were in place when the various provisions of the Constitution were enacted. All the Court can do, and is authorized to do, is interpret the Constitution. That is not what the *Casey* Court did as it attempted to mediate a national controversy, and that is why *Casey* cannot be allowed to stand. Based on the interpretation of the current Court, the right of a woman to have an abortion is not a constitutional right, as this Court, unlike its predecessors, finds no support for it in the text of the Constitution or in the Nation's history. Accordingly, rational-basis review of abortion laws is proper. Abortion presents a moral question, and the Constitution does not prohibit the citizens of each state from regulating or prohibiting abortion. *Roe* and *Casey* arrogated that authority. Therefore, those decisions are overruled.

CONCURRENCE: (Thomas, J.) Substantive due process is an oxymoron that lacks any basis in the Constitution. Because the Due Process Clause does not secure any substantive rights, it does not secure a right to abortion. Therefore, the Court should reconsider all of its substantive due process precedents, including *Griswold v. Connecticut*, 381 U.S. 479 (1965), *Lawrence v. Texas*, 539 U.S. 558 (2003), and *Obergefell v. Hodges*, 576 U.S. 644 (2015). Those were demonstrably erroneous decisions. The Court should then ask whether other constitutional provisions guarantee the myriad rights that all of the Court's substantive due process cases have generated. For example, the Court could consider whether any of the rights previously announced in the Court's substantive due process cases are "privileges or immunities of citizens of the United States" protected by the Fourteenth Amendment. To answer that question, the Court would need to decide important antecedent questions, including whether the Privileges or Immunities Clause protects any rights that are not enumerated in the Constitution and, if so, how to identify those rights.

CONCURRENCE: (Kavanaugh, J.) The Court must remain neutral regarding abortion, which presents an irreconcilable conflict between the interests of a pregnant woman who seeks an abortion and the interests in protecting the woman's fetus. The Court's job is to interpret the Constitution, and, therefore, espouses neither the position that abortion must be outlawed throughout the United States, nor that it should be legalized throughout the country. Therefore, the decision the Court announces does not prevent individual states from outlawing or permitting abortion. It is also important to emphasize that this decision does not by itself mean overruling other decisions, such as *Griswold v. Connecticut*, 381 U.S. 479 (1965), *Eisenstadt v. Baird*, 405 U.S. 438 (1972), *Loving v. Virginia*, 388 U.S. 1 (1967), or *Obergefell v. Hodges*, 576 U.S. 644 (2015). Other abortion-related legal questions that may arise are not especially difficult as a constitutional matter. For example, may a state bar a resident of that state from traveling to another state to obtain an abortion? The answer is "no." based on the constitutional right to interstate travel. May a state retroactively impose liability or punishment for an abortion that occurred prior to today's decision? "No," based on the Due Process Clause or the Ex Post Facto Clause.

CONCURRENCE IN JUDGMENT: (Roberts, C.J.) The viability line established by *Roe v. Wade*, 410 U.S. 113 (1973), and *Planned Parenthood of Southeastern Pa. v. Casey*, 505 U.S. 833 (1992), should be discarded under a straightforward stare decisis analysis because that line never made any sense. However, the Court should have not said more, out of adherence to a simple yet fundamental principle of judicial restraint: If it is not necessary to decide more to dispose of a case, then it is necessary not to decide more. The Court decides more than it needs to, especially given that the Court now repudiates a constitutional right the Court not only previously recognized, but also expressly reaffirmed applying the doctrine of stare decisis. None of the cases the Court cites as justifying the sea change it effects support the action the Court takes. Both the majority and the dissent take unwavering positions, but it seems there can be more play in the joints, for example, it is not certain that a ban on terminating a pregnancy from the moment of conception must be treated the same under the Constitution as a ban after fifteen weeks. Accordingly, the Court should have

Continued on next page.

confined itself to deciding only what was necessary to the disposition of the immediate case before it.

DISSENT: (Breyer, J.) For half a century, *Roe v. Wade*, 410 U.S. 113 (1973), and *Planned Parenthood of Southeastern Pa. v. Casey*, 505 U.S. 833 (1992), protected the liberty and equality of women. Thanks to those decisions, the government could not control a woman's body or the course of a woman's life: It could not determine what the woman's future would be. Respecting a woman as an autonomous being, and granting her full equality, those decisions gave a woman substantial choice over this most personal and most consequential of all life decisions. The majority now shreds this protection and respect. In *Roe* and *Casey*, the Court well understood the difficulty and divisiveness of the abortion issue. Therefore, the Court struck a balance, as it often does when values and goals compete. The majority now says that from the very moment of fertilization, a woman has no rights to speak of. A state can force her to bring a pregnancy to term, even at the steepest personal and familial costs. Because, as the Court has often stated, protecting fetal life is rational, states can now feel free to enact all manner of restrictions relating to abortion, even reaching inside a woman's home to criminalize the taking of medication in one's own home. Some states have passed laws without any exceptions for when the woman is the victim of rape or incest. Under those laws, a woman will have to bear her rapist's child or a young girl her father's that results from not only rape but incest—no matter if doing so will destroy her life. States can even go so far as not permitting abortion even if that means a woman's physical life or health will be at great risk or even snuffed out—and some have done so. States may now criminalize abortion—both as to providing it, and as to having it—so that women may be forced to conceive in prison. As Texas has recently shown, a state can permissibly turn neighbor against neighbor, enlisting fellow citizens in the effort to root out anyone who tries to get an abortion, or to assist another in doing so. The majority says its decision permits each state to decide the matter for itself, but that will not help poor women who cannot afford to travel to states that permit abortion. It could also be that some states will prohibit interstate travel for the purpose of receiving an abortion. Some states may criminalize efforts, including the provision of information or funding, to help women gain access to other states' abortion services. Moreover, nothing in the majority's decision stops the federal government from prohibiting abortions nationwide, once again from the moment of conception and without exceptions for rape or incest. If that happens, [the] challenge for a woman will be to finance a trip not to New York or California but to Toronto. The one sure result of the majority's decision is the curtailment of women's rights, and of their status as free and equal citizens, because now the government can force a woman to give birth, prohibiting even the earliest abortions. Regardless of the majority's attempts at assuring the Nation that only abortion rights are at risk, no one should trust that this majority is done dismantling rights that it finds repugnant. Those rights, such as the right to contraception (*Griswold v. Connecticut*, 381 U.S. 479 (1965), *Eisenstadt v. Baird*, 405 U.S. 438 (1972)), or the rights to same-sex intimacy and marriage (*Lawrence v. Texas*, 539 U.S. 558 (2003), *Obergefell v. Hodges*, 576 U.S. 644 (2015)), are all part of the same constitutional fabric, protecting autonomous decisionmaking over the most personal of life decisions. Most of the majority is eager to say that nothing it does "cast[s] doubt on precedents that do not concern abortion." But how could that be? The lone rationale for what the majority does today is that the right to elect an abortion is not "deeply rooted in history." The same could be said, though, of most of the rights the majority claims it is not tampering with. That means either the majority does not really believe in its own reasoning, or, if it does, all rights that have no history stretching back to the mid-nineteenth century are insecure. The majority simply has no good reason for the upheaval in law and society it sets off. The only reason is that the composition of the Court has changed, and the proclivities of individuals (i.e., the majority Justices) rule. Thus, the majority departs from its obligation to faithfully and impartially apply the law. *Roe* and *Casey* are part of the fabric of core constitutional concepts of individual freedom, and of the equal rights of citizens to decide on the shape of their lives. Those legal concepts have gone far toward defining what it means to be an American, because in this Nation, Americans do not believe that a government controlling all private choices is compatible with a free people. So, we as a people do not (as the majority insists today) place everything within "the reach of majorities and [government] officials." *West Virginia Bd. of Ed. v. Barnette*, 319 U.S. 624, 638 (1043). We believe in a Constitution that puts some issues off limits to majority rule. Even in the face of public opposition, we uphold the right of individuals, including women, to make their own choices and chart their own futures. The majority reaches back to a time when the Fourteenth Amendment was ratified, when women were not considered full members of the community, and when the Amendment's ratifiers—all men—did not understand reproductive rights as part of the guarantee of liberty conferred in the Fourteenth Amendment. Most women in 1868 also had a foreshortened view of their rights: If most men could not then imagine giving women control over their bodies, most women could not imagine having that kind of autonomy. But that takes away nothing from the core point. Those responsible for the original Constitution, including the Fourteenth Amendment, did not perceive women as equals, and did not recognize women's rights. When the

Continued on next page.

majority says that the Court must read the Nation's foundational charter as viewed at the time of ratification (except that we may also check it against the Dark Ages), it consigns women to second-class citizenship. Nevertheless, with time and changes in society, the Constitution now grants rights to women that it did not back in 1868. Over time, the Court (the current majority excluded) rejected the majority's pinched view of how to read the Constitution. The Founders knew they were writing a document designed to apply to ever-changing circumstances over centuries, and the Court until now has recognized that. The Framers (both in 1788 and 1868) understood that the world changes, so they did not define rights by reference to the specific practices existing at the time. Instead, the Framers defined rights in general terms, to permit future evolution in their scope and meaning. Over the course of the Nation's history, this Court has taken up the Framers' invitation. It has kept true to the Framers' principles by applying them in new ways, responsive to new societal understandings and conditions, especially when construing the majestic but open-ended words of the Fourteenth Amendment—the guarantees of "liberty" and "equality" for all. Such guarantees can evolve while remaining grounded in constitutional principles, constitutional history, and constitutional precedents. The Constitution's meaning gains content from the long sweep of the Court's decisions and successive judicial precedents—each looking to the last and each seeking to apply the Constitution's most fundamental commitments to new conditions. When the majority decimates a right that women have held for 50 years, the majority, contrary to what it asserts, is not being "scrupulously neutral." It is instead taking sides: against women who wish to exercise the right, and for states (like Mississippi) that want to bar them from doing so. The Court has until now restricted the government's power to interfere with a person's medical decisions or compel a person to undergo medical procedures, yet there are few greater incursions on a body than forcing a woman to complete a pregnancy and give birth. *Roe* and *Casey* are part of a long line of decisions protecting from government intrusion a wealth of private choices about family matters, child rearing, intimate relationships, and procreation. In numerous prior cases, the Court has repeatedly said that liberty requires such protection, even when those living in 1868 would not have recognized the claim—because they would not have seen the person making it as a full-fledged member of the community. Throughout the Nation's history, the sphere of protected liberty has expanded, bringing in individuals formerly excluded. In that way, the constitutional values of liberty and equality go hand in hand; they do not inhabit the hermetically sealed containers the majority portrays. The majority's attempts at being reassuring are unavailing. Justice Thomas makes clear he has no intention of limiting the majority's approach to just abortion rights, and even disregarding Justice Thomas's concurrence, if the majority is serious about its sole reason for overturning *Roe* and *Casey*, i.e., the legal status of abortion in the nineteenth century, the law also did not then (and would not for ages) protect a wealth of other rights that Americans have enjoyed in modern times, e.g., the right to marry across racial lines or the right to be free from government-forced sterilization. So, if the majority is right in its legal analysis, all those decisions were wrong, and all those matters properly belong to the states too. Further, the majority cannot be taken at its word, because regardless of what it says, it does not control future decisions when the composition of the Court will be different. Moreover, none of the cases the majority lists as overruling precedent came close to departing from stare decisis in the manner the majority does here. In the end, the majority says, all it must say to override stare decisis is one thing: that it believes *Roe* and *Casey* "egregiously wrong." That rule makes radical change too easy and too fast, based on nothing more than the new views of new judges. The majority has overruled *Roe* and *Casey* for one and only one reason: because it has always despised them, and now it has the votes to discard them. The majority thereby substitutes a rule by judges for the rule of law. Contrary to the majority's assertions, *Roe* and *Casey* have been workable and have been applied for decades; the undue burden standard has given rise to no unusual difficulties. Instead of removing the Court from the abortion issue, the majority puts the Court at the center of it, because its decision is sure to give rise to numerous issues regarding how far states can go in forcing a woman to give birth, and also invites a host of questions about interstate conflicts, and what is sure to be the coming "interjurisdictional abortion wars." Women living below the federal poverty line experience unintended pregnancies at rates five times higher than higher income women do, and nearly half of women who seek abortion care live in households below the poverty line. These women living in poverty will be most affected by this decision, and may lose not just their freedom, but their lives. However, the expectation of reproductive control is integral to many women's identity and their place in the Nation, as that expectation helps define a woman as an "equal citizen," with all the rights, privileges, and obligations that status entails. According to the majority, a reliance interest must be "very concrete," like those involving "property" or "contract." This unprecedented assertion is, at bottom, a radical claim to power. The interest women have in *Roe* and *Casey* are perfectly, viscerally concrete. Countless women will now make different decisions about careers, education, relationships, and whether to try to become pregnant than they would have when *Roe* served as a backstop. Because of the majority's decision, young

Continued on next page.

women will come of age with fewer rights than their mothers and grandmothers had. The majority accomplishes that result without so much as considering how women have relied on the right to choose or what it means to take that right away. The majority's refusal even to consider the life-altering consequences of reversing *Roe* and *Casey* is a stunning indictment of its decision. Power, not reason, is the new currency of this Court's decisionmaking. Nothing has changed since *Roe* and *Casey* were decided to support what the majority has done. All that has changed is the Court's composition. A new and bare majority—acting at practically the first moment possible—has converted a series of dissenting opinions expressing antipathy toward *Roe* and *Casey* into a decision greenlighting even total abortion bans. In doing so, it places in jeopardy other rights, from contraception to same-sex intimacy and marriage, and greatly undermines the Court's legitimacy. The Court's legitimacy is earned over time, but it can be destroyed much more quickly. The American public should never conclude that its constitutional protections hang by a thread—that a new majority, adhering to a new "doctrinal school," could by dint of numbers alone expunge their rights. It is impossible to conclude that anything else has happened here. In overruling *Roe* and *Casey*, the current majority has betrayed the Court's guiding principles.

ANALYSIS

Dobbs is a landmark decision. This the first time the Court has revoked a fundamental right, and the decision has raised serious questions about the current majority's integrity–as emphasized by the dissenting Justices–and raises questions about the Court's doctrinal shift and how it might impact other fundamental rights. With this decision, the United States joins just a handful of other countries that have removed legal protections to access abortion, which is at odds with the global trend of liberalizing access to abortion in the face of reproductive rights advances. Although the decision has been lauded by pro-life advocates, it has also been met with sharp criticism from legal commentators, pro-choice advocates, and from abroad. Some of the broad questions that this decision has raised follow: Will the current majority reject substantive due process precedents, as urged by Justice Thomas, and use its approach in *Dobbs* to revoke other fundamental rights, a concern raised by the dissent? How will lower courts as well as the Court handle related questions that are likely to arise from abortion regulation, such as those related to travel, free speech, interstate commerce, the dormant commerce clause, abortion by medication, insurance coverage, medical licensing across state lines, and the like? Will the Court continue to use a historical test to replace existing doctrines, and if so, how are the lower courts and the Court to apply historical tests given the limits of their capacities and training? To what extent will the Court's legitimacy suffer as a consequence of the Court's departure from stare decisis principles? The decision has raised these, as well as many other questions, many of which were touched on by the dissent. Given the magnitude of this decision, its aftermath will have to await future litigation to be determined, and its impact may last for decades to come.

Quicknotes

DUE PROCESS CLAUSE Language in the Fifth and Fourteenth Amendments to the United States Constitution providing that no person shall be deprived of "life, liberty, or property without due process of law."

EQUAL PROTECTION CLAUSE A constitutional provision that each person be guaranteed the same protection of the laws enjoyed by other persons in like circumstances.

EX POST FACTO After the fact; a law that makes subsequent activity criminal or increases the punishment for a crime that occurred, or eliminates a defense that was available to the defendant prior to its passage.

FOURTEENTH AMENDMENT Declares that no state shall make or enforce any law that shall abridge the privileges and immunities of citizens of the United States; no state shall deny to any person within its jurisdiction the equal protection of the laws.

RATIONAL-BASIS REVIEW A test employed by the court to determine the validity of a statute in equal protection actions, whereby the court determines whether the challenged statute is rationally related to the achievement of a legitimate state interest.

STARE DECISIS Doctrine whereby courts follow legal precedent unless there is good cause for departure.

SUBSTANTIVE DUE PROCESS A constitutional safeguard limiting the power of the state, irrespective of how fair its procedures may be; substantive limits placed on the power of the state.

Romer v. Evans

[Parties not identified.]

517 U.S. 620 (1996)

NATURE OF CASE: Certiorari review of constitutionality of an amendment to a state constitution.

FACT SUMMARY: A Colorado (D) constitutional amendment, Amendment 2, which struck down local antidiscrimination laws based on sexual orientation, was challenged for being violative of the Equal Protection Clause.

RULE OF LAW

Colorado's constitutional Amendment 2 violates the Equal Protection Clause because it singles out a class of citizens—homosexuals—for disfavored legal status.

FACTS: In 1992, Colorado (D) amended its state constitution by a statewide referendum. Amendment 2, as it was designated, provided that the state and local branches of government were forbidden from enacting any laws or regulations that would protect homosexuals from discrimination. Amendment 2 was challenged in court as unconstitutional for violating the Equal Protection Clause. Colorado (D) responded that Amendment 2 simply denied homosexuals any special rights given to protected classes, such as minorities. The trial court enjoined enactment of Amendment 2, the Colorado Supreme Court affirmed, and the United States Supreme Court granted certiorari to decide the issue.

ISSUE: Does Colorado's constitutional Amendment 2 violate the Equal Protection Clause because it singles out a class of citizens—homosexuals—for disfavored legal status?

HOLDING AND DECISION: (Kennedy, J.) Yes. Colorado's constitutional Amendment 2 violates the Equal Protection Clause because it singles out a class of citizens—homosexuals—for disfavored legal status. The Colorado Supreme Court's construction of Amendment 2 found that its objective was to repeal existing antidiscrimination ordinances. Thus, Amendment 2 is far-reaching in that it places homosexuals in a solitary class, withdrawing legal protection against discrimination and forbidding reinstatement of these policies except by constitutional amendment. Thus, it imposes a special disability on homosexuals, who can now change the law only by amending the state constitution, no matter how local the harm. Generally, legislative classifications are constitutional if they bear a rational relation to a legitimate end. However, Amendment 2 identifies persons by a single trait and denies them protection across the board. Therefore, it violates the principle that the government remains open on impartial terms to all who seek its assistance. Finally, equal protection means that the desire to harm a politically unpopular group is not a legitimate government interest. Amendment 2 is extraordinary and explainable only by animus toward homosexuals. Accordingly, Amendment 2 violates the Equal Protection Clause and is unconstitutional. Affirmed.

DISSENT: (Scalia, J.) Amendment 2 prohibits the special treatment of homosexuals only in that they may not obtain preferential treatment without amending the state constitution. Surely, Colorado has the right to be hostile toward homosexuals just as it may have animosity toward murderers or polygamists. In fact, laws against polygamy are the best analogy and have been ignored by the majority. Also, since homosexuals are segregated in certain communities, they possess political power much greater than their numbers. Amendment 2 seeks to counter this disproportionate political power. The majority has taken the side of the elites in this culture law.

ANALYSIS

Justice Scalia's dissenting opinion is astonishing for its not-at-all disguised animosity toward homosexuals, who will no doubt be surprised to find that they are politically powerful. The dissent is also remarkable for its tone of disgust toward the majority. At the heart of the majority decision is the recognition that homosexuality is more of a status (like sex, race, or ethnicity) than a conduct or lifestyle.

Quicknotes

EQUAL PROTECTION Guarantee under the Fourteenth Amendment to the U.S. Constitution that the government must treat each person or class of persons the same as it treats other persons or classes of persons in like circumstances.

Lawrence v. Texas

Sodomy convict (D) v. State (P)

539 U.S. 558 (2003)

NATURE OF CASE: Certiorari review of state statute prohibiting consensual sodomy.

FACT SUMMARY: When Lawrence (D) and his male partner, both adults, were prosecuted and convicted for consensual sodomy in their own private dwelling, they argued the unconstitutionality of the statute.

RULE OF LAW

Legislation that makes consensual sodomy between adults in their own dwelling criminal violates due process.

FACTS: Two Houston, Texas, police officers were dispatched to a private residence in response to a reported weapons disturbance. They entered an apartment where Lawrence (D) resided. The right of the police to enter was not an issue. The officers observed Lawrence (D) and another man engaging in sodomy. Both men were arrested, charged, and convicted before a justice of the peace of the statutory crime of "deviate sexual intercourse, namely anal sex, with a member of the same sex." Each defendant entered a plea of nolo contendere and was fined $200. Both men were adults at the time of the alleged offense. Their conduct was in private and consensual. Lawrence (D) and his partner appealed to the Supreme Court, arguing the Texas statute to be unconstitutional.

ISSUE: Does legislation that makes consensual sodomy between adults in their own dwelling criminal violate due process?

HOLDING AND DECISION: (Kennedy, J.) Yes. Legislation that makes consensual sodomy between adults in their own dwelling criminal violates due process. Liberty protects the person from unwarranted government intrusions into dwellings or other private places. In our tradition, the state is not omnipresent in the home. Furthermore, freedom extends beyond spatial bounds. Liberty presumes "autonomy of self" that includes freedom of thought, belief, expression, "and certain intimate conduct." This case involves liberty of the person in both its spatial and more transcendent dimensions. The penalties and purposes of the Texas statute in the instant case have far-reaching consequences, touching upon the most private human conduct, sexual behavior, and in the most private of places, the home. The statute seeks to control a personal relationship that, whether entitled to formal recognition in the law, is within the liberty of persons to choose without being punished as criminals. This Court acknowledges that adults may choose to enter private relationships in the confines of their own homes and their own private lives and still retain their dignity as free persons. When sexuality finds expression in intimate conduct with another person, the conduct can be but one element in a personal bond that is more enduring. The liberty protected by the Constitution allows homosexual persons the right to make this choice. Here, two adults who, with full and mutual consent from each other, engaged in sexual practices common to a homosexual lifestyle. They are entitled to respect in their private lives. The state cannot demean their existence or control their destiny by making their private sexual conduct a crime. Reversed.

CONCURRENCE: (O'Connor, J.) Rather than relying on the substantive component of the Fourteenth Amendment's Due Process Clause, as the Court does, unconstitutionality exists based on the Fourteenth Amendment's Equal Protection Clause.

DISSENT: (Scalia, J.) Homosexual sodomy is not a right "deeply rooted in our Nation's history and tradition." Constitutional entitlements do not spring into existence because some states choose to lessen or eliminate sanctions on criminal behavior. Today's opinion is the product of a Court that has largely signed on to the so-called homosexual agenda.

DISSENT: (Thomas, J.) The instant Texas statute is "uncommonly silly" and the Texas Legislature should repeal it; however, no general constitutional right of privacy was violated in this situation.

ANALYSIS

In *Lawrence*, the Supreme Court noted that of the 13 states with laws prohibiting sodomy, only four have enforced their legislation. In those states in which sodomy was still proscribed, whether for same-sex or heterosexual conduct, there was a pattern of nonenforcement with respect to consenting adults acting in private. Even Texas admitted in 1994 that as of that date it had not prosecuted anyone under those circumstances.

Quicknotes

DUE PROCESS CLAUSE Language in the Fifth and Fourteenth Amendments to the U.S. Constitution providing that no person shall be deprived of "life, liberty, or property, without due process of law."

EQUAL PROTECTION CLAUSE A constitutional provision that each person be guaranteed the same protection of the laws enjoyed by other persons in like circumstances.

United States v. Windsor

Federal government (D) v. Same-sex spouse (P)

570 U.S. 744 (2013)

NATURE OF CASE: Appeal from affirmance of judgment that § 3 of the Defense of Marriage Act, defining "marriage" and "spouse" to exclude same-sex partners, was unconstitutional.

FACT SUMMARY: The United States (D) contended that § 3 of the Defense of Marriage Act, which defined "marriage" and "spouse" to exclude same-sex partners, did not violate the Fifth Amendment's equal protection provisions.

RULE OF LAW

Section 3 of the Defense of Marriage Act, which defines "marriage" and "spouse" to exclude same-sex partners, violates the Fifth Amendment's equal protection provisions.

FACTS: New York recognized the marriage of Windsor (P) and Spyer, a same-sex couple who had wed in Canada. When Spyer died, she left her entire estate to Windsor (P). Windsor (P) sought to claim the federal estate tax exemption for surviving spouses but was barred from doing so by § 3 of the federal Defense of Marriage Act (DOMA), which amended the Dictionary Act—a law providing rules of construction for over 1,000 federal laws and the whole realm of federal regulations—to define "marriage" and "spouse" as excluding same-sex partners. Windsor (P) paid $363,053 in estate taxes and sought a refund, which the Internal Revenue Service (IRS) denied. Windsor (P) brought suit for a refund, contending that DOMA violates the principles of equal protection incorporated in the Fifth Amendment. [While the suit was pending, the Attorney General notified the Speaker of the House of Representatives that the Department of Justice would no longer defend § 3's constitutionality. In response, the Bipartisan Legal Advisory Group (BLAG) of the House of Representatives voted to intervene in the litigation to defend § 3's constitutionality. The district court permitted the intervention, held § 3 unconstitutional, and ordered the IRS to refund Windsor's (P) tax with interest. The court of appeals affirmed, but the IRS refused to pay unless ordered to do so by the United States Supreme Court, which granted certiorari.]

ISSUE: Does § 3 of the Defense of Marriage Act, which defines "marriage" and "spouse" to exclude same-sex partners, violate the Fifth Amendment's equal protection provisions?

HOLDING AND DECISION: (Kennedy, J.) Yes. Section 3 of the Defense of Marriage Act (DOMA), which defines "marriage" and "spouse" to exclude same-sex partners, violates the Fifth Amendment's equal protection provisions. By history and tradition, the definition and regulation of marriage has been treated as being within the authority and realm of the separate states. Nevertheless, Congress has enacted discrete statutes to regulate the meaning of marriage in order to further federal policy, but DOMA, with a directive applicable to over 1,000 federal statutes and the whole realm of federal regulations, has a far greater reach. Its operation is also directed to a class of persons that the laws of New York, and of several other jurisdictions, have sought to protect. Assessing the validity of that intervention requires discussing the historical and traditional extent of state power and authority over marriage. Subject to certain constitutional guarantees, regulation of domestic relations is an area that has long been regarded as a virtually exclusive province of the states. The significance of state responsibilities for the definition and regulation of marriage dates to the nation's beginning, and when the Constitution was adopted, the common understanding was that the domestic relations of husband and wife and parent and child were matters reserved to the states. While marriage laws may vary from state to state, they are consistent within each state. DOMA rejects this long-established precept. The state's decision to give this class of persons the right to marry conferred upon them a dignity and status of immense import. But the federal Government (D) uses the state-defined class for the opposite purpose—to impose restrictions and disabilities. The question is whether the resulting injury and indignity are deprivations of an essential part of the liberty protected by the Fifth Amendment, since what New York treats as alike the federal law deems unlike by a law designed to injure the same class the state seeks to protect. New York's actions were a proper exercise of its sovereign authority. They reflect both the community's considered perspective on the historical roots of the institution of marriage and its evolving understanding of the meaning of equality. By seeking to injure the very class New York seeks to protect, DOMA violates basic due process and equal protection principles applicable to the federal Government (D). The Constitution's guarantee of equality must at the very least mean that a bare congressional desire to harm a politically unpopular group cannot justify disparate treatment of that group. DOMA cannot survive under these principles. Its unusual deviation from the tradition of recognizing and accepting state definitions of marriage operates to deprive same-sex couples of the benefits and

Continued on next page.

responsibilities that come with federal recognition of their marriages. This is strong evidence of a law having the purpose and effect of disapproval of a class recognized and protected by state law. DOMA's avowed purpose and practical effect are to impose a disadvantage, a separate status, and so a stigma upon all who enter into same-sex marriages made lawful by the unquestioned authority of the states. DOMA's history of enactment and its own text demonstrate that interference with the equal dignity of same-sex marriages, conferred by the states in the exercise of their sovereign power, was more than an incidental effect of the federal statute. It was its essence. DOMA's operation in practice confirms this purpose. It frustrates New York's objective of eliminating inequality by writing inequality into the entire United States Code. DOMA's principal effect is to identify and make unequal a subset of state-sanctioned marriages. It contrives to deprive some couples married under the laws of their state, but not others, of both rights and responsibilities, creating two contradictory marriage regimes within the same state. It also forces same-sex couples to live as married for the purpose of state law but unmarried for the purpose of federal law, thus diminishing the stability and predictability of basic personal relations the state has found it proper to acknowledge and protect. DOMA places same-sex couples in an unstable position of being in a second-tier marriage, thus demeaning the couple, whose moral and sexual choices the Constitution protects, and humiliating tens of thousands of children now being raised by same-sex couples. Under DOMA, same-sex married couples have their lives burdened, by reason of government decree, in visible and public ways, and for certain married couples, DOMA's unequal effects are even more serious and bring financial harm to children of same-sex couples. For these reasons, DOMA is unconstitutional as a deprivation of the liberty of the person protected by the Fifth Amendment—as to lawful same-sex marriages recognized by state law. Affirmed.

DISSENT: (Roberts, C.J.) Congress did not act unconstitutionality in enacting the Defense of Marriage Act (DOMA). The majority makes an insufficient showing of malice on Congress's part, or an entire lack of a legitimate governmental purpose, in enacting DOMA. More importantly, it must be emphasized that the Court has not resolved the question of whether the states may continue to use the traditional definition of marriage. Instead, the majority's opinion is limited to resolving that the federal government may not intrude in this area of domestic relations, which is an area left to the states. The majority's opinion reaffirms state sovereignty in this area as well as state diversity as to same-sex marriage.

DISSENT: (Scalia, J.) The majority's decision on the merits is strikingly incorrect and inconsistent. The opinion fools its reader into believing it is about federalism but then asserts that it is unnecessary to resolve the issue of whether the federal intrusion on state power is unconstitutional. Equally perplexing is the majority's treatment of equal protection doctrine. At one point the opinion seems to say that the Equal Protection Clause is not the basis of the decision, but at another point the majority cites equal protection cases to explain why the Defense of Marriage Act (DOMA) is unconstitutional. Even if the decision is supposed to be an equal-protection opinion, it is a confusing one. The opinion does not resolve what had in the lower courts been the central question, namely whether laws restricting marriage to a man and a woman are reviewed for more than mere rationality. The majority seems to indicate that rationality review is all that is necessary but then does not apply that deferential standard. The majority avoids the tier of standards altogether by saying, effectively, that DOMA violates substantive due process, but it does not—nor could it—support this analysis with evidence that same-sex marriage is deeply rooted in the nation's history and traditions—a necessary element of substantive due process doctrine. The upshot of the opinion, which is continually shifting in its justifications, is that DOMA is invalid because it is motivated to harm couples in same-sex marriages. As to that key point, the Constitution does not forbid the government from enforcing traditional moral and sexual norm, nor does it require or prohibit society to approve of same-sex marriage. There are valid justifications, e.g., avoidance of complex choice-of-law questions—a classic purpose for a definitional provision—for DOMA. DOMA also preserves the intended effects of prior legislation against then-unforeseen changes in circumstance. Such justifications demonstrate legislative prudence rather than animus. To defend traditional marriage is not to demean, condemn, or humiliate those who would enter same-sex marriage. What is clear, despite the confusing majority opinion, is that its real rationale is that DOMA was motivated by hatred of gays and that such a rationale will be applied to state legislation that prohibits same-sex marriage. The majority will hurtle the same accusations at state legislatures that it now throws at the executive and legislative branches that enacted DOMA. The majority will declare that there is "no legitimate purpose" served by a law that prohibits same-sex marriage and will claim that the traditional definition has the purpose and effect to disparage and to injure the "personhood and dignity" of same-sex couples. The result will be a judicial distortion of our society's debate over marriage, and that is not the democratic system our founders envisioned. The Court should have let the People decide the issue, with resulting winners and losers in a democratic process.

DISSENT: (Alito, J.) Same-sex marriage is not deeply rooted in this nation's—or any other nation's—history

Continued on next page.

or tradition; it is a novel right. Windsor (P) seeks protection of this right not from elected officials but from the unelected judiciary. In the face of such innovation, the judiciary must tread very carefully, as it is not known—nor will it be for a long time to come—what the ramifications of this innovation will be, assuming same-sex marriage takes hold as an institution. Some believe that allowing same-sex marriage will seriously undermine the institution of marriage, and certainly the judiciary is ill-equipped to make such determinations, which are better left to the People and their elected officials. By arguing that the Defense of Marriage Act be subject to heightened scrutiny, Windsor (P) is asking the Court to rule that the presence of two members of the opposite sex is rationally related to marriage. The Court should not resolve the debate between two competing views of marriage. The "traditional" or "conjugal" view of marriage, which has prevailed for centuries over many cultures, is that marriage is an exclusively opposite-sex institution inextricably linked to procreation and biological kinship. The newer, "consent-based" view of marriage is that it is the solemnization of mutual commitment—marked by strong emotional attachment and sexual attraction—between two persons. Proponents of same-sex marriage argue that because gender differentiation is not relevant to this vision, the exclusion of same-sex couples from the institution of marriage is rank discrimination. The Constitution does not enshrine either of these views of marriage. This silence should end the matter as far as the judiciary is concerned. Instead, Windsor (P) implicitly asks the Court to endorse the consent-based view of marriage and to reject the traditional view. By agreeing to do so, the Court arrogates to itself the power to decide a question that others, such as philosophers, historians, social scientists, and theologians are better qualified to explore. The Constitution assigns resolution of this issue to the People, so that neither vision of marriage should be enshrined in our constitutional jurisprudence.

ANALYSIS

Two years after the Court decided *Windsor*, the Court in *Obergefell v. Hodges*, 576 U.S. 644 (2015), struck down all state bans on same-sex marriage, ruling that marriage is guaranteed to same-sex couples by both the Due Process Clause and the Equal Protection Clause. However, in his concurrence in *Dobbs v. Jackson Women's Health Organization*, 142 S. Ct. 2228 (2022)—which overruled *Roe v. Wade*, 410 U.S. 113 (1973), on the grounds that it was wrongly decided, and which is the first Supreme Court case to revoke a fundamental right—Justice Thomas invited the Court to overrule all decisions based on substantive due process on the grounds that those decisions were wrongly decided, and specifically named *Obergefell* as one of those decisions. In response to Justice Thomas, at the end of 2022, Congress enacted the Respect for Marriage Act (RFMA), which formally repealed the Defense of Marriage Act, and requires the federal government to recognize same-sex and interracial marriages, thus codifying parts of *Obergefell*, as well as *Loving v. Virginia*, 388 U.S. 1 (1967). In addition, RFMA compels all U.S. states and territories to recognize the validity of same-sex and interracial marriages if performed in a jurisdiction where such marriages are legally performed.

Quicknotes

FIFTH AMENDMENT Provides that no person shall be compelled to serve as a witness against him- or herself, be subject to trial for the same offense twice, or be deprived of life, liberty, or property without due process of law.

RATIONAL-BASIS REVIEW A test employed by the court to determine the validity of a statute in equal protection actions, whereby the court determines whether the challenged statute is rationally related to the achievement of a legitimate state interest.

STATE SOVEREIGNTY The absolute power of self-government possessed by a state.

SUBSTANTIVE DUE PROCESS A constitutional safeguard limiting the power of the state, irrespective of how fair its procedures may be; substantive limits placed on the power of the state.

Obergefell v. Hodges

[Parties not identified in casebook excerpt.]

576 U.S. 644 (2015)

NATURE OF CASE: Action challenging as unconstitutional a state's denial of the right of same sex couples to marry or to have their marriages, lawfully performed in another state, given full recognition. [The procedural posture of the case is not presented in the casebook excerpt.]

FACT SUMMARY: [The facts of the case are not presented in the casebook excerpt.]

RULE OF LAW

The Fourteenth Amendment requires a state to license a marriage between two people of the same sex and to recognize a marriage between two people of the same sex when their marriage has been lawfully licensed and performed out-of-state.

FACTS: [The facts of the case are not presented in the casebook excerpt.]

ISSUE: Does the Fourteenth Amendment require a state to license a marriage between two people of the same sex and to recognize a marriage between two people of the same sex when their marriage has been lawfully licensed and performed out-of-state?

HOLDING AND DECISION: (Kennedy, J.) Yes. The Fourteenth Amendment requires a state to license a marriage between two people of the same sex and to recognize a marriage between two people of the same sex when their marriage has been lawfully licensed and performed out-of-state. Petitioners sought to marry someone of the same sex and have their marriages deemed lawful on the same terms and conditions as marriages between persons of the opposite sex. Marriage as a union between two persons of the opposite sex has been central to the human condition and throughout the annals of human history. The institution of marriage has existed for millennia and across civilizations. This history marks the beginning of this case. To the respondents, it would demean a timeless institution if marriage were extended to same-sex couples. However, the petitioners, far from seeking to devalue marriage, seek it for themselves because of their respect—and need—for its privileges and responsibilities, as illustrated by the petitioners' own experiences. The history of marriage is one of both continuity and change. Changes, such as the decline of arranged marriages and the abandonment of the law of coverture, have worked deep transformations in the structure of marriage, affecting aspects of marriage once viewed as essential. These new insights have strengthened, not weakened, the institution. The Court has long held the right to marry is protected by the Constitution and that marriage is "one of the vital personal rights essential to the orderly pursuit of happiness by free men." The Court has reiterated that the right to marry is fundamental under the Due Process Clause. Those prior cases describing the right to marry presumed a relationship involving opposite-sex partners, but it should be kept in mind that the Court, like many institutions, has made assumptions defined by the world and time of which it is a part. Other precedents have expressed broad constitutional principles that go beyond such assumptions. In assessing whether the force and rationale of its cases apply to same-sex couples, the Court must respect the basic reasons why the right to marry has been long protected, and such an analysis compels the conclusion that same-sex couples may exercise the right to marry. Four principles and traditions demonstrate that the reasons marriage is fundamental under the Constitution apply with equal force to same-sex couples. The first premise of this Court's relevant precedents is that the right to personal choice regarding marriage is inherent in the concept of individual autonomy. This abiding connection between marriage and liberty is why the Court invalidated interracial marriage bans under the Due Process Clause. Decisions about marriage are among the most intimate that an individual can make, and this is true for all persons, whatever their sexual orientation. A second principle in this Court's jurisprudence is that the right to marry is fundamental because it supports a two-person union unlike any other in its importance to the committed individuals. Same-sex couples have the same right as opposite-sex couples to enjoy intimate association, a right extending beyond mere freedom from laws making same-sex intimacy a criminal offense. A third basis for protecting the right to marry is that it safeguards children and families and thus draws meaning from related rights of childrearing, procreation, and education. Without the recognition, stability, and predictability marriage offers, children suffer the stigma of knowing their families are somehow lesser. They also suffer the significant material costs of being raised by unmarried parents, relegated to a more difficult and uncertain family life. The marriage laws at issue thus harm and humiliate the children of same-sex couples. Fourth, and finally, this Court's cases and the nation's traditions make clear that marriage is a keystone of the nation's social order. States have contributed to the fundamental character of marriage by placing it at the center of many facets of the legal and social order. There is no difference between

Continued on next page.

same- and opposite-sex couples with respect to this principle, yet same-sex couples are denied the constellation of benefits that the states have linked to marriage and are consigned to an instability many opposite-sex couples would find intolerable. It is demeaning to lock same-sex couples out of a central institution of the nation's society, for they too may aspire to the transcendent purposes of marriage and seek fulfillment in its highest meaning. The right of same-sex couples to marry is also derived from the Fourteenth Amendment's guarantee of equal protection. The Due Process Clause and the Equal Protection Clause are connected in a profound way. Rights implicit in liberty and rights secured by equal protection may rest on different precepts and are not always co-extensive, yet each may be instructive as to the meaning and reach of the other. The Court has acknowledged the interlocking nature of these constitutional safeguards in the context of the legal treatment of gays and lesbians, and this dynamic also applies to same-sex marriage. The challenged laws burden the liberty of same-sex couples, and they abridge central precepts of equality. The marriage laws at issue are in essence unequal: Same-sex couples are denied benefits afforded opposite-sex couples and are barred from exercising a fundamental right. Especially against a long history of disapproval of their relationships, this denial works a grave and continuing harm, serving to disrespect and subordinate gays and lesbians. The right to marry is a fundamental right inherent in the liberty of the person, and under the Due Process and Equal Protection Clauses of the Fourteenth Amendment couples of the same sex may not be deprived of that right and that liberty. Same-sex couples may exercise the fundamental right to marry, and the state laws challenged by the petitioners are held invalid to the extent they exclude same-sex couples from civil marriage on the same terms and conditions as opposite-sex couples.

DISSENT: (Scalia, J.) The majority's opinion is the furthest extension imaginable of the Court's power to create so-called liberties that do not exist in the Constitution. Thus, the majority usurps the power to govern, which should remain with the People and their elected officials. A system of government that makes the People subordinate to a committee of nine unelected lawyers does not deserve to be called a democracy. The Court's Justices do not represent a cross-section of America, and to let them decide the policy question of same-sex marriage violates a fundamental tenet of democracy: no social transformation without representation. The majority's opinion is both pretentious and egotistic, and lacking in logic and precision. This decision should have been left to the People.

DISSENT: (Roberts, C.J.) The petitioners' arguments have appeal based on arguments rooted in social policy and considerations of fairness, but the Court is not a legislature, and whether same-sex marriage is a good idea should not be the Court's concern. The Court can say only what the law is, not what it should be. The majority's decision is not a pronouncement of a legal judgment, and the right it announces has no basis in the Constitution or precedent. The core meaning of marriage has been that it is a union between a man and a woman, notwithstanding that this core has changed through history. The majority's decision is bald judicial policymaking, which previously has been rejected in favor of judicial self-restraint. Implied fundamental rights must be objectively and deeply rooted in the nation's tradition and history. No precedents, including those that have guaranteed the privacy rights of same-sex couples, support the right to same-sex marriage. Unlike criminal laws banning contraceptives and sodomy, the marriage laws at issue here involve no government intrusion. They create no crime and impose no punishment. Same-sex couples remain free to live together, to engage in intimate conduct, and to raise their families as they see fit. Nothing interferes with these couples' right to be let alone. Given that the majority redefines the core meaning of marriage, its opinion invites the question of whether that core meaning can be expanded beyond just two individuals to many, since from the standpoint of history and tradition, a leap from opposite-sex marriage to same-sex marriage is much greater than one from a two-person union to plural unions, which have deep roots in some cultures around the world. Further, the opinion does not follow the usual framework for deciding equal protection cases, and in any event, the marriage laws at issue here do not violate the Equal Protection Clause, because distinguishing between opposite-sex and same-sex couples is rationally related to the states' "legitimate state interest" in "preserving the traditional institution of marriage." In sum, the Constitution had nothing to do with the majority's decision.

DISSENT: (Thomas, J.) The majority claims the petitioners are deprived of "liberty," but the majority's concept of liberty is not one that can be found in the Due Process Clauses. Based on the history of these Clauses, going back to the Magna Carta, "liberty" was construed to refer only to freedom from physical restraint. Even assuming that "liberty" goes beyond such freedom, the American legal tradition has long understood "liberty" as individual freedom from governmental action, not as a right to a particular governmental entitlement. To the extent that the Framers would have recognized a natural right to marriage that fell within the broader definition of liberty, it would not have included a right to governmental recognition and benefits. Instead, it would have included a right to engage in the very same activities that petitioners have been left free to engage in—making

Continued on next page.

vows, holding religious ceremonies celebrating those vows, raising children, and otherwise enjoying the society of one's spouse—without governmental interference. The majority emphasizes that its decision will advance the "dignity" of same-sex couples, but the Constitution does not contain a right to dignity. Even if there were a "dignity" clause in the Constitution, the government would be unable to bestow dignity, which has long been understood to be innate. Slaves did not lose their dignity because the government allowed them to be enslaved, and certainly same-sex couples do not lose their dignity because the government denies them certain benefits. Like liberty, dignity is to be shielded from government, not provided by it.

DISSENT: (Alito, J.) The majority's decision usurps the constitutional right of the People to decide whether to keep or alter the traditional understanding of marriage and violates core federalism principles. The majority, by imposing its view on the entire country, marginalizes those Americans who have traditional ideas. In attempting to make up for the harsh treatment of gays and lesbians in the past, the majority will inflict bitter and lasting wounds on the nation.

ANALYSIS

The majority's decision will require states to issue marriage licenses to same-sex couples and to recognize same-sex marriages entered in other states largely based on a constitutional provision guaranteeing "due process" before a person is deprived of his or her "life, liberty, or property." The dissent characterizes this outcome as a result of substantive due process, which has been discredited as permitting judges to stray from the Constitution's text, guided only by their personal views. The dissent (Thomas, J.) also views the majority's use of equal protection (which the majority indicates acts synergistically with due process) as only a means to shore up its substantive due process analysis, which the dissent claims is an analysis both based on an imaginary constitutional protection and a revisionist view of history and tradition.

Quicknotes

DUE PROCESS CLAUSE Language in the Fifth and Fourteenth Amendments to the U.S. Constitution, providing that no person shall be deprived of "life, liberty, or property, without due process of law."

EQUAL PROTECTION CLAUSE A constitutional provision that each person be guaranteed the same protection of the laws enjoyed by other persons in like circumstances.

FOURTEENTH AMENDMENT Declares that no state shall make or enforce any law that shall abridge the privileges and immunities of citizens of the United States; no state shall deny to any person within its jurisdiction the equal protection of the laws.

JUDICIAL RESTRAINT Self-imposed discipline by judges making decisions without indulging their own personal views or ideas that may not be consistent with existing law.

Washington v. Glucksberg

State (D) v. Doctors (P)

521 U.S. 702 (1997)

NATURE OF CASE: Certiorari review of constitutionality of state law prohibiting assisted suicide.

FACT SUMMARY: A group of Washington physicians (P) and a nonprofit organization (P) that counseled people considering physician-assisted suicide filed suit seeking a declaration that the state's assisted-suicide ban was facially unconstitutional.

RULE OF LAW

The right to assistance in committing suicide is not a fundamental liberty interest protected by the Due Process Clause.

FACTS: A Washington law stated: "a person is guilty of promoting a suicide attempt when he knowingly causes or aids another person to attempt suicide." Breaking the law was a felony punishable by up to five years' imprisonment and up to a $10,000 fine. Washington also had a Natural Death Act, which stated that withholding or withdrawal of life-sustaining treatment at a patient's discretion did not constitute a suicide. Physicians (P), who are practicing in Washington, and Compassion in Dying (P), a nonprofit organization that counseled people considering physician-assisted suicide, filed suit seeking a declaration that the ban on assisted suicide was unconstitutional. The physicians (P) who treated many terminally ill, suffering patients declared that they would have assisted some of these patients in ending their lives were it not for Washington's law. The district court found the statute invalid, and the court of appeals ultimately affirmed. The appellate court held that the Constitution encompasses a due process liberty interest in controlling the time and manner of one's death, and that the state's assisted-suicide ban was unconstitutional as applied to terminally ill competent adults who wish to hasten their deaths with medication prescribed by their physicians. The Supreme Court granted certiorari.

ISSUE: Is the right to assistance in committing suicide a fundamental liberty interest protected by the Due Process Clause?

HOLDING AND DECISION: (Rehnquist, C.J.) No. The right to assistance in committing suicide is not a fundamental liberty interest protected by the Due Process Clause. In almost every state and every western democracy, it is a crime to assist a suicide. These laws reflect a long-standing commitment to the protection and preservation of human life. In 1991, Washington voters rejected a ballot measure that would have permitted a form of physician-assisted suicide. The Court must exercise extreme prudence in expanding the Due Process Clause to include new fundamental rights and liberties. In *Cruzan v. Director, Missouri Dept. of Health*, 497 U.S. 261 (1990), the Court suggested that the Due Process Clause protects the right to refuse unwanted lifesaving medical treatment. The physicians' (P) reliance on *Cruzan* is misplaced. At common law, forced medication was a battery; however, the decision to commit suicide has never been afforded similar legal protection. Washington (D) also has a fundamental interest in protecting the integrity of the medical profession, and the American Medical Association has concluded that physician-assisted suicide is fundamentally incompatible with the physician's role as a healer. Finally, the state has an interest in protecting vulnerable groups from abuse, neglect, and mistakes. There is a very real risk of subtle coercion and undue influence in end-of-life situations that legalized physician-assisted suicide would likely exacerbate. Therefore, the statute does not violate the Fourteenth Amendment either on its face or as applied. Reversed.

CONCURRENCE: (O'Connor, J.) While the majority correctly holds that there is no generalized "right" to commit suicide, the question of whether a mentally competent person experiencing great suffering has a constitutional right to control the circumstances of his or her imminent death should not be precluded by this decision.

CONCURRENCE: (Stevens, J.) The Court's holding that Washington's statute is not invalid on its face does not foreclose the possibility that some applications of the statute might well be invalid. While the Court correctly held that *Cruzan* does not decide the issue here, *Cruzan v. Director, Missouri Dept. of Health*, 497 U.S. 261 (1990), did give recognition to an individual's interest in making decisions about how to confront an imminent death. Furthermore, the state's interest in supporting a general rule banning the practice of physician-assisted suicide does not have the same force in all cases.

CONCURRENCE: (Souter, J.) While Washington (D) has persuasively demonstrated that its ban on physician-assisted suicide should not be found facially unconstitutional, this does not preclude the possibility that the individual interests at stake here will at some point or in some cases be held "fundamental." While that day is yet to come, the Court has presently correctly deferred to Washington's institutional legislative competence.

Continued on next page.

CONCURRENCE: (Breyer, J.) The Court has misstated the claimed liberty interest. A more accurate formulation would use words like a "right to die with dignity" and would be closely linked with a right to avoid severe physical pain connected with death. Nevertheless, given the facts at hand, the Court need not decide now whether such a right is "fundamental."

ANALYSIS

The four concurring justices all left the door wide open for the Court to revisit this decision given a more fact-specific case. While they all strongly suggested that an individual under certain, limited circumstances may have a constitutionally protected right to assisted suicide, they were cautious in taking that leap given the specific question at issue here. While several states, including Washington and California, have voted down statutes permitting physician-assisted suicide, it is likely that one will eventually pass, and the Court will again be presented with these issues.

Quicknotes

ASSISTED SUICIDE The aiding of another in terminating his own life.

BATTERY Unlawful contact with the body of another person.

DUE PROCESS CLAUSE Language in the Fifth and Fourteenth Amendments to the U.S. Constitution, providing that no person shall be deprived of "life, liberty, or property, without due process of law."

LIBERTY INTEREST A right conferred by the Due Process Clauses of the state and federal constitutions.

Kelo v. City of New London

Homeowner (P) v. City (D)

545 U.S. 469 (2005)

NATURE OF CASE: Certiorari review of constitutionality of taking in underlying case involving defendant city in condemnation suit.

FACT SUMMARY: New London, Connecticut (D) condemned the private residences of Kelo (P) and others in order to use their property as part of a planned economic development.

RULE OF LAW

Governmental economic development constitutes a "public use" under the Fifth Amendment's eminent domain.

FACTS: New London, Connecticut (D) revitalized the New London Development Corp. (NLDC) to propose plans for economic development after decades of decline. Pfizer, a pharmaceutical company, also announced plans to build a $300 million facility next to Fort Trumball in the New London (D) area. The NLDC operated as a private entity, but its plans intended to benefit the city's growth. New London (D) authorized NLDC to purchase or condemn property in its name for the purpose of its approved development plan. Kelo (P) owned property in the Fort Trumball development area and refused to sell. New London (D) initiated condemnation proceedings although Kelo's (P) property was not blighted or otherwise deteriorating. Kelo (P) filed suit in state court against New London (D) claiming that the condemnation violated the taking clause's "public use" restriction. The Connecticut Supreme Court held for the defendant city and Kelo (P) appealed to the United States Supreme Court.

ISSUE: Does governmental economic development constitute a "public use" under the Fifth Amendment's eminent domain?

HOLDING AND DECISION: (Stevens, J.) Yes. Governmental economic development constitutes a "public use" under the Fifth Amendment's eminent domain. The government cannot transfer private property from one private entity to another even if the first is adequately compensated. The government can, however, take private property from one private entity with just compensation for "public use." This particular case does not fit in either scenario. New London, Connecticut (D) cannot offer a pretextual "public use" if the true benefit is to a definable class of private individuals, but no such class can be identified here. It is true that the planned development will not be completely open to the public and the stores will not act as common carriers to the public, but such a literal definition of "public use" is not required. The precedent in *Berman v. Parker*, 348 U.S. 26 (1954), and *Hawaii Housing Authority v. Midkiff*, 467 U.S. 229 (1984), supports a broad interpretation of "public use." Kelo (P) requests a bright-line rule for "public use" that would not include economic development. It is longstanding tradition of government to promote economic development and that development may be better served by using a private entity rather than government agencies. A bright-line rule cannot issue because legislatures need flexibility when determining appropriate action for the economic development of its cities. States are free to further restrict "public use" requirements beyond those of the federal government and many have already done so. Affirmed.

CONCURRENCE: (Kennedy, J.) A party may make a claim of pretextual "public use" taking that actually benefits a private entity. A presumption exists that the government acted reasonably in its taking, but courts should review all claims to the contrary by looking closely at the facts of the case. A city may take property with the public only incidentally benefiting. Here, no facts existed to show that Pfizer alone would benefit from New London (D) condemning Kelo's (P) property.

DISSENT: (O'Connor, J.) The Court's decision eliminates "for public use" from the takings clause because it allows for incidental public benefit from ordinary private use of property. The government simply cannot condemn private property when the condemnation is to benefit another private person or entity. The Court's reliance on *Berman v. Parker*, 348 U.S. 26 (1954), and *Hawaii Housing Authority v. Midkiff*, 467 U.S. 229 (1984), is misplaced because those cases actually underscore the public use versus private benefit. Both cases involved takings that directly benefited the public. Those properties were blighted and causing harm to the public in their current use. When private property is being used in its ordinary, non-harmful fashion, it cannot be taken to benefit another private user. It is nearly impossible to isolate the true motives behind a governmental taking, so the government can now condemn with near impunity. The government can also always seek to improve a property's use if the private owner is not making the most productive or attractive use of it. The facts of today's case do not justify the holding.

Continued on next page.

DISSENT: (Thomas, J.) The Court adopts the overly broad "public use" definitions of *Berman v. Parker*, 348 U.S. 26 (1954), and *Hawaii Housing Authority v. Midkiff*, 467 U.S. 229 (1984), without reasoned analysis. A legislature's determination of what constitutes "public use" is not entitled to such blind deference. The original intent of the Public Use Clause was to provide full legal rights to the public for the use of any condemned property. The Court should return to the original intent. Further, the property most likely to be taken under this new definition will be that of poor communities lacking political power and likely using their property at less than its most productive use. These communities should be protected rather than exploited.

ANALYSIS

This case caused a firestorm of fury throughout the United States. Multiple states quickly passed legislation tightening the state eminent domain laws to restrict the ability of governmental entities to take private property for anything less than blatantly public purposes. A small but vocal group of citizens began a petition to condemn Judge Breyer's private vacation residence so that the property may be put to a "better" use for the public.

Quicknotes

CONDEMNATION The taking of private property for public use as long as just compensation is paid therefor.

EMINENT DOMAIN The governmental power to take private property for public use so long as just compensation is paid therefor.

PUBLIC USE Basis for governmental taking of property pursuant to its power of eminent domain so that property taken may be utilized for the benefit of the public at large.

Pennsylvania Coal Co. v. Mahon

Coal mining company (D) v. Landowner (P)

260 U.S. 393 (1922)

NATURE OF CASE: Certiorari review of state statute.

FACT SUMMARY: A Pennsylvania statute forbade the mining of coal in such fashion as to cause the subsidence of any structure used as a human habitation.

RULE OF LAW

A state that through legislation destroys previously existing contractual and property rights between private parties that results in the severe diminution of property value must give compensation to the affected party.

FACTS: In 1878, the Pennsylvania Coal Co. (D) conveyed some land but reserved in the deed the right to remove all coal under the land. The grantee agreed to assume any resulting damage. Mahon (P), who later acquired the land, was bound by the deed. Mahon (P), wanting to prevent further mining under the land, claimed that a 1922 state law (the Kohler Act) changed Pennsylvania Coal's (D) rights. The law forbade the mining of coal in such manner as to cause the subsistence of any structure used as a human habitation with certain exceptions. Mahon's (P) injunction was denied, the trial court maintaining that the law would be unconstitutional if applied to the present case. On appeal, the state supreme court reversed, holding that the statute was a legitimate exercise of the police power.

ISSUE: Must a state that through legislation destroys previously existing contractual and property rights between private parties that results in the severe diminution of property value give compensation to the affected party?

HOLDING AND DECISION: (Holmes, J.) Yes. A state that through legislation destroys previously existing contractual and property rights between private parties that results in the severe diminution of property value must give compensation to the affected party. While private property may be regulated to a certain degree, a taking under the Fifth Amendment will be found if the regulation results in a severe diminution of value. At a certain magnitude, there must be an exercise of eminent domain and compensation to sustain the Kohler Act (the Act). While considerable deference is to be given the legislature's judgment, each case will turn upon its particular facts. Where damage is inflicted on a single private house, even if similar damage is inflicted on others in different places, there is no public interest. On the other hand, the damage to Pennsylvania Coal's (D) contractual and property rights is considerable. The act cannot be sustained where, as an exercise of the police power, it affects reserved rights. To make coal mining commercially unprofitable is, in effect, to destroy it. The rights of the public in a street purchased by eminent domain are those it has paid for. A strong public desire to improve the public condition is not enough to justify achieving it by a shorter cut than the constitutional way of paying for the charge. This is a question of degree and cannot be disposed of by general propositions. So long as private individuals or communities take the risk of contracting for or purchasing only surface rights, they must bear the loss. Reversed.

DISSENT: (Brandeis, J.) Every restriction on the use of property is an abridgment by the state of rights in property without making compensation. Here, the restriction was only against a noxious use of property that remains in Pennsylvania Coal's (D) possession. Pennsylvania Coal (D), once it discontinues its noxious use, is free to enjoy its property as before. A restriction does not cease to be public simply because some individuals may be benefited. The means chosen here may be the only way to prevent the subsistence of land. Because values are relative, the value of the coal kept in place by the restriction should be compared with the value of other parts of the land. The state should not have to follow a theory of reciprocal advantage to justify exercising its police power for the public good. The reciprocal advantage given by the law to Pennsylvania Coal (D) is that of doing business in a civilized community.

ANALYSIS

Eventually, the same analysis of the "taking" issue was used in *United States v. Causby*, 328 U.S. 265 (1946). There, a group of chicken farmers who owned land adjacent to a military airport claimed that, as a result of the noise of planes flying over their property, their chickens were literally frightened to death and egg production fell off. Rejecting the government's argument that any damage was merely consequential of the public's right of freedom of transit, Justice Douglas, writing for the majority, stated, "It is the owner's loss, not the taker's gain, which is the measure of the value of the property taken. . . . The owner's right to possess and exploit the land—that is, to say, his beneficial ownership of it—would be destroyed. . . . It would not be a case of incidental damages arising from a legalized

Continued on next page.

nuisance." In dissent, Justice Black warned "the effect of the Court's decision is to limit, by the imposition of relatively absolute constitutional barriers, possible future adjustments through legislation and regulation that might become necessary with the growth of air transportation, and [because] the Constitution does not contain such barriers."

Quicknotes

EMINENT DOMAIN The governmental power to take private property for public use so long as just compensation is paid therefor.

TAKING A governmental action that substantially deprives an owner of the use and enjoyment of his or her property, requiring compensation.

Home Building & Loan Ass'n v. Blaisdell

Mortgagee (D) v. Mortgagor (P)

290 U.S. 398 (1934)

NATURE OF CASE: Certiorari review of state statute in underlying foreclosure action.

FACT SUMMARY: During the "Great Depression," Minnesota authorized county courts to extend the redemption period from foreclosure sales.

RULE OF LAW

A state may affect the obligations between two contracting parties so long as: (1) an emergency exists; (2) the legislation is addressed to a legitimate end; (3) the relief afforded and justified by the emergency could only be of a character appropriate to that emergency; (4) the conditions upon which relief is granted do not appear to be unreasonable; and (5) the legislation is temporary in operation.

FACTS: In 1933, Minnesota enacted the Minnesota Mortgage Moratorium Law (the Act) authorizing county courts to extend the period of redemption from foreclosure sales "for such additional time as the court may deem just and equitable (but not extending beyond May 1, 1935)." The Blaisdells (P) applied for a judicial extension, and the court granted the extension but also ordered the Blaisdells (P) to pay Home Building and Loan Association (Home) (D), the mortgagee of their home, $40 a month through the extended period. Home (D) appealed on the ground that the Minnesota Act violated Article I, § 10, of the United States Constitution ("No State shall . . . pass any . . . law impairing the obligation of Contracts"). The state supreme court upheld the Act's constitutionality.

ISSUE: May a state change the existing contractual obligations between two private parties?

HOLDING AND DECISION: (Hughes, C.J.) Yes. A state may affect the obligations between two contracting parties so long as: (1) an emergency exists; (2) the legislation is addressed to a legitimate end; (3) the relief afforded and justified by the emergency could only be of a character appropriate to that emergency; (4) the conditions upon which relief is granted do not appear to be unreasonable; and (5) the legislation is temporary in operation. The reservation of the reasonable exercise of the state's protective power is read into all contracts. The prohibition embodied in the Contract Clause is not an absolute one. The state continues to possess authority to safeguard the vital interests of its people. The protection of contracts presupposes a government that views contractual obligations as worthwhile. A rational compromise must be found between public need and private rights, especially when an emergency is found to exist upon judicial review. Provisions of the Constitution must yield to interpretations that respond to current problems not envisioned by the original Framers. The Contract Clause should not be used to frustrate the states in advancing their fundamental interests. Here, the Minnesota Mortgage Moratorium Law was an appropriate response because: (1) a true emergency in Minnesota existed; (2) the legislation was for the protection of a basic interest of society rather than the advantage of a few individuals; (3) the relief afforded was geared to the emergency (mass foreclosures); (4) the mortgagee's interests are not impaired; and (5) the legislation does not outlast the emergency, being temporary in duration. Affirmed.

DISSENT: (Sutherland, J.) "The phrase 'obligation of a contract' in the constitutional sense imports a legal duty to perform the specified obligation of that contract, not to substitute and perform, against the will of one of the parties, a different, albeit equally valuable, obligation."

ANALYSIS

Despite the sweeping language of the instant opinion, the Court struck down state acts impairing contractual obligations in the following instances: exemption of payments on life insurance policies from garnishment (no time limitation, no limitation of amount to necessities); repeal of law protecting purchasers at state-conducted tax sales from attempts by the state to invalidate the transaction because of irregularities (purchaser had right to rely on earlier law so as to make land marketable) and change of procedures for enforcement of payment of benefit assessments pledged as security for Municipal Improvement District bonds. Nonetheless, the *Blaisdell* decision marked the death knell of the Contract Clause's viability as a means to assail the validity of state laws.

Quicknotes

CONTRACTS CLAUSE Article I, § 10 of the U.S. Constitution prohibiting states from passing any "law impairing the Obligation of Contracts."

FORECLOSURE An action to recover the amount due on a mortgage of real property where the owner has failed to

Continued on next page.

meet the mortgage obligations, terminating the owner's interest in the property which must then be sold to satisfy the debt.

REDEMPTION PERIOD The period during which a mortgagor has the right to reclaim forfeited property, following a default on mortgage payments, by the payment of the mortgage debt and any other interest, fees, and costs.

CHAPTER 9

Equal Protection

Quick Reference Rules of Law

Railway Express Agency v. New York

Trucking company (D) v. City (P)

336 U.S. 106 (1949)

NATURE OF CASE: Certiorari review of constitutionality of state advertising statute.

FACT SUMMARY: New York City (P) had a regulation that prohibited advertising on vehicles but allowed advertising on business vehicles so long as the vehicles are engaged in their owner's usual work and are not used mainly for advertising. Railway Express Agency (D) was convicted of violating this regulation.

RULE OF LAW

The Equal Protection Clause does not require that a statute eradicate all evils of the same type or none at all.

FACTS: A New York City (P) regulation prohibited advertising on vehicles. The statute did not prohibit, however, advertising on business vehicles so long as the vehicles are engaged in their owner's usual work and are not used merely or mainly for advertising. Railway Express Agency (D) is engaged in a nationwide express business. It operated 1,900 trucks in New York City (P). It sold space on the exterior of its trucks for advertising. Such advertising was generally unconnected with its business. The state court decided that advertising affects the safety of the public in the streets.

ISSUE: Does the Equal Protection Clause require that a statute eradicate all evils of the same type or none at all?

HOLDING AND DECISION: (Douglas, J.) No. The Equal Protection Clause does not require that a statute eradicate all evils of the same type or none at all. The court of special sessions concluded that advertising on vehicles using the streets of New York City (P) constituted a distraction to vehicle drivers and pedestrians, therefore affecting the public's safety in the use of the streets. The local authorities may well have concluded that those who advertise their own products on their trucks do not present the same traffic problem in view of the nature and extent of their advertising. The court cannot say that such a judgment is not an allowable one. The classification has a relation to the purpose for which it is made and does not contain the kind of discrimination against which the Equal Protection Clause protects. The fact that New York City (P) does not eliminate all distractions from its streets is immaterial. It is not a requirement of equal protection that all evils of the same genus be eradicated or none at all. Conviction affirmed.

CONCURRENCE: (Jackson, J.) Laws must not discriminate between among except upon some reasonable differentiation fairly related to the object of regulation. There is a real difference between doing in self-interest and doing for hire so that it is one thing to tolerate an action done in self-interest and another thing to permit the same action to be done for hire.

ANALYSIS

Traditionally, the Equal Protection Clause supported only minimal judicial intervention. During the late 1960s, however, it became the favorite and most far-reaching tool for judicial protection of fundamental rights not specified in the Constitution. For many years, the impact of the Equal Protection Clause was a very limited one. During the decades of extensive court intervention with state economic legislation, substantive due process, not equal protection, provided the means to determine a statute's constitutionality. Also, as the concurring opinion points out, equal protection demanded only a "reasonable differentiation fairly related to the object of regulation." As demonstrated by this case, the rational classification requirement could be satisfied fairly easily, as the courts were extremely deferential to legislative judgment and easily convinced that the means used might relate rationally to a plausible end.

Quicknotes

EQUAL PROTECTION Guarantee under the Fourteenth Amendment to the U.S. Constitution that the government must treat each person or class of persons the same as it treats other persons or classes of persons in like circumstances.

RATIONAL-BASIS REVIEW A test employed by the court to determine the validity of a statute in equal protection actions, whereby the court determines whether the challenged statute is rationally related to the achievement of a legitimate state interest.

Brown v. Board of Education (Brown I)

Students (P) v. School board (D)

347 U.S. 483 (1954)

NATURE OF CASE: Certiorari review of the separate-but-equal doctrine and its constitutionality.

FACT SUMMARY: Black children were denied admission to public schools attended by White children.

RULE OF LAW
The segregation of children in public schools solely on the basis of race, even though the physical facilities are equal, deprives the children of the minority group of equal protection of the law.

FACTS: Black children had been denied admission to public schools attended by White children under laws requiring or permitting segregation according to race. It was found that the Black children's schools and the White children's schools had been or were being equalized with respect to buildings, curricula, qualifications, and salaries of teachers.

ISSUE: Does segregation of children in public schools solely on the basis of race, even though the physical facilities are equal, deprive the children of the minority group of equal protection of the law?

HOLDING AND DECISION: (Warren, C.J.) Yes. The segregation of children in public schools solely on the basis of race, even though the physical facilities are equal, deprives the children of the minority group of equal protection of the law. The separate-but-equal doctrine has no application in the field of education. The segregation of children in public schools based solely on their race violates the Equal Protection Clause. First, intangible as well as tangible factors may be considered. Hence, the fact that the facilities and other tangible factors in the schools have been equalized is not controlling. Segregation of White and Black children in public schools has a detrimental effect on the Black children because the policy of separating the races is usually interpreted as denoting the inferiority of the Black children. A sense of inferiority affects children's motivation to learn. Segregation tends to deprive Black children of some of the benefits they would receive in an integrated school. Any language found in *Plessy v. Ferguson*, 163 U.S. 537 (1896), that is contrary to this is hereby rejected. The separate-but-equal doctrine has no place in the field of education. Separate facilities are inherently unequal. Such facilities deprive Black children of their right to equal protection of the laws. Remanded for further argument.

ANALYSIS

In *Plessy v. Ferguson*, 163 U.S. 537 (1896), the Court sustained a Louisiana statute requiring "equal, but separate accommodations" for Black and White railway passengers. The separate-but-equal doctrine was born and under it a long line of statutes providing separate-but-equal facilities was upheld. Justice Harlan was the only dissenter in *Plessy*. He stated, "The arbitrary separation of citizens, on the basis of race, while they are on a public highway. . .cannot be justified upon any legal grounds. The thin disguise of equal accommodations for passengers in railway cars will not mislead anyone, nor atone for the wrong done this day." After the 1954 decision in *Brown v. Board of Education*, the Court found segregation unconstitutional in other public facilities as well. Despite the emphasis on the school context in *Brown*, the later cases resulted in per curiam orders simply citing *Brown*. Facilities that were desegregated included beaches, buses, golf courses, and parks.

Quicknotes

EQUAL PROTECTION Guarantee under the Fourteenth Amendment to the U.S. Constitution that the government must treat each person or class of persons the same as it treats other persons or classes of persons in like circumstances.

PER CURIAM Denotes a decision that represents the opinion of the entire court.

SEGREGATION The use of separate institutions and facilities for persons of different races, nationalities, etc.

SEPARATE-BUT-EQUAL DOCTRINE Doctrine pursuant to the holding in *Plessy v. Ferguson*, 163 U.S. 537 (1896), that "separate but equal" facilities for persons of different races do not violate equal protection.

Loving v. Virginia

Interracial couple (D) v. State (P)

388 U.S. 1 (1967)

NATURE OF CASE: Constitutional review of state law barring interracial marriage.

FACT SUMMARY: Loving (D), a White man, and Jeter (D), a Black woman, both Virginia residents, were married in the District of Columbia. When they returned to Virginia, they were indicted for violating the state's ban on interracial marriage.

RULE OF LAW

A state law restricting the freedom to marry solely because of racial classification violates the Equal Protection Clause.

FACTS: In June 1958, Loving (D), a White man, and Jeter (D), a Black woman, both Virginia residents, were married in the District of Columbia, pursuant to its laws. Shortly after their marriage, the Lovings (D) returned to Virginia and were indicted for violating the state's law barring interracial marriage. They pleaded guilty and were sentenced to one year in jail. The trial judge suspended the sentence on the condition that the Lovings (D) leave the state and not return for 25 years. In 1963, they filed a motion to have the judgment vacated and set aside.

ISSUE: Does a state law restricting the freedom to marry solely because of racial classifications violate the Equal Protection Clause?

HOLDING AND DECISION: (Warren, C.J.) Yes. A state law restricting the freedom to marry solely because of racial classification violates the Equal Protection Clause. At the very least, the Equal Protection Clause demands that racial classifications, especially suspect in criminal statutes, be subjected to the most rigid scrutiny. If they are ever to be upheld, they must be shown to be necessary to the accomplishment of some legitimate state objective. Here, there is no question that Virginia's miscegenation statutes rest solely upon distinctions drawn according to race. The statutes proscribe generally accepted conduct if engaged in by members of different races. The fact that the statute prohibits only interracial marriages involving White persons indicates that its aim is to maintain White supremacy. There is patently no legitimate overriding purpose independent of invidious discrimination that justifies the classification. A statute restricting marriage solely because of race violates the Equal Protection Clause. These statutes also deprive the Lovings (D) of liberty without due process. Since marriage is a basic human civil right, to deny this freedom on so insupportable a basis as racial classifications deprives all the state's citizens of liberty without due process of the law. Reversed.

ANALYSIS

In *McLaughlin v. Florida*, 379 U.S. 184 (1964), a state law banning habitual nighttime cohabitation between Whites and Blacks not married to each other was held to violate the Equal Protection Clause, since other non-married couples were not subject to prosecution for the same acts. Ordinances establishing ghettos in which Blacks must reside were found to violate the Clause (*Buchanan v. Warley*, 245 U.S. 60 (1917)), as were judicial enforcement of covenants restricting ownership land to Whites (*Shelley v. Kraemer*, 334 U.S. 1 (1948)); racial discrimination in the selection of jurors (*Patton v. Mississippi*, 332 U.S. 463 (1947)); hiring Blacks for certain occupations; and establishing racial qualifications for public offices (*Anderson v. Martin*, 375 U.S. 399 (1964)).

Quicknotes

EQUAL PROTECTION CLAUSE A constitutional provision that each person be guaranteed the same protection of the laws enjoyed by other persons in like circumstances.

INVIDIOUS DISCRIMINATION Unequal treatment of a class of persons that is particularly malicious or hostile.

MISCEGENATION Marriage between persons of different races.

STRICT SCRUTINY Method by which courts determine the constitutionality of a law when a law affects a fundamental right; under the test, the legislature must have had a compelling interest to enact the law and measures prescribed by the law must be the least restrictive means possible to accomplish its goal.

SUSPECT CLASSIFICATION A class of persons that have historically been subject to discriminatory treatment; statutes drawing a distinction between persons based on a suspect classification, i.e., race, nationality or alienage, are subject to a strict scrutiny standard of review.

Washington v. Davis

Federal agency (D) v. Civil service applicants (P)

426 U.S. 229 (1976)

NATURE OF CASE: Certiorari review of constitutionality of testing requirement.

FACT SUMMARY: A qualifying test for positions as police officers in the District of Columbia was failed by a disproportionately high number of black applicants (P).

RULE OF LAW

A law or official governmental practice must have a discriminatory purpose, not merely a disproportionate effect on one race, to constitute invidious discrimination under the Fifth Amendment's Due Process Clause or the Fourteenth Amendment's Equal Protection Clause.

FACTS: To be accepted in the District of Columbia Metropolitan Police Department, all applicants must receive a grade of at least 40 on "Test 21." This test was developed by the Civil Service Commission for use throughout the federal service to test verbal ability, vocabulary, reading and comprehension. After failing this test, several Black applicants (P) brought an action against the Commissioners of the United States Civil Service Commission (D) for a declaratory judgment that "Test 21" was unconstitutional. In this action, the Black applicants (P) claimed that "Test 21" was unlawfully discriminatory against Blacks and, therefore, was in violation of the Fifth Amendment's Due Process Clause. After the test was invalidated by the court of appeals, the Commissioners (D) appealed to this court.

ISSUE: Does a law or official governmental practice constitute invidious discrimination merely because it affects a greater proportion of one race than another?

HOLDING AND DECISION: (White, J.) No. A law or official governmental practice must have a discriminatory purpose, not merely a disproportionate effect on one race, to constitute invidious discrimination under the Fifth Amendment's Due Process Clause or the Fourteenth Amendment's Equal Protection Clause. Of course, a disproportionate impact may be relevant as evidence of a discriminatory purpose. However, such impact is not the sole touchstone of invidious racial discrimination forbidden by the Constitution, and, standing alone, it does not trigger the rule that racial classifications are to be subjected to the strictest scrutiny. Here, "Test 21" is racially neutral on its face (i.e., it is designed to disqualify anyone who cannot meet the requirements of the police training program). As such, it is valid even though it has a disproportionate effect on Blacks. Reversed.

CONCURRENCE: (Stevens, J.) The line between discriminatory purpose and discriminatory impact is not nearly as bright, and perhaps not quite as critical, as the reader of the Court's opinion might assume. A constitutional issue is not presented every time some disproportionate impact is shown, but when the disproportion is especially great, it doesn't matter whether the standard is phrased in terms of purpose or effect. In the case at bar, there is no purposeful discrimination, since "Test 21" serves the neutral and legitimate purpose of requiring all applicants to meet a uniform minimum standard of literacy.

ANALYSIS

Generally, classifications based upon race are considered suspect and, therefore, subjected to strict scrutiny under the Equal Protection Clause or the Due Process Clause (i.e., such classifications must be justified by a compelling state interest). However, as this case illustrates, such strict scrutiny is applied only when there is purposeful discrimination. As such, the court (as here) can avoid applying strict scrutiny by finding that any discriminatory impact is merely incidental. Note that here the Court also avoided applying the strict standard in Title VII of the Civil Rights Act of 1964 (by saying that only the constitutional issue was raised). Under Title VII, whenever hiring and promotion practices disqualify disproportionate numbers of Blacks, the practices must be justified by more than a rational basis (i.e., they must be validated in terms of job performance) even if no discriminatory purpose is shown.

Quicknotes

DECLARATORY JUDGMENT A judgment of the court establishing the rights of the parties in a controversy that does not grant damages but is binding.

DISCRIMINATORY PURPOSE Intent to discriminate; must be show to establish an Equal Protection violation.

INVIDIOUS DISCRIMINATION Unequal treatment of a class of persons that is particularly malicious or hostile.

STRICT SCRUTINY Method by which courts determine the constitutionality of a law when a law affects a fundamental right; under the test, the legislature must have had a compelling interest to enact the law and measures prescribed by the law must be the least restrictive means possible to accomplish its goal.

Regents of Univ. of California v. Bakke

University (D) v. Applicant (P)

438 U.S. 265 (1978)

NATURE OF CASE: Certiorari review of constitutionality of admission standards.

FACT SUMMARY: Bakke (P) was denied admission to the University of California, Davis, Medical School (D) because it employed a racial quota to aid minorities.

RULE OF LAW

Race may not be made the sole criterion for an admissions decision.

FACTS: Bakke (P) applied for admission to the University of California, Davis (U.C. Davis) (D), Medical School (the School) (D). The School (D) admitted 100 students per year. However, the Regents (D) had adopted a policy of setting aside a minimum number of seats for minority applicants to increase the number of minority members in the medical profession. Members of minorities were screened by a separate admissions panel and were subject to lesser standards in the admissions. Bakke (P), a White male, was denied admission to the medical school even though his overall test scores and grade point were significantly higher than many of those admitted under the minorities program. Bakke (P) filed suit to compel his admission to the School (D). Bakke (P) alleged that the special admissions program violated the Equal Protection Clause and § 601 of Title VI of the Civil Rights Act of 1964. The court found that Bakke (P) had been discriminated against and ordered his admission, finding that the School (D) had not carried its burden of proof to establish that he would not have been admitted even without the program. The School (D) appealed, alleging that benign discrimination was not violative of the Fourteenth Amendment.

ISSUE: May race be made the sole criterion for an admissions decision?

HOLDING AND DECISION: (Powell, J.) No. Race may not be made the sole criterion for an admissions decision. Before reaching the constitutional issue, we must first determine whether the program is invalid under Title VI of the Civil Rights Act of 1964, since this would obviate the necessity of determining constitutional issues. We do not need to pass upon the issue of standing under Title VI, since this was neither briefed nor argued by the parties. Section 601 provides: "No person in the United States shall, on the ground of race, color or national origin, be excluded from participation in, be denied the benefits of, or be subjected to discrimination under any program or activity receiving Federal financial assistance." Based on its legislative history, we find that Title VI proscribes only those racial classifications that would violate the Equal Protection Clause of the Fourteenth Amendment. When racial classifications are involved, strict judicial scrutiny is required even where the class being subjected to the discrimination is White males. The Fourteenth Amendment, regardless of its original roots, is now applied to eliminate discrimination against any group. We decline to restrict its reach to encompass only minorities. Discrimination is never benign. White males may be the minority in certain areas and allegedly benign discrimination may actually have more invidious purposes. While racial classifications have been approved as remedial devices where a court has found prior racial discrimination, the University of California, Davis (U.C. Davis) (D) has no history of discrimination. To justify the use of a suspect classification such as race, a state must establish that it has a constitutionally permissible purpose or interest that is substantial, and the classification is necessary to accomplish it. The Regents (D) allege that the classification is necessary to increase the number of minority doctors, counter the effect of societal discrimination, increase the number of physicians willing to practice in minority areas, and obtain the benefit of a racially diverse student body. U.C. Davis (D) has no history of racial discrimination, and it may not employ racial quotas merely to assume that its student body will have a set percentage of students from each of the races. Racial classifications to eliminate societal discrimination have never been sanctioned. The University of California, Davis, Medical School (the School) (D) is in the business of educating, not formulating social and legislative policy. Since there is no showing that minority applicants will practice in disadvantaged areas or are in any way required to do so, the School (D) cannot justify its admission policy on this basis. While an ethnically diverse student body is a legitimate and important purpose, it is only one of the elements in the range of factors that must be considered by a school in attaining a goal of a heterogeneous student body. A school may not base its admissions policies solely on the criterion of race. Racial quotas are violative of the Equal Protection Clause. Race may be considered but only as one of the factors involved in the admissions decision. Race may be deemed a "plus" so long as all other relevant factors are considered. Affirmed.

CONCURRENCE AND DISSENT: (Brennan, J.) The central import of the opinion herein is that race may be taken into account when it does not demean or

Continued on next page.

insult any racial group but is used to remedy past disadvantages suffered by the minority or group. Based on our nation's history of discrimination, affirmative action programs are necessary to make up for past acts of societal discrimination. Title VI could not have been intended to reach such programs. This is borne out by the fact that many affirmative action programs are required as a condition to federal funding. Therefore, we find that classifications need not be color-blind where race is used to eliminate the effects of past discrimination so long as it is not the sole criterion used, i.e., racial quotas. The government must establish that no less intrusive method for accomplishing its purpose is available. U.C. Davis (D) had a sound basis for determining that minorities were seriously underrepresented and had been subjected to prior acts of societal and government discrimination. This condition would be perpetuated absent some affirmative action program. Moreover, judicial decrees in California had established discriminatory official acts, which had the effect of exacerbating the situation. We feel that the U.C. Davis (D) program was remedial. The admissions program did not stigmatize any race, minority, or majority. The number of minority applicants admitted was less than their proportion of the population in California. No quota within these minorities was established and the best qualified of minority applicants were admitted. In light of the circumstances and objectives herein, race was a reasonable criterion. We would, therefore, reverse the finding that the program was unconstitutional.

SEPARATE OPINION: (Marshall, J.) It must be remembered that during most of the past 200 years, the Constitution as interpreted by this Court did not prohibit the most ingenious and pervasive forms of discrimination against Blacks. The Thirteenth and Fourteenth Amendments were designed to eliminate discrimination against minorities. They should not be applied to benign discrimination programs.

SEPARATE OPINION: (Blackmun, J.) The Equal Protection Clause cannot be used as a shield to perpetuate the supremacy of the majority. I hope someday that affirmative action programs will become unnecessary, but we are not at that point yet. In order to get beyond racism, we must first take account of race. There is no other way.

CONCURRENCE AND DISSENT: (Stevens, J.) This is not a class action, and the scope of the opinion is far beyond that which is necessary to conclude the controversy between Bakke (P) and U.C. Davis (D). The basis of the plain language of § 601 of Title VI of the Civil Rights Act of 1964 permits affirmation. Race cannot be used under it and U.C. Davis's (D) admissions policy clearly violates this prohibition.

ANALYSIS

Bakke, based on the failure of the Court to achieve any consensus, stands merely for the proposition that racial quotas cannot be used where there is no court finding of discrimination. The loose standards enunciated herein should allow a school to establish what amounts to a racial quota merely by giving inordinate weight to race in its admissions decision; that is, of course, if any schools would want to bother if they are under no legal obligation to do so.

Quicknotes

AFFIRMATIVE ACTION PROGRAM A program designed to create benign discrimination for the purpose of remedying existing discrimination by favoring one group over another.

EQUAL PROTECTION Guarantee under the Fourteenth Amendment to the U.S. Constitution that the government must treat each person or class of persons the same as it treats other persons or classes of persons in like circumstances.

FOURTEENTH AMENDMENT Declares that no state shall make or enforce any law that shall abridge the privileges and immunities of citizens of the United States; no state shall deny to any person within its jurisdiction the equal protection of the laws.

STRICT SCRUTINY Method by which courts determine the constitutionality of a law when a law affects a fundamental right; under the test, the legislature must have had a compelling interest to enact the law and measures prescribed by the law must be the least restrictive means possible to accomplish its goal.

THIRTEENTH AMENDMENT The constitutional provision that abolished slavery in the United States.

Adarand Constructors, Inc. v. Pena

Contractor (P) v. Federal government (D)

515 U.S. 200 (1995)

NATURE OF CASE: Certiorari review of constitutionality of federal program.

FACT SUMMARY: A federal program favoring minority-owned businesses was challenged by Adarand Constructors (P), a White contractor who lost a job to a Hispanic-owned company, as violative of equal protection.

RULE OF LAW

Federal programs that set racial classifications for awarding contracts or jobs will be subject to strict judicial scrutiny.

FACTS: A general contractor to a project involving the federal government solicited bids for the subcontracts. For the guardrail portion of this highway project, Adarand Constructors (Adarand) (P), a White contractor, submitted the low bid. The general contractor, however, signed a competing Hispanic-owned company because of a congressionally created program that awarded contractors bonus monies for hiring minority-owned businesses. Adarand (P) sued in district court, contending that the program violated equal protection. The district court evaluated the program under a relaxed standard resembling intermediate scrutiny, held the program valid, and dismissed. The Tenth Circuit Court of Appeals affirmed, and the Supreme Court granted review.

ISSUE: Will federal programs that set racial classifications for awarding contracts or jobs be subject to strict judicial scrutiny?

HOLDING AND DECISION: (O'Connor, J.) Yes. Federal programs that set racial classifications for awarding contracts or jobs will be subject to strict judicial scrutiny. Three general propositions exist with respect to governmental racial classifications. The first is skepticism: all such classifications are inherently suspect. The second is consistency: the standard of review does not vary depending on race. The third proposition is congruence: that which applies to the states must apply to the national government as well. From this, the proposition naturally follows that any person of any race has the right to demand that any governmental actor explain, through the standard of strict scrutiny, why he or she is being treated differently than a person of another race. Consequently, any racial classification scheme enacted by Congress must pass strict scrutiny, which is to say, it must be narrowly tailored to serve a compelling governmental interest. This was not the standard used by the courts below. Vacated and remanded.

CONCURRENCE: (Scalia, J.) Government can never have a compelling interest in discriminating on the basis of race to "make up" for past discrimination. We are just one race in the eyes of government.

CONCURRENCE: (Thomas, J.) There is a moral and constitutional equivalence between all racial distinctions, "benign" or otherwise, that justifies subjecting them to strict scrutiny analysis.

DISSENT: (Stevens, J.) There is no moral or constitutional equivalence between a policy designed to perpetuate racial subjugation and one designed to eradicate it.

DISSENT: (Ginsburg, J.) The difficulty of this case should not obscure the Court's recognition of the persistence of racial inequality and the acknowledgment of Congress's authority to act affirmatively, not only to end discrimination but also to counteract discrimination's lingering effects. In light of the attention the political branches are currently giving to affirmative action, there is no compelling cause for the intervention the Court has made in this case.

ANALYSIS

Subjecting affirmative action policies to a rigorous examination will inevitably jeopardize a whole host of programs designed to convey special federal benefits to members of minority groups. However, Justice O'Connor stopped short of the Scalia-Thomas approach that would simply bar all racial preferences as unconstitutional. Instead, she invites the executive and legislative branches to take unspecified steps to address "the unhappy persistence of both the practice and the lingering effects of racial discrimination."

Quicknotes

AFFIRMATIVE ACTION A form of benign discrimination designed to remedy existing discrimination by favoring one group over another.

INJUNCTIVE RELIEF A court order issued as a remedy, requiring a person to do, or prohibiting that person from doing, a specific act.

STARE DECISIS Doctrine whereby courts follow legal precedent unless there is good cause for departure.

Continued on next page.

STRICT SCRUTINY Method by which courts determine the constitutionality of a law when a law affects a fundamental right; under the test, the legislature must have had a compelling interest to enact the law and measures prescribed by the law must be the least restrictive means possible to accomplish its goal.

Grutter v. Bollinger

Law school applicant (P) v. Law school (D)

539 U.S. 306 (2003)

NATURE OF CASE: Certiorari review of constitutionality of admissions policy.

FACT SUMMARY: When Grutter (P), a White applicant for admission to the University of Michigan Law School (the Law School) (D), was rejected, she argued the Law School's (D) use of race as a factor in admissions decisions resulted in discrimination against her on the basis of race in violation of the Fourteenth Amendment.

RULE OF LAW
The Equal Protection Clause does not prohibit a school's narrowly tailored use of race in admissions decisions to further a compelling interest in obtaining educational benefits flowing from a diverse student body.

FACTS: The University of Michigan Law School (the Law School) (D), as part of its admission policy, expressly seeks to admit a group of students who, among other things, will reflect "diversity." The policy reaffirms the Law School's (D) commitment to "racial and ethnic diversity" with special reference to the inclusion of students who have been historically discriminated against, such as African Americans, Hispanics, and Native Americans. Each year the Law School (D) admits a class of 350 from over 3,500 applications. Grutter (P), a White Michigan resident, applied to the Law School (D) with a 3.8 grade point average and 161 LSAT score. When her application was rejected, she sued the Law School (D) in federal district court, alleging the Law School (D) had discriminated against her on the basis of race in violation of the Fourteenth Amendment. The district court agreed, concluding that the Law School's (D) use of race as a factor in admissions decisions was unlawful. The federal court of appeals reversed, and Grutter (P) appealed to the Supreme Court.

ISSUE: Does the Equal Protection Clause prohibit a school's narrowly tailored use of race in admissions decisions to further a compelling interest in obtaining educational benefits flowing from a diverse student body?

HOLDING AND DECISION: (O'Connor, J.) No. The Equal Protection Clause does not prohibit a school's narrowly tailored use of race in admissions decisions to further a compelling interest in obtaining educational benefits flowing from a diverse student body. Here, the University of Michigan Law School's (the Law School's) (D) admission policy aspires to achieve that diversity which has the potential to enrich everyone's education and thus make a law school class stronger than the sum of its parts. By enrolling a "critical mass" of underrepresented minority students, the Law School (D) seeks to ensure their ability to make unique contributions to the character of the Law School (D). The policy does not define diversity solely in terms of racial and ethnic status. Racial classifications imposed by government must be strictly analyzed; such classifications are constitutional only if they are narrowly tailored, as here, to further compelling governmental interests. Not every decision influenced by race is equally objectionable. In keeping with the Court's tradition in giving a degree of deference to a university's academic decisions, the Law School's (D) "educational judgment" that such diversity is essential to its educational mission is one to which the Court defers. This Court has long recognized that, given the important purpose of public education and the expansive freedoms of speech and thought associated with the university environment, universities occupy a special niche in our constitutional tradition. The Court's conclusion of the Law School's (D) "compelling interest" in a diverse student body is informed by the view that attaining a diverse student body is at the heart of the Law School's (D) proper institutional mission. Furthermore, in order to cultivate national leaders with legitimacy in the eyes of the citizenry, it is necessary that the path to leadership be visibly open to talented and qualified individuals of every race and ethnicity. Affirmed.

CONCURRENCE: (Ginsburg, J.) It is well documented that conscious and unconscious race bias, even rank discrimination based on race, remain alive in our land, impeding realization of our highest values and ideals. One may hope, but not firmly forecast, that over the next generation's span, progress toward nondiscrimination and genuinely equal opportunity will make it safe to sunset affirmative action.

CONCURRENCE AND DISSENT: (Scalia, J.) Litigation can be expected on behalf of minority groups intentionally shortchanged in the institution's composition of its generic minority "critical mass." The Constitution proscribes government discrimination on the basis of race and state-provided education is no exception.

CONCURRENCE AND DISSENT: (Thomas, J.) Blacks can achieve in every avenue of American life without the meddling of university administrators. The Constitution does not tolerate institutional devotion to

Continued on next page.

the status quo in admissions policies when such devotion ripens into racial discrimination.

DISSENT: (Rehnquist, C.J.) The Law School's (D) means are not narrowly tailored to the interest it asserts. While the Law School (D) claims that it must take steps to achieve a "critical mass" of underrepresented minority students, its actual program bears no relation to this asserted goal but rather there is a direct correlation between the applicants and the admittees of a given race. This is precisely the type of racial balancing the Court calls "patently unconstitutional."

ANALYSIS

In *Grutter*, the Supreme Court noted it was true that the Court's language in some of its cases since *Regents of Univ. of California v. Bakke*, 438 U.S. 265 (1978), might be read to suggest that remedying past discrimination is the permissible justification only for race-based governmental action. Nevertheless, said the Court, it had never held that the only governmental use of race that can survive strict scrutiny is remedying past discrimination.

Quicknotes

AFFIRMATIVE ACTION A form of benign discrimination designed to remedy existing discrimination by favoring one group over another.

EQUAL PROTECTION CLAUSE A constitutional provision that each person be guaranteed the same protection of the laws enjoyed by other persons in like circumstances.

FOURTEENTH AMENDMENT Declares that no state shall make or enforce any law that shall abridge the privileges and immunities of citizens of the United States; no state shall deny to any person within its jurisdiction the equal protection of the laws.

STRICT SCRUTINY Method by which courts determine the constitutionality of a law when a law affects a fundamental right; under the test, the legislature must have had a compelling interest to enact the law and measures prescribed by the law must be the least restrictive means possible to accomplish its goal.

Gratz v. Bollinger

University applicants (P) v. University (D)

539 U.S. 244 (2003)

NATURE OF CASE: Certiorari review of constitutionality of admissions policy.

FACT SUMMARY: Gratz (P) and other "qualified" White students denied admission as undergraduates to the University of Michigan (the University) (D) sued the University (D), arguing the admission policy of automatically distributing one-fifth of the points needed to guarantee admission to every single "underrepresented minority" solely because of race constituted prohibited racial discrimination.

RULE OF LAW

A university admissions policy that automatically distributes one-fifth of the points needed to guarantee admission to every single "underrepresented minority" solely because of race is not narrowly tailored to achieve the interest in educational diversity so as to avoid violation of the Equal Protection Clause of the Fourteenth Amendment.

FACTS: Gratz (P) and other White students who were denied admission as undergraduates to the University of Michigan (the University) (D), although they were deemed qualified by the college admissions committee, brought suit against the University (D), arguing that its applicant selection method violated the Equal Protection Clause of the Fourteenth Amendment on the grounds that the University (D) automatically distributes one-fifth of the points needed to guarantee admission to every single "underrepresented minority" solely because of race.

ISSUE: Is a university admissions policy that automatically distributes one-fifth of the points needed to guarantee admission to every single "underrepresented minority" solely because of race narrowly tailored to achieve the interest in educational diversity so as to avoid violation of the Equal Protection Clause of the Fourteenth Amendment?

HOLDING AND DECISION: (Rehnquist, C.J.) No. A university admissions policy that automatically distributes one-fifth of the points needed to guarantee admission to every single "underrepresented minority" solely because of race is not narrowly tailored to achieve the interest in educational diversity so as to avoid violation of the Equal Protection Clause of the Fourteenth Amendment. This Court emphasizes the importance of considering each particular applicant as an individual, assessing all of the qualities that an individual possesses and in turn evaluating that individual's ability to contribute to the unique setting of higher education. In this regard, the Court does not contemplate that any single characteristic automatically ensures a specific and identifiable contribution to a university's diversity. Here, the University of Michigan's (the University's) (D) admission policy does not provide such individualized consideration; to the contrary, it automatically distributes 20 points to "underrepresented minority" groups, the only consideration being whether the applicant is a member of one of these minority groups. Even if a White applicant's extraordinary artistic talent rivaled that of Monet or Picasso, the applicant would receive, at most, five points under the University's (D) admissions system. Clearly, such a system does not offer applicants an individualized selection process. Nor does the fact that the implementation of a program capable of providing individualized consideration might present administrative challenges render constitutional an otherwise problematic system. The admissions policy violates the Equal Protection Clause of the Fourteenth Amendment.

CONCURRENCE: (O'Connor, J.) The selection index, by setting up automatic, predetermined point allocations for the soft variables, ensures that the diversity contributions of applicants cannot be individually assessed. This is in sharp contrast to the law school's admission plan, which enables admissions officers to make nuanced judgments as to the contributions each applicant is likely to make.

CONCURRENCE: (Thomas, J.) A state's use of racial discrimination in higher education admissions is categorically prohibited by the Equal Protection Clause.

DISSENT: (Souter, J.) On its face, the assignment of specific points does not set race apart from all other weighted considerations. Since college admission is not left entirely to inarticulate intuition, it is hard to see what is inappropriate in assigning some stated value to a relevant characteristic, whether it be reasoning ability, writing style, running speed, or minority race.

DISSENT: (Ginsburg, J.) The stain of generations of racial oppression is still visible in our society, and the determination to hasten its removal remains vital. Here, there has been no demonstration that the University of Michigan (D) unduly constricts admissions opportunities for students who do not receive special consideration based on race.

Continued on next page.

ANALYSIS

As made clear by the Supreme Court in *Gratz*, and in *Grutter v. Bollinger*, 539 U.S. 306 (2003), achieving diversity in higher education, whether it be at the undergraduate or graduate level, remains a compelling state interest sufficient to justify some degree of racial preferences without violating the Equal Protection Clause of the Fourteenth Amendment.

Quicknotes

EQUAL PROTECTION CLAUSE A constitutional provision that each person be guaranteed the same protection of the laws enjoyed by other persons in like circumstances.

Fisher v. University of Texas at Austin et al.

University applicant (P) v. State university

579 U.S. 365 (2016)

NATURE OF CASE: Appeal from judgment upholding a state university's race-conscious admissions program as constitutional under the Equal Protection Clause.

FACT SUMMARY: Fisher (P), a Caucasian who had been denied admission to the University of Texas at Austin (the University) (D), contended that the University's (D) race-conscious admissions program did not meet the requirements for being constitutional under the Equal Protection Clause.

RULE OF LAW

A state university's race-conscious admissions program is lawful under the Equal Protection Clause where it satisfies strict scrutiny and is narrowly tailored to achieve the university's permissible goals.

FACTS: The University of Texas at Austin (the University) (D) used an undergraduate admissions system containing two components. First, as required by the state's Top Ten Percent Law, it offered admission to any students who graduate from a Texas high school in the top 10 percent of their class. It then filled the remainder of its incoming freshman class, some 25 percent, by combining an applicant's Academic Achievement Index—the student's test score and high school academic performance—with the applicant's Personal Achievement Index (PAI), a holistic review containing numerous factors, including race. However, race was just one "factor of a factor of a factor" in this holistic review. The University (D) adopted its admissions process after a year-long study of its admissions process led it to conclude that its prior race-neutral system did not reach its goal of providing the educational benefits of diversity to its undergraduate students. Fisher (P), who was not in the top 10 percent of her high school class, and therefore was categorically ineligible for 75 percent of the incoming freshmen slots, was denied admission to the University's (D) freshman class after her application was reviewed through the University's (D) holistic review process. She filed suit, alleging that the University's (D) consideration of race as part of this process disadvantaged her and other Caucasian applicants, in violation of the Equal Protection Clause. In that case, *Fisher v. University of Texas at Austin*, 570 U.S. 297, 133 S. Ct. 2411 (2013) (*Fisher I*), the Supreme Court set forth three controlling principles relevant to assessing the constitutionality of a public university's affirmative action program. First, a university may not consider race unless the admissions process can withstand strict scrutiny, i.e., it must show that its purpose or interest is both constitutionally permissible and substantial and that its use of the classification is necessary to accomplish that purpose. Second, the decision to pursue the educational benefits that flow from student body diversity is, in substantial measure, an academic judgment to which some, but not complete, judicial deference is proper. Third, when determining whether the use of race is narrowly tailored to achieve the university's permissible goals, the school bears the burden of demonstrating that available and workable race-neutral alternatives do not suffice. Under these principles, a state university has a continuing obligation to satisfy the strict scrutiny burden: by periodically reassessing the admission program's constitutionality, and efficacy, in light of the school's experience and the data it has gathered since adopting its admissions plan, and by tailoring its approach to ensure that race plays no greater role than is necessary to meet its compelling interests. The court of appeals upheld the plan in light of these principles, and Fisher (P) appealed. The Supreme Court again granted certiorari in the case.

ISSUE: Is a state university's race-conscious admissions program lawful under the Equal Protection Clause where it satisfies strict scrutiny and is narrowly tailored to achieve the university's permissible goals?

HOLDING AND DECISION: (Kennedy, J.) Yes. A state university's race-conscious admissions program is lawful under the Equal Protection Clause where it satisfies strict scrutiny and is narrowly tailored to achieve the university's permissible goals. The University of Texas at Austin (the University) (D) has an ongoing obligation to satisfy the burden of strict scrutiny in light of changing circumstances, and to assess the constitutionality of its plan in light of the experience the school has accumulated and the data it has gathered since the adoption of its admissions plan. As it does so, it should remain mindful that diversity takes many forms, and that formalistic racial classifications may sometimes fail to capture diversity in all its dimensions and, when used in a divisive manner, could undermine the educational benefits the University (D) values. The compelling interest that justifies consideration of race in college admissions is not an interest in enrolling a certain number of minority students, but in promoting educational benefits that flow from student body diversity, since enrolling a diverse student body promotes cross-racial understanding, helps to break down racial stereotypes, enables students to better

Continued on next page.

understand persons of different races, and prepares students more effectively for an increasingly diverse workforce and society. Since the University (D) is prohibited from seeking a particular number or quota of minority students, it cannot be faulted for failing to specify a particular level of minority enrollment at which it believes the educational benefits of diversity will be obtained. On the other hand, asserting an interest in the educational benefits of diversity writ large is insufficient. A university's goals cannot be elusory or amorphous—they must be sufficiently measurable to permit judicial scrutiny of the policies adopted to reach them. The University (D) not only articulated concrete and precise goals, but it also gave a reasoned, principled explanation for its decision in a 39-page proposal written after a year-long study revealed that its race-neutral policies and programs did not meet its goals. Demographic data showed stagnation of minority enrollment, and anecdotal data indicated that minority students suffered from feelings of loneliness and isolation. These data were supported by quantitative data. Fisher (P) claims that it was unnecessary to consider race because such consideration had only a minor impact on the number of minority students the school admitted and therefore on the University's (D) compelling interest. However, the record shows that the consideration of race has had a meaningful, if still limited, effect on freshman class diversity. That race consciousness played a role in only a small portion of admissions decisions should be a hallmark of narrow tailoring, not evidence of unconstitutionality. Finally, Fisher (P) argues that there were numerous other race-neutral means to achieve the University's (D) goals. However, as the record reveals, none of those alternatives—such as increasing outreach to minority students—was a workable means of attaining the University's (D) educational goals as of the time of Fisher's (P) application, and her argument ignores precedent making clear that the Equal Protection Clause does not force universities to choose between a diverse student body and a reputation for academic excellence. Further, Fisher's (P) proposal to uncap the Top Ten Percent Plan overlooks the fact that the Top Ten Percent Plan, though facially neutral, cannot be understood apart from its basic purpose, which is to boost minority enrollment. Even if, as a matter of raw numbers, minority enrollment would increase under such a regime, there is little support for the proposition that college admissions would be improved if they were a function of class rank alone, since this approach would sacrifice all other aspects of diversity in pursuit of enrolling a higher number of minority students. Accordingly, the University (D) has met its burden of demonstrating that its admissions program was narrowly tailored when it rejected Fisher's (P) application. [Affirmed.]

DISSENT: (Alito, J.) *Fisher I*, 570 U.S. 297 (2013), required University of Texas at Austin (the University or UT) (D) to identify the interests justifying its plan with enough specificity to permit a reviewing court to determine whether the requirements of strict scrutiny were met and to show that those requirements were in fact satisfied. UT (D) failed to do meet these obligations. *Fisher I* rejected the argument that the courts should defer to the University (D) as to these matters, and by invoking "the educational benefits of diversity," UT (D) fails to identify any metric that would allow a court to determine whether its plan is needed to serve, or is actually serving, those interests. This amounts to nothing less than the plea for deference that was emphatically rejected in *Fisher I*. Nonetheless, it is important to keep in mind that what is not at stake in the case is whether UT (D) or any other university may adopt an admission plan that results in a student body with a broad representation of students from all racial and ethnic groups. Instead, what is at stake is whether university administrators may justify systematic racial discrimination simply by asserting that such discrimination is necessary to achieve "the educational benefits of diversity," without explaining—much less proving—why the discrimination is needed or how the discriminatory plan is well crafted to serve its objectives. Even though UT (D) has never provided any coherent explanation for its asserted need to discriminate on the basis of race, and even though UT's (D) position relies on a series of unsupported and noxious racial assumptions, the majority concludes that UT (D) has met its heavy burden. This conclusion is wrong.

ANALYSIS

Supporters of this decision hailed it as a landmark decision that will promote racial diversity and educational inclusion. Its detractors claimed that it permitted the University of Texas at Austin (D) to benefit advantaged students over impoverished ones, and even Justice Alito was reported to have told his colleagues that it was "affirmative action gone berserk." Because many colleges and universities base all their admissions decisions on academic achievement as well as factors such as race and ethnicity, this decision lets stand such admissions programs all over the nation and, importantly, recognizes that there are many ways to achieve diversity, and that some deference to an institution's particular formula for obtaining a diverse student population is necessary. The decision also emphasizes that schools will need to continually assess their admissions programs to determine whether race-conscious policies are needed in light of changing demographics and the impacts their affirmative action programs have had.

Continued on next page.

Quicknotes

AFFIRMATIVE ACTION A form of benign discrimination designed to remedy existing discrimination by favoring one group over another.

STRICT SCRUTINY Method by which courts determine the constitutionality of a law when a law affects a fundamental right; under the test, the legislature must have had a compelling interest to enact the law, and measures prescribed by the law must be the least restrictive means possible to accomplish its goal.

Parents Involved in Community Schools v. Seattle School District

Parents of unadmitted students (P) v. Public school district (D)

551 U.S. 701 (2007)

NATURE OF CASE: Certiorari review of constitutionality of school-assignment plans.

FACT SUMMARY: Two metropolitan school districts sought to assign students to schools to achieve racial balance.

RULE OF LAW

Racial balance between local high-school districts is not a compelling government interest under the Equal Protection Clause.

FACTS: The Seattle School District (Seattle) (D) implemented a student assignment plan designed to achieve numerically defined racial balance among Seattle's (D) ten public high schools. Seattle (D), however, had never been found to run racially segregated schools. The Jefferson County Public Schools in Louisville, Kentucky (Louisville), was under a desegregation order from 1975 to 2000; the order was dissolved in 2001 when a federal court ruled that Louisville (D) had reached unitary status by largely eliminating the district's earlier racial segregation. After the decree was dissolved, Louisville (D) voluntarily adopted a student assignment plan that required specific minimum and maximum enrollment percentages for Black students. Parents (P) of students who were denied admission in each school district sued their respective district, alleging, in part, violations of the Equal Protection Clause. After the intermediate appellate courts in both cases upheld the assignment plans, the parents (P) petitioned the Supreme Court for further review.

ISSUE: Is racial balance between local high-school districts a compelling government interest under the Equal Protection Clause?

HOLDING AND DECISION: (Roberts, C.J.) No. Racial balance between local high-school districts is not a compelling government interest under the Equal Protection Clause. Because both school districts (D) have apportioned government benefits on the basis of race, the applicable standard of review in these cases is strict scrutiny: Seattle (D) and Louisville (D) must show that their race-based discrimination (1) advances a compelling government interest through (2) means narrowly tailored to achieve the intended purpose. The asserted interests in both Seattle (D) and Louisville (D) reduce to nothing more than the goal of numerical racial balance between each district's (D) schools. This Court has consistently found such a purpose illegitimate. *Grutter v. Bollinger*, 539 U.S. 306 (2003), does not control here because *Grutter* involved the specific interests of higher education; it is also instructive, though, that *Grutter* upheld the law-school admission policy there because racial diversity was only one of a mix of admissions criteria. Here, on the other hand, pure numerical racial balance, by itself, is the government interest, and that interest has never been recognized as valid. The plans at issue here also fail because the school districts (D) have failed to show that they seriously considered other means besides explicit racial classifications. Reversed.

CONCURRENCE: (Thomas, J.) Racial imbalance and racial segregation are not synonymous; it is possible to have racial imbalance through no conscious decision to segregate. Further, forced racial mixing of students may or may not provide educational benefits in general or higher achievement for Black students in particular. The color-blind Constitution, then, requires that these student assignment plans be struck down.

CONCURRENCE: (Kennedy, J.) Contrary to the Chief Justice's plurality opinion, race can be considered as one among several factors in examining school enrollments. General, indirect solutions to problems of racial composition of schools are much better than the crude plans in these cases as ways to address those problems. The United States has special obligations to ensure equal opportunity for all children, and government should be permitted to consider race in its attempts to fulfill that mission. As the plurality correctly notes, though, government may not classify students based solely on race without first making a showing that such a step is necessary.

DISSENT: (Stevens, J.) In his demand of strict equality under the Constitution, the Chief Justice forgets that, before *Brown v. Board of Education of Topeka*, 347 U.S. 483 (1954), only Black students were told where they could and could not go to school. Today's plurality decision rewrites the history of our landmark school-desegregation decision.

DISSENT: (Breyer, J.) These voluntary plans bear striking resemblances to plans that this Court has long required, permitted, and encouraged local school districts to formulate and use. Every branch of government has acknowledged that government may voluntarily use race-conscious plans to address race-based problems even when such plans are not constitutionally obligatory. The plurality overlooks the fact that no case has ever decided that all racial classifications should receive precisely the same scrutiny. Actually, our decisions have

Continued on next page.

applied different standards to assess racial classifications depending on whether the government's purpose was to exclude persons from, or to include persons in, government programs. The plurality's interpretation of strict scrutiny, however, would automatically invalidate all race-conscious government action. The school districts' (D) interest here serves remedial, educational, and democratic purposes; such a multiplicity of concerns means that the rationale in *Grutter v. Bollinger*, 539 U.S. 306 (2003), controls here and requires upholding these assignment plans. Even under the strictest scrutiny, though, the plans here pass muster under the Equal Protection Clause because they are more narrowly tailored than the plan approved in *Grutter*. Accordingly, these plans are consistent with equal protection of the laws.

ANALYSIS

Chief Justice Roberts's plurality opinion in *Parents Involved* focuses on the firm percentages used by Seattle (D) and Louisville (D) in making student-assignment decisions. Despite Justice Breyer's objections in dissent, it is difficult to see how such an overtly numerical approach differs from the quota-based systems that the Court consistently has struck down under the Equal Protection Clause. See, e.g., *Regents of the University of California v. Bakke*, 438 U.S. 265, 307 (1978), "If [the University's] purpose is to assure within its student body some specified percentage of a particular group merely because of its race or ethnic origin, such a preferential purpose must be rejected not as insubstantial but as facially invalid."

Quicknotes

EQUAL PROTECTION CLAUSE A constitutional provision that each person be guaranteed the same protection of the laws enjoyed by other persons in like circumstances.

STRICT SCRUTINY Method by which courts determine the constitutionality of a law when a law affects a fundamental right; under the test, the legislature must have had a compelling interest to enact the law and measures prescribed by the law must be the least restrictive means possible to accomplish its goal.

Shaw v. Reno (Shaw I)

Voters (P) v. State (D)

509 U.S. 630 (1993)

NATURE OF CASE: Certiorari review of constitutionality of a congressional redistricting plan.

FACT SUMMARY: Shaw (P) alleged that a North Carolina reapportionment plan that included one majority-Black district with boundary lines of dramatically irregular shape constituted unconstitutional racial gerrymandering.

RULE OF LAW

An allegation that a reapportionment scheme is so irrational on its face that it can be understood only as an effort to segregate voters based on race without sufficient justification states a cognizable claim under the Fourteenth Amendment.

FACTS: North Carolina, after becoming entitled to a twelfth seat in the U.S. House of Representatives as a result of the 1990 census, enacted a reapportionment plan that included one majority-Black district with boundary lines of dramatically irregular shape. Shaw (P), on behalf of a number of voters, sued, alleging the creation of the irregular district was unconstitutional racial gerrymandering under the Fourteenth Amendment. The district court dismissed the action for failure to state a cognizable claim. Shaw (P) appealed to the Supreme Court, which granted certiorari.

ISSUE: Does an allegation that a reapportionment scheme is so irrational on its face that it can be understood only as an effort to segregate voters based on race without sufficient justification state a cognizable claim under the Fourteenth Amendment?

HOLDING AND DECISION: (O'Connor, J.) Yes. An allegation that a reapportionment scheme is so irrational on its face that it can be understood only as an effort to segregate voters based on race without sufficient justification states a cognizable claim under the Fourteenth Amendment. The Fourteenth Amendment requires that legislation that is unexplainable on grounds other than race is narrowly tailored to further a compelling governmental interest, even if facially race-neutral. An example of such unexplainable legislation would be a reapportionment plan so highly irregular on its face that it rationally cannot be understood as anything other than an effort to segregate voters on the basis of race. Such a plan perpetuates impermissible racial stereotypes by reinforcing the perception that members of the same racial group, regardless of age or economic status, share the same political ideology. Shaw's (P) complaint alleged that the North Carolina plan was such a plan and thus stated a cognizable claim. Reversed and remanded.

DISSENT: (White, J.) Shaw (P) failed to state a claim because no cognizable injury was alleged. There is neither an outright deprivation of the right to vote nor a demonstration that the challenged action had the intent and effect of unduly diminishing a group's influence on the political process.

DISSENT: (Blackmun, J.) It is ironic that today's case, in which the majority chooses to abandon settled law and for the first time to recognize this "analytically distinct" constitutional claim, is a challenge by White voters to the plan under which North Carolina has sent Black representatives to Congress for the first time since Reconstruction.

DISSENT: (Stevens, J.) The Equal Protection Clause prohibits states from creating bizarre district boundaries such as the one at issue for the sole purpose of making it more difficult for members of a minority group to win an election. However, it does not prohibit gerrymandering when the majority acts to facilitate the election of a member of a group that lacks power because it remains underrepresented in the state legislature.

DISSENT: (Souter, J.) Until today, the Court has analyzed equal protection claims involving race in electoral districting differently from equal protection claims involving other forms of governmental conduct. Unlike other contexts in which we have addressed the State's conscious use of race, electoral districting calls for decisions that nearly always require some consideration of race for legitimate reasons where there is a racially mixed population. There is no justification for treating the narrow category of bizarrely shaped district claims differently from other districting claims.

ANALYSIS

Though the holding of *Shaw* is limited, the Court spoke extensively in dicta about what constituted sufficient justification for race-based districting. If on remand a plan were found to be in fact racial gerrymandering, the plan must then be found narrowly tailored to further a compelling governmental interest. This high level of scrutiny is imposed because the Court believes racial classifications with respect to voting rights "carry particular dangers" such as compartmentalizing citizens

Continued on next page.

into competing racial factions, thus moving the country away from the goal of a political system in which race is irrelevant. In *Shaw* the challenged district was unusually long and narrow and ran along an interstate. One pundit suggested that if a driver on the interstate opened his or her car doors, the driver would risk running over every voter in the district.

Quicknotes

FOURTEENTH AMENDMENT Declares that no state shall make or enforce any law that shall abridge the privileges and immunities of citizens of the United States; no state shall deny to any person within its jurisdiction the equal protection of the laws.

GERRYMANDERING To create a civil division of an unusual shape for an improper purpose such as redistricting a state so that a maximum number of the elected representatives will be of a particular political party.

REAPPORTIONMENT PLAN The alteration of a voting district's boundaries or composition to reflect the population of that district.

Craig v. Boren

Males 18 to 20 years of age (P) v. State (D)

429 U.S. 190 (1976)

NATURE OF CASE: Certiorari review of constitutionality of state statute.

FACT SUMMARY: Craig (P) appealed after a federal district court upheld two sections of an Oklahoma statute prohibiting the sale of "nonintoxicating" 3.2 percent beer to males under the age of 21 and to females under the age of 18 on the ground that such a gender-based differential did not constitute a denial to males 18–20 years of age equal protection of the laws.

RULE OF LAW

Laws that establish classifications by gender must serve important governmental objectives and must be substantially related to achievement of those objectives to be constitutionally in line with the Equal Protection Clause.

FACTS: Craig (P) brought suit to have two sections of an Oklahoma statute, which prohibits the sale of "nonintoxicating" 3.2 percent beer to males under the age of 21 and to females under the age of 18, declared unconstitutional. Craig (P) contended that such a gender-based differential constituted a denial to males 18 to 20 years of age of the equal protection of the laws in violation of the Fourteenth Amendment. Boren (D), representing the state of Oklahoma, argued that this law was enacted as a traffic safety measure and that the protection of public health and safety was an important function of state and local governments. Boren (D) introduced statistical data demonstrating that 18–20-year-old male arrests for "driving under the influence" and "drunkenness" substantially exceeded female arrests for the same age period. The district court upheld the ordinance on the ground that it served the important governmental objective of traffic safety. Craig (P) appealed.

ISSUE: Are laws that establish classifications by gender constitutional if they do not serve important governmental objectives and are not substantially related to achievement of those objectives?

HOLDING AND DECISION: (Brennan, J.) No. Laws that establish classifications by gender must serve important governmental objectives and must be substantially related to achievement of those objectives to be constitutionally in line with the Equal Protection Clause. It appears that the objective underlying the statute in controversy is the enhancement of traffic safety. Clearly, the protection of public health and safety represents an important function of state and local governments. However, the statistics presented by Boren (D) in this Court's view cannot support the conclusion that the gender-based distinction closely serves to achieve the objective. The most relevant of the statistical surveys presented as evidence by Boren (D) in support of the statute, arrests of 18–20-year-olds for alcohol-related driving offenses, establish two percent more males than females are arrested for that offense. Such a disparity can hardly form the basis for employment of a gender line as a classifying device. Certainly, if maleness is to serve as a proxy for drinking and driving, a correlation of two percent must be considered unduly tenuous. Indeed, prior cases have consistently rejected the use of sex as a decision-making factor. Therefore, since the gender-based differential does not serve an important governmental objective, the Oklahoma statute constitutes a denial of the equal protection of the laws to males ages 18 to 20 and is unconstitutional. Reversed.

CONCURRENCE: (Powell, J.) The state legislature, by the classification it has chosen, has not adopted through the enactment of the statute a means that bears a fair and substantial relation to the objective of traffic safety.

CONCURRENCE: (Stevens, J.) It is difficult to believe that the statute in question was actually intended to cope with the problem of traffic safety, since it has only a minimal effect on access to a not-very-intoxicating beverage and does not prohibit its consumption.

DISSENT: (Rehnquist, J.) The Court's disposition of this case is objectionable on two grounds. First is its conclusion that men challenging a gender-based statute that treats them less favorably than women may invoke a more stringent standard of judicial review than pertains to most other types of classifications. Second is the Court's enunciation of this standard, without citation to any source, as being that "classifications by gender must serve important governmental objectives and must be substantially related to achievement of those objectives." The Equal Protection Clause contains no such language, and none of our previous cases adopt that standard.

ANALYSIS

Cases concerning whether males and females should be considered as reaching a majority age equally has met with some stiff opposition. In *Stanton v. Stanton*, 564 P.2d 303 (1977), a Utah justice observed: "Regardless of what a judge may think about equality, his thinking cannot change the facts of life. To judicially hold that

Continued on next page.

males and females attain their maturity at the same age is to be blind to the biological facts of life."

Quicknotes

EQUAL PROTECTION CLAUSE A constitutional provision that each person be guaranteed the same protection of the laws enjoyed by other persons in like circumstances.

FOURTEENTH AMENDMENT Declares that no state shall make or enforce any law that shall abridge the privileges and immunities of citizens of the United States; no state shall deny to any person within its jurisdiction the equal protection of the laws.

United States v. Virginia

Federal government (P) v. State (D)

518 U.S. 515 (1996)

NATURE OF CASE: Certiorari review of constitutionality of a college's male-only admission policy.

FACT SUMMARY: Virginia Military Institute (D), a state-sponsored university, had a policy of excluding women from admission or attendance.

RULE OF LAW
Public schools may not exclude women.

FACTS: Since 1839, Virginia Military Institute (VMI) (D), a Virginia (D) public institution, had been a male-only college that sought to train "citizen-soldiers." In 1990, the Attorney General (P) sued VMI (D) and Virginia (D), claiming that the admission policy violated the Equal Protection Clause. Virginia (D) eventually proposed a remedial plan under which a parallel program would be developed for women. The Virginia Women's Institute for Leadership would be created at Mary Baldwin College. The trial court and an appellate court upheld this remedial plan, but the Attorney General (P) appealed, and the Supreme Court granted a writ of certiorari.

ISSUE: May public schools exclude women?

HOLDING AND DECISION: (Ginsburg, J.) No. Public schools may not exclude women. States must show that a sex-based government action serves important governmental objectives and that the discriminatory means employed are substantially related to the achievement of those objectives. There must be an exceedingly persuasive justification for the action. This heightened review standard prevents classifications that perpetuate the legal, social, and economic inferiority of women. While single-sex education may provide benefits to some students, Virginia (D) has not shown that it pursued this option as a means to providing a diversity of educational opportunities. On the other hand, the historical record shows that Virginia (D) has systematically prevented women from obtaining higher education until relatively recently. The fact that women have been successfully integrated into the armed forces and service academies demonstrates that the Virginia Military Institute's (VMI's) (D) stature will not be downgraded by admitting women. The proposed Virginia Women's Institute for Leadership does not qualify as VMI's (D) equal in terms of faculty, facilities, course offerings, and reputation. Accordingly, since Virginia (D) is unable to provide substantial equal opportunities for women who desire to attend VMI (D), the male-only admission policy is unconstitutional. Remanded.

CONCURRENCE: (Rehnquist, C.J.) The majority decision is correct but there is no basis for stating that states must demonstrate an exceedingly persuasive justification to support sex-based classifications.

DISSENT: (Scalia, J.) The majority sweeps away an institution that has thrived for 150 years and the precedents of this Court to embark on a course of proscribing its own elite opinions on society. Virginia (D) has an important interest in providing education, and single-sex instruction is an approach substantially related to this goal.

ANALYSIS

Justice Scalia's dissent carries a tone of disgust for the majority opinion. As he did in *Romer v. Evans*, 517 U.S. 620 (1996), Justice Scalia states the majority seeks to satisfy some unidentified group of anti-majoritarian elites. This attitude is unusual for a member of the Supreme Court since dissents are usually restricted to attacks on the majority's legal reasoning.

Quicknotes

CERTIORARI A discretionary writ issued by a superior court to an inferior court in order to review the lower court's decisions; the Supreme Court's writ ordering such review.

Cleburne v. Cleburne Living Center, Inc.

Municipality (D) v. Zoning permit applicant (P)

473 U.S. 432 (1985)

NATURE OF CASE: Certiorari review of constitutionality of municipal special use permit ordinance.

FACT SUMMARY: Cleburne Living Center, Inc. (P) contended that laws impacting the mentally retarded should be given heightened constitutional scrutiny.

RULE OF LAW

Laws impacting the mentally retarded are not to be given heightened constitutional scrutiny.

FACTS: The city of Cleburne, Texas, (D) had zoned multiple-residence dwellings as R-3. Most R-3 structures required no permit; however, any proposed home for the mentally retarded did. The Cleburne Living Center, Inc. (the Center) (P) applied for such a permit. Responding to objections from nearby residents, the city council refused the application. The Center (P) challenged the ordinance as a denial of equal protection. The Fifth Circuit Court of Appeals, applying a heightened level of scrutiny toward the mentally retarded, voided the ordinance. The Supreme Court granted review.

ISSUE: Are laws impacting the mentally retarded to be given heightened constitutional scrutiny?

HOLDING AND DECISION: (White, J.) No. Laws impacting the mentally retarded are not to be given heightened scrutiny. This Court has defined certain characteristics to be so irrelevant to a person's potential contribution to society that, when combined with their political minority status, the conclusion follows that they are entitled to special protection under the Equal Protection Clause. Examples include race, alienage, and religious belief. Mental retardation does not fit this profile. The retarded person's status does relate to his or her ability to contribute to society. Second, there is ample evidence that lawmakers are responsive to retarded people's plights, showing that they are not politically powerless. Finally, if a large and amorphous class such as the mentally retarded were to be given special Fourteenth Amendment protection, it is hard to see where the process would stop. For these reasons, the Court concludes that the mentally retarded are not entitled to heightened scrutiny. [The Court went on to hold that, even under low-level scrutiny, the ordinance failed to pass constitutional scrutiny.] Affirmed.

CONCURRENCE: (Stevens, J.) The Court's equal protection analysis is better seen as a continuum than specific levels of scrutiny.

CONCURRENCE AND DISSENT: (Marshall, J.) The ordinance in question would no doubt survive the Court's classic "rational basis" test. What the Court has done is fashion a heightened level of scrutiny without so stating.

ANALYSIS

The Court's Equal Protection Clause analysis continues to evolve. As of the time of this case, three levels of scrutiny existed: rational basis, heightened, and strict. In years past, strict scrutiny automatically led to invalidation, rational basis to approval. As this case shows, this is no longer true.

Quicknotes

EQUAL PROTECTION Guarantee under the Fourteenth Amendment to the U.S. Constitution that the government must treat each person or class of persons the same as it treats other persons or classes of persons in like circumstances.

HEIGHTENED SCRUTINY A purposefully vague judicial description of all levels of scrutiny more exacting than minimal scrutiny.

QUASI-SUSPECT CLASS A class of persons who historically have been subjected to discriminatory treatment.

RATIONAL-BASIS REVIEW A test employed by the court to determine the validity of a statute in equal protection actions, whereby the court determines whether the challenged statute is rationally related to the achievement of a legitimate state interest.

STRICT SCRUTINY Method by which courts determine the constitutionality of a law when a law affects a fundamental right; under the test, the legislature must have had a compelling interest to enact the law and measures prescribed by the law must be the least restrictive means possible to accomplish its goal.

Harper v. Virginia State Board of Elections

Residents (P) v. State (D)

383 U.S. 663 (1966)

NATURE OF CASE: Certiorari review of the constitutionality of Virginia's poll tax.

FACT SUMMARY: Harper (P) and other Virginia residents brought this suit to have Virginia's (D) poll tax declared unconstitutional.

RULE OF LAW

The right to vote is a fundamental and basic right, and where such rights are asserted under the Equal Protection Clause, classifications that might restrain those rights must be closely scrutinized and carefully confined.

FACTS: Harper (P) and other Virginia residents brought these suits to have Virginia's (D) poll tax declared unconstitutional. The three-judge district court, feeling bound by the Court's decision in *Breedlove v. Suttles*, 302 U.S. 277 (1937), dismissed the complaint. Harper (P) appealed. The law at issue conditions the right to vote in state elections upon the payment of a poll tax.

ISSUE: Is the right to vote a fundamental and basic right, and where such rights are asserted under the Equal Protection Clause, must the classifications that might restrain those rights be closely scrutinized and carefully confined?

HOLDING AND DECISION: (Douglas, J.) Yes. The right to vote is a fundamental and basic right, and where such rights are asserted under the Equal Protection Clause, classifications that might restrain those rights must be closely scrutinized and carefully confined. A state violates the Equal Protection Clause whenever it makes the affluence of the voter or the payment of a fee an electoral standard. The right to vote is a basic and fundamental one, especially since it preserves other rights. Any alleged infringement of the right to vote, such as a poll tax, must be carefully scrutinized. A state's interest, when it comes to voting, is limited to the power to fix qualifications. Wealth, like race or creed or color, is irrelevant to one's ability to participate intelligently in the electoral process. Further lines drawn on the basis of wealth or property, like those of race, are traditionally disfavored. The requirement of the payment of a fee as a condition of obtaining a ballot causes invidious discrimination. *Breedlove v. Suttles*, 302 U.S. 277 (1937), sanctioned this use of the poll tax, and to that extent it is overruled. Reversed.

DISSENT: (Black, J.) So long as a distinction drawn is not irrational, unreasonable, or invidious, it must be upheld. There are certainly rational reasons for Virginia's poll tax, such as the state's desire to collect revenue and its belief that voters who pay poll tax will be interested in furthering the state's welfare. Hence, the tax must be upheld. If the tax is to be struck down, it should be done by the legislature rather than the courts.

DISSENT: (Harlan, J.) The Equal Protection Clause does not impose upon this country an ideology of unrestrained equalitarianism.

ANALYSIS

If, as the dissenters in *Harper* argue, the poll tax classification is not wholly "irrational," the case represents a greater intervention than the courts undertook under old equal protection. There is some question as to whether this greater scrutiny was because the "fundamental rights" of voting are affected or because "lines drawn on the basis of wealth" are traditionally disfavored. In *McDonald v. Board of Election Commissioners*, 394 U.S. 802 (1969), the Court sees wealth as an independent ground (apart from impact on fundamental rights) for strict scrutiny. There is a series of cases preceding and following *Harper* (among them *Reynolds v. Sims*, 377 U.S. 533 [1964]) that supports the invoking of strict scrutiny when voting rights are affected.

Quicknotes

EQUAL PROTECTION CLAUSE A constitutional provision that each person be guaranteed the same protection of the laws enjoyed by other persons in like circumstances.

FUNDAMENTAL RIGHT A liberty that is either expressly or impliedly provided for in the U.S. Constitution, the deprivation or burdening of which is subject to a heightened standard of review.

POLL TAX A tax imposed upon each person within a jurisdiction. Under the Twenty-fourth Amendment state and federal governments may not impose a poll tax as a condition to voting.

Kramer v. Union Free School District No. 15

Ineligible voter (P) v. School district (D)

395 U.S. 621 (1969)

NATURE OF CASE: Certiorari review of constitutionality of voter eligibility requirements.

FACT SUMMARY: Kramer (P) claimed that Union's (D) School District voter eligibility requirements denied him equal protection of the laws.

RULE OF LAW

Legal classifications must be tailored so that exclusion of a certain class of persons is necessary to achieve an articulated state goal.

FACTS: The New York Education Code provided that in certain school districts residents may vote in a school district election only if they or their spouse owns or leases taxable real property within the district or are parents (or have custody) of children enrolled in local public schools. Kramer (P), an unmarried man who neither owned nor leased taxable real property, argued that the voter eligibility requirements denied him equal protection. Union Free School District No. 15 (D) argued that the state has a legitimate interest in limiting the right to vote in school district elections and may reasonably conclude that parents are those primarily interested in school affairs. A three-judge federal district court dismissed Kramer's (P) complaint, and he appealed.

ISSUE: Must legal classifications be tailored so that exclusion of a certain class of persons is necessary to achieve an articulated state goal?

HOLDING AND DECISION: (Warren, C.J.) Yes. Legal classifications must be tailored so that exclusion of a certain class of person is necessary to achieve an articulated state goal. As statutes distributing voting rights are at the foundation of representative society, any unjustified discrimination in who may vote undermines the legitimacy of representative government. Thus, a statute that allows some to vote while prohibiting others must promote a compelling state interest to be valid. Assuming for purposes of argument that New York can limit the right to vote in school district elections to persons primarily interested in school affairs, that statute does not accomplish that goal. The statute excludes persons who have a distinct and direct interest in school affairs while it includes those whose interest is remote and indirect. Here, Kramer (P), who lives with his parents and pays state and federal taxes, cannot vote, while an unemployed man who pays no taxes, but who rents an apartment in the district, can vote. Reversed.

DISSENT: (Stewart, J.) The statute does not impinge on constitutionally protected rights, "for the Constitution of the United States does not confer the right of suffrage upon anyone." *Minor v. Happersett*, 21 Wall. 162, 88 U.S. 178 (1874). Accordingly, the compelling state interest test should not have been applied. The classification appeared to have been rationally related to a permissible legislative end and should have been upheld.

ANALYSIS

It appears that the Court will not be quick to sustain "interest" voting tests but will tend to uphold competency voting tests such as requirements based on age and sanity. It is not a denial of equal protection for the state to deny ex-convicts the right to vote. An interest classification that has been upheld involved allowing only landowners in a water storage district to vote. The district had a very limited purpose, *Salyer Land Co. v. Tulare Lake Basin Water Storage District*, 410 U.S. 719 (1973).

Quicknotes

EQUAL PROTECTION CLAUSE A constitutional provision that each person be guaranteed the same protection of the laws enjoyed by other persons in like circumstances.

Reynolds v. Sims

[Parties not identified.]

377 U.S. 533 (1964)

NATURE OF CASE: Certiorari review of constitutionality of one existing and two proposed plans for apportionment.

FACT SUMMARY: The federal district court held that the existing system and two proposed plans for apportionment of seats in the Alabama legislature violated the Equal Protection Clause.

RULE OF LAW

The Equal Protection Clause guarantees the opportunity for equal protection by all voters in the election of state legislators and requires that the seats in both houses of a bicameral state legislature be apportioned on a population basis.

FACTS: The federal district court for the Middle District of Alabama held that the existing and two legislatively proposed plans for the apportionment of seats in the two houses of the Alabama legislature violated the Equal Protection Clause. The court ordered into effect a temporary reapportionment plan comprised of part of the proposed plans.

ISSUE: Does the Equal Protection Clause require that seats in both houses of a bicameral state legislature be apportioned on a population basis?

HOLDING AND DECISION: (Warren, C.J.) Yes. The Equal Protection Clause guarantees the opportunity for equal protection by all voters in the election of state legislators and requires that the seats in both houses of a bicameral state legislature be apportioned on a population basis. Concededly, the basic aim of legislative apportionment is the achieving of fair and effective representation for all citizens. The Equal Protection Clause guarantees the opportunity for equal participation by all voters in the election of state legislators. Overweighting and overvaluation of the votes of persons living in one area has the effect of dilution and undervaluation of those living in another area. Diluting the weight of votes because of place of residence impairs basic constitutional rights under the Fourteenth Amendment, just as much as invidious discrimination based upon race. It is argued that the apportionment issue is a political one that the court should leave alone. However, a denial of constitutionally protected rights demands judicial protection. The weight of a citizen's vote cannot be made to depend on where he or she lives. The Equal Protection Clause requires that the seats in both houses of a bicameral state legislature must be apportioned on a population basis. Analogy to the federal system will not sustain a system not based on population. The federal system grew out of compromise and concession needed to band together states that formerly were independent. Political subdivisions of states (cities, counties) never were independent entities. The decision does not mean that the two bodies in a state legislature cannot consist of different constituencies, have different length terms, represent geographical districts of different sizes, or be of different sizes. It does mean that in apportionment's overriding objective—whatever the method used—must be substantial equality of population among the various districts. Neither history, nor economics, nor other group interests will justify disparity from population-based representation. One factor that could justify some deviation from such representation is political subdivisions. Decennial reapportionment would meet the requirement for reasonable currency. It will be for the federal courts to devise the particular remedies to be utilized in such cases. Affirmed.

DISSENT: (Harlan, J.) State legislative apportionments are wholly free of constitutional limitations save those imposed by the Republican Form of Government Clause (Article IV, § 4). This decision places basic aspects of state political systems under the overlordship of the federal judiciary, a move that is ill-advised and constitutionally impermissible.

DISSENT: (Stewart, J.) The Equal Protection Clause demands but two basic attributes of any state legislative apportionment plan. The plan must be a rational one, and it must not permit the systematic frustration of the will of a majority of the voters. Beyond this, there is nothing in the federal Constitution to prevent a state from choosing any electoral legislative plan it thinks best suited to the interests, temper, and customs of its people.

ANALYSIS

For many years, the Court refused jurisdiction of cases challenging the fairness of the representation in state legislatures, on the ground that the issue involved was a "political question." The Court abandoned this position in *Baker v. Carr*, 369 U.S. 186 (1962), and ever since has held that the federal courts have the jurisdiction to determine the fairness and validity of state legislative apportionment plans. The result has been that a traditionally political question has become justiciable, and

Continued on next page.

the courts have exerted what was traditionally deemed a legislative power in determining what is, and what is not, a fair plan of legislative apportionment.

Quicknotes

BICAMERALISM The necessity of approval by a majority of both houses of Congress when ratifying legislation or approving other legislative action.

EQUAL PROTECTION CLAUSE A constitutional provision that each person be guaranteed the same protection of the laws enjoyed by other persons in like circumstances.

INVIDIOUS DISCRIMINATION Unequal treatment of a class of persons that is particularly malicious or hostile.

POLITICAL QUESTION An issue that is more appropriately left to the determination of another governmental branch and that the court declines to hear.

REAPPORTIONMENT PLAN The alteration of a voting district's boundaries or composition to reflect the changing population of that district.

Davis v. Bandemer

State (D) v. Democrats (P)

478 U.S. 109 (1986)

NATURE OF CASE: Certiorari review of constitutionality of Indiana's 1981 state apportionment.

FACT SUMMARY: Democrats (P) challenged a state reapportionment plan that did not include exactly proportional representation.

RULE OF LAW

When determining unconstitutional vote dilution, the challenging party must show a discriminatory vote dilution to make out a prima facie case.

FACTS: In 1981, the Republican-controlled state legislature of Indiana reapportioned the state. The districts were of roughly equal population. The plan was apparently drafted without much debate due to the limited amount of information available to voting politicians. In the next election, Democrats (P) won majority popular votes but received less than half of the seats in the house and senate. The Democrats (P) then filed suit. The district court found that both discriminatory intent and actual discrimination had been proven. The decision was appealed.

ISSUE: When determining unconstitutional vote dilution, must the challenging party show a discriminatory vote dilution to make out a prima facie case?

HOLDING AND DECISION: (White, J.) Yes. When determining unconstitutional vote dilution, the challenging party must show a discriminatory vote dilution to make out a prima facie case. The Constitution mandates one-person, one-vote. However, there is no requirement that all districts in a voting region have mathematically equivalent proportional representations of the various voting populations. Here, a single election was used as evidence of an equal protection voting violation. But it would be next to impossible to conclude that actual discrimination had occurred after a single election. Since there is no requirement districts contain populations exactly proportional to the total population, the election result will most likely vary from the total popular vote. Furthermore, it would be a difficult task to ascertain how to apportion districts to even achieve exactly proportional representation of all population groups. Reversed.

CONCURRENCE: (O'Connor, J.) Political gerrymandering poses a nonjusticiable political question. Because the most easily measured indicia of political power relate solely to winning and losing elections, there is a grave risk that the plurality's various attempts to qualify and condition the group the Court has created will gradually pale in importance. What is likely to remain is a loose form of proportionality, under which some deviations from proportionality are permissible, but any significant, persistent deviations from proportionality are suspect.

DISSENT: (Powell, J.) An analysis should be used that focuses upon whether voting districts have been deliberately distorted and are arbitrary. The shape of districts is very telling when searching for an improper purpose in reapportionment. Other relevant considerations include legislative goals and procedures, evidence concerning population disparities, and statistics showing vote dilution.

ANALYSIS

Commentators have suggested that the Court opened a can of worms when it agreed that there was even a justiciable issue on the question of whether political parties deserved protection from discriminatory reapportionment. Traditionally, the focus was on protecting racial minorities. This case added yet another factor to complicate the reapportionment picture.

Quicknotes

GERRYMANDERING To create a civil division of an unusual shape for an improper purpose such as redistricting a state so that a maximum number of the elected representatives will be of a particular political party.

PRIMA FACIE CASE An action where the plaintiff introduces sufficient evidence to submit the issue to the judge or jury for determination.

PROPORTIONAL REPRESENTATION Representative bodies should be proportionally representative of the people they represent.

REAPPORTIONMENT PLAN The alteration of a voting district's boundaries or composition to reflect the population of that district.

M.L.B. v. S.L.J.

Parent (P) v. [Party not identified (D)]

519 U.S. 102 (1996)

NATURE OF CASE: Certiorari review of appeal from decree terminating parental rights and state requirements regarding appellate procedure.

FACT SUMMARY: A Mississippi court dismissed M.L.B.'s (P) appeal of the termination of her parental rights to her two minor children when she was unable to pay the required record preparation fees.

RULE OF LAW

A state may not condition appeals from trial court decrees terminating parental rights on the affected parent's ability to pay record preparation fees.

FACTS: A Mississippi court ordered M.L.B.'s (P) parental rights to her two minor children terminated. M.L.B. (P) sought to appeal the termination decree, but the state required that she pay in advance over $2,000 in record-preparation fees. Because M.L.B. (P) did not have the money to pay the fees, her appeal was dismissed. The Supreme Court granted certiorari to determine whether the Due Process and Equal Protection Clauses of the Fourteenth Amendment permitted such appeals to be conditioned on the ability to pay certain fees.

ISSUE: May a state condition appeals from trial court decrees terminating parental rights on the affected parent's ability to pay record preparation fees?

HOLDING AND DECISION: (Ginsburg, J.) No. A state may not condition appeals from trial court decrees terminating parental rights on the affected parent's ability to pay record preparation fees. Fee requirements are generally examined only for their rationality. While the Court has not prohibited state controls on every type of civil action, it has consistently distinguished those involving intrusions on family relationships. However, the stakes for M.L.B. (P), i.e., the forced dissolution of her parental rights, are far greater than any monetary loss. Mississippi's interest, on the other hand, in offsetting the costs on its court system is purely financial. Decrees forever terminating parental rights fit in the category of cases in which a state may not "bolt the door to equal justice." Reversed.

CONCURRENCE: (Kennedy, J.) The cases most on point are the decisions addressing procedures involving the rights and privileges inherent in family and personal relations, e.g., *Boddie v. Connecticut*, 401 U.S. 371 (1971), and *Lassiter v. Department of Social Services of Durham City*, 452 U.S. 18 (1981)—cases resting exclusively upon the Due Process Clause. Here, due process is a sufficient basis for the Court's holding.

DISSENT: (Thomas, J.) The majority's new-found constitutional right to free transcripts in civil appeals cannot be effectively restricted to this case. M.L.B. (P) requested relief under both the Due Process and Equal Protection Clauses, yet the majority does not specify the source of relief it has granted. Mississippi's transcript rule reasonably obliges all potential appellants to bear the cost of availing themselves of a service that the state is not constitutionally required to provide. The Equal Protection Clause is not a panacea for all perceived social and economic inequities.

ANALYSIS

While the majority's rationale in granting M.L.B. (P) relief may have been vaguely articulated, as the dissent has alleged, it would seem the issues at stake here go beyond simple textual analysis. It is not merely M.L.B.'s (P) rights that must be considered, but the impact that the termination of those rights will have on her two minor children. It will likely not be as great of a problem (as the dissent suggests) to limit the application of this holding to similarly situated parents.

Quicknotes

DUE PROCESS CLAUSE Language in the Fifth and Fourteenth Amendments to the U.S. Constitution, providing that no person shall be deprived of "life, liberty, or property, without due process of law."

EQUAL PROTECTION CLAUSE A constitutional provision that each person be guaranteed the same protection of the laws enjoyed by other persons in like circumstances.

San Antonio Independent School Dist. v. Rodriguez

School district (D) v. Students (P)

411 U.S. 1 (1973)

NATURE OF CASE: Certiorari review of constitutionality of state educational funding plan.

FACT SUMMARY: The Texas state educational system was partially funded through use of local property taxes, resulting in lower per-pupil expenditure in the poorer school districts. This system was challenged as a denial of equal protection to those students who resided in the poorer districts.

RULE OF LAW

Education is not a fundamental right, and students who live in school districts with a lower property tax base do not constitute a suspect classification, so a school financing system is not subject to a strict standard of judicial review on an equal protection challenge to the financing system.

FACTS: Public elementary schools in Texas were funded by a combination of state and district contributions. Each district supplemented the state contribution to education by a property tax on property within the district. This system resulted in significant disparities in per-pupil expenditures among the various districts that resulted from the differences in taxable property values in the district: the richer districts spent up to $594 per pupil, and the poorer districts spent $356. Rodriguez (P) was the parent of a child in a district with low per-pupil expenditure and brought a class action suit on behalf of all children similarly situated. Rodriguez (P) alleged that the state's reliance on property tax to finance education favored the more affluent districts and therefore violated the Equal Protection Clause because of the disparities in expenditures. Rodriguez (P) further alleged that this discrimination on the basis of wealth is a suspect classification, and that education is a fundamental right, requiring a strict standard of judicial review.

ISSUE: Is education a fundamental right, and do students who live in school districts with a lower property tax base constitute a suspect classification, so a school financing system is subject to a strict standard of judicial review on an equal protection challenge to the financing system?

HOLDING AND DECISION: (Powell, J.) No. Education is not a fundamental right, and students who live in school districts with a lower property tax base do not constitute a suspect classification, so a school financing system is not subject to a strict standard of judicial review on an equal protection challenge to the financing system. The strict scrutiny standard is not appropriate in this case because it involves neither a suspect classification nor a fundamental right, and the state system does not violate the Equal Protection Clause because it bears a rational relationship to a legitimate state interest. The system does not disadvantage a suspect class because there is no definable class of "poor" people that are discriminated against. The poorest families are not necessarily residents of the poorest property tax districts. The system does not result in an absolute deprivation of a desired benefit because all students in Texas get an adequate education despite the differences in per-pupil expenditures. Education is not a fundamental right. The fundamental nature of a right is established only if that right is explicitly or implicitly guaranteed by the Constitution. Rodriguez (P) argues that education is guaranteed because it is a necessary prerequisite to the exercise of other constitutionally protected rights, such as the right to free speech. This "nexus" theory is unacceptable because it is unlimited in scope. Even if it were assumed that education is constitutionally protected because it is a prerequisite to other rights, there is no evidence that the level of education given to the students in the poorer district falls short of the minimum education that would be required. Additionally, this is an inappropriate case for the use of a strict judicial scrutiny test because it is an attack on state expenditure of taxes, a field in which the Court, because of its lack of expertise, has traditionally deferred to state legislative judgments. It also involves considerations of educational policy, another area in which the Court should not interfere because of its lack of experience. The Texas system is, then, not a violation of the Equal Protection Clause because it does bear a rational relationship to a legitimate state purpose. Although the system may be imperfect and result in some inequalities, the financing system is not so irrational as to constitute invidious discrimination. Such a financing system is common practice among the states, and suggested alternatives to this system are untested. Reversed.

CONCURRENCE: (Stewart, J.) All laws have some measure of discriminatory treatment. The Equal Protection Clause is used only to test the validity of classifications created by state laws, and unless a fundamental right or suspect classification is involved, the Clause is violated only by classifications that are wholly arbitrary or capricious.

DISSENT: (White, J.) In this case, the means chosen to further a permissible state goal, local control of

Continued on next page.

education, are not rationally related to that goal. The state must establish a financing system that provides a rational basis for encouraging local control and not the current system, which gives unequal treatment to groups that are determined on the basis of criteria wholly unrelated to that goal.

DISSENT: (Marshall, J.) Rather than dividing all cases into either strict scrutiny or rational basis test, the court should adopt a sliding scale approach to testing violations of the Equal Protection Clause based on the constitutional and societal importance of the affected interest and the invidiousness of the basis on which the state has drawn the classification. The fundamental nature of a right is not entirely derived from the face of the Constitution, but the proper question is the extent to which constitutionally protected rights are dependent on interests not verbalized in the Constitution. As the connection between the two increases, the unarticulated interests become more fundamental, and the level of judicial scrutiny increases. On this basis, education is a fundamental right because of the close relationship between education and other constitutionally protected rights such as freedom of speech and the right to vote. Past cases have shown that the Court will carefully scrutinize discriminations based on wealth. Here, a careful scrutiny of the asserted state interest in local control of education shows that this interest is offered merely as an excuse for interdistrict inequality. Therefore, the financing system is a violation of the Equal Protection Clause.

ANALYSIS

Under the holding of this case, no right or interest is considered fundamental, requiring strict judicial review under the Equal Protection Clause, unless that right is explicitly or implicitly guaranteed by the Constitution. Education is not a fundamental interest because it is not so protected, and the Court also holds that wealth is not a suspect classification. Since the strict standard is not required, the classification will be upheld if it has a rational relationship to a legitimate state interest and is not invidiously discriminatory, a test that is very easy for the state to meet. This case clearly indicates that the current court will not extend the fundamental right and suspect classification analysis beyond the traditionally well-established categories, such as classification based on race.

Quicknotes

EQUAL PROTECTION CLAUSE A constitutional provision that each person be guaranteed the same protection of the laws enjoyed by other persons in like circumstances.

FUNDAMENTAL RIGHT A liberty that is either expressly or impliedly provided for in the U.S. Constitution, the deprivation or burdening of which is subject to a heightened standard of review.

HEIGHTENED SCRUTINY A purposefully vague judicial description of all levels of scrutiny more exacting than minimal scrutiny.

INVIDIOUS DISCRIMINATION Unequal treatment of a class of persons that is particularly malicious or hostile.

RATIONAL-BASIS TEST A test employed by the court to determine the validity of a statute in equal protection actions, whereby the court determines whether the challenged statute is rationally related to the achievement of a legitimate state interest.

STRICT SCRUTINY Method by which courts determine the constitutionality of a law when a law affects a fundamental right; under the test, the legislature must have a compelling interest to enact law and measures prescribed by the law must be the least restrictive means possible to accomplish goal.

SUSPECT CLASSIFICATION A class of persons that have historically been subject to discriminatory treatment; statutes drawing a distinction between persons based on a suspect classification, i.e., race, nationality, or alienage, are subject to a strict scrutiny standard of review.

CHAPTER 10

Congress's Civil Rights Enforcement Powers

Quick Reference Rules of Law

Civil Rights Cases

Citizens (P) v. Federal government (D)

109 U.S. 3 (1883)

NATURE OF CASE: Certiorari review of the constitutionality of § 1 of the Civil Rights Act of 1875.

FACT SUMMARY: Private citizens of five states who had suffered either criminal indictments or civil penalty actions for violating § 1 of the Civil Rights Act of 1875 challenged its constitutionality.

RULE OF LAW

The Fourteenth Amendment does not reach private acts of discrimination but encompasses only state action that is discriminatory.

FACTS: In § 1 of the Civil Rights Act of 1875, Congress provided that all persons were entitled to full and equal enjoyment of accommodations provided by public inns, public conveyances on land or water, theaters, and other places of public amusement, regardless of race. The statute went on to provide that violation of its provisions was a misdemeanor and also declared that aggrieved persons could recover $500 "for every such offense." Five individuals, private citizens who had excluded Black people from such facilities, challenged the constitutionality of the law and their indictments or fines.

ISSUE: Can the Fourteenth Amendment reach private acts of discrimination?

HOLDING AND DECISION: (Bradley, J.) No. The Fourteenth Amendment does not reach private acts of discrimination but encompasses only state action that is discriminatory. Since the Fourteenth Amendment is concerned with prohibiting certain types of state laws and actions, it cannot reach private acts of discrimination such as occurred in these cases. Thus, it gives Congress no power to enact laws reaching private acts of discrimination, as this law attempts to do. While the Thirteenth Amendment does reach private as well as state actions, it gives Congress power to deal only with problems of involuntary servitude and not mere racial discrimination. Thus, the challenged law is unconstitutional.

DISSENT: (Harlan, J.) The Thirteenth Amendment was designed to destroy any and all burdens and disabilities constituting badges of slavery and servitude, such as racial discrimination, and not just the institution of slavery. Furthermore, the Fourteenth Amendment affirmatively establishes the citizenship of all persons born or naturalized in the United States and is thus not limited to prohibiting certain state actions. Even if it were, railroads, inns, and public places of amusement can be seen as agents of the state whose actions are reachable anyway.

ANALYSIS

Although the Court would probably reach the opposite result were this case decided today, it continues to hold to the position that the Fourteenth Amendment can reach only state action and not private discrimination. The difference is that the Court has changed its concept of state action to include private actions attributable to the state through agency theories, etc.

Quicknotes

DISCRIMINATION Unequal treatment of a class of persons.

STATE ACTION An action taken by the state or with sufficient connection to the state so as to be attributed to it; such action is subject to judicial scrutiny for violation of due process and equal protection rights guaranteed by the Fourteenth Amendment to the U.S. Constitution.

Shelley v. Kraemer

Purchaser (D) v. Property owner (P)

334 U.S. 1 (1948)

NATURE OF CASE: Certiorari review of constitutionality of enforcing a racially related restrictive covenant in the sale of real property.

FACT SUMMARY: Kraemer (P) sought to void a sale of real property to Shelley (D) from a Mr. Fitzgerald, relying on a racially restrictive covenant.

RULE OF LAW

Judicial enforcement of a private racially restrictive covenant is considered state action for Fourteenth Amendment purposes.

FACTS: In 1911, 30 out of a total of 39 owners of area property signed an agreement, which was subsequently recorded, providing in part that the property could not be used or occupied by anyone of "the Negro or Mongolian race" for a period of 50 years. This covenant was to be valid whether it was included in future conveyances or not and was to attach to the land as a condition precedent to the sale of the property. Shelley (D), a Black man, purchased a parcel of land subject to the restrictive covenant from a Mr. Fitzgerald. Kraemer (P), an owner of other property subject to the terms of the restrictive covenant, brought suit in the circuit court of St. Louis to enjoin Shelley (D) from taking possession of the property. The trial court held for Shelley (D) and the Supreme Court granted certiorari.

ISSUE: Is judicial enforcement of a private racially restrictive covenant considered state action for Fourteenth Amendment purposes?

HOLDING AND DECISION: (Vinson, C.J.) Yes. Judicial enforcement of a private racially restrictive covenant is considered state action for Fourteenth Amendment purposes. Because the restrictive covenants did not involve any action by the state legislature or city council, the restrictive covenant itself did not violate any rights protected by the Fourteenth Amendment, since it was strictly a private covenant. But the judicial enforcement of the covenant did qualify as state action. From the time of the adoption of the Fourteenth Amendment until the present, the Court has consistently ruled that the action of the states to which the amendment has reference includes action of state courts and state judicial officers. In this case because there was a willing buyer and seller, Shelley (D) would have been able to enforce the restrictive covenants only with the active intervention of the state courts. Kraemer's (P) argument that since the state courts would enforce restrictive covenants excluding White persons from ownership of property, there was no denial of equal protection is rejected. Equal protection of the law is not achieved through indiscriminate imposition of inequalities. As to Kraemer's (P) contention that he was being denied equal protection of the laws because his restrictive covenant was not being enforced, the Constitution does not confer the right to demand action by the state that would result in the denial of equal protection of the laws to other individuals. Therefore, in granting judicial enforcement of the restrictive agreement, the state has denied Shelley (D) equal protection of the laws and the action of the state courts cannot stand. The enjoyment of property rights, free from discrimination by the states, was among the objectives sought to be effectuated by the Framers of the Fourteenth Amendment. Reversed.

ANALYSIS

The Court in its post-*Shelley v. Kraemer* decisions has given this decision a fairly narrow reading. A broad reading of this case requires that whenever a state court enforces a private racially restrictive covenant, such action constitutes state action that is forbidden by the Fourteenth Amendment. In cases where the ruling in this case could have been found to be applicable, the Court has used a different rationale. Some of the Court's statements suggest that more state involvement than evenhanded enforcement of private biases was necessary to find unconstitutional state action. Justice Black, in a dissenting opinion, stated that the decision in this case only is applicable in cases involving property rights.

Quicknotes

EQUAL PROTECTION Guarantee under the Fourteenth Amendment to the U.S. Constitution that the government must treat each person or class of persons the same as it treats other persons or classes of persons in like circumstances.

FOURTEENTH AMENDMENT Declares that no state shall make or enforce any law that shall abridge the privileges and immunities of citizens of the United States; no state shall deny to any person within its jurisdiction the equal protection of the laws.

Continued on next page.

RACIALLY RESTRICTIVE COVENANT A provision contained in a deed that discriminates on the basis of race by limiting those persons entitled to use of the property.

RESTRICTIVE COVENANT A provision contained in a deed to limit the uses to which the property will be made.

STATE ACTION An action taken by the state or with sufficient connection to the state so as to be attributed to it; such action is subject to judicial scrutiny for violation of due process and equal protection rights guaranteed by the Fourteenth Amendment to the U.S. Constitution.

Jackson v. Metropolitan Edison Co.

Customer (P) v. Utility company (D)

419 U.S. 345 (1974)

NATURE OF CASE: Certiorari review of alleged state action in violation of constitutional rights.

FACT SUMMARY: Jackson (P) claimed that the privately owned utility company Metropolitan Edison Co.'s (D) action in terminating service to her for nonpayment without notice, a hearing, or an opportunity to pay constituted state action and violated due process.

RULE OF LAW

The mere fact that a business is subject to state regulation does not necessarily transform its actions into those of the state for the purposes of the Fourteenth Amendment.

FACTS: [Metropolitan Edison Co. (Metropolitan) (D) is a privately owned utility that holds a certificate of public convenience. The certificate is issued by the state's Public Utility Commission and empowers Metropolitan (D) to deliver electricity. According to a provision of Metropolitan's (D) general tariff filed with the commission, Metropolitan's (D) has the right to terminate electricity to a customer for nonpayment. Metropolitan (D) terminated Jackson's (P) electric service for nonpayment. Jackson (P) claims that this constituted state action and because it was done without notice, a hearing, or an opportunity to pay, such action deprived her of her property (her alleged right to reasonably continuous electrical service) without due process. The lower courts dismissed Jackson's (P) complaint.]

ISSUE: Does the mere fact that a business is subject to state regulation necessarily transform its actions into those of the state for the purposes of the Fourteenth Amendment?

HOLDING AND DECISION: (Rehnquist, J.) No. The mere fact that a business is subject to state regulation does not necessarily transform its actions into those of the state for the purposes of the Fourteenth Amendment. Evidence showing a heavily regulated private utility, enjoying at least a partial monopoly in the providing of electrical service, which elected to terminate service to a customer in a manner found by the state public utilities commission to be permissible under state law, does not demonstrate a sufficiently close nexus between the state and the utility's action to make that action state action. Nor does the fact that the utility company enjoys a monopoly make its action state action. It's true that the services of Metropolitan Edison Co. (Metropolitan) (D) affect the public interest. However, the actions of all businesses that affect the public interest cannot be called state action. Metropolitan (D) is not performing a public function since state law imposes no obligation on the state to furnish utility service. Finally, the state Public Utility Commission's approval of Metropolitan's (D) tariff merely constituted a finding by the Commission that Metropolitan's (D) termination procedure was permissible under state law. It did not convert Metropolitan's (D) actions into state actions. Hence the evidence did not demonstrate a sufficiently close nexus between the state and Metropolitan's (D) action so that Metropolitan's (D) termination of services may be treated as state action. Affirmed.

DISSENT: (Marshall, J.) The Court's previous state-action cases have relied on factors that are clearly present in this case: a state-sanctioned monopoly, an extensive pattern of cooperation between the "private" entity and the state, and a service uniquely public in nature. The holding in this case would tend to repudiate these factors. State authorization and approval of "private" conduct support a finding of state action. The majority's analysis would seem to apply as well to a company that refused service to Blacks, welfare recipients, or any other group. I cannot believe this Court would hold that the state's involvement with Metropolitan Edison Co. (D) was not sufficient to require it not discriminate. However, nothing in the majority's analysis suggests otherwise.

ANALYSIS

In *Moose Lodge v. Irvis*, 407 U.S. 163 (1972), the lodge refused service to a Black guest of a lodge member. The guest claimed that although the lodge was a private club, its action was unconstitutional because it held a state liquor license. The Court held that the state was not sufficiently implicated in the lodge's discriminatory policies to make its action state action. The dissent argued that the "state was putting the weight of its liquor license, concededly a valued and important adjunct to a private club, behind racial discrimination."

Quicknotes

MONOPOLY A privilege or right conferred upon an individual or entity granting it the exclusive power to

Continued on next page.

manufacture, sell, and distribute a particular service or commodity; a market condition in which one or a few companies control the sale of a product or service thereby restraining competition in respect to that article or service.

PRIVATE FIGURE/CITIZEN An individual who does not hold a public office or who is not a member of the armed forces.

PUBLIC UTILITY A private business that provides a necessary service to the public.

STATE ACTION An action taken by the state or with sufficient connection to the state so as to be attributed to it; such action is subject to judicial scrutiny for violation of due process and equal protection rights guaranteed by the Fourteenth Amendment to the U.S. Constitution.

United States v. Guest

Federal government (P) v. Conspirators (D)

383 U.S. 745 (1966)

NATURE OF CASE: Certiorari review of dismissal of civil rights law indictment.

FACT SUMMARY: Guest (D) and others were charged with violating various civil rights of Black citizens in Georgia.

RULE OF LAW

Congress may constitutionally legislate to protect federal civil rights from private abridgment.

FACTS: Guest (D) and others were indicted under 18 U.S.C. § 241 with conspiring to deprive Black citizens of Georgia of the free exercise and enjoyment of "several specified rights secured by the Constitution and laws of the United States." Two counts of the indictment specifically charged them with: (1) preventing Black people from using public facilities maintained by the State of Georgia (protected by the Fourteenth Amendment); and (2) preventing Black people from using public highways and roads in interstate commerce (protected by the "right to travel"). From a dismissal of the indictments, the United States (P) appealed.

ISSUE: May Congress constitutionally legislate to protect federal civil rights from private abridgment?

HOLDING AND DECISION: (Stewart, J.) Yes. Congress may constitutionally legislate to protect federal civil rights from private abridgment. The Enabling Clause of the Fourteenth Amendment permits Congress to reach private action (e.g., conspiracy) that abridges Fourteenth Amendment rights so long as some active state involvement in such action is also present, but the right to travel is a right so fundamental to the concept of federal union that Congress has an inherent power to reach private action that abridges it independently. It is true that Fourteenth Amendment rights are broad and not fully delineated, but this does not justify preventing Congress from protecting those rights that are established on some kind of vagueness theory as the federal court below has done. The indictment below adequately sets out violations of federal civil rights that Congress is empowered to protect. The dismissal of the indictments below must be reversed, and the case remanded.

CONCURRENCE: (Clark, J.) The Enabling Clause of the Fourteenth Amendment permits Congress to ban wholly private action that abridges Fourteenth Amendment rights, regardless of the existence or nonexistence of state involvement.

CONCURRENCE AND DISSENT: (Brennan, J.) State action is not necessary for Congress to proscribe private conduct that abridges any "right secured by the Constitution." The Court above found that the possibility of state involvement with the alleged conspiracy to deny Black people access to Georgia public facilities was enough to sustain the indictment. Proof of such state action, difficult as it will be to provide, will undermine the ultimate prosecution of the case improperly. The Enabling Clause of the Fourteenth Amendment allows Congress to make any laws it reasonably believes necessary to the enforcement of that Amendment. Clearly, preventing private conspiracies that deny equal use of public facilities to Black people is within the scope of that clause.

ANALYSIS

This case demonstrates the continuous expansion of the Enabling Clause of the Fourteenth Amendment to permit Congress to reach wholly private acts of discrimination with its laws. In 1945, in *Screws v. United States*, 325 U.S. 91 (1945), the Court upheld federal legislation that punished state officials who acted "under color of state law." In 1966, in *United States v. Price*, 383 U.S. 787 (1966), the Court upheld federal legislation that punished private individuals who acted jointly with state officials to abridge the civil rights of others. In *Guest*, a majority of the Court (six Justices: Brennan, Warren, Douglas, Clark, Black, and Fortas) approved the power of Congress to punish wholly private action that serves to abridge civil rights of others. Note that the conduct that the Fourteenth Amendment's Enabling Clause allows Congress to proscribe is not necessarily unconstitutional itself (i.e., no state action) but merely is such as might result in deprivation of some constitutional right.

Quicknotes

ABRIDGMENT A diminishing or curtailing of rights.

ENABLING CLAUSE OF THE FOURTEENTH AMENDMENT A constitutional provision granting the power to implement and enforce the law.

FEDERAL CIVIL RIGHTS Rights protected by the U.S. Constitution.

STATE ACTION An action taken by the state or with sufficient connection to the state so as to be attributed to it; such action is subject to judicial scrutiny for violation of due process and equal protection rights guaranteed by the Fourteenth Amendment to the U.S. Constitution.

Jones v. Alfred H. Mayer Co.

Buyer (P) v. Real estate company (D)

392 U.S. 409 (1968)

NATURE OF CASE: Certiorari review of private action of refusal of property owners to sell to Black people.

FACT SUMMARY: Jones (P) brought suit in federal district court against the Alfred H. Mayer Co. (D) alleging that Mayer (D) refused to sell a home to him for the sole reason that Jones (P) was a Black man.

RULE OF LAW

Congress, pursuant to the authority vested in it by the Thirteenth Amendment, which clothes "Congress with power to pass all laws necessary and proper for abolishing all badges and incidents of slavery," may validly bar all racial discrimination, private as well as public, in the sale or rental of property.

FACTS: Relying upon 42 U.S.C. § 1982 (all citizens have the same right to inherit, purchase, lease, hold, and convey real and personal property as is enjoyed by White citizens), Jones (P) brought suit in federal district court against the Alfred H. Mayer Co. (Mayer) (D) alleging that Mayer (D) refused to sell a home to him for the sole reason that Jones (P) was a Black man. The lower courts dismissed Jones's (P) complaint.

ISSUE: May Congress, pursuant to the authority vested in it by the Thirteenth Amendment, which clothes "Congress with power to pass all laws necessary and proper for abolishing all badges and incidents of slavery," validly bar all racial discrimination, private as well as public, in the sale or rental of property?

HOLDING AND DECISION: (Stewart, J.) Yes. Congress, pursuant to the authority vested in it by the Thirteenth Amendment, which clothes "Congress with power to pass all laws necessary and proper for abolishing all badges and incidents of slavery," may validly bar all racial discrimination, private as well as public, in the sale or rental of property. 42 U.S.C. § 1982 is only a limited attempt to deal with discrimination in a select area of real estate transactions, even though, on its face, § 1982 appears to prohibit all discrimination against Black people in the sale or rental of property. If § 1982, originally enacted as § 1 of the Civil Rights Act of 1866 (the 1866 Act), had been intended to grant nothing more than an immunity from governmental interference, then much of § 2 of the 1866 Act, which provides for criminal penalties where a person has acted "under color" of any law, would have been meaningless. The broad language of § 1982 was intentional. In 1866, Congress had before it considerable evidence showing private mistreatment of Black people. The focus of Congress, then, was on private groups (e.g., the Ku Klux Klan) operating outside the law. At the very least, the Thirteenth Amendment includes the freedom to buy whatever a White person can buy, and the right to live wherever a White person can live. Reversed.

DISSENT: (Harlan, J.) The term "right" in 42 U.S.C. § 1982 operates only against state-sanctioned discrimination. There is a difference between depriving a person of a right and interfering with the enjoyment of that right in a particular case. The enforcement provisions of the Civil Rights Act of 1866 talk of "law, statute, ordinance, regulation, or custom." As for legislative history, residential racial segregation was the norm in 1866. The Court has always held that the Fourteenth Amendment reaches only "state action."

ANALYSIS

In *Sullivan v. Little Hunting Park, Inc.*, 396 U.S. 229 (1969), the Court invalidated a refusal by a homeowner's association to permit a member to assign his recreation share to a Black person. Once again, Justice Harlan in dissent questioned whether the Court should expand a century-old statute to encompass today's real estate transactions. After these two cases, it is questionable whether the Court will place any limits on its reading of the Thirteenth Amendment when reviewing legislation aimed at private discrimination.

Quicknotes

42 U.S.C. § 1982 "All citizens of the United States shall have the same right in every State and Territory, as is enjoyed by white citizens thereof to inherit, purchase, lease, sell, hold, and convey real and personal property."

STATE ACTION An action taken by the state or with sufficient connection to the state so as to be attributed to it; such action is subject to judicial scrutiny for violation of due process and equal protection rights guaranteed by the Fourteenth Amendment to the U.S. Constitution.

THIRTEENTH AMENDMENT The constitutional provision that abolished slavery in the United States.

Katzenbach v. Morgan

Voters (P) v. State (D)

384 U.S. 641 (1966)

NATURE OF CASE: Certiorari review of constitutionality of federal statute.

FACT SUMMARY: As part of the Voting Rights Act, Congress inserted a provision that prohibited restrictions on the right to register to vote and the applicant's inability to read and write English where the applicant had at least a sixth-grade education in a Puerto Rican school, where instruction was primarily in Spanish. New York had a statutory requirement of an ability to read and write English as a prerequisite to voter registration.

RULE OF LAW

A federal statute enacted pursuant to the Enabling Clause of the Fourteenth Amendment supersedes any state constitutional or statutory provision in conflict with the federal law.

FACTS: New York had a statute that required all persons seeking to register to vote be able to read and write the English language. In the Voting Rights Act of 1965, Congress inserted a provision that prohibited a requirement of the ability to read and write English where the person seeking to vote had completed at least a sixth-grade education in Puerto Rico, where the language of instruction is primarily Spanish. This suit was instituted by a group of registered voters in New York who challenged that the provision of the federal statute insofar as it would prohibit enforcement of the New York requirement. At issue were the several hundred thousand Puerto Rican immigrants in New York who were prevented from voting by the New York statute, but who would be qualified under the federal law. The Attorney General of New York filed a brief in which he argued that the federal legislation would supersede the state law only if the state law were found to violate the provisions of the Fourteenth Amendment, without reference to the federal statute. Also advanced was the argument that the federal statute violated the Equal Protection Clause of the Fourteenth Amendment since it discriminated between non-English-speaking persons from Puerto Rico and non-English-speaking persons from other countries.

ISSUE: Does a federal statute enacted pursuant to the Enabling Clause of the Fourteenth Amendment supersede any state constitutional or statutory provision in conflict with the federal law?

HOLDING AND DECISION: (Brennan, J.) Yes. A federal statute enacted pursuant to the Enabling Clause of the Fourteenth Amendment supersedes any state constitutional or statutory provision in conflict with the federal law. There is no need to determine if the New York English literacy law is violative of the Fourteenth Amendment Equal Protection Clause in order to validate the federal law respecting voter qualifications. If Congress were limited to restricting only those state laws that violated the Fourteenth Amendment, there would be no need for the federal law, since the state law could be invalidated in the courts. Rather, the test must be whether the federal legislation is appropriate to enforcement of the Equal Protection Clause. Section 5 of the Fourteenth Amendment is to be read to grant the same powers as the Necessary and Proper Clause of Article I, § 8. Therefore, the federal statute must be examined to see if it is "plainly adapted to that end" and whether it is not prohibited by but is consistent with "the letter and spirit of the Constitution." It was well within congressional authority to say that the need to vote by the Puerto Rican community warranted intrusion upon any state interests served by the English literacy test. The federal law was "plainly adapted" to furthering the aims of the Fourteenth Amendment. There is a perceivable basis for Congress to determine that this legislation was a proper way to resolve an inequity resulting from Congress's evaluation that an invidious discrimination existed. As to the contention that the federal law itself violates the Equal Protection Clause, the law does not restrict anyone's voting rights but rather extends the franchise to a previously ineligible group. This was a reform measure and Congress need not correct an entire evil with one law but may "take one step at a time, addressing itself" to that problem that seems most pressing. We hold, therefore, that the federal law was a proper exercise of the powers granted Congress by the Fourteenth Amendment and that the Supremacy Clause prevents enforcement of the New York statute insofar as it is inconsistent with the federal law. Reversed.

DISSENT: (Harlan, J.) The majority has confused the question of legislative enforcement power with the area of proper judicial review. The question here is whether the state law is so arbitrary or irrational as to violate the Equal Protection Clause. And that is a judicial, not legislative, determination. The majority has validated a legislative determination by Congress that a state law is violative of the Constitution. There is no record of any evidence secured by Congress to support this determination.

Continued on next page.

The judiciary is the ultimate arbiter of constitutionality, not Congress.

ANALYSIS

As has occurred before, there was a footnote to the decision that caused as much controversy as the decision itself. In this footnote, the Court stated that Congress could enact legislation giving force to the Fourteenth Amendment that expanded the rights provided in the Amendment but could not dilute or restrict the Amendment by legislation. In other words, Congress can make determinations of constitutionality so long as they expand rights but cannot make those determinations if they restrict rights. However, there is serious debate as to whether allowing Congress to take an independent role in interpreting the Constitution can be justified under any circumstances, in view of *Marbury v. Madison*, 5 U.S. (1 Cranch) 137 (1803). Once allowed in this area, can any restraint be thereafter imposed? Congress has traditionally tried to stay within judicially circumscribed bounds of constitutionality. But, if it has an "independent role" in this area, the restraints are removed. An example is shown in the Omnibus Crime Control Act, where Congress made legislative inroads to judicially granted rights as expressed in the *Miranda* decision, 384 U.S. 436 (1966). The Court can always rule on these inroads, but is it not better that Congress is not encouraged to embark on them in the first case?

Quicknotes

ENABLING CLAUSE OF THE FOURTEENTH AMENDMENT "The Congress shall have the power to enforce, by appropriate legislation, the provisions of this article."

SUPREMACY CLAUSE Article VI, § 2 of the Constitution, which provides that federal action must prevail over inconsistent state action.

City of Boerne v. Flores

City (D) v. Archbishop (P)

521 U.S. 507 (1997)

NATURE OF CASE: Certiorari review of the constitutionality of the Religious Freedom Restoration Act of 1993.

FACT SUMMARY: The City of Boerne (D) denied Archbishop Flores (P) a building permit to expand his church. Archbishop Flores (D) contended that the permit denial violated the Religious Freedom Restoration Act.

RULE OF LAW

The Religious Freedom Restoration Act of 1993 unconstitutionally exceeds Congress's enforcement power under the Due Process Clause of the Fourteenth Amendment.

FACTS: The Religious Freedom Restoration Act of 1993 (the RFRA) prohibited the government from substantially burdening a person's exercise of religion, even if the burden is the result of a generally applicable law, unless the government has a compelling interest and is using the least restrictive means. The City of Boerne (Boerne) (D) enacted a city ordinance requiring city preapproval for any construction on any of the city's historic landmarks. Archbishop Flores (P) sought a building permit to expand his church, a historic landmark. Boerne (D) denied the permit and Flores (P) sued, invoking the RFRA. The district court determined that the RFRA exceeded congressional power, but the Fifth Circuit Court of Appeals reversed, holding the RFRA constitutional. Boerne (D) appealed.

ISSUE: Does the Religious Freedom Restoration Act of 1993 unconstitutionally exceed Congress's enforcement power under the Due Process Clause of the Fourteenth Amendment?

HOLDING AND DECISION: (Kennedy, J.) Yes. The Religious Freedom Restoration Act of 1993 (RFRA) unconstitutionally exceeds Congress's enforcement power under the Due Process Clause of the Fourteenth Amendment. Here, Congress, with the RFRA, attempts to replace, with the compelling interest test, this Court's decision asserting that the compelling interest test is inappropriate in cases involving general prohibitions with free exercise challenges. See *Employment Div., Oregon Dept. of Human Resources v. Smith*, 494 U.S. 872 (1990). Such an action violates the long tradition of the separation of powers established by the Constitution. The judiciary is to determine the constitutionality of laws and the powers of the legislature are defined and limited. While Congress can enact remedial, preventive legislation that deters violations, the RFRA is not a preventive law. Instead, the RFRA redefines the scope of the Free Exercise Clause and nothing in our history extends to Congress the ability to take such action. The RFRA is so out of proportion to a supposed remedial or preventive object that it cannot be regarded as a response to unconstitutional behavior. Reversed.

ANALYSIS

The Religious Freedom Restoration Act of 1993 (the RFRA) was one of the four federal laws overturned by the Supreme Court during its 1997 term. Although the Court has endorsed judicial restraint in recent years, it has not hesitated to quash improper intrusions on its authority to set unconstitutional standards. The Court, however, chose not to revisit the religious freedom issue in its *Boerne* decision, leaving intact the ruling in *Employment Div., Oregon Dept. of Human Resources v. Smith*, 494 U.S. 872 (1990), which inspired Congress to pass the RFRA. In *Smith*, the Court approved Oregon's use of its ban on peyote to prohibit the drug's use in Native American religious rituals. The RFRA was intended to guarantee religious observance a higher degree of statutory protection than the *Smith* Court thought necessary.

Quicknotes

DUE PROCESS CLAUSE Language in the Fifth and Fourteenth Amendments to the U.S. Constitution providing that no person shall be deprived of "life, liberty, or property, without due process of law."

FOURTEENTH AMENDMENT Fourteenth Amendment Declares that no state shall make or enforce any law that shall abridge the privileges and immunities of citizens of the United States; no state shall deny to any person within its jurisdiction the equal protection of the laws.

FREE EXERCISE CLAUSE The guarantee of the First Amendment to the U.S. Constitution prohibiting Congress from enacting laws regarding the establishment of religion or prohibiting the free exercise thereof.

Shelby County v. Holder

State political subdivision (P) v. Federal government official (D)

570 U.S. 529 (2013)

NATURE OF CASE: Appeal from judgment upholding the constitutionality of §§ 4(b) and 5 of the Voting Rights Act of 1965.

FACT SUMMARY: Shelby County, Alabama (P), which was covered by § 4(b) of the Voting Rights Act of 1965 (the Act), contended that §§ 4(b) and 5 of the Act were facially unconstitutional.

RULE OF LAW

The coverage formula in § 4(b) of the Voting Rights Act of 1965 is facially unconstitutional.

FACTS: The Voting Rights Act of 1965 (the Act) was enacted to address entrenched racial discrimination in voting. Only some jurisdictions are covered by some of the Act's provisions. Section 4(b) of the Act provides a "coverage formula" defining the "covered jurisdictions" as states or political subdivisions that maintained tests or devices as prerequisites to voting and that had low voter registration or turnout in the 1960s and early 1970s. In those covered jurisdictions, § 5 of the Act provides that no change in voting procedures can take effect until approved by either the Department of Justice or a three-judge district court. Such approval is known as "preclearance." The coverage formula and preclearance requirement were initially set to expire after five years, but the Act has been reauthorized several times. In 2006, the Act was reauthorized for an additional 25 years, but the coverage formula was not changed. Coverage still turned on whether a jurisdiction had a voting test in the 1960s or 1970s and had low voter registration or turnout at that time. [Shortly after the 2006 reauthorization, a Texas utility district sought to bail out from the Act's coverage and, in the alternative, challenged the Act's constitutionality. In *Northwest Austin Municipal Util. Dist. No. One v. Holder*, 557 U.S. 193 (2009), the Supreme Court avoided the constitutional issue on statutory grounds but expressed serious doubts about the Act's continued constitutionality. Shelby County (P), a covered jurisdiction in Alabama, sought a declaratory judgment that §§ 4(b) and 5 are facially unconstitutional, as well as a permanent injunction against their enforcement. The court of appeals upheld those sections constitutionality, and the United States Supreme Court granted certiorari.]

ISSUE: Is the coverage formula in § 4(b) of the Voting Rights Act of 1965 facially unconstitutional?

HOLDING AND DECISION: (Roberts, C.J.) Yes. The coverage formula in § 4(b) of the Voting Rights Act of 1965 (the Act) is facially unconstitutional. A departure from the fundamental principle of equal sovereignty requires a showing that a statute's disparate geographic coverage is sufficiently related to the problem that it targets. States retain broad autonomy in structuring their governments and pursuing legislative objectives, and the Tenth Amendment reserves to the states all powers not specifically granted to the federal government, including the power to regulate elections. The states are also equally sovereign, and under the principle and tradition of equal sovereignty, there must be an exceptional circumstance justifying disparate treatment of the states. The Act sharply departs from these basic principles. It requires states to beseech the federal government for permission to implement laws that they would otherwise have the right to enact and execute on their own. Despite the tradition of equal sovereignty, the Act applies to only nine states (and additional counties). In 1966, the Court upheld the Act, concluding that such an uncommon exercise of congressional power could be justified by exceptional conditions. In 1966, these departures were justified by the blight of racial discrimination in voting that had infected the electoral process in parts of our country for nearly a century. At the time, the covered jurisdictions shared two characteristics: the use of tests and devices for voter registration, and a voting rate in the 1964 presidential election at least 12 points below the national average. Nearly 50 years later, things have changed dramatically. Largely because of the Voting Rights Act, voter turnout and registration rates in covered jurisdictions have approached parity. African American voter turnout is mostly equal to—or even exceeds—White voter turnout. Blatantly discriminatory evasions of federal decrees are rare and minority candidates hold office at unprecedented levels. The tests and devices that blocked ballot access have been forbidden nationwide for over 40 years. The Act, which undoubtedly has contributed to these significant changes, however, has not reflected the changes. It has not eased § 5's restrictions or narrowed the scope of § 4's coverage formula along the way. Instead, those extraordinary and unprecedented features have been reauthorized as if nothing has changed. Moreover, the fact that § 5's deterrence effect has contributed to salutary changes does not immunize it from scrutiny. Because § 5 applies only to those jurisdictions singled out by § 4, it must be determined whether that provision is constitutional in light of current conditions. Coverage today is based on decades-old data and eradicated practices and is no longer rational in theory and practice. The formula captures states by

Continued on next page.

reference to literacy tests and low voter registration and turnout in the 1960s and early 1970s. The literacy tests have been banned for over 40 years, and voter registration and turnout numbers in covered states have risen dramatically. The Fifteenth Amendment is not designed to punish for the past; its purpose is to ensure a better future. To serve that purpose, Congress—if it is to divide the states—must identify those jurisdictions to be singled out on a basis that makes sense in light of current conditions. The Government (D) also relies heavily on data from the record compiled by Congress before reauthorizing the Act. However, Congress did not use that record to fashion a coverage formula grounded in current conditions. It instead re-enacted a formula based on 40-year-old facts having no logical relation to the present day. Congress could have updated the formula to reflect current conditions but failed to do so. For these reasons, § 4(b) is unconstitutional and must be struck down. That conclusion, however, does not affect the Act's other provisions, and Congress is free to draft another formula based on current conditions.

CONCURRENCE: (Thomas, J.) Section 5 of the Voting Rights Act of 1965 is also unconstitutional and should be struck down. The majority opinion compellingly demonstrates that Congress has failed to justify current burdens with a record demonstrating current needs, and it is just a matter of time before § 5 will be struck down; there is no need to prolong that inevitability.

DISSENT: (Ginsburg, J.) The majority usurps Congress's power to determine whether, as currently operative, § 5 of the Voting Rights Act of 1965 (the Act) remains justifiable. Congress decided that § 5 should continue in force because it would facilitate completion of the gains made thus far, and because it would prevent backsliding. Notwithstanding that the majority acknowledges discrimination exists today, it jettisons the very remedy that proved to be best suited to block that discrimination. The Act, through the preclearance mechanism, worked where other attempted remedies failed. There also are in place numerous second-generation barriers to minority voting that go beyond voter registration and involve vote dilution, such as racial gerrymandering or the adoption of at-large voting, and the Court has long recognized that vote dilution, when adopted with a discriminatory purpose, cuts down the right to vote as certainly as denial of access to the ballot. Congress studied the problem of racial discrimination prior to reauthorizing the Act and compiled a compelling record that presents countless "examples of flagrant racial discrimination" since the last reauthorization; Congress also brought to light systematic evidence that "intentional racial discrimination in voting remains so serious and widespread in covered jurisdictions that section 5 preclearance is still needed." *Shelby County, Alabama v. Holder*, 679 F.3d 848, 866. It is well established that Congress must be given substantial deference in enforcing the Fourteenth and Fifteenth Amendments. Congress's power is at its height when dealing with invidious discrimination, and the deference it is owed is a matter of both the Constitution's text and precedent. The Civil War Amendments armed Congress with the power and authority to protect all persons within the Nation from violations of their rights by the states, and in exercising that power, Congress may use "all means which are appropriate, which are plainly adapted" to the constitutional ends declared by these Amendments. *McCulloch v. Maryland*, 4 Wheat. 316, 421 (1819). Congress may use any rational means to effectuate the constitutional prohibition of racial discrimination in voting, and if the means is rational, the Court may not question whether it is wise and substitute its judgment for Congress's. Here, Congress received considerable evidence that preclearance was still effectively preventing discriminatory changes to voting laws, as well as that § 2 alone was an inadequate substitute for preclearance in the covered jurisdictions. Because § 2 is enforced through litigation, after the fact, preclearance reduces the monetary burden on minorities of pursuing such litigation, as well as on the covered jurisdictions themselves, because the preclearance process is far less costly than defending against a § 2 claim, and clearance by the Department of Justice substantially reduces the likelihood that a § 2 claim, will be mounted. Prior to the reauthorization, there were numerous attempted electoral changes that were stopped through preclearance, suggesting that § 5 effectively protected minority voting rights. Congress appropriately considered the long history of voting discrimination in the covered jurisdictions, and to avoid rigidity, it provided a mechanism for a covered jurisdiction to bail out—upon a showing that it had complied with the Act for ten years and had engaged in efforts to eliminate intimidation and harassment of voters. Further, the majority's use of the equal sovereignty principle in this case is misplaced. That principle has been unequivocally held to apply only to the terms upon which states are admitted to the Union. The majority's unprecedented extension of the equal sovereignty principle outside its proper domain—the admission of new states—is capable of much mischief.

ANALYSIS

Although the Court purports to declare unconstitutional only the coverage formula set out in § 4(b), without that formula § 5 is effectively immobilized. Thus, this decision essentially guts the Voting Rights Act's enforcement mechanism, and with it, Congress's power (absent new legislation) to realize the goals of the Civil War Amendments.

Continued on next page.

Quicknotes

CERTIORARI A discretionary writ issued by a superior court to an inferior court in order to review the lower court's decisions; the United States Supreme Court's writ ordering such review.

DECLARATORY JUDGMENT A judgment of the court establishing the rights of the parties.

Brnovich v. Democratic National Committee

State official (D) v. Political party's national committee (P)

594 U.S.__, 2021 WL 2690267 (2021)

NATURE OF CASE: Appeal in action challenging a state's time, place, and manner voting regulations as violating § 2 of the Voting Rights Act of 1965 and the Fifteenth Amendment.

FACT SUMMARY: The Democratic National Committee (P) challenged certain time, place, and manner voting regulations enacted by Arizona (D) as violating § 2 of the Voting Rights Act of 1965 and the Fifteenth Amendment, contending that the regulations made it more difficult to vote and discriminated against minorities.

RULE OF LAW

A facially neutral state time, place, and manner voting regulation that incidentally has a disparate impact on minorities does not violate § 2 of the Voting Rights Act of 1965 or the Fifteenth Amendment.

FACTS: The Democratic National Committee (P) challenged certain time, place, and manner voting regulations enacted by Arizona (D), such as the regulation of where and how long polls are open, when voters can register, rules for absentee ballots, and voter identification requirements, as violating § 2 of the Voting Rights Act of 1965 and the Fifteenth Amendment, contending that the regulations made it more difficult to vote and discriminated against minorities. In 1982, Congress amended the language in § 2 that had been interpreted to require proof of discriminatory intent by a plurality of the Supreme Court in *Mobile v. Bolden,* 446 U.S. 55 (1980). In place of that language, § 2(a) now provides that: "No voting qualification or prerequisite to voting or standard, practice, or procedure shall be imposed or applied by any State or political subdivision in a manner which results in a denial or abridgement of the right . . . to vote on account of race or color." Section 2(b) in turn explains what must be shown to establish a § 2 violation. Section 2(b) states that § 2 is violated only where "based on the totality of the circumstances, it is shown that the political processes leading to nomination or election" are not "equally open to participation" by members of the relevant protected group "in that its members have less opportunity than other members of the electorate to participate in the political process and to elect representatives of their choice." In amending § 2, Congress sought to reject the intent test and substitute a test of fair equal opportunity to vote, focusing on the results of a state voting practice. *Thornburg v. Gingles,* 478 U.S. 30 (1986). The Supreme Court granted certiorari in the case.

ISSUE: Does a facially neutral state time, place, and manner voting regulation that incidentally has a disparate impact on minorities violate § 2 of the Voting Rights Act of 1965 or the Fifteenth Amendment?

HOLDING AND DECISION: (Alito, J.) No. A facially neutral state time, place, and manner voting regulation that incidentally has a disparate impact on minorities does not violate § 2 of the Voting Rights Act of 1965 or the Fifteenth Amendment. The size of the burden imposed by a challenged voting regulation is highly relevant to determining whether it violates § 2. Voting necessarily requires some effort and compliance with some rules; thus, the concept of a voting system that is "equally open" and that furnishes equal "opportunity" to cast a ballot must tolerate the usual burdens of voting; mere inconvenience is insufficient. Another relevant consideration is the degree to which a voting rule departs from what was standard practice when § 2 was amended in 1982. The burdens associated with the rules in effect at that time are useful in gauging whether the burdens imposed by a challenged rule are sufficient to prevent voting from being equally "open" or furnishing an equal "opportunity" to vote in the sense meant by § 2. Based on that 1982 environment, it is doubtful Congress intended to uproot facially neutral time, place, and manner regulations that have a long pedigree or are in widespread use in the United States. Another important factor to consider is the size of any disparities in a rule's impact on members of different racial or ethnic groups. To the extent that minority and non-minority groups differ with respect to employment, wealth, and education, even neutral regulations may well result in disparities in rates of voting and noncompliance with voting rules. The mere fact that there is some disparity in impact does not necessarily mean that a system is not equally open or that it does not give everyone an equal opportunity to vote. The strength of the state interests—such as the strong and entirely legitimate state interest in preventing election fraud—served by a challenged voting rule is yet another important factor to consider. In determining whether a rule goes too far "based on the totality of circumstances," rules that are supported by strong state interests are less likely to violate § 2. Further, there is no footing in the text of § 2 that requires the Court to adopt a least-restrictive means requirement that would force a state to prove that the interest served by its voting rule could not be accomplished in any other less burdensome way. To do so would

Continued on next page.

have the effect of invalidating a great many neutral voting regulations with long pedigrees that are reasonable means of pursuing legitimate interests. It would also transfer much of the authority to regulate election procedures from the states to the federal courts. Notwithstanding any disparate burden caused by Arizona's (D) law, Arizona's (D) interest in preventing election fraud would save it from § 2 liability, since a state has a compelling interest in preserving the integrity of the election process. The dissent, however, looks only at disparate impact, rather than looking at the "totality" of the circumstances. Under the dissent's approach, states would be deprived of their authority to establish nondiscriminatory voting rules, and impermissibly effect a wholesale transfer of the authority to set voting rules from the states to the federal courts.

DISSENT: (Kagan, J.) The majority undermines § 2 and the rights it was intended to provide by giving it a cramped reading. The majority then uses that very narrow reading to validate voting regulations that discriminate against minority voters. Instead of furthering the goal of § 2 to end discrimination in voting, the majority thwarts that goal. And the majority does this in an era of voting-rights retrenchment, when many states and localities are restricting voting access in ways that will predictably deprive members of minority groups of equal access to voting. The majority clearly is wrong to think that what was standard practice when § 2 was amended in 1982 is a relevant consideration in a § 2 analysis. The 1982 state of the world is no part of the § 2 test. An election rule prevalent at that time may make voting harder for minority than for White citizens, so § 2 then covers such a rule, as it is supposed to cover any other. Contrary to the majority's unsupported speculation, Congress intended exactly that; Congress wanted the Voting Rights Act (the Act) to eradicate the numerous practices and procedures that act as continued barriers to registration and voting. Section 2 was meant to disrupt the status quo, not to preserve it—to eradicate then-current discriminatory practices, not to "set them in amber." Throughout American history, election officials have asserted anti-fraud interests in using voter suppression laws. Poll taxes are a classic example. Poll taxes, which kept Black people from voting, were often justified as necessary for honest elections. There have been numerous such examples, so many, that it seems that states have always found it natural to wrap discriminatory policies in "election-integrity garb." Congress intended for § 2 to prevent such measures from working, and wanted it to apply to all laws, even facially neutral ones, that resulted in members of minority groups having unequal, and diminished, access to voting and the political process. The majority does not see it that way. Instead, it finds that a statute that would remove such discriminatory laws is "radical." It sees that such a statute would be an excessive, and undemocratic, transfer of authority to set voting rules from the states to the federal courts. However, in light of history, the majority is clearly wrong in its paean to state authority and its denigration of federal responsibility for ensuring voting rules that do not discriminate against minorities. The text of the Act does not uphold states' rights against federal courts; it upholds the right of every American, of every race, to have equal access to the ballot box. The majority undermines that right by refusing to apply the plain terms of the Act, by declaring some racially discriminatory burdens inconsequential, and by refusing to subject asserted state interests to serious means-end scrutiny. In sum, the majority enables voting discrimination.

ANALYSIS

Prior to deciding this case, the Court, in *Shelby County v. Holder,* 570 U.S. 529 (2013), held that a list of covered jurisdictions contained in § 4(b) of the Voting Rights Act of 1965 (the Act) was unconstitutional. Section 5 of the Act required that those jurisdictions, because of their history of enacting voting rules that discriminated against minorities, had to preclear any changes to their voting systems with the federal Department of Justice or a three-judge district court in Washington, D.C. By invalidating § 4(b), the Court effectively gutted § 5, which left only § 2 as a national guard against racial discrimination in voting. Justice Kagan, in her dissent, notes that almost immediately after *Shelby County* was handed down, states and localities put in place new restrictive voting laws and policies, with numerous barriers to voting, and with foreseeably adverse effects on minority voters. For these reasons, Justice Kagan sees that § 2, which Congress never meant to bear all of the weight of the Act's commitments, and which was supposed to be a backup to §§ 4(b) and 5, "is what voters have left." Given the majority's decision in *Brnovich,* it is unclear that even a weakened § 2 will be able to effectively prevent discrimination in voting throughout the nation.

Quicknotes

POLL TAX A tax imposed upon each person within a jurisdiction. Under the Twenty-fourth Amendment state and federal governments may not impose a poll tax as a condition to voting.

TIME, PLACE, AND MANNER RESTRICTION Certain types of regulations on speech that are permissible since they restrict only the time, place, and manner in which the speech may occur.

United States v. Morrison

Federal government (P) v. Students (D)

529 U.S. 598 (2000)

NATURE OF CASE: Certiorari review of the constitutionality of the federal Violence Against Women Act.

FACT SUMMARY: Brzonkala (P) brought suit against two football-playing male students (D) and Virginia Polytechnic University under the Violence Against Women Act.

RULE OF LAW

Section 13891 of the Violence Against Women Act may not be upheld as an exercise of Congress's remedial power under § 5 of the Fourteenth Amendment.

FACTS: Brzonkala (P), a student at Virginia Polytechnic Institute (Virginia Tech), complained that football-playing students Morrison (D) and Crawford (D) assaulted and repeatedly raped her. Virginia Tech's Judicial Committee found insufficient evidence to punish Crawford (D), but it found Morrison (D) guilty of sexual assault and sentenced him to immediate suspension for two semesters. The school's vice president set this aside as excessive punishment. Brzonkala (P) then dropped out of the school and brought suit against the school and the male students (D) under the Violence Against Women Act, 42 U.S.C. § 13981, providing a federal cause of action of a crime of violence motivated by gender. The Supreme Court granted certiorari in the case.

ISSUE: May § 13891 of the Violence Against Women Act be upheld as an exercise of Congress's remedial power under § 5 of the Fourteenth Amendment?

HOLDING AND DECISION: (Rehnquist, C.J.) No. Section 13891 of the Violence Against Women Act may not be upheld as an exercise of Congress's remedial power under § 5 of the Fourteenth Amendment. This case requires the Court to address the constitutionality of 42 U.S.C. § 13981. One issue presented is that § 5 of the Fourteenth Amendment authorized the statutory cause of action under Congress's remedial power. This argument is based on the assertion that there is pervasive bias in various state justice systems against victims of gender-motivated violence and that assertion is supported by a voluminous congressional record. It is argued that this bias denies victims of gender-motivated violence of equal protection of the laws, and that Congress therefore acted appropriately by providing a remedy that would address such bias by the states and deter future instances of discrimination in the state courts. While sex discrimination is one of the objects of the Fourteenth Amendment, the Amendment prohibits only state action. In two cases—*United States v. Harris*, 106 U.S. 629 (1882), and the *Civil Rights Cases*, 109 U.S. 3 (1883)—the Court interpreted the Fourteenth Amendment's provisions and concluded that laws enacted to punish private persons were beyond the scope of Congress's § 5 power. Brzonkala (P) also argued that here there has been gender-disparate treatment by state officials, whereas in those cases there was no indication of state action. Section 13891 is unlike any of the § 5 remedies that this Court has previously upheld since it has no consequence on any public official involved in investigating or prosecuting Brzonkala's (P) assault. It is aimed only at individuals who have committed criminal acts motivated by gender bias. Section 13981 is also different from previously upheld remedies in that it applies uniformly throughout the nation, even though Congress's findings indicate that the problem addressed does not exist in all, or even most, states. Congress's power under § 5 does not extend to the enactment of § 13891. Affirmed.

DISSENT: (Breyer, J.) The Court's reasoning rejecting Congress's source of authority under § 5 of the Fourteenth Amendment is questionable. This Court has held that Congress may enact remedial legislation that prohibits conduct that is not itself unconstitutional. The remedy enacted by Congress intrudes little upon states or private parties, but it may lead state actors to improve their own remedial systems. It also imposes liability for private conduct that is already outlawed by state law. Therefore, the remedy is not "disproportionate." It is also not incongruent, given that it is a substitute for constitutionally inadequate state remedies. Additionally, although the majority asserts that the inadequacy of state remedies did not exist in all states, the record nowhere revealed that Congress concluded this was not a national problem. The majority for the first time thus holds that Congress must document the existence of a certain problem in every state prior to proposing a national solution. However, such a requirement is inappropriate given that under § 5, the Court must defer to Congress's chosen remedy.

ANALYSIS

The *Morrison* decision has been criticized on grounds it failed to seriously take into account the Fourteenth Amendment's history and the objectives the Reconstruction framers meant to achieve in giving Congress the power to enforce "equal protection of the laws" as well as basic guarantees of equal citizenship.

Continued on next page.

One aspect of the Amendment's history is that it was enacted in response to states abdicating their responsibilities to ensure the most basic equality by turning a blind eye to their own laws that would have punished private violence against African Americans and those who supported them. The legislative history of the Amendment clearly indicates that the Amendment was intended to give Congress the power to stop such private violence in the face of patent state neglect.

Quicknotes

EQUAL PROTECTION Guarantee under the Fourteenth Amendment to the U.S. Constitution that the government must treat each person or class of persons the same as it treats other persons or classes of persons in like circumstances.

FOURTEENTH AMENDMENT Declares that no state shall make or enforce any law that shall abridge the privileges and immunities of citizens of the United States; no state shall deny to any person within its jurisdiction the equal protection of the laws.

STATE ACTION An action taken by the state or with sufficient connection to the state so as to be attributed to it; such action is subject to judicial scrutiny for violation of due process and equal protection rights guaranteed by the Fourteenth Amendment to the U.S. Constitution.

CHAPTER **11**

Freedom of Speech—Categories of Speech—Degrees of Protected Expression

Quick Reference Rules of Law

	PAGE
1. *Schenck v. United States.* The test to determine the constitutionality of a statute restricting free speech is whether, under the circumstances, the speech is of such a nature as to create a clear and present danger that it will bring about the substantive evils that Congress has a right to prevent.	*202*
2. *Abrams v. United States.* The United States may constitutionally restrict speech that has the intended effect of hindering the United States in a war effort by means of riots and sedition.	*203*
3. *Masses Publishing Co. v. Patten.* An opinion critical of a draft statute, no matter how seditious in nature, cannot be deemed to be advocacy of the violation of that statute unless there is a direct urging of such violation.	*204*
4. *Gitlow v. New York.* Under its police powers, a state may validly forbid any speech or publication that has a tendency to produce action dangerous to public security, even where such speech or publication presents no clear and present danger to the security of the public.	*206*
5. *Whitney v. California.* A state may, in the exercise of its police power, punish abuses of freedom of speech where such utterances are inimical to the public welfare as tending to incite crime, disturb the peace, or endanger organized government through threats of violent overthrow.	*208*
6. *Dennis v. United States.* Where an offense is specified by a statute in nonspeech or nonpress terms, a conviction relying upon speech or press as evidence of violation may be sustained only when the speech or publication created a clear and present danger of attempting or accomplishing the prohibited crime.	*210*
7. *Brandenburg v. Ohio.* The constitutional guarantees of freedom of speech and freedom of press do not permit a state to forbid or proscribe advocacy of the use of force or of law violation except where such advocacy is directed to inciting or producing imminent lawless action and is likely to produce or incite such action.	*212*
8. *Chaplinsky v. New Hampshire.* A government may proscribe language tending to incite violence.	*213*
9. *Feiner v. New York.* When clear and present danger of riot, disorder, interference with traffic on the streets, or other immediate threat to public safety, peace, or order appears, the state has the power to punish or prevent such disorder.	*214*
10. *Cohen v. California.* A state cannot bar the use of offensive words either because such words are inherently likely to cause a violent reaction or because the state wishes to eliminate such words to protect the public morality.	*215*
11. *Beauharnais v. Illinois.* A statute that makes it a crime to libel the members of any class or group is not repugnant to the Constitution.	*216*
12. *New York Times Co. v. Sullivan.* Defamatory falsehoods regarding public officials have limited protection by constitutional guarantees of freedom of speech and press.	*217*
13. *Gertz v. Robert Welch, Inc.* In an action for defamation, a private individual must show the publisher to be at fault and may recover no more than actual damages when liability is not based on a showing of knowledge of falsity or reckless disregard for the truth.	*219*

CHAPTER 11

Schenck v. United States

Publisher (D) v. Federal government (P)

249 U.S. 47 (1919)

NATURE OF CASE: Certiorari review of federal statute restricting speech.

FACT SUMMARY: During a time of war, Schenck (D) mailed to draftees circulars that were calculated to cause insubordination in the armed services and to obstruct the U.S. recruiting and enlistment program in violation of military laws.

RULE OF LAW

The test to determine the constitutionality of a statute restricting free speech is whether, under the circumstances, the speech is of such a nature as to create a clear and present danger that it will bring about the substantive evils that Congress has a right to prevent.

FACTS: During a time of war, Schenck (D) mailed circulars to draftees. The circulars stated that the Conscription Act was unconstitutional and likened conscription to conviction. They intimated that conscription was a monstrous wrong against humanity in the interest of Wall Street's chosen few and described nonconscription arguments as coming from cunning politicians and a mercenary capitalist press. They urged: "Do not submit to intimidation," but advised only peaceful actions such as a petition to repeal the Conscription Act. Schenck (D) did not deny that the jury could find that the circulars could have no purpose except to influence draftees to obstruct the carrying out of the draft. Schenck was found guilty on charges of conspiracy and unlawful use of the mail.

ISSUE: Is the test to determine the constitutionality of a statute restricting free speech whether, under the circumstances, the speech is of such a nature as to create a clear and present danger that it will bring about the substantive evils that Congress has a right to prevent?

HOLDING AND DECISION: (Holmes, J.) Yes. The test to determine the constitutionality of a statute restricting free speech is whether, under the circumstances, the speech is of such a nature as to create a clear and present danger that it will bring about the substantive evils that Congress has a right to prevent. The character of every act depends on the circumstance in which it is done. The most stringent protection of free speech would not protect a person's falsely shouting fire in a theatre and causing a panic. It is a question of proximity and degrees. During a war, things that could be said during peaceful times may be such a hindrance to the war effort that they will not be permitted. Schenck's (D) convictions are affirmed.

ANALYSIS

The Court's first significant encounter with the problem of articulating the scope of constitutionally protected speech came in a series of cases involving agitation against the draft and war during World War I, *Schenck v. United States*, *Frohwerk v. United States*, 249 U.S. 204 (1919), and *Debs v. United States*, 249 U.S. 211 (1919). *Schenck* announces the "clear and present danger" test, the test for determining the validity of legislation regulating speech. In *Schenck*, Holmes rejected perfect immunity for speech. But he also rejected a far more restrictive, far more widely supported, alternative test: that "any tendency in speech to produce bad acts, no matter how remote, would suffice to validate a repressive statute."

Quicknotes

CLEAR AND PRESENT DANGER TEST Doctrine that restraints on freedom of speech are permissible if the speech incites persons to engage in unlawful conduct.

CONSPIRACY Concerted action by two or more persons to accomplish some unlawful purpose.

FREEDOM OF SPEECH The right to express oneself without governmental restrictions on the content of that expression.

Abrams v. United States

Russian immigrants (D) v. Federal government (P)

250 U.S. 616 (1919)

NATURE OF CASE: Certiorari review of speech restriction.

FACT SUMMARY: Russian immigrants (D) issued flyers that advocated a general strike in ammunition factories to prevent ammunition from being used against Russian revolutionaries.

RULE OF LAW

The United States may constitutionally restrict speech that has the intended effect of hindering the United States in a war effort by means of riots and sedition.

FACTS: During World War I, in 1918, the United States sent forces to Russia following the overthrow of the Czarist government as part of a strategic operation against Germany on the eastern front. Russian immigrants (D) to the United States circulated literature advocating a general strike in ammunition plants to hinder the U.S. effort, as they perceived it, to crush the revolutionary struggle in Russia. The Russians (D) were charged under the Espionage Act for inciting actions that hindered the U.S. war effort. Abrams (D) and others appealed.

ISSUE: May the United States constitutionally restrict speech that has the intended effect of hindering the United States in a war effort by means of riots and sedition?

HOLDING AND DECISION: (Clarke, J.) Yes. The United States may constitutionally restrict speech that has the intended effect of hindering the United States in a war effort by means of riots and sedition. Individuals may be held accountable for the intended consequences of their actions. While speech is protected by the Constitution, it is not without limits. When speech is intended to incite riots and rebellion in such a critical time as that of war, it cannot be given the protection normally accorded to speech in the United States. Here, the Russian immigrants (D) hoped to generate a sympathetic revolution in the United States for the purpose of defeating military plans in Europe. Such a goal was so contrary to the concerns of the United States during time of war that it could not be permitted to proceed. Affirmed.

DISSENT: (Holmes, J.) This decision deeply undermines the liberties that the First Amendment was drafted to protect. Expression of dissenting opinions is the very foundation of freedom. It is only the present danger of immediate evil or intent to bring it about that warrants Congress's setting a limit to expression of opinion. These convictions on the basis of two leaflets should not be sustained.

ANALYSIS

Holmes's famous dissent sounds as though it requires greater immediacy of threat than his opinion, a few months earlier, in *Schenck v. United States*, 249 U.S. 47 (1919), which articulated the clear and present danger test. Commentators have found support for this interpretation in other writings by Holmes. It appears that he realized the need to leave some element in place to protect speech, even while permitting some level of protection against dangerous speech.

Quicknotes

ESPIONAGE ACT Federal law prohibiting spying or other crimes.

FIRST AMENDMENT Prohibits Congress from enacting any law respecting an establishment of religion or prohibiting the free exercise of religion; or abridging the freedom of speech or of the press, the right of peaceful assembly, and the right to petition for a redress of grievances.

FREEDOM OF SPEECH The right to express oneself without governmental restrictions on the content of that expression.

SEDITION Unlawful action advocating the overthrow of the government.

Masses Publishing Co. v. Patten

Publishing company (P) v. Postmaster (D)

244 Fed. 535 (S.D.N.Y. 1917)

NATURE OF CASE: Action for preliminary injunction to require postmaster to accept magazine.

FACT SUMMARY: Patten (D) refused Masses Publishing Company's (P) magazine access through mails for violating the 1917 Espionage Act.

RULE OF LAW

An opinion critical of a draft statute, no matter how seditious in nature, cannot be deemed to be advocacy of the violation of that statute unless there is a direct urging of such violation.

FACTS: Masses Publishing Co. (Masses) (P) published a monthly magazine called "The Masses," which contained cartoons and text of a politically revolutionary nature. During the First World War, Masses (P) ran political material in the magazine violently attacking the draft and the war and expressing sympathy for conscientious objectors. In July of 1917, under directions from the Postmaster General, Patten (D), Postmaster of New York, told Masses (P) that their August issue would be denied use of the mails. Patten (D) stated that the magazine violated the Espionage Act of 1917 by (1) making false statements with the intent to interfere with the operation of the military forces of the United States; (2) arousing discontent among potential draftees and thereby promoting insubordination among troops already in the war; and (3) counseling resistance and disobedience to the law. Masses (P) brought this suit for a preliminary injunction against Patten's (D) refusal to accept the magazine in the mails.

ISSUE: Can an opinion critical of a draft statute, no matter how seditious in nature, be deemed to be advocacy of the violation of that statute if there is no direct urging of such violation?

HOLDING AND DECISION: (Hand, J.) No. An opinion critical of a draft statute, no matter how seditious in nature, cannot be deemed to be advocacy of the violation of that statute unless there is a direct urging of such violation. Unless there is some direct advocacy by a person for others to resist a particular law, then that person may not be held responsible for attempting to cause a violation of the law. Here, the publications of Masses Publishing Co. (Masses) (P) may have created national dissension and thereby assisted, indirectly, the cause of the enemy. But the statute in question provides that such publications be willfully false and made with the intent to interfere with military operations. The publications were mere opinions and not publications of facts. Thus, they fall within the scope of the right to criticize, normally the privilege of individuals in countries dependent on free expression of opinions as an ultimate source of authority. The statute was intended to prevent the spreading of false rumors embarrassing to the military, not the dissemination of inflammatory public opinion. It is also contended by Patten (D) that to allow Masses (P) to arouse discontent among the public as to the conduct of the war and draft causes insubordination among wartime troops. But to interpret the word "causes" too broadly would be to suppress all hostile criticism of the war except those officially sanctioned opinions. There are recognized limits to criticisms of existing laws or policies of war. One may not counsel or advise others to violate the law as it stands. The present statute is limited to punishing direct advocacy of resistance to recruiting and enlistment, within which neither the cartoons nor text of Masses' (P) publications fall.

ANALYSIS

The present test, later supplanted with the "clear and present danger" test, as to what type of conduct constitutes advocacy of resistance to law, focuses on the speaker and the value of the speech. This decision weighs the value of content of freely spoken opinions against its impact on the orderly conduct of governmental policy. The burden is on the government, as accuser, to show that such speech or publication is so detrimental to the orderly process of government that freedom of speech should bow to governmental will. The *Masses* case takes a liberal view of First Amendment rights and allows the free expression of opinion that falls short of direct advocacy of resistance to governmental authority. Judge Hand's decision in this case was overturned by the court of appeals on the ground that a person would be held accountable for the natural consequences of his words. If his words strongly imply that a particular law should be violated, that person will not be immune from prosecution merely because he omitted a direct appeal for violations. Judge Hand later wrote to a friend that his opinion in this case had apparently received little or no professional approval.

Quicknotes

FIRST AMENDMENT Prohibits Congress from enacting any law respecting an establishment of religion or

Continued on next page.

prohibiting the free exercise of religion; or abridging the freedom of speech or of the press, the right of peaceful assembly, and the right to petition for a redress of grievances.

INJUNCTION A court order requiring a person to do, or prohibiting that person from doing, a specific act.

Gitlow v. New York

Publisher (D) v. State (P)

268 U.S. 652 (1925)

NATURE OF CASE: Certiorari review of speech restriction.

FACT SUMMARY: Gitlow (D) printed and circulated literature advocating a Communist revolt against the U.S. government.

RULE OF LAW

Under its police powers, a state may validly forbid any speech or publication that has a tendency to produce action dangerous to public security, even where such speech or publication presents no clear and present danger to the security of the public.

FACTS: Gitlow (D) was a member of the Left-Wing Section of the Socialist Party in New York (P), and he was responsible for printing the official organ of the Left Wing called the "Revolutionary Age." In this paper, Gitlow (D) printed articles advocating the accomplishment of the Communist revolution through militant revolutionary socialism. Gitlow (D) further advocated a class struggle mobilization of the proletariat through mass industrial revolts and political strikes to conquer and destroy the U.S. government and replace it with a dictatorship of the proletariat. Although there was no evidence that these writings resulted in any such action, Gitlow (D) was arrested, tried, and convicted for advocating the overthrow of the government by force under a New York (P) criminal anarchy act. At trial, Gitlow's (D) counsel urged that since there was no resulting action flowing from the publication of the Gitlow (D) "Manifesto," the statute penalized the mere utterance of doctrine having no propensity toward incitement of concrete action.

ISSUE: Under its police powers, may a state validly forbid any speech or publication that has a tendency to produce action dangerous to public security, even where such speech or publication presents no clear and present danger to the security of the public?

HOLDING AND DECISION: (Sanford, J.) Yes. Under its police powers, a state may validly forbid both speech and publication if they have a tendency to result in action that is dangerous to public security, even where such speech or publication presents no clear and present danger to the security of the public. The New York (P) criminal anarchy act did not punish the utterance of abstract doctrine, having no quality of incitement to action. It prohibits advocacy to overthrow organized government by unlawful means. These words imply advocacy of action. Clearly, Gitlow's (D) "Manifesto," which spoke in terms of "mass action" of the proletariat for the "Communist reconstruction of society—the struggle for these," is language of direct incitement. The means suggested imply force and violence and are inherently unlawful in a constitutional form of government based on law and order. Although freedom of speech and of the press are protected by the First and Fourteenth Amendments, it is fundamental that this freedom is not absolute. The police power extends to a state the right to punish those who abuse this freedom by advocating action inimical to the public welfare, tending to corrupt public morals, incite to crime, or to threaten the public security. The state need not wait for such dangers to arise. It may punish utterances likely to bring about such substantive evils. The "clear and present danger" test announced in *Schenck v. United States*, 249 U.S. 47 (1919), does not apply here since the legislature has previously determined the danger of the substantive evils that may arise from specified utterances. As long as the statute is constitutional and the use of the language sought to be penalized comes within the prohibition, the statute will be upheld. And it is not necessary that the defendant advocates some definite or immediate act of force or violence. It is sufficient if they were expressed in general terms. Affirmed.

DISSENT: (Holmes, J.) The "clear and present danger" test applies, and there was no clear and present danger here. The followers of Gitlow (D) were too few to present one. Every idea is an incitement. The only meaning of free speech is to allow everyone to have their say.

ANALYSIS

The *Gitlow* case is an example of what has been termed the "bad tendency" test. This test punishes utterances whose meaning lies somewhere between "clear and present danger" and mere advocacy of abstract ideas. The key question here is whether the language "tends" to produce action resulting in a danger to public security. The holding of the Court in this case, while recognizing Gitlow's (D) constitutional rights of free speech and press, bypassed these rights by saying that the New York (P) statute did not unduly restrict such freedom. However, in light of the modern test of "clear and present danger," it seems that the "bad tendency" test is all but dead. The "clear and present danger" test requires language that results in imminent lawless

Continued on next page.

action. Tendency is not enough. It is important to note that the "bad tendency" test has not been used by the Court since *Gitlow*.

Quicknotes

CLEAR AND PRESENT DANGER TEST Doctrine that restraints on freedom of speech are permissible if the speech incites persons to engage in unlawful conduct.

FIRST AMENDMENT Prohibits Congress from enacting any law respecting an establishment of religion or prohibiting the free exercise of religion; or abridging the freedom of speech or of the press, the right of peaceful assembly, and the right to petition for a redress of grievances.

FREEDOM OF SPEECH The right to express oneself without governmental restrictions on the content of that expression.

POLICE POWER The power of a government to impose restrictions on private persons, so long as those restrictions are reasonably related to the promotion and protection of public health, safety, morals, and the general welfare.

Whitney v. California

Communist party member (D) v. State (P)

274 U.S. 357 (1927)

NATURE OF CASE: Certiorari review of speech restriction.

FACT SUMMARY: Whitney (D), organizer and member of the Communist Labor Party of California, was convicted of aiding in that organization's violation of the California Criminal Syndicalism Act.

RULE OF LAW

A state may, in the exercise of its police power, punish abuses of freedom of speech where such utterances are inimical to the public welfare as tending to incite crime, disturb the peace, or endanger organized government through threats of violent overthrow.

FACTS: In 1919, Whitney (D) attended a convention of the Socialist Party. When the convention split into factions, Whitney (D) went with the radicals and helped form the Communist Labor Party (CLP). Later that year, Whitney (D) attended another convention to organize a new California unit of CLP. There, Whitney (D) supported a resolution that endorsed political action and urged workers to vote for CLP-member candidates at all elections. This resolution was defeated, and a more extreme program of action was adopted, over Whitney's (D) protests. At trial, upon indictment for violation of the California Criminal Syndicalism Act (the Act), which held it unlawful to organize a group that advocated unlawful acts of violence as a means of effecting change in industrial ownership and in political change, Whitney (D) contended that she never intended the CLP to become a terrorist organization. Whitney (D) further contended that since she had no intent to aid the CLP in a policy of violent political reform, her mere presence at the convention was not a crime. Whitney (D) contends that the Act thus deprived her of her liberty without due process and freedom of speech, assembly, and association. Nevertheless, she was convicted.

ISSUE: May a state, in the exercise of its police power, punish abuses of freedom of speech where such utterances are inimical to the public welfare as tending to incite crime, disturb the peace, or endanger organized government through threats of violent overthrow?

HOLDING AND DECISION: (Sanford, J.) Yes. A state may, in the exercise of its police power, punish abuses of freedom of speech where such utterances are inimical to the public welfare as tending to incite crime, disturb the peace, or endanger organized government through threats of violent overthrow. Freedom of speech, secured by the Constitution, does not confer an absolute right to speak, without responsibility. Here, the California Syndicalism Act declared that to become a knowing member of or to assist in an organization that advocates crimes involving danger to the public peace and security of the state was punishable in the exercise of the state's police powers. The essence of the offense was the combining with others to accomplish desired ends through advocacy and use of criminal means. This is in the nature of criminal conspiracy and involves an even greater danger to public security than individual acts. Miss Whitney's (D) contention the California Criminal Syndicalism Act as applied to her in this case is unconstitutional is foreclosed to the Court, since it is an effort to review a trial verdict. Affirmed.

CONCURRENCE: (Brandeis, J.) Whitney (D) is here punished for a step in the preparation of incitement that only threatens the public remotely. The California Syndicalism Act aims at punishing those who propose to preach, not put into action, criminal syndicalism. The right of freedom of speech, assembly, and association, protected by the Due Process Clause of the Fourteenth Amendment and binding on the states, is restricted if it threatens political, moral, or economic injury to the state. However, such restriction does not exist unless speech would produce a clear and imminent danger of some substantive evil to the state. The Court has not yet fixed standards in determining when a danger shall be clear. But no danger flowing from speech can be deemed clear and present unless the threatened evil is so imminent that it may strike before opportunity for discussion on it. There must be, however, probability of serious injury to the state. As to review by this Court of an allegation of unconstitutionality of a criminal syndicalism act, whenever fundamental rights of free speech and assembly are alleged to have been invaded, the defendant must be allowed to present the issue of whether a clear and present danger was made imminent by his actions. Here, mere advocacy of revolution by mass action at some future date was within the Fourteenth Amendment protection. But our power of review was lacking since there was evidence of a criminal conspiracy and such precludes review by this court of errors at a criminal trial absent a showing that constitutional rights were deprived.

Continued on next page.

ANALYSIS

The *Whitney* case is important for having added to the *Schenck* test, 249 U.S. 47 (1919), "clear and present danger," the further requirement that the danger must be "imminent." The Brandeis opinion in the *Whitney* case should be viewed as a dissenting opinion. His addition of "imminent" flies directly in the face of the majority opinion, that punished "mere advocacy" of threatened action against the state. The "mere advocacy" test has not survived. Today, through the Smith Act that continues to punish criminal syndicalism, "mere advocacy" is not punishable. The urging of action for forcible overthrow is necessary before punishment will be imposed. Thus, the "urging of action" is the modern test of "clear and present imminent danger" espoused by Justice Brandeis in *Whitney*.

Quicknotes

CRIMINAL SYNDICALISM The advocating of unlawful conduct to effect a change in ownership or control.

FREEDOM OF ASSOCIATION The right to peaceably assemble.

SMITH ACT Federal law prohibiting the violent overthrow of the U.S. government. Its formal name is the Alien Registration Act of 1940.

Dennis v. United States

Communist party leaders (D) v. Federal government (P)

341 U.S. 494 (1951)

NATURE OF CASE: Certiorari review of convictions of conspiracy to overthrow the U.S. Government (P) by force or violence.

FACT SUMMARY: Dennis (D) and other Communist Party leaders (D) were convicted for violation of the Smith Act, which is directed at conspiracy to teach or advocate the overthrow of the U.S. Government (P) by force or violence.

RULE OF LAW

Where an offense is specified by a statute in nonspeech or nonpress terms, a conviction relying upon speech or press as evidence of violation may be sustained only when the speech or publication created a clear and present danger of attempting or accomplishing the prohibited crime.

FACTS: The Smith Act made it unlawful to advocate or teach the overthrow of the U.S. Government (the Government) (P) by force or violence, or to organize people to teaching and advocating. It also prohibited a conspiracy to do any of the above. Dennis (D) and other Communist Party leaders (D) were convicted of conspiracy to overthrow the U.S. Government (P) by force or violence. The evidence showed that the Communist Party was a highly disciplined organization, adept at infiltration into strategic positions, with the use of aliases and double-meaning language. The Communist Party was rigidly controlled and tolerated no dissension. Communist Party literature and statements advocated a successful overthrow of Government (P) by force and violence.

ISSUE: Where an offense is specified by a statute in nonspeech or nonpress terms, may a conviction relying upon speech or press as evidence of violation be sustained only when the speech of publication created a clear and present danger of attempting or accomplishing the prohibited crime?

HOLDING AND DECISION: (Vinson, C.J.) Yes. Where an offense is specified by a statute in nonspeech or nonpress terms, a conviction relying upon speech or press as evidence of violation may be sustained only when the speech or publication created a clear and present danger of attempting or accomplishing the prohibited crime. In determining the constitutionality of a statute that restricts First Amendment rights, the test is this: where the offense is specified in nonspeech on nonpress terms, a conviction relying upon speech or press as evidence of violation may be sustained only when the speech or publication created a clear and present danger of attempting or accomplishing the prohibited crime. Here, the Smith Act seeks to protect the U.S. Government (the Government) (P) from overthrow by force or violence. This is certainly a substantial enough interest for the Government (P) to limit speech. Now it must be determined whether a clear and present danger existed. Success or probability of success of an attempt to overthrow the Government (P) is not a criterion of whether that attempt constitutes a clear and present danger. The question is whether the gravity of the evil, discounted by its improbability, justifies such an invasion of free speech as is necessary to avoid the danger. Here, the formation by Dennis (D) and the others (D) of such a highly organized conspiracy with rigidly disciplined members subject to call when the leaders felt the time had come, coupled with the inflammable nature of world conditions, similar uprisings in other countries, and our relations with Communist countries, convinces us that a clear and present danger existed here. Convictions affirmed.

CONCURRENCE: (Frankfurter, J.) The validity of the statute depends on a balancing of competing interests, such as the nature of the speech and the nature of the advocacy. This balancing should be done by the legislatures, not by the courts. The courts can overturn a statute, including statutes dealing with First Amendment rights, only if there is no reasonable basis for it.

CONCURRENCE: (Jackson, J.) A statute making it a criminal offense to conspire for the purpose of teaching and advocating the overthrow of the U.S. Government (P) by force or violence may be applied without infringing free speech rights even where there is no clear and present danger.

DISSENT: (Black, J.) First Amendment rights should have a preferred position in a free society. Laws restricting those rights should not be sustained by the courts on the ground of mere reasonableness.

DISSENT: (Douglas, J.) A restriction of First Amendment rights can be sustained only where there is plain and objective proof of danger that the evil advocated is imminent. This was not shown here, where it is inconceivable that Dennis (D) and other Communists (D) advocating the violent overthrow of the U.S. Government (P) have any chance of success.

Continued on next page.

ANALYSIS

After *Dennis*, the U.S. Government (P) brought Smith Act cases against a number of Communists who were lower echelon figures, rather than leaders. In *Yates v. U.S.*, 354 U.S. 298 (1957), the Court reversed the convictions of 14 defendants. It distinguished and explained *Dennis* on the ground that it had involved group indoctrination toward future violent action, under circumstances that reasonably justified the apprehension that violence would result. In *Scales v. U.S.*, 367 U.S. 203 (1961), the Court sustained the membership clause of the Smith Act, making it clear that to be convicted under that clause one must have had knowledge of an organization's illegal advocacy and must have joined the group with the specific intent of furthering its illegal aims.

Quicknotes

CONSPIRACY Concerted action by two or more persons to accomplish some unlawful purpose.

SMITH ACT Federal law prohibiting the violent overthrow of the U.S. government. Its formal name is the Alien Registration Act of 1940.

Brandenburg v. Ohio

Ku Klux Klan leader (D) v. State (P)

395 U.S. 444 (1969)

NATURE OF CASE: Certiorari review of constitutionality of state statute.

FACT SUMMARY: Brandenburg (D) was convicted under a state statute that proscribes advocacy of the duty, necessity, or propriety of crime, sabotage, violence, or unlawful methods of terrorism as a means of accomplishing reform.

RULE OF LAW

The constitutional guarantees of freedom of speech and freedom of press do not permit a state to forbid or proscribe advocacy of the use of force or of law violation except where such advocacy is directed to inciting or producing imminent lawless action and is likely to produce or incite such action.

FACTS: Brandenburg (D), a Ku Klux Klan leader, was convicted under Ohio's (P) criminal syndicalism statute. The statute prohibited advocacy of the duty, necessity, or propriety of crime, sabotage, violence, or unlawful methods of terrorism as a means of accomplishing reform, and the assembling with any group formed to teach or advocate the doctrine of criminal syndicalism. The case against Brandenburg (D) rested on some films. One film showed 12 hooded figures, some carrying firearms, gathered around a wooden cross, which they burned. Scattered words could be heard that were derogatory to Jews and African Americans. Brandenburg (D) made a speech and stated, "We are not a revengent group, but if our President, our Congress, and our Supreme Court, continues to suppress the white, Caucasian race, it's possible that there might have to be some revengence taken."

ISSUE: Do the constitutional guarantees of freedom of speech and freedom of press permit a state to forbid or proscribe advocacy of the use of force or of law violation where such advocacy is not directed to inciting or producing imminent lawless action and is not likely to produce or incite such action?

HOLDING AND DECISION: (Per curiam) No. The constitutional guarantees of free speech and free press do not permit a state to forbid or proscribe advocacy of the use of force or of law violation except where such advocacy is directed to inciting or producing imminent lawless action and is likely to incite or produce such action. The mere abstract teaching of the moral propriety or even moral necessity for a resort to force and violence is not the same as preparing a group for violent action and steering it to such action. A statute that fails to draw this distinction impermissibly intrudes upon the freedoms guaranteed by the First and Fourteenth Amendments. It sweeps within its condemnation speech that the Constitution has immunized from governmental control. The Ohio statute purports to punish mere advocacy and to forbid assembly with others merely to advocate the described type of action. Hence, it cannot be sustained. Brandenburg's (D) conviction is reversed.

CONCURRENCE: (Black, J.) The "clear and present danger" doctrine should have no place in the interpretation of the First Amendment.

CONCURRENCE: (Douglas, J.) The line between what is permissible and not subject to control and what may be made impermissible and subject to regulation is the line between ideas and overt acts. Apart from rare exceptions, speech is immune from prosecution.

ANALYSIS

This case demonstrates that imminence of danger is an essential requirement to the validity of any statute curbing freedom of speech. This requirement was reiterated in *Bond v. Floyd*, 385 U.S. 116 (1966), in which the Court reversed a state legislature's resolution excluding Bond from membership. The exclusion was based on the ground that Bond could not take the oath to support the state and U.S. Constitutions after his endorsement of a Student Nonviolent Coordinating Committee statement and his remarks criticizing the draft and the Vietnam War. The Court found no incitement to violation of law in Bond's remarks.

Quicknotes

CRIMINAL SYNDICALISM The advocating of unlawful conduct to effect a change in ownership or control.

FREEDOM OF SPEECH The right to express oneself without governmental restrictions on the content of that expression.

FREEDOM OF THE PRESS The right to publish and publicly disseminate one's views.

Chaplinsky v. New Hampshire

Jehovah's Witness (D) v. State (P)

315 U.S. 568 (1942)

NATURE OF CASE: Appeal of a conviction for violation of statute forbidding utterance of words derisive or annoying to another.

FACT SUMMARY: Chaplinsky (D), a Jehovah's Witness, first denounced all other religions as "rackets" and then called a Marshall a "fascist" and "racketeer."

RULE OF LAW

A government may proscribe language tending to incite violence.

FACTS: Chaplinsky (D), a Jehovah's Witness, had been calling other religions "rackets." An unfriendly crowd began to assemble. The City Marshal warned Chaplinsky (D) that the crowd was getting ugly, whereupon Chaplinsky (D) called the Marshal a "racketeer" and a "fascist." Chaplinsky (D) was convicted under an ordinance prohibiting the utterance of words tending to harass, annoy, or deride another. Chaplinsky (D) appealed.

ISSUE: May a government proscribe language tending to incite violence?

HOLDING AND DECISION: (Murphy, J.) Yes. A government may proscribe language tending to incite violence. It is established that words constituting a clear and present danger to the public health may be banned. So-called "fighting words" do constitute such a danger. The ordinance in question basically is a prohibition of fighting words, and therefore the ordinance is valid. Affirmed.

ANALYSIS

This case presents one of the first enunciations of the concept of "protected" and "unprotected" speech, among them libel, obscenity, and "fighting words." The scope of the former two categories has been the subject of much subsequent analysis.

Quicknotes

FIGHTING WORDS Unprotected speech that inflicts injury by its very utterance and provokes violence from the audience.

Feiner v. New York

Public speaker (D) v. State (P)

340 U.S. 315 (1951)

NATURE OF CASE: Certiorari review of conviction for speech offense.

FACT SUMMARY: Feiner (D) gave an open-air speech before a racially mixed audience. The crowd that gathered forced pedestrians into the street. Feiner (D) urged Blacks to rise up in arms against Whites and fight for equal rights. He refused to stop when asked to do so by a police officer and was arrested.

RULE OF LAW

When clear and present danger of riot, disorder, interference with traffic on the streets, or other immediate threat to public safety, peace, or order appears, the state has the power to punish or prevent such disorder.

FACTS: Feiner (D) addressed an open-air meeting. A racially mixed crowd of about 80 people gathered. The crowd forced pedestrians walking by into the street. In response to a complaint about the meeting, two police officers arrived. They heard Feiner (D) urge Blacks to take up arms and fight against Whites for equal rights. The remarks stirred up the crowd a little, and one person commented on the inability of the police to control the crowd. Another threatened violence if the police did not act. The officers finally stepped in to prevent a fight. They asked Feiner (D) to stop speaking twice. Feiner (D) ignored them, and they arrested him.

ISSUE: When clear and present danger of riot, disorder, interference with traffic on the streets, or other immediate threat to public safety, peace, or order appears, does the state have the power to punish or prevent such disorder?

HOLDING AND DECISION: (Vinson, C.J.) Yes. When clear and present danger of riot, disorder, interference with traffic on the streets, or other immediate threat to public safety, peace, or order appears, the state has the power to punish or prevent such disorder. Here, the crowd's behavior and Feiner's (D) refusal to obey the police requests presented a sufficient danger to warrant his arrest and to persuade the Court that Feiner's (D) conviction for violation of public peace, order and authority does not exceed the bounds of proper state police action. Feiner (D) was neither arrested nor convicted for the making or the content of his speech. Rather, it was the reaction it engendered. The community's interest in maintaining peace and order on its streets must be protected. Hence, Feiner's (D) conviction is affirmed.

DISSENT: (Black, J.) This decision is a long step toward totalitarian authority. Disagreement, mutterings, and objections from a crowd do not indicate imminent threat of a riot, nor does one threat to assault the speaker. Even assuming a critical situation existed, it was the duty of the police to protect Feiner's (D) right to speak, which they made no effort to do. Finally, a person making a lawful address is not required to be silent merely because an officer so directs. Here, Feiner (D) received no explanation as to why he was being directed to stop speaking. This decision means that the police have the discretion to silence minority views in any city as soon as the customary hostility to such views develops.

ANALYSIS

As *Feiner* demonstrates, free speech is not an absolute right. The conflicting interest of community order must also be considered. *Feiner* points out the question of whether the boundaries of protected speech depend on the content of the speech and the speaker's words or on the environment, the crowd reaction or potential crowd reaction. This question arose again in *Gregory v. Chicago*, 394 U.S. 111 (1969), which reversed convictions of disorderly conduct. There, participants in a "peaceful and orderly procession" to press their claims for desegregation were arrested when, after the number of bystanders increased and some became unruly, they were asked to disperse and did not. The majority asserted that this was a simple case as the marchers' peaceful conduct was a protected activity within the First Amendment. The concurring opinion saw *Gregory* as involving some complexities, since, as the judge noted, both the demonstrators and the officers had tried to restrain the hecklers but were unable to do so. He concluded that "this record is a crying example of a need for some narrowly drawn law," rather than the sweeping disorderly conduct law.

Quicknotes

CLEAR AND PRESENT DANGER A threat that is proximate and impending.

FIRST AMENDMENT Prohibits Congress from enacting any law respecting an establishment of religion or prohibiting the free exercise of religion; or abridging the freedom of speech or of the press, the right of peaceful assembly, and the right to petition for a redress of grievances.

FREEDOM OF SPEECH The right to express oneself without governmental restrictions on the content of that expression.

Cohen v. California

Defendant (D) v. State (P)

403 U.S. 15 (1971)

NATURE OF CASE: Certiorari review of state statute restricting speech.

FACT SUMMARY: Cohen (D) wore a jacket with the words "Fuck the Draft" on it in a courthouse corridor and was arrested and convicted under a disturbing the peace statute.

RULE OF LAW

A state cannot bar the use of offensive words either because such words are inherently likely to cause a violent reaction or because the state wishes to eliminate such words to protect the public morality.

FACTS: Cohen (D) was arrested in a courthouse because he was wearing a jacket bearing the words, "Fuck the Draft." Cohen (D) did not engage in any act of violence or any other unlawful act. There was also no evidence that anyone who saw the jacket became violently aroused or even protested the jacket. Cohen (D) testified that he wore the jacket to inform people of his feelings against the Vietnam War and the draft. He was convicted under a statute prohibiting "maliciously and willfully disturbing the peace or quiet . . . by offensive conduct." The state court held "offensive conduct" meant conduct that had a tendency to provoke others to disturb the peace.

ISSUE: Can a state bar the use of offensive words either because such words are inherently likely to cause a violent reaction or because the state wishes to eliminate such words to protect the public morality?

HOLDING AND DECISION: (Harlan, J.) No. A state cannot constitutionally prohibit the use of offensive words either because such words are inherently likely to cause a violent reaction or because the state wishes to eliminate such words to protect the public morality. Here, Cohen (D) could not be punished for criticizing the draft, so the statute could be upheld, if at all, only as a regulation of the manner, not the substantive content, of his speech. Cohen's (D) speech does not come within any of the exceptions to the general rule that the form and content of speech cannot be regulated: (1) this is not a prohibition designed to protect courthouse decorum because the statute is not so limited; (2) this is not an obscenity case because Cohen's (D) words were not erotic; (3) this is not a case of fighting words that are punishable as inherently likely to provoke a violent reaction because here the words were not directed as a personal insult to any person; and (4) this is not a captive audience problem since a viewer could merely avert his eyes, there is no evidence of objection by those who saw the jacket, and the statute is not so limited. The State (P) tries to justify the conviction because the words are inherently likely to cause a violent reaction, but this argument cannot be upheld because these are not fighting words and there is no evidence that words that are merely offensive would cause such a response. Next, the State (P) justifies the conviction on the ground that the State (P) is guardian of the public morality. This argument is unacceptable because "offensive" is an unlimited concept and forbidding the use of such words would also cause the risk of suppressing the accompanying ideas. Therefore, there is no valid state interest that supports the regulation of offensive words in public. Reversed.

DISSENT: (Blackmun, J.) Cohen's (D) conviction can be upheld both because his speech was fighting words and also because his act was conduct and not speech. Additionally, the state court subsequently restricted the statute in question to the fighting words context, so the case should be remanded and reconsidered under this construction.

ANALYSIS

This case reasserts the *Chaplinsky*, 315 U.S. 568 (1942), holding that fighting words are not protected by the First Amendment. Fighting words, then, are only those words that are likely to cause an immediate breach of the peace by another person and are not just offensive words. More importantly, this case holds that a state has no valid interest in preventing the use of offensive words when there is no competing privacy interest. Here, the public in general has no right to protection from hearing either offensive words or offensive ideas.

Quicknotes

DECORUM Observance of commonly accepted standards of propriety.

FIGHTING WORDS Unprotected speech that inflicts injury by its very utterance and provokes violence from the audience.

Beauharnais v. Illinois

Publisher (D) v. State (P)

343 U.S. 250 (1956)

NATURE OF CASE: Appeal from a criminal conviction.

FACT SUMMARY: Beauharnais (D) was convicted under an Illinois (P) statute making it a crime to publish any material criticizing members of a group in a way that subjects them to ridicule or invited civil unrest.

RULE OF LAW

A statute that makes it a crime to libel the members of any class or group is not repugnant to the Constitution.

FACTS: An Illinois (P) law made it a crime to publish or exhibit any lithograph, movie, play, or sketch that attributed depravity, criminality, or other conduct lacking in virtue to a racial or religious group in such a way as to expose the members of that group to derision or cause a breach of the peace. Beauharnais (D), president of the White Circle League, arranged for the distribution of lithographs that urged Whites to prevent further encroachment by Blacks and that described the alleged criminality, violence, and drug use rampant among Blacks. Beauharnais (D) was charged with violating the statute, but argued, that the enactment deprived him of freedom of speech and press and was unconstitutionally vague. Beauharnais (D) was found guilty. His conviction was affirmed by the Illinois Supreme Court, which identified the challenged statute as "a form of criminal libel law." The United States Supreme Court then agreed to review the conviction.

ISSUE: Is a statute that makes it a crime to libel the members of any class or group repugnant to the Constitution?

HOLDING AND DECISION: (Frankfurter, J.) No. A statute that makes it a crime to libel the members of any class or group is not repugnant to the Constitution. Originally, libel was a common-law crime to which even truth was not a defense. In Illinois (P), as in most states, truth is now a defense to a criminal libel charge only if publication was made "with good motives and for justifiable ends." Since Beauharnais's (D) offers of proof made no effort to establish motive or justification, the trial court properly concluded the lithographs were libelous as a matter of law and permitted the jury to decide only the issue of publication. Profane or cruelly pejorative expressions may be punished by a state without interfering with anyone's constitutionally guaranteed privileges. Historically, violence and bloodshed have accompanied racial disputes in Illinois (P). Whether or not the contested statute is the best way of dealing with the problem, it is a reasonable exercise of the legislature's power to preserve the peace and protect the public. The statute is drawn with sufficient narrowness and clarity and punishes only utterances that are indisputably libelous. Therefore, the law is constitutional, and Beauharnais's (D) conviction must be affirmed.

DISSENT: (Black, J.) This "group libel law" exemplifies an invidious form of censorship. Traditional criminal libel laws apply only to attacks upon individuals, not groups. In racial controversies, angry accusations are so prevalent virtually anyone could end up violating a statute such as enacted by Illinois (P). This law precludes free public discussion and thus stifles cherished First Amendment rights. It is argued judicial discretion could prevent Illinois (P) from abusing the statute, but the rights secured to all citizens by the Constitution should not be dispensed at the whim of an arbitrary and sometimes capricious tribunal.

ANALYSIS

Common-law criminal libel statutes were apparently designed to discourage feuding individuals from launching personal attacks upon one another in public. Such laws were not applied to punish allegedly libelous assaults upon groups. Nevertheless, some contemporary commentators argue group libel laws would be an effective and desirable method of preventing scurrilous public campaigns of hatred against particular races or religious groups. Although such laws would tend to stifle protected First Amendment rights, it may be possible to imagine situations similar to those cited by the *Beauharnais* majority in which such restraint would be justified by a need to protect against threats to the public peace and tranquility.

Quicknotes

FIRST AMENDMENT Rights conferred by the First Amendment to the U.S. Constitution prohibiting Congress from enacting any law respecting an establishment of religion or prohibiting the free exercise of religion; or abridging freedom of speech or of the press, the right of peaceful assembly, and the right to petition for a redress of grievances.

LIBEL A false or malicious publication subjecting a person to scorn, hatred or ridicule, or injuring him or her in relation to his or her occupation or business.

New York Times Co. v. Sullivan

Newspaper publisher (D) v. Public official (P)

376 U.S. 254 (1964)

NATURE OF CASE: Certiorari review of defamation judgment.

FACT SUMMARY: New York Times (D) published an editorial advertisement in which false statements were made that concerned Sullivan (P).

RULE OF LAW
Defamatory falsehoods regarding public officials have limited protection by constitutional guarantees of freedom of speech and press.

FACTS: Sullivan (P) was a commissioner in the city of Montgomery, Alabama, charged with supervision of the Police Department. During a series of civil rights demonstrations in that city in 1960, the New York Times published an editorial advertisement entitled, "Heed Their Rising Voices," in which several charges of terrorism were leveled at the Police Department. The falsity of some of these statements was uncontroverted. The advertisement charged that nine students at a local college had been expelled for leading a march on the state capitol when, in fact, the reason had been an illegal lunch counter sit-in. The advertisement charged that the police had padlocked the dining hall of the college to starve the demonstrators into submission when, in fact, no padlocking had occurred. Other false statements also were made. Sullivan (P) brought a defamation action against New York Times Co. (D) for these statements and recovered $500,000. Under Alabama law, a publication is libel per se (no special damages need be proved—general damages are presumed), whenever a defamatory falsehood is shown to have injured its subject in his public office or impute misconduct to him in his office. New York Times Co. (D) appealed the Alabama judgment, challenging this rule.

ISSUE: Do defamatory falsehoods regarding public officials have limited protection by constitutional guarantees of freedom of speech and press?

HOLDING AND DECISION: (Brennan, J.) Yes. Defamatory falsehoods regarding public officials have limited protection by constitutional guarantees of freedom of speech and press. The First Amendment requires that a public official may not recover damages for defamatory falsehoods relating to his official conduct unless he proves that the statement involved was made with "actual malice—that is, with knowledge that it was false or with reckless disregard of whether it was false or not." First Amendment protections do not turn upon the truth, popularity, or social utility of ideas and beliefs that are involved. Rather, they are based upon the theory that erroneous statements are inevitable in free debate and must be protected if such freedom is to survive. Only where malice is involved do such protections cease. Here, the Alabama rule falls short of this standard and the evidence at trial was insufficient to determine its existence. Reversed and remanded.

CONCURRENCE: (Black, J.) All statements about public officials should be constitutionally protected—even malicious ones.

ANALYSIS

New York Times Co. v. Sullivan is the landmark case in constitutional defamation law. Subsequent cases have expanded this concept even further. In *Rosenblatt v. Baer*, 383 U.S. 75 (1966), the Court defined "public official" as anyone having substantial responsibility for conduct of government affairs. In *Curtis Publishing v. Butts*, 388 U.S. 130 (1967), *New York Times* was extended to "public figures" as well as officials. In *Gertz*, 418 U.S. 323 (1974), however, the Court retreated a bit by stating that "As long as they do not impose liability without fault, the states may define for themselves the appropriate standard of liability for a publisher . . . of defamatory falsehood injurious to a private individual." Note that the Court has also taken steps to toughen the *New York Times*'s recklessness standard. In *St. Amant v. Thompson*, 390 U.S. 727 (1968), the Court ruled that recklessness was not to be measured by the reasonable man standard, but rather by the subjective standard of whether or not the defendant in the case subjectively entertained serious doubts about the truth of his statements.

Quicknotes

ACTUAL MALICE The issuance of a publication with knowledge of its falsity or with reckless disregard as to its truth.

DEFAMATION An intentional false publication, communicated publicly in either oral or written form, subjecting a person to scorn, hatred, or ridicule, or injuring the person in relation to his or her occupation or business.

FIRST AMENDMENT Prohibits Congress from enacting any law respecting an establishment of religion or

Continued on next page.

prohibiting the free exercise of religion; or abridging the freedom of speech or of the press, the right of peaceful assembly, and the right to petition for a redress of grievances.

PUBLIC FIGURE A person who has achieved or assumed a special prominence in society either willingly or by virtue of his or her social status.

REASONABLE PERSON STANDARD The standard of care exercised by one who possesses the intelligence, education, knowledge, attention, and judgment required by society of its members when governing behavior; the standard applies to a person's judgment when determining breach of a duty under the theory of negligence.

RECKLESSNESS Conduct that is conscious and that creates a substantial and unjustifiable risk of harm to others.

Gertz v. Robert Welch, Inc.

Attorney (P) v. Publisher (D)

418 U.S. 323 (1974)

NATURE OF CASE: Action for defamation.

FACT SUMMARY: Gertz (P) sued Welch (D), a publisher of a John Birch Society newsletter, when Welch (D) published an article calling Gertz (P) a long-time Communist who helped frame a Chicago policeman's conviction for murder, all of which was untrue.

RULE OF LAW

In an action for defamation, a private individual must show the publisher to be at fault and may recover no more than actual damages when liability is not based on a showing of knowledge of falsity or reckless disregard for the truth.

FACTS: Welch (D) published *American Opinion*, a monthly newsletter of the John Birch Society. An article appeared in that publication purporting to illustrate that the conviction of Nuccio, a Chicago policeman, for the murder of Nelson, a young man, was a communist frameup led by Gertz (P). It was said further that Gertz (P) had a criminal record, was an official of the Marxist League, a Leninist, and an officer of the National Lawyers Guild, which was falsely described as a communist organization in the forefront of the attack on Chicago police during the 1968 Democratic Convention. The only element of truth was that 15 years earlier Gertz (P) had been a National Lawyers Guild officer. Actually, Gertz (P) was a reputable lawyer whose only connection with the Nuccio case was to represent the Nelson family in civil litigation against Nuccio. Gertz (P) attended the coroner's inquest into Nelson's death and filed an action for damages but did not discuss the matter with the press or play any part in the criminal proceedings. At trial, the evidence showed that *American Opinion*'s managing editor knew nothing of the defamatory content but had belief in the reputation and accuracy of the author. The jury found the matter libelous per se and not privileged, and awarded a $50,000 judgment, but the judge applied the *New York Times* standard, *New York Times Co. v. Sullivan*, 376 U.S. 254 (1964), as pertaining to any discussion of a public issue without regard to the status of the person defamed. Judgment n.o.v. was entered for Welch (D). The court of appeals affirmed, and Gertz (P) appealed.

ISSUE: In an action for defamation, must a private individual show the publisher to be at fault and recover no more than actual damages when liability is not based on a showing of knowledge of falsity or reckless disregard for the truth?

HOLDING AND DECISION: (Powell, J.) Yes. In an action for defamation, a private individual must show the publisher to be at fault and may recover no more than actual damages when liability is not based on a showing of knowledge of falsity or reckless disregard for the truth. The *New York Times* standard, *New York Times Co. v. Sullivan*, 376 U.S. 254 (1964), applies to public figures and public officials, but the state interest in compensating injury to reputation of private individuals requires that a different rule should apply to them. A public figure or official has greater access to the media to counteract false statements than private individuals normally enjoy. Being more vulnerable to injury, the private individual deserves greater protection and recovery. As long as the states do not impose liability without fault, the states themselves may define the appropriate standard of liability for a publisher of defamatory matter injurious to a private person. And the states may not permit the recovery of presumed or punitive damages, at least when liability is not based on a showing of knowledge of falsity or reckless disregard for the truth. Here, Gertz (P) was not publicly involved. The public figure question should look to the nature and extent of an individual's participation in the controversy giving rise to the action. Reversed, as the jury was allowed to impose liability without fault and presume damages without proof of damages.

DISSENT: (Brennan, J.) The proper accommodation between avoidance of media self-censorship and protection of individual reputations is struck only when the states are required to apply the *New York Times*'s "knowing-or-reckless falsity" standard, *New York Times Co. v. Sullivan*, 376 U.S. 254 (1964), in civil libel actions concerning media reports of the involvement of private individuals in events of public or general interest.

DISSENT: (White, J.) Federalizing major aspects of libel law is a radical change and a severe invasion of the prerogatives of the states not shown to be necessitated by present circumstances or required by the First Amendment. Neither *New York Times Co. v. Sullivan*, 376 U.S. 254 (1964), nor the First Amendment should deprive this private citizen of his historic recourse to redress damaging falsehoods. The risk of falsehood here is shifted to the victim. While a statement may be wholly false, wrong, and unjustified, a defamation case will be dismissed if the victim cannot prove negligence or other fault.

Continued on next page.

ANALYSIS

The majority advances the view that it is necessary to restrict victims of defamation who do not prove knowledge of falsity or reckless disregard for the truth to compensation for actual injury alone. Actual injury is not limited to out-of-pocket loss. Actual harm includes impairment of reputation and standing in the community, personal humiliation, and mental anguish and suffering. While the court noted the fact that juries in the past were tempted to award excess damages, there was no proof trial judges have failed to keep judgments within reasonable bounds.

Quicknotes

DEFAMATION An intentional false publication, communicated publicly in either oral or written form, subjecting a person to scorn, hatred, or ridicule, or injuring the person in relation to his or her occupation or business.

JUDGMENT NOTWITHSTANDING THE VERDICT (JNOV) A judgment entered by the trial judge reversing a jury verdict if the jury's determination has no basis in law or fact.

PUNITIVE DAMAGES Damages exceeding the actual injury suffered for the purposes of punishment of the defendant, deterrence of the wrongful behavior, or comfort to the plaintiff. Also called "exemplary damages."

Bartnicki v. Vopper

Cell phone user (P) v. Radio commentator (D)

532 U.S. 514 (2001)

NATURE OF CASE: Appeal from decision that provisions of federal anti-wiretapping laws that prohibit disclosure of illegally intercepted communications violate the First Amendment when applied to disclosures relating to matters of public concern.

FACT SUMMARY: The cell phone conversation between two union representatives, Bartnicki (P) and Kane (P), was illegally intercepted and recorded during a period of collective-bargaining negotiations in which the union representatives were involved. Vopper (D), a radio commentator, played a tape of the intercepted conversation on his radio show in connection with news reports about the settlement. Bartnicki (P) and Kane (P) filed suit for damages, alleging, among other things, that Vopper (D) and others had repeatedly published the conversation even though they knew or had reason to know that it had been illegally intercepted. Vopper (D) claimed that the disclosures were protected by the First Amendment.

RULE OF LAW

Provisions of anti-wiretapping laws that prohibit disclosure of illegally intercepted communications violate the First Amendment when applied to disclosures of information that has been legally obtained from the intercepting party and that relates to matters of public concern.

FACTS: An unidentified person intercepted and recorded a cell phone conversation between Bartnicki (P), the chief negotiator for a local teacher's union, and Kane (P), the union president. In the conversation, Bartnicki (P) threatened violence (at least as a matter of speaking) if the union's demands were not met. After the parties accepted a proposal favorable to the teachers, Vopper (D), a radio commentator, played a tape of the intercepted conversation on his show in connection with news reports about the settlement. Vopper (D), however, had nothing to do with the interception and did not know who the responsible party was. Also, the tapes themselves had been obtained legally. Bartnicki (P) and Kane (P) filed damages suit under federal wiretapping laws, which, under 18 U.S.C. § 2511(1)(a) prohibited intercepting cell phone calls, and under § 2511(1)(c) prohibited disclosure of the contents of any illegally intercepted material. The Supreme Court granted review on appeal.

ISSUE: Do provisions of anti-wiretapping laws that prohibit disclosure of illegally intercepted communications violate the First Amendment when applied to disclosures of information that has been legally obtained from the intercepting party and that relates to matters of public concern?

HOLDING AND DECISION: (Stevens, J.) Yes. Provisions of anti-wiretapping laws that prohibit disclosure of illegally intercepted communications violate the First Amendment when applied to disclosures of information that has been legally obtained from the intercepting party and that relates to matters of public concern. First, the Court accepts Vopper's (D) assertion that he played no part in the illegal interception, that his access to the information was obtained lawfully, and that the conversations dealt with a matter of public concern. Generally, state action that punishes the publication of truthful information is usually unconstitutional. The issue here is whether a publisher of information who has obtained the information in a lawful manner from someone who has obtained it unlawfully may be punished for the ensuing publication. The government's first asserted interest served by the statute—removing an incentive for parties to intercept private conversations—does not justify applying the statute to an otherwise innocent disclosure of public information. The normal method of deterring unlawful conduct is to punish the person engaging in it. It would be remarkable to hold that speech by a law-abiding possessor of information can be suppressed in order to deter conduct by a non-law-abiding third party. The government's second interest—minimizing the harm to persons whose conversations have been illegally intercepted—is considerably stronger. Privacy of communication is an important interest. However, in this suit, privacy concerns give way when balanced against the interest in publishing matters of public importance. One of the costs associated with participation in public affairs is an attendant loss of privacy. It is clear a stranger's illegal conduct does not suffice to remove the First Amendment shield from speech about a matter of public concern. Affirmed.

CONCURRENCE: (Breyer, J.) The Court's holding is limited to the particular facts of this case and does not extend beyond these present circumstances. These facts are that (1) the broadcasters acted lawfully up to the time of final disclosure; and (2) the information involved a matter of unusual public concern—a threat of potential physical harm to others.

DISSENT: (Rehnquist, C.J.) In attempt to prevent egregious violations of privacy, the federal and state

Continued on next page.

governments have enacted laws prohibiting the intentional interception and knowing disclosure of electronic communications. The majority holds that all these statutes violate the First Amendment insofar as the illegally intercepted conversation touches upon a matter of "public concern," a concept the majority does not even attempt to define. But the majority's decision diminishes, rather than enhances, the purposes of the First Amendment and chills the speech of the millions of Americans who rely upon electronic technology to communicate. The statutes are content neutral, applying only to illegally obtained information. It is hard to imagine a more narrowly tailored prohibition of the disclosure of illegally intercepted communications, and therefore it goes contrary to precedent to review these laws under strict scrutiny. These laws should be upheld under intermediate scrutiny because they further the substantial government interest in protecting privacy; the Constitution should not be used to protect the involuntary disclosure of private conversations.

ANALYSIS

The issue in this case was one of first impression and enabled the Court to expand its jurisprudence in this area. Before this case, the Court had held that the First Amendment prevents liability for public disclosure of private facts if the information was lawfully obtained from public records, unless there was a state interest of the "highest order" justifying liability. The result in this case can be explained by the majority's emphasis on the relatively "public" nature of the communication involved, which consequently did not rise to the "highest order" that a purely private communication would have risen to.

Quicknotes

COLLECTIVE BARGAINING Negotiations between an employer and employee that are mediated by a specified third party.

FIRST AMENDMENT Prohibits Congress from enacting any law respecting an establishment of religion or prohibiting the free exercise of religion; or abridging the freedom of speech or of the press, the right of peaceful assembly, and the right to petition for a redress of grievances.

Hustler Magazine v. Falwell

Magazine publisher (D) v. Minister (P)

485 U.S. 46 (1988)

NATURE OF CASE: Review of a diversity action alleging invasion of privacy, libel, and intentional infliction of emotional distress.

FACT SUMMARY: Jury ruled in favor of Falwell (P) on intentional infliction of emotional distress claim.

RULE OF LAW

Recovery for the tort of intentional infliction of emotional distress must meet the *New York Times* standard.

FACTS: Hustler Magazine (D) published a parody of a Campari Liqueur ad featuring Jerry Falwell (P), a nationally known minister. The parody was a play on a Campari ad campaign that featured interviews with celebrities about their "first time" partaking of Campari Liqueur. The "first time" nature of the ad campaign had strong sexual undertones. The caption on the Hustler Magazine (D) fictional ad read: "Jerry Falwell talks about his first time." The ad went on to detail a fictional interview with Jerry Falwell (P) in which he states that his "first time" was during a drunken incestuous rendezvous with his mother in an outhouse. In small print on the bottom of the page, the ad contained the disclaimer "ad parody—not to be taken seriously." The magazine's (D) table of contents also listed the ad as "Fiction; Ad and Personality Parody." Following publication of this ad, Falwell (P) brought this diversity action alleging invasion of privacy, libel, and intentional infliction of emotional distress.

ISSUE: Must recovery for the tort of intentional infliction of emotional distress meet the *New York Times* standard?

HOLDING AND DECISION: (Rehnquist, C.J.) Yes. Recovery for the tort of intentional infliction of emotional distress must meet the *New York Times* standard, *New York Times Co. v. Sullivan*, 376 U.S. 254 (1964). Where a public figure or public official asserts tort claims, that figure or official must demonstrate that the publication contains a false statement of fact that was made with "actual malice." The *New York Times* standard as applied in this area reflects a First Amendment limitation upon a state's authority to protect its citizens from intentional infliction of emotional distress. Reversed.

ANALYSIS

The *Hustler Magazine* decision upholds the right and prerogative of the American citizenry to criticize public figures and measures.

Quicknotes

ACTUAL MALICE The issuance of a publication with knowledge of its falsity or with reckless disregard as to its truth.

DEFAMATION An intentional false publication, communicated publicly in either oral or written form, subjecting a person to scorn, hatred, or ridicule, or injuring the person in relation to his or her occupation or business.

Snyder v. Phelps

Parent of slain soldier (P) v. Funeral picketer (D)

562 U.S. 443 (2011)

NATURE OF CASE: Appeal by defendants from conviction in action asserting tort claims based on the defendants' speech, which the defendants claim is protected by the First Amendment as public speech.

FACT SUMMARY: Members of the Westboro Baptist Church (D) contended that they could not be held liable in tort for picketing a soldier's funeral because any tort liability would be based on their speech, which, they contended, was public speech and protected by the First Amendment.

RULE OF LAW

Speech that can be fairly characterized as public speech is shielded by the First Amendment from tort liability, even when the speech is found by a jury to be "outrageous," where the speaker is on public land and conforms to local time and place restrictions.

FACTS: For over 20 years, the congregation of the Westboro Baptist Church (Westboro) (D) picketed military funerals to communicate its belief God hates the United States for its tolerance of homosexuality, particularly in the military. Westboro's (D) picketing also condemned the Catholic Church for scandals involving its clergy. Members of Westboro (D) picketed the funeral of Matthew Snyder, a soldier killed in the line of duty. The picketing took place on public land approximately 1,000 feet from the church where the funeral was held, in accordance with guidance from local law enforcement officers. The picketers peacefully displayed their signs, that stated, e.g., "Thank God for Dead Soldiers," "Fags Doom Nations," "America is Doomed," "Priests Rape Boys," and "You're Going to Hell." They did so for about 30 minutes before the funeral began. Matthew Snyder's father (Snyder) (P), who saw the tops of the signs, brought suit against Westboro (D), alleging state tort claims of intentional infliction of emotional distress, civil conspiracy, and intrusion upon seclusion. A jury, finding that Westboro's (D) conduct was "outrageous," held Westboro (D) liable for $2.9 million in compensatory damages, and for $8 million in punitive damages. The district court reduced the punitive damages award but left the verdict otherwise intact. The Supreme Court granted certiorari.

ISSUE: Is speech that can fairly be characterized as public speech shielded by the First Amendment from tort liability, even when the speech is found by a jury to be "outrageous," where the speaker is on public land and conforms to local time and place restrictions?

HOLDING AND DECISION: (Roberts, C.J.) Yes. Speech that can be fairly characterized as public speech is shielded by the First Amendment from tort liability, even when the speech is found by a jury to be "outrageous," where the speaker is on public land and conforms to local time and place restrictions. Whether the First Amendment prohibits holding the Westboro Baptist Church (Westboro) (D) liable for its speech in this case turns largely on whether that speech is of public or private concern as determined by all the circumstances of the case, including its content, form, and context. Speech on public issues occupies the highest rung of the hierarchy of First Amendment values and is entitled to special protection. Although the boundaries of what constitutes speech on matters of public concern are not well defined, speech is of public concern when it can be fairly considered as relating to any matter of political, social, or other concern to the community, or when it is a subject of general interest and of value and concern to the public. Here, the "content" of Westboro's (D) signs plainly relates to public, rather than private, matters. The placards highlighted issues of public import—the political and moral conduct of the United States and its citizens, the fate of the Nation, homosexuality in the military, and scandals involving the Catholic clergy—and Westboro (D) conveyed its views on those issues in a manner designed to reach as broad a public audience as possible. The "context" of the speech—its connection with Matthew Snyder's funeral—cannot by itself transform the nature of Westboro's (D) speech, as the signs reflected Westboro's (D) condemnation of much in modern society, and the funeral setting does not change that conclusion. Moreover, the picketing was conducted on a public space, adjacent to a public street, which is the archetype of a public forum. While protected public speech is not beyond reasonable content-neutral time, place, and manner restrictions, Westboro's (D) conduct here complied with such restrictions. Any distress occasioned by Westboro's (D) picketing turned on the content and viewpoint of the message conveyed, rather than any interference with the funeral itself. Such speech cannot be restricted simply because it is upsetting or arouses contempt; it is a bedrock principle of First Amendment law that the government may not prohibit the expression of an idea simply because society finds the idea itself offensive or disagreeable. The special protection afforded to what Westboro (D) said, in the whole context of how and

Continued on next page.

where it chose to say it, cannot be overcome by a jury finding that the picketing was "outrageous" for purposes of applying the state law tort of intentional infliction of emotional distress, especially given that "outrageousness" is a highly malleable standard with an inherent subjectiveness about it that would pose too great a danger the jury would punish Westboro (D) for its views on matters of public concern. Such a risk is unacceptable, since in public debate we must tolerate insulting, and even outrageous, speech so sufficient breathing room can be afforded to the freedoms protected by the First Amendment. For all these reasons, Westboro (D) must be shielded in this case from tort liability for its speech, and the jury verdict imposing tort liability on Westboro (D) for intentional infliction of emotional distress must be set aside.

CONCURRENCE: (Breyer, J.) A state can sometimes regulate picketing on matters of public concern, depending on all the circumstances. Here, the majority is correct in holding that in light of those circumstances, the Westboro Baptist Church's (Westboro's) (D) means of communicating was lawful and in compliance with all police directions. Therefore, under such circumstances, to allow the application of state tort law against Westboro (D) would punish Westboro (D) for seeking to communicate its views on matters of public concern without proportionately advancing the state's interest in protecting its citizens against severe emotional harm.

DISSENT: (Alito, J.) The First Amendment does not protect the vicious speech made by the Westboro Baptist Church (Westboro) (D) at Matthew Snyder's funeral that inflicted severe and lasting emotional injury. The profound national commitment to free and open debate permits Westboro (D) to express itself in countless other ways, but it does not protect Westboro's (D) right to brutalize Snyder (P). Westboro (D) may not intentionally inflict severe emotional injury on private persons at a time of intense emotional sensitivity by launching vicious verbal attacks that make no contribution to public debate. The Court has recognized the First Amendment does not protect words that by their very utterance inflict injury and are of inconsequential social value. Notwithstanding that Westboro (D) could have delivered its message in countless other venues, it chose to conduct its brutal attack in a manner that would garner the most public attention—by inflicting the greatest amount of emotional injury and media attention. The attack on Matthew Snyder was personal, as it attacked him because he was a Catholic and a member of the military. Because Matthew and his father are not public figures, the attack on them was not one of public concern. The Court now compounds Snyder's (P) injury; it is not necessary to allow the brutalization of innocent victims in order to have a society in which public issues can be openly and vigorously debated.

ANALYSIS

In the majority opinion, Chief Justice Roberts indicates Maryland now has a law restricting funeral picketing, but he reasons that because that law was not in effect at the time of the Westboro Baptist Church's (Westboro's) (D) picketing, the Court has no occasion to consider whether that law is a reasonable time, place, or manner restriction under the standards announced by the Court. Justice Alito, in his dissent, remarks it is doubtful that the wounds inflicted by vicious verbal assaults at funerals will be prevented or at least mitigated in the future by new laws, such as Maryland's, that restrict picketing within a specified distance of a funeral. Justice Alito concludes the enactment of these laws is no substitute for the protection provided by the established intentional infliction of emotional distress (IIED) tort, since, according to the majority, Westboro's (D) speech in this case would have complied with the new Maryland law regulating funeral picketing, and since there is absolutely nothing to suggest Congress and the state legislatures, in enacting these laws, intended them to displace the protection provided by the well-established IIED tort.

Quicknotes

CONTENT-BASED STATUTES Laws that regulate speech based on its content.

FIRST AMENDMENT Prohibits Congress from enacting any law respecting an establishment of religion or prohibiting the free exercise of religion; or abridging the freedom of speech or of the press, the right of peaceful assembly, and the right to petition for a redress of grievances.

INTENTIONAL INFLICTION OF EMOTIONAL DISTRESS Intentional and extreme behavior on the part of the wrongdoer with the intent to cause the victim to suffer from severe emotional distress, or with reckless indifference, resulting in the victim's suffering from severe emotional distress.

Collin v. Smith

Head of political group (P) v. Municipal official (D)

578 F.2d 1197 (7th Cir. 1978)

NATURE OF CASE: Appeal in action challenging local ordinances on First Amendment grounds.

FACT SUMMARY: The National Socialist Party of America (NSPA) (P), a neo-Nazi group, wished to demonstrate in Skokie, Illinois (D), which included a large Jewish population, among them thousands of survivors of the Nazi Holocaust. After Skokie (D) enacted three ordinances aimed at prohibiting such demonstrations, the NSPA (P) and its leader, Collin (P), challenged the ordinances in federal district court, claiming the ordinances violated the First Amendment.

RULE OF LAW

Content legislation that does not fall within any exceptions to the rule against governmental content control violates the First Amendment, notwithstanding the speech the legislation is intended to control is generally deemed offensive and hateful.

FACTS: The National Socialist Party of America (NSPA) (P), a neo-Nazi group, wished to demonstrate in Skokie, Illinois (D), which included a large Jewish population, among them thousands of survivors of the Nazi Holocaust. The demonstration was to last about a half hour and would involve 30 to 50 demonstrators wearing uniforms including swastikas and carrying a party banner with a swastika and placards with statements thereon such as "White Free Speech," "Free Speech for the White Man," and "Free Speech for White America." Skokie (D) enacted three ordinances to prohibit such demonstrations. The first ordinance established a comprehensive permit system for all parades or public assemblies. The second ordinance prohibited within Skokie (D) the dissemination of any materials that promoted and incited hatred against persons by reason of their race, national origin, or religion. The third ordinance prohibited public demonstrations by members of political parties while wearing "military-style" uniforms. The NSPA (P) and its leader, Collin (P), challenged the ordinances in federal district court, claiming the ordinances violated the First Amendment. The court of appeals granted review.

ISSUE: Does content legislation that does not fall within any exceptions to the rule against governmental content control violate the First Amendment, notwithstanding the speech the legislation is intended to control is generally deemed offensive and hateful?

HOLDING AND DECISION: (Pell, J.) Yes. Content legislation that does not fall within any exceptions to the rule against governmental content control violates the First Amendment, notwithstanding the speech the legislation is intended to control is generally deemed offensive and hateful. While content legislation is not per se invalid, it is the most direct threat to the vitality of First Amendment rights. Here, the ordinances do not fall within the generally recognized exceptions to the rule against content control. The National Socialist Party of America's (NSPA's) (P) speech cannot be considered obscenity, which requires erotic content, and there is no indication that the demonstration will incite violence or be violent in nature. Therefore, the speech cannot be considered incitement to riot, or "fighting words." Skokie's (D) arguments in support of the ordinances are also unavailing. Skokie (D) asserts that the NSPA's (P) speech has no social content and consists of false statements of fact. To the extent the speech asserts anything it is the Nazi ideology, which cannot be treated as a mere false "fact." Under the First Amendment, there is no such thing as a false idea. However pernicious an opinion may seem, its correction does not depend on the conscience of judges and juries but on the competition of other ideas. Another argument pressed by Skokie (D) is that the ordinances are valid because they are aimed at eliminating the tendency to induce violence. Given that it is conceded that no violence from the NSPA (P) or those incited by its speech is anticipated, this argument finds no support. Skokie's (D) third argument is that it has a policy of fair housing, which the dissemination of racially defamatory material could undercut. This argument is rejected. Merely because the effective exercise of First Amendment rights may undercut a given government's policy on some issue is, indeed, one of the purposes of those rights. Skokie's (D) last argument in support of the ordinances is that the Nazi march, involving as it does the display of uniforms and swastikas, will create a substantive evil that it has a right to prohibit: the infliction of psychic trauma on resident Holocaust survivors and other Jewish residents. Such speech may not be criminalized, even if it could form the basis of a tort (i.e., intentional infliction of severe emotional distress). Although it is undeniable that the proposed demonstration would seriously disturb, emotionally and mentally, at least some, and probably many of Skokie's (D) residents, the speech at issue may not be protected by an exception to the First Amendment because such speech is indistinguishable in principle from speech that invites dispute; a state many not "make criminal the peaceful expression of unpopular views." *Edwards v. South Carolina*, 372 U.S. 229, 237. Regardless of the court's personal views of NSPA's (P) ideology—which

Continued on next page.

is that it is repugnant—its members' civil rights under the First Amendment must be upheld so that these rights remain vital for all; First Amendment rights must protect not only those society deems acceptable but also those whose ideas it quite justifiably rejects and despises.

ANALYSIS

The United States Supreme Court declined to grant certiorari in this case. Justice Blackmun, dissenting, believed this case afforded the Court an opportunity to consider whether, in the context of the unique facts presented, there is no limit whatsoever to the exercise of free speech. He indicated when citizens assert, not casually but with deep conviction, that a proposed demonstration is scheduled at a place and in a manner that is taunting and overwhelmingly offensive to the citizens of that place, that assertion, uncomfortable though it may be for judges, deserves to be examined, and upon close scrutiny, such speech just might fall into the same category as one's "right" to cry "fire" in a crowded theater, given "the character of every act depends upon the circumstances in which it is done." However, as was pointed out by concurring Judge Wood in *Collin*, since in this case there was ample warning of the proposed demonstration, this situation was not equivalent to the sudden and unfounded cry of "fire" in a crowded and unsuspecting theater to which it was sometimes analogized. As Judge Wood observed, "[r]ecognition of the full scope of freedom of speech does not compel anyone to listen, or if listening to believe."

Quicknotes

FIRST AMENDMENT Prohibits Congress from enacting any law respecting an establishment of religion or prohibiting the free exercise of religion; or abridging the freedom of speech or of the press, the right of peaceful assembly, and the right to petition for a redress of grievances.

FREEDOM OF SPEECH The right to express oneself without governmental restrictions on the content of that expression.

R.A.V. v. City of St. Paul

Teenager (D) v. Municipality (P)

505 U.S. 377 (1992)

NATURE OF CASE: Certiorari review of constitutionality of "hate crime" ordinance.

FACT SUMMARY: When R.A.V. (D) was charged with allegedly burning a cross inside the fenced yard of a Black family, the City of St. Paul (P) charged R.A.V. (D) under the Bias-Motivated Crime Ordinance.

RULE OF LAW

Where content discrimination in an ordinance is not reasonably necessary to achieve a city's compelling interests, the ordinance cannot survive First Amendment scrutiny.

FACTS: R.A.V. (D) and several other teenagers allegedly assembled a crudely made cross and burned it inside the fenced yard of a Black family. This conduct could have been punished under any of a number of laws, but the City of St. Paul (P) chose to charge R.A.V. (D) under the Bias-Motivated Crime Ordinance, which made criminally punishable conduct known as "hate crimes." R.A.V. (D) moved to dismiss on the ground that the ordinance was substantially overbroad and impermissibly content based and therefore facially invalid under the First Amendment. The trial court granted this motion, but the Minnesota Supreme Court reversed because the modifying phrase "arouses anger, alarm or resentment in others" limited the reach of the ordinance to conduct that amounted to "fighting words," and therefore the ordinance reached only expression "that the First Amendment does not protect." The court also concluded that the ordinance was not impermissibly content based because it was a narrowly tailored means toward accomplishing the compelling governmental interest of protecting the community against bias-motivated threats to public safety and order.

ISSUE: Where content discrimination in an ordinance is not reasonably necessary to achieve a city's compelling interests, can the ordinance survive First Amendment scrutiny?

HOLDING AND DECISION: (Scalia, J.) No. Where content discrimination in an ordinance is not reasonably necessary to achieve a city's compelling interests, the ordinance cannot survive First Amendment scrutiny. Assuming all expression reached by the ordinance is proscribable under the fighting words doctrine, the ordinance is nonetheless facially unconstitutional in that it prohibits otherwise permitted speech solely on the basis of the subjects the speech addresses. Some areas of speech may, consistent with the First Amendment, be regulated because of their constitutionally proscribable content, namely, obscenity, defamation, and fighting words. Although the Minnesota Supreme Court construed the modifying phrase in the ordinance to reach only those symbols or displays that amount to fighting words, the remaining, unmodified terms make clear that the ordinance applies only to fighting words that insult, or provoke violence, on the basis of race, color, creed, religion, or gender. The First Amendment does not permit St. Paul (P) to impose special prohibitions on those speakers who express views on disfavored subjects. Burning a cross in someone's front yard is reprehensible, but St. Paul (P) has sufficient means at its disposal to prevent such behavior without adding the First Amendment to the fire. Reversed.

CONCURRENCE: (White, J.) The judgment of the Minnesota Supreme Court should be reversed. However, this case could easily be decided under First Amendment law by holding that the ordinance is fatally overbroad because it criminalizes not only unprotected expression, but expression protected by the First Amendment. The Court's new "under-breadth" creation serves no desirable function.

CONCURRENCE: (Blackmun, J.) The result of the majority opinion is correct because this particular ordinance reaches beyond fighting words to speech protected by the First Amendment. However, by its decision today, the majority appears to relax the level of scrutiny applicable to content-based laws, thus weakening the traditional protections of speech.

CONCURRENCE: (Stevens, J.) The majority establishes a near-absolute ban on content-based regulation. Content-based distinctions are an inevitable and indispensable aspect of First Amendment law. On the basis of content, the First Amendment does not protect the right to fix prices, breach contracts, make false warranties, place bets, threaten, or coerce. "Unprotected" or "proscribable" categories are based on content. Courts must consider the content and context of regulated speech and the scope of restrictions. This ordinance regulates low-value speech, fighting words, and only expressive conduct, not written or spoken words. The context is confrontational and potentially violent situations. Cross-burning is not a political statement; it is the first step in an act of assault that can be no more protected than holding a gun to someone's head. The scope of the restriction is the narrow.

Continued on next page.

R.A.V. (D) is free to burn a cross or express racial supremacy, so long as the burning is not so threatening and so directed at an individual as to by its very execution inflict injury. That the ordinance singles out threats based on race, color, creed, religion, or gender is justifiable because these threats cause more harm to society and individuals than others. While not invalid as a content-based speech regulation, the ordinance is, however, overbroad.

ANALYSIS

The text of the St. Paul Bias-Motivated Crime Ordinance provides that: "Whoever places on public or private property a symbol, object, appellation, characterization or graffiti, including, but not limited to, a burning cross or Nazi swastika, which one knows or has reasonable grounds to know arouses anger, alarm or resentment in others on the basis of race, color, creed, religion or gender commits disorderly conduct and shall be guilty of a misdemeanor." The flaw in the wording of the ordinance was that it required the person who committed the hateful act to discern the reaction of the victim to the perpetrator's conduct. It is likely that hate crime ordinances that are worded to punish conduct intended by the perpetrator to frighten, anger, etc., on the basis of race, religion, etc., would be upheld. Even if no hate crime ordinance could be upheld, the hateful conduct could still be punished under criminal trespass, arson, battery, homicide statutes, etc.

Quicknotes

CONTENT-BASED STATUTES Laws that regulate speech based on its content.

CONTENT-NEUTRAL STATUTES Laws that regulate speech regardless of its content.

FIGHTING WORDS Unprotected speech that inflicts injury by its very utterance and provokes violence from the audience.

OVERBREADTH That quality or characteristic of a statute, regulation, or order that reaches beyond the problem it was meant to solve, causing it to sweep within it activity it cannot legitimately reach.

Virginia v. Black

State (P) v. Person convicted under cross-burning statute (D)

538 U.S. 343 (2003)

NATURE OF CASE: Certiorari review of constitutionality of state cross-burning statute.

FACT SUMMARY: When Black (D) was prosecuted and convicted under Virginia's (P) cross-burning statute, he argued its unconstitutionality because of a provision treating any cross burning as prima facie evidence of intent to intimidate.

RULE OF LAW

A provision in a state's cross-burning statute treating any cross burning as prima facie evidence of intent to intimidate is unconstitutional.

FACTS: Black (D) was prosecuted and convicted by a jury under Virginia's (P) cross-burning statute, which bans cross burning with intent to intimidate a person or group of persons. The statute contains a provision that any burning of a cross constitutes prima facie evidence of intent to intimidate a person or group of persons. The Supreme Court of Virginia reversed the conviction, and the United States Supreme Court granted certiorari to review the statute's constitutionality.

ISSUE: Is a provision in a state's cross-burning statute treating any cross burning as prima facie evidence of intent to intimidate unconstitutional?

HOLDING AND DECISION: (O'Connor, J.) Yes. A provision in a state's cross-burning statute treating any cross burning as prima facie evidence of intent to intimidate is unconstitutional. To this day, regardless of whether the message is a political one or whether the message is also meant to intimidate, the burning of a cross is a symbol of hate. While cross burning sometimes carries no intimidating message, at other times the intimidating message is the only message conveyed. This Court has long held that the government may regulate certain categories of expression consistent with the Constitution and that indeed intimidation in the constitutionally proscribable sense of the word is a type of true threat. The First Amendment, accordingly, permits Virginia (P) to outlaw cross burnings done with the intent to intimidate because burning a cross is a particularly virulent form of intimidation. Furthermore, instead of prohibiting all intimidating messages, Virginia (P) may choose to regulate this subset of intimidating messages in light of cross burnings' long and pernicious history as a signal of impending violence. However, this particular cross-burning statute is unconstitutionally overbroad due to its provision stating that any burning of a cross is prima facie evidence of intent to intimidate a person or group of persons. The prima facie provision strips away the very reason why a state may ban cross burning with the intent to intimidate because this provision permits a jury to convict in every cross-burning case in which defendants exercise their constitutional right not to put on a defense. It is apparent that the provision as so interpreted "would create an unacceptable risk of the suppression of ideas." Anger or hatred is not sufficient to ban all cross burnings in the absence of actual intimidation or threat. The First Amendment does not permit shortcuts. The prima facie evidence provision in this case is unconstitutional on its face.

CONCURRENCE: (Stevens, J.) Cross burning with "an intent to intimidate" unquestionably qualifies as the kind of threat that is unprotected by the First Amendment.

CONCURRENCE AND DISSENT: (Scalia, J.) While agreeing with the Court that a state may, without infringing the First Amendment, prohibit cross burning carried out with the intent to intimidate, there is no justification for the plurality's apparent decision to invalidate the prima facie evidence provision on its face.

CONCURRENCE AND DISSENT: (Souter, J.) While agreeing that the statute makes a content-based distinction within the category of punishable intimidating or threatening expression, I disagree that any exception should save the statute from unconstitutionality. No content-based statute should survive without a high probability that no official suppression of ideas is being encouraged.

DISSENT: (Thomas, J.) The majority errs in imputing an expressive component to the activity in question. In our culture, cross burning has almost invariably meant lawlessness and understandably instills in its victims a well-grounded fear of physical violence. Those who hate cannot terrorize and intimidate to make their point. The statute here addressed only conduct; there is no need for First Amendment analysis.

ANALYSIS

As articulated by the plurality in the *Black* decision, the prima facie evidence provision in the Virginia (P) cross-burning statute ignored all of the contextual factors that would be necessary in order for a court or jury to decide whether a particular cross burning was, in fact,

Continued on next page.

intended to intimidate. On the other hand, some legal commentators express the viewpoint such as that conveyed in Justice Thomas's dissent, that a cross burning always and necessarily represents intimidation.

Quicknotes

FIRST AMENDMENT Prohibits Congress from enacting any law respecting an establishment of religion or prohibiting the free exercise of religion; or abridging the freedom of speech or of the press, the right of peaceful assembly, and the right to petition for a redress of grievances.

PRIMA FACIE EVIDENCE Evidence presented by a party that is sufficient, in the absence of contradictory evidence, to support the fact or issue for which it is offered.

Roth v. United States; Alberts v. California

Publisher (D) v. Federal government (P)

354 U.S. 476 (1957)

NATURE OF CASE: Constitutional review of obscenity statutes.

FACT SUMMARY: Two defendants were convicted under obscenity statutes for selling obscene material. Roth (D) was convicted under a federal statute, Alberts (D) under a state statute.

RULE OF LAW

Obscenity is not a constitutionally protected expression and if the material, taken as a whole, has a dominant theme that appeals to prurient interest as judged by contemporary community standards, it may be proscribed.

FACTS: Roth (D) was a publisher and seller of books, magazines, and photographs. He was convicted under a federal statute for mailing obscene circulars and advertising and an obscene book. Alberts (D) was convicted under a California (P) statute that prohibited the keeping for sale of obscene and indecent books or the writing, composing, and publishing of an obscene advertisement therefor.

ISSUE: Is obscenity a constitutionally protected expression?

HOLDING AND DECISION: (Brennan, J.) No. Obscenity is not a constitutionally protected expression and if the material, taken as a whole, has a dominant theme that appeals to prurient interest as judged by contemporary community standards, it may be proscribed. The apparently unconditional phrasing of the First Amendment has been held by this Court not to protect every utterance. However, all ideas having even the slightest degree of socially redeeming value are fully protected unless they encroach upon the limited areas of more important interests. Obscenity has been held to carry no socially redeeming value and is, therefore, outside the protection of the First Amendment. A properly drawn and enforced statute outlawing obscenity will withstand the test of constitutionality. The portrayal of sex is not obscenity per se, as is evidenced by the large range of classic presentations in art, literature, and scientific works. Any attempt to proscribe obscenity must clearly define that which is prohibited. A work must be judged in its entirety, not by selected portions since many valuable and socially important materials could thereby be suppressed. The test should be whether, to the average person, applying contemporary community standards, the dominant theme of the material, taken as a whole, appeals to prurient interest. The words of this standard are sufficiently clear to give notice as to what is, or is not, permissible conduct. Both defendants were convicted under statutes applying the stated standard and both convictions are affirmed.

DISSENT: (Douglas, J.) The First Amendment is expressed in absolute terms and any law that purports to regulate material that can only produce thoughts is a clearly impermissible encroachment on these absolute guarantees. While the state and federal governments can regulate conduct, they should not be allowed to regulate the thought that precedes the conduct.

ANALYSIS

The purported standard of the *Roth* case soon became a thorn in the side of the Court. As Justice Harlan had predicted, the Court was reduced to a case-by-case review of obscenity convictions. In each case, the Court was forced to make a factual analysis of the material to determine if it was obscene. This despite the fact the same determination had already been made in every lower court. The one clarification of the *Roth* standard came in *Jacobellis v. Ohio,* 378 U.S. 184 (1964). In that case, a split Court stated the "community standard" was a national standard since a national constitution was being applied. The other noteworthy concept to come from that case was from Justice Stewart. He stated that the Court was attempting to deal with "hard core" pornography. While he admitted he could not define that term, he stated he knew it when he saw it, and the motion picture involved in that case was not it.

Quicknotes

OBSCENITY Indecency, lewdness, or offensive behavior in appearance or expression.

PRURIENT Refers to the shameful and morbid interest in nudity or sex.

Miller v. California

Bookseller (D) v. State (P)

413 U.S. 15 (1973)

NATURE OF CASE: Certiorari review of criminal prosecution for knowingly distributing obscene matter.

FACT SUMMARY: Miller (D) sent out advertising brochures for adult books to unwilling recipients.

RULE OF LAW

Material is obscene and not protected by the First Amendment if (1) the average person, applying contemporary community standards, would find that the work, taken as a whole, appeals to the prurient interest; (2) the work depicts in a patently offensive way sexual conduct specifically defined by the applicable state law; and (3) the work, taken as a whole, lacks serious literary, artistic, political, or scientific value.

FACTS: Miller (D) conducted a mass mailing campaign to advertise the sale of adult books. The advertising brochures were themselves found obscene. These brochures were sent to unwilling recipients who had not requested the material. Miller (D) was convicted of violating a statute that forbade knowingly distributing obscene matter.

ISSUE: Is material obscene and not protected by the First Amendment if (1) the average person, applying contemporary community standards, would find that the work, taken as a whole, appeals to the prurient interest; (2) the work depicts in a patently offensive way sexual conduct specifically defined by the applicable state law; and (3) the work, taken as a whole, lacks serious literary, artistic, political, or scientific value?

HOLDING AND DECISION: (Burger, C.J.) Yes. Material is obscene and not protected by the First Amendment if (1) the average person, applying contemporary community standards, would find that the work, taken as a whole, appeals to the prurient interest; (2) the work depicts in a patently offensive way sexual conduct specifically defined by the applicable state law; and (3) the work, taken as a whole, lacks serious literary, artistic, political, or scientific value. If material meets this definition of obscenity, then the state can prohibit its distribution if the mode of distribution entails the risk of offending unwilling recipients or exposing the material to juveniles. The burden of proof of the *Memoirs* test, *Memoirs v. Massachusetts*, 383 U.S. 413 (1966), that the material be utterly without redeeming value, is virtually impossible for the prosecution to meet and must be abandoned. There is no fixed national standard of "prurient interest" or "patently offensive" and these first two parts of the test are questions of fact to be resolved by the jury by applying contemporary community standards. Vacated and remanded.

DISSENT: (Douglas, J.) The test put forth by the majority offers no guidelines for defining obscenity. "Offensive" is so vague as to completely destroy the protection of the First Amendment.

DISSENT: (Brennan, J.) The statute in question is unconstitutionally overbroad and therefore invalid on its face.

ANALYSIS

The *Miller* test of obscenity is the most current test. If the three requirements are met, the material in question is considered obscene and outside the protection of the First Amendment. *Miller* is a turnaround from *Memoirs v. Massachusetts*, 383 U.S. 413 (1966), for many reasons: the *Memoirs* standard was too difficult to prove: the lower courts had no clear-cut guidelines because *Memoirs* was a plurality opinion; the Court decided to use local community standards to allow greater jury power; and the Court was beginning to feel institutional pressures, since every obscenity question was a constitutional question. Therefore, *Miller* was an attempt by the Court to decentralize decision-making.

Quicknotes

BURDEN OF PROOF The duty of a party to introduce evidence to support a fact that is in dispute in an action.

OBSCENITY Indecency, lewdness, or offensive behavior in appearance or expression.

OVERBROAD Characterization of a statute that proscribes lawful as well as unlawful conduct.

PRURIENT Refers to the shameful and morbid interest in nudity or sex.

Paris Adult Theatre I v. Slaton

Movie theatres (D) v. State (P)

413 U.S. 49 (1973)

NATURE OF CASE: Certiorari review of state statute prohibiting the showing of sexually explicit films.

FACT SUMMARY: Two adult films were shown at theatres (D) that advertised the nature of the films and required proof that all patrons were over 21.

RULE OF LAW

A state can forbid the dissemination of obscene material to consenting adults in order to preserve the quality of the community and to prevent the possibility of resulting antisocial behavior.

FACTS: Two movie theatres (D) in Atlanta showed "adult" films exclusively. The State of Georgia (P) sought to enjoin the showing of sexually explicit movies in these theatres under an obscenity statute. It was determined that the exterior advertising was not obscene or offensive, but that there were signs at the entrance stating that patrons must be 21 years of age and able to prove it. There was a further warning that those who would be offended by nudity should not enter. However, the films in question included, in addition to nudity, various simulated sex acts. The trial judge dismissed the complaint, and the Georgia Supreme Court reversed that decision.

ISSUE: Can a state forbid the dissemination of obscene material to consenting adults in order to preserve the quality of the community and to prevent the possibility of resulting antisocial behavior?

HOLDING AND DECISION: (Burger, C.J.) Yes. A state can forbid the dissemination of obscene material to consenting adults in order to preserve the quality of the community and to prevent the possibility of resulting antisocial behavior. A state has a valid interest in preventing exposure of obscene material to consenting adults. Even if exposure to juveniles and unwilling observers is prevented, the state has a further interest in preserving the quality of life, the community environment, and possible threats to public safety, which will allow the regulation of obscenity. Even if there is no conclusive scientific proof that exposure to obscenity adversely affects either an individual or society, it is for the legislature, not the courts, to resolve these empirical uncertainties. A legislature can determine that a connection between obscenity and antisocial behavior exists, even in the absence of conclusive proof. Here, even though only consenting adults are involved, the State (P) can make a judgment that public exhibition of obscenity has a tendency to injure the community and can, therefore, enjoin the distribution of obscenity. Vacated and remanded for reconsideration in light of *Miller v. California*, 413 U.S. 15 (1973).

DISSENT: (Brennan, J.) Prior obscenity standards have proved unworkable because they fail to give adequate notice of the definition of obscenity, producing a chilling effect on constitutionally protected speech. Because of the vague nature of these standards, every case is marginal, producing a vast number of constitutional questions that creates institutional stress in the judicial system. States do have a valid interest in protecting children and unconsenting adults from exposure to allegedly obscene material, but other possible state interests, as discussed in the majority opinion, are vague, speculative, and cannot be proven. Therefore, in the absence of threat of exposure to juveniles or unconsenting adults, material cannot be suppressed, but the state can regulate the manner of distribution.

ANALYSIS

The Court, in three companion cases to the principal case, also upheld obscenity convictions on seizures involving the importation of films from a foreign country, the interstate transportation of obscene materials for private use, and the sale of an obscene book that contained no pictures. In 1974, however, the Court overturned an obscenity conviction for the showing of "Carnal Knowledge," a film with a Motion Picture Association of America (MPAA) rating of "R." While asserting that the finding of obscenity was essentially a question of fact for the jury, the Court warned that the jury did not have an unbridled discretion in this area. In another case, the Court also stated that the community standard to be applied was local, not national. Justice Brennan dissented, arguing that requiring a national distributor to comply with numerous local standards was totally unreasonable.

Quicknotes

CHILLING EFFECT The result of a practice or law that discourages the exercise of a right.

OBSCENITY Indecency, lewdness, or offensive behavior in appearance or expression.

American Booksellers Ass'n v. Hudnut

Book publishers association (P) v. Mayor, City of Indianapolis (D)

771 F.2d 323 (7th Cir. 1985), *aff'd mem.*, 475 U.S. 1001 (1986)

NATURE OF CASE: Appeal from decision invalidating municipal ordinance.

FACT SUMMARY: The City of Indianapolis (D) appealed from a decision finding an Indianapolis municipal statute defining pornography in violation of the First Amendment since it discriminated on the basis of content of speech.

RULE OF LAW

Ordinances that discriminate on the basis of content of speech are unconstitutional in violation of the First Amendment.

FACTS: The City of Indianapolis (D) enacted a municipal statute defining pornography as a practice that discriminates against women and that could be redressed through the administrative and judicial methods used for other discrimination. More specifically, the statute defines pornography as the graphic sexually explicit subordination of women, whether in pictures or in words, and listed a number of examples that would qualify as pornography. The American Booksellers Association, (P) brought suit, contending that the ordinance was unconstitutional in that it discriminated on the basis of content of speech. The district court agreed, and from this decision, Indianapolis (D) appealed.

ISSUE: Are ordinances that discriminate on the basis of content of speech unconstitutional in violation of the First Amendment?

HOLDING AND DECISION: (Easterbrook, J.) Yes. Ordinances that discriminate on the basis of content of speech are unconstitutional in violation of the First Amendment. There is no question that the ordinance in question in the present case operates in this manner. Indianapolis (D) has determined what it considers the appropriate way in which to portray women. Speech that portrays women in positions of equality is allowed, and that which portrays women in positions of subservience is not, regardless of literary or artistic value. This is simply thought control, which cannot be tolerated. Even accepting the premises of the legislation, that pornographic materials, as defined, tend to perpetuate the subordination of women, this ordinance cannot stand. The fact that such speech would tend to perpetuate subordination illustrates its power as speech, and the cornerstone of our society is that our citizens have the absolute right to propagate opinions that our government finds wrongful, or even hateful. Speech is protected regardless of how insidious. This definition of pornography is unconstitutional. Affirmed.

ANALYSIS

This decision was affirmed upon appeal to the Supreme Court. Three justices of the Court would have set the case for oral arguments. The Court makes it quite clear that regulations on the content of speech, unless proper time, place, and manner restrictions are delineated, will not withstand constitutional challenge.

Quicknotes

CONTENT-BASED STATUTES Laws that regulate speech based on its content.

Erznoznik v. Jacksonville

Drive-in movie theater manager (P) v. Municipality (D)

422 U.S. 205 (1975)

NATURE OF CASE: Appeal from judgment upholding, as not violative of the First Amendment, an ordinance prohibiting drive-in movie theaters with screens visible from a public street from showing films containing nudity.

FACT SUMMARY: Erznoznik (P) challenged, as violating the First Amendment, Jacksonville's (D) ordinance prohibiting drive-in movie theaters with screens visible from the street from showing films containing nudity.

RULE OF LAW

An ordinance that prohibits drive-in movie theaters with screens visible from public streets from showing nonobscene films containing nudity is facially invalid under the First Amendment.

FACTS: Erznoznik (P) challenged, as violating the First Amendment, Jacksonville's (D) ordinance prohibiting drive-in movie theaters with screens visible from a public street from showing films containing nudity. Exhibiting nudity was defined to include exhibiting the human male or female bare buttocks, human female bare breasts, or human bare pubic areas. Jacksonville (D) conceded the ordinance applied to nonobscene movies. Jacksonville's (D) primary argument was it had the right to protect its citizens against unwilling exposure to materials that might be offensive. The ordinance was judicially upheld. The Supreme Court granted certiorari.

ISSUE: Is an ordinance that prohibits drive-in movie theaters with screens visible from public streets from showing nonobscene films containing nudity facially invalid under the First Amendment?

HOLDING AND DECISION: (Powell, J.) Yes. An ordinance that prohibits drive-in movie theaters with screens visible from public streets from showing nonobscene films containing nudity is facially invalid under the First Amendment. Although a state or municipality may protect individual privacy by enacting reasonable time, place, and manner regulations applicable to all speech irrespective of content, the First Amendment strictly limits its power when it acts as censor, undertaking selectively to shield the public from some kinds of speech on the ground they are more offensive than others. However, such censorship has been upheld only if the speech invades the privacy of the home, or the viewer cannot readily avoid exposure to it. In our pluralistic society, absent these narrow circumstances, the burden falls on the viewer to avoid exposure to the speech the viewer finds offensive. Applying these principles here, the Jacksonville (D) ordinance discriminates among movies solely on the basis of content, and it deters drive-ins from showing movies containing any nudity, no matter how innocent or educational. Viewers who happen to be on public streets and places can readily avert their eyes, because drive-in theater screens are not so obtrusive as to make viewers a captive audience. Thus, such censorship of the content of otherwise protected speech cannot be justified on the basis of the limited privacy interest of persons on the public streets. The ordinance also cannot be justified as an exercise of the city's police power for the protection of children against viewing the films. Even assuming such is its purpose, the restriction is broader than permissible since it is not directed against obscene, sexually explicit nudity or otherwise limited. Nor can the ordinance be justified as a traffic regulation. If this were its purpose, it would be invalid as a strikingly underinclusive legislative classification since it singles out movies containing nudity from all other movies that might distract a passing motorist. For these reasons, the ordinance is facially invalid under the First Amendment; where First Amendment freedoms are at stake the precision of drafting and clarity of purpose are essential, and those elements are absent from the Jacksonville (D) ordinance. Reversed.

DISSENT: (Burger, C.J.) The majority's approach is rigidly simplistic and fails to account for the diverse interests at issue here. It is unrealistic to say, as does the majority, that a passerby can avert his or her eyes when confronted with the outsize screen of a drive-in movie theater. The purpose of these screens is to attract and hold the attention of all observers, and thus, it is not unreasonable for legislators to believe that public nudity shown on these screens might distract drivers who pass by, thus causing traffic accidents. Moreover, those individuals who desire to view the films that would be banned by the ordinance may do so in indoor theaters or in drive-in movie theaters, which are shielded from public view. The ordinance does not restrict any "message," and any First Amendment interests involved are trivial, at best. It is narrowly drawn to regulate only certain unique public exhibitions of nudity, and it does not operate to suppress expression of ideas.

Continued on next page.

ANALYSIS

The Court's holding that a total ban on the display of nudity violates the First Amendment was upheld in *Schad v. Mount Ephraim,* 452 U.S. 61 (1981), which held that live entertainment may not be prohibited merely because it displays the nude human figure. Accordingly, the Court in *Schad* struck down a zoning ordinance that banned all live entertainment in a commercial zone in an attempt to outlaw nude dancing.

Quicknotes

FIRST AMENDMENT Prohibits Congress from enacting any law respecting an establishment of religion or prohibiting the free exercise of religion; or abridging the freedom of speech or of the press, the right of peaceful assembly, and the right to petition for a redress of grievances.

TIME, PLACE, AND MANNER RESTRICTION Certain types of regulations on speech that are permissible since they restrict only the time, place, and manner in which the speech may occur.

Young v. American Mini Theatres, Inc.

City (D) v. Theatre owner (P)

427 U.S. 50 (1976)

NATURE OF CASE: Review of order enjoining zoning law enforcement.

FACT SUMMARY: After Detroit enacted a zoning ordinance prohibiting the operation of "adult" theatres within 1,000 feet of any two other "regulated use" establishments, which were those showing specified sexual acts and specified anatomical areas, American Mini Theatres, Inc. (P), owner of two offending theatres, sought an injunction against enforcement of the ordinance on free speech grounds.

RULE OF LAW

A zoning ordinance may validly place reasonable limits on locations where establishments displaying sexual conduct or sexual organs may be operated within a municipality without offending the First Amendment.

FACTS: A Detroit ordinance set forth a zoning requirement that any "regulated use" establishment must be located at least 1,000 feet away from any two other such establishments. "Regulated use" establishments were those that showed sexual conduct specified by the ordinance or anatomical areas also specified in the ordinance. American Mini Theatres, Inc. (American) (P) owned two theatres that violated the ordinance by being within 1,000 feet of two other "regulated use" establishments, and American (P) sought to enjoin the municipality from enforcing the law against them on the ground that such enforcement constituted a violation of American's (P) First Amendment right to free speech. The Supreme Court granted certiorari to review the court of appeal's grant of the injunction.

ISSUE: May a zoning ordinance validly place reasonable limits on locations where establishments displaying sexual conduct or sexual organs may be operated within a municipality without offending the First Amendment?

HOLDING AND DECISION: (Stevens, J.) Yes. A zoning ordinance may validly place reasonable limits on locations where establishments displaying sexual conduct or sexual organs may be operated within a municipality without offending the First Amendment. American Mini Theatres, Inc. (American) (P) urged that the ordinance in question failed to provide adequate procedures for waiver of the 1,000-foot requirement and thus the ordinance is too vague. American (P), however, falls within the law and is not entitled to a waiver under any construction of it. The interest of the government in exhibiting material on the borderline of pornography and artistic expression is less vital than that in disseminating political ideas, and the vagueness regarding the hypothetical applicability of the ordinance to the letter will not suffice to overturn it. The ordinance is furthermore not a prior restraint on protected expression. The 1,000-foot restriction does not prevent the operation of American's (P) theatres but merely controls the locations of them. American (P) was not entitled to the injunction granted by the court of appeals. Reversed.

CONCURRENCE: (Powell, J.) This case is one of permissible land-use regulation and involves the First Amendment only incidentally. There is no restriction on the availability of adult movies. The ordinance is addressed only to the places at which this type of expression may be presented. This restriction does not interfere with content.

DISSENT: (Stewart, J.) The Court today permits a city to use a system of prior restraints and criminal sanctions to enforce a content-based restriction on the geographic location of theatres exhibiting sexually oriented films.

ANALYSIS

It seems that the Court is affording expressions of sexual content less First Amendment protection than other forms of expression, even in the absence of a finding of obscenity. As a content-based discrimination, this ordinance was subject to the constitutional argument presented here, but bolstered by the municipality's zoning power, it was nevertheless upheld.

Quicknotes

FIRST AMENDMENT Prohibits Congress from enacting any law respecting an establishment of religion or prohibiting the free exercise of religion; or abridging the freedom of speech or of the press, the right of peaceful assembly, and the right to petition for a redress of grievances.

PRIOR RESTRAINT A restriction imposed on speech prior to its communication.

ZONING ORDINANCE A statute that divides land into defined areas and that regulates the form and use of buildings and structures within those areas.

Renton v. Playtime Theatres, Inc.

Municipality (D) v. Adult movie theaters (P)

475 U.S. 41 (1986)

NATURE OF CASE: Appeal from reversal of summary judgment in an obscenity action.

FACT SUMMARY: The City of Renton (D) enacted an ordinance geographically limiting adult motion picture theaters.

RULE OF LAW

A municipality may enact zoning regulations limiting the area where adult motion picture theaters may operate.

FACTS: The City of Renton (D), concerned about the effect of adult movie houses on the surrounding areas, enacted a zoning ordinance proscribing the operation of such an establishment within 1,000 feet of certain public and private facilities and within a mile of a school. This effectively removed 95 percent of Renton (D) from such enterprises. Playtime Theaters, Inc. (P) brought an action, claiming the ordinance violated the free speech provisions of the First and Fourteenth Amendments. The district court granted summary judgment in favor of Renton (D), but the Ninth Circuit reversed. Renton (D) appealed.

ISSUE: May a municipality enact zoning regulations limiting the area where adult motion picture theaters may operate?

HOLDING AND DECISION: (Rehnquist, J.) Yes. A municipality may enact zoning regulations limiting the area where adult motion pictures theaters may operate. "Content-neutral" restrictions on speech are permissible so long as they serve a substantial interest and do not unreasonably limit alternative avenues of communication. Here, the regulations are content-neutral, as the purpose of the ordinance was to prevent the blight associated with adult theaters, not the content of the films. This is a substantial interest. Affirmed.

DISSENT: (Brennan, J.) The regulations are not content neutral, and the ordinance must be looked at much more critically.

ANALYSIS

The Court often finds itself fashioning standards of review for an issue. Historically, the Court has employed either a rubber-stamp rationality test or a very-difficult-to-meet strict scrutiny standard. The standard enunciated here seems to fall in between the two.

Quicknotes

CONTENT-BASED STATUTES Laws that regulate speech based on its content.

CONTENT-NEUTRAL STATUTES Laws that regulate speech regardless of its content.

STRICT SCRUTINY Method by which courts determine the constitutionality of a law when a law affects a fundamental right; under the test, the legislature must have had a compelling interest to enact the law and measures prescribed by the law must be the least restrictive means possible to accomplish its goal.

City of Los Angeles v. Alameda Books, Inc.

Municipality (D) v. Bookstore (P)

535 U.S. 425 (2002)

NATURE OF CASE: Appeal from a summary judgment that held unconstitutional an adult-establishment ordinance on freedom of speech grounds.

FACT SUMMARY: The owners of adult entertainment businesses sought to enjoin enforcement of an ordinance that prohibited more than one adult entertainment business in the same building on First Amendment grounds.

RULE OF LAW

A municipal ordinance that prohibits more than one adult entertainment business in the same building does not violate the First Amendment.

FACTS: A provision of the Los Angeles Municipal Code prohibits establishment or maintenance of more than one adult entertainment business in the same building or structure. Two adult establishments, one of which was Alameda Books, Inc. (P), each of which operated an adult bookstore and an adult video arcade in the same building, sued Los Angeles (D) in federal district court, seeking injunctive and declaratory relief against enforcement of the code provision, arguing the provision was unconstitutional as violating the First Amendment. The district court agreed and granted summary judgment to Alameda Books (P). The federal court of appeals affirmed, and Los Angeles (D) appealed.

ISSUE: Does a municipal ordinance that prohibits more than one adult entertainment business in the same building violate the First Amendment?

HOLDING AND DECISION: (O'Connor, J.) No. A municipal ordinance that prohibits more than one adult entertainment business in the same building does not violate the First Amendment. It is rational for a city to determine that reducing the concentration of adult operations in a neighborhood, whether within separate establishments or in one large establishment, will reduce crime rates. The record reflects that Los Angeles (D) conducted a comprehensive study of adult establishments and concluded that concentrations of adult businesses are in fact associated with higher rates of prostitution, robbery, assaults, and thefts in surrounding communities. There was evidence that the intent of the city council, when enacting the instant prohibition, was not only to disperse distinct adult establishments housed in separate buildings but also to disperse distinct adult businesses operated and housed in a single structure. The ordinance does not ban adult businesses, but merely requires that they be distanced from one another. The ordinance is not content-based and is aimed not at the content of the establishments but rather at the secondary effects of such businesses on the surrounding community. A municipality may rely on any evidence that is reasonably believed to be relevant for demonstrating a connection between speech and a substantial independent government interest. At this stage of the proceedings, Los Angeles (D) has done so. Our deference to the evidence presented by Los Angeles (D) is the product of a careful balance between competing interests. Here, there is less reason to be concerned that municipalities will use these ordinances to discriminate against unpopular speech. Reversed.

CONCURRENCE: (Kennedy, J.) The law does not require a city to ignore the consequences of adult entertainment businesses if it uses its zoning power in a reasonable way to ameliorate them without suppressing speech.

DISSENT: (Souter, J.) The government's freedom of experimentation cannot displace its burden under the intermediate scrutiny standard to show that the restriction of speech is no greater than essential to realizing an important objective.

ANALYSIS

As the *Alameda* decision makes clear, a zoning measure can be consistent with the First Amendment if it is likely to cause a significant decrease in secondary effects and a trivial decrease in the quality of speech. A dispersal ordinance causes deleterious businesses to separate rather than to close, so negative externalities are diminished but speech is not.

Quicknotes

FIRST AMENDMENT Prohibits Congress from enacting any law respecting an establishment of religion or prohibiting the free exercise of religion; or abridging the freedom of speech or of the press, the right of peaceful assembly, and the right to petition for a redress of grievances.

FREEDOM OF SPEECH The right to express oneself without governmental restrictions on the content of that expression.

SUMMARY JUDGMENT Judgment rendered by a court in response to a motion by one of the parties, claiming that the lack of a question of material fact in respect to an issue warrants disposition of the issue without consideration by the jury.

New York v. Ferber

State (P) v. Distributor (D)

458 U.S. 747 (1982)

NATURE OF CASE: Appeal from conviction under statute prohibiting persons from distributing child pornography.

FACT SUMMARY: Ferber (D) contended that a New York statute prohibiting persons from knowingly promoting sexual performances by children under the age of 16 by distributing material that depicts such performances was unconstitutional in that it encroached upon protected First Amendment interests.

RULE OF LAW

Child pornography does not constitute speech protected under the First Amendment.

FACTS: New York Criminal Code § 263.15 prohibits persons from knowingly promoting sexual performances by children under the age of 16 by distributing material that depicts such performances. A sexual performance is defined as any performance or part thereof that includes sexual conduct by a child less than 16 years of age. Criminal Code § 263.10 bans only the knowing dissemination of obscene material. Ferber (D), the proprietor of a Manhattan bookstore specializing in sexually oriented products, was indicted on two counts of violating § 263.10 and two counts of violating § 263.15 after selling two films to an undercover police officer. The films were devoted almost exclusively to depicting young boys masturbating. After a jury trial, Ferber (D) was acquitted of the two counts of promoting an obscene sexual performance but found guilty of two counts under § 263.15, which did not require proof that the films were obscene. After the New York Court of Appeals reversed the conviction, the State (P) brought this appeal.

ISSUE: Does child pornography constitute speech not protected under the First Amendment?

HOLDING AND DECISION: (White, J.) Yes. Child pornography does not constitute speech protected under the First Amendment. The states are entitled to great leeway in the regulation of pornographic depictions of children. A state's interest in safeguarding the physical and psychological well-being of a minor is compelling. The use of children as subjects of pornographic materials is harmful to the physiological, emotional, and mental health of the child. The distribution of photographs and films depicting sexual activity by juveniles is intrinsically related to the sexual abuse of children in at least two ways. First, the materials produced are a permanent record of the children's participation and the harm to the child is exacerbated by circulation of the materials. Second, the distribution network for child pornography must be closed if the production of material that requires the sexual exploitation of children is to be effectively controlled. The value of permitting live performances and photographic reproductions of children engaged in lewd sexual conduct is exceedingly modest, if not de minimis. Reversed.

CONCURRENCE: (O'Connor, J.) It is quite possible that New York's statute is overbroad because it bans depictions that do not actually threaten the harms identified by the Court. It is not necessary to address these possibilities further, however, because this potential overbreadth is not sufficiently substantial to warrant facial invalidation of New York's statute.

CONCURRENCE: (Brennan, J.) The application of § 263.15 or any similar statute to depictions of children that in themselves do have serious literary, artistic, scientific, or medical value would violate the First Amendment.

ANALYSIS

This decision separated the test for child pornography from the general standard for determining obscenity under the well-known *Miller v. California* standard, 413 U.S. 15 (1973). The *Miller* standard was adjusted in three respects: a trier of fact need not find that the material appeals to the prurient interest of the average person; it is not required that sexual conduct portrayed is done so in a patently offensive manner; and the material at issue need not be considered as a whole.

Quicknotes

DE MINIMIS Insignificant; trivial; not of sufficient significance to require legal action.

FREEDOM OF SPEECH The right to express oneself without governmental restrictions on the content of that expression.

OBSCENITY Indecency, lewdness, or offensive behavior in appearance or expression.

OVERBREADTH That quality or characteristic of a statute, regulation, or order that reaches beyond the problem it was meant to solve, causing it to sweep within it activity it cannot legitimately reach.

PRURIENT INTEREST Abnormal or obsessive interest in sex.

FCC v. Pacifica Foundation

Federal agency (P) v. Broadcasting company (D)

438 U.S. 726 (1978)

NATURE OF CASE: Certiorari review of speech restriction.

FACT SUMMARY: The Federal Communications Commission (P) disciplined Pacifica Foundation (D) for broadcasting "indecent language" over the radio airwaves.

RULE OF LAW

Government may validly regulate speech that is indecent but not obscene.

FACTS: Pacifica Foundation (D) broadcasted a monologue performed by comedian George Carlin over its radio station. The monologue sought to express Carlin's view of the public perception of "obscene" language and included the use of certain words that were considered "indecent" by a listener of the station. This listener filed a complaint with the Federal Communications Commission (FCC) (P), contending he was harmed by being exposed to Carlin's monologue. The FCC (P) found the words "indecent" and issued an order that would be considered when the station's license came up for renewal. The court of appeals overturned the order as in violation of the First Amendment freedom of speech. It held that because the FCC (P) specifically found the speech not to be obscene, it had no power to regulate it. The Supreme Court granted certiorari.

ISSUE: May government validly regulate speech that is indecent but not obscene?

HOLDING AND DECISION: (Stevens, J.) Yes. Government may validly regulate speech that is indecent yet not obscene. Government may regulate the content of speech where such speech, in context, is vulgar, offensive, and shocking. Patently offensive speech is not entitled to complete constitutional protection. It may be limited under time and place restrictions. As a result, the order was properly issued. Reversed.

CONCURRENCE: (Powell, J.) Limiting speech to appropriate times and places reduces its indecency while still affording access to willing listeners. But this is a problem where the broadcast media is involved, because during most of broadcast hours, the broadcaster cannot reach willing adults without reaching children as well. A second problem is that the broadcasts come directly into one's home. But I do not share the theory that the Justices of this Court are free generally to decide on the basis of its content which speech protected by the First Amendment is most "valuable" and hence deserving of protection. The result in this case turns not on the "value" of Carlin's monologue, but on the unique characteristics of the broadcast media and the potential harm to children and unwilling adults.

DISSENT: (Brennan, J.) The statutory term "indecent" under which the Federal Communications Commission (P) order was issued must be construed only to apply to obscene language. Because this language was held not to be obscene, the order was improper.

ANALYSIS

Justice Stevens, in this plurality decision, was careful to point out that if there had been any basis for concluding that the Federal Communications Commission's (P) characterization of Carlin's monologue rested upon its political content, First Amendment protection might be required. If it is the speaker's opinion being expressed that gives offense, constitutional protection is mandated. In this case the objection was not to Carlin's expressing his opinion but to the manner in which it was expressed.

Quicknotes

FREEDOM OF SPEECH The right to express oneself without governmental restrictions on the content of that expression.

Sable Communications, Inc. v. FCC

Communications company (P) v. Federal agency (D)

492 U.S. 115 (1989)

NATURE OF CASE: Appeal by federal government from district court's holding of the unconstitutionality of Section 223(b) of the Federal Communications Act insofar as it banned indecent telephone messages.

FACT SUMMARY: Sable Communications, Inc. (P) offered "dial-a-porn" prerecorded telephone messages through the Pacific Bell telephone system. The district court held unconstitutional legislation that placed an outright ban on indecent interstate commercial telephone messages but upheld the legislation insofar as it criminally prohibited telephone messages that were obscene.

RULE OF LAW

The Federal Communications Act's outright criminal ban on indecent interstate commercial telephone messages constitutes a First Amendment violation.

FACTS: Sable Communications, Inc. (P) began offering sexually oriented prerecorded telephone messages ("dial-a-porn") through the Pacific Bell telephone network through special phone lines requiring access codes and scrambling so that only subscribers could obtain the messages. Those who called the adult message number were charged a special fee. Section 223(b) of the Communications Act of 1934 (the Act; as amended in 1988), imposed an outright criminal ban on indecent as well as obscene interstate commercial telephone messages. The district court upheld the Act's prohibition on obscene telephone messages but enjoined enforcement of the statute insofar as it applied to indecent messages. The Supreme Court granted certiorari.

ISSUE: Does the Federal Communications Act's outright criminal ban on indecent interstate commercial telephone messages constitute a First Amendment violation?

HOLDING AND DECISION: (White, J.) Yes. The Federal Communications Act's outright criminal ban on indecent interstate commercial telephone messages constitutes a First Amendment violation. Sexual expression that is indecent but not obscene is protected by the First Amendment and may be sold to adults. However, the Government (D) has a compelling interest in protecting minors from such expression. The private telephone communications here at issue are substantially different from public radio broadcasts. In contrast to public displays, unsolicited mailings, and other means of expression the recipient has no meaningful opportunity to avoid, the dial-in medium requires the listener to take affirmative steps to receive the communication. There is no "captive audience" here; callers will generally not be unwilling listeners. Placing a telephone call is not the same thing as turning on a radio and being taken by surprise by an indecent message. The Government (D) nevertheless argues a complete ban is the only means of preventing children from gaining access to indecent messages. This argument is unpersuasive because there is evidence that the access codes, scrambling, and other technologies in place to keep such messages out of the reach of minors will be extremely effective. Accordingly, the statute is not sufficiently narrowly drawn, since its denial of adult access to indecent telephone messages is far broader than it needs to be to limit access to minors. Affirmed.

CONCURRENCE: (Scalia, J.) The majority correctly holds that the statute has the invalid effect of limiting the content of adult telephone conversations to that which is suitable for children to hear, and that the denial of adult access to telephone messages that are indecent but not obscene far exceeds that which is necessary to limit the access of minors to such messages. However, the question of how few children being able to access such messages renders the risk unacceptable depends on what "indecency" includes. Since "indecency" encompasses pornography that "obscenity" excludes, the more narrowly "obscenity" is understood, the more pornographic "indecency" becomes and the more reasonable it becomes to insist on limiting access to minors. Moreover, although the First Amendment prevents Congress from banning indecent speech in this manner, this does not mean public utilities are required to carry such speech.

CONCURRENCE AND DISSENT: (Brennan, J.) Even the criminalization of the distribution of obscene materials to consenting adults should be unconstitutional; and forbidding the transmission of all obscene telephone messages is unduly heavy handed because the statute curtails freedom of speech far more broadly than warranted by the Government's (D) interest in preventing harm to minors.

ANALYSIS

The Court noted that credit cards, access codes, and scrambling rules were a satisfactory solution to the problem of keeping indecent dial-a-porn messages out of reach of minors. The Court's reasoning in this case could be extended to the distribution of indecent,

Continued on next page.

sexually explicit materials on the Internet, where access to a particular web site could be limited to minors through the use of technology, such as blocking and filtering software. In fact, in *Ashcroft v. American Civil Liberties Union,* 542 U.S. 656 (2004), the Court ruled the Child Online Protection Act (COPA) was unconstitutional because such software was a plausible, less restrictive alternative to the statute.

Quicknotes

FREEDOM OF SPEECH The right to express oneself without governmental restrictions on the content of that expression.

OBSCENITY Indecency, lewdness, or offensive behavior in appearance or expression.

Reno v. American Civil Liberties Union

Attorney General of the United States (D) v. Civil liberties advocacy group (P)

521 U.S. 844 (1997)

NATURE OF CASE: Certiorari review of constitutionality of the Communications Decency Act of 1996.

FACT SUMMARY: The American Civil Liberties Union (P) challenged the constitutionality of provisions of the Communications Decency Act of 1996 that purported to protect minors from harmful transmissions over the Internet.

RULE OF LAW

Content-based government regulations on speech are unconstitutional unless the government can demonstrate that it has a compelling interest for the regulation and that the regulation is the least restrictive means of achieving that interest.

FACTS: The Communications Decency Act of 1996 (CDA) contained provisions designed to protect minors from "indecent" and "patently offensive" communication on the Internet. The "indecent transmission" provision prohibited the knowing transmission of obscene or indecent messages to any recipient less than 18 years of age. The "patently offensive display" provision prohibited the knowing sending or displaying of patently offensive messages to a person less than 18 years of age. The American Civil Liberties Union (P) filed an action alleging that the CDA abridged freedom of speech protected by the First Amendment. The district court found in its favor and enjoined the enforcement of the "indecent" communications provisions, but expressly preserved the government's right to investigate and prosecute the obscenity or child pornography activities prohibited by the provision. The court also issued an unqualified injunction against the enforcement of the "patently offensive displays" provision because it contained no separate reference to obscenity or child pornography.

ISSUE: Are content-based government regulations on speech unconstitutional unless the government can demonstrate that it has a compelling interest for the regulation and that the regulation is the least restrictive means of achieving that interest?

HOLDING AND DECISION: (Stevens, J.) Yes. Content-based government regulations on speech are unconstitutional unless the government can demonstrate that it has a compelling interest for the regulation and that the regulation is the least restrictive means of achieving that interest. Although the congressional goal of protecting children from harmful materials is a legitimate and important one, the Communications Decency Act of 1996 (CDA) provisions at issue here are so broad and imprecise that they cannot be upheld. The Internet is a unique medium in that it provides a relatively unlimited, low-cost capacity for communication of all kinds, including traditional print and news services, audio, video, still images, and interactive real-time dialogue. It unquestionably deserves the highest level of First Amendment protection. The breadth of the CDA's coverage is wholly unprecedented and would undoubtedly impact adult as well as minor access to such materials. It does not limit its restrictions to commercial speech or entities but encompasses anyone posting messages on a computer, regardless of time of day, website, or any other factor. The district court heard evidence that in the near future a reasonably effective and less restrictive method by which parents can prevent their children from accessing sexually explicit material will become widely available. The current provisions cannot stand as they are more likely to interfere with the free exchange of ideas than to encourage it. Affirmed.

CONCURRENCE AND DISSENT: (O'Connor, J.) The Communications Decency Act of 1996 (CDA) is little more than an attempt by Congress to create "adult zones" on the Internet. Such zoning laws are valid if (1) they do not unduly restrict adult access to materials, and (2) the materials are such that minors have no right to read or view them. The CDA "display" provision and some applications of the "indecency transmission" provision fail to adhere to the first of these requirements and should therefore be invalidated only to those extents.

ANALYSIS

Issues surrounding speech, pornography, and access to the Internet will undoubtedly be revisited often in the next several years. The issues are extremely complex because the technology is so novel and are further complicated by the fact that the Internet extends worldwide. The Court was appropriately cautious in striking down the provisions and leaving the issue in the hands of parents until further developments evolve.

Quicknotes

CONTENT-BASED STATUTES Laws that regulate speech based on its content.

FIRST AMENDMENT Prohibits Congress from enacting any law respecting an establishment of religion or

Continued on next page.

prohibiting the free exercise of religion; or abridging the freedom of speech or of the press, the right of peaceful assembly, and the right to petition for a redress of grievances.

OBSCENITY Indecency, lewdness, or offensive behavior in appearance or expression.

Ashcroft v. Free Speech Coalition

Attorney General (D) v. Trade organization (P)

535 U.S. 234 (2002)

NATURE OF CASE: Appeal from holding a federal statute unconstitutional on First Amendment grounds.

FACT SUMMARY: The Free Speech Coalition (P) argued that the federal Child Pornography Prevention Act violated the First Amendment by defining prohibited child pornography to include sexually explicit images that appear to depict minors but were produced without using any real children, such as by using computer imaging.

RULE OF LAW

The Child Pornography Prevention Act of 1996, which proscribes speech that is neither obscene nor child pornography, abridges freedom of speech and is unconstitutional.

FACTS: In 1996, Congress enacted the Child Pornography Prevention Act (CPPA), which extended the federal prohibition against child pornography to sexually explicit images that appear to depict minors but were produced without using any real children. The statute prohibits, in specific circumstances, possessing or distributing these images that may be created by using adults who look like minors or by using computer imaging. The new technology makes it possible to create realistic images of children who do not exist. The Free Speech Coalition (P), a trade organization for the adult-entertainment industry, and others brought suit in federal district court challenging the constitutionality of the CPPA and the grounds that the "appears to be" and "conveys the impression" provisions of the statute are overbroad and vague, chilling them from producing works protected by the First Amendment. The district court disagreed, granting summary judgment for the Government (D). The federal court of appeals reversed, and the Government (D) appealed.

ISSUE: Does the Child Pornography Prevention Act of 1996, which proscribes speech that is neither obscene nor child pornography, abridge freedom of speech and is it unconstitutional?

HOLDING AND DECISION: (Kennedy, J.) Yes. The Child Pornography Prevention Act (CPPA) of 1996, which proscribes speech that is neither obscene nor child pornography, abridges freedom of speech and is unconstitutional. By prohibiting child pornography that does not depict an actual child, the CPPA goes beyond this Court's decisions, which distinguish child pornography from other sexually explicit speech because of the Government's (D) interest in protecting the children exploited by the production process. Pictures of young children engaged in certain acts might be obscene while similar depictions of adults, or perhaps even older adolescents, would not. The CPPA, however, is not directed at speech that is obscene but seeks to reach beyond obscenity and makes no attempt to conform to obscenity standards. For instance, the CPPA would reach visual depictions, such as movies, even if they have redeeming social value. The statute's prohibition of "any visual depiction" does not depend at all on how the image is produced. The statute captures a range of depictions, sometimes called "virtual child pornography," including computer-generated images as well as images produced by more traditional means. The literal terms of the CPPA, therefore, would embrace a Renaissance painting depicting a scene from classical mythology, a picture that "appears to be" of a minor engaging in sexually explicit conduct, and a Hollywood movie filmed without child actors if a jury believes an actor "appears to be" a minor engaging in actual or simulated sexual intercourse. These images do not involve, let alone harm, any children in the production process. Yet under the CPPA, *any* depiction of sexually explicit activity, no matter how it is presented, is proscribed; the CPPA, for example, applies to a picture in a psychology manual as well as a movie depicting the horrors of sexual abuse. The prohibitions of the CPPA are overbroad and unconstitutional. Affirmed.

CONCURRENCE: (Thomas, J.) In the event technology evolves to the point where it becomes impossible to enforce actual child pornography laws because the Government (D) cannot prove that certain pornography images are of real children, the Government (D) should not be foreclosed from enacting a regulation of virtual child pornography that contains an appropriate affirmative defense or some other narrowly drawn restriction.

DISSENT: (Rehnquist, C.J.) This Court does not normally strike down a statute on First Amendment grounds when a limiting instruction could be placed on the challenged statute. Here, the Child Pornography Prevention Act (CPPA) could be limited so as not to reach any material that was not already unprotected before the CPPA.

ANALYSIS

In the *Free Speech Coalition* decision, the Supreme Court noted that, under the Child Pornography Prevention Act, even if a film contained no sexually explicit scenes

Continued on next page.

involving minors, it could be treated as child pornography if the title and trailers conveyed the impression that the scenes would be found in the movie. Hence, the determination of child pornography turned "on how the speech is presented, not on what is depicted."

Quicknotes

FIRST AMENDMENT Prohibits Congress from enacting any law respecting an establishment of religion or prohibiting the free exercise of religion; or abridging the freedom of speech or of the press, the right of peaceful assembly, and the right to petition for a redress of grievances.

CHILL Inhibit or discourage.

United States v. Stevens

Federal government (P) v. Purveyor of animal cruelty videos (D)

559 U.S. 460 (2010)

NATURE OF CASE: Appeal in action involving the indictment under 18 U.S.C. § 48 for creating, selling, and possessing depictions of animal cruelty.

FACT SUMMARY: Stevens (D), who was indicted under 18 U.S.C. § 48 for creating, selling, and possessing depictions of animal cruelty—specifically, for selling dogfighting videos—contended the statute was facially invalid under the First Amendment.

RULE OF LAW

A statute that criminalizes the commercial creation, sale, or possession of certain depictions of animal cruelty in which a living animal is intentionally maimed, mutilated, tortured, wounded, or killed is overbroad and facially invalid under the First Amendment as a content-based regulation of protected speech.

FACTS: Congress enacted 18 U.S.C. § 48 to criminalize the commercial creation, sale, or possession of certain depictions of animal cruelty. The statute addressed only portrayals of harmful acts, not the underlying conduct. It applied to any visual or auditory depiction "in which a living animal is intentionally maimed, mutilated, tortured, wounded, or killed," if that conduct violates federal or state law where "the creation, sale, or possession takes place." Another clause exempted depictions with "serious religious, political, scientific, educational, journalistic, historical, or artistic value." The legislative background of § 48 focused primarily on "crush videos," which feature the torture and killing of helpless animals and are said to appeal to persons with a specific sexual fetish. Stevens (D) was indicted under § 48 for selling videos depicting dogfighting, which is illegal in all states and the District of Columbia. He moved to dismiss, arguing § 48 is facially invalid under the First Amendment. The Supreme Court granted certiorari.

ISSUE: Is a statute that criminalizes the commercial creation, sale, or possession of certain depictions of animal cruelty in which a living animal is intentionally maimed, mutilated, tortured, wounded, or killed overbroad and facially invalid under the First Amendment as a content-based regulation of protected speech?

HOLDING AND DECISION: (Roberts, C.J.) Yes. A statute that criminalizes the commercial creation, sale, or possession of certain depictions of animal cruelty in which a living animal is intentionally maimed, mutilated, tortured, wounded, or killed is overbroad and facially invalid under the First Amendment as a content-based regulation of protected speech. Depictions of animal cruelty are not, as a class, categorically unprotected by the First Amendment. Since its enactment, the First Amendment has permitted restrictions on a few historic categories of speech that have never been thought to raise any constitutional problem. Depictions of animal cruelty should not be added to that list. While the prohibition of animal cruelty has a long history in American law, there is no evidence of a similar tradition prohibiting depictions of such cruelty. The Government's (P) proposed test would broadly balance the value of the speech against its societal costs to determine whether the First Amendment even applies, but the First Amendment's free speech guarantee does not extend only to categories of speech that survive an ad hoc balancing of relative social costs and benefits. The Amendment itself reflects a judgment by the American people that the benefits of its restrictions on the Government (P) outweigh the costs. Limiting 18 U.S.C. § 48's reach to crush videos and depictions of animal fighting or other extreme cruelty, as the Government (P) suggests, requires an unrealistically broad reading of the statute's exceptions clause. Nor does the Government (P) seriously contest that the presumptively impermissible applications of § 48 far outnumber any permissible ones. The Court therefore does not decide whether a statute limited to crush videos or other depictions of extreme animal cruelty would be constitutional. Section 48 is not so limited but is instead substantially overbroad and therefore invalid under the First Amendment.

DISSENT: (Alito, J.) The First Amendment does not protect criminal conduct engaged in for expressive purposes. One of the principal reasons 18 U.S.C. § 48 was enacted was to combat crush videos. Congress concluded that the only effective way of stopping the underlying criminal conduct was to prohibit the commercial exploitation of the videos of that conduct. Crush videos present a highly unusual free speech issue because they are so closely linked with violent criminal conduct: the videos record the commission of violent criminal acts, and it appears these crimes are committed for the sole purpose of creating the videos. Given these realities, the First Amendment does not require Congress to step aside and allow the underlying crimes to continue. The Court's reasoning underlying its precedents regarding child pornography applies here. As with child pornography, the conduct depicted in crush videos is criminal in every jurisdiction in the country. That conduct, which is what is

Continued on next page.

shown in the crush videos, cannot be prevented without targeting the sale of the videos. Finally, the harm caused by the underlying criminal conduct vastly outweighs any minimal value the depictions might conceivably be thought to possess.

ANALYSIS

After the Court's decision in this case, Congress enacted a much narrower version of 18 U.S.C. § 48 that was focused on just crush videos, thus eliminating the kind of overbreadth challenges accepted by the Court here. As Justice Alito pointed out in his dissent, Congress's efforts in this area seem to have been vindicated. By 2007, sponsors of § 48 declared the crush video industry dead, and even overseas websites shut down in the statute's wake. Moreover, right after the Third Circuit's decision in this case, which facially invalidated the statute, crush videos were already back online. Thus, criminalizing the display of crush videos seems to have greatly reduced, or even eliminated, the underlying animal torture.

Quicknotes

CONTENT-BASED STATUTES Laws that regulate speech based on its content.

FREEDOM OF SPEECH The right to express oneself without governmental restrictions on the content of that expression.

Brown v. Entertainment Merchants Ass'n

State official (D) v. Video game association (P)

564 U.S. 786 (2011)

NATURE OF CASE: Appeal in action to determine whether California's (D) prohibition of the sale or rental to minors of violent video games violated the First Amendment.

FACT SUMMARY: A video game association (P) brought suit challenging as violative of the First Amendment California's (D) statute prohibiting the sale or rental to minors of violent video games.

RULE OF LAW

A statute that purports to prohibit the rental or sale to minors of violent video games violates the First Amendment as being both underinclusive and overinclusive.

FACTS: California (D) enacted a statute that prohibited the sale or rental to minors of violent video games. The statute covered games "in which the range of options available to a player includes killing, maiming, dismembering, or sexually assaulting an image of a human being, if those acts are depicted" in a manner that "appeals to a deviant or morbid interest of minors," that is "patently offensive to prevailing standards in the community as to what is suitable for minors," and that "causes the game, as a whole, to lack serious literary, artistic, political, or scientific value for minors." A video game association (P) brought suit challenging the statute as violative of the First Amendment. The Supreme Court granted certiorari.

ISSUE: Does a statute that purports to prohibit the rental or sale to minors of violent video games violate the First Amendment as being both underinclusive and overinclusive?

HOLDING AND DECISION: (Scalia, J.) Yes. A statute that purports to prohibit the rental or sale to minors of violent video games violates the First Amendment as being both underinclusive and overinclusive. Video games qualify for First Amendment protection. Like protected books, plays, and movies, they communicate ideas through familiar literary devices and features distinctive to the medium, and the basic principles of freedom of speech do not vary with a new and different communication medium. A legislature cannot create new categories of unprotected speech simply by weighing the value of a particular category against its social costs and then punishing it if it fails the test. California's (D) statute does not adjust the boundaries of an existing category of unprotected speech to ensure that a definition designed for adults is not uncritically applied to children. Instead, California (D) wishes to create a wholly new category of content-based regulation that is permissible only for speech directed at children. That is unprecedented and mistaken. While a state may protect children from harm, its power to do so does not include a free-floating power to restrict the ideas to which children are exposed. This country has no tradition of specially restricting children's access to depictions of violence; in fact, numerous well-known children's stories and fairy-tales contain depictions of violence, as do books read in school through high school. Because the Act [California Assembly Bill 1179 (2005), Cal. Civ. Code Ann. §§1746–1746.5] imposes a restriction on the content of protected speech, it is invalid unless California (D) can demonstrate that it passes strict scrutiny, i.e., it is justified by a compelling government interest and is narrowly drawn to serve that interest. California (D) cannot meet that standard. Psychological studies purporting to show a connection between exposure to violent video games and harmful effects on children do not prove such exposure causes minors to act aggressively. Any demonstrated effects are both small and indistinguishable from effects produced by other media. Since California (D) has declined to restrict those other media, e.g., Saturday morning cartoons or violent comic books, its video-game regulation is wildly underinclusive, raising serious doubts about whether California (D) is pursuing the interest it invokes or is instead disfavoring a particular speaker or viewpoint. California (D) also cannot show the statute's restrictions meet the alleged substantial need of parents who wish to restrict their children's access to violent videos. The video-game industry's voluntary rating system already accomplishes that to a large extent. Moreover, as a means of assisting parents, the statute is greatly overinclusive, since not all of the children who are prohibited from purchasing violent video games have parents who disapprove of their doing so. Accordingly, because the statute is both underinclusive and overinclusive, it cannot satisfy strict scrutiny. This does not mean that the California legislature's concerns are not meritorious. Instead, it means the regulation the legislature has enacted is not justified by a compelling state interest. Even where the legislature's goal is the laudable goal of protecting children, the constitutional limits on governmental action apply.

CONCURRENCE: (Alito, J.) The statute at issue, although well intentioned, does not define "violent video games" with the precision the Constitution demands, so it violates the First Amendment by failing to provide fair

Continued on next page.

notice. That analysis should be the end of the question in this case. The majority's approach in reaching that conclusion, however, is flawed because it does not proceed with caution in the face of new technology but merely assumes that new technology is just like old technology. The majority too readily dismisses the possibility that the effect of playing video games on minors is very different from the effects of other forms of entertainment previously encountered. Some of the games contain an astounding amount of violence and antisocial content. Given that this content may be enhanced by new technologies, e.g., high-definition and 3-D, violent video games may in the near future enable troubled teens to experience in an extraordinarily personal and vivid way what it would be like to carry our unspeakable acts of violence. There are reasons to suspect that the experience of playing violent video games might be very different from reading a book, listening to the radio, or watching a movie or a television show—even if those contain elements of violence. The Court here should not have expressed its views as to whether a properly drawn statute would or would not survive constitutional scrutiny.

DISSENT: (Thomas, J.) The majority's decision does not comport with the original understanding of the First Amendment. That understanding did not encompass rights of adults to speak to minors or of minors to access speech absent approval from parents or guardians. Therefore, the statute at issue is not facially unconstitutional. This comports with evidence showing that the Founders believed parents had absolute authority over their minor children and expected parents to use that authority to direct the proper development of their children. Thus, the Framers could not possibly have understood the freedom of speech to include an unqualified right to speak to minors.

DISSENT: (Breyer, J.) The statute at issue only imposes a modest restriction on expression, as it only prevents a child or adolescent from buying a violent video game without a parent's assistance and no one is prevented from playing the game. The statute also significantly furthers the state's compelling interest, which is supported by studies and expert opinions that conclude the video games at issue are particularly likely to harm children. Here, the Court, as it has done in the past, should have deferred to the legislature and these legislative facts, especially given they involve technical matters that are beyond the Court's competence.

ANALYSIS

With this decision, the Court affirmed its holding in *United States v. Stevens*, 559 U.S. 460 (2010), where it held that new categories of unprotected speech may not be added to the list by a legislature that concludes certain speech is too harmful to be tolerated. In *Stevens*, the Court emphatically rejected the government's argument that lack of a historical warrant did not matter, and that it could create new categories of unprotected speech by applying a "simple balancing test" that weighs the value of a particular category of speech against its social costs and then punishes that category of speech if it fails the test. In both *Stevens* and this case, the majority emphasized that, based on long-standing tradition and history, obscenity is not protected speech, but non-obscene speech is protected. The Court indicated that because speech about violence is not obscene, it is protected. However, it is arguable that such a rigid, history-based approach will never permit First Amendment law to reflect changing community attitudes about non-obscene speech. Accordingly, Justice Breyer in his dissent asks "what sense does it make to forbid selling to a 13-year-old boy a magazine with an image of a nude woman, while protecting a sale to that 13-year-old of an interactive video game in which he actively, but virtually, binds and gags the woman, then tortures and kills her? What kind of First Amendment would permit the government to protect children by restricting sales of that extremely violent video game only when the woman—bound, gagged, tortured, and killed—is also topless?" The answer, according to the majority, is that regardless of the result, precedent must be adhered to, with no room for new categories of unprotected speech.

Quicknotes

FIRST AMENDMENT Prohibits Congress from enacting any law respecting an establishment of religion or prohibiting the free exercise of religion; or abridging the freedom of speech or of the press, the right of peaceful assembly, and the right to petition for a redress of grievances.

FREEDOM OF SPEECH The right to express oneself without governmental restrictions on the content of that expression.

STRICT SCRUTINY Method by which courts determine the constitutionality of a law when a law affects a fundamental right; under the test, the legislature must have had a compelling interest to enact the law and measures prescribed by the law must be the least restrictive means possible to accomplish its goal.

Virginia Pharmacy Board v. Virginia Citizens Consumer Council

State board (D) v. Residents (P)

425 U.S. 748 (1976)

NATURE OF CASE: Certiorari review of constitutionality of commercial speech restriction.

FACT SUMMARY: The Virginia Pharmacy Board (D) was charged with enforcing a state law that made it illegal for a pharmacist to advertise the prices of his or her prescription drugs.

RULE OF LAW

The First Amendment guarantee of freedom of speech extends to the recipients as well as the sources of the speech; and, as such, the consumer's interest in the free flow of advertising information brings such "commercial speech" within the protection of the First Amendment.

FACTS: Virginia law provides that licensed pharmacists are guilty of "unprofessional conduct" if they advertise "in any manner whatsoever, any amount, price, fee, premium, discount, rebate or credit terms . . . for any drugs which may be dispensed only by prescription." The Virginia Citizens Consumer Council (the Council) (P) is composed of Virginia residents who require prescription drugs. Citing statistics that show that drugs vary in price strikingly from outlet to outlet (e.g., from $2.59 to $6.00 for one drug), they filed this action to have the advertising ban declared an unconstitutional infringement on their First Amendment right to free speech. From a judgment for the Council (P), the Virginia Pharmacy Board (D) appealed, contending that "commercial speech" such as this is not protected by the First Amendment.

ISSUE: Does the First Amendment protect "commercial speech" as manifested in price advertising by professional groups?

HOLDING AND DECISION: (Blackmun, J.) Yes. The First Amendment guarantee of freedom of speech extends to the recipients as well as the sources of the speech; and, as such, the consumer's interest in the free flow of advertising information brings such "commercial speech" within the protection of the First Amendment. The traditional rule that "commercial speech" is not protected has been eroded gradually by the court and today it is set to rest. Advertising, however tasteless, is information nevertheless and entitled to constitutional deference thereby. To be sure, the holding today does not prevent reasonable regulation as to "time, place, and manner" or prevent illegal or misleading speech. It only recognizes the legitimacy of commercial speech for First Amendment purposes. Affirmed.

DISSENT: (Rehnquist, J.) The Court's decision today is troublesome for two reasons. First, it extends standing to sue to a group not asserting their right to receive information but rather the right of third parties to publish it. Second, by raising commercial speech to the level of First Amendment protection, the Court has usurped the constitutionally mandated power of state legislatures to regulate public health, etc.

ANALYSIS

Justice Burger's concurrence to the contrary notwithstanding, this case has brought many observers to the conclusion that advertising bans on professionals are no longer constitutional. Indeed, the American Bar Association and several state bar associations have begun to promulgate standards for advertising by attorneys that will protect the public from the perceived evils of a competitive bar. *Virginia Citizens Consumer Council* claims to overrule the 1951 case of *Breard v. Alexandria,* 341 U.S. 622 (1951). Note, however, that the ban on door-to-door sales upheld therein would appear to be precisely the kind of "time, place, and manner restriction" that the Court in *Virginia Citizens Consumer Council* expressly sanctioned.

Quicknotes

COMMERCIAL SPEECH Any speech that proposes a commercial transaction or promotes products or services.

TIME, PLACE, MANNER RESTRICTION Certain types of regulations on speech that are permissible since they restrict only the time, place, and manner in which the speech may occur.

Central Hudson Gas v. Public Service Comm'n

Gas company (P) v. Federal agency (D)

447 U.S. 557 (1980)

NATURE OF CASE: Certiorari review of the constitutionality of a federal regulation.

FACT SUMMARY: Central Hudson Gas (P) claimed the First Amendment prohibited the New York Public Service Commission's (D) regulation completely banning promotional advertising by an electrical utility.

RULE OF LAW

Where there is a substantial governmental interest, a restriction on commercial speech protected by the First Amendment is constitutional if it directly advances that interest and is not more extensive than is necessary to serve that interest.

FACTS: The Public Service Commission (D) banned all promotional advertising by an electrical utility as contrary to the national policy of conserving energy. Central Hudson Gas (P) challenged the regulation on First Amendment grounds.

ISSUE: Where there is a substantial governmental interest, is a restriction on commercial speech protected by the First Amendment constitutional if it directly advances that interest and is not more extensive than is necessary to serve that interest?

HOLDING AND DECISION: (Powell, J.) Yes. Where there is a substantial governmental interest, a restriction on commercial speech protected by the First Amendment is constitutional if it directly advances that interest and is not more extensive than is necessary to serve that interest. Commercial speech that concerns lawful activity and is not misleading is protected under the First Amendment, although at a lesser level than other speech. However, this protection prevents governmental restrictions on covered commercial speech unless they advance a substantial governmental interest and are not more extensive than is necessary to serve that interest. These principles produce a four-step analysis. At the outset, we must determine whether the expression is protected by the First Amendment. For commercial speech to come within that provision, it at least must concern lawful activity and not be misleading. Next, we ask whether the asserted governmental interest is substantial. If both inquiries yield positive answers, we must determine whether the regulation directly advances the governmental interest asserted, and whether it is not more extensive than is necessary to serve that interest. When applied to this case, the analysis indicates the regulation at issue is unconstitutional. It satisfies all the requirements except the last. It is so broad that it suppresses speech about electrical devices or services that would cause no increase in total energy usage and thus be unrelated to the energy conservation interest of the state. Reversed.

CONCURRENCE: (Blackmun, J.) The intermediate level of scrutiny advanced by the four-part analysis the Court sets up in this decision is appropriate for a restraint on commercial speech designed to protect consumers from misleading or coercive speech, or a regulation related to time, place, or manner of commercial speech. It is not, however, properly applied when a state seeks to suppress information about a product in order to manipulate a private economic decision that the state cannot or has not regulated or outlawed directly. No differences between commercial and other protected speech justify suppression of commercial speech in order to influence public conduct through manipulation of the availability of information.

CONCURRENCE: (Stevens, J.) This is not a "commercial speech" case, for the ban at issue would prohibit speech outside the limited boundaries of commercial speech. For example, it would seem to prohibit an electric company's advocacy of the use of electric heat for environmental reasons, as opposed to wood-burning stoves. Thus, it is not necessary to decide if the four-part analysis the Court adopts adequately protects commercial speech. This is a "regular" speech case. If the perceived harm associated with greater electrical usage is not sufficiently serious to justify direct regulation, surely it does not constitute the kind of clear and present danger that can justify the suppression of speech.

DISSENT: (Rehnquist, J.) The speech of a state-created monopoly, which is the subject of a comprehensive regulatory scheme, is not entitled to protection under the First Amendment. Furthermore, the Court errs in failing to recognize that the state law at issue in this case is most accurately viewed as an economic regulation and that the speech involved (if it falls within the First Amendment at all) occupies a significantly more subordinate position in the hierarchy of First Amendment values than the Court gives it today. Finally, in reaching its judgment, the Court improperly substitutes its own judgment for that of the state in deciding how a proper ban on promotional advertising should be drafted. On that point, in adopting a "no more extensive than necessary" analysis as the last part of its four-part test, the Court has embraced a test that will unduly impair a state legislature's ability to

Continued on next page.

adopt legislation reasonably designed to promote interests that have always been rightly thought to be of great importance to the state.

ANALYSIS

Historically, the Court had always held that commercial speech was not within the protections of the First Amendment. In the mid-1970s, however, a new trend began in which the Court recognized that the First Amendment did encompass certain commercial speech and offered it protection, although of a more limited sort than other speech. In recent years, though, there is evidence that the enthusiasm among the Justices for including commercial speech within the First Amendment is waning.

Quicknotes

COMMERCIAL SPEECH Any speech that proposes a commercial transaction or promotes products or services

44 Liquormart, Inc. v. Rhode Island

Liquor distributor (P) v. State (D)

517 U.S. 484 (1996)

NATURE OF CASE: Certiorari review of a state law prohibiting alcohol advertising.

FACT SUMMARY: Rhode Island (D) banned the advertising of retail prices of alcoholic beverages.

RULE OF LAW

Complete bans on truthful commercial advertising are unconstitutional.

FACTS: In 1956, Rhode Island (D) enacted a prohibition against advertising the retail price of any alcoholic beverage offered for sale in the state. The law also proscribed the news media from publishing this information. Rhode Island (D) claimed that the law was enacted to reduce market-wide consumption of alcohol. The law was challenged as an unconstitutional abridgement of free speech. The district court concluded that the ban was unconstitutional because liquor price advertising had no impact on levels of alcohol consumption in Rhode Island (D), and thus the ban did not directly advance the State's (D) interest. The court of appeals reversed. The Supreme Court granted certiorari to decide the issue.

ISSUE: Are complete bans on truthful commercial advertising unconstitutional?

HOLDING AND DECISION: (Stevens, J.) Yes. Complete bans on truthful commercial advertising are unconstitutional. Traditionally, commercial messages have provided consumers with information about the availability of goods and services. The common law prohibited fraudulent and misleading advertising. However, prior cases have recognized that regulation of commercial advertising is not protected to the same degree as core First Amendment speech. In *Central Hudson v. Public Service Commission of N.Y.*, 447 U.S. 557 (1980), this Court held that regulation of commercial speech had to be related to a significant state interest and that more limited alternatives are not available. When a state entirely prohibits the dissemination of truthful advertising for reasons unrelated to protecting consumers, strict scrutiny of the law is applicable. In the present case, Rhode Island (D) could reduce alcohol consumption by other methods, such as taxes, rather than through speech regulation. Thus, there is no reasonable relationship between the regulation and state objective. Accordingly, Rhode Island's (D) law is unconstitutional. Reversed.

CONCURRENCE: (Scalia, J.) Although the test enunciated in *Central Hudson v. Public Service Commission of N.Y.*, 447 U.S. 557 (1980), may not be correct, both parties argued accepting its validity so it should stand until there is a suitable replacement.

CONCURRENCE: (Thomas, J.) The government's manipulation of consumers' choices by keeping them ignorant is per se illegitimate. Thus, the balancing test of *Central Hudson v. Public Service Commission of N.Y.*, 447 U.S. 557 (1980), is not appropriate. Accurate commercial speech is entitled to full protection.

CONCURRENCE: (O'Connor, J.) Because Rhode Island's (D) regulation fails even the less stringent standard set out in *Central Hudson v. Public Service Commission of N.Y.*, 447 U.S. 557 (1980), nothing here requires adoption of a new analysis for the evaluation of commercial speech regulation.

ANALYSIS

The Court also overruled the case of *Posados de Puerto Rico Associates v. Tourism Co. of P.R.*, 478 U.S. 328 (1986), in which the Court held that a ban on casino advertising was valid since the state could choose to entirely ban casinos themselves. The decision correctly points out that banning speech may be more intrusive than banning conduct and that the speech ban is not necessarily a lesser-included state power. The Court also rejected any "vice" exception that *Posados* may have implied.

Quicknotes

BALANCING TEST A court's balancing of an individual's constitutional rights against the state's right to protect its citizens.

COMMERCIAL SPEECH Any speech that proposes a commercial transaction or promotes products or services.

STRICT SCRUTINY Method by which courts determine the constitutionality of a law when a law affects a fundamental right; under the test, the legislature must have a compelling interest to enact the law and measures prescribed by the law must be the least restrictive means possible to accomplish its goal.

CHAPTER 12

Freedom of Speech—Modes of Regulation and Standards of Review

Quick Reference Rules of Law

CHAPTER 12

Reed v. Town of Gilbert

Church official (P) v. Municipality (D)

576 U.S. 155 (2015)

NATURE OF CASE: Appeal from judgment in action challenging the constitutionality of a municipal sign code under the First Amendment.

FACT SUMMARY: A church and its pastor, Reed (P), challenged the constitutionality of the Town of Gilbert's (D) Sign Code, claiming that it was not content neutral and was not narrowly tailored to serve compelling state interests.

RULE OF LAW

A facially content-based law will not survive strict scrutiny where the government cannot prove that the law is narrowly tailored to serve compelling state interests, regardless of the government's benign motive, content-neutral justification, or lack of animus toward the ideas contained in the regulated speech.

FACTS: The Town of Gilbert (the Town) (D) had adopted a comprehensive Sign Code that prohibited the display of outdoor signs without a permit but exempted 23 categories of signs. One category was "Ideological Signs," defined as signs "communicating a message or ideas" that did not fit in any other Sign Code category. These signs could be up to 20 square feet and had no placement or time restrictions. "Political Signs," defined as signs "designed to influence the outcome of an election," could be up to 32 square feet and could be displayed only during an election season. "Temporary Directional Signs," defined as signs directing the public to a church or other "qualifying event," had even greater restrictions. As to these, no more than four of the signs, limited to six square feet, could be on a single property at any time, and signs could be displayed no more than 12 hours before the "qualifying event" and one hour after. A church and its pastor, Reed (D), held Sunday church services at various temporary locations in and near the Town (P), and their practice was to post signs early each Saturday bearing the church name and the time and location of the next service. They removed the signs around midday Sunday. The church was cited for violating the Sign Code, and the church and Reed (P) brought suit challenging the constitutionality of the Sign Code under the First Amendment, arguing that the Sign Code was not content neutral. The court of appeals concluded that the Sign Code was content neutral because it did not mention any idea or viewpoint, let alone single one out for differential treatment. The Supreme Court granted certiorari.

ISSUE: Will a facially content-based law survive strict scrutiny where the government cannot prove that the law is narrowly tailored to serve compelling state interests, regardless of the government's benign motive, content-neutral justification, or lack of animus toward the ideas contained in the regulated speech?

HOLDING AND DECISION: (Thomas, J.) No A facially content-based law will not survive strict scrutiny where the government cannot prove that the law is narrowly tailored to serve compelling state interests, regardless of the government's benign motive, content-neutral justification, or lack of animus toward the ideas contained in the regulated speech. Because content-based laws target speech based on its communicative content, they are presumptively unconstitutional and may be justified only if the government proves that they are narrowly tailored to serve compelling state interests. Speech regulation is content based if a law applies to particular speech because of the topic discussed or the idea or message expressed. The Sign Code is content based on its face. It defines the categories of temporary, political, and ideological signs on the basis of their messages and then subjects each category to different restrictions. The restrictions applied thus depend entirely on the sign's communicative content. A law that is content based on its face is subject to strict scrutiny regardless of the government's benign motive, content-neutral justification, or lack of animus toward the ideas contained in the regulated speech. The court of appeals' conclusion that the Sign Code does not single out any idea or viewpoint for discrimination conflates two distinct but related limitations that the First Amendment places on government regulation of speech. A speech regulation targeted at specific subject matter is content based even if it does not discriminate among viewpoints within that subject matter. Thus, the Sign Code is an example of content-based discrimination because it singles out specific subject matter for differential treatment, even if it does not target viewpoints within that subject matter. Also, notwithstanding that the Sign Code's distinctions are not speaker based, i.e., the restrictions in the Sign Code apply equally regardless of who sponsors the signs, this alone does not render the law content neutral. Similarly, the law is not automatically content neutral merely because its distinctions do not hinge on whether and when an event is occurring. For the Sign Code to survive strict scrutiny, the Town of Gilbert (the Town) (D) must show that it furthers compelling governmental interest and is narrowly tailored to that end. Here, the Town (D) has offered

Continued on next page.

two governmental interests that are purportedly served by the Sign Code: preserving the Town's (D) aesthetic appeal and preserving traffic safety. Even assuming these are compelling government interests, the Sign Code's distinctions are highly underinclusive. The Town (D) cannot claim that placing strict limits on temporary directional signs is necessary to beautify the Town (D) when other types of signs create the same problem, nor has it shown that temporary directional signs pose a greater threat to public safety than ideological or political signs. The Town (D) has ample content-neutral options available to resolve problems with safety and aesthetics, and it has compelling government interests, such as protecting the safety of pedestrians, drivers, and passengers, so that a sign ordinance narrowly tailored to serve such interests could survive strict scrutiny. Reversed.

CONCURRENCE: (Alito, J.) It is clear the Sign Code at issue is facially content based and must survive strict scrutiny. However, there are many types of rules that municipalities may enact that are not content based. Examples include rules that regulate the size of signs; regulate the locations in which signs may be placed; distinguish between lighted and unlighted signs; distinguish between signs with fixed messages and messages that change (such as on electronic signs); distinguish between the placement of signs on private and public property, or on commercial and residential property; restrict the total number of signs allowed per mile of roadway; or impose time restrictions on signs advertising a one-time event.

CONCURRENCE: (Kagan, J.) The majority's decision may imperil many sign ordinances that exempt certain categories of signs based on their subject matter, and it may require the repeal of exemptions that allow for helpful signs or require municipalities to lift their sign restrictions altogether, resulting in sign clutter. In some cases, where there is no possibility that official suppression of ideas is involved, it may be more realistic not to apply strict scrutiny. When a regulation facially differentiates on the basis of viewpoint, there is always the possibility that governmental suppression of ideas is involved, and in such cases, strict scrutiny is warranted. However, when there is no realistic possibility that such suppression is motivating the regulation, strict scrutiny should be relaxed in favor of less stringent review so that "entirely reasonable" laws may survive. Here, however, the Town of Gilbert's (D) defense does not pass even a very relaxed level of scrutiny, so there is no need to decide in this case whether strict scrutiny should apply to every sign ordinance that contains a subject-matter exemption.

ANALYSIS

It should be remembered that not all content-neutral restrictions on speech are necessarily consistent with the First Amendment. Time, place, and manner restrictions, for example, must be narrowly tailored to serve the government's legitimate, content-neutral interests. However, such restrictions need not meet the high standard imposed by strict scrutiny on viewpoint- and content-based restrictions. Instead, such restrictions may survive if they meet the standards of intermediate scrutiny.

Quicknotes

CONTENT-BASED STATUTES Laws that regulate speech based on its content.

CONTENT-NEUTRAL STATUTES Laws that regulate speech regardless of its content.

FACIALLY NEUTRAL ORDINANCE A statute that appears to be neutral on its face and does not appear to have a disproportionate impact on a particular class of individuals.

STRICT SCRUTINY Method by which courts determine the constitutionality of a law when a law affects a fundamental right; under the test, the legislature must have had a compelling interest to enact the law and measures prescribed by the law must be the least restrictive means possible to accomplish its goal.

City of Austin, Texas v. Reagan National Advertising of Austin

Municipality (D) v. Billboard advertising company (P)

597 U.S. ___, 142 S. Ct. 1464 (2022)

NATURE OF CASE: Appeal from judgment in action challenging the constitutionality of a municipality's regulation of off-premises signs differently from on-premises signs.

FACT SUMMARY: The City of Austin (D) regulated off-premises signs, which advertise things that are not located on the same premises as the sign, as well as signs that direct people to offsite locations, most notably billboards. Reagan National Advertising of Austin (P) challenged the regulation as violating the First Amendment, contending that under the Court's precedents, the regulation was not content neutral, so that strict scrutiny would apply.

RULE OF LAW

A municipality's regulation of signs that treats on-premises signs differently from off-premises signs is not per se subject to strict scrutiny where the regulation is agnostic as to content.

FACTS: The City of Austin (the City) (D) regulated off-premises signs, which advertise things that are not located on the same premises as the sign, as well as signs that direct people to offsite locations, most notably billboards. Reagan National Advertising of Austin (P) challenged the regulation as violating the First Amendment, contending that under the Court's precedents, the regulation was not content neutral, so that strict scrutiny would apply. The Fifth Circuit Court of Appeals agreed, interpreting *Reed v. Town of Gilbert,* 576 U.S. 155 (2015), to mean that if "a reader must ask: who is the speaker and what is the speaker saying" to apply a regulation, then the regulation is automatically content based, and, therefore, subject to strict scrutiny. The City (D) appealed, and the Supreme Court granted certiorari.

ISSUE: Is a municipality's regulation of signs that treats on-premises signs differently from off-premises signs per se subject to strict scrutiny where the regulation is agnostic as to content?

HOLDING AND DECISION: (Sotomayor, J.) No. A municipality's regulation of signs that treats on-premises signs differently from off-premises signs is not per se subject to strict scrutiny where the regulation is agnostic as to content. *Reed v. Town of Gilbert,* 576 U.S. 155 (2015), held that a regulation of speech is content based under the First Amendment if it targets speech based on its communicative content, i.e., if it applies to particular speech because of the topic discussed or the idea or message expressed. That interpretation of *Reed*—to mean that a regulation cannot be content neutral if its application requires reading the sign at issue—is too extreme an interpretation of the Court's precedent. Unlike the sign code in *Reed,* the City of Austin's (the City's) (D) sign ordinances here do not single out any topic or subject matter for differential treatment; they are agnostic as to content. A sign's message matters only to the extent that it informs the sign's relative location. Thus, the City's (D) on-/off-premises distinction is more like ordinary time, place, or manner restrictions, which do not require the application of strict scrutiny. The Court's precedents and doctrines have consistently recognized that restrictions on speech may require some evaluation of the speech and, nonetheless, remain content neutral. Most relevant here, the First Amendment allows for regulations of solicitation, and speech must be read or heard to determine whether it entails solicitation. Moreover, the Court has previously understood distinctions between on-premises and off-premises signs to be content neutral. Underlying these cases and others is a rejection of the view that any examination of speech or expression inherently triggers heightened First Amendment concern. Rather, content-based regulations are those that discriminate based on the topic discussed or the idea or message expressed. *Reed* did not depart from this understanding, and it effectively held that a regulation of speech cannot escape classification as facially content based simply by swapping an obvious subject-matter distinction for a "function or purpose" proxy that achieves the same result. However, that does not mean that any classification that considers function or purpose is always content based. Such a reading of "function or purpose" would contravene numerous precedents, on which *Reed* did not purport to cast doubt. Nor did *Reed* cast doubt on the nation's history of regulating off-premises signs. The dissent would hold that tens of thousands of jurisdictions have presumptively violated the First Amendment, some for more than half a century, and that they have done so by use of an on-/off-premises distinction the Court has repeatedly reviewed and never previously questioned. The Constitution does not require that bizarre result. Instead, the result reached is one of common sense: a location-based and content-agnostic on-/off-premises distinction does not, on its face, single out specific subject matter for differential treatment. The determination that the City's (D) on-/off-premises distinction is facially content neutral does not end the First Amendment inquiry. Evidence that an impermissible purpose or justification underpins

Continued on next page.

a facially content-neutral restriction may mean that the restriction is nevertheless content based. Moreover, to survive intermediate scrutiny, a restriction on speech or expression must be narrowly tailored to serve a significant governmental interest. Because the Court of Appeals did not address these issues, the Court leaves them for remand and expresses no view on the matters. Reversed and remanded.

CONCURRENCE: (Breyer, J.) Although the result reached by the majority is correct, the reasoning in *Reed v. Town of Gilbert*, 576 U.S. 155 (2015), was wrong. When it comes to categories such as "content discrimination," the First Amendment is better served if such categories are treated as rules of thumb. Thus, if *Reed* is interpreted to mean that courts must strictly scrutinize regulations simply because they refer to particular content, there is good reason to fear that courts will strike down entirely reasonable regulations. If that happens, the Court's content-based line-drawing will substitute judicial for democratic decisionmaking and threaten the ability of the people to translate their ideas into policy. Or courts may instead dilute the stringent strict-scrutiny standard in an effort to avoid striking down reasonable regulations. Doing so would weaken the First Amendment's protection in instances where strict scrutiny should apply in full force. A third possibility is that courts will develop a matrix of formal subsidiary rules and exceptions that seek to distinguish between reasonable and unreasonable content-based regulations. Such a patchwork, however, may prove overly complex, unwieldy, or unworkable, thus weakening First Amendment protections and values.

CONCURRENCE AND DISSENT: (Alito, J.) The Court of Appeals erred in its application of the test that must be met before a law is held to be facially unconstitutional. Most of the situations to which the City of Austin's (D) regulations apply involve commercial speech, and commercial speech regulations are analyzed differently from other regulations that implicate the First Amendment. Thus, on remand, the lower courts should determine whether those regulations are unconstitutional as applied to each of the billboards at issue. The majority, however, goes too far by holding that the regulations are not facially discriminatory as to content, because there is real possibility that signs posted on a premises that are political or ideological or in any way not related to the type of commerce transacted on those premises would be deemed off-premises advertising, and, therefore, disallowed. This would constitute disparate treatment on the basis of topic or subject matter.

DISSENT: (Thomas, J.) The off-premises regulations at issue clearly draw distinctions based on a sign's communicative content, notwithstanding that the location of a given sign is content-neutral. Therefore, the regulations are impermissibly content based under *Reed v. Town of Gilbert*, 576 U.S. 155 (2015). To reach the opposite result, the majority implicitly rewrites *Reed* by reasoning that a regulation based on a sufficiently general or broad category of communicative content is not actually content based. The only historical support the majority musters for its conclusion is that regulations like those of the City of Austin (the City) (D) proliferated following the enactment of the Highway Beautification Act of 1965. Relying on only a few decades of regulation, rather than reaching back two centuries to the founding is dangerous because with such a relatively short time of regulation, the Court can subject new categories of speech to less exacting First Amendment scrutiny. In any event, historical regulation is irrelevant to the question before the Court. Even if the City (D) had met its burden of identifying a historical tradition of analogous regulation—as can be done, say, for obscenity or defamation—that would not make the off-premises rule content neutral. It might simply mean that the off-premises rule is a constitutional form of content-based discrimination. However, content neutrality under *Reed* is an empirical question, not a historical one. Thus, the majority's historical argument is not only meritless but misguided.

ANALYSIS

In *Reed v. Town of Gilbert*, 576 U.S. 155 (2015), the town of Gilbert, Arizona, adopted a comprehensive sign code that applied distinct size, placement, and time restrictions to 23 different categories of signs, giving more favorable treatment to some categories (such as ideological signs or political signs) and less favorable treatment to others (such as temporary directional signs relating to religious events, educational events, or other similar events). The Court rejected the contention that the restrictions were content neutral because they did not discriminate on the basis of particular viewpoints, reasoning that a speech regulation targeted at specific subject matter is content based even if it does not discriminate among viewpoints within that subject matter. In *Reed*, the Court also announced the sweeping rule that a law is presumed to be unconstitutional if it regulates speech "based on the message a speaker conveys." As the district court in this case observed, such a broad rule would apply strict scrutiny to all regulations for signs with written text, even stop signs. With *City of Austin*, the Court narrowed *Reed*'s reach, at least as to off-premises sign regulations. Nonetheless, the "clear and firm" rule set forth in *Reed* remains applicable to many regulations that, as Justice Breyer said, may be "entirely reasonable," and the courts will have to figure out how to apply *Reed* to such regulations, perhaps, as Justice Breyer urges, by

Continued on next page.

applying the rule in *Reed* as a rule of thumb, rather than an unbending, categorical rule.

Quicknotes

CONTENT-NEUTRAL STATUTES Laws that regulate speech regardless of its content.

INTERMEDIATE SCRUTINY A standard of reviewing the propriety of classifications pertaining to gender or legitimacy under the Equal Protection Clause of the U.S. Constitution that requires a court to ascertain whether the classification furthers an important state interest and is substantially related to the attainment of that interest.

STRICT SCRUTINY Method by which courts determine the constitutionality of a law when a law affects a fundamental right; under the test, the legislature must have had a compelling interest to enact the law and measures prescribed by the law must be the least restrictive means possible to accomplish its goal.

United States v. O'Brien

Federal government (P) v. Demonstrator (D)

391 U.S. 367 (1968)

NATURE OF CASE: Certiorari review of speech restriction with nonspeech aspect of conduct.

FACT SUMMARY: O'Brien (D) was convicted of a violation of a federal statute after he publicly burned his draft card during a demonstration against the compulsory draft and the war in Vietnam.

RULE OF LAW

When both speech and nonspeech elements are combined in the same conduct, sufficiently important governmental interest in regulating the nonspeech element can justify incidental limitations of First Amendment freedoms.

FACTS: During a public demonstration directed against the compulsory draft and the war in Vietnam, O'Brien (D) and several others burned their Selective Service Registration Certificates. Several agents of the Federal Bureau of Investigation (P) witnessed his act and arrested him. The arrest was for violating a federal statute prohibiting the knowing destruction or knowing mutilation of a Selective Service Certificate. The statute also prohibited any changes, alterations, or forgeries of the Certificates. O'Brien (D) was convicted and appealed, contending a violation of his First Amendment right to free speech.

ISSUE: When both speech and nonspeech elements are combined in the same conduct, can sufficiently important governmental interest in regulating the nonspeech element justify incidental limitations of First Amendment freedoms?

HOLDING AND DECISION: (Warren, C.J.) Yes. When both speech and nonspeech elements are combined in the same conduct, sufficiently important governmental interest in regulating the nonspeech element can justify incidental limitations of First Amendment freedoms. The Court considered two aspects of O'Brien's (D) appeal. First, it considered that the statute was unconstitutional in its application to him, and secondly, that the statute was unconstitutional as enacted. Where conduct is composed of speech and nonspeech elements, the speaker can invoke his freedom of speech rights to defend against unwarranted governmental interference. What must be determined is whether the attempted regulation of the nonspeech element also impermissibly inhibits the speech aspect. An incidental restriction on speech can be justified where the government can show a substantial interest in furthering a constitutional power that is not directed at the suppression of speech. In order to facilitate the implementation of the power to raise and support armies, Congress has enacted a system for classifying individuals as to eligibility for military service. The Selective Service cards provide an efficient and reasonable method for identifying those persons previously deemed fit for military service should a national emergency arise. The Court found the requirement that the card be in the possession of the holder to be a valid requirement. The Court also found an independent justification for both the possession requirement and the prohibition against mutilation or destruction. While admitting some overlap, the possession requirement was intended for a smooth functioning of the draft system, while the prohibition against mutilation was a sabotage prevention measure. A person could destroy another's card while retaining his own intact. The statute was intended as a necessary and proper method to carry out a vital governmental interest. No reasonable alternative is apparent, and the narrow construction of the statute indicates it was not intended to suppress communication. As to the contention the statute was unconstitutional on its face, the Court found congressional intent to be the smooth functioning of the draft system, not the suppression of anti-war sentiment. Reversed.

ANALYSIS

Many articles written about this decision have been critical of the court's superficial analysis of the interests involved on both sides of this case. The commentators felt that O'Brien's (D) contention that the draft card was not a vital document was dismissed out of hand. They also felt there should have been a more probing analysis of the operation of the Selective Service System and an examination of the actual, not supposed, importance of the draft card in that system. The strongest criticism of this case has been that the Court justified the suppression of expression, not on the basis of a compelling interest but on a bureaucratic system designed for convenience. There was no analysis of alternative systems. Finally, some observers saw in this decision a desire to counterbalance the long string of cases decided by the Warren Court upholding individual rights in the face of much stronger governmental interests.

Continued on next page.

Quicknotes

CONSCRIPTION Compulsory service in the military; the state of being drafted.

FIRST AMENDMENT Prohibits Congress from enacting any law respecting an establishment of religion or prohibiting the free exercise of religion; or abridging freedom of speech or the press, the right of peaceful assembly, and the right to petition for a redress of grievances.

SYMBOLIC SPEECH Communication of ideas through conduct.

Texas v. Johnson

State (P) v. Flag owner (D)

491 U.S. 397 (1989)

NATURE OF CASE: Certiorari review of constitutionality of state statute criminalizing flag-burning.

FACT SUMMARY: Johnson (D), who burned a U.S. flag as a means of political protest, was convicted under Texas (P) law of desecrating a venerated object.

RULE OF LAW

Burning a U.S. flag as a means of political protest may not be criminalized.

FACTS: Johnson (D) joined a protest at the site of the 1984 Republican National Convention. Except for some minor vandalism in which Johnson (D) took no part, the protest was peaceful. At one-point Johnson burned a U.S. flag. He was convicted under a state law criminalizing the desecration of a venerated object. The state court of criminal appeals reversed, holding Johnson's (D) actions protected under the First Amendment. The Supreme Court granted review.

ISSUE: May burning the U.S. flag as a means of political protest be criminalized?

HOLDING AND DECISION: (Brennan, J.) No. Burning a U.S. flag as a means of political protest may not be criminalized. While the First Amendment literally protects only "speech," it has long been the rule that conduct that is meant to express an idea also raises First Amendment concerns. Johnson's (D) behavior undoubtedly was so meant, and Texas (P) conceded this. This being so, the prosecution of Johnson (D) could be upheld only if Texas (P) could show an interest therein unrelated to the suppression of ideas. Two have been offered: keeping the peace and preserving the flag as a symbol of national unity. Here, no breach of the peace occurred, and this Court is unwilling to presume that symbolic conduct not directed at any person or group in particular constitutes such a danger to public tranquility that a state may proscribe such conduct. As to the latter justification, it is a core principle of the First Amendment that government may not prohibit expression of an idea because it finds the idea disagreeable. While the Court does not doubt that government is free to promote respect for the flag as a symbol of national unity, it may not compel how a flag, or any symbol, is used. All this being so, the conclusion must be that the law under which Johnson (D) was prosecuted constitutes an abridgment of expressive conduct for which no justification separate from such abridgment can be found, and the statute violates the First Amendment. Affirmed.

DISSENT: (Rehnquist, C.J.) The flag does not represent any idea or point of view. It is a unique symbol of our national heritage and deserves special protection. Beyond that, the acts of Johnson (D) did have a tendency to incite a breach of the peace. It is more likely to antagonize others than to communicate an idea.

DISSENT: (Stevens, J.) Due to the unique value of the flag as a symbol, the government's interest in preserving that value is significant and legitimate.

ANALYSIS

This was one of the most controversial decisions of the Supreme Court in decades. Almost immediately, calls for a constitutional amendment to overturn the decision were made. Within the year of its decision, Congress had passed a statute, rather than an amendment, in a response that was hoped would pass First Amendment scrutiny. The amendment movement faltered because never in history has the Bill of Rights been amended.

Quicknotes

FIRST AMENDMENT Prohibits Congress from enacting any law respecting an establishment of religion or prohibiting the free exercise of religion; or abridging the freedom of speech or of the press, the right of peaceful assembly, and the right to petition for a redress of grievances.

SYMBOLIC CONDUCT Conduct that is expressive of a person's thoughts or opinions.

SYMBOLIC SPEECH Communication of ideas through conduct.

Holder v. Humanitarian Law Project

U.S. Attorney General (D) v. Activists (P)

561 U.S. 1 (2010)

NATURE OF CASE: Appeal from Ninth Circuit Court of Appeals.

FACT SUMMARY: Members of the Humanitarian Law Project (P) sought an injunction against the federal Government (D) to prevent the enforcement of 18 U.S.C.A. § 2339B(a)(1), which prohibits providing nonviolent material support for organizations that engage in terrorism.

RULE OF LAW

The federal government may prohibit providing nonviolent material support for terrorist organizations, including legal services and advice, without violating the Free Speech Clause of the First Amendment.

FACTS: Under U.S.C.A. § 2339B(a)(1), the Secretary of State has the authority to designate any particular group as a "foreign terrorist organization." The law makes it a crime for anyone to provide "material support or resources" to even the nonviolent activities of a designated organization. Supporters of the Kurdistan Workers Party and the Liberation Tigers of Tamil Eelam, both of which were identified by the Secretary of State as terrorist groups, sought an injunction to prevent the U.S. Government (D) from enforcing the law. The Government (D) moved for summary judgment, arguing that the challenged provisions of the law were not unconstitutionally vague. The district court granted a partial motion for summary judgment but held that some parts of the law were unconstitutionally vague. The United States Court of Appeals for the Ninth Circuit affirmed, holding that the terms "service," "training," or "other specialized knowledge" within the statute in question as applied to the plaintiffs were unconstitutionally vague.

ISSUE: May the federal government prohibit providing nonviolent material support for terrorist organizations, including legal services and advice, without violating the Free Speech Clause of the First Amendment?

HOLDING AND DECISION: (Roberts, C.J.) Yes. The federal government may prohibit providing nonviolent material support for terrorist organizations, including legal services and advice, without violating the Free Speech Clause of the First Amendment. The statute may not be clear in every respect, but it is sufficiently clear with respect to the Humanitarian Law Project (P). The material support provision of the statute is not vague as applied to the specific kinds of support that the Humanitarian Law Project (P) seeks to provide to terrorist organizations, and it is not unconstitutional. The statutory terms at issue—"training," "expert advice or assistance," "service," and "personnel"—are not similar to terms like "annoying" and "indecent" that have been struck down in the past as being too vague. Reversed.

DISSENT: (Breyer, J.) The statute is not unconstitutionally vague; but the Constitution does not permit the Government (D) to prosecute the Humanitarian Law Project (P) criminally for engaging in teaching and advocacy that advances the so-called terrorist groups' lawful political objectives. The Government (D) failed to meet its burden to show that the speech prohibited by the statute served a compelling governmental interest.

ANALYSIS

This case marks the first time the Supreme Court has held that abridgment of political speech – which is ordinarily protected by the First Amendment, no matter the content – passed the strict scrutiny test. To fully understand the Court's decision, consider the legislative history of U.S.C.A. §§ 2339A and 2339B. Congress enacted § 2339A as part of a wide-ranging crime package, the Violent Crime Control and Law Enforcement Act of 1994, and at the time it generated little notice. Congress then amended § 2339A and supplemented it with § 2339B as part of the Antiterrorism and Effective Death Penalty Act of 1996. New § 2339B reflected Congress's belief that the supply of funds, goods, or services by individuals or organizations to terrorist groups helps to mitigate the costs to the terrorist organization of running its legitimate activities, which in turn frees an equal sum that can then be spent on terrorist activities. After the terrorist attacks on 9/11, the USA PATRIOT Act was passed, and it amended both §§ 2339A and 2339B by increasing prison sentences and adding "expert advice or assistance" to forms of proscribed material support or resources. And finally, the Intelligence Reform and Terrorism Prevention Act of 2004 amended the definition of "material support or resources" that applies to both sections. The specific forms of support that had been used to define the term became examples of a more general definition that covers "any property, tangible or intangible, or service." Clarifying definitions of the examples "training" and "expert advice or assistance"

Continued on next page.

were added as was a clarifying explanation of the term "personnel."

Quicknotes

FIRST AMENDMENT RIGHTS Rights conferred by the First Amendment to the U.S. Constitution prohibiting Congress from enacting any law respecting an establishment of religion or prohibiting the free exercise of religion; or abridging freedom of speech or of the press, the right of peaceful assembly, and the right to petition for a redress of grievances.

Barnes v. Glen Theatre, Inc.

State official (D) v. Adult entertainment establishment (P)

501 U.S. 560 (1991)

NATURE OF CASE: Appeal from judgment invalidating as violative of the First Amendment a state indecency law prohibiting total nudity in public places.

FACT SUMMARY: Adult entertainment establishments (P) wishing to provide completely nude dancing challenged as violative of the First Amendment a State (D) indecency law that prohibited total nudity in public places and required dancers to wear pasties and G-strings. The State (D) contended that the law was justified as furthering societal order and morality.

RULE OF LAW

An indecency law that prohibits total nudity in public places, including adult entertainment establishments, does not violate the First Amendment's guarantee of freedom of expression.

FACTS: Adult entertainment establishments (P) and some of their dancers (P), who wished to provide completely nude dancing, challenged the State's (D) indecency law, which banned total nudity in public places and required dancers to wear pasties and G-strings, as violating the First Amendment's guarantee of freedom of expression. The State (D) contended that the law protected societal order and morality and therefore did not violate the First Amendment because its impact on expression was minimal, and it furthered substantial governmental interests. The federal court of appeals ruled that the law was unconstitutional, and the State (D) appealed. The Supreme Court granted certiorari.

ISSUE: Does an indecency law that prohibits total nudity in public places, including adult entertainment establishments, violate the First Amendment's guarantee of freedom of expression?

HOLDING AND DECISION: (Rehnquist, C.J.) No. An indecency law that prohibits total nudity in public places, including adult entertainment establishments, does not violate the First Amendment's guarantee of freedom of expression. Nude dancing of the kind sought to be performed here is expressive conduct within the outer perimeters of the First Amendment, although only marginally so. The State's (D) indecency law is justified notwithstanding that it incidentally limits some expressive activity. The law is clearly within the State's (D) constitutional power since it furthers a substantial governmental interest in protecting societal order and morality. Public indecency statutes reflect moral disapproval of people appearing in the nude among strangers in public places, and this particular law follows a long line of state laws banning public nudity. The states' traditional police power is defined as the authority to provide for the public health, safety, and morals, and such a basis for legislation has been upheld. Moreover, this governmental interest is unrelated to the suppression of free expression, since it can be argued that almost limitless types of conduct—including appearing in the nude in public—are "expressive," and in one sense of the word this is true. People who go about in the nude in public may be expressing something about themselves by so doing. However, such an expansive view of "expressive conduct" has been rejected, since not every type of conduct can be labeled "speech" whenever the person engaging in the conduct intends thereby to express an idea. Reversed.

CONCURRENCE: (Scalia, J.) The indecency law at bar must be upheld, not because it survives First Amendment scrutiny, but because it is a general law regulating conduct that is not specifically directed at expression, so the First Amendment is not implicated at all. The statute is in the line of a long tradition of laws against public nudity, which have never been thought to run afoul of traditional understanding of "the freedom of speech," and public indecency—including public nudity—has long been an offense at common law. Regardless of whether public nudity offends anyone, it has been through the ages deemed immoral so that it does not matter whether the viewer of the nudity has consented to see it. Because virtually every law regulating conduct can be seen as incidentally regulating expression, it cannot reasonably be demanded that every restriction of expression incidentally produced by a general law regulating conduct pass normal First Amendment scrutiny, or even that it be justified by an "important or substantial" government interest. Moreover, none of the Court's precedents require as much.

CONCURRENCE: (Souter, J.) The State's (D) asserted interest in preventing the secondary effects of adult entertainment establishments—prostitution, sexual assaults, and other criminal activity—is sufficient to justify the law's enforcement against nude dancing, as the prevention of such effects clearly falls within the State's (D) constitutional power. Moreover, the interest is unrelated to the suppression of free expression since the pernicious effects are merely associated with nude dancing establishments and are not the result of the expression inherent in nude dancing.

Continued on next page.

DISSENT: (White, J.) The purpose of forbidding people to appear nude in parks, beaches, hot dog stands, and like public places is to protect others from offense, but that could not possibly be the purpose of preventing nude dancing in theaters and barrooms since the viewers are exclusively consenting adults who pay money to see these dances. The purpose of the proscription in these contexts is to protect the viewers from what the State (D) believes is the harmful message that nude dancing communicates. The emotional or erotic impact of the dance is intensified by the nudity of the performers, and the sight of a fully clothed, or even a partially clothed, dancer generally will have a far different impact on a spectator than that of a nude dancer, even if the same dance is performed. Thus, the nudity is itself an expressive component of the dance, not merely incidental "conduct." Accordingly, the statutory prohibition is of necessity related to expressive conduct. Since the State (D) permits the dancers to perform if they wear pasties and G-strings but forbids nude dancing, it is precisely because of the distinctive, expressive content of nude dancing performances that the State (D) seeks to apply the statutory prohibition. It is only because nude dancing performances may generate emotions and feelings of eroticism and sensuality among the spectators that the State (D) seeks to regulate such expressive activity, apparently on the assumption that creating or emphasizing such thoughts and ideas in the minds of the spectators may lead to increased prostitution and the degradation of women. However, generating thoughts, ideas, and emotions is the essence of communication protected by the First Amendment. Therefore, the statute at issue must pass exacting scrutiny and may be upheld only if it serves a compelling State (D) interest and is narrowly drawn to further that interest. Here, even if the State (D) had a compelling interest, the statute is overbroad.

ANALYSIS

The plurality in the *Barnes* decision effectively holds that morality alone is a good enough content-neutral state interest to support the regulation of speech. As Justice Scalia posits, "The purpose of Indiana's nudity law would be violated, I think, if 60,000 fully consenting adults crowded into the Hoosier Dome to display their genitals to one another, even if there were not an offended innocent in the crowd. Our society prohibits, and all human societies have prohibited, certain activities not because they harm others but because they are considered, in the traditional phrase, 'contra bonos mores,' i.e., immoral." In response, Justice White counters that "the plurality and Justice Scalia's simple references to the State's (D) general interest in promoting societal order and morality are not sufficient justification for a statute that concededly reaches a significant amount of protected expressive activity." Justice White, in arguing that the statute at bar is not a general law, as Justice Scalia insists, expands on Justice Scalia's hypothetical, saying: "We agree with Justice Scalia that the Indiana statute would not permit 60,000 consenting Hoosiers to expose themselves to each other in the Hoosier Dome. No one can doubt, however, that those same 60,000 Hoosiers would be perfectly free to drive to their respective homes across all Indiana and, once there, to parade around, cavort, and revel in the nude for hours in front of relatives and friends. It is difficult to see why the State's (D) interest in morality is any less in that situation, especially if, as Justice Scalia seems to suggest, nudity is inherently evil." These disparate views on the government's proper role in promoting "morality," as well as what is moral and what is expression, might explain why the Court's decisions on nude dancing have mustered only pluralities, rather than majorities.

Quicknotes

FREEDOM OF EXPRESSION The guarantee of the First Amendment to the U.S. Constitution prohibiting Congress from enacting any law respecting an establishment of religion, prohibiting the free exercise of religion, or abridging freedom of speech or the press.

POLICE POWER The power of a government to impose restrictions on the rights of private persons, so long as those restrictions are reasonably related to the promotion and protection of public health, safety, morals, and the general welfare.

PUBLIC POLICY Policy administered by the state with respect to the health, safety, and morals of its people in accordance with common notions of fairness and decency.

Members of City Council v. Taxpayers for Vincent

City council (D) v. Campaign supporters (P)

466 U.S. 789 (1984)

NATURE OF CASE: Certiorari review of constitutionality of a law prohibiting the posting of signs on public property.

FACT SUMMARY: A Los Angeles Municipal Code prohibited the posting of signs on public property, and supporters of Vincent (P), a political candidate, challenged the removal of their signs from utility poles.

RULE OF LAW

It is not an unconstitutional infringement of speech to prevent political messages from being posted on public property.

FACTS: The Los Angeles City Council (D) passed an ordinance prohibiting the posting of signs on public property. Pursuant to the ordinance, city workers removed signs attached to power poles. Some of the signs removed were political message signs for Vincent. Taxpayers for Vincent (P) filed suit, alleging an infringement of speech. The suit was dismissed. The appellate court reversed, and the City of Los Angeles (D) appealed to the Supreme Court.

ISSUE: Is it an unconstitutional infringement of speech to prevent political messages from being posted on public property?

HOLDING AND DECISION: (Stevens, J.) No. It is not an unconstitutional infringement of speech to prevent political messages from being posted on public property. So long as the state's interest is sufficiently substantial to justify the effect of an ordinance, and the effect is no greater than necessary, the state may restrict the posting of messages on public property. A city has a justified interest in reducing visual blight. To this end, the posting of signs can be regulated within certain bounds. In this case, the City of Los Angeles (D) removed signs from power poles to limit the visual discordance caused by haphazard posting. Since numerous other avenues existed for political speech, the ordinance was not overly restrictive. The ordinance was content neutral and impartially administered. Reversed.

DISSENT: (Brennan, J.) The Court has undermined the First Amendment with its lenient approach toward an argument of aesthetics. The presence of so many signs in the City of Los Angeles indicates that it may be the only avenue of communication feasibly available to many. Such a complete restriction should not be upheld.

ANALYSIS

Evidently, aesthetic concerns are an important matter for government. Given the much grander matters treated in many free speech cases, it seems unusual that aesthetics would receive such supportive treatment. However, such treatment has been used in several Supreme Court decisions, including *Metromedia, Inc. v. San Diego*, 453 U.S. 490 (1981), so evidently there is harmony on this matter.

Quicknotes

CONTENT-NEUTRAL STATUTES Laws that regulate speech regardless of its content.

Clark v. Community for Creative Non-Violence

Secretary of the U.S. Department of the Interior (D) v. Organization (P)

468 U.S. 288 (1984)

NATURE OF CASE: Certiorari review of constitutionality of a state regulation limiting political demonstrations.

FACT SUMMARY: Community for Creative Non-Violence (P) contended that the application of a National Park Service regulation prohibiting camping in certain parks to its demonstration in protest of the plight of the homeless was a violation of their freedom of speech.

RULE OF LAW

Expression may be constitutionally restricted to reasonable times, places, and manners.

FACTS: Community for Creative Non-Violence (CCNV) (P) received a permit from the National Park Service allowing them to set up tents in Lafayette Park (across the street from the White House) to protest the plight of the nation's homeless. The permit denied CCNV (P) the right to have its members sleep in the tents. This denial was made pursuant to a National Park Service regulation prohibiting camping in Lafayette Park. CCNV (P) sued, contending the application of the regulation to its demonstration violated its right to free speech. The district court upheld the regulation, and the court of appeals reversed. The Supreme Court took jurisdiction.

ISSUE: May expression be subjected to reasonable time, place, and manner restrictions?

HOLDING AND DECISION: (White, J.) Yes. Expression may be subject to reasonable time, place, and manner restrictions. Assuming that sleeping, within the context of this case, constitutes expression, it is subject to reasonable time, place, and manner restrictions. The application of the National Park Service regulation had nothing to do with the content of the expression. The ban on sleeping was a restriction on the manner of expression. As a result, the application of the regulation did not violate freedom of speech. Reversed.

DISSENT: (Marshall, J.) Sleep in this context went beyond mere conduct. It was symbolic speech, and its ban served no substantial government interest. Therefore, it should not have been suppressed.

ANALYSIS

The threshold question in cases of this sort is whether the action at issue can be considered speech in a constitutional context. The majority assumed that sleeping in this context was expression, but it failed to hold as such. Chief Justice Burger would deny the Community for Creative Non-Violence's (P) claim by finding that sleeping was conduct and not entitled to First Amendment protection. Justice Marshall on the other hand would characterize sleeping as symbolic speech and worthy of protection.

Quicknotes

SYMBOLIC SPEECH Communication of ideas through conduct.

Shurtleff v. City of Boston, Massachusetts

Director of religious organization (P) v. Municipality (D)

596 U.S. ___, 142 S. Ct. 1583 (2022)

NATURE OF CASE: Appeal in action challenging as an unconstitutional violation of the First Amendment a city's refusal to allow an organization to raise its self-described "Christian flag" under the city's program allowing private groups to use a flagpole on the plaza in front of city hall to fly the flag of their choosing in connection with events sponsored by the groups.

FACT SUMMARY: The City of Boston, Massachusetts, (Boston) (D) allowed private groups to request use of a flagpole that was on City Hall Plaza to raise flags of their choosing. When Boston (D) denied such a request, for the first time ever, made by Harold Shurtleff (Shurtleff) (P), the director of a Christian organization, to fly a Christian flag, Shurtleff (P) claimed the denial was an unconstitutional violation of the First Amendment, raising the issue as to whether Boston's (D) flag-raising program constituted government speech.

RULE OF LAW

Where a municipality has a flag-raising program whereby the municipality allows private groups to raise flags of their choosing on a municipal flagpole without reviewing the flags raised, the municipality's flag-raising program does not constitute government speech.

FACTS: For years, the City of Boston, Massachusetts, (Boston) (D) allowed private groups to request use of a flagpole that was on City Hall Plaza to raise flags of their choosing. As part of this program, Boston (D) approved hundreds of requests to raise dozens of different flags in connection with various events. It did not deny a single request to raise a flag until Harold Shurtleff (Shurtleff) (P), the director of a Christian organization, asked to fly a Christian flag. Boston (D) refused, even though it had no written policy limiting use of the flagpole based on a flag's content, and in no way had controlled the flag raisings or shaped the messages the flags sent. Until Shurtleff's (P) request, Boston (D) never requested to review a flag or requested changes to a flag in connection with approval, and its practice had been to approve flag raisings, without exception. Shurtleff (P) sued, challenging the denial as an unconstitutional violation of the First Amendment, raising the issue as to whether Boston's (D) flag-raising program constituted government speech. [The District Court held that flying private groups' flags from the flagpole amounted to government speech, so Boston could refuse Shurtfleff's (P) request without running afoul of the First Amendment. The First Circuit Court of Appeals affirmed.] The Supreme Court granted certiorari in the case.

ISSUE: Where a municipality has a flag-raising program whereby the municipality allows private groups to raise flags of their choosing on a municipal flagpole without reviewing the flags raised, does the municipality's flag-raising program constitute government speech?

HOLDING AND DECISION: (Breyer, J.) No. Where a municipality has a flag-raising program whereby the municipality allows private groups to raise flags of their choosing on a municipal flagpole without reviewing the flags raised, the municipality's flag-raising program does not constitute government speech. When the government wishes to state an opinion, to speak for the community, to formulate policies or to implement programs, what it says constitutes government speech. To determine whether the government intends to speak for itself or to regulate private expression, the Court looks to the context in which the expression at issue occurs. In reviewing that context, the Court has looked to the history of the expression, the public's likely perception as to who (the government or a private person) is speaking, and the extent to which the government has actively shaped or controlled the expression. Here, Boston (D) did not at all shape the messages sent by raised flags and did not consider the flag's viewpoints. It did nothing to control the flag's content. Boston (D) could have done more to make clear it wished to speak for itself by raising flags, but it did not, and, going forward, Boston (D) may change its flag-raising policies if it so desires. However, until it does so, its flag-raising program does not constitute government speech.

CONCURRENCE IN JUDGMENT: (Alito, J.) The majority's use of history, the public's perception of who is speaking, and the extent to which the government has exercised control over speech to determine whether the government is speaking is misplaced. Treating this triad of factors obscures the question of whether the government is speaking instead of regulating private expression. Instead, courts should focus on the identity of the speaker, as the ultimate question is whether the government is actually expressing its own views, or the real speaker is a private party, and the government is surreptitiously engaged in the regulation of private speech. Government speech occurs if—but only if—(1) a

Continued on next page.

government purposefully expresses a message of its own through persons authorized to speak on its behalf, and (2) in doing so, does not rely on a means that abridges private speech. In other words, the government must set the overall message to be communicated through official action. The government-speech doctrine is not based on the view that governmental entities have First Amendment rights. Instead, the doctrine is based on the notion that governmental communication does not normally restrict the activities of persons acting as private individuals. The government can speak using private assistance in two ways. First, it can prospectively enlist private entities to convey its own message by deputizing private persons as its agents, as long as it does so without coercion. Second, the government can adopt a medium of expression created by a private party and use it to express a government message. For the adopted expression to qualify as the government's, the private party must give up control over the medium of expression to the government, which must put the medium to use to intentionally express a government message. When the government provides a forum for private-party expression without either of these conditions being met, the expression is not government speech. The government can speak as a participant in a forum, but the creation of a space for private discourse does not involve expressing a governmental message, deputizing private parties to express it, or adopting a private party's contribution as a vehicle of government speech. Therefore, in such a case, there is no need to consider history, public perception, or control in the abstract.

ANALYSIS

In this case, Boston (D) refused Shurtleff's (P) request out of concern that it not violate the Establishment Clause. However, as the Court has held more recently, a government does not violate the Establishment Clause merely because it treats religious persons, organizations, and speech equally with secular persons, organizations, and speech in public programs, benefits, facilities, and the like. *See, e.g., Zelman v. Simmons-Harris*, 536 U.S. 639 (2002). And, the Court has held that, to the contrary, a government violates the Constitution when, as in the case at bar, it excludes religious persons, organizations, or speech because of religion from public programs, benefits, facilities, and the like. *See, e.g., Espinoza v. Montana Dept. of Revenue*, 140 S. Ct. 2246 (2020). Thus, under contemporary precedent, local governments have sometimes violated the First Amendment in the name of protecting it, thus illustrating the fine line that government must sometimes walk between running afoul of the Establishment Clause and suppressing religious speech and exercise.

Quicknotes

ESTABLISHMENT CLAUSE The constitutional provision prohibiting the government from favoring any one religion over others or engaging in religious activities or advocacy.

Mahanoy Area School District v. B. L., a Minor

Public school district (D) v. Student (P)

141 S. Ct. 2038 (2021)

NATURE OF CASE: Appeal in action challenging as unconstitutional a school's punishing a student for the student's off-campus expression on social media, using some vulgarity, of the student's frustration with the school.

FACT SUMMARY: After B. L. (P), a student at Mahanoy Area High School, was punished by the school for using profanity in off-campus social media posts to her friends, B. L. (P) and her parents (P) challenged the punishment as an unconstitutional violation of B. L.'s (P) First Amendment rights of free speech.

RULE OF LAW

A public school's interest in prohibiting students from using vulgar language to criticize a school activity or faculty or staff is not sufficient to overcome a student's First Amendment free speech rights when the student uses profanity in off-campus social media posts to express such criticism.

FACTS: Mahanoy Area High School student B. L. (P) failed to make the school's varsity cheerleading squad. Over the weekend, B. L. (P) posted two images on Snapchat, a social media application for smartphones that allows users to share temporary images with selected friends. B. L.'s (P) posts expressed frustration with the school and the school's cheerleading squad, and one contained vulgar language (she used the word "fuck") and gestures (raised middle finger). When school officials learned of the posts, they suspended B. L. (P) from the junior varsity cheerleading squad for the upcoming year based on her use of profanity, and B. L. (P) and her parents (P) challenged the punishment as an unconstitutional violation of B. L.'s (P) First Amendment rights of free speech. The Supreme Court granted certiorari in the case.

ISSUE: Is a public school's interest in prohibiting students from using vulgar language to criticize a school activity or faculty or staff sufficient to overcome a student's First Amendment free speech rights when the student uses profanity in off-campus social media posts to express such criticism?

HOLDING AND DECISION: (Breyer, J.) No. A public school's interest in prohibiting students from using vulgar language to criticize a school activity or faculty or staff is not sufficient to overcome a student's First Amendment free speech rights when the student uses profanity in off-campus social media posts to express such criticism. The special characteristics that give schools additional license to regulate student speech do not always disappear when that speech takes place off campus. Circumstances that may implicate a school's regulatory interests include serious or severe bullying or harassment targeting particular individuals; threats aimed at teachers or other students; the failure to follow rules concerning lessons, the writing of papers, the use of computers, or participation in other online school activities; and breaches of school security devices. Nevertheless, three features of off-campus speech often, even if not always, distinguish schools' efforts to regulate off-campus speech. First, a school will rarely stand in loco parentis when a student speaks off campus. Second, from the student speaker's perspective, regulations of off-campus speech, when coupled with regulations of on-campus speech, include all the speech a student utters during the full 24-hour day. That means courts must be more skeptical of a school's efforts to regulate off-campus speech, for doing so may mean the student cannot engage in that kind of speech at all. Third, the school itself has an interest in protecting a student's unpopular expression, especially when the expression takes place off campus, because America's public schools are the nurseries of democracy. Taken together, these three features of much off-campus speech mean that the leeway the First Amendment grants to schools in light of their special characteristics is diminished. Applying these considerations to the case at bar and putting aside the vulgarity used by B. L. (P), a listener would hear criticism of the team, the team's coaches, and the school—in a few words, criticism of the rules of a community of which B. L. (P) forms a part. This criticism did not involve features that would place it outside the First Amendment's ordinary protection. B. L.'s (P) posts, while crude, did not amount to fighting words, nor was her speech obscene under the Court's precedents. The circumstances of B. L.'s (P) speech also diminish the school's interest in regulation. B. L.'s (P) posts appeared outside of school hours from a location outside the school. She did not identify the school in her posts or target any member of the school community with vulgar or abusive language. B. L. (P) also transmitted her speech through a personal cellphone, to an audience consisting of her private circle of Snapchat friends. On the other hand, the school's interest in punishing the use of vulgar language aimed at part of the school community is weakened considerably by the fact that B. L. (P) spoke outside the school on her own time; B. L. (P) spoke under circumstances where the school did not stand in loco parentis; and the vulgarity in

Continued on next page.

B. L.'s (P) posts encompassed a message of criticism. In addition, the school presented no evidence of any general effort to prevent students from using vulgarity outside the classroom. Moreover, there was no evidence of substantial disruption of a school activity or a threatened harm to the rights of others that might justify the school's action. Although it might be tempting to dismiss B. L.'s (P) words as unworthy of robust First Amendment protections, in essence, sometimes it is necessary to protect the superfluous to preserve the necessary.

CONCURRENCE: (Alito, J.) Parents relinquish the quantum of authority that schools need to exercise to carry out their state-mandated educational mission, as well as the authority to perform any other functions to which parents expressly or implicitly agree. Thus, it is reasonable to infer that this authority extends to periods when students are in school but are not in class. However, a public school's regulation of off-premises student speech is a different matter because parents do not implicitly relinquish all that authority when they send their children to a public school. There are areas of off-premises student speech that have given rise to the most litigation. One involves perceived threats to school administrators, teachers, other staff members, or students. Another involves speech that criticizes or derides school administrators, teachers, or other staff members. With regard to this category of speech, parents do not relinquish their children's ability to complain in an appropriate manner about wrongdoing, dereliction, or even plain incompetence. The most difficult category involves criticism or hurtful remarks about other students. Though bullying and severe harassment are serious and age-old problems, these concepts are difficult to define with the precision required for a regulation of speech.

DISSENT: (Thomas, J.) The assessment of the scope of free speech rights incorporated against the states should be conducted by looking to what ordinary citizens at the time of the Fourteenth Amendment's ratification would have understood the right to encompass. Cases and treatises from that era reveal that public schools retained substantial authority to discipline students. Although schools at that time had less authority after a student returned home, it was well settled that they still could discipline students for off-campus speech or conduct that had a proximate tendency to harm the school environment. Although modern doctrine draws a clear line between speech and conduct, cases in the 19th century did not. And, although some courts made statements that, if read in isolation, could suggest that schools had no authority at all to regulate off-campus speech, those courts made it clear that the rule against regulating off-campus speech applied only when that speech was not connected with the management or successful operation of a school. If there is a good constitutional reason to depart from this historical rule, the majority and the parties fail to identify it.

ANALYSIS

The Court noted that given the advent of computer-based learning, it declined with this case to determine precisely which of many school-related off-campus activities a school may regulate without violating students" constitutional rights, especially since permitted school regulation might vary, depending upon a student's age, the nature of the school's off-campus activity, or the impact upon the school itself. Thus, the Court emphasized that it was not setting forth a broad, highly general First Amendment rule stating just what counts as "off campus" speech and whether or how ordinary First Amendment standards must give way off campus to a school's special need to prevent, e.g., substantial disruption of learning-related activities or the protection of those who make up a school community. It left the resolution of these issues for the future.

Connick v. Myers

Employer (D) v. Employee (P)

461 U.S. 138 (1983)

NATURE OF CASE: Certiorari review of speech restriction in employment context.

FACT SUMMARY: Myers (P) alleged that her employment was wrongfully terminated because she had exercised her constitutionally protected right of free speech by preparing and circulating a questionnaire soliciting the views of fellow staff members concerning office transfer policy and related matters.

RULE OF LAW

When a public employee speaks not as a citizen upon matters of public interest but instead as an employee upon matters only of personal interest, any personnel decision taken as a result by a public agency should not be a matter for the courts to review.

FACTS: Myers (P), who had some opposition to her impending transfer to prosecute cases in another section of the criminal court, prepared a questionnaire soliciting the views of her fellow assistant district attorneys concerning office transfer policy, office morale, the need for a grievance committee, the level of confidence in supervisors, and whether employees felt pressured to work in political campaigns. She was told that her distribution of the questionnaire was an act of insubordination and that she was terminated because of her refusal to accept the transfer. Myers (P) sued, alleging that her employment had been wrongfully terminated because she had exercised her right of free speech. The district court found that her distribution of the questionnaire was the actual reason for her termination and then held that the questionnaire involved matters of public concern and that the state had not "clearly demonstrated" that the survey "substantially interfered" with the operations of the District Attorney's office, as District Attorney Connick (D) had claimed. The Fifth Circuit Court of Appeals affirmed.

ISSUE: When a public employee speaks not as a citizen upon matters of public interest but instead as an employee upon matters only of personal interest, should any personnel decision taken as a result by a public agency be a matter for the courts to review?

HOLDING AND DECISION: (White, J.) No. When a public employee speaks not as a citizen upon matters of public interest but instead as an employee upon matters only of personal interest, any personnel decision taken as a result by a public agency should not be a matter for the courts to review. This means that when employee expression cannot be fairly considered as relating to any matter of political, social, or other concern to the community, governmental officials should enjoy wide latitude in managing their offices, without intrusive oversight by the judiciary in the name of the First Amendment. Thus, if Myers's (P) questionnaire cannot be fairly characterized as constituting speech on a matter of public concern, it is unnecessary for this Court to scrutinize the reasons for her discharge. Whether an employee's speech addresses a matter of public concern must be determined by the content, form, and context of a given statement, as revealed by the whole record. In this case, with the exception of the question regarding being pressured to work in political campaigns, the questions Myers (P) posed to her coworkers do not fall under the rubric of matters of "public concern" but rather reflect her dissatisfaction with her transfer and an attempt to turn that displeasure into a cause célèbre. Since one of the questions she touched on in her survey does, however, touch upon a matter of public concern and contributed to her discharge, the Court must determine whether District Attorney Connick (D) was justified in discharging Myers (P). The district court erred in this phase by imposing an unduly onerous burden on the state to justify her discharge, making the government bear the burden of "clearly demonstrating" that the speech in question "substantially interfered" with official responsibilities. Yet, as the *Pickering v. Board of Education*, 391 U.S. 563 (1968), case unmistakably states, the state's burden in justifying a particular discharge varies depending upon the nature of the employee's expression. The Court must, in such cases, reach the most appropriate possible balance of the competing interests of the employee, a citizen, in commenting upon the matters of public concern and the interest of the state, as an employer, in promoting the efficiency of the public services it performs through its employees. When close working relationships are essential to the fulfilling of public responsibilities, a wide degree of deference to the employer's judgment is appropriate. It is not necessary for an employer to allow events to unfold to the extent that the disruption of the office and the destruction of working relationships is manifest before acting. However, the Court cautions that a stronger showing may be necessary if the employee's speech more substantially involved matters of public concern. Also relevant are the manner, time, and place in which the questionnaire was distributed. Here, the questionnaire was prepared and distributed at the office, with the manner of distribution requiring not only Myers (P) but others to leave their

Continued on next page.

work in order to tend to it. The fact that Myers (P) exercised her rights to speech at the office supports Connick's (D) fears that the functioning of his office was endangered, even if that potential outcome never actually came about. Finally, the context in which the dispute arose is significant; it came upon the heels of an unwelcome transfer notice. Although Myers's (P) survey touched upon matters of public concern in a most limited sense, it is most accurately characterized as an employee grievance concerning internal office policy. Thus, the limited First Amendment interest involved here does not require that Connick (D) tolerate action that he reasonably believed would disrupt the office, undermine his authority, and destroy close working relationships. Accordingly, his discharge of Myers (P) did not offend the First Amendment. Reversed.

DISSENT: (Brennan, J.) Most of Myers's (P) questionnaire, and not just one question thereon, addressed matters of public concern because it discussed subjects that could reasonably be expected to be of interest to persons seeking to develop informed opinions about the manner in which the Orleans Parish District Attorney, an elected official charged with managing a vital government agency, discharges his responsibilities. The Court misapplied the *Pickering* test, *Pickering v. Board of Education*, 391 U.S. 563 (1968), by effectively deciding, contrary to prior authority, that a public employer's mere apprehension that speech will be disruptive justifies suppression of that speech when all the objective evidence suggests that those fears are essentially unfounded.

ANALYSIS

It was not until the 1950s and 1960s that the Court began to cast doubt on the theretofore unchallenged dogma that a public employee had no right to object to conditions placed upon the terms of employment—including those restricting his or her exercise of constitutional rights. While sitting on the Supreme Judicial Court of Massachusetts, Justice Holmes made the following statement expressing this position: "A policeman may have a constitutional right to talk politics, but he has no constitutional right to be a policeman." *McAuliffe v. Mayor of New Bedford*, 155 Mass. 216 (1892).

Quicknotes

FIRST AMENDMENT Prohibits Congress from enacting any law respecting an establishment of religion or prohibiting the free exercise of religion; or abridging the freedom of speech or of the press, the right of peaceful assembly, and the right to petition for a redress of grievances.

LIBEL A false or malicious publication subjecting a person to scorn, hatred or ridicule, or injuring him or her in relation to his or her occupation or business.

TIME, PLACE, AND MANNER RESTRICTION Certain types of regulations on speech that are permissible since they restrict only the time, place, and manner in which the speech may occur.

WRONGFUL TERMINATION Unlawful termination of an individual's employment.

Agency for International Development v. Alliance for Open Society International, Inc.

Federal agency (D) v. Non-governmental organization (P)

570 U.S. 205 (2013)

NATURE OF CASE: Appeal in action challenging a funding requirement in the United States Leadership Against HIV/AIDS Act as violative of the First Amendment.

FACT SUMMARY: Nongovernmental organizations (P) that had been awarded funding under the United States Leadership Against HIV/AIDS Act (Leadership Act) challenged as unconstitutional a condition in the Leadership Act that provided that no funds would be made available to any group or organization that did not have a policy explicitly opposing, inter alia, prostitution (the Policy Requirement), arguing that this condition violated their free speech rights.

RULE OF LAW

A statute's conditioning the receipt of funding for a government program on a recipient's affirmation of a belief that by its nature cannot be confined within the scope of the program violates First Amendment free speech protections.

FACTS: In 2003, in the United States Leadership Against HIV/AIDS Act (Leadership Act), Congress authorized the appropriation of billions of dollars to fund efforts by nongovernmental organizations (P) to combat HIV/AIDS worldwide. Congress determined that it should be the nation's policy to eradicate prostitution and other sexual victimization, as it determined that these contributed to the HIV/AIDS epidemic. Accordingly, the Leadership Act imposed two related conditions: (1) No funds "may be used to promote or advocate the legalization or practice of prostitution;" and (2) no funds may be used by an organization "that does not have a policy explicitly opposing prostitution." To enforce the second condition, known as the Policy Requirement, the Government (D) through the Department of Health and Human Services (HHS) (D) and the United States Agency for International Development (USAID) (D) required funding recipients to agree in their award documents that they opposed prostitution. Some of the organizations (P) feared that adopting a policy explicitly opposing prostitution could alienate certain host governments and could diminish the effectiveness of some of their programs by making it more difficult to work with prostitutes in the fight against HIV/AIDS. They were also concerned that the Policy Requirement could require them to censor their privately funded discussions in publications, at conferences, and in other forums about how best to prevent the spread of HIV/AIDS among prostitutes. On the grounds that the Policy Requirement violated their First Amendment rights to free speech, the organizations (P) sought and obtained a preliminary injunction barring HHS (D) and USAID (D) from cutting off their Leadership Act funding during the litigation or from otherwise acting based on their privately funded speech. The Government (D) appealed, and while the appeal was pending, the agencies issued guidelines on how recipients of Leadership Act funds could retain funding while working with affiliated organizations not bound by the Policy Requirement. The court of appeals summarily remanded the case to the district court to consider whether the preliminary injunction was still appropriate in light of the new guidelines. On remand, the district court issued a new preliminary injunction along the same lines as the first, and the Government (D) renewed its appeal. The Supreme Court granted certiorari in the case.

ISSUE: Does a statute's conditioning the receipt of funding for a government program on a recipient's affirmation of a belief that by its nature cannot be confined within the scope of the program violate First Amendment free speech protections?

HOLDING AND DECISION: (Roberts, C.J.) Yes. A statute's conditioning the receipt of funding for a government program on a recipient's affirmation of a belief that by its nature cannot be confined within the scope of the program violates First Amendment free speech protections. The Policy Requirement mandates that recipients of federal funds explicitly agree with the Government's (D) policy to oppose prostitution. The First Amendment, however, "prohibits the government from telling people what they must say." As a direct regulation, the Policy Requirement would clearly violate the First Amendment. The question is whether the Government (D) may nonetheless impose that requirement as a condition of federal funding. If a party objects to conditions on federal funding, its usual recourse is to decline the funds. In some cases, however, a funding condition can result in an unconstitutional burden on First Amendment rights. The distinction that has emerged is between conditions that define the limits of the Government (D) spending program—those that specify the activities Congress wants to subsidize—and conditions that seek to leverage funding to regulate speech

Continued on next page.

outside the contours of the federal program itself. The line separating these is not always clear. While the definition of a program may be manipulated to subsume the challenged condition, the Court has held that Congress cannot recast a condition on funding as a mere definition of its program. Otherwise, the First Amendment would be reduced to a simple semantic exercise. Here, the Policy Requirement falls on the unconstitutional side of the line. The United States Leadership Against HIV/AIDS Act's (Leadership Act's) other funding condition, which prohibits Leadership Act funds from being used to promote or advocate the legalization or practice of prostitution or sex trafficking, ensures that federal funds will not be used for prohibited purposes. The Policy Requirement thus must be doing something more—and it is. By demanding that funding recipients adopt and espouse, as their own, the Government's (D) view on an issue of public concern, the Policy Requirement by its very nature affects protected conduct outside the scope of the federally funded program. A recipient cannot avow the belief dictated by the condition when spending Leadership Act funds and assert a contrary belief when participating in activities on its own time and dime. Thus, by requiring recipients to profess a specific belief, the Policy Requirement goes beyond defining the limits of the federally funded program to defining the recipient. The affiliate guidelines also do not save the program. The use of affiliates does not violate the First Amendment when the affiliates permit an organization bound by a funding condition to exercise its free speech rights outside the federal program's scope. Affiliates cannot serve that purpose when the condition is that a funding recipient espouse a specific belief as its own. If the affiliate is distinct from the recipient, the arrangement does not afford a means for the recipient to express its beliefs. If the affiliate is more clearly identified with the recipient, the recipient can express those beliefs only at the price of evident hypocrisy. Here, the Policy Requirement goes beyond preventing recipients from using private funds in a way that would undermine the federal program. It requires them to pledge allegiance to the Government's (D) policy of eradicating prostitution. That condition on funding violates the First Amendment.

DISSENT: (Scalia, J.) The Policy Requirement is a constitutionally permissible means of selecting suitable organizations to implement the Government's (D) chosen strategy to eradicate HIV/AIDS, since the First Amendment does not mandate a viewpoint-neutral government. The Government (D) may enlist the assistance of those who believe in its ideas to carry them to fruition, and it does not have to enlist those who do not support its ideas. So long as the unfunded organization remains free to engage in its activities without federal assistance, the Government's (D) refusal to make use of the organization's assistance for an enterprise to which it is opposed does not abridge its speech. Adhering to this principle does not violate the Constitution, since the constitutional prohibition at issue is not a prohibition against discriminating against or injuring opposing points of view (which permissibly occurs any time a Government (D) program takes a position on a controversial issue), but the First Amendment's prohibition against the coercing of speech. Even if the program disadvantages those who do not support the Government's (D) position, that does not amount to coercion. Here the views that the Government (D) demands an applicant forswear—or favor—are relevant to the program in question. The program is valid only if the Government (D) is entitled to disfavor the opposing view (i.e., advocacy of or toleration of prostitution). Thus, if the program can disfavor this view, so can the selection of those who will administer the program. There is no risk that this principle will enable the Government (D) to discriminate arbitrarily against positions it disfavors, because it is permissible to admit to participation in the program only those who believe in the program's goals. The line that the majority draws, between conditions that operate inside a spending program and those that control speech outside of it, is inapposite. Here, elimination of prostitution is an objective of the HIV/AIDS program, and any promotion of prostitution—whether made inside or outside the program—does harm the program. The admission to a program of an ideological opponent can frustrate the purpose of the program by freeing up the opponent's funds for use in its ideological opposition. Because money is fungible, when organizations can conduct their AIDS work through federal funding, they can expand greater resources on policies that undercut the United States Leadership Against HIV/AIDS Act. The Government (D) does not have to prove by record evidence that this will actually happen; it is enough that this is a real and obvious risk. Although the majority invokes the unconstitutional conditions doctrine, that doctrine is inapplicable here, since it has never been held that a condition that is relevant to a statute's valid purpose and that is not in itself unconstitutional violates the doctrine. Finally, the condition imposed by the Policy Requirement is not coercive, even though the majority implies that it is. Compelling as a condition of federal funding the affirmation of a belief is not a compulsion at all. Organizations remain free to accept or reject the condition, so that the condition defines the recipient only to the extent that the recipient decides that it is in its interest to be so defined. The Government's (D) choosing between competing applicants on relevant ideological grounds is common and constitutional. Unfortunately, the majority's opinion will lead to frequent challenges to the denial of government funding for relevant ideological reasons.

Continued on next page.

ANALYSIS

The majority draws on *Rust v. Sullivan*, 500 U.S. 173 (1991), for support of its holding. In *Rust*, the Court considered Title X of the Public Health Service Act, which authorized grants to health-care organizations offering family planning services but prohibited federal funds from being "used in programs where abortion is a method of family planning." To enforce the provision, Department of Health and Human Services regulations barred Title X projects from advocating abortion and required grantees to keep their Title X projects separate from their other projects. The regulations were valid, the Court explained, because they governed only the scope of the grantee's Title X projects, leaving the grantee free to engage in abortion advocacy through programs that were independent from its Title X projects. Because the regulations did not prohibit speech "outside the scope of the federally funded program," they did not run afoul of the First Amendment. In his dissent, Justice Scalia points out that the fact that the pro-abortion speech prohibition was limited to "inside the program" speech was relevant in *Rust* because the program itself was not an anti-abortion program, and that the statutory objective could not be impaired by "outside the program" pro-abortion speech, thus distinguishing *Rust* from the case at bar.

Quicknotes

COERCION The overcoming of a person's free will as a result of threats, promises, or undue influence.

Matal v. Tam

Patent and Trademark Office Official (D) v. Trademark applicant (P)

581 U.S. ___, 137 S. Ct. 1744 (2017)

NATURE OF CASE: Appeal in action challenging the facial constitutionality of the Lanham Act's disparagement clause, 15 U.S.C. § 1052(a).

FACT SUMMARY: Tam (P), the leader of an Asian-American band who unsuccessfully sought to register the trademark "The Slants" as a result of the Lanham Act's disparagement clause, challenged the clause as facially invalid under the First Amendment's Free Speech Clause.

RULE OF LAW

The disparagement clause of the Lanham Act, prohibiting federal trademark registration for marks that might disparage any persons, living or dead, is facially invalid under the First Amendment's Free Speech Clause.

FACTS: Tam (P), lead singer of the rock group "The Slants," whose members were Asian-Americans, chose this moniker to "reclaim" the term and drain its denigrating force as a derogatory term for Asian persons. Tam (P) sought federal registration of the mark "THE SLANTS." The Patent and Trademark Office (P) denied the application under a Lanham Act provision prohibiting the registration of trademarks that may "disparage . . . or bring . . . into contemp[t] or disrepute" any "persons, living or dead." 15 U.S.C. § 1052(a). Tam (P) eventually sued in federal court, contending the disparagement clause was facially unconstitutional under the First Amendment's Free Speech Clause and the court agreed. The Supreme Court granted certiorari in the case.

ISSUE: Is the disparagement clause of the Lanham Act, prohibiting federal trademark registration for marks that might disparage any persons, living or dead, facially invalid under the First Amendment's Free Speech Clause?

HOLDING AND DECISION: (Alito, J.) Yes. The disparagement clause of the Lanham Act, prohibiting federal trademark registration for marks that might disparage any persons, living or dead, is facially invalid under the First Amendment's Free Speech Clause. As a threshold matter, the disparagement clause applies to marks that disparage the members of a racial or ethnic group. Tam's (P) view—that the clause applies only to natural or juristic persons—is refuted by the plain terms of the clause, which uses the word "persons." A mark that disparages a "substantial" percentage of the members of a racial or ethnic group necessarily disparages many "persons," namely, members of that group. Turning to whether the disparagement clause violates the First Amendment's Free Speech Clause, the Government's (D) first contention, that trademarks are government speech, is rejected. Instead, trademarks are private speech. Because the Free Speech Clause does not regulate government speech, the Government (D) is not required to maintain viewpoint neutrality on its own speech. This Court exercises great caution in extending its government-speech precedents, for if private speech could be passed off as government speech by simply affixing a government seal of approval, government could silence or muffle the expression of disfavored viewpoints. The federal Government (D) does not dream up the trademarks registered by the Patent and Trademark Office (PTO). Except as required by § 1052(a), an examiner may not reject a mark based on the viewpoint that it appears to express. If the mark meets the Lanham Act's viewpoint-neutral requirements, registration is mandatory. Once a mark is registered, the PTO is not authorized to remove it from the register unless a party moves for cancellation, the registration expires, or the Federal Trade Commission initiates proceedings based on certain grounds. It is thus far-fetched to suggest that the content of a registered mark is government speech, especially given the fact that if trademarks become government speech when they are registered, the federal Government (D) is babbling prodigiously and incoherently. Moreover, none of the Court's government-speech cases supports the idea that registered trademarks are government speech. If a trademark were deemed to be government speech, that would constitute a huge and dangerous extension of the government-speech doctrine because other systems of government registration (such as copyright) could easily be characterized in the same way. Similarly, the Government's (D) second argument, that this case is governed by the Court's subsidized-speech cases, is unpersuasive. Those cases all involved cash subsidies or their equivalent, e.g., funds to private parties for family planning services and cash grants. The federal registration of a trademark is nothing like these programs, since the PTO does not pay money to parties seeking registration of a mark. Likewise, unpersuasive is the Government's (D) third key argument, that the disparagement clause is constitutional under a "government-program" doctrine, an argument that is based on a merger of the Court's government-speech cases and subsidy cases. However, those cases occupy a special area of First Amendment case law that is far removed from the registration of trademarks. Cases in which government creates a limited public forum for private speech, thus

Continued on next page.

allowing for some content- and speaker-based restrictions, are potentially more analogous, but even in those cases, viewpoint discrimination is forbidden. The disparagement clause denies registration to any mark that is offensive to a substantial percentage of the members of any group. That is viewpoint discrimination in the sense relevant here: Giving offense is a viewpoint. The parties also dispute whether trademarks are commercial speech subject to relaxed scrutiny, but the disparagement clause cannot withstand even such review. Under the Court's precedent regarding such review, a restriction of speech must serve "a substantial interest" and be "narrowly drawn." One purported interest is in preventing speech expressing ideas that offend, but that idea strikes at the heart of the First Amendment. The second interest asserted is protecting the orderly flow of commerce from disruption caused by trademarks that support invidious discrimination; but the clause, which reaches any trademark that disparages any person, group, or institution, is not narrowly drawn. A deeper problem with the argument that commercial speech may be cleansed of any expression likely to cause offense is that the commercial market is full of merchandise that disparages prominent figures and groups, and the line between commercial and non-commercial speech is not always clear, as this case illustrates. If affixing the commercial label permits the suppression of any speech that may lead to political or social "volatility," free speech would be endangered. For these reasons, the disparagement clause is facially invalid under the First Amendment. [Affirmed.]

CONCURRENCE: (Kennedy, J.) With few narrow exceptions, a fundamental principle of the First Amendment is that the government may not punish or suppress speech based on disapproval of the ideas or perspectives the speech conveys. The test for viewpoint discrimination is whether—within the relevant subject category—the government has singled out a subset of messages for disfavor based on the views expressed. Here, the disparagement clause identifies the relevant subject as "persons, living or dead, institutions, beliefs, or national symbols," § 1052(a); and within that category, an applicant may register a positive or benign mark but not a derogatory one. The law thus reflects the Government's (D) disapproval of a subset of messages it finds offensive, the essence of viewpoint discrimination. A subject that is first defined by content and then regulated or censored by mandating only one sort of comment is not viewpoint neutral. To prohibit all sides from criticizing their opponents makes a law more viewpoint based, not less so. The logic of the Government's (D) rule is that a law would be viewpoint neutral even if it provided that public officials could be praised but not condemned. The First Amendment's viewpoint neutrality principle protects more than the right to identify with a particular side. It protects the right to create and present arguments for particular positions in particular ways, as the speaker chooses. By mandating positivity, the law here might silence dissent and distort the marketplace of ideas. The Government's (D) arguments in defense of the statute are unpersuasive. Regardless of whether trademarks are commercial speech, the viewpoint-based discrimination here necessarily invokes heightened scrutiny. To the extent trademarks qualify as commercial speech, they are an example of why that category does not serve as a blanket exemption from the First Amendment's requirement of viewpoint neutrality. In the realm of trademarks, the metaphorical marketplace of ideas becomes a tangible, powerful reality. To permit viewpoint discrimination in this context is to permit Government (D) censorship.

ANALYSIS

This case makes clear, without deciding whether all trademarks are commercial speech, that the Government (D) may not insulate a law from charges of viewpoint discrimination by tying censorship to the reaction of the speaker's audience, since the danger of viewpoint discrimination is that the Government (D) is attempting to remove certain ideas or perspectives from a broader debate. That danger is all the greater if the ideas or perspectives are ones a particular audience might think offensive, at least at first hearing. An initial reaction may prompt further reflection, leading to a more reasoned, more tolerant position. Indeed, a speech burden based on audience reactions is simply Government (D) hostility and intervention in a different guise. The speech is targeted, after all, based on the Government's (D) disapproval of the speaker's choice of message. Moreover, in this case it is the Government (D) itself that is attempting to decide whether the relevant audience would find the speech offensive. For reasons like these, the Court's cases have long prohibited the Government (D) from justifying a First Amendment burden by pointing to the offensiveness of the speech to be suppressed.

Quicknotes

LANHAM ACT Name of the Trademark Act of 1946 that governs federal law regarding trademarks.

VIEWPOINT DISCRIMINATION Impermissible restriction on speech by the state that discriminates on the basis of the viewpoint being espoused.

Near v. Minnesota ex rel. Olson

Publisher (D) v. State (P)

283 U.S. 697 (1931)

NATURE OF CASE: Certiorari review of constitutionality of state statute.

FACT SUMMARY: Minnesota (P) sought to have an injunction issued against the Saturday Press (D), which was publishing articles charging public officials with dereliction and complicity in dealing with gangsters.

RULE OF LAW

A state statute that authorizes previous restraints on publication violates the liberty of the press guaranteed by the Fourteenth Amendment if such publication relates to the malfeasance of public officials.

FACTS: A Minnesota statute authorized the abatement as a public nuisance of a "malicious, scandalous and defamatory" newspaper. The law permitted the defense of good motives and justifiable ends. The Saturday Press (the Press) (D) had published a series of articles that charged that gangsters were in control of gambling, bootlegging, and racketeering in Minneapolis, and that public officials were either derelict in their duties or had illicit relations with the gangsters. Minnesota (P) sought to abate further publication of the Press (D) that is "malicious, scandalous, or defamatory." The trial court issued a permanent injunction, and the Press (D) appealed.

ISSUE: Is a state statute that authorizes abatement of a newspaper publication dealing with the corruption of public officials unconstitutional?

HOLDING AND DECISION: (Hughes, C.J.) Yes. A state statute that authorizes previous restraints on publication violates the liberty of the press guaranteed by the Fourteenth Amendment if such publication relates to the malfeasance of public officials. It is the chief purpose of the constitutional guaranty of freedom of press to prevent previous restraint on publication. Placing previous restraints on the press endangers the very nature of a free state. Only in exceptional circumstances may previous restraints be imposed. These would include where a government seeks to prevent actual obstruction to its recruiting service or the publication of the sailing dates of transports or the number and location of troops. Similarly, obscene publications and incitements to acts of violence or the overthrow by force of orderly government may be enjoined. However, previous restraint on a publication that seeks to expose the malfeasance of public officials is prohibited by the Fourteenth Amendment. Public officials have recourse against false accusations under the libel law. Finally, requiring newspapers to present proof of their good intentions is merely an additional step to a complete system of censorship. So far as the Minnesota statute authorized the abatement proceedings against the Saturday Press (D), it is unconstitutional. Reversed.

DISSENT: (Butler, J.) The Minnesota statute does not operate as a "previous restraint on publication within the proper meaning of that phrase." It does not authorize administrative control in advance such as was formerly exercised by the licensers and censors but prescribes a remedy to be enforced by a suit in equity. Existing libel laws are ineffective to suppress the evils occasioned by false and malicious publications.

ANALYSIS

"The issue is not whether the government may impose a particular restriction of substance in an area of public expression, such as forbidding obscenity in newspapers, but whether it may do so by a particular method, such as advance screening of newspaper copy. In other words, restrictions which could be validly imposed when enforced by subsequent punishment are, nevertheless, forbidden if attempted by prior restraint." Emerson, "The Doctrine of Prior Restraint," 20 *L. & Contemp. Prob.* 648 (1956). Traditionally, the judicial concern in prior restraint cases is on the broad discretion over free expression vested in administrative officers.

Quicknotes

FOURTEENTH AMENDMENT Declares that no state shall make or enforce any law that shall abridge the privileges and immunities of citizens of the United States; no state shall deny to any person within its jurisdiction the equal protection of the laws.

42 U.S.C. § 1983 Defamation by state officials in connection with a discharge implies a violation of a liberty interest protected by the due process requirements of the U.S. Constitution.

FREEDOM OF THE PRESS The right to publish and publicly disseminate one's views.

PRIOR RESTRAINT A restriction imposed on speech imposed prior to its communication.

New York Times Co. v. United States (The Pentagon Papers Case)

News publisher (D) v. Federal government (P)

403 U.S. 713 (1971)

NATURE OF CASE: Certiorari review of injunction request regarding publication of government paper.

FACT SUMMARY: The Government (P) sought to enjoin the New York Times (D) and the Washington Post (D) from publishing The Pentagon Papers.

RULE OF LAW
Any system of prior restraints of expression comes to the Court bearing a heavy presumption against its constitutional validity.

FACTS: The Government (P) sought to enjoin the New York Times (D) and the Washington Post (D) from publishing the contents of a classified study entitled "History of U.S. Decision-Making Process on Vietnam Policy" (The Pentagon Papers). The Government (P) sought temporary restraining orders and injunctions, and these actions progressed through two district courts and two courts of appeals. The Supreme Court granted certiorari.

ISSUE: Does any system of prior restraints of expression come to the Court bearing a heavy presumption against its constitutional validity?

HOLDING AND DECISION: (Per curiam) Yes. Any system of prior restraints of expression comes to the court bearing a heavy presumption against its constitutional validity. Here, the Government (P) carried a heavy burden of showing justification for the enforcement of such a restraint. It did not meet that burden. The denial of injunctive relief is affirmed, and the stays entered by the Second Circuit Court of Appeals are vacated.

CONCURRENCE: (Black, J.) The cases should have been dismissed and relief denied when they were first presented to the Court. Every moment's continuance of the injunctions against the newspapers amounts to a flagrant, indefensible violation of the First Amendment. To find that the President has "inherent power" to halt the publication of news by resort to the courts would wipe out the First Amendment.

CONCURRENCE: (Douglas, J.) The First Amendment leaves no room for government restraint on the press. Its dominant purpose was to prohibit the widespread practice of governmental suppression of embarrassing information.

CONCURRENCE: (Brennan, J.) The error that has pervaded these cases was the granting of any injunctive relief whatsoever since the entire thrust of the Government's (P) claim was that publication of the material "could" or "might" or "may" prejudice the national interest. Only governmental allegation and proof that publication must inevitably, directly, and immediately cause the occurrence of an event kindred to imperiling the safety of a transport already at sea can support even the issuance of an interim restraining order.

CONCURRENCE: (Stewart, J.) Publication of this material will not necessarily result in direct, immediate, and irreparable damage to the nation, so the relief sought must be denied.

CONCURRENCE: (White, J.) Publication will do substantial damage to public interests, but the United States (P) has not met its heavy burden. However, failure by the United States (P) to justify prior restraints does not measure its constitutional entitlement to a conviction for criminal publication. That the Government (P) mistakenly chose to proceed by injunction does not mean it could not successfully proceed in another way.

CONCURRENCE: (Marshall, J.) The issue in this case is whether this Court or Congress has the power to make law. Congress has specifically rejected passing legislation that would have clearly given the President the power he seeks here and make the New York Times' (D) current activities unlawful. When Congress has specifically declined to make conduct unlawful it is not for this Court to redecide those issues—to overrule Congress. This Court has no authority to grant the requested relief.

DISSENT: (Harlan, J.) The doctrine of prior restraints does not prevent the courts from maintaining the status quo long enough to act responsibly. The separation of powers requires that the judicial function in passing upon the activities of the executive in foreign affairs be narrowly restricted. Even if there is some room for the judiciary to override executive determinations of the probable impact of disclosure on national security, the scope of review must be very narrow. Here, the executive's conclusions were not given even the deference owing to an administrative agency, much less a coequal branch of the government.

DISSENT: (Blackmun, J.) The First Amendment is not absolute. There is a danger that publication would result in the death of soldiers, the destruction of alliances, the greatly increased difficulty of negotiation with our

Continued on next page.

enemies, the prolongation of the war, and further delay in the freeing of U.S. prisoners.

ANALYSIS

On June 13, 1971, the New York Times (D) began publishing parts of the Pentagon Papers. On June 18, the Washington Post also began publishing parts of the papers. The Government (P) brought an action to restrain publication. Between June 15 and June 28, two district courts and two courts of appeals considered the case. On June 25, the Supreme Court granted certiorari. Restraining orders were continued in effect pending a decision, which was handed down on June 30. Four Justices – Brennan, Marshall, Douglas, and Black – dissented from the grants of certiorari, urging summary action and stating that they would not continue the restraint on the newspapers.

Quicknotes

PRIOR RESTRAINT A governmental restriction placed on communication before it is made.

CHAPTER 13

Beyond Speaking—Compelled Speech, Association, Money and the Media

Quick Reference Rules of Law

National Institute of Family and Life Advocates v. Becerra

Pregnancy center (P) v. State official (D)

138 S. Ct. 2361 (2018)

NATURE OF CASE: Appeal in action challenging as violating the First Amendment's Free Speech Clause guarantees a state law requiring licensed and unlicensed pregnancy centers to provide certain notices.

FACT SUMMARY: "Crisis pregnancy centers" (P), which sought to discourage pregnant women from obtaining abortions, challenged California's Reproductive Freedom, Accountability, Comprehensive Care, and Transparency Act, which required licensed and unlicensed pregnancy centers to provide certain notices to pregnant women, on the grounds that the notice requirements abridged the freedom of speech protected by the First Amendment.

RULE OF LAW

A state law requiring licensed pregnancy-related clinics to disseminate a notice stating the existence of publicly funded family-planning services, including contraception and abortions, and requiring unlicensed pregnancy-related clinics to disseminate a notice stating that they are not licensed violates the First Amendment rights to free speech.

FACTS: The California Reproductive Freedom, Accountability, Comprehensive Care, and Transparency Act (the Act) required clinics that primarily served pregnant women to provide certain notices. Clinics that were licensed were required to notify women that the State (D) provides free or low-cost services, including abortions, and give them a phone number to call. Unlicensed clinics were required to notify women that the State (D) had not licensed the clinics to provide medical services. "Crisis pregnancy centers" (P), whose mission was to discourage pregnant women from obtaining abortions, challenged the Act, alleging that both the licensed and the unlicensed notices abridged the freedom of speech protected by the First Amendment. The Supreme Court granted certiorari in the case.

ISSUE: Does a state law requiring licensed pregnancy-related clinics to disseminate a notice stating the existence of publicly funded family-planning services, including contraception and abortions, and requiring unlicensed pregnancy-related clinics to disseminate a notice stating that they are not licensed violate the First Amendment rights to free speech?

HOLDING AND DECISION: (Thomas, J.) Yes. A state law requiring licensed pregnancy-related clinics to disseminate a notice stating the existence of publicly funded family-planning services, including contraception and abortions, and requiring unlicensed pregnancy-related clinics to disseminate a notice stating that they are not licensed violates the First Amendment rights to free speech. The licensed notice is a content-based regulation. By compelling certain pregnancy clinics to speak a particular message, the notice alters the content of their speech. For example, one of the state-sponsored services that the licensed notice requires petitioners to advertise is abortion—the very practice that the plaintiffs (P) are devoted to opposing. Although less protection is sometimes afforded to professional speech—e.g., where a law requires professionals to disclose factual, noncontroversial information in their commercial speech and where states regulate professional conduct that incidentally involves speech—neither of these situations is implicated here. Instead of regulating factual information or professional conduct, the California Reproductive Freedom, Accountability, Comprehensive Care, and Transparency Act regulates speech as speech. The risk of such regulation is the same as the risk posed by the regulation of any speech content: that the Government seeks not to advance a legitimate regulatory goal, but to suppress unpopular ideas or information. Moreover, because professional speech is a difficult category to define with precision, if states could choose the protection that speech receives simply by requiring a license, they would have a powerful tool to impose invidious discrimination of disfavored subjects. The State (D) has not provided a persuasive reason for applying different rules to professional speech. Even if, as the State (D) asserts, its interest in educating low-income women about state-sponsored service is substantial, the licensed notice here is not sufficiently drawn to promote it. The notice is underinclusive because it applies only to clinics that have a "primary purpose" of providing family planning or pregnancy-related services while excluding several other types of clinics that also serve low-income women and could educate them about the State's (D) services. Additionally, the State (D) could inform the women about its services, without burdening a speaker with unwanted speech, through a public-information campaign. The unlicensed notice requirement unduly burdens protected speech since it imposes a government-scripted, speaker-based disclosure requirement that is wholly disconnected from the State's (D) informational interest and that drowns out the speaker's own message. [Reversed.]

Continued on next page.

CONCURRENCE: (Kennedy, J.) The State's (D) notice requirements represent serious viewpoint discrimination and are a paradigmatic example of the serious threat presented when government seeks to impose its own message in the place of individual speech, thought, and expression. Here, the State (D) requires primarily pro-life pregnancy centers to promote the State's (D) own preferred message advertising abortions. This compels individuals to contradict their most deeply held beliefs—beliefs grounded in basic philosophical, ethical, or religious precepts, or all of these.

DISSENT: (Breyer, J.) By finding the statute at bar to be content based and thus meriting heightened scrutiny, the majority threatens to create serious problems and potential litigation over much, if not most, government regulation. Virtually every disclosure law could be considered "content based," since virtually every disclosure law requires individuals to speak a particular message. Thus, the majority's view, if taken literally, could radically change prior law, perhaps placing much securities law or consumer protection law at constitutional risk, depending on how broadly its exceptions are interpreted. Many ordinary disclosure laws would fall outside the majority's exceptions for disclosures related to the professional's own services or conduct, and the majority fails to explain why the California Reproductive Freedom, Accountability, Comprehensive Care, and Transparency Act (the Act), which implicates health and safety concerns, does not come within a long-recognized exception for health and safety warnings. The majority departs significantly from precedent, too, since historically, the Court has been wary of claims that regulation of business activity, particularly health-related activity, violates the Constitution. Effectively, the majority goes where the Court has never gone before but without any defining standard or explanation for its severe departure from precedent. The Court previously held constitutional a law requiring doctors to inform women considering abortions about adoption services and the risks of abortions. Accordingly, if a state can lawfully require a doctor to tell a woman seeking an abortion about adoption services, why should it not be able, as here, to require a medical counselor to tell a woman seeking prenatal care or other reproductive healthcare about childbirth and abortion services? As the question suggests, there is no convincing reason to distinguish between information about adoption and information about abortion in this context. As to the unlicensed notice, there was significant record evidence that the legislature enacted this provision in response to information-related delays in qualified healthcare that affected women seeking to terminate their pregnancies as well as women carrying their pregnancies to term, with delays in qualified prenatal care causing life-long health problems for infants. The majority also wrongly suggests that the Act is suspect because it covers some speakers but not others. In fact, however, there is no basis for such concern, since the Act does not, on its face, distinguish between facilities that favor pro-life and those that favor pro-choice points of view. Nor is there any convincing evidence that discrimination was the purpose or the effect of the statute. Finally, whatever burdens the Act imposes are not burdens that accompany the Act on its face but would derive from potentially burdensome applications of the Act in particular circumstances.

ANALYSIS

Some federal courts of appeals have recognized "professional speech" as a separate category of speech that is excepted from the rule that content-based regulations of speech are subject to strict scrutiny under the First Amendment. These courts define "professionals" as individuals who provide personalized services to clients and who are subject to a generally applicable licensing and regulatory regime. "Professional speech" is then defined as any speech by these individuals that is based on their expert knowledge and judgment or that is within the confines of the professional relationship. Nevertheless, the Supreme Court itself has not recognized "professional speech" as a separate category of speech, and speech is not unprotected merely because it is uttered by "professionals." As the majority in this opinion noted, however, the Supreme Court has afforded less protection for professional speech in two circumstances: where professionals are required to disclose, factual, noncontroversial information; and where professionals' conduct is regulated, notwithstanding that the conduct incidentally involves speech. Because professionals might have a host of good-faith disagreements, both with each other and with the government, on many topics in their respective fields, the majority believes that permitting the government to police the content of these professionals' speech could result in the suppression of truth and minorities at the expense of increasing state powers. Accordingly, the majority finds no persuasive reasons for treating professional speech as a unique category that is exempt from ordinary First Amendment principles.

Quicknotes

FIRST AMENDMENT Prohibits Congress from enacting any law respecting an establishment of religion or prohibiting the free exercise of religion; or abridging the freedom of speech or of the press, the right of peaceful assembly, and the right to petition for a redress of grievances.

Continued on next page.

HEIGHTENED SCRUTINY A purposefully vague judicial description of all levels of scrutiny more exacting than minimal scrutiny.

STRICT SCRUTINY Method by which courts determine the constitutionality of a law when a law affects a fundamental right; under the test, the legislature must have had a compelling interest to enact the law and measures prescribed by the law must be the least restrictive means possible to accomplish its goal.

Hurley v. Irish-American Gay, Lesbian and Bisexual Group of Boston (GLIB)

Parade sponsor (D) v. Permit applicants (P)

515 U.S. 557 (1995)

NATURE OF CASE: Review of order mandating parade permit.

FACT SUMMARY: The sponsors (D) of a parade in Boston contended that a law compelling them to issue a permit to an organization they found repugnant violated the First Amendment.

RULE OF LAW

Private citizens organizing a parade may not be forced to include groups whose message they do not wish to convey.

FACTS: Since 1947, Boston's annual St. Patrick's Day parade had been organized by the South Boston Allied War Veterans Council (D). In 1983 the Irish-American Gay, Lesbian and Bisexual Group of Boston (GLIB) (P) applied for and was refused a permit. It filed suit. The trial court held that the parade was a public accommodation subject to Massachusetts's antidiscrimination laws and ordered GLIB (P) admitted. The Massachusetts Supreme Judicial Court affirmed. The United States Supreme Court granted review.

ISSUE: May private citizens organizing a parade be forced to include groups whose message they do not wish to convey?

HOLDING AND DECISION: (Souter, J.) No. Private citizens organizing a parade may not be forced to include groups whose message they do not wish to convey. A parade is a collection of marchers who make a collective point. A parade's dependence on watchers is so extreme that a parade without spectators and media coverage is arguably not a parade at all. Consequently, a parade is without question a form of expressive conduct protected by the First Amendment. Expression in the context of a parade is more than banners and speeches; the type of participants is also part of the overall message. Free speech in the demonstration/parade context necessarily involves the right on the part of the parade organizer not to include those whose inclusion would send a message the organizer does not wish said. Here, the South Boston Allied War Veterans Council (D) was of the opinion inclusion of the Irish-American Gay, Lesbian and Bisexual Group of Boston (GLIB) (P) in its parade conveyed an unwanted message. It was therefore acting within its rights not to allow GLIB (P) to march. Reversed.

ANALYSIS

A conceptually similar case, which came out differently, was *Turner Broadcasting Systems, Inc. v. F.C.C.*, 512 U.S. 622 (1994). In that case, FCC regulations mandated that cable operators include certain types of programming. This was held constitutional.

Quicknotes

FIRST AMENDMENT Prohibits Congress from enacting any law respecting an establishment of religion or prohibiting the free exercise of religion; or abridging the freedom of speech or of the press, the right of peaceful assembly, and the right to petition for a redress of grievances.

PLACE OF PUBLIC ACCOMMODATION A business providing food, lodging or entertainment to customers that either has an effect on interstate commerce or is supported by state action and in which racial discrimination is prohibited pursuant to the Civil Rights Act of 1964.

NAACP v. Alabama

Association (D) v. State (P)

357 U.S. 449 (1958)

NATURE OF CASE: Certiorari review of conviction for contempt for failure to obey state court order to produce records.

FACT SUMMARY: The National Association for the Advancement of Colored People (D), in a hearing initiated by the State of Alabama (P) to oust it from the state for failure to comply with incorporation requirements, refused to obey a state court order to produce its membership lists.

RULE OF LAW

A state must demonstrate a controlling justification for the deterrent effect on the free enjoyment of the right to associate that disclosure of membership lists is likely to have.

FACTS: [Alabama (P) brought proceedings against the National Association for the Advancement of Colored People (NAACP) (D) to oust it from the state for failure to comply with a state statute setting forth requirements governing foreign corporations. The NAACP (D) claimed it was exempt. A state court issued an order restraining the NAACP (D) from continuing to engage in further activities or to attempt to qualify itself while the action was pending. Before the hearing began, the state moved for production of the NAACP's (D) membership lists, alleging that the documents were necessary for adequate preparation for the hearing. The court granted the motion and issued an order to that effect. The NAACP (D) thereupon complied with the requirements of the statute but did not produce the lists. The NAACP (D) was held in civil contempt, fined, and prevented from obtaining a hearing on the merits of the ouster action until it produced the records.]

ISSUE: Must a state demonstrate a controlling justification for the deterrent effect on the free enjoyment of the right to associate that disclosure of membership lists is likely to have?

HOLDING AND DECISION: (Harlan, J.) Yes. A state must demonstrate a controlling justification for the deterrent effect on the free enjoyment of the right to associate that disclosure of membership lists is likely to have. Group association is an effective means to further advocacy of both public and private viewpoints. The fact that Alabama (P) has taken no direct steps to interfere with the National Association for the Advancement of Colored People's (D) freedom of association does not end the question because it may have engaged in more subtle intimidation. There is a vital relationship between the freedom to associate and privacy in one's associations. Here, there is a good possibility that disclosure would expose members to economic reprisal, loss of employment, and threat of physical coercion, thus having a deterrent effect on continued membership and discouraging others from joining. It is insufficient to answer that the pressure comes from the private community and not the State (P) as there is interplay between the two. Having found the potential for deterrence, the next inquiry is whether the State (P) was justified in seeking the lists. The disclosure of the lists has no substantial bearing on the issue of compliance with the state statute. This case differs substantially from an earlier Supreme Court decision involving the Ku Klux Klan and its failure to produce membership lists in violation of a New York law. There, the nature of the Ku Klux Klan—its violent tendencies, which the Court took notice of, and its failure to comply with any conditions, unlike in the instant situation—distinguish the two groups. Reversed.

ANALYSIS

At the same time that state investigations seeking public disclosure were prevailing over countervailing claims of First Amendment freedoms in other contexts, the Court, as evidenced in *NAACP v. Alabama* above and *Shelton v. Tucker*, 364 U.S. 479 (1960), required the state to produce a relevant justification for its probe and the collateral effect of disclosure on First Amendment freedoms. *NAACP v. Alabama* thus portends a shift in the Court's focus to greater scrutiny of reasons for state inquiries that have deterrent or "chilling" effects, on freedom of speech, association, or expression. The new approach would gain wider application in the 1960s where the state's interest in seeking information was pitted against the individual's right to privacy.

Quicknotes

CIVIL CONTEMPT One party's failure to comply with a court order requiring that party to undertake an action for the benefit of another party to the action.

DUE PROCESS CLAUSE Language in the Fifth and Fourteenth Amendments to the U.S. Constitution providing that no person shall be deprived of "life, liberty, or property, without due process of law."

Continued on next page.

FREEDOM OF ASSOCIATION The right to peaceably assemble.

RIGHT TO PRIVACY The violation of an individual's right to be protected against unwarranted interference in his or her personal affairs, falling into one of four categories: (1) appropriating the individual's likeness or name for commercial benefit; (2) intrusion into the individual's seclusion; (3) public disclosure of private facts regarding the individual; and (4) disclosure of facts placing the individual in a false light.

Americans for Prosperity Foundation v. Bonta

Charitable organization (P) v. State official (D)

141 S. Ct. 2373 (2021)

NATURE OF CASE: Appeal in action challenging a state requirement that charitable organizations disclose their largest donors as a violation of the First Amendment right to association.

FACT SUMMARY: California required that charitable organizations soliciting contributions in California disclose their largest donors to the state's Attorney General (D). Charitable organizations (P) challenged the requirement as a violation of the First Amendment right to association.

RULE OF LAW

A state requirement that charitable organizations soliciting contributions in the state must disclose their largest donors to the state is a facially unconstitutional violation of the First Amendment association right.

FACTS: Charitable organizations (P) soliciting funds in California had to disclose the identities of their major donors to the state Attorney General's Office (D). Charities generally had to register with the Attorney General (D) and renew their registrations annually. The Attorney General (D) required charities (P) renewing their registrations to file copies of their Internal Revenue Service Form 990. Schedule B to Form 990 requires organizations to disclose the names and addresses of their major donors. California contended that having this information readily available furthered its interest in policing misconduct by charities. Charities (P) that solicited contributions in California, to preserve their donors' anonymity, declined to file unredacted Schedule Bs, and the Attorney General (D), after several years of not enforcing the requirement, ultimately threatened them with suspension of their registrations and fines for noncompliance. The charities (P) challenged the compelled disclosure requirement as violating their First Amendment association rights and those of their donors. The Supreme Court granted certiorari in the case.

ISSUE: Is a state requirement that charitable organizations soliciting contributions in the state must disclose their largest donors to the state a facially unconstitutional violation of the First Amendment association right?

HOLDING AND DECISION: (Roberts, C.J.) Yes. A state requirement that charitable organizations soliciting contributions in the state must disclose their largest donors to the state is a facially unconstitutional violation of the First Amendment association right. The compelled disclosure of affiliation with groups engaged in advocacy may constitute as effective a restraint on freedom of association as other forms of governmental action, and such disclosure is subject to an "exacting scrutiny" standard of review, which requires a substantial relation, and narrow tailoring, between the disclosure requirement and a sufficiently important governmental interest. Here, the Court does not doubt the importance of California's interest in preventing charitable fraud and self-dealing. However, the enormous amount of sensitive information collected through Schedule Bs does not form an integral part of California's fraud detection efforts. California does not rely on Schedule Bs to initiate investigations, and evidence at trial did not support California's concern that alternative means of obtaining Schedule B information—such as a subpoena or an audit letter—are inefficient and ineffective compared to up-front collection. In reality, California's interest is less in investigating fraud and more in ease of administration. In the First Amendment context, the Court has recognized a type of facial challenge, whereby a law may be invalidated as overbroad if a substantial number of its applications are unconstitutional, judged in relation to the statute's plainly legitimate sweep. The compelled disclosure requirement at issue is plainly overbroad under that standard. The regulation lacks any tailoring to California's investigative goals, and California's interest in administrative convenience is weak. As a result, every demand that might deter association creates an unnecessary risk of chilling in violation of the First Amendment. For these reasons, the up-front collection of Schedule Bs is facially unconstitutional.

CONCURRENCE: (Thomas, J.) Although the Court reaches the correct result, it should have approached three issues differently. First, the text and history of the Assembly Clause suggest that the right to assemble includes the right to associate anonymously. Laws directly burdening the right to associate anonymously, including compelled disclosure laws, should be subject to the same strict scrutiny as laws directly burdening other First Amendment rights. Second, the origins and application of the Court's overbreadth doctrine are questionable. Third, and relatedly, a declaration that the law is "facially" unconstitutional seems to be no more than an advisory opinion—which a federal court should never issue at all.

CONCURRENCE: (Alito, J.) The exacting scrutiny standard has real teeth because it requires both narrow tailoring and consideration of alternative means

Continued on next page.

of obtaining the sought-after information. California's approach to charitable disclosures without a doubt fails exacting scrutiny and is facially unconstitutional. However, because the choice between exacting and strict scrutiny has no effect on the decision in these cases, there was no need to decide which standard should be applied here or whether the same level of scrutiny should apply in all cases in which the compelled disclosure of associations is challenged under the First Amendment.

DISSENT: (Sotomayor, J.) Instead of requiring and obtaining proof that the disclosure requirement actually burdens charities' (P) associational rights, by exposing them to objective harms, such as threats, harassment, or reprisals, the Court presumes (contrary to the evidence, precedent, and common sense) that all disclosure requirements impose associational burdens. This would be less troubling if the Court still required means-end tailoring commensurate to the actual burden imposed. Under a First Amendment analysis that is faithful to the Court's precedents, California's Schedule B requirement is constitutional. Although the charities (P) have presented evidence that their donors face a reasonable probability of threats, harassment, and reprisals if their affiliations are made public, California's Schedule B regulation is a nonpublic reporting requirement, and California has implemented security measures to ensure that Schedule B information remains confidential. The charities (P) also have failed to show that their donors, or any organization's donors, will face threats, harassment, or reprisals if their names remain in the hands of a few California state officials. Given the modesty of the First Amendment burden, California may justify its Schedule B requirement with a correspondingly modest showing that the means achieve its ends. California easily meets this standard, and the Schedule B reporting requirement is properly tailored to further California's efforts to police charitable fraud. To add insult to injury, the Court concludes that the disclosure requirement is unconstitutional not just as applied to the charities (P), but on its very face, even though the Court points to not a single piece of record evidence showing that California's reporting requirement will chill "a substantial number" of top donors from giving to their charities (P) of choice. Instead of striking down every application of the disclosure requirement, the answer is to proceed on a case-by-case basis, and to ensure that the state's confidentiality measures are sound or, in the case of public disclosures, to require a procedure for governments to address requests for exemptions in a timely manner. It is not to hamper all government law enforcement efforts by forbidding confidential disclosures en masse.

ANALYSIS

Some of the charities (P) argued that the Court should apply strict scrutiny, not exacting scrutiny, to the disclosure requirement, contending that only strict scrutiny would adequately protect the associational rights of charities. Under strict scrutiny, the government must adopt the least restrictive means of achieving a compelling state interest, rather than a means substantially related to a sufficiently important interest. On the other hand, the Attorney General (D) argued that exacting scrutiny was the correct standard of review, but also argued that exacting scrutiny demands no additional tailoring beyond the "substantial relation" requirement. As the case illustrates, the Court adopted a middle ground, whereby it applied an exacting scrutiny standard that does not require that disclosure regimes be the least restrictive means of achieving their ends but does require that they be narrowly tailored to the government's asserted interest. Thus, under the Court's exacting scrutiny standard, a substantial relation to an important interest is not enough to save a disclosure regime that is insufficiently tailored.

Quicknotes

EXACTING SCRUTINY An intermediate form of judicial review used in reviewing restrictions on speech in the area of campaign finance, election law, and compelled disclosures, with parameters that lie between strict scrutiny and intermediate scrutiny; at a minimum it requires that the government's interest be substantial, but it does not require that the government adopt the least restrictive means of achieving that interest.

INTERMEDIATE SCRUTINY A standard of reviewing the propriety of classifications pertaining to gender or legitimacy under the Equal Protection Clause of the U.S. Constitution that requires a court to ascertain whether the classification furthers an important state interest and is substantially related to the attainment of that interest.

STRICT SCRUTINY Method by which courts determine the constitutionality of a law when a law affects a fundamental right; under the test, the legislature must have had a compelling interest to enact the law and measures prescribed by the law must be the least restrictive means possible to accomplish its goal.

NAACP v. Button

Association (D) v. State (P)

371 U.S. 415 (1963)

NATURE OF CASE: Certiorari review of finding of a violation of American Bar Association Canons of Professional Ethics.

FACT SUMMARY: Virginia amended its bar regulations to ban the mass counseling and soliciting techniques of the National Association for the Advancement of Colored People (D).

RULE OF LAW

A state statute regulating the practice of law constitutionally may not be used to prevent minority groups from associating to seek legal redress.

FACTS: As a part of their statewide school desegregation program, National Association for the Advancement of Colored People (NAACP) (D) lawyers held regular meetings with Black parents to explain legal steps necessary to achieve such desegregation. After such meetings, forms were provided to the parents authorizing the NAACP (D) to represent them. With such authorization, NAACP (D) attorneys would then commence action. In response to this practice, Virginia added a Chapter 33 to its code of conduct for lawyers, which prohibited solicitation of legal action by agents of any organization that employs lawyers to carry out such actions. The Virginia Supreme Court of Appeals found the NAACP (D) in violation of this chapter as well as American Bar Association Canons of Professional Ethics 35 (prohibiting the control of legal services by intermediary lay agencies) and 47 (prohibiting any lawyer from assisting such an intermediary lay agency). This appeal followed.

ISSUE: May a state statute regulating the practice of law constitutionally be used to prevent minority groups from associating to seek legal redress?

HOLDING AND DECISION: (Brennan, J.) No. A state statute regulating the practice of law constitutionally may not be used to prevent minority groups from associating to seek legal redress. It is well settled that states have an inherent power to regulate the practice of law in their courts, but where solicitation and counseling activities by lawyers attain the status of political expression and association, free exercise of these rights may not be chilled by vague and overbroad bar regulations that lend themselves to selective enforcement against unpopular causes. Virginia (P) claims that solicitation, a crime, is outside the protections of the First Amendment, but First Amendment protection of vigorous advocacy may not be so inhibited by such labeling. Association for litigation (and thereby expression) may be the most effective way to protect minority rights. Proscribing it requires a compelling state interest that Virginia (P) has failed to demonstrate here. Virginia (P) claims that its interest in regulating the practice of law is sufficient. However, the purpose behind anti-solicitation rules has traditionally been to prevent improper private gain by attorneys. No such situation exists here. The ban is unconstitutional. Ruling is reversed.

DISSENT: (Harlan, J.) While the Court is correct in saying that association for litigation is a form of political expression and association, it should have balanced the state interests to reach a contrary outcome. Over and above the anti-private-gain purposes of the regulation of the bar, there is a deeper and more fundamental purpose of preventing outside interference with the attorney-client relationship. Here, even though the interests of the National Association for the Advancement of Colored People (D) and the parents were identical and the rights involved were fundamental, Virginia's attempt to so preserve the attorney-client relationship should have been upheld.

ANALYSIS

This case points up the now generally recognized view that state regulation of the practice of law may not be used to interfere with any group's freedom of expression or association. This principle has been extended by the Court to cover associations less unpopular than the National Association for the Advancement of Colored People as well. In *Brotherhood of Railroad Trainmen v. Virginia*, 377 U.S. 1 (1964), the Court held that a labor union had a right to set up a system of referrals of members to selected attorneys as a part of its freedom of association and expression in union-related activities. In *U.M.W. v. Illinois Bar*, 389 U.S. 217 (1967), the Court similarly held that a union had the right to hire a lawyer (on salary) to represent members before a state workmen's compensation board.

Quicknotes

ATTORNEY-CLIENT RELATIONSHIP The confidential relationship established when a lawyer enters into employment with a client.

Continued on next page.

COMPELLING STATE INTEREST Defense to an alleged Equal Protection Clause violation that a state action was necessary in order to protect an interest the government is under a duty to protect.

SOLICITATION Contact initiated by an attorney for the purpose of obtaining employment.

VAGUENESS AND OVERBREADTH Characteristics of a statute that make it difficult to identify the limits of the conduct being regulated.

Boy Scouts of America v. Dale

Nonprofit organization (D) v. Member (P)

530 U.S. 640 (2000)

NATURE OF CASE: Review of the constitutionality of a private organization's membership policies.

FACT SUMMARY: Dale's (P) membership in the Boy Scouts of America (the Boy Scouts) (D) was revoked when the Boy Scouts (D) learned that he was an avowed homosexual and gay rights activist.

RULE OF LAW

A group may constitutionally exclude an unwanted person if forced inclusion would infringe the group's freedom of expressive association by affecting in a significant way the group's ability to advocate public or private viewpoints.

FACTS: James Dale (P) is a former Eagle Scout whose adult membership in the Boy Scouts of America (the Boy Scouts) (D) was revoked when the Boy Scouts (D) learned that he was a homosexual and gay rights activist. The New Jersey Supreme Court held that the Boy Scouts (D) must admit Dale (P) and the Boy Scouts (D) appealed.

ISSUE: May a group constitutionally exclude an unwanted person if forced inclusion would infringe the group's freedom of expressive association by affecting in a significant way the group's ability to advocate public or private viewpoints?

HOLDING AND DECISION: (Rehnquist, C.J.) Yes. A group may constitutionally exclude an unwanted person if forced inclusion would infringe the group's freedom of expressive association by affecting in a significant way the group's ability to advocate public or private viewpoints. The New Jersey Supreme Court held that the state's public accommodations law requires that the Boy Scouts of America (the Boy Scouts) (D) admit Dale (P). Application of the law in this way, however, violates the Boy Scouts' (D) First Amendment right of expressive association. The statute prohibits in part discrimination on the basis of sexual orientation in places of public accommodation. The Supreme Court held that the Boy Scouts (D) was a place of public accommodation subject to the law, that the organization was not exempt from the law under any of its express exemptions, and that the Boy Scouts (D) violated the law by revoking Dale's (P) membership based on his homosexuality. The forced inclusion of an unwanted person in a group infringes the group's freedom of expressive association if that person's presence affects in a significant way the group's ability to advocate public or private viewpoints. However, the freedom of expression is not absolute. It may be overridden by regulations enacted to serve compelling state interests, unrelated to the suppression of ideas that cannot be achieved through means significantly less restrictive of associational freedoms. In determining whether a group is protected by the First Amendment's expressive associational right, it must first be determined whether the group engaged in "expressive association." Given that the Boy Scouts (D) engages in expressive activity, it must be determined whether the forced inclusion of Dale (P) as assistant scoutmaster would significantly affect the Boy Scouts' (D) ability to advocate public or private viewpoints. The Boy Scouts (D) asserts that homosexual conduct is inconsistent with the values instilled in the Scout Oath—"To keep myself physically strong, mentally awake, and morally straight." The Boy Scouts (D) asserts that it does not wish to promote homosexual conduct as a legitimate form of behavior. Thus, we must determine whether Dale's (P) presence as an assistant scoutmaster would significantly burden this goal. The Court must give deference both to an association's assertions regarding the nature of its expression as well as the association's view of what would impair its expression. Dale's (P) presence would force the organization to send a message that it accepts homosexual conduct as a legitimate form of behavior. Reversed.

DISSENT: (Stevens, J.) The law does not impose any serious burdens on the Boy Scouts of America's (the Boy Scouts) (D) "collective effort on behalf of its shared goals," nor does it force the Boy Scouts (D) to communicate any message that it does not wish to advocate. Thus, it does not infringe any constitutional right of the Boy Scouts (D).

ANALYSIS

Public accommodation laws, such as the one here, were initially promulgated in order to prevent discrimination in public places of accommodation. Such laws have gradually expanded to include many other forms of accommodation.

Quicknotes

FREEDOM OF ASSOCIATION The right to peaceably assemble.

PUBLIC ACCOMMODATION LAWS Laws passed pursuant to the Civil Rights Act of 1964 prohibiting discrimination in business establishments that are related to interstate commerce.

Buckley v. Valeo

Congressman (P) v. Federal government (D)

424 U.S. 1 (1976)

NATURE OF CASE: Certiorari review of constitutionality of Federal Election Campaign Act.

FACT SUMMARY: Senator Buckley (P) and others challenged the Federal Election Campaign Act's contribution and expenditure limitation, reporting and disclosure requirements, and public financing of presidential elections.

RULE OF LAW

The strong governmental interest in preventing election corruption does not justify imposition of substantial restrictions on the effective ability of any individual to express his or her political beliefs and engage in political association.

FACTS: In order to curtail political corruption, Congress in the Federal Election Campaign Act of 1971 (FECA), as amended in 1974, developed an intricate statutory scheme for the regulation of federal political campaigns. Among other provisions, Congress imposed a $1,000 limitation on individual contributions "to a single candidate" in § 608(b)(1), a $5,000 limitation on "contributions" to a single candidate by political committees in § 608(b)(2), a $25,000 limitation on total "contributions" by any individual in one year to political candidates in § 608(b)(3), a $1,000 ceiling on "expenditures" relative to a known candidate in § 608(e)(1), and similar ceilings on "expenditures" by the candidate and the candidate's family and on overall campaign "expenditures" § 608(a) and (c). In addition, Congress required disclosure by candidates of all "contributions" greater than $10, and by individuals of all "contributions and expenditures" aggregating over $1,000—§ 434. In a separate action, Congress provided for federal financing of presidential elections. Senator Buckley (P) and others, pursuant to a special section in FECA, brought this action to have all the above-mentioned sections declared an unconstitutional violation of their First Amendment rights of freedom of expression and association. This appeal followed.

ISSUE: Does the strong governmental interest in preventing election corruption justify imposition of substantial restrictions on the effective ability of any individual to express his or her political beliefs and engage in political association?

HOLDING AND DECISION: (Per curiam) No. The strong governmental interest in preventing election corruption does not justify imposition of substantial restrictions on the effective ability of any individual to express his or her political beliefs and engage in political association. Although the First Amendment protects political association as well as political expression, a limitation upon the amount that any one person or group may contribute to (and associate with) a candidate or a political committee entails only a marginal restriction on the contributor's ability to engage in free communication (and association); but, a restriction on the amount of money a person or group can spend on political communication (as a whole during a campaign reduces the quantity of expression by restricting the number of issues discussed, the depth of their exploration, and the size of the audience reached. As such, the so-called contribution limitations here (§ 608(b)1-3) may be upheld as valid means for limiting political corruption by donors.The expenditure limitations (§ 608(a), (c), (e)), however, place too broad a restriction on the individual's ability to speak out and must therefore be voided. As for the reporting and disclosure requirements, broad as they are, they are clearly upheld by the "compelling government interest" in deterring corruption by getting important information to the voters and providing records for enforcement of the law. Finally, the challenge to the public financing of presidential elections is simply unfounded since it entails no abridgment of speech whatsoever. Affirmed in part; reversed in part.

CONCURRENCE AND DISSENT: (Burger, C.J.) I agree with the part of the Court's opinion that holds unconstitutional the limitations the Federal Election Campaign Act of 1971 (FECA) puts on campaign expenditures. But the disclosure requirements for small contributions are unnecessarily broad intrusions into First Amendment rights since only large contributions are likely to cause the corruption FECA is supposed to remedy. The contribution limitations upheld by the Court place just as great a burden on political expression as expenditure limitations. Finally, there is no constitutional justification for the "incestuous" relationship between government and politics that the public financing law, upheld by the Court, creates.

CONCURRENCE AND DISSENT: (White, J.) Since the expenditure limitations, struck down by the Court, are neutral as to the content of speech, are not motivated by the fear of political expression, and reflect the well-founded conclusion of Congress that regulation

Continued on next page.

of campaign finances is essential to protect the integrity of the system, the First Amendment is not violated by them.

DISSENT: (Blackmun, J.) There is no principled constitutional distinction between limits on contributions and limits on expenditures.

DISSENT: (Marshall, J.) I dissent from the invalidation of the limits on the amount a candidate may spend from his own funds. The perception that personal wealth wins elections may not only discourage potential candidates without significant person wealth from entering the political arean, but also undermine public confidence in the integrity of the electoral process.

DISSENT: (Rehnquist, J.): Congress has enshrined the Republican and Democratic parties in a permanently preferred position.

ANALYSIS

In this case, the Court has identified one of the few compelling governmental interests that may be employed to justify congressional regulation of an area subject to strict judicial scrutiny. This interest is the interest in maintaining the integrity of the political process. Note, however, that even though the interest is held as compelling, the Court does not automatically affirm its imposition. Note that the Court's decision left the Federal Election Campaign Act of 1971 rife with loopholes. Perhaps the most exploited was that which permitted individuals to "expend" (i.e., separately from any candidate or the candidate's organization) large sums to endorse a vote for a particular candidate.

McConnell v. Federal Election Commission

Election contributor (P) v. Federal commission (D)

540 U.S. 93 (2003)

NATURE OF CASE: Certiorari review of constitutionality of Federal Election Campaign Act of 1971.

FACT SUMMARY: Several provisions of the Federal Election Campaign Act of 1971, as amended, were attacked as abridging First Amendment rights.

RULE OF LAW

The Federal Election Campaign Act of 1971 as amended does not abridge First Amendment rights.

FACTS: The Federal Election Campaign Act of 1971 (FECA), as amended, contains a wide variety of limits on political contributions, including limits on so-called soft money contributions. Suit was brought attacking the constitutionality of many of FECA's provisions on the grounds that they abridged First Amendment rights.

ISSUE: Does the Federal Election Campaign Act of 1971 (FECA) as amended abridge First Amendment rights?

HOLDING AND DECISION: (Stevens, J.) No. The Federal Election Campaign Act of 1971 (FECA) as amended does not abridge First Amendment rights. A contribution limit or restriction involving even "significant interference" with associational rights is valid if it is being "closely drawn" to match a "sufficiently important interest." This Court's treatment of contribution restrictions reflects more than the limited burdens they impose on First Amendment freedoms. It also reflects the importance of the interests that underlie contribution limits: interests in preventing both the actual corruption threatened by large financial contributions and the eroding of public confidence in the electoral process through the appearance of corruption. When this Court reviews a congressional decision to enact contribution limits, there is no place for a strong presumption against constitutionality of the sort often thought to accompany the words "strict scrutiny." The less rigorous standard of review that this Court has applied to contribution limits shows proper deference to Congress's ability to weigh competing constitutional interests in an area in which it enjoys particular expertise. It also provides Congress with sufficient room to anticipate and respond to concerns about circumvention of regulations designed to protect the integrity of the political process. Here, FECA's restrictions have only a "marginal impact" on the ability of contributors, candidates, officeholders, and parties to engage in effective political speech; the regulations simply limit the source and individual amount of donations. Furthermore, the solicitation provisions leave open ample opportunities for soliciting federal funds on behalf of entities subject to FECA's source and amount restrictions. Restrictions on national party committees, for example, simply affect a return to schemes approved by this Court in earlier cases; the idea that large soft-money contributions to a national party can corrupt is neither novel nor implausible. Both common sense and the ample record confirm the belief of Congress that they do. So too, FECA's amendments restricting corporations' and labor unions' funding of electioneering communications do not violate First Amendment free speech since the statute is not overbroad and the government has a compelling interest in eliminating corruption in use of such funds. [Rehnquist, C.J., delivered the portion of the Court's opinion holding invalid a section of the statute prohibiting individuals 17 years old or younger from making contributions to candidates and political parties, on the grounds that "Minors enjoy the protection of the First Amendment." Breyer, J., upheld requirements that broadcasters maintain records for political advertisements.] Affirmed in part and reversed in part.

DISSENT: (Rehnquist, C.J.) The statute does not regulate only donations given to influence a particular federal election; it regulates all donations to national political committees, no matter the use to which the funds are put. The statute is overinclusive.

CONCURRENCE AND DISSENT: (Thomas, J.) Rather than permit the never-ending and self-justifying process of upholding this legislation, the federal government should explain why proposed speech restrictions are needed in light of actual government interests, and, in particular, why the bribery laws are not sufficient. Today's holding continues a disturbing trend: the steady decrease in the level of scrutiny applied to "restrictions on core political speech."

CONCURRENCE AND DISSENT: (Kennedy, J.) The plurality here ignores constitutional bounds and in effect interprets the anticorruption rationale to allow regulation, not just of actual or apparent quid pro quo arrangements, but of any conduct that wins goodwill from or influences a member of Congress. This generic influence theory is at odds with standard First Amendment analysis because it is "unbounded" and susceptible to no limiting principle.

Continued on next page.

ANALYSIS

As made clear by the Supreme Court in *McConnell*, just as troubling to a functioning democracy as classic quid pro quo corruption is the danger that officeholders will decide issues, not on the merits or the desires of their constituents, but according to the wishes of those who have made large financial contributions valued by the officeholder. Stating that the best means of prevention is to identify and to remove the temptation, the *McConnell* court accordingly rejected nearly all the First Amendment challenges to the Federal Election Campaign Act of 1971.

Quicknotes

FIRST AMENDMENT Prohibits Congress from enacting any law respecting an establishment of religion or prohibiting the free exercise of religion; or abridging the freedom of speech or of the press, the right of peaceful assembly, and the right to petition for a redress of grievances.

Federal Election Comm'n v. Wisconsin Right to Life

Government agency (D) v. Nonprofit advocacy group (P)

551 U.S. 449 (2007)

NATURE OF CASE: Certiorari review of constitutionality of Section 203 of the federal Bipartisan Campaign Reform Act.

FACT SUMMARY: During the Bipartisan Campaign Reform Act's blackout period, a nonprofit advocacy group (P) wanted to run broadcast ads encouraging listeners to "call Senator Feingold" to object to the U.S. Senate's filibuster of judicial nominees.

RULE OF LAW

A broadcast ad urging listeners to "call Senator Feingold" is not the functional equivalent of express advocacy.

FACTS: Section 203 of the Bipartisan Campaign Reform Act (BCRA) criminalizes any corporate broadcast of any communication near the time of a federal election if the communication names a candidate for a federal elected office and is directed toward voters. A nonprofit corporation that served as an advocacy group, Wisconsin Right to Life (WRTL) (P), ran several broadcast ads suggesting that listeners "call Senator Feingold" to complain about the U.S. Senate's filibuster of judicial nominees. WRTL (P) wanted to run similar ads near the time of the 2004 election. It therefore filed suit against the Federal Election Commission (D), seeking a declaration that § 203 permits the broadcast of similar ads during the BCRA's blackout period near the time of the federal election.

ISSUE: Is a broadcast ad urging listeners to "call Senator Feingold" the functional equivalent of express advocacy?

HOLDING AND DECISION: (Roberts, C.J.) No. A broadcast ad urging listeners to "call Senator Feingold" is not the functional equivalent of express advocacy. In *McConnell v. Federal Election Commission*, 540 U.S. 93 (2003), this Court held that § 203 does not facially violate the First Amendment's overbreadth requirement; this case presents the as-applied question that *McConnell* reserved. *McConnell* held that § 203 can survive the strict scrutiny required for regulation of political speech if the regulated speech is express advocacy or its functional equivalent. Thus, if Wisconsin Right to Life's (WRTL's) (P) ads here are not express advocacy or its functional equivalent, the Federal Election Committee (FEC) (D) must show that prohibiting these ads near the time of a federal election is a narrowly tailored way to advance a compelling government interest. *McConnell*, however, did not articulate a standard for deciding whether an ad is the functional equivalent of express advocacy. Because such a standard should be both objective and accommodating of political speech, we hold that an ad is the functional equivalent of express advocacy only if it cannot be reasonably interpreted as anything but an appeal to vote for or against a specific candidate. The focus of this inquiry should be on the ads themselves and seldom on the context in which the ads appear. WRTL's (P) ads clearly are not the functional equivalent of express advocacy under this standard: they are similar to an issue ad, and they do not contain the common indicia of express advocacy (such as naming a specific candidate or political party). The FEC (D) therefore must show that banning these ads is a narrowly tailored way to advance a compelling government interest. These ads are not like campaign contributions, and they therefore do not implicate the government interest of "preventing corruption and the appearance of corruption" in campaigns. Similarly, these ads do not implicate the interest in preventing the effects of aggregated wealth on the political process. As applied to WRTL's (P) ads, then, § 203 of the BCRA violates the First Amendment.

CONCURRENCE: (Scalia, J.) *McConnell*'s holding on § 203 was wrong, and it should be overruled. Leaving § 203 facially intact has only had the ironic effect of concentrating even more power in the country's wealthiest persons while restricting a genuinely politically involved group such as Wisconsin Right to Life (P).

DISSENT: (Souter, J.) The practical effect of this decision is that *McConnell*'s holding on § 203 has been overruled. What is now lost is the realistic means of limiting the effect that large corporations can have on the political process by opening their treasuries for electoral purposes. In this case, the corporation is itself largely funded by other organizations, and the context rejected by the Chief Justice clearly shows that the ads here were the functional equivalents of express advocacy. In that essential context, there is no reasonable doubt that the ads are subject to regulation under § 203 following the rationale of *McConnell*.

ANALYSIS

Federal Election Comm'n v. Wisconsin Right to Life illustrates the special place of political speech in U.S. constitutional law. Such speech has been called the "core" of the speech guaranteed by the First Amendment. In this case, Chief Justice Roberts deferred to the fundamental

Continued on next page.

importance of that speech by "giv[ing] the benefit of the doubt to speech, not censorship."

Quicknotes

FIRST AMENDMENT Prohibits Congress from enacting any law respecting an establishment of religion or prohibiting the free exercise of religion; or abridging the freedom of speech or of the press, the right of peaceful assembly, and the right to petition for a redress of grievances.

POLITICAL SPEECH Speech pertaining to the political process that is afforded the greatest amount of protection under the First Amendment.

Citizens United v. Federal Election Commission

Non-profit organization (D) v. Government agency (P)

558 U.S. 310 (2010)

NATURE OF CASE: Supreme Court review of a lower court decision denying Citizens United's motion for a preliminary injunction to stop the Federal Election Commission from enforcing provisions of the Bipartisan Campaign Reform Act of 2002, which would prevent the airing of a film criticizing a presidential candidate.

FACT SUMMARY: During the presidential campaign for the 2008 election, Citizens United (D), a conservative, nonprofit organization, sought to advertise and then air a movie that was critical of then-Senator Hillary Clinton.

RULE OF LAW

The government may not suppress political speech on the basis of the speaker's corporate identity.

FACTS: In January 2008, Citizens United (D), a nonprofit organization, released a 90-minute documentary highly critical of then-Senator Hillary Clinton. The movie mentioned Clinton by name and featured interviews with commentators who were highly critical of the candidate. The movie was released in theatres, and Citizens United (D) attempted to increase distribution by making it available through video-on-demand. To do this, Citizens United (D) created advertisements containing short, pejorative statements about Clinton. It then wanted to promote the video-on-demand offering by running ads on broadcast and cable television. The Federal Election Commission (FEC) (P), using provisions of the Bipartisan Campaign Reform Act of 2002, stopped Citizens United (D) from running the film within 30 days of the 2008 Democratic primaries. Citizens United (D) tried unsuccessfully in district court to get a restraining order against the FEC's (P) action. The Supreme Court heard the appeal.

ISSUE: May the government suppress political speech on the basis of the speaker's corporate identity?

HOLDING AND DECISION: (Kennedy, J.) No. The government may not suppress political speech on the basis of the speaker's corporate identity. There is no basis for the proposition that the government may impose restrictions on certain disfavored speakers, and this First Amendment protection extends to corporations as well. In *Austin v. Michigan Chamber of Commerce*, 494 U.S. 652 (1990), the Court identified a new governmental interest in preventing the "corrosive distorting effects of immense aggregations of wealth that are accumulated with the help of the corporate form and that have little or no correlation to the public's support for the corporation's political ideas." The Court's anti-distortion rationale thus states that the corporate form of an entity is the problem to be feared, yet media corporations, which can aggregate huge wealth as well, are exempt from the ban on corporate expenditures. Thus, the anti-distortion rationale of *Austin* seems to be undercut by this exemption. Next, the Government (P) says that corporate political speech can be banned in order to prevent "corruption or its appearance." The anticorruption interest, however, is not sufficient to displace the speech in question. Furthermore, the Government (P) says that corporate expenditures can be limited because of its interest in protecting dissenting shareholders from being compelled to fund corporate political speech. The First Amendment does not allow that power, and additionally, nothing prevents shareholders from exercising their powers, which includes the possibility of removing board members, through the corporate process. *Austin* is not well reasoned, and for this reason, it must be and is now overruled. Reversed.

CONCURRENCE: (Scalia, J.) The dissent tries to show that today's decision is not supported by the original understanding of the First Amendment. It contends that the Framers were concerned about the free speech rights belonging to individuals. But the individual person's right to speak includes the right to speak in association with other individual persons. The Amendment is written in terms of "speech," not speakers.

DISSENT: (Stevens, J.) In the context of election to public office, the distinction between corporate and human speakers is significant. Corporations are not truly members of our society, despite the significant contributions that they make to it. The financial resources and legal structure of the corporate entity raise complicated questions about its proper role in the election process. Since they are not natural persons, it does not make sense to treat corporations as such when one considers the role they can play when making expenditures to support or attack a political candidate. Today's decision marks a troubling departure from this Court's previous rulings.

ANALYSIS

This five-to-four decision stands one of the most important First Amendment cases in years. Section 441b of the Bipartisan Campaign Reform Act of 2002 (BCRA) (commonly known as the McCain-Feingold Act) made

Continued on next page.

it a felony for corporations to expressly advocate the election or defeat of a political candidate or to broadcast electioneering communications within 30 days of an election. There was an exemption for political action committees created by a corporation, and the dissent noted this fact to rebut the argument that it was opposed to all forms of corporate speech. The dissent was troubled by the fact that a corporation, due to its structure, can marshal huge amounts of wealth and resources and thus distort the nature of the election discourse in ways that are not available to the individual advocate. The majority seemed less troubled by this fact and claimed it was simply ridding this issue of contradictions inherent in previous rulings.

Quicknotes

FIRST AMENDMENT Prohibits Congress from enacting any law respecting an establishment of religion or prohibiting the free exercise of religion; or abridging the freedom of speech or of the press, the right of peaceful assembly, and the right to petition for a redress of grievances.

McCutcheon v. F.E.C.

Campaign contributor (P) v. Federal agency (D)

572 U.S. 185 (2014)

NATURE OF CASE: Appeal in action challenging the aggregate limits on political contributions in 2 U.S.C. § 441a(a)(1) [the Federal Election Campaign Act of 1971].

FACT SUMMARY: McCutcheon (P), who wished to make political contributions to more candidates and political committees than he had already but was barred from doing so by the aggregate limits on such contributions in 2 U.S.C. § 441a(a)(1) [the Federal Election Campaign Act of 1971], challenged the aggregate limits as unconstitutional under the First Amendment.

RULE OF LAW

The aggregate limits on political contributions to candidates and political committees in 2 U.S.C. § 441a(a)(1) [the Federal Election Campaign Act of 1971] violate speech and association rights under the First Amendment.

FACTS: There are two types of political contribution limits in 2 U.S.C. § 441a [the Federal Election Campaign Act of 1971]: (1) base limits restrict how much money a donor may contribute to a particular candidate or committee while (2) aggregate limits restrict how much money a donor may contribute in total to all candidates or committees. During an election cycle, McCutcheon (P) contributed to 16 different federal candidates, complying with the base limits applicable to each. However, the aggregate limits prevented him from contributing to 12 additional candidates and to a number of additional political committees. He brought suit, alleging that the aggregate limits violated his speech and association rights under the First Amendment. The Supreme Court granted certiorari in the case.

ISSUE: Do the aggregate limits on political contributions to candidates and political committees in 2 U.S.C. § 441a(a)(1) [the Federal Election Campaign Act of 1971] violate speech and association rights under the First Amendment?

HOLDING AND DECISION: (Roberts, C.J.) Yes. The aggregate limits on political contributions to candidates and political committees in 2 U.S.C. § 441a(a)(1) [the Federal Election Campaign Act of 1971] violate speech and association rights under the First Amendment. The Government (D) contends that the aggregate limits prevent evasion of the base limits. However, even under a "closely drawn" standard of review, there is a substantial mismatch between the Government's (D) stated objective and the means used to achieve it. The limits deny the individual all ability to exercise his or her expressive and associational rights by contributing to someone who will advocate for the individual's policy preferences. A donor must limit the number of candidates he or she supports and may have to choose which of several policy concerns he or she will advance. It is no answer to say that the individual can simply contribute less money to more people. To require one person to contribute at lower levels than others because he or she wants to support more candidates or causes is to impose a special burden on broader participation in the democratic process. The only legitimate governmental interest for restricting campaign finances is the prevention of quid pro quo corruption or the appearance thereof. Spending large sums of money in connection with elections, but not in connection with an effort to control the exercise of an officeholder's official duties, does not give rise to quid pro quo corruption nor does the possibility that an individual who spends large sums, may garner influence over or access to elected officials or political parties. The line between quid pro quo corruption and general influence must be respected in order to safeguard basic First Amendment rights. The Government (D) bears the burden of proving that the aggregate limits are constitutional, but once the aggregate limits kick in, they ban all contributions of any amount, even though Congress's selection of a base limit indicates its belief that contributions beneath that amount do not create a cognizable risk of corruption. The Government (D) must thus defend the aggregate limits by demonstrating that they prevent circumvention of the base limits, a function they do not serve in any meaningful way. The fear, expressed in *Buckley v. Valeo*, 424 U.S. 1 (1976), that an individual might contribute massive amounts of money to a particular candidate through unearmarked contributions to entities likely to support the candidate, is far too speculative given the statutes and regulations that control such contributions. The aggregate limits also violate the First Amendment because they are not closely drawn to avoid unnecessary abridgment of associational freedoms. The Government (D) argues that the aggregate limits prevent an individual from giving to too many initial recipients who might then recontribute a donation, but experience suggests that the vast majority of contributions are retained and spent by their recipients. Importantly, there are multiple alternatives available to Congress that would serve the Government's (D) interest in preventing circumvention while avoiding unnecessary abridgment of First Amendment rights. Such alternatives might include targeted restrictions on

Continued on next page.

transfers among candidates and political committees or tighter earmarking rules. Disclosure of contributions also reduces the potential for abuse of the campaign finance system. Disclosure requirements may burden speech, but they often represent a less restrictive alternative to flat bans on certain types or quantities of speech, such as the bans inherent in the aggregate limits. With the advent of modern technology, such as the Internet, disclosure now offers more robust protections against corruption than previously possible. Finally, the Government (D) argues that the aggregate limits deter corruption by checking widely distributed support within all applicable base limits. However, recasting as corruption a donor's widely distributed support for a political party would dramatically expand government regulation of the political process.

CONCURRENCE: (Thomas, J.) *Buckley v. Valeo*, 424 U.S. 1 (1976), should be overruled, thus subjecting the aggregate limits to strict scrutiny, which the limits would not survive.

DISSENT: (Breyer, J.) The plurality is wrong to overrule *Buckley v. Valeo*, 424 U.S. 1 (1976), as to the aggregate limits. First, the plurality defines "corruption" too narrowly. The anticorruption interest is significantly broader than suggested by the plurality and encompasses maintaining the integrity of governmental institutions. The political speech protected by the First Amendment is communication that seeks to secure government action. Corruption breaks this speech-to-government tie, since the general public will not be heard where large donations are speaking. Also, the appearance of corruption can lead the public to believe that it has no say, thus leading it to lose interest in participating in the political process altogether. Thus, the anticorruption interest is rooted in the First Amendment itself and in the constitutional effort to create a democracy that is responsive to the people. The plurality also errs in concluding that the aggregate limits are no longer needed to prevent the circumvention of limits on direct contributions. In the absence of the aggregate limits, donors can and likely will find ways to channel very large sums of money to parties and to individual candidates, producing precisely the kind of "corruption" or "appearance of corruption" that previously led the Court to hold aggregate limits constitutional. Thus, the plurality's opinion will help certain donors to evade individual contribution limits. Further, contrary to the plurality's conclusion, there is no substantial mismatch between Congress's legitimate objective and the means chosen to achieve it. Finally, a determination of whether anticorruption objectives justify a particular set of contribution limits should be made on the basis of an empirically based evidentiary record, and such determinations are better left for Congress, which is more suited to resolving such questions than are judges. In the absence of a more fully developed record, the plurality lacks grounds for overturning *Buckley*.

ANALYSIS

The Court's decision effectively struck down limits on the total amount that a single donor can give to candidates, party committees, and political action committees in an election cycle. The Court also ruled that government regulation may not target the general gratitude a candidate may feel toward those who support him or his allies, or the political access such support may afford, saying that ingratiation and access are not corruption but instead embody a central feature of democracy—that constituents support candidates who share their beliefs and interests, and candidates who are elected can be expected to be responsive to those concerns. Justice Breyer, dissenting, observed that the plurality's conception of corruption failed to recognize the difference between influence resting upon public opinion and influence bought by money alone, and would eviscerate the nation's campaign finance laws.

Quicknotes

FIRST AMENDMENT Prohibits Congress from enacting any law respecting an establishment of religion or prohibiting the free exercise of religion; or abridging the freedom of speech or of the press, the right of peaceful assembly, and the right to petition for a redress of grievances.

POLITICAL SPEECH Speech pertaining to the political process that is afforded the greatest amount of protection under the First Amendment.

QUID PRO QUO Something for something. In contract law, the consideration, something of value, passed between the parties to render the contract binding.

Branzburg v. Hayes

News reporters (D) v. State and federal government (P)

408 U.S. 665 (1972)

NATURE OF CASE: Certiorari review of appeal from contempt citations for failure to testify before state and federal grand juries.

FACT SUMMARY: Journalists refused to testify before state and federal grand juries, claiming that their news sources were confidential.

RULE OF LAW

The First Amendment's freedom of press does not exempt a journalist from disclosing to a grand jury information he or she has received in confidence.

FACTS: Branzburg (D), who had written articles for a newspaper about drug activities he had observed, refused to testify before a state grand jury regarding his information. Pappas (D), a television reporter, even though he wrote no story, refused to testify before a state grand jury on his experiences inside Black Panther headquarters. Caldwell (D), a reporter who had interviewed several Black Panther leaders and then written stories, refused to testify before a federal grand jury that was investigating violations of criminal statutes dealing with threats against the President and traveling interstate to incite a riot. Branzburg (D) and Pappas (D) were held in contempt.

ISSUE: Does the First Amendment's freedom of press exempt a journalist from disclosing to a grand jury information he or she has received in confidence?

HOLDING AND DECISION: (White, J.) No. The First Amendment's freedom of press does not exempt a journalist from disclosing to a grand jury information he or she has received in confidence. The First Amendment does not invalidate every incidental burdening of the press that may result from the enforcement of civil or criminal statutes of general applicability. Journalists cannot invoke a testimonial privilege not enjoined by other citizens. The Constitution should not shield criminals who wish to remain anonymous from prosecution through disclosure. Forcing journalists to testify will not impede the flow of news. The journalists may never be called. Many political groups will still turn to a reporter because they are dependent on the media for exposure. Grand jury proceedings are secret, and the police are experienced in protecting informants. More important, the public's interest in news flow does not override the public's interest in deterring crime. Here, the grand juries were not probing at will without relation to existing need; the information sought was necessary to the respective investigations. A grand jury is not restricted to seeking information from nonnewsmen—it may choose the best method for its task. The contempt citations are affirmed.

CONCURRENCE: (Powell, J.) The journalist always has to resort to the courts to quash subpoenas where his or her testimony bears only a remote and tenuous relationship to the subject of the investigation.

DISSENT: (Stewart, J.) The press should not be treated as an investigating tool of the government. Concrete evidence exists proving that fear of an unbridled subpoena power deters sources. The Court's inquiry should be (1) whether there is a rational connection between the government's and the deterrence of First Amendment activity and (2) whether the effect would occur with some regularity. The government has the burden of showing that (1) the information sought is clearly relevant to a precisely defined subject of governmental inquiry, (2) it is reasonable to think the witness in question has that information, and (3) there is no other means of obtaining that information less destructive of First Amendment freedoms.

DISSENT: (Douglas, J.) A journalist has an absolute right not to appear before a grand jury so as to have absolute privacy in uncovering information in the course of testing his or her hunches. Effective government depends upon a free flow of opinion and reporting.

ANALYSIS

Guidelines promulgated by the Attorney General for federal officials to follow when subpoenaing members of the press to testify before grand juries or at criminal trials included the following test for information: (1) whether there is "sufficient reason to believe that the information sought is essential to a successful investigation" and (2) whether the information cannot be obtained from non-press sources. However, in "emergencies and other unusual situations, subpoenas that do not conform to the guidelines may be issued."

Quicknotes

CONTEMPT Conduct that interferes with the proper administration of justice by a court or legislature.

Continued on next page.

FREEDOM OF THE PRESS The right to publish and publicly disseminate one's views.

GRAND JURY A group summoned to investigate, inform, and accuse persons of crimes when sufficient evidence exists to do so.

SUBPOENA A court-issued mandate to compel a witness to appear at trial.

Minneapolis Star & Tribune Co. v. Minnesota Comm'r of Revenue

Newspaper publisher (P) v. State (D)

460 U.S. 575 (1983)

NATURE OF CASE: Certiorari review of constitutionality of state use tax statute.

FACT SUMMARY: The Minneapolis Star & Tribune Co. (P) contended that Minnesota (D) had acted unconstitutionally in imposing a four percent use tax on the cost of ink and paper consumed in the production of any publication and then enacting an exemption that effectively resulted in only a few of the biggest newspapers having to pay any such use tax.

RULE OF LAW

In order to be constitutionally permissible, any differential taxation of the press must be necessary to the achievement of a state interest of compelling importance.

FACTS: Under the tax scheme set up by the Minnesota legislature, newspapers were exempt from the four percent sales tax. However, a four percent use tax on the costs of ink and paper consumed in the production of any publication was imposed. In addition, an exemption was provided for the first $100,000 worth of ink and paper consumed by a publication in any calendar year, which amounted to giving each publication an annual tax credit of $4,000. Only eleven papers, one of them the Star Tribune (P), used sufficient quantities of ink and paper to become liable for payment of use taxes beyond the amount of the tax credit in 1974. Only thirteen papers had to pay actual use taxes in 1975. In challenging the constitutionality of the use tax and seeking a refund of the use taxes it had paid, the Minneapolis Star & Tribune Co. (P) argued that there had been a violation of the guarantees of freedom of the press and equal protection found in the First and Fourteenth Amendments. The Minnesota Supreme Court upheld the tax against this constitutional challenge.

ISSUE: In order to be constitutionally permissible, must any differential taxation of the press be necessary to the achievement of a state interest of compelling importance?

HOLDING AND DECISION: (O'Connor, J.) Yes. In order to be constitutionally permissible, any differential taxation of the press must be necessary to the achievement of a state interest of compelling importance. Differential taxation of the press places such a burden on the interests protected by the First Amendment that it is not constitutionally permissible unless the state asserts a counterbalancing interest of compelling importance that cannot be achieved without differential taxation. By creating this special use tax, Minnesota (D) singled out the press for special tax treatment. It justifies such by its need to raise revenue. Yet, that goal could be attained by taxing businesses generally, thus avoiding the censorial threat implicit in a tax that singles out the press. Minnesota (D) offers the counterargument that the use tax actually favors the press. However, the very selection of the press for special treatment threatens the press not only with the current differential treatment but with the possibility of subsequent differentially more burdensome treatment. Thus, this Court would hesitate to fashion a rule that automatically allowed the state to single out the press for a different method of taxation as long as the effective burden on the press was lighter than that on other businesses. Such a rule should also be avoided because the courts as institutions are poorly equipped to evaluate with precision the relative burdens of various methods of taxation. Minnesota's (D) ink and paper tax would not survive anyway because it violates the First Amendment for another reason other than its singling out of the press. It also violates the First Amendment because it targets a small group of newspapers. Recognizing a power in the state not only to single out the press but also to tailor the tax so that it singles out a few members of the press presents such a potential for abuse that no interest suggested by Minnesota (D) can justify the scheme. When, as in this case, a tax exemption operates to select such a narrowly defined group to bear the full burden of the tax, the tax begins to resemble more a penalty for a few of the largest newspapers than an attempt to favor struggling smaller enterprises. There having been no satisfactory justification offered for this tax on the use of ink and paper, it must be held to violate the First Amendment. Reversed.

DISSENT: (Rehnquist, J.) The $1,224,747 the Minneapolis Star & Tribune Co. (P) actually paid in use taxes over the years in question is significantly less burdensome than the $3,685,092 that it would have had to pay were the sales of its newspapers subject to the sales tax. Thus, the tax scheme, which allowed newspapers to pay a use tax in return for being free of sales tax, actually benefited, not burdened, the freedom of speech and the press. If there was no burden, there was no "abridgment" of these freedoms of speech and the press. Without such an "abridgment" there is no violation of the First Amendment.

Continued on next page.

ANALYSIS

In *Washington v. United States*, 460 U.S. 536 (1983), the Court was dealing with a state tax that singled out federal contractors as a separate category. It did not evidence any reluctance in that case to assess the impact of the tax, finding it was not impermissibly discriminatory on the United States because it imposed a tax burden no greater than what the contractors would have had to otherwise pay in state taxes were they treated the same as everyone else.

Quicknotes

DIFFERENTIAL TAXATION A marked disparity in tax rates between parties where such rates should be uniform.

FIRST AMENDMENT Prohibits Congress from enacting any law respecting an establishment of religion or prohibiting the free exercise of religion; or abridging the freedom of speech or of the press, the right of peaceful assembly, and the right to petition for a redress of grievances.

CHAPTER 14

The Religion Clauses: Free Exercise and Establishment

Quick Reference Rules of Law

Church of the Lukumi Babalu Aye v. City of Hialeah

Church (P) v. Municipality (D)

508 U.S. 520 (1993)

NATURE OF CASE: Certiorari review of constitutionality of an ordinance prohibiting ritual animal sacrifice.

FACT SUMMARY: A church (P) that performed the sacrificial killing of animals as required by the Santeria religion challenged various Hialeah (D) ordinances prohibiting such killings as a violation of the Free Exercise Clause of the First Amendment.

RULE OF LAW

If a law's object is to infringe upon or restrict religious practices, it must be justified by a compelling interest and be narrowly tailored to advance that interest.

FACTS: The Church of the Lukumi Babalu Aye (P) (the Church) and its members practiced the religion of Santeria. An integral part of the religion was the sacrificial killing of animals for certain events. In 1987, the Church (P) leased land in the city of Hialeah (D) on which it planned to build various structures including a house of worship. Distressed by the Church's (P) plans, Hialeah (D) called an emergency public session during which it passed various ordinances that essentially prohibited the type of sacrifices required in Santeria. The Church (P) thereafter filed suit, arguing that the ordinances violated the Free Exercise Clause of the First Amendment by targeting its religious practices. The district court disagreed and upheld the ordinances with the court of appeals affirming. The Supreme Court granted review.

ISSUE: If a law's object is to infringe upon or restrict religious practices, must it be justified by a compelling interest and be narrowly tailored to advance that interest?

HOLDING AND DECISION: (Kennedy, J.) Yes. If a law's object is to infringe upon or restrict religious practices, it must be justified by a compelling interest and be narrowly tailored to advance that interest. Neutral and generally applicable laws need not meet this higher level of scrutiny. The ordinances at issue, however, were not neutral and generally applicable. They restricted the practices because of their religious motivation. Though not evident on the face of the ordinances, their nonneutrality is clear from the expressed concerns of residents and citizens, the expressed motive of council members, and the ordinances' operation. Practically the only conduct prohibited by the ordinances is that exercised by Santeria church members. In addition, the ordinances in no way promoted the legitimate concerns of public morals, peace, or safety advanced in their support. Thus, since the ordinances were not neutral and were not narrowly tailored to serve compelling interests, they were unconstitutional. Reversed.

CONCURRENCE: (Scalia, J.) The ordinances violate the Free Exercise Clause simply because they prohibit the free exercise of religion, regardless of the good, bad, or nonexistent motives of the lawmakers.

CONCURRENCE: (Souter, J.) Hialeah (D) has enacted a rare example of a law actually aimed at suppressing religious exercise. Such a law is nearly always invalid.

ANALYSIS

Though a majority of the Court agree that the correct result was reached, the concurring opinions evidence the hostility of many justices to the rule announced in *Employment Div., Dept. of Human Resources of Oregon v. Smith*, 494 U.S. 872 (1992), just one year earlier, that neutral laws of general applicability are not subject to a high level of scrutiny. Thus, its continued viability is questionable as the makeup of the Court changes.

Quicknotes

COMPELLING STATE INTEREST Defense to an alleged Equal Protection Clause violation that a state action was necessary in order to protect an interest the government is under a duty to protect.

FREE EXERCISE OF RELIGION The right to practice one's religious beliefs free from governmental conduct or interference.

Sherbert v. Verner

Applicant for unemployment (P) v. Employment Security Commission (D)

374 U.S. 398 (1963)

NATURE OF CASE: Certiorari review of constitutionality of state unemployment benefit program.

FACT SUMMARY: Sherbert (P) was discharged by her employer because she would not work on her religion's Sabbath.

RULE OF LAW

It is unconstitutional for a state to refuse unemployment benefits to a worker who was discharged because of his or her refusal to work on his or her religion's Sabbath.

FACTS: Sherbert (P) was discharged by her employer because she refused to work on Saturday, her religion's Sabbath. She could not find other employment because she would not work on Saturday. The South Carolina Employment Security Commission (the Commission) (D) found Sherbert (P) ineligible for unemployment compensation because her refusal to work on Saturday was failure without good cause to accept available work. The state law provides that no employee shall be required to work on Sunday. The South Carolina Supreme Court sustained the Commission's decision.

ISSUE: Is it unconstitutional for a state to refuse unemployment benefits to a worker who was discharged because of his or her refusal to work on his or her religion's Sabbath?

HOLDING AND DECISION: (Brennan, J.) Yes. It is unconstitutional for a state to refuse unemployment benefits to a worker who was discharged because of his or her refusal to work on his or her religion's Sabbath. It is an unconstitutional burden on a worker's free exercise of religion for a state to apply eligibility requirements for unemployment benefits so as to force a worker to abandon her religious principles respecting her religion's Sabbath. Sherbert (P) was forced to choose between following her religion and obtaining unemployment benefits. Such a choice puts the same kind of burden on her free exercise of religion as would a fine imposed for Saturday worship. Further, by expressly providing that no one will be compelled to work on Sunday, the State (D) saves the Sunday worshipper from having to make such a choice. The State (D) has shown no compelling state interest to justify this burden on Sherbert's (P) free exercise of religion. Hence, the burden is unconstitutional. This case is distinguishable from *Braunfeld v. Brown*, 366 U.S. 599 (1961). There, the state showed a strong state interest in providing one uniform day of rest for all workers. Reversed and remanded.

CONCURRENCE: (Stewart, J.) The cases dealing with the Establishment Clause have been wrongly decided, and this case is in conflict with them. They hold that the government must blind itself to differing religious traditions and beliefs. Yet here the Court holds that because Sherbert's (P) refusal to work Saturdays is religiously motivated, she is entitled to unemployment benefits. If she was unable to work Saturdays due to indolence or lack of a babysitter, she would not be entitled to benefits. Also, this case is in conflict with *Braunfeld v. Brown*, 366 U.S. 599 (1961). The criminal statute involved there made the burden on religious freedom much greater than here. *Braunfeld* should be overruled.

DISSENT: (Harlan, J.) The purpose of unemployment benefits was to tide people over while work was unavailable. It was not to provide relief for those who for personal reasons became unavailable for work. Secondly, this decision conflicts with and overrules *Braunfeld v. Brown*, 366 U.S. 599 (1961).

ANALYSIS

The Court has encountered many situations unlike Sherbert's (P), in which the individual's right to freedom of religious belief and practices is subordinated to other community interests. Freedom of religion is not absolute and does not extend to situations where its practice would jeopardize public health, safety, or morals, or the rights of third persons. Hence, laws prohibiting polygamy and bigamy have been upheld, as well as those requiring compulsory vaccination and X-rays, in spite of allegations that such laws required action in violation of the Mormon and Christian Science religions. The conscientious objector's right to avoid military service has been said to rest upon legislative grace rather than constitutional right.

Quicknotes

COMPELLING STATE INTEREST Defense to an alleged Equal Protection Clause violation that a state action was necessary in order to protect an interest the government is under a duty to protect.

ESTABLISHMENT CLAUSE The constitutional provision prohibiting the government from favoring any one religion over others or engaging in religious activities or advocacy.

FREE EXERCISE OF RELIGION The right to practice one's religious beliefs free from governmental conduct or interference.

Employment Division, Dept. of Human Resources v. Smith

State (P) v. Applicant for unemployment compensation (D)

494 U.S. 872 (1990)

NATURE OF CASE: Certiorari review of constitutionality of an Oregon statute prohibiting the sacramental use of peyote.

FACT SUMMARY: After Smith (D) ingested peyote during a ceremony of the Native American Church, he was terminated from his job as a drug counselor.

RULE OF LAW

An individual's religious beliefs do not excuse noncompliance with an otherwise valid law prohibiting conduct that the state is free to regulate.

FACTS: Smith (D) was fired from his job with a private drug rehabilitation organization because he ingested peyote for sacramental purposes during a ceremony of the Native American Church. Oregon law classifies peyote as a controlled substance. Persons convicted of possessing peyote are guilty of a felony. Smith (D) was deemed ineligible for unemployment compensation benefits after it was determined that he was discharged for "misconduct." The Oregon Court of Appeals and the Oregon Supreme Court reversed that determination on the basis that the Oregon prohibition of the sacramental use of peyote violated Smith's (D) free exercise of religion. The United States Supreme Court granted certiorari.

ISSUE: Do an individual's religious beliefs excuse noncompliance with an otherwise valid law prohibiting conduct that the state is free to regulate?

HOLDING AND DECISION: (Scalia, J.) No. An individual's religious beliefs do not excuse noncompliance with an otherwise valid law prohibiting conduct that the state is free to regulate. The free exercise of religion means the right to believe and profess whatever religious doctrine one desires. The exercise of religion often involves not only belief and profession but also the performance of physical acts. A state would be prohibiting the free exercise if it seeks to ban acts that are only engaged in for religious reasons. Smith (D) contends that his religious motivation for using peyote places its use beyond the reach of a criminal law not specifically directed at religious practice even though the law is constitutional when applied against nonreligious use of a controlled substance. This Court's decisions have consistently held that the right of free exercise does not relieve an individual of the obligation to comply with a valid and neutral law of general applicability on the ground that the law proscribes conduct that his or her religion prescribes. Smith (D) contends that rejection of his claim for religious exemption for peyote use may be justified only by a balancing compelling state interest. The compelling state interest test is inapplicable to validate challenges to criminal prohibitions on a particular form of conduct. Application of the compelling interest standard in this context would open the prospect of constitutionally required religious exemptions from civic obligations of almost every conceivable kind—ranging from compulsory military service to the payment of taxes. Reversed.

CONCURRENCE: (O'Connor, J.) Oregon has a compelling state interest in regulating peyote use by its citizens and accommodating Smith's (D) religiously motivated conduct will unduly interfere with the fulfillment of the government interest.

DISSENT: (Blackmun, J.) The critical question in this case is whether exempting Smith (D) from Oregon's general prohibition on peyote use will unduly interfere with fulfillment of the governmental interest. It is not Oregon's broad interest in fighting the critical war on drugs that must be weighed against Smith's (D) claim, but Oregon's narrow interest in refusing to make an exception for the religious, ceremonial use of peyote. The state's asserted interest amounts to the symbolic preservation of an unenforced prohibition. Almost half the states and the federal government have maintained an exemption for religious peyote use and have not found themselves overwhelmed by claims to other religious exemptions. Also, the courts should not turn a blind eye to the severe impact of a state's restrictions on the adherents of a minority religion. Oregon's interest in enforcing its drug laws against religious use of peyote is not sufficiently compelling to outweigh Smith's (D) right to the free exercise of religion.

ANALYSIS

Selective service laws have traditionally exempted from military service conscientious objectors opposed to war in any form on religious grounds. However, the Court has traditionally held that the exemption is a product of the legislature rather than compelled by the constitutional prohibition on the free exercise of religion. See, for example, the *Selective Draft Law Cases*, 245 U.S. 366 (1918).

Continued on next page.

Quicknotes

COMPELLING STATE INTEREST Defense to an alleged Equal Protection Clause violation that a state action was necessary in order to protect an interest the government is under a duty to protect.

FELONY A criminal offense of greater seriousness than a misdemeanor; felonies are generally defined pursuant to statute as any crime that is punishable by death or by a term of imprisonment exceeding one year.

FREE EXERCISE OF RELIGION The right to practice one's religious beliefs free from governmental conduct or interference.

Everson v. Board of Education

Taxpayer (P) v. School board (D)

330 U.S. 1 (1947)

NATURE OF CASE: Certiorari review of taxpayer's suit challenging the constitutionality of a state statute.

FACT SUMMARY: Acting pursuant to a state statute authorizing local boards to make rules and contracts for the transportation of school children, a Board of Education (D) authorized the reimbursement to parents of money spent on their children's transportation to school, including parochial schools.

RULE OF LAW

A state statute authorizing that parents be reimbursed for money spent on their children's transportation to parochial schools does not violate the First Amendment.

FACTS: A state statute authorizes local school boards to make rules and contracts for the transportation of school children. A Board of Education (D), acting pursuant to this statute, authorized reimbursement to parents of money spent on their children's transportation to school on the public transportation system. Part of this money was for the payment of transportation of children to Catholic parochial schools. At these schools, the children received religious instruction as well as a secular education. Everson (P) brought this taxpayer's suit challenging the statute's constitutionality. He contended that the statute violated the First Amendment in that it forced its citizens to pay taxes to help support and maintain schools that taught the Catholic faith.

ISSUE: Does a state statute authorizing that parents be reimbursed for money spent on their children's transportation to parochial schools violate the First Amendment?

HOLDING AND DECISION: (Black, J.) No. A state statute authorizing that parents be reimbursed for money spent on their children's transportation to parochial schools does not violate the First Amendment. The First Amendment forbids a state to exclude any of its citizens, because of their religious faith or lack of it, from receiving the benefits of public welfare legislation. A statute authorizing the spending of tax-raised funds to pay the bus fares of parochial school children as part of a general program under which it pays the fares of children attending public and other schools is public welfare legislation. The First Amendment, which is made applicable to the states by the Fourteenth Amendment, commands that a state shall make no law respecting an establishment of religion or prohibiting the free exercise thereof. A state cannot, consistent with the First Amendment, contribute tax-raised funds to any institution that teaches the tenets and faith of any church. On the other hand, neither can a state hamper its citizens in the free exercise of their own religion. Hence, it cannot exclude members of any faith, because of their faith or lack of it, from receiving the benefits of public welfare legislation. State power is no more to be used so as to handicap religions than it is to favor them. Parents would be less willing to send their children to parochial schools if such children were not to be protected by police employed to protect them from traffic dangers, or if such schools were cut off from government services such as police and fire protection, sewage disposal, highways, and sidewalks. Likewise, such parents might be less willing to permit their children to attend parochial schools if they were thereby cut off from state reimbursement for their children's school transportation. A statute authorizing the spending of tax-raised funds to pay the bus fares of parochial school children as a part of a general program under which it pays the fares of children attending public and other schools is public welfare legislation and does not violate the First Amendment. Affirmed.

DISSENT: (Jackson, J.) There are no good grounds on which to support this legislation. The undertones of the opinion that advocate complete and uncompromising separation of Church and State seem discordant with its conclusion yielding support to their commingling in educational matters.

DISSENT: (Rutledge, J.) The purpose of the First Amendment was the creation of a permanent and complete separation of the spheres of civil authority and religious activity by "comprehensively forbidding" every form of public aid or support for religion. Money taken by taxation (in this case by New Jersey) from one person is not to be used or given to support another's religious training or belief, or indeed even one's own. The prohibition is absolute.

ANALYSIS

The First Amendment guarantees that neither the federal nor any state government may establish an official religion and that every person is free to practice his or her faith as he or she chooses. The former involves the Establishment Clause and the latter the Free Exercise Clause. These clauses protect overlapping values, but they may exert conflicting pressures. Under the Establishment Clause, the Supreme Court has ruled

Continued on next page.

against the giving of any state assistance to religious causes, even though it may be nondiscriminatory as between different faiths. Although the Court's attention to financial assistance involving religious groups is long-standing, it did not become intense and controversial until recently with the increasing demand for federal spending for education.

Quicknotes

ESTABLISHMENT CLAUSE The constitutional provision prohibiting the government from favoring any one religion over others or engaging in religious activities or advocacy.

FREE EXERCISE OF RELIGION The right to practice one's religious beliefs free from governmental conduct or interference.

PAROCHIAL SCHOOL A school affiliated with a parish or other religious body.

Mueller v. Allen

Taxpayer (P) v. State (D)

463 U.S. 388 (1983)

NATURE OF CASE: Certiorari review of the constitutionality of a state tax deduction law.

FACT SUMMARY: Mueller (P) instituted suit challenging the constitutionality of a Minnesota law allowing taxpayers, in computing their state income tax, to deduct certain expenses incurred in providing for their children's education, whether the children attended public schools or private parochial schools.

RULE OF LAW

The three-prong test for determining whether a program aiding parochial schools violates the Establishment Clause is the following: (1) Does it have a secular purpose? (2) Does it have "the primary effect of advancing the sectarian aims of the nonpublic schools?" and (3) Does it "excessively entangle" the state in religion?

FACTS: Minnesota passed a law allowing taxpayers, in figuring their state income tax, to deduct actual expenses incurred for the "tuition, textbooks and transportation" of dependents attending elementary or secondary schools, whether they are nonsectarian or sectarian. A maximum of $500 deduction for each dependent in grades K through 6 and $700 for each dependent in grades 7 through 12 was permitted. Mueller (P) brought suit challenging the validity of the law under the Establishment Clause. The court of appeals held that the Clause was not offended by this argument.

ISSUE: Is the three-prong test for determining whether a program aiding parochial schools violates the Establishment Clause the following: (1) Does it have a secular purpose? (2) Does it have "the primary effect of advancing the sectarian aims of the nonpublic schools?" and (3) Does it "excessively entangle" the state in religion?

HOLDING AND DECISION: (Rehnquist, J.) Yes. A three-part test was laid down in *Lemon v. Kurtzman*, 403 U.S. 602, and is the means by which it can be ascertained whether a particular program that in some manner aids parochial schools (either directly or indirectly) violates the Establishment Clause. The three-prong test for determining if a program aiding parochial schools violates the Establishment Clause is the following: (1) Does it have a secular purpose? (2) Does it have "the primary effect of advancing the sectarian aims of the nonpublic schools?" and (3) Does it "excessively entangle" the state in religion? The first part inquires whether the program has a secular purpose. In this case, the answer is yes. The tax deduction attempts to give parents an incentive to educate their children, and this serves the secular purpose of ensuring a well-educated citizenry. The second part of the test asks the related question of whether the program has "the primary effect of advancing the sectarian aims of the nonpublic schools." Here, the answer is no. The deduction is available to all parents, including those sending their children to public schools, and it channels whatever funds available to such schools only as a result of numerous, private choices of individual parents of school-age children. The third part of the test to which this program must be put inquires whether the program "excessively entangles" the state in religion. It does not. The only decision that might remotely involve state officials in state surveillance of religious-type issues would be the decisions state officials have to make in determining whether particular textbooks qualify for the deduction. In making this decision, they must disallow deductions taken from "instructional materials used in the teaching of religious tenets, doctrines or worship, the purpose of which is to inculcate such tenets, doctrines or worship." Minn. Stat. § 290.09, subd. (1982). Making this type of decision does not differ substantially from making the types of decisions approved in early opinions of this Court. Thus, the program at issue here must be considered constitutional, as it has passed the three parts of the appropriate test. Affirmed.

DISSENT: (Marshall, J.) As this Court requoted in *Committee for Public Education v. Nyquist*, 413 U.S. 756 (1973), indirect assistance in the form of financial aid to parents for tuition payments is impermissible because it is not "subject to . . . restrictions" that "guarantee the separation between secular and religious educational functions and . . . ensure that state financial aid supports only the former." The Minnesota statute at hand here is little more than a subsidy of tuition masquerading as a subsidy of general education expenses. While tax deductions are ostensibly available to parents sending their children to public schools, most such parents have no tuition payments to make and would be able to deduct only what they pay for such things as gym clothes, pencils, notebooks, etc. These deductible expenses are de minimis in comparison to tuition expenses paid by most parents sending their children to parochial schools. Thus, the parochial schools are the ones benefited. In this case, the Court for the first time approves a program providing financial support for religious schools without any reason at all to assume that the support will be restricted to the secular functions of those schools and will not be used to

Continued on next page.

support religious instruction. This result is flatly at odds with the fundamental principle that a state may provide no financial support whatsoever to promote religion.

ANALYSIS

In the previously decided *Committee for Public Education v. Nyquist*, 413 U.S. 756 (1973), case, on which the constitutional challenge to this tax deduction program relied heavily, New York had passed a statute that gave the parents of children attending private schools thinly disguised "tax benefits" that actually amounted to tuition grants. This was found to violate the Establishment Clause. By simply providing in its tax deduction statute that all parents could take such tuition deductions, Minnesota kept its tax deduction scheme from being declared unconstitutional. Yet it is really a change in form more than substance, for most public-school parents do not have to pay tuition. So, giving them the opportunity to deduct tuition expenses is of little practical consequence and does little to change the effect of the program in providing indirect aid mostly to parochial schools.

Quicknotes

ESTABLISHMENT CLAUSE The constitutional provision prohibiting the government from favoring any one religion over others or engaging in religious activities or advocacy.

Lee v. Weisman

School officials (D) v. Parent (P)

505 U.S. 577 (1992)

NATURE OF CASE: Certiorari review of permanent injunction against public school religious invocations and benedictions.

FACT SUMMARY: Daniel Weisman (P), father of student Deborah (P), sought a permanent injunction barring the Providence public school officials (D) from inviting clergy to deliver invocations and benedictions at graduation ceremonies.

RULE OF LAW

Religious invocations and benedictions may not be given at a public primary or secondary school graduation ceremony.

FACTS: As allowed by the Providence School Committee (D), Principal Lee (D) invited Rabbi Gutterman to give the invocation and benediction at Lee's (D) middle school's graduation. Attendance at graduation exercises at Providence public schools is voluntary. Following school procedure, Lee (D) gave Rabbi Gutterman written guidelines for nonsectarian prayers. David Weisman (P), on behalf of himself and his daughter Deborah (P), sought a temporary restraining order (TRO) against school officials (D) to prevent Rabbi Gutterman from delivering prayers at Deborah's (P) graduation. The TRO was denied, and Deborah (P) went through the ceremonies. The students stood for a few minutes while Rabbi Gutterman delivered prayers. The Weismans' (P) suit continued since Deborah (P) was a student at a Providence public high school and would likely face the same situation at high school graduation. The district court held the prayers violated the Establishment Clause and permanently enjoined school officials (D) from inviting clergy to give invocations and benedictions at future graduations. The court of appeals affirmed.

ISSUE: May religious invocations and benedictions be given at a public primary or secondary school graduation ceremony?

HOLDING AND DECISION: (Kennedy, J.) No. Religious invocations and benedictions may not be given at a public primary or secondary school graduation ceremony. Here, state officials (D) directed the performance of a formal, explicit religious exercise at public school graduation. Principal Lee (D) decided which prayers should be given, selected the cleric, and gave written guidelines for the prayer. Even for students who objected to religious exercise, attendance and participation was in every practical sense obligatory. High school graduation is one of life's most significant occasions. To say that attendance is "voluntary" is formalistic in the extreme. Such prayers in public schools carry a particular risk of coercion. There is public and peer pressure on attending students to stand as a group or maintain respectful silence. A dissenter is injured by his reasonable perception that others view his standing as approval and that he is being forced by the state to pray. The First Amendment protects the objector from having to take unilateral, private action to avoid compromising religious principles at a state function. The fact that the prayer was "nonsectarian" does not make government involvement acceptable. Affirmed.

CONCURRENCE: (Blackmun, J.) The Establishment Clause not only prohibits government coercion but also any government engagement in religious practices. The simple issue is whether the state placed a stamp of approval on a religious activity. Here, it did.

CONCURRENCE: (Souter, J.) The history of the First Amendment supports the settled principle that the Establishment Clause prohibits support for religion in general as much as support for a particular religion. A distinction between "sectarian" and "nonsectarian" prayers would involve courts in an unconstitutional inquiry as to whether particular prayers are ecumenical enough. A showing of coercion is not necessary to establish a violation of the Establishment Clause. Were coercion a requirement under the Establishment Clause, the Clause would be redundant. The Framers' writings and practices indicate a much broader reading than a mere ban on state coercion.

DISSENT: (Scalia, J.) Nonsectarian prayers at graduations and other public celebrations are a long-standing American tradition. From the Framers to our current President, Congress, and Supreme Court, government leaders have opened public functions with prayer. No one here was forced to pray. Standing is not necessarily a sign of approval; more likely it is a sign of respect for religious beliefs of others, a civic virtue that our schools should cultivate. The Establishment Clause bars only state religious activity backed by threat of penalty for nonparticipation.

ANALYSIS

The dissent claimed that the Court's failure to apply the three-part test of *Lemon v. Kurtzman*, 403 U.S. 602 (1971), means the test is no longer good law. However, Justice Kennedy in his opinion for the Court expressly declined to reconsider *Lemon*. Justices Kennedy and

Continued on next page.

Souter both cited *Lemon* with approval, though they did not apply the test. Justice Blackmun's concurrence, joined by Justices Stevens and O'Connor, expressed the view that *Lemon* still applies in all Establishment Clause cases.

Quicknotes

ESTABLISHMENT CLAUSE The constitutional provision prohibiting the government from favoring any one religion over others or engaging in religious activities or advocacy.

TEMPORARY RESTRAINING ORDER A court order preserving the status quo pending a hearing regarding injunctive relief.

Kennedy v. Bremerton School District

High school coach (P) v. School district (D)

597 U.S. ___, 142 S. Ct. 2407 (2022)

NATURE OF CASE: Appeal in action challenging as an unconstitutional violation of the First Amendment the termination of a public-school football coach because he prayed on the football field after each game.

FACT SUMMARY: Joseph Kennedy (Kennedy) (P), who lost his job as a public high school football coach in the Bremerton School District (District) (D) after he knelt at midfield after games to pray, contended that his termination violated the First Amendment's Free Speech and Free Exercise Clauses.

RULE OF LAW

The Free Exercise and Free Speech Clauses of the First Amendment protect from termination a public-school coach who visibly engages in a personal religious observance at the center of a public school's playing field after each school sporting event.

FACTS: Joseph Kennedy (Kennedy) (P) lost his job as a public high school football coach in the Bremerton School District (the District) (D) after he knelt at midfield after games to pray. Apparently, Kennedy (P) had a long-standing practice of conducting demonstrative prayers on the 50-yard line of the football field. Kennedy (P) consistently invited others to join his prayers and for years led student athletes in prayer at the same time and location. The federal District Court found that the District (D) terminated Kennedy (P) because it did not want to violate the Constitution's Establishment Clause. However, there was also record evidence that the District (D) terminated Kennedy (P) because his religious activities during school were highly disruptive. Kennedy (P) alleged that the District's (D) actions violated the First Amendment's Free Speech and Free Exercise Clauses. The Supreme Court granted certiorari in the case.

ISSUE: Do the Free Exercise and Free Speech Clauses of the First Amendment protect from termination a public-school coach who visibly engages in a personal religious observance at the center of a public school's playing field after each school sporting event?

HOLDING AND DECISION: (Gorsuch, J.) Yes. The Free Exercise and Free Speech Clauses of the First Amendment protect from termination a public-school coach who visibly engages in a personal religious observance at the center of a public school's playing field after each school sporting event. Kennedy's (P) prayers were speech of a private citizen, not that of a school or government official. He was not engaged in speech that was ordinarily within the scope of his duties as a coach, so he did not speak pursuant to government policy and was not seeking to convey a government-created message. He was not instructing players, discussing strategy, encouraging better on-field performance, or engaged in any other speech the Bremerton School District (the District) (D) paid him to produce as a coach. Simply put: his prayers were not part of Kennedy's (P) responsibilities as a public employee. The timing and circumstances of Kennedy's (P) prayers—during the postgame period when coaches were free to attend briefly to personal matters and students were engaged in other activities—confirms that he did not pray while acting within the scope of his duties as a coach. Finding that Kennedy's (P) prayers represented his own private speech does not end the inquiry, however, since it also must be determined whether the District's (D) interests as a public employer outweigh its employee's private speech. The District (D) argued that its suspension of Kennedy (P) was essential to avoid a violation of the Establishment Clause. The Court has recently decided that the Establishment Clause does not include anything like a "modified heckler's veto," in which religious activity can be proscribed based on others" perceptions or discomfort. Instead, the Court has instructed that historical practice and understandings should be the guides in this area, so as to adhere to the founding fathers" values. In keeping with a historical understanding of the Establishment Clause, the Court has long held that government may not make a religious observance compulsory. Here, Kennedy's (P) private religious exercise did not come close to crossing any line one might imagine separating protected private expression from impermissible government coercion. Any offense his conduct created is not dispositive since such offense does not equate to coercion. Also rejected is the District's (D) suggestion that any visible religious conduct by a teacher or coach should be deemed—without more and as a matter of law—impermissibly coercive on students. Such a rule would conflict with the Court's traditional understanding that permitting private speech is not the same thing as coercing others to participate in it.

CONCURRENCE: (Thomas, J.) The Court leaves two unresolved issues. First, the Court does not decide whether or how public employees' rights under the Free Exercise Clause may or may not be different from those

Continued on next page.

enjoyed by the general public. The First Amendment protects public employee speech only when it falls within the core of First Amendment protection—speech only as to matters of public concern. It remains an open question, however, if a similar analysis can or should apply to free-exercise claims in light of the "history" and "tradition" of the Free Exercise Clause. Second, the Court does not decide what burden a government employer must bear to justify restricting an employee's religious expression. A government employer's burden therefore might differ depending on which First Amendment guarantee a public employee invokes.

CONCURRENCE: (Alito, J.) The Court does not decide what standard applies under the Free Speech Clause to private religious expression by a public employee when the employee is not on work time, but it holds only that retaliation for this expression is unconstitutional.

DISSENT: (Sotomayor, J.) This case is about whether a public school must permit a school official to kneel, bow his head, and say a prayer at the center of a school event. The Constitution does not authorize, let alone require, public schools to embrace this conduct. The majority gives short shrift to the Establishment Clause. In doing so, it ignores the facts, which are that Kennedy (P) had a long-standing practice of conducting demonstrative prayers on the 50-yard line of the football field; that he consistently invited others to join his prayers; and that for years he led student athletes in prayer at the same time and location. The Court also ignores the severe disruption to school events caused by Kennedy's (P) conduct. In the process, the Court rejects long-standing concerns surrounding government endorsement of religion and replaces the standard for reviewing such questions with a new "history and tradition" test. In addition, although the Court reaffirms that the Establishment Clause prohibits the government from coercing participation in religious exercise, it applies a nearly toothless version of the coercion analysis, failing to acknowledge the unique pressures faced by students when participating in school-sponsored activities. Contrary to the majority's characterization, this case is not about the limits on an individual's ability to engage in private prayer at work, but it is about whether a school district is required to allow one of its employees to incorporate a public, communicative display of the employee's personal religious beliefs into a school event, where that display is recognizable as part of a long-standing practice of the employee ministering religion to students as the public watched. The Establishment Clause prohibits a school from permitting such conduct. Kennedy's (P) tradition of a 50-yard line prayer thus strikes at the heart of the Establishment Clause's concerns about endorsement. The majority also ignores how such conduct by a coach, who is deemed to be a role-model for students, implicates coercion concerns at the center of the Court's Establishment Clause jurisprudence. Regardless, whether students look up to a coach, they do depend on a coach for tangible benefits, such as playing time or letters of recommendation. Public school faculty members accept certain limitations on their freedom of speech when they accept government employment, so that Kennedy's (P) right to pray at any time and in any manner he wished while exercising his professional duties was not absolute. The Bremerton School District (the District) (D) has a strong argument that Kennedy's (P) speech, formally integrated into the center of a District (D) event, was speech in his official capacity as an employee that was not entitled to First Amendment protections at all, and that the District (D) had a responsibility under the Establishment Clause to restrict his conduct. With this decision, the majority crafts an entirely novel Religion Clauses jurisprudence, all the while proclaiming that nothing has changed at all. The majority now says for the first time that endorsement simply does not matter, and completely repudiates the test established. Precedent long has recognized that endorsement concerns under the Establishment Clause, properly understood, bear no relation to a heckler's veto. Endorsement inquiry is not about the perceptions of particular individuals or saving isolated nonadherents from discomfort but concern with the political community writ large. The majority overrules *Lemon v. Kurtzman*, 403 U. S. 602 (1971), and replaces it with a new history-and-tradition that it fails to explain, all the while claiming that it is established law. The problems with elevating history and tradition over purpose and precedent are well documented. Leaving those aside, the majority provides almost no guidance for school administrators or lower courts.

ANALYSIS

Before this decision, the Court had held that religious activity in public schools was not permitted under the Establishment Clause if it could reasonably be interpreted as a school endorsement of religion, or if it tended to "coerce" student participation in religious activity. In *Kennedy*, the majority rejected the traditional "endorsement" and "coercion" tests in favor of an "analysis focused on original meaning and history" and "reference to historical practices and understandings." However, as Justice Sotomayor observes in dissent, if fully briefed judges who are not experts in history regularly disagree and err in their "amateur" efforts at history, how are school administrators, faculty, and staff supposed to adapt to the Court's novel and unprecedented approach? The majority's new history-and-tradition standard offers very little practical guidance to schools, and as such guidance is not forthcoming from

Continued on next page.

the Court, schools will have to wait at least until the lower courts start to flesh out the standard's contours to get a better sense of how to proceed when faced with conduct like that of coach Kennedy (P).

Quicknotes

ESTABLISHMENT CLAUSE The constitutional provision prohibiting the government from favoring any one religion over others or engaging in religious activities or advocacy.

FREE EXERCISE CLAUSE The guarantee of the First Amendment to the U.S. Constitution prohibiting Congress from enacting laws regarding the establishment of religion or prohibiting the free exercise thereof.

Edwards v. Aguillard

[Parties not identified.]

482 U.S. 578 (1987)

NATURE OF CASE: Certiorari review of constitutionality of an education statute.

FACT SUMMARY: Louisiana (D) contended its statute requiring the teaching of evolution and creationism together, if either was taught, was constitutional.

RULE OF LAW

Any statute requiring the teaching of a religious theory whenever a scientific theory is taught violates the Establishment Clause.

FACTS: Louisiana (the State) (D) enacted the "Balanced Treatment for Creation-Science and Evolution-Science in Public School Instruction Act, which required the teaching of creationism if the theory of evolution was taught. The statute was challenged as contrary to the Establishment Clause. The State (D) defended it, saying it promoted academic freedom. The trial court held the statute unconstitutional. The court of appeals affirmed, and the Supreme Court granted certiorari.

ISSUE: Does any statute requiring the teaching of a religious theory whenever a scientific theory is taught violate the Establishment Clause?

HOLDING AND DECISION: (Brennan, J.) Yes. Any statute requiring the teaching of religious theory whenever a scientific theory is taught violates the Establishment Clause. The "Balanced Treatment for Creation-Science and Evolution-Science in Public School Instruction Act" required public schools to advance a religious doctrine. It thus clearly had a nonsecular purpose and violated the Constitution. Affirmed.

CONCURRENCE: (Powell, J.) The "Balanced Treatment for Creation-Science and Evolution-Science in Public School Instruction Act" was clearly passed to advance a religious purpose. It thus was invalid.

DISSENT: (Scalia, J.) There was no evidence the "Balanced Treatment for Creation-Science and Evolution-Science in Public School Instruction Act" was primarily motivated by a desire to advance a particular religious theory.

ANALYSIS

The Court pointed out that religious freedom was not advanced by this statute. Because this was the stated rationale for its passage, it could not survive. It did not promote religious freedom because it deterred the teaching of one theory by requiring the simultaneous teaching of the other.

Quicknotes

ESTABLISHMENT CLAUSE The constitutional provision prohibiting the government from favoring any one religion over others or engaging in religious activities or advocacy.

Lynch v. Donnelly

Municipality (D) v. Union/residents (P)

465 U.S. 668 (1984)

NATURE OF CASE: Certiorari review of constitutionality of religious display.

FACT SUMMARY: The district court held that the City of Pawtucket's (D) display of a nativity scene on public property violated the Establishment Clause.

RULE OF LAW

The Establishment Clause does not prohibit a municipality from including a religious display in its annual Christmas display.

FACTS: The City of Pawtucket (D), Rhode Island, included a nativity scene in its annual Christmas display. It had done so for over 40 years. The American Civil Liberties Union (ACLU) (P) and certain residents of Pawtucket sued, contending the inclusion of the scene violated the Establishment Clause. The district court found for the ACLU (P), holding the scene conferred a substantial benefit on religion. The court of appeals affirmed, and the City (D) appealed.

ISSUE: Does the Establishment Clause prohibit a municipality from including a religious display in its annual Christmas display?

HOLDING AND DECISION: (Burger, C.J.) No. The Establishment Clause does not prohibit a municipality from including a religious display in its annual Christmas display. The Establishment Clause has historically not been interpreted in a strict manner. The inclusion of the nativity scene conferred no discernible advantage on religion that exceeded that resulting from the inclusion of "In God We Trust" on money and other permissible religious references. As a result, the display did not violate the Establishment Clause. Reversed.

CONCURRENCE: (O'Connor, J.) In this case there was no impermissible government entanglement in religion and no municipal endorsement of religion. Therefore, it did not violate the Establishment Clause.

DISSENT: (Brennan, J.) This display is a re-creation of an event that lies at the heart of the Christian religion. As a result, it promotes that religion and religion in general and violated the Clause.

DISSENT: (Blackmun, J.) The Court ignored the established precedents in upholding the display.

ANALYSIS

This case represents the trend in the Supreme Court's handling of Establishment Clause cases, in contrast to its previous application of the three-prong analysis used in many cases, such as *Larkin v. Grendel's Den, Inc.*, 454 U.S. 116 (1982), where a statute or other governmental action is evaluated for its effect on religion and government. In *Marsh v. Chambers*, 463 U.S. 783 (1983), the Court, again with Chief Justice Burger writing for the majority, failed to apply the three-prong analysis and upheld a government prayer observance.

Quicknotes

ESTABLISHMENT CLAUSE The constitutional provision prohibiting the government from favoring any one religion over others or engaging in religious activities or advocacy.

McCreary County v. ACLU of Kentucky

Kentucky county (D) v. Civil liberties group (P)

545 U.S. 844 (2005)

NATURE OF CASE: Certiorari review of constitutional challenges to postings of the Ten Commandments in county courthouses.

FACT SUMMARY: Two Kentucky counties posted the Ten Commandments in their respective courthouses.

RULE OF LAW

Government action that has the ostensible and predominant purpose of advancing religion violates the Establishment Clause.

FACTS: Two Kentucky counties, McCreary County (D) and Pulaski County (D) (Counties), placed gold-framed copies of the Ten Commandments in their respective courthouses; each display contained only the Ten Commandments and included a citation to the Book of Exodus. The American Civil Liberties Union of Kentucky (the ACLU) (P) sued Counties (D), [seeking injunctive relief and] alleging violations of the Establishment Clause. Counties (D) then altered their displays to include a statement that the Ten Commandments served as a foundation for the civil and criminal codes of Kentucky. The trial court ordered that the displays be removed. Counties (D) then altered their displays a second time, this time putting up new displays in their respective courthouses that included the Ten Commandments within a group of documents presented under the title of "Foundations of American Law and Government." [The trial court granted the ACLU's (P) request to supplement the original injunction to include the third display, and the intermediate appellate court affirmed.] Counties (D) petitioned the Supreme Court for further review.

ISSUE: Does government action that has the ostensible and predominant purpose of advancing religion violate the Establishment Clause?

HOLDING AND DECISION: (Souter, J.) Yes. Government action that has the ostensible and predominant purpose of advancing religion violates the Establishment Clause. Government action for a predominant religious purpose violates the cardinal principle of Establishment Clause jurisprudence—that government must maintain neutrality toward religion, that is, between one religion and another and between religion and irreligion. In any given case, details in the record are crucial in determining the government's purpose in the Establishment Clause analysis. Here, the first display of the plainly religious Ten Commandments, with the Commandments standing apart from any secular context, clearly furthered a religious purpose. The second display also demonstrated a religious purpose because the statement about the Commandments' foundational status for Kentucky law was based on the Commandments' religious content. The third display, with the Ten Commandments included in and among several other documents, still demonstrates a religious purpose in this case, given the full context of the repeated efforts of McCreary County (D) and Pulaski County (D) to post the Ten Commandments. This holding should not be interpreted as prohibiting all integrated displays of the Ten Commandments; this decision is only that this particular integrated display violates the Establishment Clause on this case's specific facts. Affirmed.

CONCURRENCE: (O'Connor, J.) As a nation, we have no reason to trade a system based on government neutrality toward religion for a system like so many others around the world that cause so much strife. The displays of McCreary County (D) and Pulaski County (D) in this case clearly violated the Establishment Clause because the displays unmistakably endorsed religion. The Framers did not foresee the multiplicity of religious belief in today's America. They did see, though, that choosing between religions is an enterprise that government should avoid.

DISSENT: (Scalia, J.) The Constitution has never required the complete exclusion of religion from public life. The founding generation made multiple official references to and recognitions of religion. That generation believed that morality was crucial for the social order and that fostering religion promoted morality. In the United States, government can favor religion over irreligion. It also can favor one religion—specifically, monotheistic religion—over another. Today's opinion thus only increases this Court's hostility toward religion by now requiring that a secular purpose must "predominate" in government action. The displays in this case were constitutional, though, even under the majority's misguided analysis. The third, integrated "foundations" display served precisely the secular purpose that McCreary County (D) and Pulaski County (D) had advanced: to show that the Ten Commandments have influenced our system of law. The Court has no basis for conflating the purposes for the first two displays into the analysis of the purpose behind the third display.

Continued on next page.

ANALYSIS

As the *McCreary County* majority notes, a government's purpose in actions involving religion is a firmly developed part of the Court's Establishment Clause jurisprudence. Regardless of the general understanding of the Establishment Clause held by some individual members of the founding generation, it is worth noting that none of Justice Scalia's examples from the founding period arose in a specifically framed case or controversy in which a litigant sought to enforce the Establishment Clause against the actions that Justice Scalia recites. In the case or controversy in *McCreary County*, the majority correctly saw through McCreary County's (D) and Pulaski County's (D) belated defenses of their efforts to do nothing more than to promote the plainly religious Ten Commandments.

Quicknotes

ESTABLISHMENT CLAUSE The constitutional provision prohibiting the government from favoring any one religion over others or engaging in religious activities or advocacy.

INJUNCTION A court order requiring a person to do, or prohibiting that person from doing, a specific act.

INJUNCTIVE RELIEF A court order issued as a remedy, requiring a person to do, or prohibiting that person from doing, a specific act.

Van Orden v. Perry

User of state capitol grounds (P) v. Governor of Texas (D)

545 U.S. 677 (2005)

NATURE OF CASE: Certiorari review of constitutional challenge to the placement of a Ten Commandments monument in an integrated display of monuments and historical markers on the grounds of the Texas State Capitol.

FACT SUMMARY: The State of Texas (D) created a display, on the grounds of its State Capitol, of monuments and historical markers to commemorate "Texan identity." One of the monuments was a large monolith depicting the Ten Commandments.

RULE OF LAW

Government action that has religious content or that promotes a religious message does not necessarily violate the Establishment Clause.

FACTS: On the 22 acres surrounding the Texas State Capitol, the State of Texas (D) placed 17 monuments and 21 historical markers to honor various aspects of "Texan identity." One of the 17 monuments was a six-by-three-foot monolith of the Ten Commandments. Van Orden (P) was offended by the monolith when he had to walk past it to reach the Texas Supreme Court Library. He sued the State of Texas (D), alleging that the use of the Ten Commandments violated the Establishment Clause.

ISSUE: Does government action that has religious content or that promotes a religious message necessarily violate the Establishment Clause?

HOLDING AND DECISION: (Rehnquist, C.J.) No. Government action that has religious content or that promotes a religious message does not necessarily violate the Establishment Clause. The three-factor test announced in *Lemon v. Kurtzman*, 403 U.S. 602 (1971), does not apply here because the case is more appropriately analyzed by considering the nature of the Ten Commandments monument and American history. The Ten Commandments are religious, but the person whom Judeo-Christians believe to have delivered the Commandments, Moses, was also a lawgiver. Here, the State of Texas (D) has treated the display involving the Ten Commandments as an expression of the State's (D) political and legal history. That display therefore does not violate the Establishment Clause. Affirmed.

CONCURRENCE: (Scalia, J.) This decision accurately represents the Court's Establishment Clause jurisprudence. Consistent with the Establishment Clause, government can promote religion in general, conduct public prayer, or neutrally respect the Ten Commandments.

CONCURRENCE: (Thomas, J.) The original understanding of the Establishment Clause means that the Clause should not be incorporated against the states at all. Even if it is incorporated, the Court should adopt the original meaning of "establishment," a term that the Framers understood to mean "necessarily [to] involve actual legal coercion." Under that correct understanding of establishment, the State of Texas's (D) use of the Ten Commandments here clearly comports with the Establishment Clause because Texas (D) has not compelled Van Orden (P) in any way.

CONCURRENCE: (Breyer, J.) This borderline case requires an exercise of legal judgment more than it requires a legal test. The key inquiry here is how the Ten Commandments are used, and that consideration in turn requires the further consideration of the context in which the Commandments appear. The circumstances suggest that the State of Texas (D) intended a predominantly secular purpose. That no one has challenged the Commandments in 40 years, until this case, only buttresses the conclusion that visitors to the grounds themselves have seen a predominant secular purpose. Invalidating Texas's (D) use of the Ten Commandments in this case, merely because the Ten Commandments are religious, could well lead to the very religious strife that the Establishment Clause was adopted to avoid.

DISSENT: (Stevens, J.) The State of Texas (D) has placed the Ten Commandments on its Capitol grounds solely for the Decalogue's religious content. The State's (D) message is therefore clear: Texas (D) endorses the "Judeo-Christian" God. Texas (D) can use secular means to legitimately combat juvenile delinquency (which was one purpose that informed the original decision to place the Ten Commandments on the grounds 40 years ago). The message in the monument, however, is a plainly religious text, indeed an inherently sectarian text, and Texas's (D) use of the monument is therefore unconstitutional. The beliefs of the individual members of the founding generation are irrelevant; it is also easy to contradict views of Founders who favored fusing church and state with, for example, the views of Jefferson and Madison, who advocated strictly separated church and state. Regardless of individual Framers' beliefs, though, this Court is bound, not by the Framers' individual expectations, but by the text of the Constitution that they adopted and

Continued on next page.

ratified. That text prohibits Texas's (D) use of the Ten Commandments in this case.

DISSENT: O'Connor, J.) The majority is incorrect for the reasons stated in Justice Souter's dissent in this case and stated in my concurrence in *McCreary County v. ACLU of Kentucky*, 545 U.S. 844 (2005).

DISSENT: (Souter, J.) Neutrality can be reconciled with a government's display of an indisputably religious text only if the display's predominant purpose is not to promote the religious message. The Ten Commandments can be depicted with a predominant secular purpose, as in their depiction, and the depictions of Moses, in and around this Court. In this case, though, people strolling through the Texas State Capitol grounds would be hard-pressed to find a non-religious reason for the State of Texas's (D) use of the Ten Commandments: there is no readily discernible theme linking the Ten Commandments to the other displays scattered across the 22 acres of the grounds. A state's Capitol, however, should represent all the state's citizens, not only the ones who agree with a religious perspective promoted by the state.

ANALYSIS

An important point to note in this difficult, intensely fragmented decision is that five members of the Court applied some form of the "predominant purpose" test used in *McCreary County v. ACLU of Kentucky*, 545 U.S. 844 (2005). The four dissenters here use that test (with Justice O'Connor using the "endorsement" language that she long preferred in Establishment Clause cases). Despite his protestations that he favors legal judgment over a legal test in this case, Justice Breyer, in his concurrence, also examines the State of Texas's (D) predominant purpose in its use of the Ten Commandments. Even after *Van Orden*, then, some form of the "predominant purpose" test still seems to be the law.

Quicknotes

ESTABLISHMENT CLAUSE The constitutional provision prohibiting the government from favoring any one religion over others or engaging in religious activities or advocacy.

The American Legion v. American Humanist Association

Veterans' group (D) v. Secular group (P)

588 U.S. ___, 139 S. Ct. 2067 (2019)

NATURE OF CASE: Appeal from judgment that a World War I monument in the shape of a Latin cross on public land, and the expenditure of public funds to maintain it, violated the Establishment Clause.

FACT SUMMARY: The American Legion (D), a veterans' group, contended that a World War I monument in the shape of a Latin cross on public land, and the expenditure of public funds to maintain it, did not violate the Establishment Clause.

RULE OF LAW

A World War I monument in the shape of a Latin cross on public land, and the expenditure of public funds to maintain it, does not violate the Establishment Clause.

FACTS: In 1918, residents of Prince George's County, Maryland, formed a committee for the purpose of erecting a memorial for the county's soldiers who fell in World War I. The committee decided that the memorial should be a cross, which was not surprising since the plain Latin cross had become a central symbol of the war. The image of row after row of plain white crosses marking the overseas graves of soldiers was emblazoned on the minds of Americans at home. The memorial would stand at the terminus of another World War I memorial—the National Defense Highway connecting Washington to Annapolis. The memorial, known as the Bladensburg Cross (the Cross), was completed in 1925. The 32-foot Latin cross sits on a large pedestal bearing, inter alia, a bronze plaque that lists the names of the 49 county soldiers who had fallen in the war. In 1961, the Maryland-National Capital Park and Planning Commission (the Commission) acquired the Cross and the land where it sits, and the Commission has used public funds to maintain the monument ever since. Almost 90 years after the Cross was dedicated, the American Humanist Association (AHA) (P) brought suit asserting that the Cross's presence on public land and the Commission's maintenance of the memorial violated the Establishment Clause of the First Amendment. The court of appeals agreed with the AHA (P). The Supreme Court granted certiorari.

ISSUE: Does a World War I monument in the shape of a Latin cross on public land, and the expenditure of public funds to maintain it, violate the Establishment Clause?

HOLDING AND DECISION: (Alito, J.) No. A World War I monument in the shape of a Latin cross on public land, and the expenditure of public funds to maintain it, does not violate the Establishment Clause. The cross at issue, as well as similar monuments throughout the country, must be considered in historical context. Although the cross has long been a preeminent Christian symbol, its use in the Bladensburg memorial has a special significance. After the First World War, the picture of row after row of plain white crosses marking the overseas graves of soldiers who had lost their lives in that horrible conflict was emblazoned on the minds of Americans at home, and the adoption of the cross as the Bladensburg memorial must be viewed in that context. Moreover, there are many contexts in which the cross has taken on a secular meaning or is primarily secular to begin with. One of many examples is the Red Cross symbol, which was intended to convey the neutrality of Switzerland, since the Swiss flag consists of a white cross on a red background (the Red Cross symbol is a red cross on a white background). At least four considerations show that retaining established, religiously expressive monuments, symbols, and practices is quite different from erecting or adopting new ones. First, these cases often concern monuments, symbols, or practices that were first established long ago, and thus identifying their original purpose or purposes may be especially difficult. Second, as time goes by, the purposes associated with an established monument, symbol, or practice often multiply. Even if the monument's original purpose was infused with religion, the passage of time may obscure that sentiment and the monument may be retained for the sake of its historical significance or its place in a common cultural heritage. Third, the message of a monument, symbol, or practice may evolve. Familiarity itself can become a reason for preservation. Fourth, when time's passage imbues a religiously expressive monument, symbol, or practice with this kind of familiarity and historical significance, removing it may no longer appear neutral, especially to the local community. The passage of time thus gives rise to a strong presumption of constitutionality. This is especially true since tearing down monuments with religious symbolism and scrubbing away any reference to the divine will strike many as aggressively hostile to religion. The role of the cross in World War I memorials is illustrative of each of these considerations. The cross is a symbol closely linked to World War I. The United States adopted it as part of its military honors, establishing the Distinguished Service Cross and the Navy Cross in 1918 and 1919, respectively. Also, the fallen soldiers" final resting places abroad were marked by white crosses or Stars of David, solemn images

Continued on next page.

that became inextricably linked with and symbolic of the ultimate price paid by 116,000 soldiers. This relationship between the cross and the war may not have been the sole or dominant motivation for the design of the many war memorials that sprang up across the nation, but that is all but impossible to determine today. The passage of time means that testimony from the decisionmakers may not be available. Regardless of the original purposes for erecting the monument, a community may wish to preserve it for very different, non-religious reasons, such as historic preservation. The area surrounding a monument like the Bladensburg Cross (the Cross) may also have been altered in ways that change its meaning and provide new reasons for its preservation; it now sits at a very busy traffic intersection. Finally, as World War I monuments have endured through the years and become a familiar part of the physical and cultural landscape, requiring their removal or alteration would not be viewed by many as a neutral act. All these considerations apply to the Bladensburg Cross. Thus, although the cross is undoubtedly a Christian symbol, that should not blind one to everything else that the Bladensburg Cross has come to represent: a symbolic resting place for ancestors who never returned home, a place for the community to gather and honor all veterans and their sacrifices for this nation, and a historical landmark. For many, destroying or defacing the Cross would not be neutral and would not further the ideals of respect and tolerance embodied in the First Amendment. Accordingly, the Bladensburg Cross and its maintenance do not violate the Establishment Clause. [Reversed and remanded.]

CONCURRENCE: (Breyer, J.) There is no single formula for resolving Establishment Clause challenges, and therefore the Court must consider each case in light of the basic purposes that the Religion Clauses were meant to serve: assuring religious liberty and tolerance for all, avoiding religiously based social conflict, and maintaining that separation of church and state that allows each to flourish in its separate sphere. Here, the Bladensburg Cross (the Cross) cannot be understood as a government effort to favor a particular religious sect or religion over non-religion, for all the reasons elaborated by the Court. It would be a different case, for example, if there were evidence that the organizers of the monument had deliberately disrespected members of minority faiths or if the Cross had been erected only recently, rather than in the aftermath of World War I. Additionally, the Court's opinion does not adopt a "history and tradition test" that would permit any newly constructed religious memorial on public land, so that a newer memorial, erected under different circumstances, would not necessarily be permissible under this approach.

CONCURRENCE: (Kavanaugh, J.) The Court's opinion, by applying a history and tradition test, acts in accord with precedent. The opinion also is relevant to five categories of Establishment Clause cases: (1) religious symbols on government property and religious speech at government events; (2) religious accommodations and exemptions from generally applicable laws; (3) government benefits and tax exemptions for religious organizations; (4) religious expression in public schools; and (5) regulation of private religious speech in public forums. Although the Bladensburg Cross (the Cross) does not violate the Establishment Clause because it is not reflective of government coercion, but rather is rooted in history and tradition, respect must be given to those who object to seeing a cross on public land, or those like Jewish war veterans who see it as sending a message of exclusion. Their sense of distress and alienation must be recognized and acknowledged. The interests on both sides are genuine and deeply held, and it is important to reaffirm that all citizens are equally American, no matter what religion they are or whether they have no religion at all. In addition, it should be noted that those who object to the Cross have other avenues of recourse: the Court's ruling allows the state to maintain the cross on public land but does not require it to do so. Thus, for example the state's legislature could enact laws requiring removal of the Cross, or transfer of the land. This illustrates that in the nation's republican form of government, entities other than the Court, which safeguards rights secured by the Constitution, can also safeguard individual rights above and beyond those found in the Constitution.

CONCURRENCE: (Thomas, J.) The text and history of the Establishment Clause, which reads "Congress shall make no law respecting an establishment of religion," suggest that it should not be incorporated against the states. Even if it is enforceable against the states, it is limited by its text to laws passed by a legislature. Thus, it is unclear whether the Cross would implicate any incorporated right. However, even if the Bladensburg Cross did implicate such rights, this religious display does not involve the type of actual legal coercion that was a hallmark of historical establishments of religion.

CONCURRENCE AND DISSENT: (Kagan, J.): Although a rigid application of the *Lemon* test does not solve every Establishment Clause problem, the test's focus on purposes and effects is crucial in evaluating government action in this sphere. This case clearly demonstrates that, and the test should be applied on a case-by-case base. However, any broader statements about history's role in Establishment Clause analysis is questionable.

CONCURRENCE: (Gorsuch, J.) This case should have been dismissed for lack of standing. Although there is no reason to doubt that members of the American Humanist Association (P) are genuinely offended by the

Continued on next page.

Bladensburg Cross, the "offended observer" theory of standing has no basis in federal law. In fact, the Court has already rejected mere offense as a qualifier for "concrete and particularized" injury sufficient to confer standing. In a large and diverse country, offense can be easily found. Really, most every governmental action probably offends somebody. Nonetheless, recourse for disagreement and offense does not lie in federal litigation. Instead, in a society that holds among its most cherished ambitions mutual respect, tolerance, self-rule, and democratic responsibility, an "offended viewer" may "avert his eyes," or pursue a political solution.

DISSENT: (Ginsburg, J.) The cross at issue is immense and highly visible in its community. The plurality's decision, therefore, disserves the Constitution's commitment to governmental neutrality respecting religion, since the Latin cross is the foremost symbol of Christianity. Precisely because the cross symbolizes these sectarian beliefs, it is a common marker for the graves of Christian soldiers. For the same reason, using the cross as a war memorial does not transform it into a secular symbol. Just as a Star of David is not suitable to honor Christians who died serving their country, so a cross is not suitable to honor those of other faiths who died defending their nation. By maintaining the Bladensburg Cross (the Cross) on a public highway, the Commission elevates Christianity over other faiths and religion over non-religion. Memorializing the service of American soldiers is an admirable and unquestionably secular objective, but the Commission does not serve that objective by displaying a symbol that bears a starkly sectarian message. To hold the Cross unconstitutional here would not require the destruction of other cross-shaped memorials throughout the country, since the matter would be context-specific. For example, such memorials in a public cemetery would not send the message that the government seeks either to adopt the religious message they hold or to urge its acceptance by others, since they would be viewed as private speech of each veteran. Moreover, recognizing that a Latin cross does not belong on a public highway or building does not mean the monument must be destroyed. There could be alternatives to tearing the monument down, depending on the specifics of the case. In some instances, the violation could be cured by relocating the monument to private land or by transferring ownership of the land and monument to a private party.

ANALYSIS

With this decision, the Court in large measure has abandoned its decision in *Lemon v. Kurtzman,* 403 U.S. 602 (1971), which held that whether governmental action violates the Establishment Clause depends on its (1) purpose, (2) effect, and (3) potential to excessively entangle church and state. The Court came to understand this standard as prohibiting the government from doing anything that a reasonable observer might perceive as "endorsing" religion. Justice Alito noted that the *Lemon* decision ambitiously attempted to fashion a test for all Establishment Clause cases, but that the expectation of a ready framework had not been met and that the Court many times either expressly declined to apply the test or simply ignored it. Instead, the Court, according to Justice Alito, has taken a more modest approach that focuses on the particular issue at hand and looks to history for guidance—as in *American Legion.* Justice Thomas would overrule the *Lemon* test in all contexts, finding that the test has no basis in the original meaning of the Constitution; that it has been manipulated to fit whatever result the Court aimed to achieve; and that it continues to cause enormous confusion in the states and the lower courts. Justice Gorsuch, who believes there should be no "offended observer" standing in federal law, blamed *Lemon* on creating such standing in the first place, concluding that lower courts invented offended observer standing for Establishment Clause cases in response to *Lemon,* reasoning that if the Establishment Clause forbids anything that a reasonable observer would view as an endorsement of religion, then such an observer must be able to sue. To these justices, *Lemon* was a judicial "misadventure."

Quicknotes

ESTABLISHMENT CLAUSE The constitutional provision prohibiting the government from favoring any one religion over others or engaging in religious activities or advocacy.

Trinity Lutheran Church of Columbia, Inc. v. Comer

Church (P) v. State official (D)

582 U.S. ___, 137 S. Ct. 2012 (2017)

NATURE OF CASE: Appeal in action challenging the disqualification of a church from receiving public funds for an allegedly secular purpose as unconstitutional under the Free Exercise Clause.

FACT SUMMARY: After Trinity Lutheran Church of Columbia, Inc. (P) was categorically denied an application for participation in a competitive program that provided public state funds for rubber surfaces for its preschool and day care center's playground, merely on the grounds that it was a religious organization, it sued the State (D), claiming that such denial violated the Free Exercise Clause of the First Amendment.

RULE OF LAW

The denial to a religious organization of public funds for playground resurfacing, merely because of the organization's religious identity, violates the Free Exercise Clause of the First Amendment.

FACTS: The State (D) had a program whereby it provided public funds, on a competitive basis, to schools and nonprofit organizations, other than those with religious affiliations, for installing rubber surfaces on playgrounds. After Trinity Lutheran Church of Columbia, Inc. (P) was categorically denied an application for such funds for its preschool and day care center's playground, it sued the State (D), claiming that such denial violated the Free Exercise Clause of the First Amendment. The Supreme Court granted certiorari in the case.

ISSUE: Does the denial to a religious organization of public funds for playground resurfacing, merely because of the organization's religious identity, violate the Free Exercise Clause of the First Amendment?

HOLDING AND DECISION: (Roberts, C.J.) Yes. The denial to a religious organization of public funds for playground resurfacing, merely because of the organization's religious identity, violates the Free Exercise Clause of the First Amendment. The State's (D) policy expressly discriminates against otherwise eligible recipients by disqualifying them from a public benefit solely because of their religious character. Thus, the State (D) has imposed a penalty on the free exercise of religion that must withstand the most exacting scrutiny. The parties agree that the Establishment Clause would not prevent the State (D) from including Trinity Lutheran Church of Columbia, Inc. (the Church) (P) in its resurfacing program, but the State (D) emphasizes its long antiestablishment tradition of not providing taxpayer money directly to churches. However, in this case, this antiestablishment policy forces the Church (P) to choose between being a church or receiving public funds. Such discrimination must withstand the strictest scrutiny by being supported by a state interest of the "highest order." The only interest the State (D) asserts is its antiestablishment interest. Because of the clear infringement of the State's (D) policy on the free exercise of religion, such an interest is not sufficiently compelling. [Reversed.]

CONCURRENCE AND DISSENT: (Thomas, J.) Any endorsement of discrimination against religion, no matter how mild the discrimination, is troubling. However, because the Court's endorsement of such discrimination is confined to very limited circumstances (e.g., it is constitutional to deny public funds to a student studying to join the clergy), such endorsement itself does not taint the Court's decision.

CONCURRENCE AND DISSENT: (Gorsuch, J.) The Court leaves open the possibility a useful distinction might be drawn between laws that discriminate on the basis of religious status and religious use. However, it is doubtful that this line can withstand blurring, since it can be difficult, if not impossible, to actually draw such a line, e.g., is it a religious group that built the playground (religious status), or did a group build the playground so it might be used to advance a religious mission (religious use)? Often enough the same facts can be described both ways. The Court's statement (in its footnote 3) that the case "involves express discrimination based on religious identity with respect to playground resurfacing" is stated too narrowly and might be misconstrued as not announcing a general principle. That principle is that discrimination against religious exercise is prohibited.

CONCURRENCE: (Breyer, J.) What needs to be emphasized is the public benefit at issue. The Court has previously announced the principle that religious organizations may not be cut off from general government services. Here, the playground resurfacing program is such a general program, in line with services such as fire and police protection. Thus, the application of the Free Exercise Clause to other kinds of public benefits should be left to a different case.

DISSENT: (Sotomayor, J.) The Court, for the first time, requires government to provide public funds to a church. The case is about whether a State (D) can decline to fund improvements to the facilities Trinity Lutheran Church of Columbia, Inc. (the Church) (P) uses to practice and

Continued on next page.

spread its religious views. The Court has repeatedly warned that funding of exactly this kind—payments from the government to a house of worship—would cross the line drawn by the Establishment Clause. Here, the Establishment Clause does not allow the State (D) to grant the Church's (P) funding request because the Church (P) uses its learning center, including its playground, in conjunction with its religious mission. The Court may simply disagree with this account of the facts and think that the Church (P) does not put its playground to religious use. If so, its mistake is limited to this case. However, if it agrees that the State's (D) funding would further religious activity and sees no Establishment Clause problem, then it must be implicitly applying a rule that is a radical departure from precedent. Not only does the Court err in failing to apply the Establishment Clause, it errs in its application of the Free Exercise Clause. The Court claims that the government may not draw lines based on an entity's religious "status," but that claim wrongfully ignores a long line of precedents where the Court has repeatedly said that government can draw such lines. A state is permitted to avoid the historic "antiestablishment interests" raised by use of taxpayer funds to support a church. Here, the State (D) has permissibly decided that the unique status of houses of worship requires a special rule when it comes to public funds. This decision has deep roots in the nation's history and constitutional jurisprudence. The great majority of states (38) have rules in their constitutions, similar to the State's (D), prohibiting public funding for houses of worship. This principle has a pedigree that goes back to or before the states' original constitutions were enacted and reflects the nation's understanding of how best to foster religious liberty. Thus, the Court's characterization of the policy as "discriminatory" is wrong. In this area of the law, a decision to treat entities differently based on distinctions that the Religion Clauses make relevant does not amount to discrimination. The Court's rule, at heart, is that the government may draw lines on the basis of religious status to grant a benefit to religious persons or entities, but it may not draw lines on that basis when doing so would further the interests the Religion Clauses protect in other ways. Nothing supports this lopsided outcome.

ANALYSIS

Chief Justice Roberts says in his opinion that the parties agree that the Establishment Clause does not prevent the State (D) from including Trinity Lutheran Church of Columbia, Inc. (the Church) (P) in the playground resurfacing program. However, Justice Sotomayor disagrees, pointing out that constitutional questions are decided by the Court, not the parties' concessions. Moreover, she argues that it is beyond dispute that there is an Establishment Clause issue presented, since a house of worship exists to foster and further religious exercise. According to Justice Sotomayor, the Church (P) seeks state funds to improve its learning center's facilities, which, by the Church's (P) own avowed description, are used to assist the spiritual growth of the children of its members and to spread the Church's (P) faith to the children of nonmembers. Thus, the Church's (P) playground surface—like a Sunday School room's walls or the sanctuary's pews—are integrated with and integral to its religious mission. The conclusion that the funding the Church (P) seeks would impermissibly advance religion is thus inescapable. From this, Justice Sotomayor concludes the plurality's silence on these front signals either its misunderstanding of the facts of the case or a startling departure from the Court's precedents.

Quicknotes

ESTABLISHMENT CLAUSE The constitutional provision prohibiting the government from favoring any one religion over others or engaging in religious activities or advocacy.

FREE EXERCISE CLAUSE The guarantee of the First Amendment to the U.S. Constitution prohibiting Congress from enacting laws regarding the establishment of religion or prohibiting the free exercise thereof.

STRICT SCRUTINY Method by which courts determine the constitutionality of a law when a law affects a fundamental right; under the test, the legislature must have had a compelling interest to enact the law and measures prescribed by the law must be the least restrictive means possible to accomplish its goal.

Carson v. Makin

Parent of student at religious school (P) v. State official (D)

596 U.S. ___, 142 S. Ct. 1987 (2022)

NATURE OF CASE: Appeal from judgment that a state's tuition assistance program, which did not pay for private religious schools but did pay for other private schools, was not unconstitutional under the Free Exercise Clause.

FACT SUMMARY: Maine (D) offered its citizens tuition assistance payments for any family whose school district did not provide a public secondary school, but Maine (D) did not offer such assistance for private religious schools. The program was challenged as violating the Free Exercise Clause on the grounds that it discriminated against religion.

RULE OF LAW

A state's "nonsectarian" requirement for otherwise generally available tuition assistance payments violates the Free Exercise Clause.

FACTS: Maine (D) offered its citizens tuition assistance payments for any family whose school district did not provide a public secondary school, but Maine (D) did not offer such assistance for private religious schools. The program was challenged as violating the Free Exercise Clause on the grounds that it discriminated against religion. The First Circuit Court of Appeals upheld the program on the ground that the funding restriction imposed was a permissible use-based restriction, rather than a status-based restriction. The Supreme Court granted certiorari.

ISSUE: Does a state's "nonsectarian" requirement for otherwise generally available tuition assistance payments violate the Free Exercise Clause?

HOLDING AND DECISION: (Roberts, C.J.) Yes. A state's "nonsectarian" requirement for otherwise generally available tuition assistance payments violates the Free Exercise Clause. Maine's (D) tuition assistance program specifically carved out private religious schools from those eligible to receive such funds, but a neutral benefit program in which public funds flow to religious organizations through the independent choices of private benefit recipients does not offend the Establishment Clause. Moreover, an interest in separating church and state more fiercely than the Constitution cannot qualify as compelling in the face of the infringement of free exercise. Here, there is nothing neutral about Maine's (D) program, which discriminates against religion. The Court of Appeals and the dissent attempt to uphold the program on the ground that it presents a use-based restriction, rather than a restriction that is status-based, but such a distinction does not have support in the Court's precedents, which never suggested that use-based discrimination is any less offensive to the Free Exercise Clause. Because educating young people in their religious faith lies at the very core of the mission of a private religious school, any attempt to give effect to such a distinction by scrutinizing whether and how a religious school pursues its educational mission would raise serious concerns about state entanglement with religion and denominational favoritism. Thus, the prohibition on status-based discrimination under the Free Exercise Clause is not a permission to engage in use-based discrimination. Finally, there is no historic and substantial tradition against aiding private religious schools comparable to the tradition against state-supported clergy, which is prohibited by the Court's precedents.

DISSENT: (Breyer, J.) The majority treats the Religion Clauses as though they must work in tandem. However, such treatment will work against their fundamental purposes: to enable people with multiple religious beliefs, and those who do not practice religion, to coexist without serious risk of religion-based social divisions. The majority holds for the first time that a state must use state funds to pay for religious education as part of a tuition program designed to ensure the provision of free statewide public-school education. Here, Maine (D) chose not to fund only those schools that promote the faith or belief system with which the schools are associated and/or present the academic material taught through the lens of this faith, thus excluding schools from its tuition program not because of the schools" religious character but because the schools would use the funds to teach and promote religious ideals. The very point of the Establishment Clause is to prevent the government from sponsoring religious activity itself. The majority, by requiring the funding of religious activity risks the very social conflict based upon religion that the Religion Clauses were designed to prevent.

DISSENT: (Sotomayor, J.) First, the majority's analysis leaves Maine (D) with some options, namely, that under state law, school administrative units (SAUs) that cannot feasibly operate their own schools may contract directly with a public school in another SAU, or with an approved private school, to educate their students. The majority's decision does not mandate that SAUs contract directly with schools that teach religion, which would go beyond the Court's private-choice doctrine and blatantly violate the Establishment Clause. Second, with this

Continued on next page.

decision, the majority makes "separation of church and state" a constitutional violation, rather than honoring its intent to make such separation a guarantee.

ANALYSIS

From a practical perspective, this decision directs Maine (D) and, by extension, its taxpaying citizens, to subsidize institutions that undisputedly engage in religious instruction. In addition, while purporting to protect against discrimination of one kind, the Court requires Maine (D) to fund what many of its citizens believe to be discrimination of other kinds. The upshot is that Maine (D) must choose between giving subsidies to its residents or refraining from financing religious teaching and practices. Thus, as a result of this decision, if a state cannot offer subsidies to its citizens without being required to fund religious exercise, any state that values its historic anti-establishment interests will have to curtail the support it offers to its citizens for public school education.

Quicknotes

ESTABLISHMENT CLAUSE The constitutional provision prohibiting the government from favoring any one religion over others or engaging in religious activities or advocacy.

FREE EXERCISE CLAUSE The guarantee of the First Amendment to the U.S. Constitution prohibiting Congress from enacting laws regarding the establishment of religion or prohibiting the free exercise thereof.

Glossary

Common Latin Words and Phrases Encountered in the Law

A FORTIORI: Because one fact exists or has been proven, therefore a second fact that is related to the first fact must also exist.

A PRIORI: From the cause to the effect. A term of logic used to denote that when one generally accepted truth is shown to be a cause, another particular effect must necessarily follow.

AB INITIO: From the beginning; a condition that has existed throughout, as in a marriage that was void ab initio.

ACTUS REUS: The wrongful act; in criminal law, such action as is sufficient to trigger criminal liability.

AD VALOREM: According to value; an ad valorem tax is imposed upon an item located within the taxing jurisdiction calculated by the value of such item.

AMICUS CURIAE: Friend of the court. Its most common usage takes the form of an amicus curiae brief, filed by a person who is not a party to an action but is nonetheless allowed to offer an argument supporting his or her legal interests.

ARGUENDO: In arguing. A statement, possibly hypothetical, made for the purpose of argument.

BILL QUIA TIMET: A bill to quiet title (establish ownership) to real property.

BONA FIDE: True, honest, or genuine. May refer to a person's legal position based on good faith or lacking notice of fraud (such as a bona fide purchaser for value) or to the authenticity of a particular document (such as a bona fide last will and testament).

CAUSA MORTIS: With approaching death in mind. A gift causa mortis is a gift given by a party who feels certain that death is imminent.

CAVEAT EMPTOR: Let the buyer beware. This maxim is reflected in the rule of law that a buyer purchases at his or her own risk because it is the buyer's responsibility to examine, judge, test, and otherwise inspect what he or she is buying.

CERTIORARI: A writ of review. Petitions for review of a case by the United States Supreme Court are most often done by means of a writ of certiorari.

CONTRA: On the other hand. Opposite. Contrary to.

CORAM NOBIS: Before us; a writ of error directed to the court that originally rendered the judgment.

CORAM VOBIS: Before you; a writ of error directed by an appellate court to a lower court to correct a factual error.

CORPUS DELICTI: The body of the crime; the requisite elements of a crime amounting to objective proof that a crime has been committed.

CUM TESTAMENTO ANNEXO, ADMINISTRATOR (ADMINISTRATOR C.T.A.): With will annexed; an administrator c.t.a. settles an estate pursuant to a will in which he or she is not appointed.

DE BONIS NON, ADMINISTRATOR (ADMINISTRATOR D.B.N.): Of goods not administered; an administrator d.b.n. settles a partially settled estate.

DE FACTO: In fact; in reality; actually. Existing in fact but not officially approved or engendered.

DE JURE: By right; lawful. Describes a condition that is legitimate "as a matter of law," in contrast to the term "de facto," which connotes something existing in fact but not legally sanctioned or authorized. For example, de facto segregation refers to segregation brought about by housing patterns, etc., whereas de jure segregation refers to segregation created by law.

DE MINIMUS: Of minimal importance; insignificant; a trifle; not worth bothering about.

DE NOVO: Anew; a second time; afresh. A trial de novo is a new trial held at the appellate level as if the case originated there and the trial at a lower level had not taken place.

DICTA: Generally used as an abbreviated form of obiter dicta, a term describing those portions of a judicial opinion incidental or not necessary to resolution of the specific question before the court. Such nonessential statements and remarks are not considered to be binding precedent.

DUCES TECUM: Refers to a particular type of writ or subpoena requesting a party or organization to produce certain documents in their possession.

EN BANC: Full bench. Where a court sits with all justices present rather than the usual quorum.

EX PARTE: For one side or one party only. An ex parte proceeding is one undertaken for the benefit of only one party, without notice to, or an appearance by, an adverse party.

EX POST FACTO: After the fact. An ex post facto law is a law that retroactively changes the consequences of a prior act.

EX REL.: Abbreviated form of the term "ex relatione," meaning upon relation or information. When the state brings an action in which it has no interest against an individual at the instigation of one who has a private interest in the matter.

FORUM NON CONVENIENS: Inconvenient forum. Although a court may have jurisdiction over the case, the action should be tried in a more conveniently located court, one to which parties and witnesses may more easily travel, for example.

GUARDIAN AD LITEM: A guardian appointed by the court to represent a minor or incompetent person in a legal action.

HABEAS CORPUS: You have the body. The modern writ of habeas corpus is a writ directing that a person (body) being detained (such as a prisoner) be brought before the court so that the legality of his or her detention can be judicially ascertained.

IN CAMERA: In private, in chambers. When a hearing is held before a judge in his or her chambers or when all spectators are excluded from the courtroom.

IN FORMA PAUPERIS: In the manner of a pauper. A party who proceeds in forma pauperis because of his or her poverty is one who is allowed to bring suit without liability for costs.

INFRA: Below, under. A word referring the reader to a later part of a book. (The opposite of supra.)

IN LOCO PARENTIS: In the place of a parent.

IN PARI DELICTO: Equally wrong; a court of equity will not grant requested relief to an applicant who is in pari delicto, or as much at fault in the transactions giving rise to the controversy as is the opponent of the applicant.

IN PARI MATERIA: On like subject matter or upon the same matter. Statutes relating to the same person or things are said to be in pari materia. It is a general rule of statutory construction that such statutes should be construed together, i.e., looked at as if they together constituted one law.

IN PERSONAM: Against the person. Jurisdiction over the person of an individual.

IN RE: In the matter of. Used to designate a proceeding involving an estate or other property.

IN REM: Signifies an action against the res, or thing. An action in rem is basically one that is taken directly against property, as distinguished from an action in personam, i.e., against the person.

INTER ALIA: Among other things. Used to show that the whole of a statement, pleading, list, statute, etc., has not been set forth in its entirety.

INTER PARTES: Between the parties. May refer to contracts, conveyances, or other transactions having legal significance.

INTER VIVOS: Between the living. An inter vivos gift is a gift made by a living grantor, as distinguished from bequests contained in a will, which pass upon the death of the testator.

IPSO FACTO: By the mere fact itself.

JUS: Law or the entire body of law.

LEX LOCI: The law of the place; the notion that the rights of parties to a legal proceeding are governed by the law of the place where those rights arose.

MALUM IN SE: Evil or wrong in and of itself; inherently wrong. Describes an act that is wrong by its very nature, as opposed to one which would not be wrong but for the fact that there is a specific legal prohibition against it (malum prohibitum).

MALUM PROHIBITUM: Wrong because prohibited, but not inherently evil. Describes something that is wrong because it is expressly forbidden by law but that is not in and of itself evil, e.g., speeding.

MANDAMUS: We command. A writ directing an official to take a certain action.

MENS REA: A guilty mind; a criminal intent. A term used to signify the mental state that accompanies a crime or other prohibited act. Some crimes require only a general mens rea (general intent to do the prohibited act), but others, like assault with intent to murder, require the existence of a specific mens rea.

MODUS OPERANDI: Method of operating; generally refers to the manner or style of a criminal in committing crimes, admissible in appropriate cases as evidence of the identity of a defendant.

NEXUS: A connection to.

NISI PRIUS: A court of first impression. A nisi prius court is one where issues of fact are tried before a judge or jury.

N.O.V. (NON OBSTANTE VEREDICTO): Notwithstanding the verdict. A judgment n.o.v. is a judgment given in favor of one party despite the fact that a verdict was returned in favor of the other party, the justification being that the verdict either had no reasonable support in fact or was contrary to law.

NUNC PRO TUNC: Now for then. This phrase refers to actions that may be taken and will then have full retroactive effect.

PENDENTE LITE: Pending the suit; pending litigation underway.

PER CAPITA: By head; beneficiaries of an estate, if they take in equal shares, take per capita.

PER CURIAM: By the court; signifies an opinion ostensibly written "by the whole court" and with no identified author.

PER SE: By itself, in itself; inherently.

PER STIRPES: By representation. Used primarily in the law of wills to describe the method of distribution where a person, generally because of death, is unable to take that which is left to him or her by the will of another, and therefore his or her heirs divide such property between them rather than take under the will individually.

PRIMA FACIE: On its face, at first sight. A prima facie case is one that is sufficient on its face, meaning that the evidence supporting it is adequate to establish the case until contradicted or overcome by other evidence.

PRO TANTO: For so much; as far as it goes. Often used in eminent domain cases when a property owner receives partial payment for his or her land without prejudice to his or her right to bring suit for the full amount he or she claims the land to be worth.

QUANTUM MERUIT: As much as the party deserves. Refers to recovery based on the doctrine of unjust enrichment in those cases in which a party has rendered valuable services or furnished materials that were accepted and enjoyed by another under circumstances that would reasonably notify the recipient that the rendering party expected to be paid. In essence, the law implies a contract to pay the reasonable value of the services or materials furnished.

QUASI: Almost like; as if; nearly. Essentially used to signify that one subject or thing is almost analogous to another but that material differences between them do exist. For example, a quasi-criminal proceeding is one that is not strictly criminal but shares enough of the same characteristics to require some of the same safeguards (e.g., procedural due process must be followed in a parole hearing).

QUID PRO QUO: Something for something. In contract law, the consideration, something of value, passed between the parties to render the contract binding.

RES GESTAE: Things done. In evidence law, this principle justifies the admission of a statement that would otherwise be hearsay when it is made so closely to the event in question as to be said to be a part of it, or with such spontaneity as not to have the possibility of falsehood.

RES IPSA LOQUITUR: The thing speaks for itself. This doctrine gives rise to a rebuttable presumption of negligence when the instrumentality causing the injury was within the exclusive control of the defendant, and the injury was one that does not normally occur unless a person has been negligent.

RES JUDICATA: A matter adjudged. Doctrine that provides that once a court of competent jurisdiction has rendered a final judgment or decree on the merits, that judgment or decree is conclusive upon the parties to the case and prevents them from engaging in any other litigation on the points and issues determined therein.

RESPONDEAT SUPERIOR: Let the master reply. This doctrine holds the master liable for the wrongful acts of his or her servant (or the principal for his or her agent) in those cases in which the servant (or agent) was acting within the scope of his or her authority at the time of the injury.

STARE DECISIS: To stand by or adhere to that which has been decided. The common law doctrine of stare decisis attempts to give security and certainty to the law by following the policy that once a principle of law as applicable to a certain set of facts has been set forth in a decision, it forms a precedent that will subsequently be followed, even though a different decision might be made were it the first time the question had arisen. Of course, stare decisis is not an inviolable principle and is departed from in instances where there is good cause (e.g., considerations of public policy led the Supreme Court to disregard prior decisions sanctioning segregation).

SUPRA: Above. A word referring a reader to an earlier part of a book. (The opposite of infra.)

ULTRA VIRES: Beyond the power. This phrase is most commonly used to refer to actions taken by a corporation that are beyond the power or legal authority of the corporation.

Addendum of French Derivatives

CHATTEL: Tangible personal property.

CY PRES: Doctrine permitting courts to apply trust funds to purposes not expressed in the trust but necessary to carry out the settlor's intent.

IN PAIS: Not pursuant to legal proceedings.

PER AUTRE VIE: For another's life; during another's life. In property law, an estate may be granted that will terminate upon the death of someone other than the grantee.

PROFIT A PRENDRE: A license to remove minerals or other produce from land.

VOIR DIRE: Process of questioning jurors as to their predispositions about the case or parties to a proceeding in order to identify those jurors displaying bias or prejudice.